Marxist Literary Theory
A Reader

Edited by

Terry Eagleton
and
Drew Milne

BLACKWELL
Publishers

First published 1996

Reprinted 1996 (twice), 1999

Blackwell Publishers Ltd
108 Cowley Road
Oxford OX4 1JF, UK

Blackwell Publishers Inc.
238 Main Street
Cambridge, Massachusetts 02142, USA

British Library Cataloguing in Publication Data
A CIP catalogue record for this book is available from the British Library

Library of Congress Cataloging in Publication Data
Marxist literary theory : a reader/edited by Terry Eagleton and Drew Milne.
p.   cm.
Includes bibliographical references and index.
ISBN 0–631–18579–8 — ISBN 0–631–18581–X (pbk)
1. Marxist literary criticism. I. Eagleton, Terry, 1943–
II. Milne, Drew.
PN98.C6M28   1996   95–21024
801'.95—dc20   CIP

Typeset in 10 on 12pt Ehrhardt
by Pure Tech Corporation, Pondicherry, India
Printed and bound in Great Britain by T J International Ltd, Padstow, Cornwall

This book is printed on acid-free paper

Contents

Acknowledgements

The editors and publishers wish to thank the following for permission to use extracts:

Blackwell Publishers for an excerpt from Alex Callinicos, *Against Postmodernism*, Polity Press (1989), pp. 9–28.

Lawrence & Wishart Ltd for excerpts from Marx and Engels, *On Literature and Art* (1967), pp. 41–4, 82–4, 90–2, 64–8; Christopher Caudwell, *Illusion and Reality* (1977), pp. 85–100; and Alick West, *Crisis and Criticism and Selected Literary Essays* (1975), pp. 99–103.

The Merlin Press Ltd for an excerpt from Georg Lukács, *The Meaning of Contemporary Realism*, trans. John and Necke Mander (1963), pp. 17–46.

The MIT Press for an excerpt from Ernst Bloch, *Utopian Function of Art and Literature*, trans. J. Zipes and F. Meckleburg (1988), pp. 156–62.

The Oxford Literary Review for Etienne Balibar and Pierre Macherey, 'On Literature as an Ideological Form: Some Marxist Propositions', *Oxford Literary Review*, 3 (1978), pp. 4–12. Copyright © 1978 *Oxford Literary Review*.

Oxford University Press for an excerpt from Raymond Williams, *Marxism and Literature* (1977), pp. 45–54. Copyright © 1977 Oxford University Press.

Random House UK Ltd on behalf of the Estate of the author for an excerpt from Raymond Williams, *Modern Tragedy*, Chatto & Windus (1966), pp. 61–84.

Reed Consumer Books Ltd and Hill and Wang, a division of Farrar Strauss & Giroux, Inc. for Bertolt Brecht, 'A Short Organum for the Theatre', from *Brecht on Theatre*, ed. and trans. John Willett, Methuen London (1964). Translation copyright © 1964 and renewed © 1992 by John Willett.

Routledge, with Editions Gallimard for an excerpt from Lucien Goldmann, *Towards a Sociology of the Novel*, trans. Alan Sheridan, Tavistock Publications (1964), pp. 1–17. Copyright © 1964 Editions Gallimard; and with Cornell University Press for an excerpt from Fredric Jameson, *The Political Unconscious: Narrative as a Socially Symbolic Act*, Methuen & Co. (1981), pp. 74–103. Copyright © 1981 by Cornell University Press; The University of Chicago Press for an excerpt from Jean-Paul Sartre, *The Family Idiot: Gustave Flaubert, 1821–1857*, Vol. V, trans. Carol Cosman (1981–93), pp. 33–56.

Verso for excerpts from Walter Benjamin, *One-Way Street and Other Writings*, trans. Edmund Jephcott and Kingsley Shorter, New Left Books, (1979), pp. 225–39. Copyright © Suhrkamp Verlag, trans. copyright © 1979 New Left Books; Walter Benjamin, *Charles Baudelaire*, trans. Harry Zohn, New Left Books (1973), pp. 103–6. Copyright © 1969, 1971 Suhrkamp Verlag trans. copyright © 1973 New Left Books; Galvano Della Volpe, *Critique of Taste*, trans. Michael Caesar, New Left Books (1978), pp. 173–201. Copyright © 1960 Feltrinelli, trans. copyright © 1978 New Left Books; T. W. Adorno, 'Commitment', trans. Francis McDonagh, from Ernst Bloch and others, *Aesthetics and Politics*, New Left Books (1977), pp. 177–95. Copyright © Suhrkamp Verlag. trans. copyright © 1977 New Left Books; Louis Althusser, *Lenin and Philosophy and Other Essays*, trans. Ben Brewster, New Left Books (1971), pp. 221–7; Terry Eagleton, *Criticism and Ideology*, New Left Books (1976), pp. 64–101. Copyright © 1975, Terry Eagleton; Aijaz Ahmad, *In Theory: Classes, Nations, Literatures*, Verso (1992), pp. 95–122. Copyright © 1992 Aijaz Ahmad; Zed Books Ltd for an excerpt from *The Theory of African Literature*, by Chidi Amuta (1989), pp. 130–6.

Every effort has been made to trace all the copyright holders, but if any have been inadvertently overlooked the publishers will be pleased to make the necessary arrangement at the first opportunity.

Introduction Part I
Terry Eagleton

It is no longer possible, if it ever really was, to take the word 'Marxist' in the phrase 'Marxist criticism' for granted, and turn instead to the critical issues at stake. For Marxism is at present enduring the most grievous crisis of its fraught career – a crisis which involves nothing less than the question of its very survival. If this has never quite been true before, the fact is not necessarily to Marxism's credit. The long night of Stalinism did more to discredit the doctrine, not least in the eyes of those working people in the West who might have stood to gain something by it, than all the polemics of the right-wing intelligentsia put together; but at least Stalinism and its progeny seemed to mean that Marxism of some species was here to stay, as a fact if not as a value. Ironically, what discredited it at one level served to entrench it at another. It may not have been to one's taste, but one couldn't ignore it – whereas today, in the turbulent aftermath of all that, it is possible for some to find virtue in Marxist thought exactly because it can be easily enough sidelined in political reality.

But it was not the collapse of neo-Stalinism, or however the political taxonomists choose to label whatever was under way in eastern Europe, which first plunged Marxism into crisis. The chronology here is simply false, for Marxism was already in deep trouble before the first brick of the Berlin wall had been loosened. It was not the implosion of the Soviet world, but the quickening contradictions of the Western one, which first began to undermine historical materialism. If, as Fredric Jameson has maintained, the 1960s came to an end in 1973–4 with the international oil crisis, then the heady Althusserian heyday of the early and mid-1970s, when something like a Marxist *culture* last existed in the West, was already, unbeknown to itself, the beginnings of a political downturn. The same period witnessed the end of the great wave of national liberation movements throughout the world, movements which had dealt international capitalism a series of staggering rebuffs. A few years later, high Althusserianism had veered on its axis and worked its way through to so-called post-Marxism, as the ice age of Reagan-Thatcherism set in. Under mounting economic pressure, the political regimes of the West shifted sharply to the right, and Marxism was one casualty of this carnival of reaction.

In what exact sense, though? For it is not as though anyone actually *disproved* the doctrine. It is not as though they needed to. In the new ambience of political cynicism, cultural philistinism and economic self-interest, Marxism was less and less even *in question*, as quaintly antiquarian a pursuit for some as Ptolemaic cosmology or the scholasticism of Duns Scotus. One no more needed to refute it than one would waste time refuting a fakir or a flat-earther. For many, Marxism, in Foucauldian phrase, was less and less 'in the truth', no longer quite the kind of epistemic object which might seriously qualify for debate as to its truth-value. It was becoming less false than irrelevant, a question on which it was no more necessary to have a firm opinion than it was on crop circles or poltergeists. One might have thought that if Marxism was true in 1975, as many then claimed it was, then – short of some immense sea-change in the world itself – it would also have been true in 1985. But in 1985 it was mattering less whether it was true or not, just as the existence of God was a burning issue in 1860 but hardly so one century later. Marxism was now less a discomforting challenge than the irritating or endearing idiosyncrasy of those unable to relinquish an imaginary selfhood inherited from the past. It belonged irrevocably to the great epoch of modernity, within which, whether true or false, it figured as an entirely intelligible project. Once that age had passed into a different problematic, Marxism could be seen as at best a set of valid responses to a set of questions which were no longer on the agenda. It thus crossed over, in the eyes of some, from being false but relevant, to true but superfluous. And the line between claiming that it was superfluous because capitalism *should* not be defeated, and asserting that it was redundant because the system *could* not be defeated, became easy enough to cross.

Marxism, then, was taken to be less disproved than discredited, out of the question rather than out of arguments. But quite *what* had been discredited was not entirely clear. Did the fall of the Berlin wall mean that Georg Lukács's remarks on Balzac were now valueless? Did the rise of market relations in Poland mean that nobody involved in the celebrated 'transition from feudalism to capitalism' debate had uttered a single illuminating word? This, indeed, would be the unity of theory and practice with a vengeance, outmarxizing the Marxists themselves! It would, to be sure, be singularly unMarxist to regard Marxism itself as politically bankrupt while still a useful tool of intellectual analysis. The American professor who remarked of Marxism in my hearing that of course the economics were up the spout but it could still throw a lot of light on Chaucer was not just being a selective Marxist, he was being no sort of Marxist at all. For whatever else Marxists may disagree upon, they are agreed that the term 'Marxist' functions more like the word 'carpenter' than it does like the word 'Cartesian'. But this is not to claim, even so, that theory and practice always dance harmoniously together. Marxist theory may be ultimately for the sake of political practice; but it would be a brand of Marxist pragmatism (commonly known as Stalinism or historicism) to hold that the truth-value of the theory is determined by its success in a particular political conjuncture. For one thing, it is not easy to know whether it was the theory which brought about the success; perhaps the very fact that you were in error allowed you to achieve what you wanted. For another thing, Marxist theory itself contains explanations of why theory and practice do not always slide together quite so symmetrically. And if theory exists now for the sake of practice, that practice exists for the sake of some future condition in which we would not need to rationalize the pleasures of thought at the tribunal of some instrumental reason.

But there is another consideration at stake here. Part of the crisis of Marxism would seem to be that it is no longer easy to say what *counts* as being a Marxist, if indeed it ever was. In our own time, it has proved possible for individuals to discount many of the classical doctrines of the creed – the labour theory of value, the notion of historical laws, the contradiction between the forces and relations of production, the model of base and superstructure, the idea of 'class identity', the supposedly scientific basis of Marxist epistemology, the concept of false consciousness, the philosophy of 'dialectical materialism' – and still lay claim to the name of Marxist. Whether it is possible for someone to renounce *all* of these tenets and still remain in some meaningful sense a Marxist is rather less obvious; but it has certainly become less clear just how many of the 39 articles, so to speak, one needs to subscribe to in order to lay claim to the title. There are 'Marxists' these days – to continue the ecclesiastical analogy – who resemble the kind of extreme-liberal Anglican who has no time for the doctrines of the existence of God, the divinity of Christ, heaven and hell, the sacraments, the Ten Commandments or the resurrection. Such a faith is not even precise enough to be wrong. Of course, if the word 'Marxist' is to have meaning, then there must logically be something which is incompatible with it – just as one can find all kinds of feminists, but not feminists who think male dominance of women an excellent thing. But it is likely, even so, that the word 'Marxist' works to denote a set of family resemblances rather than some immutable essence. Certainly Marx and Engels themselves repudiated the idea that social class, or even class struggle, was original to their way of thinking. What they considered innovative about their theory was the claim that the rise and fall of social classes is bound up with the rise and fall of historical modes of production. There seems no epistemological doctrine which Marxism does not share with a host of other realisms, so that those unwary Marxists who believe they are unique in holding to the objective independent existence of the material world have obviously not been chatting to conservative middle-class philosophers. The 'last-instance' determination of the economic would appear a peculiarly

Marxist claim, but it is one that Freud, no particular friend of Marxism, subscribed to himself, when he remarked that the motive of all social life was finally an economic one. As for more narrowly political beliefs – equality, common ownership, self-government and the rest – it is hard to think of any which Marxists do not share in common with other types of radicals or revolutionaries. And this has a bearing on the issue of validation. For the *distinctive* focus of Marxism, as opposed to some other styles of socialism, is not the 'political conjuncture', but the *longues durées* of – for example – the conflict between the forces and relations of material production. The validity or otherwise of its claims about such epochal questions cannot be decided by the political short term, which is not to say that they cannot be determined at all – that Marxism is, as Popper would have it, inherently unfalsifiable and so intrinsically unscientific. It is just that you cannot determine the truth of such broad claims in the same way as you can the truth of the charge that Stalin murdered kulaks.

But surely, it will be objected, almost a century of botched Marxist experiment is *longue durée* enough. If *that* isn't enough to demonstrate that the theory simply doesn't work in practice, then what would conceivably count as conclusive evidence? But assessing the success of a theory involves taking into account what *it* would count as success; we do not upbraid Einstein for failing to find a cure for cancer. And none of the founding theorists of Marxism imagined for a moment that it could provide the means by which desperately backward societies could throw off their oppressors, catapult themselves single-handed into the twentieth century and construct socialism in a besieged and isolated state. This would involve the backbreaking task of developing the productive forces from a very low level – a task which capitalism had cannily entrusted to individual self-interest, and so had magnificently accomplished. But if men and women in post-capitalist conditions proved understandably reluctant to submit themselves freely to such a dispiriting labour, then an authoritarian state would have to step in and do it on their behalf, thus undermining the political content of socialism (popular participatory democracy) in the very process of striving to lay down its economic base. Building socialism takes time – time for the complex business of democratic self-management; and this in turn requires a shortening of the working day impossible if people have no food or shoes. It also helps if you inherit a wealth of cultural resources, sophisticated institutions of civil society and a flourishing tradition of bourgeois liberalism, for socialism is of course the 'sublation' of such a precious liberal humanist heritage and not simply its antithesis. But these resources, not to speak of the basic educational skills essential for socialist democracy, are scarcely likely to thrive in conditions of economic backwardness. One of the tragic ironies of the twentieth century, then, is that socialism has proved least possible where it has been most urgently necessary. It was this, no doubt, that Lenin had in mind when he remarked with dialectical deftness that it was the relative absence of culture (in the sense of an elaborate realm of 'civil society') which had made the revolution in Russia possible to achieve, but the very same absence of culture (in the sense of spiritual and material resources) which had made it so hard to sustain.

Is this to claim, then, that only the well-heeled can go socialist, abandoning the Third World to its fate? Not at all; it is to claim rather, as did the Bolsheviks, that socialist change can surely be initiated in such conditions, but that unless the richer nations come to its aid it is very likely to be forced down the Stalinist path. There can be no socialism in one country in an interdependent world, even if the process has to start somewhere. All this has long been understood by the Marxist tradition itself. If one wants a critique of neo-Stalinism which is materially based, historically rooted and implacably critical, then one has to turn to key aspects of the Marxist heritage, rather than to the middle-class liberal one. Liberalism has properly defended civil liberties in the neo-Stalinist societies, but this, for a Marxist, was never really radical enough. What happened in eastern Europe a few years ago – the overthrow of the ruling bureaucracies by popular power, in a gratifyingly bloodless series of revolutions – was what many currents of Marxism had been calling for for well over half a century. If it arrived a little later than, say, the incurably hopeful Trotsky had expected, it was better late than never. It also took place, by a pleasing irony, at just the historical point when sophisticated Western leftists everywhere had abandoned the whole notion of popular revolution as incorrigibly naïve. And what happened in the wake of those revolutions – a reversion to, or inauguration of, capitalist social relations – was a development which key currents of modern Marxism had also for a long time foreseen as an ominous possibility. The downfall of the ruling bureaucracies was a necessary, but by no means sufficient, condition of constructing democratic socialism.

If Marxism is in crisis, then, it is not on account of some pervasive left disillusionment over the disintegration of the post-capitalist countries. You can, after all, suffer disillusion only if you were illusioned in the first place; and the last time that the Western left harboured widespread illusions about the Soviet Union was the 1930s. If the left is in some disarray, it is not in the first place to do with Marxism, but with a far more general sense of impotence and frustration consequent on the fact that capitalism for the moment lacks an effective, concerted political challenge. In that sense, the system can be said to be currently victorious – but the very word has something of a grotesque ring to it. For how can a global system which is at once the most productive history has ever witnessed, yet which needs to keep the great majority of men and women in a state of spiritual and material deprivation, possibly be described as successful? To this extent, the rancour of the socialist contains an implicit hope: what is so bad about this system is exactly the fact that it doesn't and can't work. Socialism may be pitched into crisis for this or that reason from time to time; but capitalism exists in a state of chronic neurosis, and could not do otherwise.

It is typical of Marxism, as opposed to other styles of socialist belief, to have paid special attention to the *contradictions* of capitalism – to the ways that it can't help producing wealth and poverty at a stroke, as material conditions of one another. And this, in turn, lends it a peculiar stance towards the question of modernity. Modern radicalisms have tended on the whole to divide between nostalgic-regressive and progressive-technological strains: between romantic anti-capitalism and Fabianism, the potter's wheel and the Futurist machine, Lukács and Brecht. Marxism, however, at once outdoes the Futurists in its praise for the mighty achievements of modernity, and outflanks the romantic anti-capitalists in its remorseless denunciation of the very same era. As both the offspring of Enlightenment and its immanent critique, it cannot be readily categorized in the facile pro- and anti-modernist terms now fashionable in Western cultural debate. Whereas modernism proper was really just confused on this score, never really able to square its revolt against modernity with its dependence upon it, and whereas postmodernism either commodifies the past or erases it, Marxism alone has sustained the eminently dialectical belief, inimical at once to romantic nostalgia and modernizing triumphalism, that modern history has been inseparably civilization and barbarism. This dialect-ical view can in turn be rephrased as another. Marxism gives immense weight to culture, social construction, historical change, sceptical as it is of the supposedly natural and immutable; and to this extent it has something in common with postmodernism. Unlike postmodernism, however, it is at the same time deeply suspicious of the cultural, which it views as in the end the offspring of labour, as well as, often enough, a disownment of it; and since the historical narrative it has to deliver is one of recurrent struggle, scarcity and suffering, as well as of dynamism, open-endedness and variety, it is less likely to be seduced by some modish notion of an endlessly pluralist history. The story which Marxism has to tell is more tedious, but also more true to the humdrum, vulnerable nature of humanity, than exotic tales of difference, multiplicity and mutability. It is not that Marxism does not *wish* such fables to be true; it is rather that they can only be true of some transformed future, when History (or, as Marx puts it, pre-history) would be thankfully over, and real histories might consequently begin. Marxism is all about how to get from the kingdom of identity to the realm of difference; it is just that it is wary of the kind of callow idealism that believes you can do this by studying Derrida rather than Aristotle, or more generally by adopting a different outlook on life.

If socialism were just an outlook on life, then one might well expect it to go under, disabled by its Stalinist distortions and crippled by the onslaughts of the free marketeers. But socialism is more than just a good idea, like brushing one's teeth or wrapping Westminster bridge in crêpe paper; it is arguably the greatest reform movement in the history of humanity, and one well accustomed to serious set-backs. If it is aware of the formidable power of what it opposes, it is equally conscious of how quickly and unpredictably history can alter. And even if it does not do so – even if 'late' capitalism turns out to mean a long way from the beginning rather than anywhere near the end – there is no reason why this sobering thought should change what one strives for, which remains true and valuable whether or not it can be realized in the here and now.

Culture for Marxism is at once absolutely vital and distinctly secondary: the place where power is crystallized and submission bred, but also somehow 'superstructural', something which in its more narrow sense of specialized artistic institutions can only be fashioned out of a certain economic surplus and division of labour, and which even in its more generous anthropological sense of a 'form of life' risks papering over certain important conflicts and distinctions. Culture is more than just ideology, but it is not a neutral or transcendent entity either; and any Marxist criticism worth the name must thus adopt a well-nigh impossible double optic, seeking on the one hand to take the full pressure of a cultural artefact while striving at the same time to displace it into its enabling material conditions and set it within a complex field of social power. What this means in effect is that one will find oneself bending the stick too far towards formalism and then too far towards contextualism, in search of that ever-receding discourse which would in allegorical manner speak simultaneously of an artistic device and a whole material history, of a turn of narrative and a style of social consciousness.

Very schematically, it is possible to distinguish four broad kinds of Marxist criticism, each of which corresponds to a certain 'region' within Marxist theory, and also (very roughly speaking) to a particular historical period. These are the *anthropological, political, ideological* and *economic* – modes which in their various intricate permutations go to make up the corpus of criticism recorded in this book. '*Anthropological*' criticism (the term needs its qualifying quotation marks) is the most ambitious and far-reaching of all four approaches, seeking as it does to raise some awesomely fundamental questions. What is the function of art within social evolution? What are the material and biological bases of 'aesthetic' capacities? What are the relations between art and human labour? How does art relate to myth, ritual, religion and language, and what are its social functions? These and cognate questions are not on the whole ones with which we feel terribly comfortable today, smacking as they do of the compulsively synthetic vision of the late nineteenth-century human sciences. The postmodern sensibility is allergic to such embarrassingly large issues, which stride briskly across epochs and civilizations, assume certain abiding identities ('art', 'labour'), and tend to substitute evolution for history. But from G. V. Plekhanov to Christopher Caudwell, and with the odd late flowering like Ernst Fischer's *The Necessity of Art*, this has formed one important current of Marxist cultural enquiry. It represents a materialism of a somewhat fundamentalist but none the less interesting kind – an attempt to demystify idealist notions of art by situating it in the context of what the young Marx himself called our 'species being', of the natural history, so to speak, of the species. Positivist, functionalist and biologistic in bent, it nevertheless contrasts tellingly in its scope and intellectual energy with the dwindled vistas of contemporary left-historicism, for which phenomena would seem to live and die in their punctual historical moments, reducing all generality or persisting identity to so much metaphysical or ideological baggage. But as Francis Mulhern has well argued, this is to reduce *history* to *change*, whereas history 'is also – and decisively, for its greater part – *continuity*. The historical process is differential: it is patterned by a plurality of rhythms and tempos, some highly variable, some very little so, some measured by clocks and calendars, others belonging to the practical eternity of "deep time".'[1] The time of a literary work is not the time of the human body, which has altered very little in the course of evolution; but neither is it the time of an ephemeral event like a handshake. Texts persist as well as mutate, strike correspondences as well as enforce differences, 'constellate' distinct historical moments as well as measure their mutual estrangement. The brand of extreme historicism which imprisons works within their historical context, or the kind of new historicism which incarcerates them in our own, are then perpetually liable to raise a set of problems which are in part pseudo-problems, such as 'how come that I, a twentieth-century non-believer in the Furies with liberal views on incest, can respond as I do to ancient Greek tragedy?' It is, famously, the kind of question which lost Karl Marx some sleep as well. But Marxism is not just an historicism, and neither should one assume that all historicisms are radical. Many of them are anything but. Transhistorical concepts have their place in historical materialism, since transhistorical activities play a key role in human history. And it is one of the virtues of 'anthropological' Marxist criticism, for all its limitations, to remind us of the fact. The realm of culture is changing, whereas that of the biological species is a good deal more stable; but this antithesis obscures as much as it illuminates. For culture, in the broadest sense of the term, is also a permanent necessity of our material being, without which we would quickly die. Our 'species being' brings with it a kind of structural gap or absence where culture of some kind must be implanted if we are to survive and flourish; and though *what* kind of culture is of course highly variable, the *necessity* of culture is not. It is not so much, then, the culturalist doctrine that 'the nature of humanity is culture' as the rather more dialectical point that we are cultural beings of our very nature.

Anthropological criticism belongs above all to the period of the Second International, with its encyclopaedic scholarship and confidently totalizing vision, its positivist assurance of certain progressive historical laws which render socialism inevitable, its curious blending of mechanical materialism and neo-Kantianism which allows it to speak in one breath of the opposing thumb and in the next of the faculty for appreciating beauty. From the time of the Bolsheviks, however, a *political* criticism comes to the fore, which addresses a quite different set of issues. With Plekhanov and his colleagues, Marxist criticism had been a contemplative, largely academic affair; now, from Lenin's pamphlets on Tolstoy to Trotsky's *Literature and Revolution*, criticism becomes a matter of polemic and intervention, of seeking to shape state cultural policy or confound some opposing cultural-political tendency, of winning over the fellow travellers or fighting off the Mensheviks. Cultural questions become, in part, code for much deeper political matters; where your stand on art reflects your position on the working class, on bourgeois democracy, on socialism in one country or the relative importance of peasant and urban proletariat. What is at stake is no longer the biological basis of the aesthetic faculty but whether art should be openly tendentious or 'objectively' partisan, whether avant-garde experiment is a way of figuring the revolutionary future or merely of alienating the unsophisticated masses, whether art should tell it as it is or as it should be, whether it should be mirror or hammer, cognitive or affective, beamed in unabashed class terms at the proletariat or imaging forth the 'universal' socialist being already in the making. Should the literature of class society be dumped, re-fashioned or disseminated amongst the people in cheap popular editions? Was a bad poem by a worker better than a good one by a bourgeois? Should art be scaled down to the present level of the masses, or the masses elevated to the current level of art? Was it elitist to use pen and paper rather than scribbling your poems on people's shirt-fronts in the street? Was any literary form compatible with a committed art, or was realism to be given a special privilege?

All of these issues belonged to the great ferment of activity around the years of the Russian revolution, when an entirely new cultural project, apparently without precedent, was in train, when it was as though the whole of familiar history had gone into the melting pot and the answers to some urgent questions had to be improvised as one went along. If it is impossible for us now to recapture that vertiginous mixture of anxiety and euphoria, it is nevertheless possible to trace the marks of it in the critical debates of the time, which still resound today with a vigour and audaciousness we have yet to reattain. And these great electrifying currents of energy, as new critical concepts are invented on the wing and as theory must hobble hard to keep up with artistic practice, belong not just to the world's first workers' state but to the wider context of radical European modernism, to the world of Dada, Surrealism, Brecht and Weimar. The role of culture is now nothing less than to fashion the forms of subjectivity appropriate to a revolutionized reality. It is not, as in our own time, that a radical culture overshoots a conservative reality;

on the contrary, the problem is that reality is shifting before one's eyes but human consciousness is unable or unwilling to keep pace with it. Just as industrial capitalism required a whole new human sensorium, so industrial socialism is in hot pursuit of a subjectivity adequate to its new social relations, and it is to this task, rather than to the annotation of colour symbolism in Pushkin, that the Soviet critic is dedicated. Literary critic and literary practitioner will hammer out a new relationship, as in the liaison between the Formalist Osip Brik and the Futurist Mayakovsky, or later between Benjamin and Brecht – a relationship in which the critic is, as it were, tester, analyst and supplier of linguistic techniques and materials to the artist himself. And we are speaking in any case not of isolated academic critics but of movements, journals, collectives: of agit-prop and the Left Front in Art, Proletkult and RAPP.

The triumph of the doctrine of so-called socialist realism, and the rolling back of the more militant artistic projects, will finally put paid to this great epoch of cultural experiment, as a Soviet Union confronted by the rise of fascism feels the need to downplay an aggressive cultural proletarianism for the sake of an alliance with the progressive bourgeoisie of other nations. With the exception of the school of Bakhtin, which is itself forced underground, all the most creative developments in Marxist criticism will then shift elsewhere – to the so-called Western Marxist lineage of Lukács, Gramsci, Bloch, Adorno, Brecht, Benjamin, Marcuse, Caudwell, Sartre, Goldmann, Althusser. Most of these theorists are either quite outside official Soviet ideology or in some notably oblique relationship with it – relentless critics of orthodox Marxism, maverick fellow-travellers like Benjamin or Sartre, or (like Lukács and Althusser) party members whose cultural or theoretical work runs implicitly against the grain of the political establishment. All of them, as supposedly materialist thinkers, grant a remarkably high priority to culture and philosophy, and do so in part as a substitute for a politics that has failed.[2] For Georg Lukács, a dialectical totality which refuses to be realized in political reality is kept alive instead in the realist work of art. For Ernst Bloch, aesthetic utopia keeps open a perspective which Stalinism has closed off, whereas for Adorno and Marcuse 'high' culture, for all its objectionable privilege and anodyne harmonies, lingers on as the best that we can now do by way of political critique. Gramsci will harness culture to a resourceful new theory of power ('hegemony'), while Sartre will discover in the very act of writing a mode of freedom which implicitly rebukes Soviet as well as capitalist reality. Meanwhile, with Benjamin, Adorno and others of the Frankfurt school, a new and momentous field is delineated, that of popular culture in its structural opposition to high modernism.

Criticism, in other words, is now politics by other means, encompassing as it does questions of mass culture, literacy, popular education, power formations and forms of subjectivity as well as, more narrowly, the artistic text. But if this third wave of Marxist criticism can best be dubbed *ideological*, it is because its theoretical strengths lie above all in exploring what might be called the *ideology of form*, and so avoiding at once a mere formalism of the literary work and a vulgar sociologism of it. The wager here is that it is possible to find the material history which produces a work of art somehow inscribed in its very texture and structure, in the shape of its sentences or its play of narrative viewpoints, in its choice of a metrical scheme or its rhetorical devices. So it is that Lukács will trace the bourgeoisie's loss of historical direction in the disintegration of its narrative methods, or Walter Benjamin will detect the invisible presence of the Parisian crowd in the very perceptual strategies of Baudelaire's poetry. Lucien Goldmann will unearth from the work of Racine and Pascal an abiding structure of categories which binds them to the fortunes of an ousted social class, while Theodor Adorno detects in the conflictive, fragmentary nature of the modernist work of art an ultimately self-thwarting attempt to hold out against the miseries of ideological closure and economic commodification.

This studied avoidance of mere 'content analysis' reaches a point of self-parody in the work of the Althusserian critic Pierre Macherey, for whom what a literary work does *not* say – its eloquent silences, significant elisions, half-muttered ambiguities – are far more revealing of its relation to social ideologies than anything it may happen to utter. All of this intense preoccupation with literary form is not much remembered about Marxist criticism by its political opponents, who find it on the whole more convenient to believe that Marxist critics are only bothered about whether the author was progressive or reactionary, how many copies the novel sold and whether it mentions the working class. It is as though one were to judge the rich inheritance of psychoanalytic criticism by its speculations about phallic symbolism. Critics of Marxism still regularly accuse Marxist critics of paying scant attention to the 'words on the page' in their rush to read some ulterior political meaning into them. They cannot have read Trotsky's *Literature and Revolution*, Adorno's literary essays, Bakhtin's reflections on Dostoevsky, Benjamin's work on Baudelaire, Della Volpe's Marxist-semiotic studies of poetry, Sartre's writings on Flaubert, Fredric Jameson on Balzac or Conrad, or a host of similar studies. In general, the charge that Marxist criticism deals for the most part in unwieldy generalities is quite insupportable. And it is worth remembering in any case that not to attend to a work's historical range of reference is hardly to do justice to the 'words on the page'.

'Ideological' criticism has busied itself in the main with the relation between literary works and forms of social consciousness. It has also involved some subtle epistemological reflections: is art reflection, displacement, projection, refraction, transformation, reproduction, production? Is it an embodiment of social ideology or a critique of it? Or does it, as the Althusserians thought, critically 'distantiate' that ideology while remaining caught up in its logic?

Would a 'revolutionary' artwork be one which had risen above ideology altogether, or one which transformed its readers' relations to that ideology? And which of the twenty different meanings of the term 'ideology' is at stake here? These and parallel questions have been the occasion for some of the most *intellectually* resourceful work in Marxist criticism; but it has not on the whole been the most *politically* productive. Indeed one might almost risk the formulation that the theoretical strengths of Marxist criticism have been more or less proportionate to its political weaknesses. The claim requires instant qualification: it is hardly true of the Left Front in Art, André Breton, Bertolt Brecht, Christopher Caudwell. But it remains true that much of the best Marxist criticism has been the product of a cultural displacement occasioned by political deadlock. Georg Lukács's turning from direct political engagement to literary criticism, under the shadow of Stalinism, is an exemplary moment here, as are Gramsci's reflections on language and philosophy in a fascist prison cell, or Benjamin's esoteric researches on Baudelaire in political exile. The fluctuating interests of the Frankfurt school, as it veers from the political-economic to the cultural-philosophical during the long freeze of fascism, world war and cold war, is another case in point. And the Althusserian concern for culture springs from a belief in the 'relative autonomy' of such areas which forms part of a critique of a repressive Marxist orthodoxy. It may well be, then, by a choice historical irony, that one effect of political downturn for the left was to wonderfully concentrate the critical mind, or at least to creatively deflect it.

Yet this deflection was not without its penalties. It is hard to concern yourself with ideologies, even from a materialist standpoint, without slipping unconsciously into the idealist faith that ideas are what finally count. It is a fallacy to which academics, even radical ones, are an easy prey by virtue of their profession; and part of what we observe happening in this third great wave of Marxist critical writing, roughly from Lukács's studies of the novel to, say, the contemporary work of a Williams or a Jameson, is the steady academicization of what for Trotsky, Breton, Caudwell and Brecht had been a mode of political intervention. This is not a cheap gibe at 'armchair Marxists': it is not the fault of the left that it has been deprived of political outlets, and it is preferable for radical ideas to survive in an armchair than to go under altogether. Part of the task of socialist intellectuals is to preserve precious traditions, which is for the most part more a matter of reflection than of action. Even so, the intellectual apogee of Marxist criticism corresponded with a certain political declension, and a preoccupation with 'marginal' areas like literature and philosophy reflected in part the social marginality of radical thinkers themselves. Marxist criticism was now an isolated theoretical enquiry rather than part of a political or institutional process, a fact which reflected the dwindling of a left 'public sphere' in society as a whole.

There had always been, however, a counter-movement to this trend, one which constitutes our fourth, *economic* (the term is grossly inadequate) dimension of Marxist criticism. Unlike the previous currents, this one is much harder to periodize: it has cropped up in one guise or another throughout the history of Marxist cultural theory, weaving its way in and out of other kinds of approach. Its topic is what might be called *modes of cultural production*: its primary concern is neither with the concrete literary work, nor with the abstractions of a social fomation, but with that whole intermediary space which is the material apparatuses of cultural production, all the way from theatres and printing presses to literary coteries and institutions of patronage, from rehearsing and reviewing to the social context of producers and recipients. Described in this way, the area is hard to distinguish from the so-called sociology of literature, and indeed is often distinctive only by virtue of its political assumptions and anti-empiricist methods. As with any major shift of theoretical interest, this one had its material conditions: the fact that what was emerging from the high-modernist period onwards, but at greatly accelerated speed in the post-war decades, was a new form of culture whose material apparatuses (film, radio, television, sound recording) were not only the most striking and novel thing about them, but had as media of communication an obvious and intimate relation to their 'content'. Much the same might be said about books, which are of course quite as much material media, social institutions and nodes of social relations as television; but all of this had been long since 'naturalized', as we came to stare through the stubborn material fact of a book to its etherial sense, no longer intrigued by the mystery of how these little black marks on the page could actually be meanings. It was then as though modern cultural technology violently estranged these familiar perceptions, forcing us once again to register the way a particular medium generates specific sorts of meanings, confronting us once more with the social or collective nature of a long-privatized 'art' in the form of (say) cinema audiences, and making dramatically clear the interpenetration between these cultural institutions and the power of capital itself. In other words, one no longer had to argue so strenuously for the material nature of culture when it leapt out at you on the flick of a switch, or for its economic basis when it came wrapped in advertising.

Much of this was already obvious to the early revolutionary avant-garde, the Futurists, Constructivists and Surrealists who recognized that a revolutionary culture could not consist of pumping different materials down the same channels but meant a transformation in the means of communication themselves. Brecht's so-called epic theatre is an inheritor of this lineage, and its major theorist is his colleague Walter Benjamin, not least in his seminal essay 'The Author as Producer'. In Britain, it was a form of criticism already adumbrated in the early 1960s in Raymond Williams's *The Long Revolution*, a work which can now be seen as laying the ground for what the later Williams will come to describe as 'cultural materialism'. The phrase offers to resolve the paradox we have touched on before – that culture for Marxism is at once central and secondary. On the one hand, culture is no more than a sector of the wider field of materialism in general; on the other hand, by being thus 'materialized', it comes to assume a force and reality of which aesthetic idealism had deprived it. What is now at stake, in other words, is not just an alternative reading of literary works but a materialist re-reading of the culture of which they are part; and this allows the 'economic' approach to art to draw together something of the other procedures we have outlined. For cultural materialism depends to some extent on certain broader 'anthropological' categories of labour, production, communication and so on; it examines the relations between material media and meaning, and thus learns from the formal concerns of ideological criticism; and by carrying materialism directly, so to speak, into enemy territory – into a 'culture' which was constructed as idealist in the first place, and which figures for its apologists as the last bastion of 'spirit' in a degraded world – it lends Marxist criticism a keener political edge. Nobody is much bothered by materialist readings of *Titus Andronicus*, or indeed by materialist theories of politics and economics, where one would expect such views to be relevant; but a materialist theory of culture – a theory of culture as production before it is expression – sounds, in the spontaneously idealist milieu of middle-class society, something of a category mistake or a contradiction in terms.

We may return, finally, to where we began – with the perilous future of Marxism itself. What would the 'death of Marxism' actually mean? For Marxism is as inseparable from modern civilization as Darwinism or Freudianism, as much part of our 'historical unconscious' as Newton was for the Enlightenment. One does not need to *agree* with all or even most of the doctrines of Newton or Freud to accept their utter centrality to modernity. So it is difficult to see how Marxism could simply 'die' without modernity dying too, which of course is what postmodernism exists to proclaim. If postmodernism is right – if modernity is effectively over – then Marxism is most certainly superannuated along with it. If, however, we are still struggling within the contradictions of modernity, and if it will not be over until we resolve them, and if its regular obituary notices have thus been greatly exaggerated, then Marxism remains as relevant as it ever was, which is not the same as claiming it as true. The 'end of modernity' is in any case a performative act masquerading as a constative proposition: who precisely wants to call off modernity, who has the title to do so, who is blowing the whistle on it for what purposes? Is the 'end of modernity' just a cryptic way of announcing that its contradictions have turned out to be insoluble, and that we therefore might as well move on to something else? Who precisely has the privilege to make this move, and who does not?

If postmodernism is right, then Marxism is wrong – *pace* those brands of postmodern Marxism which bear about the same relation to the classical tradition as guitar-toting vicars do to the Desert Fathers. But in another sense the proposition is misleading. For it is not as though one is being asked to choose between Marx and, say, Lyotard or Baudrillard. The very idea of such a choice involves, for a Marxist at least, a grotesque kind of category mistake, as though one were being asked to choose between a turkey sandwich and the concept of entropy. Marxism is not the body of work of an individual; it belongs to a much wider movement, that of socialism, which has in its time involved some millions of men and women across the nations and the centuries, a movement to which many have devoted themselves with impressive courage and for which some of them have been occasionally prepared to die. The practical transformations socialism envisages – the production of a new kind of human being who would find violence and exploitation abhorrent – would no doubt take several centuries to complete, though certain other vital changes would need to be carried through in a much shorter period. However much one might admire the ideas of Lyotard or Baudrillard, one is discussing an essentially different kind of reality, as only intellectuals could fail to realize.

It is surely not enough, however, that Marxism should survive only as part of our historical unconscious. For it is clear that capital is incapable of solving the human suffering it causes, and that its early emancipatory promise has long been exhausted. As more and more pre- or non-capitalist societies are drawn inexorably into its wake, the social devastation which ensues will make socialism more urgent and relevant a proposal than ever. The role that the specifically Marxist tradition might play in that broader project cannot be determined in advance. But the materials in this book alone reveal a wisdom, insight and imaginative flair which it is not only hard to see being simply written off, but which will surely play its part in any future change.

NOTES

1 Francis Mulhern (ed.), *Contemporary Marxist Literary Criticism* (London: Longman, 1992), 22.
2 See Perry Anderson, *Considerations on Western Marxism* (London: Verso, 1979).

Introduction Part II: Reading Marxist Literary Theory

Drew Milne

Like Marxism, literature and literary criticism are also in crisis. This crisis reflects capitalism's capacity to melt all that seems solid into air, a capacity which dissolves spiritual and utilitarian claims for the values of literature into hot air. Capitalism is the most developed and contradictory mode of production. Liberating vast human potential while enslaving the world to a logic of capital divorced from human interests, capitalism creates profound socio-economic and ecological problems. The crisis of capitalism's permanent revolution is, if anything, as severe as that facing Marxism. In such conditions of antagonism, arguments about Marxism are notoriously contentious, particularly within Marxism. The other terms in the title of this book are also contentious, not least the status of 'a reader' as an anthology which invites the participation of different readers in new social networks. This anthology offers a resource for different readers to enable new ways of reading Marxism, literature, theory and the social possibilities of writing. How might these new ways of reading be approached?

The death of literature as a significant social form has been predicted since Hegel, even before widespread literacy was a significant social force. As Raymond Williams observed, whatever the glories of six centuries of English literature, we have had barely two centuries of English literacy. The struggle to socialize this contradiction is central to the struggle for socialism. Within the secular world of modernity, however, expressive social forms are continually made over into forms whose ideal is the triumph of capital over any language which resists financial exchange. New media and information technology also make the continuing relevance of literature increasingly precarious. Despite the widespread development of access to writing, notably through printing technology, the emancipatory potential of literature is engulfed by a global culture industry which reads such potential as a currency of information to be rendered unto capital. Class conflict often takes the form of a struggle for power over such different forms of literacy and literature, from tablets of stone to the microchip.

One form of this struggle is the attempt to silence the conceptions of writing developed by Marxism, whose death, like that of literature, has been foretold for as long as Marxism has haunted the capitalist imaginary. The struggle to become writers of our own worlds, rather than readers of a capitalist script whose hieroglyphic form is the money sign, is central to the emancipatory aims of Marxism. This struggle, however, is continually marginalized by the struggle to create material conditions for writing as something more than imaginative potential. Marxism tries to offer a critique of the ideological distortion of human interests, recognizing the relation between civilization and barbarity in literature, but without simply mirroring the current system of production. As such, Marxism threatens to become merely critical criticism, a negative expression of capitalism which affirms the illusions of culture, rather than a social praxis of freedom in culture and freedom from culture.

Marxism has also been at the centre of debates in literary theory for almost a century. It offers sustained and differentiated engagements with literature, and that against which most other forms of literary theory have defined themselves. The struggles for hegemony between Marxism, formalism and what became known as New Criticism were particularly intense in the period after the Russian Revolution through to the economic depression of the 1930s.[1] Raymond Williams suggests that the disconnected positions of the Bloomsbury class fraction in effect defined themselves as alternatives to a general theory of the kind articulated by Marxism.[2] Such resistances to Marxism have been of profound ideological significance, especially in English and American culture. From the 1930s onwards, traditions of thought associated with existentialism, structuralism, psychoanalysis, feminism, post-structuralism and postcolonial theory have all developed through critical dialogues with Marxism. Such traditions have borrowed from Marxism, defining themselves either through reductive critiques or without making antagonisms explicit. The significance of Marxism in such ideological formations is not just that it challenges the eclectic hegemony of ruling-class ideas. Marxism also provides anti-Marxists with a structure of resistance for the vacuum at the centre of divided intellectual labours, a vacuum which lacks positive beliefs or a coherent general ideology. To fill the absence of viable theodicy with which to defend capitalism, Marxism has been used as that against which ideological legitimation defines itself. This structure of negativity often does not directly engage with or refute Marxism, but uses Marxism as a political scarecrow. Such structural negativities in the legitimation crises of capitalism were particularly evident during the cold war. The implicit history of these antagonistic negativities means that Marxism is significant for literary theory, whether Marxist or anti-Marxist.

Literary theory itself marks a tension between resistances to theory – the value of literature seen as its autonomy from other forms of writing; and theoretical resistances to literature – the subsumption of literature within broader conceptions of writing or other cultural media. Indeed, literary theory is often only a euphemism for critical theory. This anthology, however, offers Marxist writings with an evident relation to literature and the analysis of writing. Preference is given to theories which develop specifically Marxist conceptions, such as the determining status of the forces and relations of production and the historical centrality of class struggle. Within the available space many approaches with Marxist affinities are not represented, either because similar theories are articulated elsewhere in the anthology, or, more contentiously, because Marxist theory is often not evident in writing by avowed Marxists save as a political or materialist orientation. A stress on theoretical contributions also limits presentation of the more empirical and historical work needed to substantiate different theories.

Marxism is, however, a revolutionary theory of the practice of social and political transformation. Implicit in this anthology is the attempt to discern what has been historically significant in Marxist literary theory, but also what might remain relevant for the theory and practice of socialism. In a cruel turn on Marx's thesis on Feuerbach, it would seem that Marxists have thus far failed to change the world: the point now is to interpret this failure.

Central to such interpretation is the relation between Marx's writing and Marxism. Marx shares with Freud the historically distinct status of being what Michel Foucault calls a founder of discursivity.[3] As Foucault suggests, Marx is an author whose writing establishes open possibilities of discourse, possibilities which go beyond any simple causal relation to Marx as their origin, but which nevertheless refer back to Marx. As with Freud, the extent to which Marx might be critical of those who claim his name and authority is itself part of the creative range of contested influence generated by his work. Engels reports in a letter that even when Marx was alive he used to say, 'All I know is that I am not a Marxist.'[4] *Capital* has not been widely or carefully read, even by professed Marxists, and much of Marx's work was not published or translated until long after his death. Nevertheless, Marxism is in part a struggle between readings of Marx and attempts to interpret and change the world. The problem of reading Marx is then central to Marxism, and a problem not just for Marxists, but for any attempt to understand the power of writing. Trying to understand the production and reception of Marx's writing suggests that a literary theory of Marxism and a fully developed mode of Marxist literary theory may have more than a family resemblance. The reception of Marx's writing could be seen as a problem with which to test the explanatory power of any literary theory. Indeed, the difference between a Marxist theory of Marx and a literary theory which could provide a critical account of the history of Marx and Marxism may be immaterial.

An aspiring poet in his youth, Marx maintained literary ambitions for the quality of his writing throughout his life, in journalism, political polemic or the more scientific mode of critique. Committed to writing as both a mode of reason with practical purpose and a pleasurable means of human liberation, Marx was an admirer of Shakespeare, a friend of Heinrich Heine, and planned, according to Paul Lafargue's reminiscences of Marx, to write a critique of Balzac's *La Comédie humaine* once he finished his economic studies. But if literary quality is not an optional varnish on the serious business of prose, what is the place of literature in Marxism? As S. S. Prawer has shown, Marx's work is immersed in literature.[5] Nevertheless, his writing on literature is fragmented and only suggestive in the context of readings of Marx's work as a whole. On the one hand, then, theories of how to read Marx are integral to most forms of Marxism. On the other hand, Marxist theories of literature bear little relation to Marx's tantalizingly brief comments on literature. Thus Marxism has generated literary theories whose sympathy with Marx needs careful analysis, while also being a discourse of modernity whose literary status and reception requires similarly careful analysis.

With regard to the simultaneous production and reception of Marxism as a way of reading Marx and the world, there are analogies in the reinvention of the authority of texts such as the Koran or Shakespeare. Religions seek to mediate between new historical situations, vernacular translations, authorized or otherwise, and the laws of founding texts. Shakespeare's plays exist in a struggle between the possibility of new performances and attempts to stabilize an authorized version of Shakespeare. Literary texts such as the Bible, *Pilgrim's Progress* and *Paradise Lost* can be refigured in radical traditions, as E. P. Thompson suggests in *The Making of the English Working Class* (1963); or refashioned in critical public spheres of the kind described by Jürgen Habermas in *The Structural Transformation of the Public Sphere* (1962). But Marxism attempts new relations between theory, writing and social praxis, relations in which successful revolutionary transformations would render Marxism itself redundant, part of a prehistory it helped to overcome. Marx authorizes a socialist reading of his work such that new situations necessarily rewrite its significance. And Marx continues to indicate horizons for discourses which seek to go beyond Marx, partly because Marx offers one of the few theoretical and historical perspectives whose practical problems cannot be assigned to an intellectual pigeon-hole, and partly because his modes of critical reading are exemplary.

Marxism, then, exists in a dialectical movement between historical challenges to Marx's terms and theories and new forms of thinking which claim Marx's authority. As with Freud, sects and parties compete for copyright on the living testament, a struggle embodied in the disintegration of the First, Second, Third and Fourth Internationals. Some major Marxist theoreticians, notably Lukács, Gramsci and Althusser, have sought to transform Marxist parties from within through revisionary readings of Marx. For some time now, however, Marxism has also informed intellectual traditions and autonomous socialist groupings with a shared theoretical orientation which is critical of orthodox Marxism and Communist Party ideology. This more dispersed theoretical orientation offers modes of Marxism which articulate themselves less in relation to Marxist parties than to academic or intellectual theory. Such modes might be called neo-Marxist, but the revisionary and often defeatist impetus in such readings of Marx and Marxism may be so tenuous as to suggest the end of the discourse founded by Marx, or at least the end of personality cults of Marx. Indeed, it is incongruous that the historical and collective struggle for socialism should invest so much authority in one man. This returns us to the problem of a literary theory of Marxism, a problem sharpened by reflecting on Stalin, Stalinism and the relation between theory and practice.

To what extent does the way Marxism reads Marx reflect Marx's own methods of reading and writing? A feature of the struggle between orthodox and revisionist Marxist traditions – a struggle aptly pickled in the pejorative use of the term 'vulgar' – is the way readings of Marx have been demonstrably reductive, with positions and propositions quoted schematically, and without recognition of the processes of critical reading in Marx's own work. From his early critiques of Hegel, Marx explores arguments in an immanent process of critical exposition. The quantity of detailed criticisms in texts such as *The Holy Family*, *The German Ideology* and *Theories of Surplus Value* develops into the more integrated quality of argument in *Capital*. As such, Marx's method of critique is exemplary for literary-critical reading as a necessary component of intellectual labour, combining the close reading of details, an acute sense of historical context and an ability to conceptualize and co-ordinate general theories. Rather than scattered intimations of a Marxist aesthetic, it is the way Marx's work embodies both critique and criticism which makes Marx's work important for critical theory and for specifically literary criticism. 'The Critique of the Gotha Programme' reveals Marx's skill in reading the ambiguous structure of complex words such as 'labour', exemplifying the merits of so-called practical criticism with more obviously practical intent. Indeed, Marx develops close reading as a theoretical resistance to the inflationary rhetoric of theory itself, often to devastating effect in the dialectics of chiasmic reversal, as in *The Poverty of Philosophy*, Marx's answer to Proudhon's *Philosophy of Poverty*. As such, Marx's work understands theory through critique and historical materialism rather than as a transcendent rhetoric of abstraction.

Marx's most sustained combination of detailed criticism, immanent exposition and integrated theory is in *Capital*, but *Capital* has rarely been read with Marx's own methods of critique. More commonly, general theories are abstracted by reducing the dialectical dynamic of *Capital* to stable positions or propositions. The texts posing the most significant problems in Marxist debates are often those which are easily quoted and lend themselves to dogmatic reproduction. One such text is the 'Preface' to *A Contribution to the Critique of Political Economy*, which contains Marx's most quoted summary of the materialist conception of history:

> With the change of the economic foundations the entire immense superstructure is more or less rapidly transformed. In considering such transformations a distinction should always be made between the material transformation of the economic conditions of production, which can be determined with the precision of natural science, and the legal, political, religious, aesthetic, or philosophic – in short, ideological forms in which men become conscious of this conflict and fight it out.[6]

The way this much debated formulation is read is decisive for Marxist literary theory, not least because Marx's distinction between base and superstructure does not of itself explain *how* the distinction is to be made, or how base and superstructure mutually determine each other. The distinction is metaphorical. Marx himself does not isolate the terms as static categories but analyses their dialectical interrelation. As Jameson suggests in *Late Marxism*:

> we must initially separate the figuration of the terms base and superstructure – only the initial shape of the problem – from the type of efficacity or causal law it is supposed to imply. *Uberbau* and *Basis*, for example, which so often suggest to people a house and its foundations, seem in fact to have been railroad terminology and to have designated the rolling stock and the rails respectively, something which suddenly jolts us into a rather different picture of ideology and its effects.[7]

Most accounts of the base/superstructure metaphor have proceeded, however, as though the distinction were more self-evident and could be determined with the precision of a science, natural or otherwise, rather than as a problem of how we become conscious of the ideological figuration of conflict. The opposition of science and ideology – with law, politics, religion, art and philosophy lined up on the side of ideology – is similarly ambiguous in Marx's formulation, but has been dogmatically deployed as if Marxism were scientific and all other discourses ideological. The possibility of a science of textuality has often tempted Marxist criticism, just as Marx's own work claims scientific authority for a new conception of human and socialized science. This tension runs through the various understandings of writing offered in this anthology, and is especially marked in conflicting accounts of the value of literature.

Hegelian Marxists seek to understand literature as an illusory but cognitive mode akin to the ideology of religion. As such, literature is an opiate of the people which expresses and protests against reality. The ideological power of religion is understood as being secularized in the authority of literature as part of the fetishized culture of commodities. However self-estranged, literature has a certain truth-value in such understandings. Thus Marx, Lenin and Lukács recognized the value of literary realism in writers such as Shakespeare, Tolstoy and Balzac as dramatic or fictional ways of mirroring and reflecting the world. By contrast, anti-Hegelian Marxists offer more positivist accounts of literature as a distorted ideology of the practice of writing. As such, literature is no more inherently significant or illuminating than any other signifying practice. Marxists in this tradition have often placed literature within accounts of the sociology of culture or semiotic analysis. The contrast here is between the canons of imaginative potential represented by literature and the ideological illegitimacy of the privileged status of literature as it has been deployed and developed by the ruling class. The complexity of this contrast can be traced through the work of Raymond Williams, who sought to broaden the understanding of writing within culture, and yet continued to use literature as a privileged mode of access to social understanding. This difficulty is encapsulated in Williams's concept of structures of feeling and his critique of 'literature' in the chapter in this anthology excerpted from *Marxism and Literature* (1977). Ultimately there is no clear epistemological break between Hegelian, dialectical or humanist types of Marxism and more Leninist, materialist or scientific types of Marxism, despite the claims of Althusserians criticized by E. P. Thompson in *The Poverty of Theory* (1978). What is significant, however, is that different conceptions of the ideology of literature produce different types of argument.

For some Marxists the quality of realism in literary representation, whether understood as an expression, reflection or reproduction of critical responses to reality, means that literature continues to have an aesthetic truth content, however distorted. For other Marxists it has no such truth. Critique and historical analysis can be directed to the production or to the reception of literature. Literature can be read as a way of understanding the past or as a way of rewriting the present. It can be seen as a human resource which speaks of resistances to the alienation and reification of human labour. Or it can be figured as the ideological legitimation of such alienation and reification. Some theories stress formal or aesthetic qualities, while others stress the material and educational dissemination of literature. The struggle for social articulacy links these different approaches, but often the relation between literacy and literature is torn between the attempt to salvage the aesthetics of ideology and the complete rejection of the ideology of the aesthetic. These conflicting approaches need to be traced back to the ambiguous productivity of Marx's understanding of science and ideology, and forward to modern literary study.

Marx's 'Theses on Feuerbach' have also been deployed in the discourse of Marxism with scant regard for what it would mean to deploy quotations critically or to construe appropriate contexts for interpretation. Written in a condensed aphoristic form, the 'Theses on Feuerbach' were not intended for publication but have been treated as propositions to be deployed like magic wands. Marx's claim in the second thesis – 'The question whether objective truth can be attributed to human thinking is not a question of theory but is a *practical question*' – sits uneasily next to claims for the scientific status of Marx's theory. A conception of ideology which denies the objective status of true and false consciousness can hardly claim a scientific status for its own capacity to offer true representations of reality. Some account is needed of the quality of representation in discourse, writing and ideology, a problem for which literature is central.[8] Marx's account of the secular basis of religion has encouraged Marxists to reduce religion and other forms of spirit, such as literature and culture, to the status of mere practices but without articulating why certain practices, such as Marxism itself, are more ideologically significant than other practices. Even if Marxism aspires to applicability, the objective truth of Marxist theory is a practical question which requires theoretical reflection. The 'Theses on Feuerbach' also deploy an opposition between materialism and idealism often used to legitimate dogmatic Marxist polemics against philosophy, such as Lenin's *Materialism and Empirio-criticism* (1908), a text Althusser tried in vain to salvage.[9]

A further problem suggested by reading Marx is the way Marx's comments about turning Hegel on his head have been taken as gospel for leaps into new modes of unreflective epistemology.[10] Adorno suggests rethinking Marx's relation to Hegel's *Phenomenology of Spirit* by considering *Capital* as the phenomenology of anti-spirit. Accordingly, inversion involves not just opposition, but a dialectical critique developed through the whole argument and exposition. As such, Hegel's account of spirit is understood, sublated and reconfigured as the logic of capital. Accordingly, Marx's mode of critique would reveal the mistake of reducing understanding to isolated positions and propositions, rather than understanding the struggle between different traditions of thought in the dialectics of reading. Particular metaphors are especially vulnerable to such isolation. To do justice to Marx, Marxist literary theory would involve immanent critique as the dynamic rearticulation of figures and claims, rather than the isolation of particulars or the abstract use of critical categories. To judge a writer against a given schema or class origin as being idealist, bourgeois or racist – or alternatively as materialist, progressive or transgressive – may serve as polemical shorthand. But this amounts to a reductive mode of judgement if taken as the end of the analysis, hence the importance of the way Marx and Engels read Balzac against the grain of his class allegiances and political beliefs.

Further readings of Marx can be developed to criticize the use of static categories in Marxism. Key oppositions, such as base/superstructure, science/ideology, theory/practice, idealism/materialism, could be extended to include the opposition between use-value and exchange-value central to

Marx's critique of political economy and the labour theory of value. Indeed the history of Marxism could be deconstructed as the attempt to keep such oppositions in play, as dynamic and dialectical terms of analysis rather than as a crude catechism. As Marx suggests, however, such oppositions do not produce history and historical discourse, but are rather the ideological figures through which social and class struggles becomes conscious.

Perhaps the most significant problem for Marxist literary theory, then, is to theorize the way particular conceptual and rhetorical figures function as units of ideology. Such units might be called ideologemes, as Vološinov suggests, and understood as ways in which discourse mediates social relations. The struggle over particular terms both determines and is determined by social relations, such that particular words or tropes are figured as litmus tests of class conflict. In the history of poetic theory, class struggle has often been articulated through the ideologemes of different metres, from classical metres to free verse, as forms which reflect and shape different class registers and experiences. In modern literary theory a significant ideologeme is the term 'post-'. 'Post' appears in numerous novelty compound terms as an empty signifier which marks the site of ideological conflicts. Major paradigm shifts attempt to become hegemonic through the strategic dissemination of this prefix. 'Post-' paralyses debate around the significance of the term to which the prefix is added, often without respecting the complexity of the existing term: post-modernism, post-structuralism, post-colonial theory, post-feminism, post-Marxism, and co. The need to debate the prefix merely compounds the abstract relation to existing social formations, forcing opponents of the critiques left implicit in such hegemonic discourses into ever more reductive arguments about the labels used to control debate. The term 'Marxist' also functions as a badge of honour and abuse which holds debate within the ideologeme rather than enabling discussion. Much of the terminology in Marx's writing, however, is not invented by Marx but reworked through critique and dialectical exposition. A similar approach to critical jargon might guard against the industrial production of academic discourse offering novelty wares for the conspicuous consumption of thought.

The way Marxism has read Marx through crudely formulated structural oppositions suggests that more sophisticated methods of reading are necessary if Marxism is to determine its own mediation. Marx's writings may be too suggestive or indeterminate to resist the abuses of selective quotation. A Marxist reading of Marx needs to show how specific contradictions and polemical strains in Marx's writing might enable such abuses. In short, literary theory, Marxist or anti-Marxist, needs to determine the extent to which Marx's writings have determined their reception or have been mediated by the productive forces determining this reception. Was Stalinism implicit in Marx's writing, or the consequence of the overdetermination of Soviet Russia by its pre-capitalist history and the isolation of socialism within a state mediated by global capitalism? Given the authority accorded to writing by Marx and Lenin, how might we now read not just Marx but Stalin? Would a deconstruction of Lenin's final testament make any difference? A fully developed critique of Marxism would necessarily reveal reflexive affinities between Marxist literary theory and a literary theory of Marxism.

To develop such reflexive affinities is to trace these problems through the highly abbreviated history of Marxist literary theory offered in this anthology. Introductory notes provide indications of the contexts from which each essay or article has been taken and suggestions for further reading. To articulate broader contexts of analysis is more difficult. It is possible, for example, to trace the attenuation of explicit affiliation to Marxist parties in the writing presented in this anthology, a development also evident in increasingly specialized registers of address. This might be defended as the growing sophistication and reflexivity of Marxist literary theory. But it might also mark a developing gulf between the speech and writing of the working class and that of Marxists. The idea of a 'common reader' is part of the ideology of literature in bourgeois society, since the terms of access and ownership with regard to what is held in common reflect the political and economic conditions which Marxism seeks to criticize. Students confronted with Marxism for the first time often express disbelief that the language of Marxism should be so inaccessible, without reflecting on the extent to which they have been denied access to this language by processes of education and by what Chomsky has called the manufacture of consent by the media.

Nevertheless, Marxism needs to articulate itself beyond the terms dictated by the combination of market forces in the culture industry and the mystified rhetorics of power deployed within academic divisions of intellectual labour. This difficulty has led some socialists, such as Orwell, to insist on plain speaking while at the same time falling foul of the abuses of simplistic terms in newspeak. But norms of 'standard' language invariably reflect the exclusion of the majority of existing language communities from such norms. This is often evident in the apostrophes used to represent the supposed abnormality of working-class speech. Such modes of representation reflect class struggle and express different relations both between speech and writing, and between class identity and cultural capital.

Important consequences follow from how we understand the contradictory levels of access to literacy and literature, and the value of more or less literary modes of expression. Some Marxists seek to redeem bourgeois culture by making it available in new ways, while others seek to redeem aspects of culture denigrated by the bourgeoisie, such as popular song. The meaning of 'popular', however, needs to be analysed with regard to whether popularity is an expression of different forms of social articulacy or whether it is the product of mass marketing in which individuals are constructed as 'the masses', a distinction marked in different conceptions of popular culture and mass culture.[11] The culture industry divides culture into art and mass culture, and the torn halves of such cultural divisions cannot be put back together by assuming the validity of one half in isolation. Poetry, for example, is sometimes assumed to be an elitist art form, despite its long popular history, the popularity of lyric poetry in music and the large quantity of poetry which continues to be written by the working class even if it is not published. Such profound alienations in the resources of poetry cannot easily be reconciled.

Accordingly, the attempt to forge populist and radical readings of literature is caught between the rejection of literature as an expression of social privilege, and the rejection of the very quality of articulacy which such readings might popularize. Contradictions run right through the choice of particular texts, forms and languages as sites of struggle. Texts articulate different qualities of reception, both actual and potential, according to the way their form and content might resist assimilation within the terms of bourgeois culture. Significance does not reside only in what is done with texts in their reception any more than the significance of people resides in what is done to them. Given the increasingly commodified languages of capital, and the way capital ceaselessly revolutionizes the ownership and exchange of meaning, it may no longer make sense to talk of bourgeois culture as though it existed. But literary theory which denies the articulacy of writing, whatever its context or origin, threatens to eradicate the resources for articulating different modes of production. Many modernist texts, for example, seek to liberate new ways of making reading an active process of writing which resists bourgeois culture, only to find their democratic potential assimilated or controlled by social networks of access and education. New struggles over the radical potential of information technology suggest similar contradictions in the form and content of social access.

The contradictions of radical or anti-authoritarian textuality are also reflected in the way that the populist and revolutionary intent of Marxist writing is often inaccessible without careful study. Given the complexity of capitalism as a humanly produced social system which defies individual understanding and social control, it is hardly surprising that Marxism insists on the complexity of social analysis. Reductive abuses of populist Marxism indicate that without such complexity Marxism can all too easily become an ideology of state oppression. But if Marxism cannot develop popular forms, the prospects for successful revolutionary politics are bleak.

Many Marxists have written in a range of registers and forms to bridge the gulf between specialized modes of research and enquiry and more general readerships, sometimes to the extent of writing literature rather than argumentative prose. A number of writers, from William Morris to Ngugi wa Thiong'o, have wrestled with the problem of developing popular modes of writing directly influenced by Marxism and socialist theories of literary practice. The complexity of political interventions in literature is perhaps best exemplified by the popular realism of Bertolt Brecht, whose work has inspired writers as diverse as Walter Benjamin, Roland Barthes, John Berger and Augusto Boal to develop ways of combining Marxist theory with new modes of writing, analysis and political theatre. Other Marxists have operated almost entirely within the local institutions and international markets of academic theory. One of the more startling contrasts revealed by this anthology is the way Marxists such as Lenin and Trotsky were directly engaged by the values of literature. More recent academic Marxists have been concerned with theory as such, rather than literature, or with the problems of the culture industry and media such as film, redefining literary study as the study of rhetorics in history, or as cultural materialism. Francis Mulhern suggests that the progressive components in such redefinitions are often more negligible than its rhetoric suggests, pointing out that: 'The "political" posture of radical literary studies is, at worst, a residual group mannerism.'[12]

One of the identifiable group mannerisms in supposedly radical literary studies is the meagre respect shown for the aspirations and struggles which continue to be expressed through literature, both through its history and in the continuing search for forms to articulate the voices of the oppressed. This search has been a priority in working-class cultures, feminism, black politics and other oppressed social groups. However much it remains necessary to show that there is a politics to culture, it also remains necessary to develop new forms with which to articulate cultures of resistance. The history of literature remains one of those resources which should not be surrendered to the ruling class or to the instrumental reason of communication, even if the history of literature is as much a record of civilization as it is of barbarity. An image ban on the articulation of beauty bodes ill for writing which might prefigure a better world. Nevertheless, the hopefulness of writers such as Ernst Bloch needs to be assessed in the light of the Marxist critique of utopian blueprints which block the possibility of utopia by deflecting attention from the already existing conditions for change. Marxism remains a theory of the material conditions of joy rather than a short-cut to ecstasies of literary transcendence. But writing remains one of the most transgressive and most easily exchanged cultural forms through which dissidence can be articulated, not least because the material prerequisites of pen and paper are relatively easy to acquire. The persistence of literary aspiration evident in the way millions write without necessarily thinking of material gain suggests that the idealism of creativity also harbours expressive potentials within the material conditions of everyday life. If radical literary studies are to offer more than a group mannerism they need to be able to develop these expressive resources of literacy and literature, by making the traditions of literature and Marxist literary theory available for new contexts and struggles.

Evidence of the attempt to develop Marxist literary theory in new contexts is provided by writers, of a kind that Marx and Lenin might not have recognized, seeking to bring the insights of Marxism to bear on areas such as feminism, poststructuralism, postmodernism and postcolonial theories of literature.[13] Within the global political economy and the ideologies of nationalism, patriarchy, colonization, race, ecology, religion, human rights and 'free' trade, Marxism retains its critical force as an internationalist description of the world and as a theory of how the world might be changed. And the need for new ways of reading both Marxism and literature suggests the continuing importance of Marxist literary theory for what some recent Marxists have called 'open Marxism'.[14] Perhaps the most significant components are: the critique of literature as a historical phenomenon; the critique of the reproduction and educational dissemination of 'literature'; and the critique of literature as an ideological form whose social physiognomy provides cognitive, utopian or aesthetic insights. The development of a Marxist conception of writing as a mode of representing reality and as a liberating expression of qualitative articulacy requires the renewal of all of these different and conflicting components of critique. The influence of Marxism on literary theory and the reception of Marx's work in Marxism suggests the need to develop modes of critical theory which can understand the reflexive affinities between Marxist literary theory and Marxism, between writing and social change. It may be immaterial whether such critical theory continues to be called Marxism. Nevertheless, Marx provides one of the most developed examples of a materialist dialectics of reading. And Marx's work continues to suggest critical horizons for the revolutionary transformation of a world which has yet to articulate what Marx called the poetry of the future.

NOTES

1 See Christopher Pike (ed.), *The Futurists, the Formalists and the Marxist Critique* (London: Verso, 1979); Francis Mulhern, *The Moment of 'Scrutiny'* (London: Verso, 1979); and Ernst Bloch et al., *Aesthetics and Politics* (London: NLB, 1977).

2 Raymond Williams, 'The Bloomsbury Fraction', *Problems in Materialism and Culture* (London: Verso, 1980), 148–69.

3 Michel Foucault, 'What Is an Author?', *The Foucault Reader*, ed. P. Rabinow (Harmondsworth: Penguin, 1984), 101–20.

4 Karl Marx and Frederick Engels, *Selected Correspondence*, trans. I. Lasker (Moscow: Progress Publishers, 1965), 415.

5 S. S. Prawer, *Karl Marx and World Literature* (Oxford: Oxford University Press, 1978); see also, K. Marx and F. Engels, *On Literature and Art* (Moscow: Progress Publishers, 1976).

6 Karl Marx, *Selected Writings*, ed. David McLellan (Oxford: Oxford University Press, 1977), 389–90.

7 F. Jameson, *Late Marxism* (London: Verso, 1990), 46.

8 Compare, for example, the accounts of the aesthetics of ideology in G. Lukács, 'Art and Objective Truth', *Writer and Critic*, trans. A. Kahn (London: Merlin, 1970), 25–60; T. W. Adorno, *Aesthetic Theory*, trans. C. Lenhardt (London: RKP, 1984); and Terry Eagleton, *The Ideology of the Aesthetic* (Oxford: Blackwell, 1990).

9 See *Lenin and Philosophy, and Other Essays*, trans. B. Brewster (London: NLB, 1971). M. Merleau-Ponty, *Adventures of the Dialectic*, trans. J. Bien (London and Evanston: Northwestern University Press, 1974), offers a salutary critique of opportunist use of materialist dialectics, for example by Trotsky. David-Hillel Ruben, *Marxism and Materialism* (Brighton: Harvester, 1979) offers some challenging reflections on this subject. The most sustained example of a Marxist dialectics of knowledge is probably T. W. Adorno, *Negative Dialectics*, trans. E. B. Ashton (London: RKP, 1973).

10 For a survey of some of the problems raised by the relationship between Marx and Hegel, see Lucio Colletti, 'Introduction' to Karl Marx, *Early Writings*, trans. R. Livingstone and G. Benton (Harmondsworth: Penguin, 1975), 7–56.

11 Such different conceptions can be traced in Raymond Williams, *Culture and Society 1780–1950* (London: Hogarth, 1958); Theodor W. Adorno, *The Culture Industry*, ed. J. M. Bernstein (London: Routledge, 1991); and John Frow, *Cultural Studies and Cultural Value* (Oxford: Oxford University Press, 1995).

12 Francis Mulhern (ed.), *Contemporary Marxist Literary Criticism* (London: Longman, 1992), 17.

13 See *Contemporary Marxist Literary Criticism*, ed. Francis Mulhern; and *Marxism and the Interpretation of Culture*, eds Cary Nelson and Lawrence Grossberg (Urbana and Chicago: University of Illinois Press, 1988). Some earlier useful anthologies include: *Marxists on Literature: An Anthology*, ed. David Craig (Harmondsworth: Penguin, 1975); *Marxism and Art*, eds Berel Lang and Forrest Williams (New York, 1972); *Marxism and Art: Essays Classic and Contemporary*, ed. Maynard Solomon (New York: Vintage, 1973); and *Weapons of Criticism: Marxism in America and the Literary Tradition*, ed. Rudich Norman (Palo Alto, California: Stanford University Press, 1976). A further helpful resource is *A Dictionary of Marxist Thought*, ed. Tom Bottomore (Oxford: Blackwell, 1983).

14 *Open Marxism*, 2 vols, eds Werner Bonefeld, Richard Gunn and Kosmas Psychopedis (London: Pluto, 1992).

1 Karl Marx and Friedrich Engels

a) Marx/Engels, 'Social Being and Social Consciousness' (1859/1845–6)
b) Marx, 'Uneven Character of Historical Development and Questions of Art' (1857–8)
c) Marx, 'Poetry of the Future' (1852)
d) Engels, 'Against Vulgar Marxism' (1890)
e) Engels, 'On Realism' (1888)*

These brief extracts from Karl Marx (1818–83) and Friedrich Engels (1820–95) provide some of the passages which have figured prominently in Marxist discussions of literature. 'Social Being and Social Consciousness' brings together two extracts, the first from Marx's 'Preface to *A Contribution to the Critique of Political Economy*', published in 1859; and a section from *The Germany Ideology*, which Marx and Engels wrote together, *circa* 1845–6, but which was not published until 1932. 'Uneven Character of Historical Development and Questions of Art' comes from the notebooks known as the *Grundrisse*, written by Marx *circa* 1857–8 but not published until 1939. 'Poetry of the Future' consists of the opening paragraphs of *The Eighteenth Brumaire* (1852) which, as Marx puts it, was written under the immediate pressure of events in 1852, partly as a polemic against superficial transhistorical analogies. 'Against Vulgar Marxism' (1890) and 'On Realism' (1888) are from letters written by Engels. These texts need to be read both in relation to the fragments collected in Marx/Engels, *On Literature and Art* (1976), and in the context of Marx and Engels, *Collected Works* (1975–). See also *Marx/Engels on Literature and Art*, edited by L. Baxandall and S. Morawski (1973). For discussions of Marx on literature see M. Lifshitz, *The Philosophy of Art of Karl Marx* (1933; trans. 1973); P. Demetz, *Marx, Engels and the Poets* (1959; trans. 1967); and S. S. Prawer, *Karl Marx and World Literature* (1976). A succinct introduction is provided by Georg Lukács, 'Marx and Engels on Aesthetics', *Writer and Critic* (1970). The complexity of debates generated by figures in Marx's writing can be sampled by comparing the discussion of passages from *The Eighteenth Brumaire* in J. Derrida, *Specters of Marx* (1993; trans. 1994) with F. Jameson, 'Marx's Purloined Letter', *New Left Review* 209 (1995).

* a) From Marx/Engels, *On Literature and Art* (London: Lawrence & Wishart, 1976), 41–4; (b) from Marx/Engels, *On Literature and Art*, 82–4; (c) from Marx, *Surveys from Exile* (Harmondsworth: Penguin, 1973), 146–9; (d) from Marx/Engels, *On Literature and Art*, 57; (e) from Marx/Engels, *On Literature and Art*, 90–2.

a) Marx and Engels, 'Social Being and Social Consciousness'

1 [from 'Preface to *A Contribution to the Critique of Political Economy*']

In the social production of their life, men enter into definite relations that are indispensable and independent of their will, relations of production which correspond to a definite stage of development of their material productive forces. The sum total of these relations of production constitutes the economic structure of society, the real foundation, on which rises a legal and political superstructure and to which correspond definite forms of social consciousness. The mode of production of material life conditions the social, political and intellectual life process in general. It is not the consciousness of men that determines their being, but, on the contrary, their social being that determines their consciousness. At a certain stage of their development, the material productive forces of society come in conflict with the existing relations of production, or – what is but a legal expression for the same thing – with the property relations within which they have been at work hitherto. From forms of development of the productive forces these relations turn into their fetters. Then begins an epoch of social revolution. With the change of the economic foundation the entire immense superstructure is more or less rapidly transformed. In considering such transformations a distinction should always be made between the material transformation of the economic conditions of production, which can be determined with the precision of natural science, and the legal, political, religious, aesthetic or philosophic – in short, ideological forms in which men become conscious of this conflict and fight it out. Just as our opinion of an individual is not based on what he thinks of himself, so can we not judge of such a period of transformation by its own consciousness; on the contrary, this consciousness must be explained rather from the contradictions of material life, from the existing conflict between the social productive forces and the relations of production. No social order ever perishes before all the productive forces for which there is room in it have developed; and new, higher relations of production never appear before the material conditions of their existence have matured in the womb of the old society itself. Therefore mankind always sets itself only such tasks as it can solve; since, looking at the matter more closely, it will always be found that the task itself arises only when the material conditions for its solution already exist or are at least in the process of formation. In broad outline Asiatic, ancient, feudal, and modern bourgeois modes of production can be designated as progressive epochs in the economic formation of society. The bourgeois relations of production are the last antagonistic form of the social process of production – antagonistic not in the sense of individual antagonism, but of one arising from the social conditions of life of the individuals; at the same time the productive forces developing in the womb of bourgeois society create the material conditions for the solution of that antagonism. This social formation brings, therefore, the prehistory of human society to a close.

2 [from *The German Ideology*]

The production of ideas, of conceptions, of consciousness, is at first directly interwoven with the material activity and the material intercourse of men – the language of real life. Conceiving, thinking, the mental intercourse of men at this stage still appear as the direct efflux of their material behaviour. The same applies to mental production as expressed in the language of the politics, laws, morality, religion, metaphysics, etc., of a people. Men are the producers of their conceptions, ideas, etc., that is, real, active men, as they are conditioned by a definite development of their productive forces and of the intercourse corresponding to these, up to its furthest forms.[1] Consciousness [*das Bewusstsein*] can never be anything else than conscious being [*das bewusste Sein*], and the being of men is their actual life-process. If in all ideology men and their relations appear upside-down as in a *camera obscura*, this phenomenon arises just as much from their historical life-process as the inversion of objects on the retina does from their physical life-process.

In direct contrast to German philosophy which descends from heaven to earth, here it is a matter of ascending from earth to heaven. That is to say, not of setting out from what men say, imagine, conceive, nor from men as narrated, thought of, imagined, conceived, in order to arrive at men in the flesh; but of setting out from real, active men, and on the basis of their real life-process demonstrating the development of the ideological reflexes and echoes of this life-process. The phantoms formed in the brains of men are also, necessarily, sublimates of their material life-process, which is empirically verifiable and bound to material premises. Morality, religion, metaphysics, and all the rest of ideology as well as the forms of consciousness corresponding to these, thus no longer retain the semblance of independence. They have no history, no development; but men, developing their material production and their material intercourse, alter, along with this their actual world, also their thinking and the products of their thinking. It is not consciousness that determines life, but life that determines consciousness. For the first manner of approach the starting-point is consciousness taken as the living individual; for the second manner of approach, which conforms to real life, it is the real living individuals themselves, and consciousness is considered solely as *their* consciousness.

This manner of approach is not devoid of premises. It starts out from the real premises and does not abandon them for a moment. Its premises are men, not in any fantastic isolation and fixity, but in their actual, empirically perceptible process of development under definite conditions. As soon as this active life-process is described, history ceases to be a collection of dead facts, as it is with the empiricists (themselves still abstract), or an imagined activity of imagined subjects, as with the idealists.

Where speculation ends, where real life starts, there consequently begins real, positive science, the expounding of the practical activity, of the practical process of development of men. Empty phrases about consciousness end, and real knowledge has to take their place. When the reality is described, a self-sufficient philosophy [*die selbständige Philosophie*] loses its medium of existence. At the best its place can only be taken by a summing-up of the most general results, abstractions which are derived from the observation of the historical development of men. These abstractions in themselves, divorced from real history, have no value whatsoever. They can only serve to facilitate the arrangement of historical material, to indicate the sequence of its separate strata. But they by no means afford a recipe or schema, as does philosophy, for neatly trimming the epochs of history. On the contrary, the difficulties begin only when one sets about the examination and arrangement of the material – whether of a past epoch or of the present – and its actual presentation.

NOTE

1 [The manuscript originally had:] Men are the producers of their conceptions, ideas, etc., and they are precisely men conditioned by the mode of production of their material life, by their material intercourse and its further development in the social and political structure.

b) Marx, 'Uneven Character of Historical Development and Questions of Art' (from *Grundrisse*)

6 *The unequal development of material production and, e.g., that of art.* The concept of progress is on the whole not to be understood in the usual abstract form. Modern art, etc. This disproportion is not as important and difficult to grasp as within concrete social relations, e.g., in education. Relations of the United States to Europe. However, the really difficult point to be discussed here is how the relations of production as legal relations take part in this uneven development. For example the relation of Roman civil law (this applies in smaller measure to criminal and constitutional law) to modern production. 7 *This conception appears to be an inevitable development.* But vindication of chance. How? (Freedom, etc., as well.) (Influence of the means of communication. World history did not always exist; history as world history is a result.) 8 *The starting-point is of course the naturally determined factors*; both subjective and objective. Tribes, races, etc.

As regards art, it is well known that some of its peaks by no means correspond to the general development of society; nor do they therefore to the material substructure, the skeleton as it were of its organization. For example the Greeks compared with modern [nations], or else Shakespeare. It is even acknowledged that certain branches of art, *e.g.*, the *epos*, can no longer be produced in their epoch-making classic form after artistic production as such has begun; in other words, that certain important creations within the compass of art are only possible at an early stage in the development of art. If this is the case with regard to different branches of art within the sphere of art itself, it is not so remarkable that this should also be the case with regard to the entire sphere of art and its relation to the general development of society. The difficulty lies only in the general formulation of these contradictions. As soon as they are reduced to specific questions they are already explained.

Let us take, for example, the relation of Greek art, and that of Shakespeare, to the present time. We know that Greek mythology is not only the arsenal of Greek art, but also its basis. Is the conception of nature and of social relations which underlies Greek imagination and therefore Greek [art] possible when there are self-acting mules, railways, locomotives and electric telegraphs? What is a Vulcan compared with Roberts and Co., Jupiter compared with the lightning conductor, and Hermes compared with the *Crédit mobilier*? All mythology subdues, controls and fashions the forces of nature in the imagination and through imagination; it disappears therefore when real control over these forces is established. What becomes of Fama side by side with Printing

House Square? Greek art presupposes Greek mythology, in other words that natural and social phenomena are already assimilated in an unintentionally artistic manner by the imagination of the people. This is the material of Greek art, not just any mythology, *i.e.*, not every unconsciously artistic assimilation of nature (here the term comprises all physical phenomena, including society); Egyptian mythology could never become the basis of or give rise to Greek art. But at any rate [it presupposes] a mythology; on no account however a social development which precludes a mythological attitude towards nature, *i.e.*, any attitude to nature which might give rise to myth; a society therefore demanding from the artist an imagination independent of mythology.

Regarded from another aspect: is Achilles possible when powder and shot have been invented? And is the *Iliad* possible at all when the printing press and even printing machines exist? Is it not inevitable that with the emergence of the press bar the singing and the telling and the muse cease, that is the conditions necessary for epic poetry disappear?

The difficulty we are confronted with is not, however, that of understanding how Greek art and epic poetry are associated with certain forms of social development. The difficulty is that they still give us aesthetic pleasure and are in certain respects regarded as a standard and unattainable ideal.

An adult cannot become a child again, or he becomes childish. But does the naïveté of the child not give him pleasure, and does not he himself endeavour to reproduce the child's veracity on a higher level? Does not the child in every epoch represent the character of the period in its natural veracity? Why should not the historical childhood of humanity, where it attained its most beautiful form, exert an eternal charm because it is a stage that will never recur? There are rude children and precocious children. Many of the ancient peoples belong to this category. The Greeks were normal children. The charm their art has for us does not conflict with the immature stage of the society in which it originated. On the contrary its charm is a consequence of this and is inseparably linked with the fact that the immature social conditions which gave rise, and which alone could give rise, to this art cannot recur.

c) Marx, 'Poetry of the Future' (from *The Eighteenth Brumaire*)

Hegel remarks somewhere that all the great events and characters of world history occur, so to speak, twice.[1] He forgot to add: the first time as tragedy, the second as farce. Caussidière in place of Danton, Louis Blanc in place of Robespierre, the Montagne of 1848–51 in place of the Montagne of 1793–5, the Nephew in place of the Uncle.[2] And we can perceive the same caricature in the circumstances, surrounding the second edition of the eighteenth Brumaire![3]

Men make their own history, but not of their own free will; not under circumstances they themselves have chosen but under the given and inherited circumstances with which they are directly confronted. The tradition of the dead generations weighs like a nightmare on the minds of the living. And, just when they appear to be engaged in the revolutionary transformation of themselves and their material surroundings, in the creation of something which does not yet exist, precisely in such epochs of revolutionary crisis they timidly conjure up the spirits of the past to help them; they borrow their names, slogans and costumes so as to stage the new world-historical scene in this venerable disguise and borrowed language. Luther put on the mask of the apostle Paul; the Revolution of 1789–1814 draped itself alternately as the Roman republic and the Roman empire; and the revolution of 1848 knew no better than to parody at some points 1789 and at others the revolutionary traditions of 1793–5. In the same way, the beginner who has learned a new language always retranslates it into his mother tongue: he can only be said to have appropriated the spirit of the new language and to be able to express himself in it freely when he can manipulate it without reference to the old, and when he forgets his original language while using the new one.

If we reflect on this process of world-historical necromancy, we see at once a salient distinction. Camille Desmoulins, Danton, Robespierre, Saint-Just and Napoleon, the heroes of the old French Revolution, as well as its parties and masses, accomplished the task of their epoch, which was the emancipation and establishment of modern *bourgeois* society, in Roman costume and with Roman slogans. The first revolutionaries smashed the feudal basis to pieces and struck off the feudal heads which had grown on it. Then came Napoleon. Within France he created the conditions which first made possible the development of free competition, the exploitation of the land by small peasant property, and the application of the unleashed productive power of the nation's industries. Beyond the borders of France he swept away feudal institutions so far as this was necessary for the provision on the European continent of an appropriate modern environment for the bourgeois society in France. Once the new social formation had been established, the antediluvian colossi disappeared along with the resurrected imitations of Rome – imitations of Brutus, Gracchus, Publicola, the tribunes, the senators, and Caesar himself. Bourgeois society in its sober reality had created its true interpreters and spokesmen in such people as Say,[4] Cousin,[5] Royer-Collard,[6] Benjamin Constant[7] and Guizot. The real leaders of the bourgeois army sat behind office desks while the fathead Louis XVIII served as the bourgeoisie's political head. Bourgeois society was no longer aware that the ghosts of Rome had watched over its cradle, since it was wholly absorbed in the production of wealth and the peaceful struggle of economic competition. But unheroic as bourgeois society is, it still required heroism, self-sacrifice, terror, civil war, and battles in which whole nations were engaged, to bring it into the world. And its gladiators found in the stern classical traditions of the Roman republic the ideals, art forms and self-deceptions they needed in order to hide from themselves the limited bourgeois content of their struggles and to maintain their enthusiasm at the high level appropriate to great historical tragedy. A century earlier, in the same way but at a different stage of development, Cromwell and the English people had borrowed for their bourgeois revolution the language, passions and illusions of the Old Testament. When the actual goal had been reached, when the bourgeois transformation of English society had been accomplished, Locke drove out Habakkuk.

In these revolutions, then, the resurrection of the dead served to exalt the new struggles, rather than to parody the old, to exaggerate the given task in the imagination, rather than to flee from solving it in reality, and to recover the spirit of the revolution, rather than to set its ghost walking again.

For it was only the ghost of the old revolution which walked in the years from 1848 to 1851, from Marrast, the *républicain en gants jaunes*[8] who disguised himself as old Bailly,[9] right down to the adventurer who is now hiding his commonplace and repulsive countenance beneath the iron death-mask of Napoleon.

An entire people thought it had provided itself with a more powerful motive force by means of a revolution; instead, it suddenly found itself plunged back into an already dead epoch. It was impossible to mistake this relapse into the past, for the old dates arose again, along with the old chronology, the old names, the old edicts, long abandoned to the erudition of the antiquaries, and the old minions of the law, apparently long decayed. The nation might well appear to itself to be in the same situation as that mad Englishman in Bedlam, who thought he was living in the time of the pharaohs. He moaned every day about the hard work he had to perform as a gold-digger in the Ethiopian mines, immured in his subterranean prison, by the exiguous light of a lamp fixed on his own head. The overseer of the slaves stood behind him with a long whip, and at the exits was a motley assembly of barbarian mercenaries, who had no common language and therefore understood neither the forced labourers in the mines nor each other. 'And I, a freeborn Briton,' sighed the mad Englishman, 'must bear all this to make gold for the old pharaohs.' 'To pay the debts of the Bonaparte family,' sighed the French nation. As long as he was in his right mind, the Englishman could not free himself of the obsession of making gold. As long as the French were engaged in revolution, they could not free themselves of the memory of Napoleon. The election of 10 December 1848[10] proved this. They yearned to return from the dangers of revolution to the fleshpots of Egypt, and 2 December 1851 was the answer. They have not merely acquired a caricature of the old Napoleon, they have the old Napoleon himself, in the caricature form he had to take in the middle of the nineteenth century.

The social revolution of the nineteenth century can only create its poetry from the future, not from the past. It cannot begin its own work until it has sloughed off all its superstitious regard for the past. Earlier revolutions have needed world-historical reminiscences to deaden their awareness of their own content. In order to arrive at its own content the revolution of the nineteenth century must let the dead bury their dead. Previously the phrase transcended the content; here the content transcends the phrase.

NOTES

1 It is doubtful whether Hegel ever wrote these words. This theme, which Marx elaborates on in the ensuing paragraphs, is an expansion of a number of hints thrown out by Engels in his letter to Marx of 3 December 1851. See Marx and Engels, *Selected Correspondence*, trans. I. Lasker (Moscow: Progress, 1965), 62: 'It really seems as if old Hegel in his grave were acting as World Spirit and directing history, ordaining most conscientiously that it should all be unrolled twice over, once as a great tragedy and once as a wretched farce.'

2 Louis Bonaparte was the nephew of Napoleon I.

3 Napoleon I's *coup d'état* against the Directory took place on 9 November 1799, i.e. on 18 Brumaire of the year VIII by the revolutionary calendar. Marx therefore described Louis Bonaparte's *coup* of 2 December 1851 as the second edition of the eighteenth Brumaire.

4 Jean-Baptiste Say was a French economist, who popularized the doctrines of Adam Smith in the early nineteenth century.

5 Victor Cousin was a French philosopher, appointed Minister of Education in Thiers's short-lived cabinet of 1840. He endeavoured to combine the ideas of Descartes, Hume and Kant into a system he himself described as 'eclecticism'.

6 Pierre-Paul Royer-Collard was a political theorist and politician under the Restoration and the July monarchy. He supported constitutional monarchy as, quite explicitly, the organ of bourgeois rule.

7 Benjamin Constant was a liberal writer and politician, a leading figure in the opposition of the 1820s to the rule of Charles X and the ultras.

8 Yellow-gloved republican.

9 Jean-Sylvain Bailly was a leader of the liberal and constitutionalist bourgeoisie in the first French revolution; guillotined in 1793.

10 On 10 December 1848 Louis Bonaparte was elected President of the French Republic by a large majority.

d) Engels, 'Against Vulgar Marxism'

Engels to Joseph Bloch, 21–2 Sept. 1890

According to the materialist conception of history, the *ultimately* determining factor in history is the production and reproduction of real life. Neither Marx nor I have ever asserted more than this. Hence if somebody twists this into saying that the economic factor is the *only* determining one, he transforms that proposition into a meaningless, abstract, absurd phrase. The economic situation is the basis, but the various elements of the superstructure – political forms of the class struggle and its results, such as constitutions established by the victorious class after a successful battle, etc., juridical forms, and especially the reflections of all these real struggles in the brains of the participants, political, legal, philosophical theories, religious views and their further development into systems of dogmas – also exercise their influence upon the course of the historical struggles and in many cases determine their *form* in particular. There is an interaction of all these elements in which, amid all the endless host of accidents (that is, of things and events whose inner interconnection is so remote or so impossible of proof that we can regard it as non-existent and neglect it), the economic movement is finally bound to assert itself. Otherwise the application of the theory to any period of history would be easier than the solution of a simple equation of the first degree.

e) Engels, 'On Realism'

Engels to Margaret Harkness in London, April 1888

[Rough copy]

Dear Miss Harkness,
I thank you very much for sending me your *City Girl*[1] through Messrs Vizetelly. I have read it with the greatest pleasure and avidity. It is indeed, as my friend Eichhoff your translator calls it, *ein kleines Kunstwerk*; . . .[2]
  If I have anything to criticize, it would be that perhaps, after all, the tale is not quite realistic enough. Realism, to my mind, implies, besides truth of detail, the truthful reproduction of typical characters under typical circumstances.

Now your characters are typical enough, as far as they go; but the circumstances which surround them and make them act, are not perhaps equally so. In the *City Girl* the working class figures as a passive mass, unable to help itself and not even showing (making) any attempt at striving to help itself. All attempts to drag it out of its torpid misery come from without, from above. Now if this was a correct description about 1800 or 1810, in the days of Saint-Simon and Robert Owen, it cannot appear so in 1887 to a man who for nearly fifty years has had the honour of sharing in most of the fights of the militant proletariat. The rebellious reaction of the working class against the oppressive medium which surrounds them, their attempts – convulsive, half conscious or conscious – at recovering their status as human beings, belong to history and must therefore lay claim to a place in the domain of realism.

I am far from finding fault with your not having written a point-blank socialist novel, a 'Tendenzroman',[3] as we Germans call it, to glorify the social and political views of the authors. That is not at all what I mean. The more the opinions of the author remain hidden, the better for the work of art. The realism I allude to may crop out even in spite of the author's opinions. Let me refer to an example. Balzac whom I consider a far greater master of realism than all the Zolas *passés, présents et à venir*,[4] in *La Comédie humaine* gives us a most wonderfully realistic history of French 'Society', especially of *le monde parisien*, describing, chronicle-fashion, almost year by year from 1816 to 1848 the progressive inroads of the rising bourgeoisie upon the society of nobles, that reconstituted itself after 1815 and that set up again, as far as it could, the standard of *la vieille politesse française*.[5] He describes how the last remnants of this, to him, model society gradually succumbed before the intrusion of the vulgar moneyed upstart, or were corrupted by him; how the grande dame whose conjugal infidelities were but a mode of asserting herself in perfect accordance with the way she had been disposed of in marriage, gave way to the bourgeoisie, who horned her husband for cash or cashmere; and around this central picture he groups a complete history of French Society from which, even in economic details (for instance the rearrangement of real and personal property after the Revolution) I have learned more than from all the professed historians, economists and statisticians of the period together. Well, Balzac was politically a Legitimist; his great work is a constant elegy on the irretrievable decay of good society, his sympathies are all with the class doomed to extinction. But for all that his satire is never keener, his irony never bitterer, than when he sets in motion the very men and women with whom he sympathizes most deeply – the nobles. And the only men of whom he always speaks with undisguised admiration, are his bitterest political antagonists, the republican heroes of the Cloître Saint-Méry, the men, who at that time (1830–6) were indeed the representatives of the popular masses. That Balzac thus was compelled to go against his own class sympathies and political prejudices, that he *saw* the necessity of the downfall of his favourite nobles, and described them as people deserving no better fate; and that he *saw* the real men of the future where, for the time being, they alone were to be found – that I consider one of the greatest triumphs of Realism, and one of the grandest features in old Balzac.

I must own, in your defence, that nowhere in the civilized world are the working people less actively resistant, more passively submitting to fate, more *hébétés*[6] than in the East End of London. And how do I know whether you have not had very good reasons for contenting yourself, for once, with a picture of the passive side of working-class life, reserving the active side for another work?

NOTES

1 A novel by Margaret Harkness.
2 A small work of art.
3 Problem novel.
4 Past, present and yet to come.
5 Old French refinement.
6 Bewildered.

2 V. I. Lenin

Leo Tolstoy and His Epoch (1911)[*]

After Marx, Lenin, pseudonym of Vladimir Ilich Ulyanov (1870–1924), remains the most influential political leader and theorist of Marxism. From his *Collected Works*, Lenin's most important books include *Development of Capitalism in Russia* (1899); *What Is To Be Done?* (1902); *Imperialism, the Highest Stage of Capitalism* (1916); and *State and Revolution* (1917). Evidence of Lenin's processes of reading are provided by his *Philosophical Notebooks*. Like Marx, Lenin's discussions of literature, collected in *On Literature and Art* (1967), are mostly fragmentary and occasional, with the exception of 'Party Organization and Party Literature' (1905) and his articles on Tolstoy. Lenin attempted to wrest the popular authority of Tolstoy for revolutionary purposes, reading his work as a mirror of the Russian revolution of 1905, and as an ideological camera obscura of an upside-down world. The metaphors in such models of mirroring and reflection have been much argued with regard to the relation between base and superstructure. Discussion of Lenin's approach to literature is provided by Pierre Macherey, *A Theory of Literary Production* (1966; trans. 1978), which, in the English translation, includes Lenin's articles on Tolstoy in an appendix. Macherey's approach to Lenin has affinities with Althusser's reworking of Lenin, notably in *Lenin and Philosophy* (1968; trans. 1971). Georg Lukács, *Lenin: A Study in the Unity of his Thought* (1924; trans. 1967) provides one of the most succinct and engaged introductions to Lenin's work; T. Cliff, *Lenin*, 4 vols (1975–9) provides one of the more exhaustive and engaged accounts of Lenin's life and work.

The epoch to which Leo Tolstoy belongs and which is reflected in such bold relief both in his brilliant literary works and in his teachings began after 1861 and lasted until 1905. True, Tolstoy commenced his literary career earlier and it ended later, but it was during this period, whose transitional nature gave rise to *all* the distinguishing features of Tolstoy's works and of Tolstoyism, that he fully matured both as an artist and as a thinker.

---

[*] From V. I. Lenin, *On Literature and Art* (London: Lawrence & Wishart, 1967), 64–8.

Through Levin, a character in *Anna Karenina*, Tolstoy very vividly expressed the nature of the turn in Russia's history that took place during this half-century.

> Talk about the harvest, hiring labourers, and so forth, which, as Levin knew, it was the custom to regard as something very low, . . . now seemed to Levin to be the only important thing. 'This, perhaps, was unimportant under serfdom, or is unimportant in England. In both cases the conditions are definite; but here today, when everything has been turned upside down and is only just taking shape again, the question of how these conditions will shape is the only important question in Russia,' mused Levin.

'Here in Russia everything has now been turned upside down and is only just taking shape', – it is difficult to imagine a more apt characterization of the period 1861–1905. What 'was turned upside down' is familiar, or at least well known, to every Russian. It was serfdom, and the whole of the 'old order' that went with it. What 'is just taking shape' is totally unknown, alien and incomprehensible to the broad masses of the population. Tolstoy conceived this bourgeois order which was 'only just taking shape' vaguely, in the form of a bogey-England. Truly, a bogey, because Tolstoy rejects, on principle, so to speak, any attempt to investigate the features of the social system in this 'England', the connection between this system and the domination of capital, the role played by money, the rise and development of exchange. Like the Narodniks, he refuses to see, he shuts his eyes to, and dismisses the thought that what is 'taking shape' in Russia is none other than the bourgeois system.

It is true that, if not the 'only important' question, then certainly one of the most important from the standpoint of the immediate tasks of all social and political activities in Russia in the period of 1861–1905 (and in our times, too), was that of 'what shape' this system would take, this bourgeois system that had assumed extremely varied forms in 'England', Germany, America, France, and so forth. But such a definite, concretely historical presentation of the question was something absolutely foreign to Tolstoy. He reasons in the abstract, he recognizes only the standpoint of the 'eternal' principles of morality, the eternal truths of religion, failing to realize that this standpoint is merely the ideological reflection of the old ('turned upside down') order, the feudal order, the way of the life of the Oriental peoples.

In *Lucerne* (written in 1857), Tolstoy declares that to regard 'civilization' as a boon is an 'imaginary concept' which 'destroys in human nature the instinctive, most blissful primitive need for good'. 'We have only one infallible guide,' exclaims Tolstoy, 'the Universal Spirit that permeates us'.

In *The Slavery of Our Times* (written in 1900), Tolstoy, repeating still more zealously these appeals to the Universal Spirit, declares that political economy is a 'pseudoscience' because it takes as the 'pattern' 'little England, where conditions are most exceptional', instead of taking as a pattern 'the conditions of men in the whole world throughout the whole of history'. What this 'whole world' is like is revealed to us in the article 'Progress and the Definition of Education' (1862). Tolstoy counters the opinion of the 'historians' that progress is 'a general law for mankind' by referring to 'the whole of what is known as the Orient'. 'There is no general law of human progress,' says Tolstoy, 'and this is proved by the quiescence of the Oriental peoples.'

Tolstoyism, in its real historical content, is an ideology of an Oriental, an Asiatic order. Hence the asceticism, the non-resistance to evil, the profound notes of pessimism, the conviction that 'everything is nothing, everything is a material nothing' ('The Meaning of Life', p. 52), and faith in the 'Spirit', in 'the beginning of everything', and that man, in his relation to this beginning, is merely a 'labourer . . . allotted the task of saving his own soul', etc. Tolstoy is true to this ideology in his *Kreutzer Sonata* too when he says: 'the emancipation of woman lies not in colleges and not in parliaments, but in the bedroom', and in the article written in 1862, in which he says that universities train only 'irritable, debilitated liberals' for whom 'the people have no use at all', who are 'uselessly torn from their former environment', 'find no place in life', and so forth.

Pessimism, non-resistance, appeals to the 'Spirit' constitute an ideology inevitable in an epoch when the whole of the old order 'has been turned upside down', and when the masses, who have been brought up under this old order, who imbibed with their mother's milk the principles, the habits, the traditions and beliefs of this order, do not and cannot see *what kind* of a new order is 'taking shape', *what* social forces are 'shaping' it and how, what social forces are *capable* of bringing release from the incalculable and exceptionally acute distress that is characteristic of epochs of 'upheaval'.

The period of 1862–1904 was just such a period of upheaval in Russia, a period in which before everyone's eyes the old order collapsed, never to be restored, in which the new system was only just taking shape; the social forces shaping the new system first manifested themselves on a broad, nation-wide scale, in mass public action in the most varied fields only in 1905. And the 1905 events in Russia were followed by analogous events in a number of countries in that very 'Orient' to the 'quiescence' of which Tolstoy referred in 1862. The year 1905 marked the beginning of the end of 'Oriental' quiescence. Precisely for this reason that year marked the historical end of Tolstoyism, the end of an epoch that could give rise to Tolstoy's teachings and in which they were inevitable, not as something individual, not as a caprice or a fad, but as the ideology of the conditions of life under which millions and millions actually found themselves for a certain period of time.

Tolstoy's doctrine is certainly utopian and in content is reactionary in the most precise and most profound sense of the word. But that certainly does not mean that the doctrine was not socialistic or that it did not contain critical elements capable of providing valuable material for the enlightenment of the advanced classes.

There are various kinds of socialism. In all countries where the capitalist mode of production prevails there is the socialism which expresses the ideology of the class that is going to take the place of the bourgeoisie; and there is the socialism that expresses the ideology of the classes that are going to be replaced by the bourgeoisie. Feudal socialism, for example, is socialism of the latter type, and the nature of *this* socialism was appraised long ago, over sixty years ago, by Marx, simultaneously with his appraisal of other types of socialism.

Furthermore, critical elements are inherent in Tolstoy's utopian doctrine, just as they are inherent in many utopian systems. But we must not forget Marx's profound observation to the effect that the value of critical elements in utopian socialism 'bears an inverse relation to historical development'. The more the activities of the social forces which are 'shaping' the new Russia and bringing release from present-day social evils develop and assume a definite character, the more rapidly is critical-utopian socialism 'losing all practical value and all theoretical justification'.

A quarter of a century ago, the critical elements in Tolstoy's doctrine might at times have been of practical value for some sections of the population *in spite of* its reactionary and utopian features. This could not have been the case during, say, the last decade, because historical development had made considerable progress between the eighties and the end of the last century. In our days, since the series of events mentioned above has put an end to 'Oriental' quiescence, in our days, when the consciously reactionary ideas of *Vekhi* (reactionary in the narrow-class, selfishly-class sense) have become so enormously widespread among the liberal bourgeoisie and when these ideas have infected even a section of those who were almost Marxists and have created a liquidationist trend – in our days, the most direct and most profound harm is caused by every attempt to idealize Tolstoy's doctrine, to justify or to mitigate his 'non-resistance', his appeals to the 'Spirit', his exhortations for 'moral self-perfection', his doctrine of 'conscience' and universal 'love', his preaching of asceticism and quietism, and so forth.

3   Leon Trotsky

The Formalist School of Poetry and Marxism (1923)*

Lyov Davidovich Bronstein (1879–1940), pen-name 'Trotsky', was a leading figure in the Russian Revolutions of 1905 and 1917. After 1923 until his assassination by an agent of Stalin he led the left opposition to Stalin and Soviet bureaucracy, forming the Fourth International in the 1930s. His theoretical influence is as a critic of Stalinism who developed a theory of uneven economic development and permanent revolution. After 1917, Trotsky took sides against the concept of 'proletarian culture', and maintained a keen interest in bourgeois and *avant-garde* movements. *Literature and Revolution* (1923) discusses pre-revolutionary art; literary 'fellow-travellers' of the revolution; contemporary developments in futurism; and communist policy towards art. 'The Formalist School of Poetry and Marxism' defends a Marxist account of the relative autonomy of art against vulgar materialism and formalism, a position echoed by the Bakhtin circle and P. N. Medvedev, *The Formal Method in Literary Scholarship* (1928; trans. 1978). Trotsky's interest in culture and political hegemony was shared by Gramsci, whose letter to Trotsky on Italian Futurism was printed in the Russian edition of *Literature and Revolution*, but not in the English translation (see A. Gramsci, *Selections from Cultural Writings* (1985)). Trotsky continued to pursue his interest in politics and aesthetics in the 1930s, writing a manifesto for revolutionary art with Diego Rivera and Andre Breton while in Mexico. This and other essays can be found in *Leon Trotsky on Literature and Art*, ed. P. N. Siegel (1970). Trotsky's major works include *History of the Russian Revolution*, 3 vols (1932–3); *The Revolution Betrayed* (1937); and *The Permanent Revolution* and *Results and Prospects* (1962). For a philosophical critique of Trotsky see M. Merleau-Ponty, *Adventures of the Dialectic* (1955; trans. 1973). For context see Victor Erlich, *Russian Formalism: History – Doctrine* (1955; trans. 1980); and I. Deutscher, *The Prophet Unarmed: Trotsky 1921–1929* (1959).

* From Leon Trotsky, *Literature and Revolution* (Ann Arbor: University of Michigan Press, 1960), 162–83

The Formalist opposition to Marxism. – the reduction of poetry to etymology and syntax. – art for art's sake and the materialist dialectics. – The argumentations of shklovsky and others. – an analogy with the theologic argument against darwinism.

Leaving out of account the weak echoes of pre-revolutionary ideologic systems, the only theory which has opposed Marxism in Soviet Russia these years is the Formalist theory of Art. The paradox consists in the fact that Russian Formalism connected itself closely with Russian Futurism, and that while the latter was capitulating politically before Communism, Formalism opposed Marxism with all its might theoretically.

Victor Shklovsky is the theorist of Futurism, and at the same time the head of the Formalist school. According to his theory, art has always been the work of self-sufficient pure forms, and it has been recognized by Futurism for the first time. Futurism is thus the first conscious art in history, and the Formalist school is the first scientific school of art. Owing to the efforts of Shklovsky – and this is not an insignificant virtue! – the theory of art, and partly art itself, have at last been raised from a state of alchemy to the position of chemistry. The herald of the Formalist school, the first chemist of art, gives a few friendly slaps in passing to those Futurist 'conciliators' who seek a bridge to the Revolution, and who try to find this bridge in the materialistic conception of history. Such a bridge is unnecessary; Futurism is entirely sufficient unto itself.

There are two reasons why it is necessary to pause a little before this Formalist school. One is for its own sake; in spite of the superficiality and reactionary character of the Formalist theory of art, a certain part of the research work of the Formalists is useful. The other reason is Futurism itself; however unfounded the claims of the Futurists to a monopolistic representation of the new art may be, one cannot thrust Futurism out of that process which is preparing the art of the future.

What is the Formalist school?

As it is represented at present by Shklovsky, Zhirmunsky, Jacobson and others, it is extremely arrogant and immature. Having declared form to be the essence of poetry, this school reduces its task to an analysis (essentially descriptive and semi-statistical) of the etymology and syntax of poems, to the counting of repetitive vowels and consonants, of syllables and epithets. This analysis which the Formalists regard as the essence of poetry, or poetics, is undoubtedly necessary and useful, but one must understand its partial, scrappy, subsidiary and preparatory character. It can become an essential element of poetic technique and of the rules of the craft. Just as it is useful for a poet or a writer to make lists of synonyms for himself and increase their number so as to expand his verbal keyboard, so it is useful, and quite necessary for a poet, to estimate a word not only in accord with its inner meaning, but also in accord with its acoustics, because a word is passed on from man to man, first of all by acoustics. The methods of Formalism, confined within legitimate limits, may help to clarify the artistic and psychologic peculiarities of form (its economy, its movement, its contrasts, its hyperbolism, etc.). This, in turn, may open a path – one of the paths – to the artist's feeling for the world, and may facilitate the discovery of the relations of an individual artist, or of a whole artistic school, to the social environment. In so far as we are dealing with a contemporary and living school which is still developing, there is an immediate significance in our transitional stage in probing it by means of a social probe and in clarifying its class roots, so that not only the reader, but the school itself could orientate itself, that is, know itself, purify and direct itself.

But the Formalists are not content to ascribe to their methods a merely subsidiary, serviceable and technical significance – similar to that which statistics has for social science, or the microscope for the biological sciences. No, they go much further. To them verbal art ends finally and fully with the word, and depictive art with colour. A poem is a combination of sounds, a painting is a combination of colour spots and the laws of art are the laws of verbal combinations and of combinations of colour spots. The social and psychologic approach which, to us, gives a meaning to the microscopic and statistical work done in connection with verbal material, is, for the Formalists, only alchemy.

'Art was always free of life, and its color never reflected the color of the flag which waved over the fortress of the City.' (Shklovsky.) 'Adjustment to the expression, the verbal mass, is the one essential element of poetry.' (R. Jacobson, in his 'Recent Russian Poetry'.) 'With a new form comes a new content. Form thus determines content.' (Kruchenikh.) 'Poetry means the giving of form to the word, which is valuable in itself' (Jacobson), or, as Khlebnikov says, 'The word which is something in itself', etc.

True, the Italian Futurists have sought in the word a means of expressing the locomotive, the propeller, electricity, the radio, etc., for their own age. In other words, they sought a new form for the new content of life. But it turned out that 'this was a reform in the field of reporting, and not in the field of poetic language'. (Jacobson.) It is quite different with Russian Futurism; it carries to the end 'the adjustment to verbal mass'. For Russian Futurism, form determines content.

True, Jacobson is compelled to admit that 'a series of new poetic methods finds application (?) for itself in urbanism' (in the culture of the city). But this is his conclusion: 'Hence the urban poems of Mayakovsky and Khlebnikov.' In other words: not city culture, which has struck the eye and the ear of the poet and which has re-educated them, has inspired him with new form, with new images, new epithets, new rhythm, but, on the contrary, the new form, originating arbitrarily, forced the poet to seek appropriate material and so pushed him in the direction of the city! The development of the 'verbal mass' went on arbitrarily from the 'Odyssey' to 'A Cloud in Trousers', the torch, the wax candle, the electric lamp, had nothing to do with it! One has only to formulate this point of view clearly to have its childish inadequacy strike the eye. But Jacobson tries to insist; he replies in advance that the same Mayakovsky has such lines as these: 'Leave the cities, you silly people.' And the theorist of the Formalist school reasons profoundly: 'What is this, a logical contradiction? But let others fasten on the poet thoughts expressed in his works. To incriminate a poet with ideas and feelings is just as absurd as the behaviour of the medieval public which beat the actor who played Judas.' And so on.

It is quite evident that all this was written by a very capable high-school boy who had a very evident and quite 'self-significant' intention to 'stick the pen into our teacher of literature, a notable pedant'. At sticking the pen, our bold innovators are masters, but they do not know how to use their pen theoretically or grammatically. This is not hard to prove.

Of course Futurism felt the suggestions of the city – of the tram-car, of electricity, of the telegraph, of the automobile, of the propeller, of the night cabaret (especially of the night cabaret) much before it found its new form. Urbanism (city culture) sits deep in the subconsciousness of Futurism, and the epithets, the etymology, the syntax and the rhythm of Futurism are only an attempt to give artistic form to the new spirit of the cities which has conquered consciousness. And when Mayakovsky exclaims: 'Leave the cities, you silly people', it is the cry of a man citified to the very marrow of his bones, who shows himself strikingly and clearly a city person, especially when he is outside the city, that is, when he 'leaves the city' and becomes an inhabitant of a summer resort. It is not at all a question of 'incriminating' (this word misses something!) a poet with the ideas and feelings which he expresses. Of course the way he expresses them makes the poet. But after all, a poet uses the language of the school which he has accepted or which he has created to fulfil tasks which lie outside of him. And this is even true also when he limits himself to lyricism, to personal love and personal death. Though individual shadings of poetic form correspond to individual makeup, they do go hand in hand with imitation and routine, in the feeling itself, as well as in the method of its expression. A new artistic form, taken in a large historic way, is born in reply to new needs. To take an example from intimate lyric poetry, one may say that between the physiology of sex and a poem about love there lies a complex system of psychological transmitting mechanisms in which there are individual, racial and social elements. The racial foundation, that is, the sexual basis of man, changes slowly. The social forms of love change more rapidly. They affect the psychologic superstructure of love, they produce new shadings and intonations, new spiritual demands, a need of a new vocabulary, and so they present new demands on poetry. The poet can find material for his art only in his social environment and transmits the new impulses of life through his own artistic consciousness. Language, changed and complicated by urban conditions, gives the poet a new verbal material, and suggests or facilitates new word combinations for the poetic formulation of new thoughts or of new feelings, which strive to break through the dark shell of the subconscious. If there were no changes in psychology produced by changes in the social environment, there would be no movement in art; people would continue from generation to generation to be content with the poetry of the Bible, or of the old Greeks.

But the philosopher of Formalism jumps on us, and says it is merely a question of a new form 'in the field of reporting and not in the field of poetic language'. There he struck us! If you will, poetry is reporting, only in a peculiar, grand style.

The quarrels about 'pure art' and about art with a tendency took place between the liberals and the 'populists'. They do not become us. Materialistic dialectics are above this; from the point of view of an objective historical process, art is always a social servant and historically utilitarian. It finds the necessary rhythm of words for dark and vague moods, it brings thought and feeling closer or contrasts them with one another, it enriches the spiritual experience of the individual and of the community, it refines feeling, makes it more flexible, more responsive, it enlarges the volume of thought in advance and not through the personal method of accumulated experience, it educates the individual, the social group, the class and the nation. And this it does quite independently of whether it appears in a given case under the flag of a 'pure' or of a frankly tendentious art. In our Russian social development tendentiousness was the banner of the intelligentsia which sought contact with the people. The helpless intelligentsia, crushed by Tsarism and deprived of a cultural environment, sought support in the lower strata of society and tried to prove to the 'people' that it was thinking only of them, living only for them and that it loved them 'terribly'. And just as the 'populists' who went to the people were ready to do without clean linen and without a comb and without a toothbrush, so the intelligentsia was ready to sacrifice the 'subtleties' of form in its art, in order to give the most direct and spontaneous expression to the sufferings and hopes of the oppressed. On the other hand, 'pure' art was the banner of the rising bourgeoisie, which could not openly declare its bourgeois character, and which at the same time tried to keep the intelligentsia in its service. The Marxist point of view is far removed from these tendencies, which were historically necessary, but which have become historically *passé*. Keeping on the plane of scientific investigation, Marxism seeks with the same assurance the social roots of the 'pure' as well as of the tendentious art. It does not at all 'incriminate' a poet with the thoughts and feelings which he expresses, but raises questions of a much more profound significance, namely, to which order of feelings does a given artistic work correspond in all its peculiarities? What are the social conditions of these thoughts and feelings? What place do they occupy in the historic development of a society and of a class? And, further, what literary heritage has entered into the elaboration of the new form? Under the influence of what historic impulse have the new complexes of feelings and thoughts broken through the shell which divides them from the sphere of poetic consciousness? The investigation may become complicated, detailed or individualized, but its fundamental idea will be that of the subsidiary role which art plays in the social process.

Each class has its own policy in art, that is, a system of presenting demands on art, which changes with time; for instance, the Maecenas-like protection of court and grand seigneur, the automatic relationship of supply and demand which is supplemented by complex methods of influencing the individual, and so forth, and so on. The social and even the personal dependence of art was not concealed, but was openly announced as long as art retained its court character. The wider, more popular, anonymous character of the rising bourgeoisie led, on the whole, to the theory of 'pure art', though there were many deviations from this theory. As indicated above, the tendentious literature of the 'populist' intelligentsia was imbued with a class interest; the intelligentsia could not strengthen itself and could not conquer for itself a right to play a part in history without the support of the people. But in the revolutionary struggle, the class egotism of the intelligentsia was turned inside out, and in its left wing, it assumed the form of highest self-sacrifice. That is why the intelligentsia not only did not conceal art with a tendency, but proclaimed it, thus sacrificing art, just as it sacrificed many other things.

Our Marxist conception of the objective social dependence and social utility of art, when translated into the language of politics, does not at all mean a desire to dominate art by means of decrees and orders. It is not true that we regard only that art as new and revolutionary which speaks of the worker, and it is nonsense to say that we demand that the poets should describe inevitably a factory chimney, or the uprising against capital! Of course the new art cannot but place the struggle of the proletariat in the centre of its attention. But the plough of the new art is not limited to numbered strips. On the contrary, it must plow the entire field in all directions. Personal lyrics of the very smallest scope have an absolute right to exist within the new art. Moreover, the new man cannot be formed without a new lyric poetry. But to create it, the poet himself must feel the world in a new way. If Christ alone or Sabaoth himself bends over the poet's embraces (as in the case of Akhmatova, Tsvetaeva, Shkapskaya and others), then this only goes to prove how much behind the times his lyrics are and how socially and aesthetically inadequate they are for the new man. Even where such terminology is not a survival of experience so much as of words, it shows psychologic inertia and therefore stands in contradiction to the consciousness of the new man. No one is going to prescribe themes to a poet or intends to prescribe them. Please write about anything you can think of! But allow the new class which considers itself, and with reason, called upon to build a new world, to say to you in any given case: It does not make new poets of you to translate the philosophy of life of the Seventeenth Century into the language of the Acméists. The form of art is, to a certain and very large degree, independent, but the artist who creates this form, and the spectator who is enjoying it, are not empty machines, one for creating form and the other for appreciating it. They are living people, with a crystallized psychology representing a certain unity, even if not entirely harmonious. This psychology is the result of social conditions. The creation and perception of art forms is one of the functions of this psychology. And no matter how wise the Formalists try to be, their whole conception is simply based upon the fact that they ignore the psychological unity of the social man, who creates and who consumes what has been created.

The proletariat has to have in art the expression of the new spiritual point of view which is just beginning to be formulated within him, and to which art must help him give form. This is not a state order, but an historic demand. Its strength lies in the objectivity of historic necessity. You cannot pass this by, nor escape its force.

The Formalist school seems to try to be objective. It is disgusted, and not without reason, with the literary and critical arbitrariness which operates only with tastes and moods. It seeks precise criteria for classification and valuation. But owing to its narrow outlook and superficial methods, it is constantly falling into superstitions, such as graphology and phrenology. These two 'schools' have also the task of establishing purely objective tests for determining human character; such as the number of the flourishes of one's pen and their roundness, and the peculiarities of the bumps on the back of one's head. One may assume that pen-flourishes and bumps do have some relation to character; but this relation is not direct, and human character is not at all exhausted by them. An apparent objectivism based on accidental, secondary and inadequate characteristics leads inevitably to the worst subjectivism. In the case of the Formalist school it leads to the superstition of the word. Having counted the adjectives, and weighed the lines, and measured the rhythms, a Formalist either stops silent with the expression of a man who does not know what to do with himself, or throws out an unexpected generalization which contains five per cent of Formalism and ninety-five per cent of the most uncritical intuition.

In fact, the Formalists do not carry their idea of art to its logical conclusion. If one is to regard the process of poetic creation only as a combination of sounds or words, and to seek along these lines the solution of all the problems of poetry, then the only perfect formula of 'poetics' will be this: Arm yourself with a dictionary and create by means of algebraic combinations and permutations of words, all the poetic works of the world which have been created and which have not yet been created. Reasoning 'formally' one may produce *Eugene Onegin* in two ways: either by subordinating the selection of words to a preconceived artistic idea (as Pushkin himself did), or by solving the problem algebraically. From the 'Formal' point of view, the second method is more correct, because it does not depend upon mood, inspiration, or other unsteady things, and has besides the advantage that while leading to *Eugene Onegin* it may bring one to an incalculable number of other great works. All that one needs is infinity in time, called eternity. But as neither mankind nor the individual poet have eternity at their disposal, the fundamental source of poetic words will remain, as before, the preconceived artistic idea understood in the broadest sense, as an accurate thought and as a clearly expressed personal or social feeling and as a vague mood. In its striving towards artistic materialization, this subjective idea will be stimulated and jolted by form and may be sometimes pushed on to a path which was entirely unforeseen. This simply means that verbal form is not a passive reflection of a preconceived artistic idea, but an active element which influences the idea itself. But such an active mutual relationship – in which form influences and at times entirely transforms content – is known to us in all fields of social and even biologic life. This is no reason at all for rejecting Darwinism and Marxism and for the creation of a Formalist school either in biology or sociology.

Victor Shklovsky, who flits lightly from verbal Formalism to the most subjective valuations, assumes a very uncompromising attitude towards the historico-materialistic theory of art. In a booklet which he published in Berlin, under the title of 'The March of the Horse', he formulates in the course of three small pages – brevity is a fundamental and, at any rate, an undoubted merit of Shklovsky – five (not four and not six, but five) exhaustive arguments against the materialist conception of art. Let us examine these arguments, because it won't harm us to take a look and see what kind of chaff is handed out as the last word in scientific thought (with the greatest variety of scientific references on these same three microscopic pages).

'If the environment and the relations of production,' says Shklovsky, 'influenced art, then would not the themes of art be tied to the places which would correspond to these relations? But themes are homeless.' Well, and how about butterflies? According to Darwin, they also 'correspond' to definite relations, and yet they flit from place to place, just like an unweighted litterateur.

It is not easy to understand why Marxism should be supposed to condemn themes to a condition of serfdom. The fact that different peoples and different classes of the same people make use of the same themes, merely shows how limited the human imagination is, and how man tries to maintain an economy of energy in every kind of creation, even in the artistic. Every class tries to utilize, to the greatest possible degree, the material and spiritual heritage of another class. Shklovsky's argument could be easily transferred into the field of productive technique. From ancient times on, the wagon has been based on one and the same theme, namely, axles, wheels and a shaft. However, the chariot of the Roman patrician was just as well adapted to his tastes and needs as was the carriage of Count Orlov, fitted out with inner comforts, to the tastes of this favourite of Catherine the Great. The wagon of the Russian peasant is adapted to the needs of his household, to the strength of his little horse, and to the peculiarities of the country road. The automobile, which is undoubtedly a product of the new technique, shows, nevertheless, the same 'theme', namely, four wheels on two axles. Yet every time a peasant's horse shies in terror before the blinding lights of an automobile on the Russian road at night, a conflict of two cultures is reflected in the episode.

'If environment expressed itself in novels,' so runs the second argument, 'European science would not be breaking its head over the question of where the stories of "A Thousand and One Nights" were made, whether in Egypt, India, or Persia.' To say that man's environment, including the artist's, that is, the conditions of his education and life, find expression in his art also, does not mean to say that such expression has a precise geographic, ethnographic and statistical character. It is not at all surprising that it is difficult to decide whether certain novels were made in Egypt, India or Persia, because the social conditions of these countries have much in common. But the very fact that European science is 'breaking its head' trying to solve this question from these novels themselves, shows that these novels reflect an environment, even though unevenly. No one can jump beyond himself. Even the ravings of an insane person contain nothing that the sick man had not received before from the outside world. But it would be an insanity of another order to regard his ravings as the accurate reflection of an external world. Only an experienced and thoughtful psychiatrist, who knows the past of the patient, will be able to find the reflected and distorted bits of reality in the contents of his ravings. Artistic creation, of course, is not a raving, though it is also a deflection, a changing and a transformation of reality, in accordance with the peculiar laws of art. However fantastic art may be, it cannot have at its disposal any other material except that which is given to it by the world of three dimensions and by the narrower world of class society. Even when the artist creates heaven and hell, he merely transforms the experience of his own life into his phantasmagorias, almost to the point of his landlady's unpaid bill.

'If the features of class and caste are deposited in art,' continues Shklovsky, 'then how does it come that the various tales of the Great Russians about their nobleman are the same as their fairy tales about their priest?'

In essence, this is merely a paraphrase of the first argument. Why cannot the fairy tales about the nobleman and about the priest be the same, and how does this contradict Marxism? The proclamations which are written by well-known Marxists not infrequently speak of landlords, capitalists, priests, generals and other exploiters. The landlord undoubtedly differs from the capitalist, but there are cases when they are considered under one head. Why, then, cannot folk-art in certain cases treat the nobleman and the priest together, as the representatives of the classes which stand above the people and which plunder them? In the cartoons of Moor and of Deni, the priest often stands side by side with the landlord, without any damage to Marxism.

'If ethnographic traits were reflected in art,' Shklovsky goes on, 'the folk-lore about the peoples beyond the border would not be interchangeable and could not be told by any one folk about another.'

As you see, there is no letting up here. Marxism does not maintain at all that ethnographic traits have an independent character. On the contrary, it emphasizes the all-determining significance of natural and economic conditions in the formation of folk-lore. The similarity of conditions in the development of the herding and agricultural and primarily peasant peoples, and the similarity in the character of their mutual influence upon one another, cannot but lead to the creation of a similar folk-lore. And from the point of view of the question that interests us here, it makes absolutely no difference whether these homogeneous themes arose independently among different peoples, as the reflection of a life-experience which was homogeneous in its fundamental traits and which was reflected through the homogeneous prism of a peasant imagination, or whether the seeds of these fairy tales were carried by a favourable wind from place to place, striking root wherever the ground turned out to be favourable. It is very likely that, in reality, these methods were combined.

And finally, as a separate argument – 'The reason (*i.e.*, Marxism) is incorrect in the fifth place' – Shklovsky points to the theme of abduction which goes through Greek comedy and reaches Ostrovsky. In other words, our critic repeats, in a special form, his very first argument (as we see, even in so far as formal logic is concerned, all is not well with our Formalist). Yes, themes migrate from people to people, from class to class, and even from author to author. This means only that the human imagination is economical. A new class does not begin to create all of culture from the beginning, but enters into possession of the past, assorts it, touches it up, rearranges it, and builds on it further. If there were no such utilization of the 'second-hand' wardrobe of the ages, historic processes would have no progress at all. If the theme of Ostrovsky's drama came to him through the Egyptians and through Greece, then the paper on which Ostrovsky developed his theme came to him as a development of the Egyptian papyrus through the Greek parchment. Let us take another and closer analogy: the fact that the critical methods of the Greek Sophists, who were the pure Formalists of their day, have penetrated the theoretic consciousness of Shklovsky, does not in the least change the fact that Shklovsky himself is a very picturesque product of a definite social environment and of a definite age.

Shklovsky's destruction of Marxism in five points reminds us very much of those articles which were published against Darwinism in the magazine *The*

Orthodox Review in the good old days. If the doctrine of the origin of man from the monkey were true, wrote the learned Bishop Nikanor of Odessa thirty or forty years ago, then our grandfathers would have had distinct signs of a tail, or would have noticed such a characteristic in their grandfathers and grandmothers. Second, as everybody knows, monkeys can only give birth to monkeys. . . . Fifth, Darwinism is incorrect, because it contradicts Formalism – I beg your pardon, I meant to say the formal decisions of the universal church conferences. The advantage of the learned monk consisted, however, in the fact that he was a frank *passéist* and took his cue from the Apostle Paul and not from physics, chemistry or mathematics, as the Futurist, Shklovsky, does.

It is unquestionably true that the need for art is not created by economic conditions. But neither is the need for food created by economics. On the contrary, the need for food and warmth creates economics. It is very true that one cannot always go by the principles of Marxism in deciding whether to reject or to accept a work of art. A work of art should, in the first place, be judged by its own law, that is, by the law of art. But Marxism alone can explain why and how a given tendency in art has originated in a given period of history; in other words, who it was who made a demand for such an artistic form and not for another, and why.

It would be childish to think that every class can entirely and fully create its own art from within itself, and, particularly, that the proletariat is capable of creating a new art by means of closed art guilds or circles, or by the Organization for Proletarian Culture, etc. Generally speaking, the artistic work of man is continuous. Each new rising class places itself on the shoulders of its preceding one. But this continuity is dialectic, that is, it finds itself by means of internal repulsions and breaks. New artistic needs or demands for new literary and artistic points of view are stimulated by economics, through the development of a new class, and minor stimuli are supplied by changes in the position of the class, under the influence of the growth of its wealth and cultural power. Artistic creation is always a complicated turning inside out of old forms, under the influence of new stimuli which originate outside of art. In this large sense of the word, art is a handmaiden. It is not a disembodied element feeding on itself, but a function of social man indissolubly tied to his life and environment. And how characteristic it is – if one were to reduce every social superstition to its absurdity – that Shklovsky has come to the idea of art's absolute independence from the social environment at a period of Russian history when art has revealed with such utter frankness its spiritual, environmental and material dependence upon definite social classes, subclasses and groups!

Materialism does not deny the significance of the element of form, either in logic, jurisprudence, or art. Just as a system of jurisprudence can and must be judged by its internal logic and consistency, so art can and must be judged from the point of view of its achievements in form, because there can be no art without them. However, a juridical theory which attempted to establish the independence of law from social conditions would be defective at its very base. Its moving force lies in economics – in class contradictions. The law gives only a formal and an internally harmonized expression of these phenomena, not of their individual peculiarities, but of their general character, that is, of the elements that are repetitive and permanent in them. We can see now with a clarity which is rare in history how new law is made. It is not done by logical deduction, but by empirical measurement and by adjustment to the economic needs of the new ruling class. Literature, whose methods and processes have their roots far back in the most distant past and represent the accumulated experience of verbal craftsmanship, expresses the thoughts, feelings, moods, points of view and hopes of the new epoch and of its new class. One cannot jump beyond this. And there is no need of making the jump, at least, for those who are not serving an epoch already past nor a class which has already outlived itself.

The methods of formal analysis are necessary, but insufficient. You may count up the alliterations in popular proverbs, classify metaphors, count up the number of vowels and consonants in a wedding song. It will undoubtedly enrich our knowledge of folk-art, in one way or another; but if you don't know the peasant system of sowing, and the life that is based on it, if you don't know the part the scythe plays, and if you have not mastered the meaning of the church calendar to the peasant, of the time when the peasant marries, or when the peasant women give birth, you will have only understood the outer shell of folk art, but the kernel will not have been reached. The architectural scheme of the Cologne cathedral can be established by measuring the base and the height of its arches, by determining the three dimensions of its naves, the dimensions and the placement of the columns, etc. But without knowing what a medieval city was like, what a guild was, or what was the Catholic Church of the Middle Ages, the Cologne cathedral will never be understood. The effort to set art free from life, to declare it a craft self-sufficient unto itself, devitalizes and kills art. The very need of such an operation is an unmistakable symptom of intellectual decline.

The analogy with the theological arguments against Darwinism which was made above may appear to the reader external and anecdotal. That may be true, to some extent. But a much deeper connection exists. The Formalist theory inevitably reminds a Marxist who has done any reading at all of the familiar tunes of a very old philosophic melody. The jurists and the moralists (to recall at random the German Stammler, and our own subjectivist Mikhailovský) tried to prove that morality and law could not be determined by economics, because economic life was unthinkable outside of juridical and ethical norms. True, the formalists of law and morals did not go so far as to assert the complete independence of law and ethics from economics. They recognized a certain complex mutual relationship of 'factors', and these 'factors', while influencing one another, retained the qualities of independent substances, coming no one knew whence. The assertion of complete independence of the aesthetic 'factor' from the influence of social conditions, as is made by Shklovsky, is an instance of specific hyperbole whose roots, by the way, lie in social conditions too; it is the megalomania of aesthetics turning our hard reality on its head. Apart from this peculiarity, the constructions of the Formalists have the same kind of defective methodology that every other kind of idealism has. To a materialist, religion, law, morals and art represent separate aspects of one and the same process of social development. Though they differentiate themselves from their industrial basis, become complex, strengthen and develop their special characteristics in detail, politics, religion, law, ethics and aethetics remain, none the less, functions of social man and obey the laws of his social organization. The idealist, on the other hand, does not see a unified process of historic development which evolves the necessary organs and functions from within itself, but a crossing or combining and interacting of certain independent principles – the religious, political, juridical, aesthetic and ethical substances, which find their origin and explanation in themselves. The (dialectic) idealism of Hegel arranges these substances (which are the eternal categories) in some sequence by reducing them to a genetic unity. Regardless of the fact that this unity with Hegel is the absolute spirit, which divides itself in the process of its dialectic manifestation into various 'factors', Hegel's system, because of its dialectic character, not because of its idealism, gives an idea of historic reality which is just as good as the idea of a man's hand that a glove gives when turned inside out. But the Formalists (and their greatest genius was Kant) do not look at the dynamics of development, but at a cross-section of it, on the day and at the hour of their own philosophic revelation. At the crossing of the line they reveal the complexity and multiplicity of the object (not of the process, because they do not think of processes). This complexity they analyse and classify. They give names to the elements, which are at once transformed into essences, into sub-absolutes, without father or mother; to wit, religion, politics, morals, law, art. Here we no longer have a glove of history turned inside out, but the skin torn from the separate fingers, dried out to a degree of complete abstraction, and this hand of history turns out to be the product of the 'inter-action' of the thumb, the index, the middle finger, and all the other 'factors'. The aesthetic 'factor' is the little finger, the smallest, but not the least beloved.

In biology, vitalism is a variation of the same fetish of presenting the separate aspects of the world-process, without understanding its inner relation. A creator is all that is lacking for a super-social, absolute morality or aesthetics, or for a super-physical absolute 'vital force'. The multiplicity of independent factors, 'factors' without beginning or end, is nothing but a masked polytheism. Just as Kantian idealism represents historically a translation of Christianity into the language of rationalistic philosophy, so all the varieties of idealistic formalization, either openly or secretly, lead to a God, as the Cause of all causes. In comparison with the oligarchy of a dozen sub-absolutes of the idealistic philosophy, a single personal Creator is already an element of order. Herein lies the deeper connection between the Formalist refutations of Marxism and the theological refutations of Darwinism.

The Formalist school represents an abortive idealism applied to the questions of art. The Formalists show a fast ripening religiousness. They are followers of St John. They believe that 'In the beginning was the Word'. But we believe that in the beginning was the deed. The word followed, as its phonetic shadow.

4 V. N. Vološinov

Concerning the Relationship of the Basis and Superstructures (1929)[*]

V. N. Vološinov (1895–?) (sometimes spelt Voloshinov) was a member of the Bakhtin Circle, which included M. M. Bakhtin and P. N. Medvedev, who were active in Russia in the 1920s developing new modes of sociological poetics and discourse theory. Controversy about Bakhtin's contribution to the writings produced by this group has largely overshadowed discussion of Vološinov. This stems in part from the intellectual ice age of Stalinism and the 'disappearance' of Vološinov in the 1930s. But the controversy also involves the more explicitly Marxist orientation of writing by Vološinov and Medvedev, as compared with Bakhtin's work. Bakhtin developed a range of themes relating to discourse, dialogism and carnival which have been eagerly appropriated by academic literary criticism. Vološinov's key works, *Freudianism: A Marxist Critique* (1927; trans. 1976) and *Marxism and the Philosophy of Language* (1929; trans. 1973), have been less eagerly appropriated, perhaps because of his stress on class struggle in linguistic conflicts. Although *Marxism and the Philosophy of Language* had some influence on the Prague School associated with Jakobson, it remained largely unknown until its translation in the 1970s. Chapter 2, 'Concerning the Relationship of the Basis and Superstructures', provides an introduction to Vološinov's main themes. His approach to ideology and language is distinct from traditions associated with Saussure or Wittgenstein, and suggests modes of semiotics and discourse theory which might integrate Marxism and literary criticism in correspondingly distinct ways. Further essays by Vološinov can be found in *Bakhtin School Papers*, ed. Ann Shukman (*Russian Poetics in Translation*, vol. 10, 1983). For context, see also P. N. Medvedev, *The Formal Method in Literary Scholarship* (1928; trans. 1978); and *The Futurists, the Formalists and the Marxist Critique*, ed. C. Pike (1979).

[*] From V. N. Vološinov, *Marxism and the Philosophy of Language*, trans. Ladislav Matejka and I. R. Titunik (Cambridge, Mass. and London: Harvard University Press, 1986), 17–24.

Inadmissibility of the category of mechanistic causality in the study of ideologies. The generative process of society and the generative process of the word. The semiotic expression of social psychology. The problem of behavioural speech genres. Forms of social intercourse and forms of signs. The theme of a sign. The class struggle and the dialectics of signs. Conclusions.

The problem of the *relationship of basis and superstructures* – one of the fundamental problems of Marxism – is closely linked with questions of philosophy of language at a number of crucial points and could benefit considerably from a solution to those questions or even just from treatment of them to some appreciable extent and depth.

When the question is posed as to how the basis determines ideology, the answer given is: *causally*; which is true enough, but also far too general and therefore ambiguous.

If what is meant by causality is mechanical causality (as causality has been and still is understood and defined by the positivistic representatives of natural scientific thought), then this answer would be essentially incorrect and contradictory to the very fundaments of dialectal materialism.

The range of application for the categories of mechanical causality is extremely narrow, and even within the natural sciences themselves it grows constantly narrower the further and more deeply dialectics takes hold in the basic principles of these sciences. As regards the fundamental problems of historical materialism and of the study of ideologies altogether, the applicability of so inert a category as that of mechanical causality is simply out of the question.

No cognitive value whatever adheres to the establishment of a connection between the basis and some isolated fact torn from the unity and integrity of its ideological context. It is essential above all to determine the *meaning of any, given ideological change in the context of ideology appropriate to it*, seeing that every domain of ideology is a unified whole which reacts with its entire constitution to a change in the basis. Therefore, any explanation must preserve *all the qualitative differences* between interacting domains and must trace all the various stages through which a change travels. Only on this condition will analysis result, not in a mere outward conjunction of two adventitious facts belonging to different levels of things, but in the process of the actual dialectical generation of society, a process which emerges from the basis and comes to completion in the superstructures.

If the specific nature of the semiotic–ideological material is ignored, the ideological phenomenon studied undergoes simplification. Either only its rationalistic aspect, its content side, is noted and explained (for example, the direct, referential sense of an artistic image, such as 'Rudin as superflous man'), and then that aspect is correlated with the basis (e.g., the gentry class degenerates; hence the 'superflous man' in literature); or, oppositely, only the outward, technical aspect of the ideological phenomenon is singled out (e.g., some technicality in building construction or in the chemistry of colouring materials) and then this aspect is derived directly from the technological level of production.

Both these ways of deriving ideology from the basis miss the real essence of an ideological phenomenon. Even if the correspondence established is correct, even if it is true that 'superfluous men' did appear in literature in connection with the breakdown of the economic structure of the gentry, still, for one thing, it does not at all follow that related economic upsets mechanically cause 'superfluous men' to be produced on the pages of a novel (the absurdity of such a claim is perfectly obvious); for another thing, the correspondence established itself remains without any cognitive value until both the specific role of the 'superfluous man' in the artistic structure of the novel and the specific role of the novel in social life as a whole are elucidated.

Surely it must be clear that between changes in the economic state of affairs and the appearance of the 'superfluous man' in the novel stretches a long, long road that crosses a number of qualitatively different domains, each with its own specific set of laws and its own specific characteristics. Surely it must be clear that the 'superfluous man' did not appear in the novel in any way independent of and unconnected with other elements of the novel, but that, on the contrary, the whole novel, as a single organic unity subject to its own specific laws, underwent restructuring, and that, consequently, all its other elements – its composition, style, etc. – also underwent re-structuring. And what is more, this organic restructuring of the novel came about in close connection with changes in the whole field of literature, as well.

The problem of the interrelationship of the basis and superstructures – a problem of exceptional complexity, requiring enormous amounts of preliminary data for its productive treatment – can be elucidated to a significant degree through the material of the word.

Looked at from the angle of our concerns, the essence of this problem comes down to *how* actual existence (the basis) determines sign and *how* sign reflects and refracts existence in its process of generation.

The properties of the word as an ideological sign (properties discussed in the preceding chapter) are what make the word the most suitable material for viewing the whole of this problem in basic terms. What is important about the word in this regard is not so much its sign purity as its *social ubiquity*. The word is implicated in literally each and every act or contact between people – in collaboration on the job, in ideological exchanges, in the chance contacts of ordinary life, in political relationships, and so on. Countless ideological threads running through all areas of social intercourse register effect in the word. It stands to reason, then, that the word is the most sensitive *index of social changes*, and what is more, of changes still in the process of growth, still without definitive shape and not as yet accommodated into already regularized and fully defined ideological systems. The word is the medium in which occur the slow quantitative accretions of those changes which have not yet achieved the status of a new ideological quality, not yet produced a new and fully-fledged ideological form. The word has the capacity to register all the transitory, delicate, momentary phases of social change.

That which has been termed 'social psychology' and is considered, according to Plexanov's theory and by the majority of Marxists, as the transitional link between the socio-political order and ideology in the narrow sense (science, art, and the like), is, in its actual, material existence, *verbal interaction*. Removed from this actual process of verbal communication and interaction (of semiotic communication and interaction in general), social psychology would assume the guise of a metaphysical or mythic concept – the 'collective soul' or 'collective inner psyche', the 'spirit of the people', etc.

Social psychology in fact is not located anywhere within (in the 'souls' of communicating subjects) but entirely and completely *without* – in the word, the gesture, the act. There is nothing left unexpressed in it, nothing 'inner' about it – it is wholly on the outside, wholly brought out in exchanges, wholly taken up in material, above all in the material of the word.

Production relations and the socio-political order shaped by those relations determine the full range of verbal contacts between people, all the forms and means of their verbal communication – at work, in political life, in ideological creativity. In turn, from the conditions, forms, and types of verbal communication derive not only the forms but also the themes of speech performances.

Social psychology is first and foremost an atmosphere made up of multifarious *speech performances* that engulf and wash over all persistent forms and kinds of ideological creativity: unofficial discussions, exchanges of opinion at the theatre or a concert or at various types of social gatherings, purely chance exchanges of words, one's manner of verbal reaction to happenings in one's life and daily existence, one's inner-word manner of identifying oneself and identifying one's position in society, and so on. Social psychology exists primarily in a wide variety of forms of the 'utterance', of little *speech genres* of internal and external kinds – things left completely unstudied to the present day. All these speech performances are, of course, joined with other types of semiotic manifestation and interchange – with miming, gesturing, acting out, and the like.

All these forms of speech interchange operate in extremely close connection with the conditions of the social situation in which they occur and exhibit an extraordinary sensitivity to all fluctuations in the social atmosphere. And it is here, in the inner workings of this verbally materialized social psychology, that the barely noticeable shifts and changes that will later find expression in fully fledged ideological products accumulate.

From what has been said, it follows that social psychology must be studied from two different viewpoints: first, from the viewpoint of content, i.e., the themes pertinent to it at this or that moment in time; and second, from the viewpoint of the forms and types of verbal communication in which the themes in question are implemented (i.e., discussed, expressed, questioned, pondered over, etc.).

Up till now the study of social psychology has restricted its task to the first viewpoint only, concerning itself exclusively with definition of its thematic makeup. Such being the case, the very question as to where documentation – the concrete expressions – of this social psychology could be sought was not posed with full clarity. Here, too, concepts of 'consciousness', 'psyche', and 'inner life' played the sorry role of relieving one of the necessity to try to discover clearly delineated material forms of expression of social psychology.

Meanwhile, this issue of concrete forms has significance of the highest order. The point here has to do, of course, not with the sources of our knowledge about social psychology at some particular period (e.g., memoirs, letters, literary works), nor with the sources for our understanding of the 'spirit of the age' – the point here has to do with the forms of concrete implementation of this spirit, that is, precisely with the very forms of semiotic communication in human behaviour.

A typology of these forms is one of the urgent tasks of Marxism. Later on, in connection with the problem of the utterance and dialogue, we shall again touch upon the problem of speech genres. For the time being, let us take note at least of the following.

Each period and each social group has had and has its own repertoire of speech forms for ideological communication in human behaviour. Each set of cognate forms, i.e., each behavioural speech genre, has its own corresponding set of themes.

An interlocking organic unity joins the form of communication (for example, on-the-job communication of the strictly technical kind), the form of the utterance (the concise, businesslike statement) and its theme. Therefore, *classification of the forms of utterance must rely upon classification of the forms of verbal communication*. The latter are entirely determined by production relations and the socio-political order. Were we to apply a more detailed analysis, we would see what enormous significance belongs to *the hierarchical factor* in the processes of verbal interchange and what a powerful influence is exerted on forms of utterance by the hierarchical organization of communication. Language etiquette, speech tact, and other forms of adjusting an

utterance to the hierarchical organization of society have tremendous importance in the process of devising the basic behavioural genres.[1]

Every sign, as we know, is a contruct between socially organized persons in
the process of their interaction. Therefore, *the forms of signs are conditioned
above all by the social organization of the participants involved and also by the
immediate conditions of their interaction*. When these forms change, so does sign.
And it should be one of the tasks of the study of ideologies to trace this social
life of the verbal sign. Only so approached can the *problem of the relationship
between sign and existence* find its concrete expression; only then will the
process of the causal shaping of the sign by existence stand out as a process
of genuine existence-to-sign transit, of genuine dialectical refraction of existence in the sign.

To accomplish this task certain basic, methodological prerequisites must be
respected:

1   *Ideology may not be divorced from the material reality of sign* (i.e., by locating
    it in the 'consciousness' or other vague and elusive regions);
2   *The sign may not be divorced from the concrete forms of social intercourse*
    (seeing that the sign is part of organized social intercourse and cannot
    exist, as such, outside it, reverting to a mere physical artefact);
3   *Communication and the forms of communication may not be divorced from the
    material basis*.

Every ideological sign – the verbal sign included – in coming about through
the process of social intercourse, is defined by the *social purview* of the given
time period and the given social group. So far, we have been speaking about
the form of the sign as shaped by the forms of social interaction. Now we shall
deal with its other aspect – the *content* of the sign and the evaluative
accentuation that accompanies all content.

Every stage in the development of a society has its own special and
restricted circle of items which alone have access to that society's attention
and which are endowed with evaluative accentuation by that attention. Only
items within that circle will achieve sign formation and become objects in
semiotic communication. What determines this circle of items endowed with
value accents?

In order for any item, from whatever domain of reality it may come, to enter
the social purview of the group and elicit ideological semiotic reaction, it must
be associated with the vital socio-economic prerequisites of the particular
group's existence; it must somehow, even if only obliquely, make contact with
the bases of the group's material life.

Individual choice under these circumstances, of course, can have no
meaning at all. The sign is a creation between individuals, a creation within a
social milieu. Therefore the item in question must first acquire interindividual

significance, and only then can it become an object for sign formation. In other words, *only that which has acquired social value can enter the world of ideology, take shape, and establish itself there.*

For this reason, all ideological accents, despite their being produced by the individual voice (as in the case of word) or, in any event, by the individual organism – all ideological accents are social accents, ones with claim to *social recognition* and, only thanks to that recognition, are made outward use of in ideological material.

Let us agree to call the entity which becomes the object of a sign the *theme* of the sign. Each fully fledged sign has its theme. And so, every verbal performance has its theme.

An ideological theme is always socially accentuated. Of course, all the social accents of ideological themes make their way also into the individual consciousness (which, as we know, is ideological through and through) and there take on the semblance of individual accents, since the individual consciousness assimilates them as its own. However, the source of these accents is not the individual consciousness. Accent, as such, is interindividual. The animal cry, the pure response to pain in the organism, is bereft of accent; it is a purely natural phenomenon. For such a cry, the social atmosphere is irrelevant, and therefore it does not contain even the germ of sign formation.

The theme of an ideological sign and the form of an ideological sign are inextricably bound together and are separable only in the abstract. Ultimately, the same set of forces and the same material prerequisites bring both the one and the other to life.

Indeed, the economic conditions that inaugurate a new element of reality into the social purview, that make it socially meaningful and 'interesting', are exactly the same conditions that create the forms of ideological communication (the cognitive, the artistic, the religious, and so on), which in turn shape the forms of semiotic expression.

Thus, the themes and forms of ideological creativity emerge from the same matrix and are in essence two sides of the same thing.

The process of incorporation into ideology – the birth of theme and birth of form – is best followed out in the material of the word. This process of ideological generation is reflected two ways in language: both in its large-scale, universal-historical dimensions as studied by semantic palaeontology, which has disclosed the incorporation of undifferentiated chunks of reality into the social purview of prehistoric man, and in its small-scale dimensions as constituted within the framework of contemporaneity, since, as we know, the word sensitively reflects the slightest variations in social existence.

Existence reflected in sign is not merely reflected but *refracted.* How is this refraction of existence in the ideological sign determined? By an intersecting of differently oriented social interests within one and the same sign community, i.e., *by the class struggle.*

Class does not coincide with the sign community, i.e., with the community which is the totality of users of the same set of signs for ideological communication. Thus various different classes will use one and the same language. As a result, differently oriented accents intersect in every ideological sign. Sign becomes an arena of the class struggle.

This social *multiaccentuality* of the ideological sign is a very crucial aspect. By and large, it is thanks to this intersecting of accents that a sign maintains its vitality and dynamism and the capacity for further development. A sign that has been withdrawn from the pressures of the social struggle – which, so to speak, crosses beyond the pale of the class struggle – inevitably loses force, degenerating into allegory and becoming the object not of live social intelligibility but of philological comprehension. The historical memory of mankind is full of such worn out ideological signs incapable of serving as arenas for the clash of live social accents. However, inasmuch as they are remembered by the philologist and the historian, they may be said to retain the last glimmers of life.

The very same thing that makes the ideological sign vital and mutable is also, however, that which makes it a refracting and distorting medium. The ruling class strives to impart a supraclass, eternal character to the ideological sign, to extinguish or drive inward the struggle between social value judgements which occurs in it, to make the sign uniaccentual.

In actual fact, each living ideological sign has two faces, like Janus. Any current curse word can become a word of praise, any current truth must inevitably sound to many other people as the greatest lie. This *inner dialectic quality* of the sign comes out fully in the open only in times of social crises or revolutionary changes. In the ordinary conditions of life, the contradiction embedded in every ideological sign cannot emerge fully because the ideological sign in an established, dominant ideology is always somewhat reactionary and tries, as it were, to stabilize the preceding factor in the dialectical flux of the social generative process, so accentuating yesterday's truth as to make it appear today's. And that is what is responsible for the refracting and distorting peculiarity of the ideological sign within the dominant ideology.

This, then, is the picture of the problem of the relation of the basis to superstructures. Our concern with it has been limited to concretization of certain of its aspects and elucidation of the direction and routes to be followed in a productive treatment of it. We made a special point of the place philosophy of language has in that treatment. The material of the verbal sign allows one most fully and easily to follow out the continuity of the dialectical process of change, a process which goes from the basis to superstructures. The category of mechanical causality in explanations of ideological phenomena can most easily be surmounted on the grounds of philosophy of language.

NOTE

1 The problem of behavioural speech genres has only very recently become a topic of discussion in linguistic and philosophical scholarship. One of the first serious attempts to deal with these genres, though, to be sure, without any clearly defined sociological orientation, is Leo Spitzer's *Italienische Umgangssprache* (1922).

5 Walter Benjamin

a) Surrealism: The Last Snapshot of the European
Intelligentsia (1929)
b) Addendum to 'The Paris of the Second Empire in
Baudelaire' (1938)*

Walter Benjamin (1892–1940) lived mostly in Germany and, after 1933, in France. Attempting to escape the Nazis, he killed himself in 1940. His major early work, *The Origin of German Tragic Drama* (1928; trans. 1977) failed to establish him within the German university system. Thereafter he worked as a writer, translator, journalist and, from 1933 onwards, with the financial support of the so-called Frankfurt School. Some of his wide range of writing is translated in the collections *Illuminations* (1973); *Charles Baudelaire* (1973); *Reflections* (1978); and *One-Way Street* (1979). Benjamin never joined the Communist Party and the extent of his Marxism has always been controversial. Written through deceptively simple constellations or fragments, rather than elaborated arguments, Benjamin's work resists systematic exposition or critique. Running through his work, however, is an approach to interpretation which combines Marxism and theology and seeks to redeem the significance of particulars as dialectical images of a revealed world. Influenced by the early Lukács and Bloch, his friends included Brecht, Adorno, and Gershom Scholem, whose conflicting interests in literature, critical theory and Judaism represent the main lines of interpretation of Benjamin's work. Whether as Marxist materialist or negative theologian, Benjamin's distinctive theoretical contributions concern history and historicism; literary forms such as tragedy, translation and allegory; and the impact of modernity and technology on experience. The suggestive style of 'Surrealism' (1929) illustrates Benjamin's affinities with surrealism and his distinct approach to the emancipatory illumination of everyday life. This essay prefigures Benjamin's unfinished work on the prehistory of modernity known as the *Passagenwerk* or Arcades project, from which 'Addendum to "The Paris of the Second Empire in Baudelaire" ' provides a brief introduction. For discussion, see R. Wolin, *Walter Benjamin* (1982); M. W. Jennings, *Dialectical Images: Walter Benjamin's Theory of Literary Criticism* (1987); *On Walter Benjamin*, ed. G. Smith (1988); and S. Buck-Morss, *The Dialectics of Seeing: Walter Benjamin and the Arcades Project* (1989).

---

* a) From Walter Benjamin, *One-Way Street and Other Writings*, trans. Edmund Jephcott and Kingsley Shorter (London: NLB, 1979), 225–39; (b) from Walter Benjamin, *Charles Baudelaire*, trans. Harry Zohn (London: NLB, 1973), 103–6.

a) Surrealism: The Last Snapshot of the European Intelligentsia

Intellectual currents can generate a sufficient head of water for the critic to install his power station on them. The necessary gradient, in the case of Surrealism, is produced by the difference in intellectual level between France and Germany. What sprang up in 1919 in France in a small circle of literati – we shall give the most important names at once: André Breton, Louis Aragon, Philippe Soupault, Robert Desnos, Paul Eluard – may have been a meagre stream, fed on the damp boredom of post-war Europe and the last trickle of French decadence. The know-alls who even today have not advanced beyond the 'authentic origins' of the movement, and even now have nothing to say about it except that yet another clique of literati is here mystifying the honourable public, are a little like a gathering of experts at a spring who, after lengthy deliberation, arrive at the conviction that this paltry stream will never drive turbines.

The German observer is not standing at the head of the stream. That is his opportunity. He is in the valley. He can gauge the energies of the movement. As a German he is long acquainted with the crisis of the intelligentsia, or, more precisely, with that of the humanistic concept of freedom; and he knows how frantic is the determination that has awakened in the movement to go beyond the stage of eternal discussion and, at any price, to reach a decision; he has had direct experience of its highly exposed position between an anarchistic *fronde* and a revolutionary discipline, and so has no excuse for taking the movement for the 'artistic', 'poetic' one it superficially appears. If it was such at the outset, it was, however, precisely at the outset that Breton declared his intention of breaking with a praxis that presents the public with the literary precipitate of a certain form of existence while withholding that existence itself. Stated more briefly and dialectically, this means that the sphere of poetry was here explored from within by a closely knit circle of people pushing the 'poetic life' to the utmost limits of possibility. And they can be taken at their word when they assert that Rimbaud's *Saison en enfer* no longer had any secrets for them. For this book is indeed the first document of the movement (in recent times; earlier precursors will be discussed later). Can the point at issue be more definitively and incisively presented than by Rimbaud himself in his personal copy of the book? In the margin, beside the passage 'on the silk of the seas and the arctic flowers', he later wrote, 'There's no such thing.'

In just how inconspicuous and peripheral a substance the dialectical kernel that later grew into Surrealism was originally embedded, was shown by Aragon in 1924 – at a time when its development could not yet be foreseen –

in his *Vague de rêves*. Today it can be foreseen. For there is no doubt that the heroic phase, whose catalogue of heroes Aragon left us in that work, is over. There is always, in such movements, a moment when the original tension of the secret society must either explode in a matter-of-fact, profane struggle for power and domination, or decay as a public demonstration and be transformed. Surrealism is in this phase of transformation at present. But at the time when it broke over its founders as an inspiring dream wave, it seemed the most integral, conclusive, absolute of movements. Everything with which it came into contact was integrated. Life only seemed worth living where the threshold between waking and sleeping was worn away in everyone as by the steps of multitudinous images flooding back and forth, language only seemed itself where sound and image, image and sound interpenetrated with automatic precision and such felicity that no chink was left for the penny-in-the-slot called 'meaning'. Image and language take precedence. Saint-Pol Roux, retiring to bed about daybreak, fixes a notice on his door: 'Poet at work.' Breton notes: 'Quietly. I want to pass where no one yet has passed, quietly! – After you, dearest language.' Language takes precedence.

Not only before meaning. Also before the self. In the world's structure dream loosens individuality like a bad tooth. This loosening of the self by intoxication is, at the same time, precisely the fruitful, living experience that allowed these people to step outside the domain of intoxication. This is not the place to give an exact definition of Surrealist experience. But anyone who has perceived that the writings of this circle are not literature but something else – demonstrations, watchwords, documents, bluffs, forgeries if you will, but at any rate not literature – will also know, for the same reason, that the writings are concerned literally with experiences, not with theories and still less with phantasms. And these experiences are by no means limited to dreams, hours of hashish eating, or opium smoking. It is a cardinal error to believe that, of 'Surrealist experiences', we know only the religious ecstasies or the ecstasies of drugs. The opium of the people, Lenin called religion, and brought the two things closer together than the Surrealists could have liked. I shall refer later to the bitter, passionate revolt against Catholicism in which Rimbaud, Lautréamont and Apollinaire brought Surrealism into the world. But the true, creative overcoming of religious illumination certainly does not lie in narcotics. It resides in a *profane illumination*, a materialistic, anthropological inspiration, to which hashish, opium, or whatever else can give an introductory lesson. (But a dangerous one; and the religious lesson is stricter.) This profane illumination did not always find the Surrealists equal to it, or to themselves, and the very writings that proclaim it most powerfully, Aragon's incomparable *Paysan de Paris* and Breton's *Nadja*, show very disturbing symptoms of deficiency. For example, there is in *Nadja* an excellent passage on the 'delightful days spent looting Paris under the sign of Sacco and

Vanzetti'; Breton adds the assurance that in those days Boulevard Bonne-Nouvelle fulfilled the strategic promise of revolt that had always been implicit in its name. But Madame Sacco also appears, not the wife of Fuller's victim but a *voyante*, a fortune-teller who lives at 3 rue des Usines and tells Paul Eluard that he can expect no good from Nadja. Now I concede that the breakneck career of Surrealism over rooftops, lightning conductors, gutters, verandas, weathercocks, stucco work – all ornaments are grist to the cat burglar's mill – may have taken it also into the humid backroom of spiritualism. But I am not pleased to hear it cautiously tapping on the window-panes to inquire about its future. Who would not wish to see these adoptive children of revolution most rigorously severed from all the goings-on in the conventicles of down-at-heel dowagers, retired majors and *émigré* profiteers?

In other respects Breton's book illustrates well a number of the basic characteristics of this 'profane illumination'. He calls *Nadja* 'a book with a banging door'. (In Moscow I lived in a hotel in which almost all the rooms were occupied by Tibetan lamas who had come to Moscow for a congress of Buddhist churches. I was struck by the number of doors in the corridors that were always left ajar. What had at first seemed accidental began to be disturbing. I found out that in these rooms lived members of a sect who had sworn never to occupy closed rooms. The shock I had then must be felt by the reader of *Nadja*.) To live in a glass house is a revolutionary virtue par excellence. It is also an intoxication, a moral exhibitionism, that we badly need. Discretion concerning one's own existence, once an aristocratic virtue, has become more and more an affair of petty-bourgeois parvenus. *Nadja* has achieved the true, creative synthesis between the art novel and the *roman-à-clef*.

Moreover, one need only take love seriously to recognize in it, too – as *Nadja* also indicates – a 'profane illumination'. 'At just that time' (i.e., when he knew Nadja), the author tells us, 'I took a great interest in the epoch of Louis VII, because it was the time of the "courts of love", and I tried to picture with great intensity how people saw life then.' We have from a recent author quite exact information on Provençal love poetry, which comes surprisingly close to the Surrealist conception of love. 'All the poets of the "new style",' Erich Auerback points out in his excellent *Dante: Poet of the Secular World*, 'possess a mystical beloved, they all have approximately the same very curious experience of love; to them all Amor bestows or withholds gifts that resemble an illumination more than sensual pleasure; all are subject to a kind of secret bond that determines their inner and perhaps also their outer lives.' The dialectics of intoxication are indeed curious. Is not perhaps all ecstasy in one world humiliating sobriety in that complementary to it? What is it that courtly *Minne* seeks – and it, not love, binds Breton to the telepathic girl – if not to make chastity, too, a transport? Into a world that borders not only on tombs of the Sacred Heart or altars to the Virgin, but also on the morning before a battle or after a victory.

The lady, in esoteric love, matters least. So, too, for Breton. He is closer to the things that Nadja is close to than to her. What are these things? Nothing could reveal more about Surrealism than their canon. Where shall I begin? He can boast an extraordinary discovery. He was the first to perceive the revolutionary energies that appear in the 'outmoded', in the first iron constructions, the first factory buildings, the earliest photos, the objects that have begun to be extinct, grand pianos, the dresses of five years ago, fashionable restaurants when the vogue has begun to ebb from them. The relation of these things to revolution – no one can have a more exact concept of it than these authors. No one before these visionaries and augurs perceived how destitution – not only social but architectonic, the poverty of interiors, enslaved and enslaving objects – can be suddenly transformed into revolutionary nihilism. Leaving aside Aragon's *Passage de l'Opéra*, Breton and Nadja are the lovers who convert everything that we have experienced on mournful railway journeys (railways are beginning to age), on Godforsaken Sunday afternoons in the proletarian quarters of the great cities, in the first glance through the rain-blurred window of a new apartment, into revolutionary experience, if not action. They bring the immense forces of 'atmosphere' concealed in these things to the point of explosion. What form do you suppose a life would take that was determined at a decisive moment precisely by the street song last on everyone's lips?

The trick by which this world of things is mastered – it is more proper to speak of a trick than a method – consists in the substitution of a political for a historical view of the past. 'Open, graves, you, the dead of the picture galleries, corpses behind screens, in palaces, castles, and monasteries, here stands the fabulous keeper of keys holding a bunch of the keys to all times, who knows where to press the most artful lock and invites you to step into the midst of the world of today, to mingle with the bearers of burdens, the mechanics whom money ennobles, to make yourself at home in their automobiles, which are beautiful as armour from the age of chivalry, to take your places in the international sleeping cars, and to weld yourself to all the people who today are still proud of their privileges. But civilization will give them short shrift.' This speech was attributed to Apollinaire by his friend Henri Hertz. Apollinaire originated this technique. In his volume of novellas, *L'hérésiarque*, he used it with Machiavellian calculation to blow Catholicism (to which he inwardly clung) to smithereens.

At the centre of this world of things stands the most dreamed-of of their objects, the city of Paris itself. But only revolt completely exposes its Surrealist face (deserted streets in which whistles and shots dictate the outcome). And no face is surrealistic in the same degree as the true face of a city. No picture by de Chirico or Max Ernst can match the sharp elevations of the city's inner strongholds, which one must overrun and occupy in order to master their fate and, in their fate, in the fate of their masses, one's own.

Nadja is an exponent of these masses and of what inspires them to revolution: 'The great living, sonorous unconsciousness that inspires my only convincing acts, in the sense that I always want to prove that it commands forever everything that is mine.' Here, therefore, we find the catalogue of these fortifications, from Place Maubert, where as nowhere else dirt has retained all its symbolic power, to the 'Théâtre Moderne', which I am inconsolable not to have known. But in Breton's description of her bar on the upper floor – 'it is quite dark, with arbours like impenetrable tunnels – a drawing room on the bottom of a lake' – there is something that brings back to my memory that most uncomprehended room in the old Princess Café. It was the back room on the first floor, with couples in the blue light. We called it the 'anatomy school'; it was the last restaurant designed for love. In such passages in Breton, photography intervenes in a very strange way. It makes the streets, gates, squares of the city into illustrations of a trashy novel, draws off the banal obviousness of this ancient architecture to inject it with the most pristine intensity toward the events described, to which, as in old chambermaids' books, word-for-word quotations with page numbers refer. And all the parts of Paris that appear here are places where what is between these people turns like a revolving door.

The Surrealists' Paris, too, is a 'little universe'. That is to say, in the larger one, the cosmos, things look no different. There, too, are crossroads where ghostly signals flash from the traffic, and inconceivable analogies and connections between events are the order of the day. It is the region from which the lyric poetry of Surrealism reports. And this must be noted if only to counter the obligatory misunderstanding of *l'art pour l'art*. For art's sake was scarcely ever to be taken literally; it was almost always a flag under which sailed a cargo that could not be declared because it still lacked a name. This is the moment to embark on a work that would illuminate as has no other the crisis of the arts that we are witnessing: a history of esoteric poetry. Nor is it by any means fortuitous that no such work yet exists. For written as it demands to be written – that is, not as a collection to which particular 'specialists' all contribute 'what is most worth knowing' from their fields, but as the deeply grounded composition of an individual who, from inner compulsion, portrays less a historical evolution than a constantly renewed, primal upsurge of esoteric poetry – written in such a way it would be one of those scholarly confessions that can be counted in every century. The last page would have to show an X-ray picture of Surrealism. Breton indicates in his *Introduction au discours sur le peu de réalité* how the philosophical realism of the Middle Ages was the basis of poetic experience. This realism, however – that is, the belief in a real, separate existence of concepts whether outside or inside things – has always very quickly crossed over from the logical realm of ideas to the magical realm of words. And it is as magical experiments with words, not as artistic dabbling, that we must understand the passionate phonetic and graphical transformational games that have run through the whole literature of the avant-garde for the past fifteen years, whether it is called Futurism, Dadaism, or Surrealism. How slogans, magic formulas, and concepts are here intermingled is shown by the following words of Apollinaire's from his last manifesto, *L'esprit nouveau et les poètes*. He says, in 1918: 'For the speed and simplicity with which we have all become used to referring by a single word to such complex entities as a crowd, a nation, the universe, there is no modern equivalent in literature. But today's writers fill this gap; their synthetic works create new realities the plastic manifestations of which are just as complex as those referred to by the words standing for collectives.' If, however, Apollinaire and Breton advance even more energetically in the same direction and complete the linkage of Surrealism to the outside world with the declaration, 'The conquests of science rest far more on a surrealistic than on a logical thinking' – if, in other words, they make mystification, the culmination of which Breton sees in poetry (which is defensible), the foundation of scientific and technical development, too – then such integration is too impetuous. It is very instructive to compare the movement's over-precipitate embrace of the uncomprehended miracle of machines – 'the old fables have for the most part been realized, now it is the turn of poets to create new ones that the inventors on their side can then make real' (Apollinaire) – to compare these overheated fantasies with the well-ventilated utopias of a Scheerbart.

'The thought of all human activity makes me laugh.' This utterance of Aragon's shows very clearly the path Surrealism had to follow from its origins to its politicization. In his excellent essay '*La révolution et les intellectuals*', Pierre Naville, who originally belonged to this group, rightly called this development dialectical. In the transformation of a highly contemplative attitude into revolutionary opposition, the hostility of the bourgeoisie toward every manifestation of radical intellectual freedom played a leading part. This hostility pushed Surrealism to the left. Political events, above all the war in Morocco, accelerated this development. With the manifesto 'Intellectuals Against the Moroccan War', which appeared in *L'Humanité*, a fundamentally different platform was gained from that which was characterized by, for example, the famous scandal at the Saint-Pol Roux banquet. At that time, shortly after the war, when the Surrealists, who deemed the celebration for a poet they worshipped compromised by the presence of nationalistic elements, burst out with the cry 'Long live Germany', they remained within the boundaries of scandal, toward which, as is known, the bourgeoisie is as thick-skinned as it is sensitive to all action. There is remarkable agreement between the ways in which, under such political auspices, Apollinaire and Aragon saw the future of the poet. The chapters 'Persecution' and 'Murder' in Apollinaire's *Poète assassiné* contain the famous description of a program against poets. Publishing houses are stormed, books of poems thrown on the fire, poets lynched. And the same scenes are taking place at the same time all over the world. In Aragon, 'Imagination', in anticipation of such horrors, calls its company to a last crusade.

To understand such prophecies, and to assess strategically the line arrived at by Surrealism, one must investigate the mode of thought widespread among the so-called well-meaning left-wing bourgeois intelligentsia. It manifests itself clearly enough in the present Russian orientation of these circles. We are not of course referring here to Béraud, who pioneered the lie about Russia, or to Fabre-Luce, who trots behind him like a devoted donkey, loaded with every kind of bourgeois ill-will. But how problematic is even the typical mediating book by Duhamel. How difficult to bear is the strained uprightness, the forced animation and sincerity of the Protestant method, dictated by embarrassment and linguistic ignorance, of placing things in some kind of symbolic illumination. How revealing his résumé: 'the true, deeper revolution, which could in some sense transform the substance of the Slavonic soul itself, has not yet taken place.' It is typical of these left-wing French intellectuals – exactly as it is of their Russian counterparts, too – that their positive function derives entirely from a feeling of obligation, not to the Revolution, but to traditional culture. Their collective achievement, as far as it is positive, approximates conservation. But politically and economically they must always be considered a potential source of sabotage.

Characteristic of this whole left-wing bourgeois position is its irremediable coupling of idealistic morality with political practice. Only in contrast to the helpless compromises of 'sentiment' are certain central features of Surrealism, indeed of the Surrealist tradition, to be understood. Little has happened so far to promote this understanding. The seduction was too great to regard the Satanism of a Rimbaud and a Lautrémont as a pendant to art for art's sake in an inventory of snobbery. If, however, one resolves to open up this romantic dummy, one finds something usable inside. One finds the cult of evil as a political device, however romantic, to disinfect and isolate against all moralizing dilettantism. Convinced of this, and coming across the scenario of a horror play by Breton that centres about a violation of children, one might perhaps go back a few decades. Between 1865 and 1875 a number of great anarchists, without knowing of one another, worked on their infernal machines. And the astonishing thing is that independently of one another they set its clock at exactly the same hour, and forty years later in western Europe the writings of Dostoevsky, Rimbaud, and Lautrémont exploded at the same time. One might, to be more exact, select from Dostoevsky's entire work the one episode that was actually not published until about 1915, 'Stavrogin's Confession' from *The Possessed*. This chapter, which touches very closely on the third canto of the *Chants de Maldoror*, contains a justification of evil in which certain motifs of Surrealism are more powerfully expressed than by any of its present spokesmen. For Stavrogin is a Surrealist *avant la lettre*. No one else understood, as he did, how naïve is the view of the Philistines that goodness, for all the manly virtue of those who practise it, is God-inspired; whereas evil stems entirely from our spontaneity, and in it we are independent and self-sufficient beings. No one else saw inspiration, as he did, in even the most ignoble actions, and precisely in them. He considered vileness itself as something preformed, both in the course of the world and also in ourselves, to which we are disposed if not called, as the bourgeois idealist sees virtue. Dostoevsky's God created not only heaven and earth and man and beast, but also baseness, vengeance, cruelty. And here, too, he gave the devil no opportunity to meddle in his handiwork. That is why all these vices have a pristine vitality in his work; they are perhaps not 'splendid', but eternally new, 'as on the first day', separated by an infinity from the clichés through which sin is perceived by the Philistine.

The pitch of tension that enabled the poets under discussion to achieve at a distance their astonishing effects is documented quite scurrilously in the letter Isidore Ducasse addressed to his publisher on 23 October 1869, in an attempt to make his poetry look acceptable. He places himself in the line of descent from Mickiewicz, Milton, Southey, Alfred de Musset, Baudelaire, and says: 'Of course, I somewhat swelled the note to bring something new into this literature that, after all, only sings of despair in order to depress the reader and thus make him long all the more intensely for goodness as a remedy. So that in the end one really sings only of goodness, only the method is more philosophical and less naïve than that of the old school, of which only Victor Hugo and a few others are still alive.' But if Lautréamont's erratic book has any lineage at all, or, rather, can be assigned one, it is that of insurrection. Soupault's attempt, in his edition of the complete works in 1927, to write a political curriculum vitae for Isidore Ducasse was therefore a quite understandable and not unperceptive venture. Unfortunately, there is no documentation for it, and that adduced by Soupault rests on a confusion. On the other hand, and happily, a similar attempt in the case of Rimbaud was successful, and it is the achievement of Marcel Coulon to have defended the poet's true image against the Catholic usurpation by Claudel and Berrichon. Rimbaud is indeed a Catholic, but he is one, by his own account, in the most wretched part of himself, which he does not tire of denouncing and consigning to his own and everyone's hatred, his own and everyone's contempt: the part that forces him to confess that he does not understand revolt. But that is the concession of a communard dissatisfied with his own contribution who, by the time he turned his back on poetry, had long since – in his earliest work – taken leave of religion. 'Hatred, to you I have entrusted my treasure', he writes in the *Saison en enfer*. This is another dictum around which a poetics of Surrealism might grow like a climbing plant, to sink its roots deeper than the theory of 'surprised' creation originated by Apollinaire, to the depth of the insights of Poe.

Since Bakunin, Europe has lacked a radical concept of freedom. The Surrealists have one. They are the first to liquidate the sclerotic liberal-moral-humanistic ideal of freedom, because they are convinced that 'freedom, which on this earth can only be bought with a thousand of the hardest sacrifices, must be enjoyed unrestrictedly in its fullness without any kind of pragmatic calculation, as long as it lasts.' And this proves to them that 'mankind's struggle for liberation in its simplest revolutionary form (which, however, is liberation in every respect), remains the only cause worth serving.' But are they successful in welding this experience of freedom to the other revolutionary experience that we have to acknowledge because it has been ours, the constructive, dictatorial side of revolution? In short, have they bound revolt to revolution? How are we to imagine an existence oriented solely toward Boulevard Bonne-Nouvelle, in rooms by Le Corbusier and Oud?

To win the energies of intoxication for the revolution – this is the project about which Surrealism circles in all its books and enterprises. This it may call its most particular task. For them it is not enough that, as we know, an ecstatic component lives in every revolutionary act. This component is identical with the anarchic. But to place the accent exclusively on it would be to subordinate the methodical and disciplinary preparation for revolution entirely to a praxis oscillating between fitness exercises and celebration in advance. Added to this is an inadequate, undialectical conception of the nature of intoxication. The aesthetic of the painter, the poet, *en état de surprise*, of art as the reaction of one surprised, is enmeshed in a number of pernicious romantic prejudices. Any serious exploration of occult, surrealistic, phantasmagoric gifts and phenomena presupposes a dialectical intertwinement to which a romantic turn of mind is impervious. For histrionic or fanatical stress on the mysterious side of the mysterious takes us no further; we penetrate the mystery only to the degree that we recognize it in the everyday world, by virtue of a dialectical optic that perceives the everyday as impenetrable, the impenetrable as everyday. The most passionate investigation of telepathic phenomena, for example, will not teach us half as much about reading (which is an eminently telepathic process), as the profane illumination of reading about telepathic phenomena. And the most passionate investigation of the hashish trance will not teach us half as much about thinking (which is eminently narcotic), as the profane illumination of thinking about the hashish trance. The reader, the thinker, the loiterer, the *flâneur*, are types of illuminati just as much as the opium eater, the dreamer, the ecstatic. And more profane. Not to mention that most terrible drug – ourselves – which we take in solitude.

'To win the energies of intoxication for the revolution' – in other words, poetic politics? 'We have tried that beverage. Anything, rather than that!' Well, it will interest you all the more how much an excursion into poetry clarifies things. For what is the programme of the bourgeois parties? A bad poem on springtime, filled to bursting with metaphors. The socialist sees that 'finer future of our children and grandchildren' in a condition in which all act 'as if they were angels', and everyone has as much 'as if he were rich', and everyone lives 'as if he were free'. Of angels, wealth, freedom, not a trace. These are mere images. And the stock imagery of these poets of the social-democratic associations? Their *gradus ad parnassum*? Optimism. A very different air is breathed in the Naville essay that makes the 'organization of pessimism' the call of the hour. In the name of his literary friends he delivers an ultimatum in face of which this unprincipled, dilettantish optimism must unfailingly show its true colours: where are the conditions for revolution? In the changing of attitudes or of external circumstances? That is the cardinal question that determines the relation of politics to morality and cannot be glossed over. Surrealism has come ever closer to the Communist answer. And that means pessimism all along the line. Absolutely. Mistrust in the fate of literature, mistrust in the fate of freedom, mistrust in the fate of European humanity, but three times mistrust in all reconciliation: between classes, between nations, between individuals. And unlimited trust only in I. G. Farben and the peaceful perfection of the air force. But what now, what next?

Here due weight must be given to the insight that in the *Traité du style*, Aragon's last book, required in distinction between metaphor and image, a happy insight into questions of style that needs extending. Extension: nowhere do these two – metaphor and image – collide so drastically and so irreconcilably as in politics. For to organize pessimism means nothing other than to expel moral metaphor from politics and to discover in political action a sphere reserved one hundred per cent for images. This image sphere, however, can no longer be measured out by contemplation. If it is the double task of the revolutionary intelligentsia to overthrow the intellectual predominance of the bourgeoisie and to make contact with the proletarian masses, the intelligentsia has failed almost entirely in the second part of this task because it can no longer be performed contemplatively. And yet this has hindered hardly anybody from approaching it again and again as if it could, and calling for proletarian poets, thinkers and artists. To counter this, Trotsky had to point out – as early as *Literature and Revolution* – that such artists would only emerge from a victorious revolution. In reality it is far less a matter of making the artist of bourgeois origin into a master of 'proletarian art' than of deploying him, even at the expense of his artistic activity, at important points in this sphere of imagery. Indeed, might not perhaps the interruption of his 'artistic career' be an essential part of his new function?

The jokes he tells are the better for it. And he tells them better. For in the joke, too, in invective, in misunderstanding, in all cases where an action puts forth its own image and exists, absorbing and consuming it, where nearness looks with its own eyes, the long-sought image sphere is opened, the world of universal and integral actualities, where the 'best room' is missing – the sphere, in a word, in which political materialism and physical nature share the inner man, the psyche, the individual, or whatever else we wish to throw to them, with dialectical justice, so that no limb remains unrent. Nevertheless – indeed, precisely after such dialectical annihilation – this will still be a sphere of images and, more concretely, of bodies. For it must in the end be admitted: metaphysical materialism, of the brand of Vogt and Bukharin, as is attested by the experience of the Surrealists, and earlier of Hebel, Georg Büchner, Nietzsche and Rimbaud, cannot lead without rupture to anthropological materialism. There is a residue. The collective is a body, too. And the *physis* that is being organized for it in technology can, through all its political and factual reality, only be produced in that image sphere to which profane illumination initiates us. Only when in technology body and image so interpenetrate that all revolutionary tension becomes bodily collective innervation, and all the bodily innervations of the collective become revolutionary discharge, has reality transcended itself to the extent demanded by the *Communist Manifesto*. For the moment, only the Surrealists have understood its present commands. They exchange, to a man, the play of human features for the face of an alarm clock that in each minute rings for sixty seconds.

b) Addendum to 'The Paris of the Second Empire in Baudelaire'

Sundering truth from falsehood is the goal of the materialist method, not its point of departure. In other words, its point of departure is the object riddled with error, with $\delta o \xi \alpha$ [conjecture]. The distinctions with which the materialist method, discriminative from the outset, starts are distinctions within this highly mixed object, and it cannot present this object as mixed or uncritical enough. If it claimed to approach the object the way it is 'in truth', it would only greatly reduce its chances. These chances, however, are considerably augmented if the materialist method increasingly abandons such a claim, thus preparing for the insight that 'the matter in itself' is not 'in truth'.

It is, to be sure, tempting to pursue the 'matter in itself'. In the case of Baudelaire, it offers itself in profusion. The sources flow to one's heart's content, and there they converge to form the stream of tradition; this stream flows along as far as the eye can reach between well-laid-out slopes. Historical materialism is not diverted by this spectacle. It does not seek the reflection of the clouds in this stream, but it also does not turn away from the stream to drink 'from the source' and pursue the 'matter itself' behind men's backs. Whose mills does this stream activate? Who is utilizing its power? Who dammed it? These are the questions which historical materialism asks, and it changes the picture of the landscape by naming the forces which have been operative in it.

This seems like a complicated process, and it is. Is there not a more direct, a more decisive one? Why not simply confront the poet Baudelaire with present-day society and answer the question as to what he has to say to this society's progressive cadres by referring to his works – without, to be sure, ignoring the question whether he has anything to say to them at all? What speaks against this is precisely that when we read Baudelaire we are given a course of historical lessons by bourgeois society. These lessons can never be ignored. A critical reading of Baudelaire and a critical revision of this course of lessons are one and the same thing. For it is an illusion of vulgar Marxism that the social function of a material or intellectual product can be determined without reference to the circumstances and the bearers of its tradition. 'As the aggregate of objects which are viewed independently (if not of the production process in which they originated, then of the production process in which they survive), the concept of culture . . . has something fetishistic about it.'[1] The tradition of Baudelaire's works is a very short one, but it already bears historical scars which must be of interest to critical observers.

Taste

Taste develops with the definite preponderance of commodity production over any other kind of production. As a consequence of the manufacture of products as commodities for the market, people become less and less aware of the conditions of their production – not only of the social conditions in the form of exploitation, but of the technical conditions as well. The consumer, who is more or less expert when he gives an order to an artisan – in individual cases he is advised by the master craftsman himself – is not usually knowledgeable when he appears as a buyer. Added to this is the fact that mass production, which aims at turning out inexpensive commodities, must be bent upon disguising bad quality. In most cases it is actually in its interest that the buyer have little expertise. The more industry progresses, the more perfect are the imitations which it throws on the market. The commodity is bathed in a profane glow; this glow has nothing in common with the glow that produces its 'theological capers', yet it is of some importance to society. In a speech about trademarks Chaptal said on 17 July 1824: 'Do not tell me that in the final analysis a shopper will know about the different qualities of a material. No, gentlemen, a consumer is no judge of them; he will go only by the appearance of the commodity. But are looking and touching enough to determine the permanence of colours, the fineness of a material, or the quality and nature of its finish?' In the same measure as the expertness of a customer declines, the importance of his taste increases – both for him and for the manufacturer. For the consumer it has the value of a more or less elaborate masking of his lack of expertness. Its value to the manufacturer is a fresh stimulus to consumption which in some cases is satisfied at the expense of other requirements of consumption the manufacturer would find more costly to meet.

It is precisely this development which literature reflects in *l'art pour l'art*. This doctrine and its corresponding practice for the first time give taste a dominant position in poetry. (To be sure, taste does not seem to be the object there; it is not mentioned anywhere. But this proves no more than does the fact that taste was often discussed in the aesthetic debates of the eighteenth century. Actually, these debates centred on the content.) In *l'art pour l'art* the poet for the first time faces language the way the buyer faces the commodity on the open market. He has lost his familiarity with the process of its production to a particularly high degree. The poets of *l'art pour l'art* are the last about whom it can be said that they come 'from the people'. They have nothing to formulate with such urgency that it could determine the *coining* of their words. Rather, they have to choose their words. The 'chosen word' soon became the motto of the *Jugendstil* literature.[2] The poet of *l'art pour l'art* wanted to bring to language above all himself – with all the idiosyncrasies, nuances and imponderables of his nature. These elements are reflected in taste. The poet's taste guides him in his choice of words. But the choice is made only among words which have not already been coined by the *object* itself – that is, which have not been included in its process of production.

In point of fact, the theory of *l'art pour l'art* assumed decisive importance around 1852, at a time when the bourgeoisie sought to take its 'cause' from the hands of the writers and the poets. In *The Eighteenth Brumaire* Marx recollects this moment, when 'the extra-parliamentary masses of the bourgeoisie . . . through the brutal abuse of their own press', called upon Napoleon 'to destroy their speaking and writing segment, their politicians and literati, so that they might confidently pursue their private affairs under the protection of a strong and untrammelled government'. At the end of this development may be found Mallarmé and the theory of *poésie pure*. There the cause of his own class has become so far removed from the poet that the problem of a literature without an object becomes the centre of discussion. This discussion takes place not least in Mallarmé's poems, which revolve about *blanc*, *absence*, *silence*, *vide*. This, to be sure – and particularly in Mallarmé – is the face of a coin whose other side is by no means insignificant. It furnishes evidence that the poet no longer undertakes to support any of the causes that are pursued by the class to which he belongs. To build a production on this basic renunciation of all manifest experiences of this class, causes specific and considerable difficulties. These difficulties turn this poetry into an esoteric poetry. Baudelaire's works are not esoteric. The social experiences which are reflected in his work are, to be sure, nowhere derived from the production process – least of all in its most advanced form, the industrial process – but all of them originated in extensive roundabout ways. But these roundabout ways are quite apparent in his works. The most important among them are the experiences of the neurasthenic, of the big-city dweller, and of the customer.

NOTES

1 The incalculable consequences of the more resolute procedure are rather forbidding in other respects as well. There is little point in trying to include the position of a Baudelaire in the fabric of the most advanced position in mankind's struggle of liberation. From the outset it seems more promising to investigate his machinations where he undoubtedly is at home – in the enemy camp. Very rarely are they a blessing for the opposite side. Baudelaire was a secret agent – an agent of the secret discontent of his class with its own rule.
2 'Pierre Louys écrit: le throne: on trouve partout des abymes, des ymages, ennuy des fleurs, etc. . . . Triomphe de l'y.'

6 Ernst Bloch
Marxism and Poetry (1935)*

Ernst Bloch (1885–1977) lived through a complicated and contradictory political trajectory. He developed his unorthodox mode of Marxist thinking out of utopian
and expressionist influences in Berlin. In political exile from Germany after 1933 he
became an important Marxist critic both of the cultural politics of the Soviet Union
and of Lukács, his friend and a major influence on his work. Having lived in the
United States from 1938–49, he moved to East Germany in 1949, became a critic
of 'fascist America' and a defender of Stalinist East Germany, only then to move to
West Germany as the Berlin Wall was being built. Given these shifts, Bloch has
been criticized for the political indeterminacy and naïve idealism of his interest in
wishful thinking. Nevertheless, Bloch's work is a remarkably persistent attempt to
realize philosophy as a collective praxis and to trace utopian intimations of a
better world. 'Marxism and Poetry' (1935) provides a brief introduction to
Bloch's theoretical attempt to understand the 'not-yet-conscious' and the 'not-yet-
become' in order to develop anticipatory illuminations of a classless society. Bloch
pursued this Marxist aesthetics of hope through a vast range of materials, from
aydreams and fairy tales to music and philosophy, notably in *The Principle of
Hope (1959, trans. 1986). Other works translated include Man on His Own* (1970);
A Philosophy of the Future (1970); *On Karl Marx* (1971); *Natural Law and
Human Dignity (1986); and Heritage of Our Times* (1990). Two collections of
Bloch's essays – *Essays on the Philosophy of Music* (1985) and *The Utopian
Function of Art and Literature* (1988) – provide helpful introductions and biblio-
graphical material. For discussion see F. Jameson, 'Ernst Bloch and the Future',
Marxism and Form (1971); and Wayne Hudson, *The Marxist Philosophy of Ernst Bloch*
(1982).

Nowadays a dream has a hard time in the world outside. That is the
lament particularly of those writers whose inner life is not in mere disarray.
They distrust sheer private humbug, and they have the will to express their

* From Ernst Bloch, *Utopian Function of Art and Literature: Selected Essays*, trans. J. Zipes and
F. Mecklenburg (Cambridge, Mass.: MIT Press, 1988), 156–62. The translation of this essay is
from the revised version published in *Literarische Aufsätze*.

common truth. They are thus led to socialist thought, which alone provides them with direction. But many writers touched by Marxism tend to consider themselves handicapped by this cold touch. The inner life does not come out well this way: the feeling and careful desire to articulate it are not always noticed. Each flower figures as a lie, and the intellect appears dried out or, if it has any juice at all, it is acidic. Many a pen becomes helpless by writing fiction while wanting to write the truth, or by looking for subjects that do not only let themselves be described or even narrated, but, in an honest way, let themselves be coloured in an imaginative way or their story be continued. Those who are handicapped say that Marx stole their good conscience of invention. It is amazing how much Marx is blamed for everything. But even a good story often no longer knows where to begin.

Not long ago it seemed easier to start. That was the time when feeble talents dressed themselves up. Now the more gifted ones draw what they can from the dream. Thirty years ago bells still resounded everywhere. Dehmel praised the *working man*. Poets made off to socialism like going off on adventure, none for the better. There is no doubt about it: the competent but small battle cry for revolution exaggerated its virility, excluded objects that could have invigorated it. Marxism keeps greater distance from experimental poets, especially those with grotesque imaginations, than the cynical bourgeoisie, which accepts them as clowns for their private amusement and understands or misunderstands them as diversions. The 'need of the moment' does not favour the broader, more creative and real poetic production any more. The motto for our day is, Make the most of your opportunities! Journalism or worse appears more readily to be tolerated: people as well as plots are conceived in accordance with flat, prearranged clichés. Naturalistic directness is praised as a manner of writing and as subject matter, the simple realism that kills the spirit, love, and the same without much ado. Such writing and subject matter confine reality mainly to what has become real for the proletariat these days, and neither acknowledges any historical remains nor any dream, even if it existed objectively. Thus, many young people, who have the strong urge to compose, to tell tales, to express their inborn imaginations, to temper them and have an effect, face the revolution as if it demanded the sacrifice of all imagination whatsoever, just as the obscurantists demanded the sacrifice of intellect. Hate all of Proust, even Kafka: 'Leave everything behind' appears as a permanent inscription above the door to Marxism.

But it is a distorted concern and in the long run no concern at all. Especially not when the confusing of teacher with disciplinarian, learning with draining the mind of imagination might ultimately stop. Sobriety and knowledge remain the spice of good dreams. And, if the dreams cannot bear knowledge, then they are self-deception or swindle. Marxist terminology leads beyond private or homeless curiosities. It is *real* and *great* and does not extract the true poetic correlate. Marx once called it the 'dream of a thing' in the world. Marxist terminology connects, directs, and corrects the surplus of the writer's material, connects him with the *surplus of tendency and latency* that reality produces about the so-called facts. Naturalism may describe these so-called facts. They are as valuable and as superficial as naturalism itself. Genuine realistic poetry deals with *process*, isolating and manipulating the facts. The process requires a precise imagination to portray it and is connected concretely with the imagination. Once one has tasted Marxist criticism, all ideological hogwash becomes repulsive, and one will discard it. The true poetic aura, the only one remaining and possible, imagination without lie, appears all the more distinctly and does not envy any former era for its subjects. Marxism remains as clarity, non-deceptive even poetically. It sheds light on the bourgeois writers of decline such as Green, Proust and Joyce, who reflect the mixed darkness and bleakness of the time. Marxism monitors and certifies their crypto-dialectics for posterity. Marxism predicted the capitalist 'frigidization' of existence long before the first fascist was born, and now the fascists have increased it by necrophilia à la Benn. The Marxist writer does not adhere to archaic methods of nothingness when he deals with nihilism but to the dialectical process. In western Europe the subjects of the dialectical process are still at least subversive and fermenting. But in the Soviet Union they are open and active, open to change. They are so abundant, and there is so much fresh material that literature could readily drown in subjects than die of thirst.

Therefore, the concern of writers, to be red and also mature, is distorted and is in the long run no concern at all. The time will come when the art of writing a story is no longer suspicious and when a mind with ideas will almost be busy not to have any; when having imagination is no longer a crime or treated largely as idealistic, as if there were no subjective factor at all; when the surface of things no longer stands for their totality, their cliché no longer for their reality; when little red Babbit's world no longer determines everything he ever saw. The long lasting praise of a realism, castrated by classicistic formulas, as the only genuine one is, from a Marxist point of view, an anomaly, both narrow-minded and dilettantish. But if one chooses to accept Marxism, then it opens gates to poetry where the bleakness, solitude and disorientation of late capitalism are pressing concerns. It shows movement and landscape being newly formed that lose nothing of their abundance and aspirations through exact topography. Instead of sterility and the non-existence of problems, which had become a stigma of the congealed, bourgeois-rationalistic Enlightenment (from Friedrich Nicolai, the publisher, to the philistine of culture who claimed to know everything and to have advanced magnificently far), Marxism shows countless problems of motion and incompleteness within a reality whose tendency and utopian backgrounds require more geniuses to express it than there are muses. The so-called poetic journalism and the so-called literature of the fact, praised between 1921 and

1929, are receding now. The problem of heritage moves forward, the heritage of Pushkin, Tolstoy, the great realism emerging from great poetry, certainly not through the imitation of epigones. Even apparent irregularity gains objective space as in times when mountains turn around. Then even the 'golden dragons and crystal spirits of the human soul' appear, says Gottfried Keller, the realist, in *Ursula*, part of the *Züricher Novellas*. Keller was not influenced by Jean Paul for nothing; he speaks of times of change when mountains move. The world was not built by schoolteachers, neither its poetry nor its forming-transforming forces that provide the basis for a poetry of universal style. Marxism's sole theme is that of forming-transforming, and it scares away the dreamers but not the precise imagination. It is this imagination, which is dialectically trained and mediated with tendency and latency of existence, with those time-spaces of real possibility. In brief, if imagination can find at best only hollow spaces in the late capitalist world in which to hide, it can find subjects, work and blessings to help it in the socialist world, the more the better. The imagination is no longer the social outcast.

The poetic inner life does not disclose at all what it is. That question is as idle and abstract as the related higher one about the meaning of the 'human' as such, the so-called universality of it. Nevertheless, the 'human' genuinely does exist within Marxist thought as the 'oppressed, alienated human being'. This way of thinking is the most real one, and Marxism does not know any other way than the real, i.e., human beings historically determined by class. The Marxist concept of the 'human', related to the poetic one, is not completely absorbed by its hitherto existing historical appearances so that it is still floating in them and seems unfulfilled. The poetic concept, although it is only comprehensible as it is expressed, only exists that way. There is no doubt that all inner life, especially when it is 'spiritual', is dangerously close to idealism, both overlapping with each other and almost more with objective idealism than with subjective. But Lenin noted, 'Philosophical idealism is nonsense *only* when viewed from the standpoint of crude, simple materialism. When viewed from the standpoint of dialectical materialism, on the other hand, philosophical idealism is a *one-sided*, exaggerated, extravagant inflation of one feature of knowledge.' Thus, it is mere 'one-sidedness', but not nonsense or total non-reality. After all, it is a relative and peculiar kind of reality that belongs as one of the 'features of knowledge' to the inner life of poetic consciousness, given that it is not completely detached from material existence. At the very least, 'idealism' exists at the starting point of anything 'human', and also in all 'formative, constructive, and creative forces'. When this factor is not put to use, it can only lead to non-expression, non-creation and non-representation. It is only in this way that the undeniable reality of human products would subsequently be little more than idealism in reality. Here consciousness and existence, ideology and base have a mutual effect on each other. The 'poetic' never entered the formations of ideology formally or without contents of its own so that it overlaps with mere 'false consciousness' – without 'productive additives' of its own. Ideology has been created by the 'poetic' in the superstructure of former civilizations. The poetic is not just a formal treatment. It is also an objective piece of work with material that leads to its condensation and brings out its essence. It shows itself most clearly in dramatic form through experimental isolation and elucidation of the conflicts, through intensification of the figures so that they capture the role of their characters and reveal their essence only when *driven to the very heights* in a poetic way. Thus, Lessing's phrase becomes clear: 'On stage we do not want to learn what this or that person did, but what everybody might do with a given character under certain given circumstances.' Thus Aristotle's famous phrase, which was obviously Lessing's reference, also takes on significance: 'The historiographer and the poet do not distinguish themselves from one another through the use of verse or prose. Their difference consists in the fact that one expresses what really happened; the other one, what might well happen. Therefore, poetry is more philosophical than historiography because it shows the universal more.' Consequently, the poetical depiction of the essential is based on something fundamental that does not appear at all so clearly in the empirical substance or has not become obvious in any way whatsoever. The subjective factor of the poetical is then the midwife of the artistic anticipatory illumination. Given the amazing superiority of philosophical truth – in particular, the truth given by Aristotelian poetics in preference to poetry rather than to so-called naturalistic history – it becomes clear at the same time that the case of realism is not as simple as it seems to the elemental or schematic *Weltanschauung*. Or, not everything remains idealistic – in the sense of the unreal – which is added to the subject while it is being driven away; rather, the most important element of reality might comply with it – the not yet lived possibility. In such a manner meaningful poetry makes the world become aware of an *accelerated flow of action*, an *elucidated waking dream of the essential*. The world wants to be changed in this way. Therefore, the *correlate of the world* to the poetically appropriate action is precisely the *tendency*. To the poetically appropriate waking dream it is precisely the *latency* of existence. And especially today the poetically precise dream does not die because of truth, for truth is not the portrayal of facts, but of processes. Truth is ultimately the demonstration of tendency and latency of what has not yet developed and needs its agent.

There is childhood or the fairy tale as material that constantly refreshes itself. There are the rebellious dream images in oppressed classes or the barely re-utilized treasures of cheap and popular literature. The uprisings of the people await their realization in 'red' epic poems, in the kind of 'historical' poetry that the bourgeoisie did not have and could not have. There is the history of heresy, a storehouse of brothers, enemies, symbols, which concern us in a powerful way – and which are poetically almost undiscovered, despite the Faust material. In our own time there is a world with fighting, corpses, victors, horrors, dangers, decisions, with the gloom and gaiety of Shakespearian dimension. There is a kind of nature to which no response has been given since Rimbaud, and, without an evocative qualitative language of latency, there is no answer whatsoever that can be given in a poetic way. All that, of course, denies the beautifully completed coherences in poetry since they are only possible idealistically. On the other hand, when observed from a Marxist perspective, reality is more coherent than ever, but only as *mediated interruption*, and the process of reality as such, traced by Marxism, is still open, therefore objectively fragmentary. It is only because of the really possible that the world is not made into a sophisticated book, but into a process dialectically mediated, therefore dialectically open. And realism, too, reveals itself poetically time and again as created in a rough and extended way. One might even say that wherever realism appears as a complete portrayal of reality without interruption and openness, then it is not realism but rather the remains of the old idealistic structure of beauty as such. Whereas in terms of realism, in particular, one finds significantly less 'complete, coherent reality' in Goethe's *Wilhelm Meister* and in Keller's *Grüner Heinrich* than neo-classicism would like. There, too, we find Shakespeare everywhere, this one and only classical stumbling block of the real. Only the artificial and abstract viewpoint produces continuity – it does not objectively engender breaks in style, which has led to montage. There is a fine saying by a French poet that applies to all art that does not try to pass off cheap imitation for genuine reflection: a masterpiece never looks like one. In any case, great poetry is driven more to extremities, built with more that is essential than its subject *ante formam*, but that is why the dawn and the sea are beyond that fortress. That is why there is the sea of the process in which the depths of reality are most incomplete. Marxism relates to this so closely that it could provide access to this *subject pending in process* – minus ideological lies, plus concrete utopia. That is, access to poetry that has nothing in common with self-satisfaction and illusion, nor with false, i.e., artificial, classicism. In contrast, there is genuine classicism, as Goethe says, the classicism that is often rounded out but never closed. Creative poetry never approaches truth without pressure or demands; it toils toward the end and seeks to transcend even if the manner is not beautiful. All great writers want to become like Faust.

In many of these writers, especially in Brecht, there is even a bit of restless contempt for art and therefore the desire to destroy the saying that all poetry is false. Therefore, Marxism is the weapon that first gives the imagination a guilty conscience and also the same weapon that heals the affected imagination. The disenchantment of the lies, the separation of appearance from the potential, aesthetic anticipatory illumination will enhance the function of poetry, which feels itself as a force of production, and make poetry even more meaningful. Marxism does not in the least separate the world from the freedom of inner life, nor does it, as Sartre once did, posit the inner life as simply isolated. On the contrary, Marxism wants to create a new interplay between the world and the inner life and overcome alienation and reification. This intention is completely realistic, but surely not in the sense of a banal or even schematic cliché. On the contrary, Marxist reality means: reality plus the future within it. Marxism proves by bringing about concrete changes that are left open: there is still an immeasurable amount of unused dreams, of unsettled historical content, of unsold nature in the world. Those who have taught through poetry have rarely found any subject more excellent than our adventurously moving, latently expectant world – the most real thing there is.

7   Christopher Caudwell

English Poets: The Period of Primitive Accumulation (1937)*

Christopher St John Sprigg (1907–37), who wrote as Christopher Caudwell, joined the British Communist Party in 1934 and was killed in action in the Spanish Civil War. His early death spoke volumes about the tragic unity of theory and practice, and cut short a promising career. Except for his novel *This My Hand* (1935), Caudwell's books were published posthumously, including two essay collections, *Studies in a Dying Culture* (1938) and *Further Studies in a Dying Culture* (1949); a book on science, *The Crisis in Physics* (1939); and *Poems* (1939). *Illusion and Reality* (1937), in press when he left for Spain, is probably his most significant contribution to Marxist literary theory. Subtitled 'A Study of the Sources of Poetry', the book attempts a comprehensive Marxist theory of the history of poetry. Caudwell situates his work against idealism and mechanical materialism, arguing for a historical-materialist conception of poetry from early human society to the present. For Caudwell, the truth of poetry is its dynamic role in society as the content of collective emotion in social images. 'English Poets: The Period of Primitive Accumulation' offers a highly condensed description of this dynamic in one period. Although it is one of the landmarks of British Marxist literary criticism, Caudwell's work has been dismissed more than admired. Raymond Williams, for example, commented that Caudwell was often not specific enough to be wrong. Others have suggested that Caudwell's work suffers from its English isolation from European intellectual and political currents. Previously unpublished material by Caudwell is published in *Scenes and Actions* (1986). For discussion of Caudwell's work, see E. P. Thompson, 'Caudwell', *Socialist Register (1977)*; F. Mulhern, 'The Marxist Aesthetics of Christopher Caudwell', *New Left Review*, 85 (1974); D. N. Margolies, *The Function of Literature: A Study of Caudwell's Aesthetics* (1969); and *Christopher Caudwell*, eds D. Margolies and L. Peach (1989).

* From Christopher Caudwell, *Illusion and Reality* (London: Lawrence & Wishart, 1977), 85–100.

1

Capitalism requires two conditions for its existence – masses of capital and 'free' – i.e. expropriated – wage-labourers. Once the movement has started, capitalism generates its own conditions for further development. The sum of constant capital grows by accumulation and aggregates by amalgamation, and this amalgamation, by continually expropriating artisans and other petty bourgeoisie, produces the necessary supply of wage-labourers.

A period of primitive accumulation is therefore necessary before these conditions can be realized. This primitive accumulation must necessarily be violent and forcible, for the bourgeoisie, not yet a ruling class, has not yet created the political conditions for its own expansion: the State is not yet a bourgeois state.

In England during this period the bourgeoisie and that section of the nobility which had gone over to the bourgeoisie, seized the Church lands and treasure and created a horde of dispossessed vagrants by the enclosure of common lands, the closing of the monasteries, the extension of sheep-farming, and the final extinction of the feudal lords with their retainers. The seizure of gold and silver from the New World also played an important part in providing a base for capitalism. This movement was possible because the monarchy, in its fight with the feudal nobility, leant on the bourgeois class and in turn rewarded them for their support. The Tudor monarchs were autocrats in alliance with the bourgeoisie and bourgeoisified nobility.

In this period of primitive accumulation the conditions for the growth of the bourgeois class are created lawlessly. To every bourgeois it seems as if his instincts – his 'freedom' are intolerably restricted by laws, rights and restraints, and that beauty and life can only be obtained by the violent expansion of his desires.

Intemperate will, 'bloody, bold and resolute', without norm or measure, is the spirit of this era of primitive accumulation. The absolute-individual will overriding all other wills is therefore the principle of life for the Elizabethan age. Marlowe's Faust and Tamburlaine express this principle in its naïvest form.

This life principle reaches its highest embodiment in the Renaissance 'prince'. In Italy and England – at this time leaders in primitive accumulation – life reaches its most poignant issue in the absolute will of the prince – this figure of the prince expresses most clearly the bourgeois illusion, just as in real society the prince is the necessary means of realizing the conditions for bourgeois expansion. To break the moulds of feudalism and wrench from them capital requires the strength and remorselessness of an absolute monarch.

Any established bound or let to the divine right of his will would be wrong, for such bounds or lets, being established and traditional, could only be feudal, and would therefore hold back the development of the bourgeois class.

Elizabethan poetry in all its grandeur and insurgence is the voice of this princely will, the absolute bourgeois will whose very virtue consists in breaking all current conventions and realizing itself. That is why all Shakespeare's heroes are princely; why kingliness is the ideal type of human behaviour at this time.

Marlowe, Chapman, Greene, but above all Shakespeare, born of bourgeois parents, exactly express the cyclonic force of the princely bourgeois will in this era, in all its vigour and recklessness. Lear, Hamlet, Macbeth, Antony, Troilus, Othello, Romeo and Coriolanus, each in his different way knows no other obligation than to be the thing he is, to realize himself to the last drop, to give out in its purest and most exquisite form the aroma of self. The age of chivalry appears, not as it sees itself, but discredited and insulted, as the bourgeois class sees it, in the person of Hotspur, Falstaff and Armado, English cousins of Don Quixote.

Even the meanest creature, the empty, discredited, braggart Parolles, realizes this unbounded self-realization to be the law of his stage existence and in some sort the justification of his character:

> Simply to be the thing I am
> Shall make me live.

In this intemperate self-expression, by which they seem to expand and fill the whole world with their internal phantasmagoria, lies the significance of Shakespeare's heroes. That even death does not end their self-realization, that they are most essentially themselves in death – Lear, Hamlet, Cleopatra and Macbeth – in this too is both the secret of their death and the solution of the tragedy.

The depth with which Shakespeare moved in the bourgeois illusion, the greatness of his grasp of human society, is shown by the fact that he is ultimately a tragedian. This unfettered realization of human individualities involves for him the equally unfettered play of Necessity. The contradiction which is the driving force of capitalism finds its expression again and again in Shakespeare's tragedies. In *Macbeth* the hero's ambitions are realized – inverted. In *King Lear* the hero wrecks himself against the equally untempered expression of his daughters' will and also against Nature, whose necessity is expressed in a storm. The power of the storm symbolism lies in the fact that in a thunderstorm Nature seems to conduct herself, not as an inexorable machine but like a human being in an ungovernable passion. In *Othello* man's love realizes the best in himself, yet by the free play of that realization 'kills the thing it loves'. In *Hamlet* the problem of a conflict of unmeasured wills is posed in yet another form – here a man's will is divided against itself, and therefore even though nothing 'external' can oppose or reflect it, it can yet struggle with itself and be wrecked. This 'doubleness' of a single will is aptly symbolized by the poisoned swords and goblet in which the one aim is as it were two-faced, and secures opposite ends. In *Antony and Cleopatra* and in *Romeo and Juliet* the fulfilment of the simplest and most violent instinct is to love without bound or compass, and this love ensures the destruction of the lovers, who are justified simply because the love is unbounded, and scorns patriotism, family loyalty, reason and self-interest Such deaths are tragic because at this era the intemperate realization of the self is heroic; it is the life principle of history. We feel that the death is necessary and is what must have been: 'Nothing is here for tears.'

At this stage the strength and vigour of the bourgeois depends on his cohesion as a class under monarchist leadership. In many parts already a self-armed, self-acting commune, the bourgeoisie in England, has as its spearhead the court. The court is the seat of progress, and its public collective life is for the moment the source of bourgeois progress and fountain of primitive accumulation. The court itself is not bourgeois: it seeks the coercive imposition of its will like a feudal overlord, but it can only do so by allying itself with the bourgeoisie for whom the 'absoluteness' of the monarch, although feudal in its essence, is bourgeois in its outcome because it is creating the conditions for their development.

Hence we find Shakespeare, although expressing the bourgeois illusion, is an official of the court or of the bourgeois nobility. Players are the 'Queen's Servants'. He is not a producer for the bourgeois market or 'public'. He has a feudal *status*. Hence his art is not in its form individualistic: it is still collective. It breathes the collective life of the court. As player and as dramatist he lived with his audience in one simultaneous public world of emotion. That is why Elizabethan poetry is, in its greatest expression, drama – real, acted drama. It can still remain social and public and yet be an expression of the aspirations of the bourgeois class because of the alliance of the monarchy with the bourgeoisie.

Elizabethan poetry tells a story. The story always deals with men's individualities as realized in economic functions – it sees them from the outside as 'characters' or 'types'. It sites them in a real social world seen from the outside. But in the era of primitive accumulation, bourgeois economy has not differentiated to an extent where social 'types' or 'norms' have been stabilized. Bourgeois man believes himself to be establishing an economic role by simply realizing his character, like a splay foot. The instinctive and the economic seem to him naturally one: it is only the feudal roles which seem to him forced and 'artificial'. Hence the story and poetry are not yet antagonistic: they have not yet separated out.

In this era of primitive accumulation all is fluid and homogeneous. Bourgeois society has not created its elaborate division of labour, to which the elaborate complexity of culture corresponds. Today psychology, biology, logic, philosophy, law, poetry, history, economics, novel-writing, the essay, are all separate spheres of thought, each requiring specialization for their exploration and each using a specialized vocabulary. But men like Bacon and Galileo and da Vinci did not specialize, and their language reflects this lack of differentiation. Elizabethan tragedy speaks a language of great range and compass, from the colloquial to the sublime, from the technical to the narrative, because language itself is as yet undifferentiated.

Like all great language, this has been bought and paid for. Tyndale paid for it with his life; the English prose style as a simple and clear reality, fit for poetry, was written in the fear of death, by heretics for whom it was a religious but also a revolutionary activity demanding a bareness and simplicity which scorned all trifling ornament and convention. Nothing was asked of it but the truth.

These facts combined make it possible for Elizabethan poetry to be drama and story, collective and undifferentiated, and yet express with extraordinarypower the vigour of the bourgeois illusion in the era of primitive accumulation.

Shakespeare could not have achieved the stature he did if he had not exposed, at the dawn of bourgeois development, the whole movement of the capitalist contradiction, from its tremendous achievement to its mean decline. His position, his feudal 'perspective', enabled him to comprehend in one era all the trends which in later eras were to separate out and so be beyond the compass of one treatment.[1] It was not enough to reveal the dewy freshness of bourgeois love in *Romeo and Juliet*, its fatal empire-shattering drowsiness in *Antony and Cleopatra*, or the pageant of individual human wills in conflict in *Macbeth, Hamlet, Lear* and *Othello*. It was necessary to taste the dregs, to anticipate the era of *surréalisme* and James Joyce and write *Timon of Athens*, to express the degradation caused by the whole movement of capitalism, which sweeps away all feudal loyalties in order to realize the human spirit, only to find this spirit the miserable prisoner of the cash-nexus – to express this not symbolically, but with burning precision:

> Gold! yellow, glittering, precious gold! No, gods,
> I am no idle votarist. Roots, you clear heavens!
> Thus much of this will make black white, foul fair,
> Wrong right, base noble, old young, coward valiant.
> Ha! you gods, why this? What this, you gods? Why this
> Will lug your priests and servants from your sides,
> Pluck stout men's pillows from below their heads:
> This yellow slave
> Will knit and break religions; bless the accurs'd;
> Make the hoar leprosy ador'd; place thieves,

> And give them title, knee, and approbation,
> With senators on the bench; this is it
> That makes the wappen'd widow wed again;
> She, whom the spital-house and ulcerous sores
> Would cast the gorge at, this embalms and spices
> To the April day again. Come, damned earth,
> Thou common whore of mankind, that putt'st odds
> Among the rout of nations, I will make thee
> Do thy right nature.

James Joyce's characters repeat the experience of Timon:

> all is oblique,
> There's nothing level in our cursed natures
> But direct villainy. Therefore, be abhorred
> All feasts, societies, and throngs of men!
> His semblable, yea, *himself*, Timon disdains.
> Destruction, fang mankind!

From the life-thoughts of Elizabethan poetry to the death-thoughts of the age of imperialism is a tremendous period of development but all are comprehended and cloudily anticipated in Shakespeare's plays.

Before he died Shakespeare had cloudily and phantastically attempted an *un*tragic solution, a solution without death. Away from the rottenness of bourgeois civilization, in the island of *The Tempest*, man attempts to live quietly and nobly, alone with his thoughts. Such an existence still retains an Elizabethan reality; there is an exploited class – Caliban, the bestial serf – and a 'free' spirit who serves only for a time – Ariel, apotheosis of the free wage-labourer. This heaven cannot endure. The actors return to the real world. The magic wand is broken. And yet, in its purity and childlike wisdom, there is a bewitching quality about *The Tempest* and its magic world, in which the forces of Nature are harnessed to men's service in a bizarre forecast of communism.

2

As primitive accumulation gradually generates a class of differentiated bourgeois producers, the will of the monarch, which in its absoluteness had been a creative force, now becomes anti-bourgeois and feudal. Once primitive accumulation has reached a certain point, what is urgently desired is not capital but a set of conditions in which the bourgeois can realize the development of his capital. This is the era of 'manufacture' – as opposed to factory development.

The absolute monarchy, by its free granting of monopolies and privileges, becomes as irksome as the old network of feudal loyalties. It is, after all, itself feudal. A cleavage appears between the monarchy and the class of artisans, merchants, farmers and shopkeepers.

The court supports the big landowner or noble who is already parasitic. He is allied with the court to exploit the bourgeoisie and the court rewards him with monopolies, privileges or special taxes which hamper the development of the overwhelming majority of the rising bourgeois class. Thus the absolute 'will' of the prince, now that the era of primitive accumulation is over, no longer expresses the life principle of the bourgeois class at this stage.

On the contrary the court appears as the source of evil. Its glittering corrupt life has a smell of decay; foulness and mean deeds are wrapped in silk. Bourgeois poetry changes into its opposite and by a unanimous movement puritanically draws its skirt's hem away from the dirt of the court life. The movement which at first was a reaction of the Reformed Church against the Catholic Church is now a reaction of the puritan against the Reformed Church.

The Church, expressing the absolute will of the monarch and the privileges of the nobility, is met by the individual 'conscience' of the puritan, which knows no law but the Spirit – his own will idealized. His thrift reflects the need, now that primitive accumulation is over, to mass the capital in which freedom and virtue inheres by 'saving' and not by gorgeous and extravagant robbery.

Donne expresses the transition, for he is torn by it. At first, captivated by the sensuality and glittering brilliance of the court, the insolent treatment he receives produces a movement away from it, into repentance. The movement is not complete. In Donne's last years, filled as they are with death-thoughts and magniloquent hatred of life, the pride of the flesh still tears at his heart.

Poetry, drawing away from the collective life of the court, can only withdraw into the privacy of the bourgeois study, austerely furnished, shared only with a few chosen friends, surroundings so different from the sleeping and waking publicity of court life that it rapidly revolutionizes poetic technique. Crashaw, Herrick, Herbert, Vaughan – all the poetry of this era seems written by shy, proud men writing alone in their studies – appealing from court life to the country or to heaven. Language reflects the change. Lyrics no longer become something that a gentleman could sing to his lady; conceits are no longer something which could be tossed in courtly conversation. Poetry is no longer something to be roared out to a mixed audience. It smells of the library where it was produced. It is a learned man's poetry: student's poetry. Poetry is read, not declaimed: it is correspondingly subtle and intricate.

But Suckling and Lovelace write court poetry, the simple, open poetry of their class. They stand in antagonism to puritan poetry, and maintain the tradition of the Elizabethan court lyric.

The collective drama, born of the collective spirit of the court, necessarily perishes. Webster and Tourneur express the final corruption, the malignantly evil and Italianate death of the first stage of the bourgeois illusion.

3

The transitional period moves towards Revolution. The bourgeoisie revolt against the monarchy and the privileged nobility in the name of Parliament, liberty and the 'Spirit' which is nothing but the bourgeois will challenging the monarchical. This is the era of armed revolution, of civil war, and with it emerges England's first openly revolutionary poet, Milton.

Revolutionary in style, revolutionary in content. The bourgeois now enters a stage of the illusion where he sees himself as defiant and lonely, challenging the powers that be. With this therefore goes an artificial and *consciously* noble style, an isolated style, the first of its kind in English poetry.

Bourgeois revolutions, which are only accomplished by the help of the people as a whole, always reach a stage where it is felt that they have 'gone too far'. The bourgeois demand for unlimited freedom is all very well until the 'have-nots' too demand unlimited freedom, which can only be obtained at the expense of the 'haves'. Then a Cromwell or Robespierre steps in to hold back coercively the progress of the Revolution.

Such a bourgeois halt must always lead to a reaction, for the bourgeois class thus destroys its own mass basis. A Robespierre gives place to a Directory and then a Napoleon; at an earlier stage a Cromwell gives place to a Monk and a Charles II. The wheel does not come back full circle: there is a compromise.

To those who expressed directly the interests of the petty bourgeois, the puritans, this final stage of reaction is a betrayal of the Revolution. Therefore in *Paradise Lost* Milton sees himself as Satan overwhelmed and yet still courageous: damned and yet revolutionary. In *Paradise Regained* he has already rejected power in this world in exchange for power in the next. He scorns the temples and towers of this world; his reward is in the next because he will not compromise. Hence this poem is defeatist, and lacks the noble defiance of *Paradise Lost*. In *Samson Agonistes* Milton recovers his courage. He hopes for the day when he can pull the temple down on the luxury of his wanton oppressors and wipe out the Philistine court.

Did he consciously figure himself as Satan, Jesus and Samson? Only consciously perhaps as Samson. But when he came to tackle the bourgeois theme of how man, naturally good, is everywhere bad, and to give the familiar, answer – because of Adam's fall from natural goodness as a result of temptation – he was led to consider the tempter, Satan and *his* fall. And Satan's struggle being plainly a revolution, he filled it with his revolutionary experience and made the defeated revolutionary a puritan, and the reactionary

God a Stuart. Thus emerged the towering figure of Satan, which by its unexpected disproportion shows that Milton's theme had 'run away with him'.

In *Paradise Regained* Milton tries to believe that to be defeated temporally is to win spiritually, to win 'In the long run'. But Milton was a real active revolutionary and in his heart he finds this spiritual satisfaction emptier than real defeat – as the unsatisfactoriness of the poem shows. In *Samson Agonistes* he tries to combine defeat and victory.

Of course the choice was already made in *Comus*, where the Lady spurns the luxury of the court and allies herself with the simple virtue of the people.

Note how already the bourgeois illusion is a little self-conscious. Milton is consciously noble – Shakespeare never. The Elizabethans are heroic: the Puritans are not, and therefore have to see themselves as heroic, in an archaistic dress. The Verse and vocabulary of the Latin secretary to the Provisional Government well expresses this second movement of the illusion. The theme of the poems cannot at once be noble and in any sense contemporary. Poetry is already isolating itself from the collective daily life, which makes it inevitable that the prose 'story' now begins to appear as an opposite pole.

Of course the transition from the court, like all other movements of the bourgeois illusion, is foreshadowed in Shakespeare. In *The Tempest* Prospero withdraws from corrupt court life to the peace of his island study, like a Herbert or a Milton. Shakespeare did the same in life when he retired to Stratford-on-Avon.

But he could not write there. His magic wand was a collective one. He had broken it with the breaking of his tie with the court, and the cloud-capp'd palaces of his fancy became empty air.

4

The atmosphere of a period of reaction such as that which followed the Puritan Revolution is of good-humoured cynicism. A betrayal of the extreme 'ideals' for which the battle had been fought appeared prudent to the majority. Unrestrained liberty and the free following of the spirit, excellent in theory, had in practice been proved to involve awkwardnesses for the very class of whom it was the battle-cry. The bourgeois illusion went through a new stage, that of the Restoration.

Such a movement is cynical, because it is the outcome of a betrayal of 'ideals' for earthly reasons. It is luxurious because the class with whom the bourgeoisie, having taught it a sharp lesson, now allies itself again – the landed nobility – has no need of thrift to acquire capital. It is collective because there is a return to the public court life and the play. It is not decadent in any real sense; true, the bourgeoisie has allied itself with the old doomed class – but it has breathed new life into that class. Webster, expressing the decadence of the court, gives way to Dryden, expressing its vigour. And Dryden, with his turn-coat life, so different from Milton's rectitude, exactly expresses the confused and rapid movement of the bourgeoisie of the time, from Cromwell to Charles II and from James II to William III. It is a real alliance – there is no question of the feudal regime returning. James II's fate in the 'Glorious Revolution' clearly shows the bourgeoisie have come to rule.

The poet must return from his study to court, but it is now a more cityfied, sensible, less romantic and picturesque court. The court itself has become almost burgher. The language shows the same passage from study to London street, from conscious heroism to business-like common sense. The sectarian bourgeois revolutionary, a little inclined to pose, becomes the sensible man-of-the-world. This is the transition from Milton to Dryden. The idealization of compromise between rival classes as 'order' and 'measure' – a familiar feature of reaction – leads to the conception of the Augustan age, which passes by an inevitable transition into eighteenth-century nationalism, once the Glorious Revolution has shown that the bourgeoisie are dominant in the alliance.

The self-valuation of this age as Augustan is in fact singularly fitting. Caesar played the role of Cromwell, and Augustus of Charles II in a similar movement in Rome, where the knightly class at first rebelled against the senatorial and, when it became dangerous to go farther, entered on a road of compromise and reaction.

Elizabethan insurgence, the voice of primitive accumulation, thus turns into its opposite, Augustan propriety, the voice of manufacture, Individualism gives place to good taste. In its early stages bourgeoisdom requires the shattering of all feudal forms, and therefore its illusion is a realization of the instincts in freedom. In the course of this movement, first to acquire capital, and then to give capital free play, it leans first on the monarchy – Shakespeare – and then on the common people – Milton. But because it is the interests of a class it dare not go too far in its claims, for to advance the interests of all society is to deny its own. It must not only shatter the old forms which maintained the rule of the feudal class, but it must create the new forms which will ensure its own development as a ruling class. This is the epoch of manufacture and of agricultural capitalism. Land, not factories, is still the pivot.

This epoch is not only opposed to that of primitive accumulation, it is also opposed to that of free trade. Capital exists, but the proletariat is as yet barely in existence. The numerous artisans and peasants are not yet proletarianized by the very movemment of capital: the State must therefore be invoked to assist the process. The expansive period of capitalism, in which the rapid expropriation of the artisan hurls thousands of free labourers on to the market, has not yet arrived. The vagrants of Elizabethan days have already been absorbed. The bourgeoisie finds that there is a shortage of wage-labour which might lead to a rise in the price of labour-power over and above its value (i.e. its cost of reproduction in food and rent).

Hence there is need for a network of laws to keep down wages and prices and regulate labour in order to secure for the bourgeois class the conditions of its development. It now sees the 'impracticable idealism' of its revolutionary demands for liberty. Order, measure, law, good taste and other imposed forms are necessary. Tradition and convention are valuable. Now that the feudal State has perished, these restraints ensure the development of bourgeois economy. Free trade seems the very opposite of desirable to the economists of this era. The bourgeois illusion betrays itself.

5

Therefore, during the eighteenth century, bourgeois poetry expresses the spirit of manufacture, of the petty manufacturing bourgeoisie, beneath the wings of the big landowning capitalists, giving birth to industrial capitalism. The shattering expansion of capitalism has not yet begun. Capitalism still approximates to those economies where 'conservation is the first condition of existence' and has not yet fully entered into the state where it 'cannot exist without constantly revolutionizing the means of production'. Capitalism is revolutionizing itself, but like a slowly growing plant that needs protection, instead of like an explosion in which the ignition of one part detonates the rest. By the compromise of the Glorious Revolution, the Whig landed aristocracy were prepared to give that protection because they had themselves become bourgeoisified.

It was only when the separation between agricultural and industrial capitalism took place as a result of the rise of the factory that the cleavage between the aristocracy and the bourgeoisie began to have a determining effect on the bourgeois illusion. While the woollen-mill was still no more than a hand-loom and an appendage of the agricultural capitalist's sheep-farm there was no direct antagonism between the classes: it was only as the woollen-mill became a cotton-mill, depending for its raw material on outside sources, and when sheep-farming developed in Australia and provided wool for English mills, that there arose a direct antagonism between agricultural and industrial capitalism which expressed itself ultimately on the side of the industrialists as a demand for Free Trade and the repeal of the Corn Laws.

Pope's poetry, and its 'reason' – a reason moving within singularly simple and shallow categories but moving accurately – with its polished language and metre and curt antitheses, is a reflection of that stage of the bourgeois illusion where freedom for the bourgeoisie can only be 'limited' – man must be prudent in his demands, and yet there is no reason for despair, all goes well. Life is on the up-grade, but it is impossible to hurry. The imposition of outward forms on the heart is necessary and accepted. Hence the contrast between the elegant corset of the eighteenth-century heroic couplet and the natural luxuriance of Elizabethan blank verse, whose sprawl almost conceals the bony structure of the iambic rhythm inside it.

Pope perfectly expresses the ideals of the bourgeois class in alliance with a bourgeoisified aristocracy in the epoch of manufacture.

It is important to note that even now the poet himself has not been bourgeoisified as a producer. He does not produce as yet for the free market. Almost a court or aristocratic official in the time of Shakespeare, poet is a parson's or scholar's occupation in the ensuing period, and even as late as Pope he is dependent on being patronized, i.e. he has a 'patriarchal' or 'idyllic' relation to the class of whom he is the spokesman in the time of Pope.

Such an 'idyllic' relation means that the poet writes non-idyllic poetry. He still sees himself as a man playing a social role. This was the case with the primitive poet; it remains true of Pope. It imposes on him the obligation to speak the language of his paymasters or co-poets – in the primitive tribe these constitute the whole tribe, in Augustan society these are the men who form his patron's circle – the ruling class. Johnson – dependent on subscribers – bridges the gap between the poet by status and the poet as producer. Thus poetry remains in this sense collective. It talks a more or less current language, and the poet writes for an audience he has directly in mind, to whom perhaps he will presently read his poems and so be able to watch their effect. Poetry is still for him not so much a poem – a self-subsisting work of art – as a movement from writer to reader, like the movement of emotion in a publicly acted drama or the movement of a Muse in the minds of men. Hence he realizes himself as playing a social role: inspirer of humanity or redresser of the follies of mankind. He has not yet become a self-conscious artist.

NOTE

1 In the same way More, from his feudal perspective, anticipates the development of capitalism into communism in his *Utopia*.

8 Alick West
The Relativity of Literary Value (1937)[*]

Alick West joined the British Communist Party in 1934 and became one of the Communist Party literary critics associated with *Left Review*. This group included Christopher Caudwell, Edgell Rickword, Douglas Garman, Cecil Day Lewis, Edward Upward, Ralph Fox, Jack Lindsay and George Thomson. Compromised by the cultural politics of Stalinism, this group were hegemonically defeated by the more formally acute 'new' criticism associated with I. A. Richards, F. R. Leavis and William Empson. What remains of value in British Communist Party literary criticism is its materialist orientation and specific critical readings (notably in George Thomson's work), rather than its theoretical contribution. Arnold Kettle, in his 'Foreword' (1973) to *Crisis and Criticism*, notes West's suspicion of the kind of ideological criticism found in the work of continental Marxists trained in the Hegelian tradition. But this suspicion owes more to the insular peculiarities of English Marxism than to explicitly theorized resistance. 'The Relativity of Literary Value' is a chapter from West's *Crisis and Criticism* (1937), which, along with Caudwell's *Illusion and Reality*, represents the strengths and weaknesses of this tradition. Approaching literature as a mode of heightened consciousness embedded in social conflict, the theoretical difficulty is the judgement of value in the relation between aesthetic form and class struggle. West translated F. Engels, *The Origin of the Family, Private Property and the State* (1942). He also wrote *A Good Man Fallen among Fabians: A Study of George Bernard Shaw* (1950); *The Mountain in the Sunlight* (1958); and his autobiography, *One Man in His Time* (1969).

But it may be objected that, although literary judgement is a proper study for Marxist criticism, value is here made into something absolute. A work of literature, it is said, embodies a particular social attitude; in certain social conditions this attitude can be advantageously advanced by certain social classes, and the work is then said to have value. When those conditions change, it loses its value. The vicissitudes of Shakespeare's fame are adduced

---

[*] From Alick West, *Crisis and Criticism and Selected Literary Essays* (London: Lawrence & Wishart, 1975), 99–103.

as proof. Value, it is said, is a purely subjective judgement; any distinction between this changing popularity and value makes value a metaphysical absolute.

The position maintained here is that the popularity or unpopularity of a work of literature does not create or destroy its value; it is a sign, in the case of such work as Shakespeare's, that the value is operative or non-operative. The existence of those qualities in Shakespeare's plays which make them valuable, no more depends on us than does the existence of the plays themselves. What depends on us, is how we feel those qualities. Marx said that a railway is only potentially a railway if nobody travels on it. In the same way, it may be said that Shakespeare is only potentially Shakespeare if nobody reads him with appreciation. But the act of appreciation no more creates his valuable work than the travelling on the railway creates the railway. The statement that value is a mere elevation of popularity into the absolute, leads to the position that we create our own Shakespeares.

It resembles a standpoint that says the same thing in terms of cultures, instead of classes: that cultures arise and disappear, that each culture interprets previous cultures as suits itself, and that its interpretation is only another expression of itself, containing no truth about what the previous culture actually was. The standpoint that the value of literature lies in the popularity accorded to it by a class and not in the work itself, also sees only a succession of classes without continuity, each class expressing only its own attitude to the world, but making no statement about it with objective validity.

This standpoint also is a method of avoiding the vital question of aesthetics. The criticism founded on it confines itself to registering the relation between the manifest tendency of a work of literature, regardless of the particular form and style of its expression, and the social tendencies of the class with whom it is popular or unpopular. The judgement that it is beautiful it dismisses as the idealistic formulation of a class prejudice, thereby implying that the critic himself is in some way above class and above aesthetic appreciation – 'above love', as the mouldy student says in *The Cherry Orchard*. This standpoint would destroy the possibility of aesthetic enjoyment; by denying the objective existence of Shakespeare's value apart from his popularity, it isolates the pleasure we actually have in it from the material practical activity by which we live, and in which, instead of thinking with this superior relativity, we know that our judgements are not only temporary class prejudices, but contain truth. And that material practical activity is the only source of power of aesthetic enjoyment.

At the same time, while denying the existence of value in literature, this standpoint indirectly retains the conception of literature as 'pure art'. For it implies that there is no truth in it, only the beauty which is created by the class looking at it. But the beauty of literature is the felt truth that we live through organized productive activity, and it makes true statements about the phases of that activity.

We value literature as we value our lives, for it is a part of our lives; and as long as the second phrase retains sense, so will the first. Any suggestion that the value of literature is unreal or unimportant, either says that the value we give our lives is unreal and unimportant, or it cuts off literature from our lives.

The question of what possible reason we have, in view of the changes in literary reputation, for trusting our perception of value is the same error in another form. The undertone of scepticism, that we cannot trust our taste, denies the experience of valuing. We cannot at one and the same moment like a poem and disable our judgement. To discuss the relativity of value from the standpoint that we have no reason whatever for believing in ourselves, is useless metaphysics; for we do believe in ourselves.

But we may be, and often are, wrong. The only profitable way to put the question of the relativity of value is to ask: What must we do to improve our perception of it? The answer is evident from the analysis of value given. The value of literature springs from the fact that it continues and changes the organization of social energy; we perceive value through the awakening of the same kind of energy in ourselves. Just as the writer sees life more vividly, the more he identifies himself with the most active group and tendency of his time, so the same act of identification in our own circumstances intensifies our pleasure and our power of criticism. If we realize in our own lives that we have to contribute to making society, we like the literature which embodies that creation. If we are content to exploit society, we have no possibility of interest in literature; we prefer the printed matter which, like ourselves, uses language and life as mere given facts; if we read good literature, we degrade it to bad.

It should perhaps be pointed out that the analysis of value given here cannot be used as a touchstone. The theory of value depending on the expression of the alternations in fundamental social experience does not enable us to read a poem with a blank mind, note the alternations and then pass judgement. The heightening of social energy has to be felt before the means by which it was aroused can be studied. The stir of emotion is prior to analysis, and the condition of it. Criticism can then help us to decide whether we were stirred through the excitement of our productive energy or the satisfaction of our consumer's appetite. But criticism does not decide whether we were stirred; our lives do that. And if they are such that we are stirred by what is bad, no critical theory is proof against being twisted into self-justification.

Consequently, the criticism of our lives, by the test of whether we are helping forward the most creative movement in our society, is the only effective foundation of the criticism of literature. The results of both kinds of criticism have the same validity.

The most creative movement is socialism. Its theory and practice define a term which has been hitherto used in this book without further specification. We have been speaking of the 'social organism'. Which social organism is meant?

Humanity is meant. There is no other social unit in terms of which any social activity can be fully understood. Capitalism has created the world market, and economic, social and political interactions are so close that what happens in one country can only be understood in relation to what is happening in the whole world.

For the same reasons, action to change society has to be planned in reference to the world situation.

The time has gone by when we could speak, like Bishop Hurd, of a European criticism based on the practice of the Greeks and Romans. Already the statement was rapidly losing its justification when he made it, owing to the growing importance of colonization; its principle can only be applied to western Europe till the time of the crusades, when large parts of the world had not been discovered and the intercourse with what was known was slight. Such a position now is untenable. To say, with Mr Eliot, that we must think and write as parts of an English or European mind, is only a means of obscuring the economic and social facts which demonstrate the necessity of thinking and acting as members of humanity. It is propaganda against socialized humanity.

The same applies to such ideas as Spengler's, that cultures are mutually incomprehensible to one another, that we can never understand Chinese thought, but only project our own into it. This conception also, by making west Europe today a distinct social entity and thus returning to a position only true of the early stages of feudalism, wants to preserve capitalism from the consequences of its own action in creating a world market. By these cultural barriers against socialized humanity it also makes propaganda for capitalism.

Instead of eternal misunderstanding, the co-operation of Chinamen and Englishmen now in working for socialized humanity will make possible the mutual appreciation of the literatures even from the time when one country did not know of the other's existence.

The social organism to which literature has to be related, is humanity in its advance to socialism. The function of criticism is to judge literature, both content and form, as a part of this movement. It can only fulfil this function if it takes part in this movement itself on the side of the workers of the world.

It is in this sense that its aesthetics are not static, but dynamic.

9 Bertolt Brecht

A Short Organum for the Theatre (1949)[*]

Bertolt Brecht (1898–1956), playwright, poet and theatre director, lived mostly in Germany. In exile in Europe and America during the Hitler years, he returned to East Berlin in 1949. Like his friend Walter Benjamin, Brecht never joined the Communist Party, but from the late 1920s onwards his work exemplifies the theory and practice of socialist aesthetics. Bourgeois criticism has usually proceeded as if this combination of theory and practice could be severed in order to 'redeem' his plays from their political praxis. Brecht's approach to epic theatre developed the work of Piscator and Meyerhold with collaborators such as Hans Eisler, Caspar Neher and Helene Weigel. Epic theatre, in Brecht's theory and practice, is a modern theatrical mode in which popular realism combines avant-garde techniques with accessible entertainment. Brecht sought to engage actors and audience in more active and critical roles in both production and reception. Using stylized techniques – usually known as 'alienation-effects', but better thought of as estrangement or distanciation processes – he sought to open out structures of theatrical artifice to focus analysis on social and political questions, often through parables. Brecht's modernist realism made him exemplary in the resistance to socialist realism, and brought him into sharp conflict with Lukács. His theories of dialectical theatre are best understood through his plays and processes of production. However, 'The Short Organum', written in 1948 and published in 1949, is the most sustained, if provisional, representation of his theoretical approach. Brecht's materialist and experimental practice remains an important influence on socialist approaches to literature. But his work has also been criticized for the quality of 'crude thinking' which is central in Brecht's approach to translating complicated social analyses into critical signifying practices. *Brecht on Theatre*, ed. John Willett (1964) provides useful selections and contextual materials. For discussion see the essays by Barthes and Adorno in this anthology; Walter Benjamin, *Understanding Brecht* (1973); Ernst Bloch and others, *Aesthetics and Politics* (1977); E. Lunn, *Modernism and Marxism* (1985); and P. Brooker, *Bertolt Brecht* (1987).

[*] From *Brecht on Theatre*, ed. and trans. John Willett (New York and London: Hill & Wang and Methuen, 1964), 179–205.

Prologue

The following sets out to define an aesthetic drawn from a particular kind of theatrical performance which has been worked out in practice over the past few decades. In the theoretical statements, excursions, technical indications occasionally published in the form of notes to the writer's plays, aesthetics have only been touched on casually and with comparative lack of interest. There you saw a particular species of theatre extending or contracting its social functions, perfecting or sifting its artistic methods and establishing or maintaining its aesthetics – if the question arose – by rejecting or converting to its own use the dominant conventions of morality or taste according to its tactical needs. This theatre justified its inclination to social commitment by pointing to the social commitment in universally accepted works of art, which only fail to strike the eye because it was the accepted commitment. As for the products of our own time, it held that their lack of any worthwhile content was a sign of decadence: it accused these entertainment emporiums of having degenerated into branches of the bourgeois narcotics business. The stage's inaccurate representations of our social life, including those classed as so-called Naturalism, led it to call for scientifically exact representations; the tasteless rehashing of empty visual or spiritual palliatives, for the noble logic of the multiplication table. The cult of beauty, conducted with hostility towards learning and contempt for the useful, was dismissed by it as itself contemptible, especially as nothing beautiful resulted. The battle was for a theatre fit for the scientific age, and where its planners found it too hard to borrow or steal from the armoury of aesthetic concepts enough weapons to defend themselves against the aesthetics of the Press they simply threatened 'to transform the means of enjoyment into an instrument of instruction, and to convert certain amusement establishments into organs of mass communication' i.e. to emigrate from the realm of the merely enjoyable. Aesthetics, that heirloom of a by now depraved and parasitic class, was in such a lamentable state that a theatre would certainly have gained both in reputation and in elbowroom if it had rechristened itself thaëter. And yet what we achieved in the way of theatre for a scientific age was not science but theatre, and the accumulated innovations worked out during the Nazi period and the war – when practical demonstration was impossible – compel some attempt to set this species of theatre in its aesthetic background, or anyhow to sketch for it the outlines of a conceivable aesthetic. To explain the theory of theatrical alienation except within an aesthetic framework would be impossibly awkward.

Today one could go so far as to compile an aesthetics of the exact sciences. Galileo spoke of the elegance of certain formulae and the point of an experiment; Einstein suggests that the sense of beauty has a part to play in the making of scientific discoveries; while the atomic physicist R. Oppenheimer praises the scientific attitude, which 'has its own kind of beauty and seems to suit mankind's position on earth'.

Let us therefore cause general dismay by revoking our decision to emigrate from the realm of the merely enjoyable, and even more general dismay by announcing our decision to take up lodging there. Let us treat the theatre as a place of entertainment, as is proper in an aesthetic discussion, and try to discover which type of entertainment suits us best.

1

'Theatre' consists in this: in making live representations of reported or invented happenings between human beings and doing so with a view to entertainment. At any rate that is what we shall mean when we speak of theatre, whether old or new.

2

To extend this definition we might add happenings between humans and gods, but as we are only seeking to establish the minimum we can leave such matters aside. Even if we did accept such an extension we should still have to say that the 'theatre' set-up's broadest function was to give pleasure. It is the noblest function that we have found for 'theatre'.

3

From the first it has been the theatre's business to entertain people, as it also has of all the other arts. It is this business which always gives it its particular dignity; it needs no other passport than fun, but this it has got to have. We should not by any means be giving it a higher status if we were to turn it e.g. into a purveyor of morality; it would on the contrary run the risk of being debased, and this would occur at once if it failed to make its moral lesson enjoyable, and enjoyable to the senses at that: a principle, admittedly, by which morality can only gain. Not even instruction can be demanded of it: at any rate, no more utilitarian lesson than how to move pleasurably, whether in the physical or in the spiritual sphere. The theatre must in fact remain something entirely superfluous, though this indeed means that it is the superfluous for which we live. Nothing needs less justification than pleasure.

4

Thus what the ancients, following Aristotle, demanded of tragedy is nothing higher or lower than that it should entertain people. Theatre may be said to be derived from ritual, but that is only to say that it becomes theatre once the two have separated; what it brought over from the mysteries was not its former ritual function, but purely and simply the pleasure which accompanied this. And the catharsis of which Aristotle writes – cleansing by fear and pity, or from fear and pity – is a purification which is performed not only in a pleasurable way, but precisely for the purpose of pleasure. To ask or to accept more of the theatre is to set one's own mark too low.

5

Even when people speak of higher and lower degrees of pleasure, art stares impassively back at them; for it wishes to fly high and low and to be left in peace, so long as it can give pleasure to people.

6

Yet there are weaker (simple) and stronger (complex) pleasures which the theatre can create. The last-named, which are what we are dealing with in great drama, attain their climaxes rather as cohabitation does through love: they are more intricate, richer in communication, more contradictory and more productive of results.

7

And different periods' pleasures varied naturally according to the system under which people lived in society at the time. The Greek demos [literally: the demos of the Greek circus] ruled by tyrants had to be entertained differently from the feudal court of Louis XIV. The theatre was required to deliver different representations of men's life together: not just representations of a different life, but also representations of a different sort.

8

According to the sort of entertainment which was possible and necessary under the given conditions of men's life together the characters had to be given varying proportions, the situations to be constructed according to varying points of view. Stories have to be narrated in various ways, so that these particular Greeks may be able to amuse themselves with the inevitability of divine laws where ignorance never mitigates the punishment; these French with the graceful self-discipline demanded of the great ones of this earth by a courtly code of duty; the Englishmen of the Elizabethan age with the self-awareness of the new individual personality which was then uncontrollably bursting out.

9

And we must always remember that the pleasure given by representations of such different sorts hardly ever depended on the representation's likeness to the thing portrayed. Incorrectness, or considerable improbability even, was hardly or not at all disturbing, so long as the incorrectness had a certain consistency and the improbability remained of a constant kind. All that mattered was the illusion of compelling momentum in the story told, and this was created by all sorts of poetic and theatrical means. Even today we are happy to overlook such inaccuracies if we can get something out of the spiritual purifications of Sophocles or the sacrificial acts of Racine or the unbridled frenzies of Shakespeare, by trying to grasp the immense, or splendid feelings of the principal characters in these stories.

10

For of all the many sorts of representation of happenings between humans which the theatre has made since ancient times, and which have given entertainment despite their incorrectness and improbability, there are even today an astonishing number that also give entertainment to us.

11

In establishing the extent to which we can be satisfied by representations from so many different periods – something that can hardly have been possible to the children of those vigorous periods themselves – are we not at the same time creating the suspicion that we have failed to discover the special pleasures, the proper entertainment of our own time?

12

And our enjoyment of the theatre must have become weaker than that of the ancients, even if our way of living together is still sufficiently like theirs for it to be felt at all. We grasp the old works by a comparatively new method – empathy – on which they rely little. Thus the greater part of our enjoyment is drawn from other sources than those which our predecessors were able to exploit so fully. We are left safely dependent on beauty of language, on elegance of narration, on passages which stimulate our own private imaginations: in short, on the incidentals of the old works. These are precisely the poetical and theatrical means which hide the imprecisions of the story. Our theatres no longer have either the capacity or the wish to tell these stories, even the relatively recent ones of the great Shakespeare, at all clearly: i.e. to make the connection of events credible. And according to Aristotle – and we agree there – narrative is the soul of drama. We are more and more disturbed to see how crudely and carelessly men's life together is represented, and that not only in old works but also in contemporary ones constructed according to the old recipes. Our whole way of appreciation is starting to get out of date.

13

It is the inaccurate way in which happenings between human beings are represented that restricts our pleasure in the theatre. The reason: we and our forebears have a different relationship to what is being shown.

14

For when we look about us for an entertainment whose impact is immediate, for a comprehensive and penetrating pleasure such as our theatre could give us by representations of men's life together, we have to think of ourselves as children of a scientific age. Our life as human beings in society – i.e. our life – is determined by the sciences to a quite new extent.

15

A few hundred years ago a handful of people, working in different countries but in correspondence with one another, performed certain experiments by which they hoped to wring from Nature her secrets. Members of a class of craftsmen in the already powerful cities, they transmitted their discoveries to people who made practical use of them, without expecting more from the new sciences than personal profit for themselves.

Crafts which had progressed by methods virtually unchanged during a thousand years now developed hugely; in many places, which became linked by competition, they gathered from all directions great masses of men, and these, adopting new forms of organization, started producing on a giant scale. Soon mankind was showing powers whose extent it would till that time scarcely have dared to dream of.

16

It was as if mankind for the first time now began a conscious and co-ordinated effort to make the planet that was its home fit to live on. Many of the earth's components, such as coal, water, oil, now became treasures. Steam was made to shift vehicles; a few small sparks and the twitching of frogs' legs revealed a natural force which produced light, carried sounds across continents, etc. In all directions man looked about himself with a new vision, to see how he could adapt to his convenience familiar but as yet unexploited objects. His surroundings changed increasingly from decade to decade, then from year to year, then almost from day to day. I who am writing this write it on a machine which at the time of my birth was unknown. I travel in the new vehicles with a rapidity that my grandfather could not imagine; in those days nothing moved so fast. And I rise in the air: a thing that my father was unable to do. With my father I already spoke across the width of a continent, but it was together with my son that I first saw the moving pictures of the explosion at Hiroshima.

17

The new sciences may have made possible this vast alteration and all-important alterability of our surroundings, yet it cannot be said that their spirit determines everything that we do. The reason why the new way of thinking and feeling has not yet penetrated the great mass of men is that the sciences, for all their success in exploiting and dominating nature, have been stopped by the class which they brought to power – the bourgeoisie – from operating in another field where darkness still reigns, namely that of the relations which people have to one another during the exploiting and dominating process. This business on which all alike depended was performed without the new intellectual methods that made it possible ever illuminating the mutual relationships of the people who carried it out. The new approach to nature was not applied to society.

18

In the event people's mutual relations have become harder to disentangle than ever before. The gigantic joint undertaking on which they are engaged seems more and more to split them into two groups; increases in production lead to increases in misery; only a minority gain from the exploitation of nature, and they only do so because they exploit men. What might be progress for all then becomes advancement for a few, and an ever-increasing part of the productive process gets applied to creating means of destruction for mighty wars. During these wars the mothers of every nation, with their children pressed to them, scan the skies in horror for the deadly inventions of science.

19

The same attitude as men once showed in face of unpredictable natural catastrophes they now adopt towards their own undertakings. The bourgeois class, which owes to science an advancement that it was able, by ensuring that it alone enjoyed the fruits, to convert into domination, knows very well that its rule would come to an end if the scientific eye were turned on its own undertakings. And so that new science which was founded about a hundred years ago and deals with the character of human society was born in the struggle between rulers and ruled. Since then a certain scientific spirit has developed at the bottom, among the new class of workers whose natural element is large-scale production; from down there the great catastrophes are spotted as undertakings by the rulers.

20

But science and art meet on this ground, that both are there to make men's life easier, the one setting out to maintain, the other to entertain us. In the age to come art will create entertainment from that new productivity which can so greatly improve our maintenance, and in itself, if only it is left unshackled, may prove to be the greatest pleasure of them all.

21

If we want now to surrender ourselves to this great passion for producing, what ought our representations of men's life together to look like? What is that productive attitude in face of nature and of society which we children of a scientific age would like to take up pleasurably in our theatre?

22

The attitude is a critical one. Faced with a river, it consists in regulating the river; faced with a fruit tree, in spraying the fruit tree; faced with movement, in constructing vehicles and aeroplanes; faced with society, in turning society upside down. Our representations of human social life are designed for river-dwellers, fruit farmers, builders of vehicles and upturners of society, whom we invite into our theatres and beg not to forget their cheerful occupations while we hand the world over to their minds and hearts, for them to change as they think fit.

23

The theatre can only adopt such a free attitude if it lets itself be carried along by the strongest currents in its society and associates itself with those who are necessarily most impatient to make great alterations there. The bare wish, if nothing else, to evolve an art fit for the times must drive our theatre of the scientific age straight out into the suburbs, where it can stand as it were wide open, at the disposal of those who live hard and produce much, so that they can be fruitfully entertained there with their great problems. They may find it hard to pay for our art, and immediately to grasp the new method of entertainment, and we shall have to learn in many respects what they need and how they need it; but we can be sure of their interest. For these men who seem so far apart from natural science are only apart from it because they are being forcibly kept apart; and before they can get their hands on it they have first to develop and put into effect a new science of society; so that these are the true children of the scientific age, who alone can get the theatre moving if it is to move at all. A theatre which makes productivity its main source of entertainment has also to take it for its theme, and with greater keenness than ever now that man is everywhere hampered by men from self-production: i.e. from maintaining himself, entertaining and being entertained. The theatre has to become geared into reality if it is to be in a position to turn out effective representations of reality, and to be allowed to do so.

24

But this makes it simpler for the theatre to edge as close as possible to the apparatus of education and mass communication. For although we cannot bother it with the raw material of knowledge in all its variety, which would stop it from being enjoyable, it is still free to find enjoyment in teaching and inquiring. It constructs its workable representations of society, which are then in a position to influence society, wholly and entirely as a game: for those who are constructing society it sets out society's experiences, past and present alike, in such a manner that the audience can 'appreciate' the feelings, insights and impulses which are distilled by the wisest, most active and most passionate among us from the events of the day or the century. They must be entertained with the wisdom that comes from the solution of problems, with the anger that is a practical expression of sympathy with the underdog, with the respect due to those who respect humanity, or rather whatever is kind to humanity; in short, with whatever delights those who are producing something.

25

And this also means that the theatre can let its spectators enjoy the particular ethic of their age, which springs from productivity. A theatre which converts the critical approach – i.e. our great productive method – into pleasure finds nothing in the ethical field which it must do and a great deal that it can. Even the wholly anti-social can be a source of enjoyment to society so long as it is presented forcefully and on the grand scale. It then often proves to have considerable powers of understanding and other unusually valuable capacities, applied admittedly to a destructive end. Even the bursting flood of a vast catastrophe can be appreciated in all its majesty by society, if society knows how to master it; then we make it our own.

26

For such an operation as this we can hardly accept the theatre as we see it before us. Let us go into one of these houses and observe the effect which it has on the spectators. Looking about us, we see somewhat motionless figures in a peculiar condition: they seem strenuously to be tensing all their muscles, except where these are flabby and exhausted. They scarcely communicate with each other; their relations are those of a lot of sleepers, though of such as dream restlessly because, as is popularly said of those who have nightmares, they are lying on their backs. True, their eyes are open, but they stare rather than see, just as they listen rather than hear. They look at the stage as if in a trance: an expression which comes from the Middle Ages, the days of witches and priests. Seeing and hearing are activities, and can be pleasant ones, but these people seem relieved of activity and like men to whom something is being done. This detached state, where they seem to be given over to vague but profound sensations, grows deeper the better the work of the actors, and so we, as we do not approve of this situation, should like them to be as bad as possible.

27

As for the world portrayed there, the world from which slices are cut in order to produce these moods and movements of the emotions, its appearance is such, produced from such slight and wretched stuff as a few pieces of cardboard, a little miming, a bit of text, that one has to admire the theatre folk who, with so feeble a reflection of the real world, can move the feelings of their audience so much more strongly than does the world itself.

28

In any case we should excuse these theatre folk, for the pleasures which they sell for money and fame could not be induced by an exacter representation of the world, nor could their inexact renderings be presented in a less magical way. Their capacity to represent people can be seen at work in various instances; it is especially the rogues and the minor figures who reveal their knowledge of humanity and differ one from the other, but the central figures have to be kept general, so that it is easier for the onlooker to identify himself with them, and at all costs each trait of character must be drawn from the narrow field within which everyone can say at once: that is how it is.

For the spectator wants to be put in possession of quite definite sensations, just as a child does when it climbs on to one of the horses on a roundabout: the sensation of pride that it can ride, and has a horse; the pleasure of being carried, and whirled past other children; the adventurous daydreams in which it pursues others or is pursued, etc. In leading the child to experience all this the degree to which its wooden seat resembles a horse counts little, nor does it matter that the ride is confined to a small circle. The one important point for the spectators in these houses is that they should be able to swap a contradictory world for a consistent one, one that they scarcely know for one of which they can dream.

29

That is the sort of theatre which we face in our operations, and so far it has been fully able to transmute our optimistic friends, whom we have called the children of the scientific era, into a cowed, credulous, hypnotized mass.

30

True, for about half a century they have been able to see rather more faithful representations of human social life, as well as individual figures who were in revolt against certain social evils or even against the structure of society as a whole. They felt interested enough to put up with a temporary and exceptional restriction of language, plot and spiritual scope; for the fresh wind of the scientific spirit nearly withered the charms to which they had grown used. The sacrifice was not especially worthwhile. The greater subtlety of the representations subtracted from one pleasure without satisfying another. The field of human relationships came within our view, but not within our grasp. Our feelings, having been aroused in the old (magic) way, were bound themselves to remain unaltered.

31

For always and everywhere theatres were the amusement centres of a class which restricted the scientific spirit to the natural field, not daring to let it loose on the field of human relationships. The tiny proletarian section of the public, reinforced to a negligible and uncertain extent by renegade intellectuals, likewise still needed the old kind of entertainment, as a relief from its predetermined way of life.

32

So let us march ahead! Away with all obstacles! Since we seem to have landed in a battle, let us fight! Have we not seen how disbelief can move mountains? Is it not enough that we should have found that something is being kept from us? Before one thing and another there hangs a curtain: let us draw it up!

33

The theatre as we know it shows the structure of society (represented on the stage) as incapable of being influenced by society (in the auditorium). Oedipus, who offended against certain principles underlying the society of his time, is executed: the gods see to that; they are beyond criticism. Shakespeare's great solitary figures, bearing on their breast the star of their fate, carry through with irresistible force their futile and deadly outbursts; they prepare their own downfall; life, not death, becomes obscene as they collapse; the catastrophe is beyond criticism. Human sacrifices all round! Barbaric delights! We know that the barbarians have their art. Let us create another.

34

How much longer are our souls, leaving our 'mere' bodies under cover of the darkness, to plunge into those dreamlike figures up on the stage, there to take part in the crescendos and climaxes which 'normal' life denies us? What kind of release is it at the end of all these plays (which is a happy end only for the conventions of the period – suitable measures, the restoration of order –), when we experience the dreamlike executioner's axe which cuts short such crescendos as so many excesses? We slink into *Oedipus*; for taboos still exist and ignorance is no excuse before the law. Into *Othello*; for jealously still causes us trouble and everything depends on possession. Into *Wallenstein*; for we need to be free for the competitive struggle and to observe the rules, or it would peter out. This deadweight of old habits is also needed for plays like *Ghosts* and *The Weavers*, although there the social structure, in the shape of a 'setting', presents itself as more open to question. The feelings, insights and impulses of the chief characters are forced on us, and so we learn nothing more about society than we can get from the 'setting'.

35

We need a type of theatre which not only releases the feelings, insights and impulses possible within the particular historical field of human relations in which the action takes place, but employs and encourages those thoughts and feelings which help transform the field itself.

36

The field has to be defined in historically relative terms. In other words we must drop our habit of taking the different social structures of past periods, then stripping them of everything that makes them different; so that they all look more or less like our own, which then acquires from this process a certain air of having been there all along, in other words of permanence pure and simple. Instead we must leave them their distinguishing marks and keep their impermanence always before our eyes, so that our own period can be seen to be impermanent too. (It is of course futile to make use of fancy colours and folklore for this, such as our theatres apply precisely in order to emphasize the similarities in human behaviour at different times. We shall indicate the theatrical methods below.)

37

If we ensure that our characters on the stage are moved by social impulses and that these differ according to the period, then we make it harder for our spectator to identify himself with them. He cannot simply feel: that's how I would act, but at most can say: if I had lived under those circumstances. And if we play works dealing with our own time as though they were historical, then perhaps the circumstances under which he himself acts will strike him as equally odd; and this is where the critical attitude begins.

38

The 'historical conditions' must of course not be imagined (nor will they be so constructed) as mysterious Powers (in the background); on the contrary, they are created and maintained by men (and will in due course be altered by them): it is the actions taking place before us that allow us to see what they are.

39

If a character responds in a manner historically in keeping with his period, and would respond otherwise in other periods, does that mean that he is not simply 'Everyman'? It is true that a man will respond differently according to his circumstances and his class; if he were living at another time, or in his youth, or on the darker side of life, he would infallibly give a different response, though one still determined by the same factors and like anyone else's response in that situation at that time. So should we not ask if there are any further differences of response? Where is the man himself, the living, unmistakeable man, who is not quite identical with those identified with him? It is clear that his stage image must bring him to light, and this will come about if this particular contradiction is recreated in the image. The image that gives historical definition will retain something of the rough sketching which indicates traces of other movements and features all around the fully-worked-out figure. Or imagine a man standing in a valley and making a speech in which he occasionally changes his views or simply utters sentences which contradict one another, so that the accompanying echo forces them into confrontation.

40

Such images certainly demand a way of acting which will leave the spectator's intellect free and highly mobile. He has again and again to make what one might call hypothetical adjustments to our structure, by mentally switching off the motive forces of our society or by substituting others for them: a process which leads real conduct to acquire an element of 'unnaturalness', thus allowing the real motive forces to be shorn of their naturalness and become capable of manipulation.

41

It is the same as when an irrigation expert looks at a river together with its former bed and various hypothetical courses which it might have followed if there had been a different tilt to the plateau or a different volume of water. And while he in his mind is looking at a new river, the socialist in his is hearing new kinds of talk from the labourers who work by it. And similarly in the theatre our spectator should find that the incidents set among such labourers are also accompanied by echoes and by traces of sketching.

42

The kind of acting which was tried out at the Schiffbauerdamm Theater in Berlin between the First and Second World Wars, with the object of producing such images, is based on the 'alienation effect' (A-effect). A representation that alienates is one which allows us to recognize its subject, but at the same time makes it seem unfamiliar. The classical and medieval theatre alienated its characters by making them wear human or animal masks; the Asiatic theatre even today uses musical and pantomimic A-effects. Such devices were certainly a barrier to empathy, and yet this technique owed more, not less, to hypnotic suggestion than do those by which empathy is achieved. The social aims of these old devices were entirely different from our own.

43

The old A-effects quite remove the object represented from the spectator's grasp, turning it into something that cannot be altered; the new are not odd in themselves, though the unscientific eye stamps anything strange as odd. The new alienations are only designed to free socially-conditioned phenomena from that stamp of familiarity which protects them against our grasp today.

44

For it seems impossible to alter what has long not been altered. We are always coming on things that are too obvious for us to bother to understand them. What men experience among themselves they think of as 'the' human experience. A child, living in a world of old men, learns how things work there. He knows the run of things before he can walk. If anyone is bold enough to want something further, he only wants to have it as an exception. Even if he realizes that the arrangements made for him by 'Providence' are only what has been provided by society he is bound to see society, that vast collection of beings like himself, as a whole that is greater than the sum of its parts and therefore not in any way to be influenced. Moreover, he would be used to things that could not be influenced; and who mistrusts what he is used to? To transform himself from general passive acceptance to a corresponding state of suspicious inquiry he would need to develop that detached eye with which the great Galileo observed a swinging chandelier. He was amazed by this pendulum motion, as if he had not expected it and could not understand its occurring, and this enabled him to come on the rules by which it was governed. Here is the outlook, disconcerting but fruitful, which the theatre must provoke with its representations of human social life. It must amaze its public, and this can be achieved by a technique of alienating the familiar.

45

This technique allows the theatre to make use in its representations of the new social-scientific method known as dialectical materialism. In order to unearth society's laws of motion this method treats social situations as processes, and traces out all their inconsistencies. It regards nothing as existing except in so far as it changes, in other words is in disharmony with itself. This also goes for those human feelings, opinions and attitudes through which at any time the form of men's life together finds its expression.

46

Our own period, which is transforming nature in so many and different ways, takes pleasure in understanding things so that we can interfere. There is a great deal to man, we say; so a great deal can be made out of him. He does not have to stay the way he is now, nor does he have to be seen only as he is now, but also as he might become. We must not start with him; we must start on him. This means, however, that I must not simply set myself in his place, but must set myself facing him, to represent us all. That is why the theatre must alienate what it shows.

47

In order to produce A-effects the actor has to discard whatever means he has learnt of getting the audience to identify itself with the characters which he plays. Aiming not to put his audience into a trance, he must not go into a trance himself. His muscles must remain loose, for a turn of the head, e.g. with tautened neck muscles, will 'magically' lead the spectators' eyes and even their heads to turn with it, and this can only detract from any speculation or reaction which the gesture may bring about. His way of speaking has to be free from parsonical sing-song and from all those cadences which lull the spectator so that the sense gets lost. Even if he plays a man possessed he must not seem to be possessed himself, for how is the spectator to discover what possessed him if he does?

48

At no moment must he go so far as to be wholly transformed into the character played. The verdict: 'he didn't act Lear, he was Lear' would be an annihilating blow to him. He has just to show the character, or rather he has to do more than just get into it; this does not mean that if he is playing passionate parts he must himself remain cold. It is only that his feelings must not at bottom be those of the character, so that the audience's may not at bottom be those of the character either. The audience must have complete freedom here.

49

This principle – that the actor appears on the stage in a double role, as Laughton and as Galileo; that the showman Laughton does not disappear in the Galileo whom he is showing; from which this way of acting gets its name of 'epic' – comes to mean simply that the tangible, matter-of-fact process is no longer hidden behind a veil; that Laughton is actually there, standing on the stage and showing us what he imagines Galileo to have been. Of course the audience would not forget Laughton if he attempted the full change of personality, in that they would admire him for it; but they would in that case miss his own opinions and sensations, which would have been completely swallowed up by the character. He would have taken its opinions and sensations and made them his own, so that a single homogeneous pattern would emerge, which he would then make ours. In order to prevent this abuse the actor must also put some artistry into the act of showing. An illustration may help: we find a gesture which expresses one-half of his attitude – that of showing – if we make him smoke a cigar and then imagine him laying it down now and again in order to show us some further characteristic attitude of the figure in the play. If we then subtract any element of hurry from the image and do not read slackness into its refusal to be taut we shall have an actor who is fully capable of leaving us to our thoughts, or to his own.

50

There needs to be yet a further change in the actor's communication of these images, and it too makes the process more 'matter-on-fact'. Just as the actor no longer has to persuade the audience that it is the author's character and not himself that is standing on the stage, so also he need not pretend that the events taking place on the stage have never been rehearsed, and are now happening for the first and only time. Schiller's distinction is no longer valid: that the rhapsodist has to treat his material as wholly in the past: the mime his, as wholly here and now.[1] It should be apparent all through his performance that 'even at the start and in the middle he knows how it ends' and he must 'thus maintain a calm independence throughout'. He narrates the story of his character by vivid portrayal, always knowing more than it does and treating its 'now' and 'here' not as a pretence made possible by the rules of the game but as something to be distinguished from yesterday and some other place, so as to make visible the knotting-together of the events.

51

This matters particularly in the portrayal of large-scale events or ones where the outside world is abruptly changed, as in wars and revolutions. The spectator can then have the whole situation and the whole course of events set before him. He can for instance hear a woman speaking and imagine her speaking differently, let us say in a few weeks' time, or other women speaking differently at that moment but in another place. This would be possible if the actress were to play as though the woman had lived through the entire period and were now, out of her memory and her knowledge of what happened next, recalling those utterances of hers which were important at the time; for what is important here is what became important. To alienate an individual in this way, as being 'this particular individual' and 'this particular individual at this particular moment', is only possible if there are no illusions that the player is identical with the character and the performance with the actual event.

52

We shall find that this has meant scrapping yet another illusion: that everyone behaves like the character concerned. 'I am doing this' has become 'I did this', and now 'he did this' has got to become 'he did this, when he might have done something else'. It is too great a simplification if we make the actions fit the character and the character fit the actions: the inconsistencies which are to be found in the actions and characters of real people cannot be shown like this. The laws of motion of a society are not to be demonstrated by 'perfect examples', for 'imperfection' (inconsistency) is an essential part of motion and of the thing moved. It is only necessary – but absolutely necessary – that there should be something approaching experimental conditions, i.e. that a counter-experiment should now and then be conceivable. Altogether this is a way of treating society as if all its actions were performed as experiments.

53

Even if empathy, or self-identification with the character, can be usefully indulged in at rehearsals (something to be avoided in a performance) it has to be treated just as one of a number of methods of observation. It helps when rehearsing, for even though the contemporary theatre has applied it in an indiscriminate way it has none the less led to subtle delineation of personality. But it is the crudest form of empathy when the actor simply asks: what should I be like if this or that were to happen to me? what would it look like if I were to say this and do that? – instead of asking: have I ever heard somebody saying this and doing that? in order to piece together all sorts of elements with which to construct a new character such as would allow the story to have taken place – and a good deal else. The coherence of the character is in fact shown by the way in which its individual qualities contradict one another.

54

Observation is a major part of acting. The actor observes his fellow men with all his nerves and muscles in an act of imitation which is at the same time a process of the mind. For pure imitation would only bring out what had been observed; and this is not enough, because the original says what it has to say with too subdued a voice. To achieve a character rather than a caricature, the actor looks at people as though they were playing him their actions, in other words as though they were advising him to give their actions careful consideration.

55

Without opinions and objectives one can represent nothing at all. Without knowledge one can show nothing; how could one know what would be worth knowing? Unless the actor is satisfied to be a parrot or a monkey he must master our period's knowledge of human social life by himself joining in the war of the classes. Some people may feel this to be degrading, because they rank art, once the money side has been settled, as one of the highest things; but mankind's highest decisions are in fact fought out on earth, not in the heavens; in the 'external' world, not inside people's heads. Nobody can stand above the warring classes, for nobody can stand above the human race. Society cannot share a common communication system so long as it is split into warring classes. Thus for art to be 'unpolitical' means only to ally itself with the 'ruling' group.

56

So the choice of viewpoint is also a major element of the actor's art, and it has to be decided outside the theatre. Like the transformation of nature, that of society is a liberating act; and it is the joys of liberation which the theatre of a scientific age has got to convey.

57

Let us go on to examine how, for instance, this viewpoint affects the actor's interpretation of his part. It then becomes important that he should not 'catch on' too quickly. Even if he straightaway establishes the most natural cadences for his part, the least awkward way of speaking it, he still cannot regard its actual pronouncement as being ideally natural, but must think twice and take his own general opinions into account, then consider various other conceivable pronouncements; in short, take up the attitude of a man who just wonders. This is not only to prevent him from 'fixing' a particular character prematurely, so that it has to be stuffed out with after-thoughts because he has not waited to register all the other pronouncements, and especially those of the other characters; but also and principally in order to build into the character that element of 'Not – But' on which so much depends if society, in the shape of the audience, is to be able to look at what takes place in such a way as to be able to affect it. Each actor, moreover, instead of concentrating on what suits him and calling it 'human nature', must go above all for what does not suit him, is not his speciality. And along with his part he must commit to memory his first reactions, reserves, criticisms, shocks, so that they are not destroyed by being 'swallowed up' in the final version but are preserved and perceptible; for character and all must not grow on the audience so much as strike it.

58

And the learning process must be co-ordinated so that the actor learns as the other actors are learning and develops his character as they are developing theirs. For the smallest social unit is not the single person but two people. In life too we develop one another.

59

Here we can learn something from our own theatres' deplorable habit of letting the dominant actor, the star, 'come to the front' by getting all the other actors to work for him: he makes his character terrible or wise by forcing his partners to make theirs terrified or attentive. Even if only to secure this advantage for all, and thus to help the story, the actors should sometimes swap roles with their partners during rehearsal, so that the characters can get what they need from one another. But it is also good for the actors when they see their characters copied or portrayed in another form. If the part is played by somebody of the opposite sex the sex of the character will be more clearly brought out; if it is played by a comedian, whether comically or tragically, it will gain fresh aspects. By helping to develop the parts that correspond to his own, or at any rate standing in for their players, the actor strengthens the all-decisive social standpoint from which he has to present his character. The master is only the sort of master his servant lets him be, etc.

60

A mass of operations to develop the character are carried out when it is introduced among the other characters of the play, and the actor will have to memorize what he himself has anticipated in this connection from his reading of the text. But now he finds out much more about himself from the treatment which he gets at the hands of the characters in the play.

61

The realm of attitudes adopted by the characters towards one another is what we call the realm of gest. Physical attitude, tone of voice and facial expression are all determined by a social gest: the characters are cursing, flattering, instructing one another, and so on. The attitudes which people adopt towards one another include even those attitudes which would appear to be quite private, such as the utterances of physical pain in an illness, or of religious faith. These expressions of a gest are usually highly complicated and contra- dictory, so that they cannot be rendered by any single word and the actor must take care that in giving his image the necessary emphasis he does not lose anything, but emphasizes the entire complex.

62

The actor masters his character by paying critical attention to its manifold utterances, as also to those of his counterparts and of all the other characters involved.

63

Let us get down to the problem of gestic content by running through the opening scenes of a fairly modern play, my own *Life of Galileo*. Since we wish at the same time to find out what light the different utterances cast on one another we will assume that it is not our first introduction to the play. It begins with the man of 46 having his morning wash, broken by occasional browsing in books and by a lesson on the solar system for Andrea Sarti, a small boy. To play this, surely you have got to know that we shall be ending with the man of 78 having his supper, just after he has said good-bye for ever to the same pupil? He is then more terribly altered than this passage of time could possibly have brought about. He wolfs his food with unrestrained greed, no other idea in his head; he has rid himself of his educational mission in shameful circumstances, as though it were a burden: he, who once drank his morning milk without a care, greedy to teach the boy. But does he really drink it without care? Isn't the pleasure of drinking and washing one with the pleasure which he takes in the new ideas? Don't forget: he thinks out of self-indulgence. . . . Is that good or bad? I would advise you to represent it as good, since on this point you will find nothing in the whole play to harm society, and more especially because you yourself are, I hope, a gallant child of the scientific age. But take careful note: many horrible things will happen in this connection. The fact that the man who here acclaims the new age will be forced at the end to beg this age to disown him as contemptible, even to dispossess him; all this will be relevant. As for the lesson, you may like to decide whether the man's heart is so full that his mouth is overflowing, so that he has to talk to anybody about it, even a child, or whether the child has first to draw the knowledge out of him, by knowing him and showing interest. Again, there may be two of them who cannot restrain themselves, the one from asking, the other from giving the answer: a bond of this sort would be interesting, for one day it is going to be rudely snapped. Of course you will want the demonstration of the earth's rotation round the sun to be conducted quickly, since it is given for nothing, and now the wealthy unknown pupil appears, lending the scholar's time a monetary value. He shows no interest, but he has to be served; Galileo lacks resources, and so he will stand between the wealthy pupil and the intelligent one, and sigh as he makes his choice. There is little that he can teach his new student, so he learns from him instead; he hears of the telescope which has been invented in Holland: in his own way he gets something out of the disturbance of his morning's work. The Rector of the university arrives. Galileo's application for an increase in salary has been turned down; the university is reluctant to pay so much for the theories of physics as for those of theology; it wishes him, who after all is operating on a generally accepted low level of scholarship, to produce something useful here and now. You will see from the way in which he offers his thesis that he is used to being refused and corrected. The Rector reminds him that the Republic guarantees freedom of research even if she doesn't pay; he replies that he cannot make much of this freedom if he lacks the leisure which good payment permits. Here you should not find his impatience too peremptory, or his poverty will not be given due weight. For shortly after that you find him having ideas which need some explanation: the prophet of a new age of scientific truth considers how he can swindle some money out of the Republic by offering her the telescope as his own invention. All he sees in the new invention, you will be surprised to hear, is a few scudi, and he examines it simply with a view to annexing it himself. But if you move on to the second scene you will find that while he is selling the invention to the Venetian Signoria with a speech that disgraces him by its falsehoods he has already almost forgotten the money, because he has realized that the instrument has not only military but astronomical significance. The article which he has been blackmailed – let us call it that – into producing proves to have great qualities for the very research which he had to break off in order to produce it. If during the ceremony, as he complacently accepts the undeserved honours paid him, he outlines to his learned friend the marvellous discoveries in view – don't overlook the theatrical way in which he does this – you will find in him a far more profound excitement than the thought of monetary gain called forth. Perhaps, looked at in this way, his charlatanry does not mean much, but it still shows how determined this man is to take the easy course, and to apply his reason in a base as well as a noble manner. A more significant test awaits him, and does not every capitulation bring the next one nearer?

64

Splitting such material into one gest after another, the actor masters his character by first mastering the 'story'. It is only after walking all round the entire episode that he can, as it were by a single leap, seize and fix his character, complete with all its individual features. Once he has done his best to let himself be amazed by the inconsistencies in its various attitudes, knowing that he will in turn have to make them amaze the audience, then the story as a whole gives him a chance to pull the inconsistencies together; for the story, being a limited episode, has a specific sense, i.e. only gratifies a specific fraction of all the interests that could arise.

65

Everything hangs on the 'story'; it is the heart of the theatrical performance. For it is what happens *between* people that provides them with all the material that they can discuss, criticize, alter. Even if the particular person represented by the actor has ultimately to fit into more than just the one episode, it is mainly because the episode will be all the more striking if it reaches fulfilment in a particular person. The 'story' is the theatre's great operation, the complete fitting together of all the gestic incidents, embracing the communications and impulses that must now go to make up the audience's entertainment.

66

Each single incident has its basic gest: *Richard Gloster courts his victim's widow. The child's true mother is found by means of a chalk circle. God has a bet with the Devil for Dr Faustus's soul. Woyzeck buys a cheap knife in order to do his wife in*, etc. The grouping of the characters on the stage and the movements of the groups must be such that the necessary beauty is attained above all by the elegance with which the material conveying that gest is set out and laid bare to the understanding of the audience.

67

As we cannot invite the audience to fling itself into the story as if it were a river and let itself be carried vaguely hither and thither, the individual episodes have to be knotted together in such a way that the knots are easily noticed. The episodes must not succeed one another indistinguishably but must give us a chance to interpose our judgement. (If it were above all the obscurity of the original interrelations that interested us, then just this circumstance would have to be sufficiently alienated.) The parts of the story have to be carefully set off one against another by giving each its own structure as a play within the play. To this end it is best to agree to use titles like those in the preceding paragraph. The titles must include the social point, saying at the same time something about the kind of portrayal wanted, i.e. should copy the tone of a chronicle or a ballad or a newspaper or a morality. For instance, a simple way of alienating something is that normally applied to customs and moral principles. A visit, the treatment of an enemy, a lovers' meeting, agreements about politics or business, can be portrayed as if they were simply illustrations of general principles valid for the place in question. Shown thus, the particular and unrepeatable incident acquires a disconcerting look, because it appears as something general, something that has become a principle. As soon as we ask whether in fact it should have become such, or what about it should have done so, we are alienating the incident. The poetic approach to history can be studied in the so-called panoramas at sideshows in fairs. As alienation likewise means a kind of fame certain incidents can just be represented as famous, as though they had for a long while been common knowledge and care must be taken not to offer the least obstacle to their further transmission. In short: there are many conceivable ways of telling a story, some of them known and some still to be discovered.

68

What needs to be alienated, and how this is to be done, depends on the exposition demanded by the entire episode; and this is where the theatre has to speak up decisively for the interests of its own time. Let us take as an example of such exposition the old play Hamlet. Given the dark and bloody period in which I am writing – the criminal ruling classes, the widespread doubt in the power of reason, continually being misused – I think that I can read the story thus: It is an age of warriors. Hamlet's father, king of Denmark, slew the king of Norway in a successful war of spoliation. While the latter's son Fortinbras is arming for a fresh war the Danish king is likewise slain: by his own brother. The slain king's brothers, now themselves kings, avert war by arranging that the Norwegian troops shall cross Danish soil to launch a predatory war against Poland. But at this point the young Hamlet is summoned by his warrior father's ghost to avenge the crime committed against him. After at first being reluctant to answer one bloody deed by another, and even preparing to go into exile, he meets young Fortinbras at the coast as he is marching with his troops to Poland. Overcome by this warrior-like example, he turns back and in a piece of barbaric butchery slaughters his uncle, his mother and himself, leaving Denmark to the Norwegian. These events show the young man, already somewhat stout, making the most ineffective use of the new approach to Reason which he has picked up at the university of Wittenberg. In the feudal business to which he returns it simply hampers him. Faced with irrational practices, his reason is utterly unpractical. He falls a tragic victim to the discrepancy between such reasoning and such action. This way of reading the play, which can be read in more than one way, might in my view interest our audience.

69

Whether or no literature presents them as successes, each step forward, every emancipation from nature that is scored in the field of production and leads to a transformation of society, all those explorations in some new direction which mankind has embarked on in order to improve its lot, give us a sense of confidence and triumph and lead us to take pleasure in the possibilities of change in all things. Galileo expresses this when he says: 'It is my view that the earth is most noble and wonderful, seeing the great number and variety of changes and generations which incessantly take place on it.'

70

The exposition of the story and its communication by suitable means of alienation constitute the main business of the theatre. Not everything depends on the actor, even though nothing may be done without taking him into account. The 'story' is set out, brought forward and shown by the theatre as a whole, by actors, stage designers, mask-makers, costumiers, composers and choreographers. They unite their various arts for the joint operation, without of course sacrificing their independence in the process.

71

It emphasizes the general gest of showing, which always underlies that which is being shown, when the audience is musically addressed by means of songs. Because of this the actors ought not to 'drop into' song, but should clearly mark it off from the rest of the text; and this is best reinforced by a few theatrical methods such as changing the lighting or inserting a title. For its part, the music must strongly resist the smooth incorporation which is generally expected of it and turns it into an unthinking slavey. Music does not 'accompany' except in the form of comment. It cannot simply 'express itself' by discharging the emotions with which the incidents of the play have filled it. Thus Eisler, for example, helped admirably in the knotting of the incidents when in the carnival scene of *Galileo* he set the maskedprocession of the guilds to a triumphant and threatening music which showed what a revolutionary twist the lower orders had given to the scholar's astronomical theories. Similarly in *The Caucasian Chalk Circle* the singer, by using a chilly and unemotional way of singing to describe the servant-girl's rescue of the child as it is mimed on the stage, makes evident the terror of a period in which motherly instincts can become a suicidal weakness. Thus music can make its point in a number of ways and with full independence, and can react in its own manner to the subjects dealt with; at the same time it can also quite simply help to lend variety to the entertainment.

72

Just as the composer wins back his freedom by no longer having to create atmosphere so that the audience may be helped to lose itself unreservedly in the events on the stage, so also the stage designer gets considerable freedom as soon as he no longer has to give the illusion of a room or a locality when he is building his sets. It is enough for him to give hints, though these must make statements of greater historical or social interest than does the real setting. At the Jewish Theatre in Moscow *King Lear* was alienated by a structure that recalled a medieval tabernacle; Neher set *Galileo* in front of projections of maps, documents and Renaissance works of art; for *Haitang erwacht* at the Piscator-Theater Heartfield used a background of reversible flags bearing inscriptions, to mark changes in the political situation of which the persons on the stage were sometimes unaware.

73

For choreography too there are once again tasks of a realistic kind. It is a relatively recent error to suppose that it has nothing to do with the representation of 'people as they really are'. If art reflects life it does so with special mirrors. Art does not become unrealistic by changing the proportions but by changing them in such a way that if the audience took its representations as a practical guide to insights and impulses it would go astray in real life. It is of course essential that stylization should not remove the natural element but should heighten it. Anyhow, a theatre where everything depends on the gest cannot do without choreography. Elegant movement and graceful grouping, for a start, can alienate, and inventive miming greatly helps the story.

74

So let us invite all the sister arts of the drama, not in order to create an 'integrated work of art' in which they all offer themselves up and are lost, but so that together with the drama they may further the common task in their different ways; and their relations with one another consist in this: that they lead to mutual alienation.

75

And here once again let us recall that their task is to entertain the children of the scientific age, and to do so with sensuousness and humour. This is something that we Germans cannot tell ourselves too often, for with us everything easily slips into the insubstantial and unapproachable, and we begin to talk of *Weltanschauung* when the world in question has already dissolved. Even materialism is little more than an idea with us. Sexual pleasure with us turns into marital obligations, the pleasures of art subserve general culture, and by learning we mean not an enjoyable process of finding out, but the forcible shoving of our nose into something. Our activity has none of the pleasure of exploration, and if we want to make an impression we do not say how much fun we have got out of something but how much effort it has cost us.

76

One more thing: the delivery to the audience of what has been built up in the rehearsals. Here it is essential that the actual playing should be infused with the gest of handing over a finished article. What now comes before the spectator is the most frequently repeated of what has not been rejected, and so the finished representations have to be delivered with the eyes fully open, so that they may be received with the eyes open too.

77

That is to say, our representations must take second place to what is represented, men's life together in society; and the pleasure felt in their perfection must be converted into the higher pleasure felt when the rules emerging from this life in society are treated as imperfect and provisional. In this way the theatre leaves its spectators productively disposed even after the spectacle is over. Let us hope that their theatre may allow them to enjoy as entertainment that terrible and never-ending labour which should ensure their maintenance, together with the terror of their unceasing transformation. Let them here produce their own lives in the simplest way; for the simplest way of living is in art.

NOTES [by John Willett]

The 'Short Organum' was written in Switzerland in 1948, while Brecht was staying outside Zurich. 'More or less finished with Organum – short condensation of the Messingkauf', says a diary note of 18 August. But if the 'Messingkauf' was derived from Galileo the new work seems to relate both formally and stylistically to the *Novum Organum* of Francis Bacon, the other great Renaissance scientist whose name occurs a number of times in Brecht's writings. (On this point, see Dr Reinhold Grimm's essay in the symposium *Das Ärgernis Brecht*, Basle: Basilius Presse, 1961, where he suggests that Bacon's book attracted Brecht because it was directed against the *Organum* of Aristotle, Aristotle being of course not only the implied enemy of the non-aristotelian drama but also the ideological villain of *Galileo*.)

When the 'Short Organum' was reprinted in 1953 in *Versuche 12* a covering note called it 'a description of a theatre of the scientific age'. Later Brecht wrote a number of appendices to it and linked it to his last collection of notes, 'Die Dialektik auf dem Theater', which he derived from the short reference to dialectical materialism in paragraph 45. Failing completion of 'Der Messingkauf', the 'Short Organum' became (and remained) Brecht's most important theoretical work.

[1] Letter to Goethe, 26 Dec. 1797.

10 Roland Barthes
The Tasks of Brechtian Criticism (1956)*

Roland Barthes (1915–80) was influential in what became known as poststructuralism. His earlier work, however, developed a more Marxist approach to literary critique which owed much to Brecht. *Mythologies* (1957; trans. 1972) exemplifies this Brechtian political demystification of signs as a structuralist mode of Marxist semiotics. Barthes, however, also responded to moves away from structuralism, moves which can be traced through his books *Writing Degree Zero* (1953; trans. 1967) and *Elements of Semiology* (1964; trans. 1967), to works such as *S/Z* (1970; trans. 1974) and *The Pleasure of the Text* (1973; trans. 1975). These later works offer a materialist erotics of avant-garde textuality. Indeed, *Roland Barthes by Roland Barthes* (1975; trans. 1977) suggests the vertiginous pleasures of a self-reflexively Proustian Marxist: gay, witty and transgressive, if distanced from the immediacy of class conflict. Primarily an essayist, Barthes' work is suggestive in ways similar to Benjamin. Much of his most important work appeared as essays, notably in *Critical Essays* (1964; trans. 1972) in which 'The Tasks of Brechtian Criticism' (1956) was collected. This essay, along with a number of essays Barthes wrote for *Théâtre populaire*, attempts to rethink the possibilities of Brechtian theatre and criticism. This was later developed in *Screen* by Stephen Heath, whose book *Vertige du déplacement* (1974) remains one of the best books on Barthes. Recent critical accounts are provided by Annette Lavers, *Roland Barthes* (1982) and Michael Moriarty, *Roland Barthes* (1991).

It is safe to predict that Brecht's work will become increasingly important for us; not only because it is great, but because it is exemplary as well; it shines, today at least, with an exceptional lustre amid two deserts: the desert of our contemporary theatre, where aside from his there are no great names to cite; and the desert of revolutionary art, sterile since the beginnings of the Zhdanovian impasse. Any reflection on theatre and on revolution must come

* From Roland Barthes, *Critical Essays*, trans. R. Howard (Evanston, ll.: Northwestern University Press, 1972), 71–6.

to terms with Brecht, who brought about this situation himself: the entire force of his work opposes the reactionary myth of unconscious genius; its greatness is the kind which best suits our period, the greatness of responsibility; it is a work which is in a state of 'complicity' with the world, with our world: a knowledge of Brecht, a reflection on Brecht, in a word, Brechtian criticism is by definition extensive with the problematics of our time. We must tirelessly repeat this truth: knowing Brecht is of a different order of importance from knowing Shakespeare or Gogol; because it is for us, precisely, that Brecht has written his plays, and not for eternity. Brechtian criticism will therefore be written by the spectator, the reader, the consumer, and not the exegete: it is a criticism of a *concerned* man. And if I myself were to write the criticism whose context I am sketching here, I should not fail to suggest, at the risk of appearing indiscreet, how this work touches me and helps me, personally, as an individual. But to confine myself here to the essentials of a programme of Brechtian criticism, I shall merely suggest the levels of analysis which such criticism should successively investigate.

(1) *Sociology*. Generally speaking, we do not yet have adequate means of investigation to define the theatre's public, or publics. Furthermore, in France at least, Brecht has not yet emerged from the experimental theatres (except for the TNP's *Mother Courage*, a production so misconceived that the case is anything but instructive). For the moment, therefore, we can study only the press reactions.

There are four types to distinguish. By the extreme right, Brecht's work is totally discredited because of its political commitment: Brecht's theatre is mediocre *because* it is communist. By the right (a more complicated right, which can extend to the 'modernist' bourgeoisie of *L'Express*), Brecht is subjected to the usual political denaturation: the man is dissociated from the work, the former consigned to politics (emphasizing successively and contradictorily his independence and his servility with regard to the Party), and the latter enlisted under the banners of an eternal theatre: Brecht's work, we are told, is great in spite of Brecht, against Brecht.

On the left, there is first of all a humanist reading: Brecht is made into one of those giant creative figures committed to a humanitarian promotion of man, like Romain Rolland or Barbusse. This sympathetic view unfortunately disguises an anti-intellectualist prejudice frequent in certain far-left circles: in order to 'humanize' Brecht, the theoretical part of his work is discredited or at least minimized: the plays are great *despite* Brecht's systematic views on epic theatre, the actor, alienation, etc.: here we encounter one of the basic theorems of *petit-bourgeois* culture, the romantic contrast between heart and head, between intuition and reflection, between the ineffable and the rational – an opposition which ultimately masks a magical conception of art. Finally, the communists themselves express certain reservations (in France, at least) with regard to Brecht's opposition to the positive hero, his epic conception of theatre, and the 'formalist' orientation of his dramaturgy. Apart from the contestation of Roger Vailland, based on a defence of French tragedy as a dialectical art of crisis, these criticisms proceed from a Zhdanovian conception of art.

I am citing a dossier from memory; it should be examined in detail. The point, moreover, is not to refute Brecht's critics, but rather to approach Brecht by the means our society spontaneously employs to digest him. Brecht reveals whoever speaks about him, and this revelation naturally concerns Brecht to the highest degree.

(2) *Ideology*. Must we oppose the 'digestions' of the Brechtian canon by a canonical truth of Brecht? In a sense and within certain limits, yes. There is a specific ideological content, coherent, consistent and remarkably organized, in Brecht's theatre, one which protests against abusive distortions. This content must be described.

In order to do this, we possess two kinds of texts: first of all, the theoretical texts, of an acute intelligence (it is no matter of indifference to encounter a man of the theatre who is intelligent), of a great ideological lucidity, and which it would be childish to underrate on the pretext that they are only an intellectual appendage to an essentially *creative* body of work. Of course Brecht's theatre is made to be performed. But before performing it or seeing it performed, there is no ban on its being understood: this intelligence is organically linked to its constitutive function, which is to transform a public even as it is being entertained. In a Marxist like Brecht, the relations between theory and practice must not be underestimated or distorted. To separate the Brechtian theater from its theoretical foundations would be as erroneous as to try to understand Marx's action without reading *The Communist Manifesto* or Lenin's politics without reading *The State and the Revolution*. There is no official decree or supernatural intervention which graciously dispenses the theatre from the demands of theoretical reflection. Against an entire tendency of our criticism, we must assert the capital importance of Brecht's systematic writings: it does not weaken the creative value of this theatre to regard it as a reasoned theatre.

Moreover, the plays themselves afford the chief elements of Brechtian ideology. I can indicate here only the principal ones: the historical and not 'natural' character of human misfortunes; the spiritual contagion of economic alienation, whose final effect is to blind the very men it oppresses as to the causes of their servitude; the correctible status of Nature, the tractability of the world; the necessary adequation of means and situations (for instance, in a bad society, the law can be reestablished only by a reprobate judge); the transformation of ancient psychological 'conflicts' into historical contradictions, subject as such to the corrective power of men.

We must note here that these truths are never set forth except as the consequence of concrete situations, and these situations are infinitely plastic. Contrary to the rightist prejudice, Brecht's theatre is not a thesis theatre, not a propaganda theatre. What Brecht takes from Marxism are not slogans, an articulation of arguments, but a general method of explanation. It follows that in Brecht's theatre the Marxist elements always seem to be recreated. Basically, Brecht's greatness, and his solitude, is that he keeps inventing Marxism. The ideological theme, in Brecht, could be precisely defined as a dynamic of events which combines observation and explanation, ethics and politics: according to the profoundest Marxist teaching, each theme is at once the expression of what men want to be and of what things are, at once a protest (because it unmasks) and a reconciliation (because it explains).

(3) *Semiology*. Semiology is the study of signs and significations. I do not want to engage here in a discussion of this science, which was postulated some forty years ago by the linguist Saussure and which is generally accused of formalism. Without letting ourselves be intimidated by the words, we might say that Brechtian dramaturgy, the theory of *Episierung*, of alienation, and the entire practice of the Berliner Ensemble with regard to sets and costumes, propose an explicit semiological problem. For what Brechtian dramaturgy postulates is that today at least, the responsibility of a dramatic art is not so much to express reality as to signify it. Hence there must be a certain distance between signified and signifier: revolutionary art must admit a certain arbitrary nature of signs, it must acknowledge a certain 'formalism', in the sense that it must treat form according to an appropriate method, which is the semiological method. All Brechtian art protests against the Zhdanovian confusion between ideology and semiology, which has led to such an aesthetic impasse.

We realize, moreover, why this aspect of Brechtian thought is most antipathetic to bourgeois and Zhdanovian criticism: both are attached to an aesthetic of the 'natural' expression of reality: art for them is a false Nature, a *pseudo-Physis*. For Brecht, on the contrary, art today – i.e., at the heart of a historical conflict whose stake is human disalienation – art today must be an *anti-Physis*. Brecht's formalism is a radical protest against the confusions of the bourgeois and *petit-bourgeois* false Nature: in a still-alienated society, art must be critical, it must cut off all illusions, even that of 'Nature': the sign must be partially arbitrary, otherwise we fall back on an art of expression, an art of essentialist illusion.

(4) *Morality*. Brechtian theatre is a moral theatre, that is, a theatre which asks, with the spectator: what is to be done in such a situation? At this point we should classify and describe the archetypical situations of the Brechtian theatre; they may be reduced, I think, to a single question: how to be good in a bad society? It seems to me very important to articulate the moral structure of Brecht's theatre: granted that Marxism has had other more urgent tasks than to concern itself with problems of individual conduct; none the less capitalist society endures, and communism itself is being transformed: revolutionary action must increasingly cohabit, and in an almost institutional

fashion, with the norms of bourgeois and *petit-bourgeois* morality: problems of conduct, and no longer of action, arise. Here is where Brecht can have a great cleansing power, a pedagogical power.

Especially since his morality has nothing catechistic about it, being for the most part strictly interrogative. Indeed, some of his plays conclude with a literal interrogation of the public, to whom the author leaves the responsibility of finding its own solution to the problem raised. Brecht's moral role is to infiltrate a question into what seems self-evident (this is the theme of the exception and the rule). For what is involved here is essentially a morality of invention. Brechtian invention is a tactical process to unite with revolutionary correction. In other words, for Brecht the outcome of every moral impasse depends on a more accurate analysis of the concrete situation in which the subject finds himself: the issue is joined by representing in explicit terms the historical particularity of this situation, its artificial, purely conformist nature. Essentially, Brecht's morality consists of a correct reading of history, and the plasticity of the morality (*to change Custom when necessary*) derives from the very plasticity of history.

11 Georg Lukács
The Ideology of Modernism (1957)*

Georg Lukács (1885–1971) joined the Hungarian Communist Party in 1918, and, although imprisoned, exiled and expelled at various times, he remained loyal to the Party. His most influential philosophical contribution, *History and Class Consciousness* (1923; trans. 1971), argued for a Hegelian Marxist approach to class consciousness, alienation and reification. Like Karl Korsch's *Marxism and Philosophy* (1923; trans. 1970) this proved unacceptable to Communist Party orthodoxy. With the defeat of his 'Blum Theses' (1928), Lukács retreated to literature and aesthetics. Refining theories of reflection, typicality and representation, his most sophisticated work differentiates the form and content of realism and aesthetic objectivity. He defended a conception of critical realism through Marxist readings of novels: from Scott, Balzac and Tolstoy to the present. 'The Ideology of Modernism', from *The Meaning of Contemporary Realism* (1957; trans. 1963), exemplifies his critique of socialist realism and of modernist redefinitions of realism. Compromised by Stalinism, Lukács has often been dismissed for his failure to appreciate modernist literature. While this aspect of Lukács's work has been considered reductive, however, analogous and even more reductive antipathies to modernism have become hegemonic via debates associated with postmodernism. Indeed, if Lukács is seen as prefiguring critiques of the ideology of postmodernism of the kind offered by Jameson, then his insistence on critical realism requires reassessment. Arrested by the Communist Party in 1956, deported, locked up in a castle and held without trial in Rumania, Lukács is reputed to have said that Kafka was a realist after all. Other works translated include *The Historical Novel* (1969); *Writer and Critic* (1970); *Studies in European Realism* (1972); and *Essays on Realism* (1980). Lukács also wrote a number of influential pre-Marxist works, notably *Soul and Form* (1910; trans. 1974) and *The Theory of the Novel* (1916; trans. 1971). For discussion see E. Bloch and others, *Aesthetics and Politics* (1977); F. Jameson, *Marxism and Form* (1971); J. M. Bernstein, *The Philosophy of the Novel* (1984) and A. Kadarkay, *Georg Lukács* (1991).

* From Georg Lukács, *The Meaning of Contemporary Realism*, trans. John and Necke Mander (London: Merlin, 1963), 17–46.

It is in no way surprising that the most influential contemporary school of writing should still be committed to the dogmas of 'modernist' anti-realism. It is here that we must begin our investigation if we are to chart the possibilities of a bourgeois realism. We must compare the two main trends in contemporary bourgeois literature, and look at the answers they give to the major ideological and artistic questions of our time.

We shall concentrate on the underlying ideological basis of these trends (ideological in the above-defined, not in the strictly philosophical, sense). What must be avoided at all costs is the approach generally adopted by bourgeois-modernist critics themselves: that exaggerated concern with formal criteria, with questions of style and literary technique. This approach may appear to distinguish sharply between 'modern' and 'traditional' writing (i.e. contemporary writers who adhere to the styles of the last century). In fact it fails to locate the decisive formal problems and turns a blind eye to their inherent dialectic. We are presented with a false polarization which, by exaggerating the importance of stylistic differences, conceals the opposing principles actually underlying and determining contrasting styles.

To take an example: the *monologue intérieur*. Compare, for instance, Bloom's monologue in the lavatory or Molly's monologue in bed, at the beginning and at the end of *Ulysses*, with Goethe's early-morning monologue as conceived by Thomas Mann in his *Lotte in Weimar*. Plainly, the same stylistic technique is being employed. And certain of Thomas Mann's remarks about Joyce and his methods would appear to confirm this.

Yet it is not easy to think of any two novels more basically dissimilar than *Ulysses* and *Lotte in Weimar*. This is true even of the superficially rather similar scenes I have indicated. I am not referring to the – to my mind – striking difference in intellectual quality. I refer to the fact that with Joyce the stream-of-consciousness technique is no mere stylistic device; it is itself the formative principle governing the narrative pattern and the presentation of character. Technique here is something absolute; it is part and parcel of the aesthetic ambition informing *Ulysses*. With Thomas Mann, on the other hand, the *monologue intérieur* is simply a technical device, allowing the author to explore aspects of Goethe's world which would not have been otherwise available. Goethe's experience is not presented as confined to momentary sense-impressions. The artist reaches down to the core of Goethe's personality, to the complexity of his relations with his own past, present, and even future experience. The stream of association is only apparently free. The monologue is composed with the utmost artistic rigour: it is a carefully plotted sequence gradually piercing to the core of Goethe's personality. Every person or event, emerging momentarily from the stream and vanishing again, is given a specific weight, a definite position, in the pattern of the whole. However unconventional the presentation, the compositional principle is that of the traditional epic; in the way the pace is controlled, and the transitions and climaxes are organized, the ancient rules of epic narration are faithfully observed.

It would be absurd, in view of Joyce's artistic ambitions and his manifest abilities, to qualify the exaggerated attention he gives to the detailed recording of sense-data, and his comparative neglect of ideas and emotions, as artistic failure. All this was in conformity with Joyce's artistic intentions; and, by use of such techniques, he may be said to have achieved them satisfactorily. But between Joyce's intentions and those of Thomas Mann there is a total opposition. The perpetually oscillating patterns of sense- and memory-data, their powerfully charged – but aimless and directionless – fields of force, give rise to an epic structure which is *static*, reflecting a belief in the basically static character of events.

These opposed views of the world – dynamic and developmental on the one hand, static and sensational on the other – are of crucial importance in examining the two schools of literature I have mentioned. I shall return to the opposition later. Here, I want only to point out that an exclusive emphasis on formal matters can lead to serious misunderstanding of the character of an artist's work.

What determines the style of a given work of art? How does the intention determine the form? (We are concerned here, of course, with the intention realized in the work; it need not coincide with the writer's conscious intention). The distinctions that concern us are not those between stylistic 'techniques' in the formalistic sense. It is the view of the world, the ideology or *Weltanschauung* underlying a writer's work, that counts. And it is the writer's attempt to reproduce this view of the world which constitutes his 'intention' and is the formative principle underlying the style of a given piece of writing. Looked at in this way, style ceases to be a formalistic category. Rather, it is rooted in content; it is the specific form of a specific content.

Content determines form. But there is no content of which Man himself is not the focal point. However various the *données* of literature (a particular experience, a didactic purpose), the basic question is, and will remain: what is Man?

Here is a point of division: if we put the question in abstract, philosophical terms, leaving aside all formal considerations, we arrive – for the realist school – at the traditional Aristotelian dictum (which was also reached by other than purely aesthetic considerations): Man is *zoon politikon*, a social animal. The Aristotelian dictum is applicable to all great realistic literature. Achilles and Werther, Oedipus and Tom Jones, Antigone and Anna Karenina: their individual existence – their *Sein an sich*, in the Hegelian terminology; their 'ontological being', as a more fashionable terminology has it – cannot be distinguished from their social and historical environment. Their human significance, their specific individuality cannot be separated from the context in which they were created.

The ontological view governing the image of man in the work of leading modernist writers is the exact opposite of this. Man, for these writers, is by nature solitary, asocial, unable to enter into relationships with other human beings. Thomas Wolfe once wrote: 'My view of the world is based on the firm conviction that solitariness is by no means a rare condition, something peculiar to myself or to a few specially solitary human beings, but the inescapable, central fact of human existence.' Man, thus imagined, may establish contact with other individuals, but only in a superficial, accidental manner; only, ontologically speaking, by retrospective reflection. For 'the others', too, are basically solitary, beyond significant human relationship.

This basic solitariness of man must not be confused with that individual solitariness to be found in the literature of traditional realism. In the latter case, we are dealing with a particular situation in which a human being may be placed, due either to his character or to the circumstances of his life. Solitariness may be objectively conditioned, as with Sophocles' Philoctetes, put ashore on the bleak island of Lemnos. Or it may be subjective, the product of inner necessity, as with Tolstoy's Ivan Ilyitsch or Flaubert's Frédéric Moreau in the *Education Sentimentale*. But it is always merely a fragment, a phase, a climax or anticlimax, in the life of the community as a whole. The fate of such individuals is characteristic of certain human types in specific social or historical circumstances. Beside and beyond their solitariness, the common life, the strife and togetherness of other human beings, goes on as before. In a word, their solitariness is a specific social fate, not a universal *condition humaine*.

The latter, of course, is characteristic of the theory and practice of modernism. I would like, in the present study, to spare the reader tedious excursions into philosophy. But I cannot refrain from drawing the reader's attention to Heidegger's description of human existence as a 'thrownness-into-being' (*Geworfenheit ins Dasein*). A more graphic evocation of the ontological solitariness of the individual would be hard to imagine. Man is 'thrown-into-being'. This implies, not merely that man is constitutionally unable to establish relationships with things or persons outside himself; but also that it is impossible to determine theoretically the origin and goal of human existence.

Man, thus conceived, is an ahistorical being. (The fact that Heidegger does admit a form of 'authentic' historicity in his system is not really relevant. I have shown elsewhere that Heidegger tends to belittle historicity as 'vulgar'; and his 'authentic' historicity is not distinguishable from ahistoricity.) This negation of history takes two different forms in modernist literature. First, the hero is strictly confined within the limits of his own experience. There is not for him – and apparently not for his creator – any pre-existent reality beyond his own self, acting upon him or being acted upon by him. Secondly, the hero himself is without personal history. He is 'thrown-into-the-world': meaninglessly, unfathomably. He does not develop through contact with the world; he neither forms nor is formed by it. The only 'development' in this literature is the gradual revelation of the human condition. Man is now what he has always been and always will be. The narrator, the examining subject, is in motion; the examined reality is static.

Of course, dogmas of this kind are only really viable in philosophical abstraction, and then only with a measure of sophistry. A gifted writer, however extreme his theoretical modernism, will in practice have to compromise with the demands of historicity and of social environment. Joyce uses Dublin, Kafka and Musil the Hapsburg Monarchy, as the locus of their masterpieces. But the locus they lovingly depict is little more than a backcloth; it is not basic to their artistic intention.

This view of human existence has specific literary consequences. Particularly in one category, of primary theoretical and practical importance, to which we must now give our attention: that of *potentiality*. Philosophy distinguishes between *abstract* and *concrete* (in Hegel, 'real') *potentiality*. These two categories, their interrelation and opposition, are rooted in life itself. *Potentiality* – seen abstractly or subjectively – is richer than actual life. Innumerable possibilities for man's development are imaginable, only a small percentage of which will be realized. Modern subjectivism, taking these imagined possibilities for actual complexity of life, oscillates between melancholy and fascination. When the world declines to realize these possibilities, this melancholy becomes tinged with contempt. Hofmannsthal's Sobeide expressed the reaction of the generation first exposed to this experience:

> The burden of those endlessly pored-over
> And now forever perished possibilities . . .

How far were those possibilities even concrete or 'real'? Plainly, they existed only in the imagination of the subject, as dreams or day-dreams. Faulkner, in whose work this subjective potentiality plays an important part, was evidently aware that reality must thereby be subjectivized and made to appear arbitrary. Consider this comment of his: 'They were all talking simultaneously, getting flushed and excited, quarrelling, making the unreal into a possibility, then into a probability, then into an irrefutable fact, as human beings do when they put their wishes into words.' The possibilities in a man's mind, the particular pattern, intensity and suggestiveness they assume, will of course be characteristic of that individual. In practice, their number will border on the infinite, even with the most unimaginative individual. It is thus a hopeless undertaking to define the contours of individuality, let alone to come to grips with a man's actual fate, by means of potentiality. The *abstract* character of potentiality is clear from the fact that it cannot determine development – subjective mental states, however permanent or profound, cannot here be decisive. Rather, the development of personality is determined by inherited gifts and qualities; by the factors, external or internal, which further or inhibit their growth.

But in life potentiality can, of course, become reality. Situations arise in which a man is confronted with a choice; and in the act of choice a man's character may reveal itself in a light that surprises even himself. In literature – and particularly in dramatic literature – the denouement often consists in the realization of just such a potentiality, which circumstances have kept from coming to the fore. These potentialities are, then, 'real' or concrete potentialities. The fate of the character depends upon the potentiality in question, even if it should condemn him to a tragic end. In advance, while still a subjective potentiality in the character's mind, there is no way of distinguishing it from the innumerable abstract potentialities in his mind. It may even be buried away so completely that, before the moment of decision, it has never entered his mind even as an abstract potentiality. The subject, after taking his decision, may be unconscious of his own motives. Thus Richard Dudgeon, Shaw's Devil's Disciple, having sacrificed himself as Pastor Andersen, confesses: 'I have often asked myself for the motive, but I find no good reason to explain why I acted as I did.'

Yet it is a decision which has altered the direction of his life. Of course, this is an extreme case. But the qualitative leap of the denouement, cancelling and at the same time renewing the continuity of individual consciousness, can never be predicted. The concrete potentiality cannot be isolated from the myriad abstract potentialities. Only actual decision reveals the distinction.

The literature of realism, aiming at a truthful reflection of reality, must demonstrate both the concrete and abstract potentialities of human beings in extreme situations of this kind. A character's concrete potentiality once revealed, his abstract potentialities will appear essentially inauthentic. Moravia, for instance, in his novel *The Indifferent Ones*, describes the young son of a decadent bourgeois family, Michel, who makes up his mind to kill his sister's seducer. While Michel, having made his decision, is planning the murder, a large number of abstract – but highly suggestive – possibilities are laid before us. Unfortunately for Michel the murder is actually carried out; and, from the sordid details of the action, Michel's character emerges as what it is – representative of that background from which, in subjective fantasy, he had imagined he could escape.

Abstract potentiality belongs wholly to the realm of subjectivity; whereas concrete potentiality is concerned with the dialectic between the individual's subjectivity and objective reality. The literary presentation of the latter thus implies a description of actual persons inhabiting a palpable, identifiable world. Only in the interaction of character and environment can the concrete potentiality of a particular individual be singled out from the 'bad infinity' of purely abstract potentialities, and emerge as the determining potentiality of just this individual at just this phase of his development. This principle alone enables the artist to distinguish concrete potentiality from a myriad abstractions.

But the ontology on which the image of man in modernist literature is based invalidates this principle. If the 'human condition' – man as a solitary being, incapable of meaningful relationships – is identified with reality itself, the distinction between abstract and concrete potentiality becomes null and void. The categories tend to merge. Thus Cesare Pavese notes with John Dos Passos, and his German contemporary, Alfred Döblin, a sharp oscillation between 'superficial *verisme*' and 'abstract, Expressionist schematism'. Criticizing Dos Passos, Pavese writes that fictional characters 'ought to be created by deliberate selection and description of individual features' – implying that Dos Passos' characterizations are transferable from one individual to another. He describes the artistic consequences: by exalting man's subjectivity, at the expense of the objective reality of his environment, man's subjectivity itself is impoverished.

The problem, once again, is ideological. This is not to say that the ideology underlying modernist writings is identical in all cases. On the contrary: the ideology exists in extremely various, even contradictory forms. The rejection of narrative objectivity, the surrender to subjectivity, may take the form of Joyce's stream of consciousness, or of Musil's 'active passivity', his 'existence without quality', or of Gide's '*action gratuite*', where abstract potentiality achieves pseudo-realization. As individual character manifests itself in life's moments of decision, so too in literature. If the distinction between abstract and concrete potentiality vanishes, if man's inwardness is identified with an abstract subjectivity, human personality must necessarily disintegrate.

T. S. Eliot described this phenomenon, this mode of portraying human personality, as

> Shape without form, shade without colour,
> Paralysed force, gesture without motion.

The disintegration of personality is matched by a disintegration of the outer world. In one sense, this is simply a further consequence of our argument. For the identification of abstract and concrete human potentiality rests on the assumption that the objective world is inherently inexplicable. Certain leading modernist writers, attempting a theoretical apology, have admitted this quite frankly. Often this theoretical impossibility of understanding reality is the point of departure, rather than the exaltation of subjectivity. But in any case the connection between the two is plain. The German poet Gottfried Benn, for instance, informs us that 'there is no outer reality, there is only human consciousness, constantly building, modifying, rebuilding new worlds out of its own creativity'. Musil, as always, gives a moral twist to this line of thought. Ulrich, the hero of his *The Man without Qualities*, when asked what he would do if he were in God's place, replies: 'I should be compelled to abolish reality.'

Subjective existence 'without qualities' is the complement of the negation of outward reality.

The negation of outward reality is not always demanded with such theoretical rigour. But it is present in almost all modernist literature. In conversation, Musil once gave as the period of his great novel, 'between 1912 and 1914'. But he was quick to modify this statement by adding: 'I have not, I must insist, written a historical novel. I am not concerned with actual events. . . . Events, anyhow, are interchangeable. I am interested in what is typical, in what one might call the ghostly aspect of reality.' The word 'ghostly' is interesting. It points to a major tendency in modernist literature: the attenuation of actuality. In Kafka, the descriptive detail is of an extraordinary immediacy and authenticity. But Kafka's artistic ingenuity is really directed towards substituting his *angst*-ridden vision of the world for objective reality. The realistic detail is the expression of a ghostly un-reality, of a nightmare world, whose function is to evoke *angst*. The same phenomenon can be seen in writers who attempt to combine Kafka's techniques with a critique of society – like the German writer, Wolfgang Koeppen, in his satirical novel about Bonn, *Das Treibhaus*. A similar attenuation of reality underlies Joyce's stream of consciousness. It is, of course, intensified where the stream of consciousness is itself the medium through which reality is presented. And it is carried *ad absurdum* where the stream of consciousness is that of an abnormal subject or of an idiot – consider the first part of Faulkner's *Sound and Fury* or, a still more extreme case, Beckett's *Molloy*.

Attenuation of reality and dissolution of personality are thus interdependent: the stronger the one, the stronger the other. Underlying both is the lack of a consistent view of human nature. Man is reduced to a sequence of unrelated experiential fragments; he is as inexplicable to others as to himself. In Eliot's *Cocktail Party* the psychiatrist, who voices the opinions of the author, describes the phenomenon:

> Ah, but we die to each other daily
> What we know of other people
> Is only our memory of the moments
> During which we knew them. And they have changed
>   since then.
> To pretend that they and we are the same
> Is a useful and convenient social convention
> Which must sometimes be broken. We must also remember
> That at every meeting we are meeting a stranger.

The dissolution of personality, originally the unconscious product of the identification of concrete and abstract potentiality, is elevated to a deliberate principle in the light of consciousness. It is no accident that Gottfried Benn called one of his theoretical tracts '*Doppelleben*'. For Benn, this dissolution of personality took the form of a schizophrenic dichotomy. According to him, there was in man's personality no coherent pattern of motivation or behaviour. Man's animal nature is opposed to his denaturized, sublimated thought processes. The unity of thought and action is 'backwoods philosophy'; thought and being are 'quite separate entities'. Man must be either a moral or a thinking being – he cannot be both at once.

These are not, I think, purely private, eccentric speculations. Of course, they are derived from Benn's specific experience. But there is an inner connection between these ideas and a certain tradition of bourgeois thought. It is more than a hundred years since Kierkegaard first attacked the Hegelian view that the inner and outer world form an objective dialectical unity, that they are indissolubly married in spite of their apparent opposition. Kierkegaard denied any such unity. According to Kierkegaard, the individual exists within an opaque, impenetrable 'incognito'.

This philosophy attained remarkable popularity after the Second World War – proof that even the most abstruse theories may reflect social reality. Men like Martin Heidegger, Ernst Jünger, the lawyer Carl Schmitt, Gottfried Benn and others passionately embraced this doctrine of the eternal incognito which implies that a man's external deeds are no guide to his motives. In this case, the deeds obscured behind the mysterious incognito were, needless to say, these intellectuals' participation in Nazism: Heidegger, as Rector of Freiburg University, had glorified Hitler's seizure of power at his Inauguration; Carl Schmitt had put his great legal gifts at Hitler's disposal. The facts were too well-known to be simply denied. But, if this impenetrable incognito were the true '*condition humaine*', might not – concealed within their incognito – Heidegger or Schmitt have been secret opponents of Hitler all the time, only supporting him in the world of appearances? Ernst von Salomon's cynical frankness about his opportunism in *The Questionnaire* (keeping his reservations to himself or declaring them only in the presence of intimate friends) may be read as an ironic commentary on this ideology of the incognito as we find it, say, in the writings of Ernst Jünger.

This digression may serve to show, taking an extreme example, what the social implications of such an ontology may be. In the literary field, this particular ideology was of cardinal importance; by destroying the complex tissue of man's relations with his environment, it furthered the dissolution of personality. For it is just the opposition between a man and his environment that determines the development of his personality. There is no great hero of fiction – from Homer's Achilles to Mann's Adrian Leverkühn or Sholochov's Grigory Melyekov – whose personality is not the product of such an opposition. I have shown how disastrous the denial of the distinction between abstract and concrete potentiality must be for the presentation of character. The destruction of the complex tissue of man's interaction with his environment likewise saps the vitality of this opposition. Certainly, some writers who adhere to this ideology have attempted, not unsuccessfully, to portray this opposition in concrete terms. But the underlying ideology deprives these contradictions of their dynamic, developmental significance. The contradictions coexist, unresolved, contributing to the further dissolution of the personality in question.

It is to the credit of Robert Musil that he was quite conscious of the implications of his method. Of his hero Ulrich he remarked: 'One is faced with a simple choice: either one must run with the pack (when in Rome, do as the Romans do); or one becomes a neurotic.' Musil here introduces the problem, central to all modernist literature, of the significance of psychopathology.

This problem was first widely discussed in the Naturalist period. More than fifty years ago, that doyen of Berlin dramatic critics, Alfred Kerr, was writing: 'Morbidity is the legitimate poetry of Naturalism. For what is poetic in everyday life? Neurotic aberration, escape from life's dreary routine. Only in this way can a character be translated to a rarer clime and yet retain an air of reality.' Interesting, here, is the notion that the poetic necessity of the pathological derives from the prosaic quality of life under capitalism. I would maintain – we shall return to this point – that in modern writing there is a continuity from Naturalism to the Modernism of our day – a continuity restricted, admittedly, to underlying ideological principles. What at first was no more than dim anticipation of approaching catastrophe developed, after 1914, into an all-pervading obsession. And I would suggest that the ever-increasing part played by psychopathology was one of the main features of the continuity. At each period – depending on the prevailing social and historical conditions – psychopathology was given a new emphasis, a different significance and artistic function. Kerr's description suggests that in naturalism the interest in psychopathology sprang from an aesthetic need; it was an attempt to escape from the dreariness of life under capitalism. The quotation from Musil shows that some years later the opposition acquired a moral slant. The obsession with morbidity had ceased to have a merely decorative function, bringing colour into the greyness of reality, and become a moral protest against capitalism.

With Musil – and with many other modernist writers – psychopathology became the goal, the *terminus ad quem*, of their artistic intention. But there is a double difficulty inherent in their intention, which follows from its underlying ideology. There is, first, a lack of definition. The protest expressed by this flight into psychopathology is an abstract gesture; its rejection of reality is wholesale and summary, containing no concrete criticism. It is a gesture, moreover, that is destined to lead nowhere; it is an escape into nothingness. Thus the propagators of this ideology are mistaken in thinking that such a protest could ever be fruitful in literature. In any protest against particular social conditions, these conditions themselves must have the central place. The bourgeois protest against feudal society, the proletarian against bourgeois society, made their point of departure a criticism of the old order. In both cases the protest – reaching out beyond the point of departure – was based on a concrete *terminus ad quem*: the establishment of a new order. However indefinite the structure and content of this new order, the will towards its more exact definition was not lacking.

How different the protest of writers like Musil! The *terminus a quo* (the corrupt society of our time) is inevitably the main source of energy, since the *terminus ad quem* (the escape into psychopathology) is a mere abstraction. The rejection of modern reality is purely subjective. Considered in terms of man's relation with his environment, it lacks both content and direction. And this lack is exaggerated still further by the character of the *terminus ad quem*. For the protest is an empty gesture, expressing nausea, or discomfort, or longing. Its content – or rather lack of content – derives from the fact that such a view of life cannot impart a sense of direction. These writers are not wholly wrong in believing that psychopathology is their surest refuge; it is the ideological complement of their historical position.

This obsession with the pathological is not only to be found in literature. Freudian psychoanalysis is its most obvious expression. The treatment of the subject is only superficially different from that in modern literature. As everybody knows, Freud's starting point was 'everyday life'. In order to explain 'slips' and day-dreams, however, he had to have recourse to psychopathology. In his lectures, speaking of resistance and repression, he says: 'Our interest in the general psychology of symptom-formation increases as we understand to what extent the study of pathological conditions can shed light on the workings of the normal mind.' Freud believed he had found the key to the understanding of the normal personality in the psychology of the abnormal. This belief is still more evident in the typology of Kretschmer, which also assumes that psychological abnormalities can explain normal psychology. It is only when we compare Freud's psychology with that of Pavlov, who takes the Hippocratic view that mental abnormality is a deviation from a norm, that we see it in its true light.

Clearly, this is not strictly a scientific or literary-critical problem. It is an ideological problem, deriving from the ontological dogma of the solitariness of man. The literature of realism, based on the Aristotelean concept of man as *zoon politikon*, is entitled to develop a new typology for each new phase in the evolution of a society. It displays the contradictions within society and within the individual in the context of a dialectical unity. Here, individuals embodying violent and extraordinary passions are still within the range of a socially normal typology (Shakespeare, Balzac, Stendhal). For, in this literature, the average man is simply a dimmer reflection of the contradictions always existing in man and society; eccentricity is a socially conditioned distortion. Obviously, the passions of the great heroes must not be confused with 'eccentricity' in the colloquial sense: Christian Buddenbrook is an 'eccentric'; Adrian Leverkühn is not.

The ontology of *Geworfenheit* makes a true typology impossible; it is replaced by an abstract polarity of the eccentric and the socially average. We have seen why this polarity – which in traditional realism serves to increase our understanding of social normality – leads in modernism to a fascination with morbid eccentricity. Eccentricity becomes the necessary complement of the average; and this polarity is held to exhaust human potentiality. The implications of this ideology are shown in another remark of Musil's: 'If humanity dreamt collectively, it would dream Moosbrugger.' Moosbrugger, you will remember, was a mentally retarded sexual pervert with homicidal tendencies.

What served, with Musil, as the ideological basis of a new typology – escape into neurosis as a protest against the evils of society – becomes with other modernist writers an immutable *condition humaine*. Musil's statement loses its conditional 'if' and becomes a simple description of reality. Lack of objectivity in the description of the outer world finds its complement in the reduction of reality to a nightmare. Beckett's *Molloy* is perhaps the *ne plus ultra* of this development, although Joyce's vision of reality as an incoherent stream of consciousness had already assumed in Faulkner a nightmare quality. In Beckett's novel we have the same vision twice over. He presents us with an image of the utmost human degradation – an idiot's vegetative existence. Then, as help is imminent from a mysterious unspecified source, the rescuer himself sinks into idiocy. The story is told through the parallel streams of consciousness of the idiot and of his rescuer.

Along with the adoption of perversity and idiocy as types of the *condition humaine*, we find what amounts to frank glorification. Take Montherlant's *Pasiphae*, where sexual perversity – the heroine's infatuation with a bull – is presented as a triumphant return to nature, as the liberation of impulse from the slavery of convention. The chorus – i.e. the author – puts the following question (which, though rhetorical, clearly expects an affirmative reply): 'Si l'absence de pensée et l'absence de morale ne contribuent pas beaucoup à la dignité des bêtes, des plantes et des eaux . . . ?' Montherlant expresses as plainly as Musil, though with different moral and emotional emphasis, the hidden – one might say repressed – social character of the protest underlying this obsession with psychopathology, its perverted Rousseauism, its anarchism. There are many illustrations of this in modernist writing. A poem of Benn's will serve to make the point:

> O that we were our primal ancestors,
> Small lumps of plasma in hot, sultry swamps;
> Life, death, conception, parturition
> Emerging from those juices soundlessly.

A frond of seaweed or a dune of sand,
Formed by the wind and heavy at the base;
A dragonfly or gull's wing – already, these
Would signify excessive suffering.

This is not overtly perverse in the manner of Beckett or Montherlant. Yet, in his primitivism, Benn is at one with them. The opposition of man as animal to man as social being (for instance, Heidegger's devaluation of the social as '*das Man*', Klages' assertion of the incompatibility of *Geist* and *Seele*, or Rosenberg's racial mythology) leads straight to a glorification of the abnormal and to an undisguised anti-humanism.

A typology limited in this way to the *homme moyen sensuel* and the idiot also opens the door to 'experimental' stylistic distortion. Distortion becomes as inseparable a part of the portrayal of reality as the recourse to the pathological. But literature must have a concept of the normal if it is to 'place' distortion correctly; that is to say, to see it *as* distortion. With such a typology this placing is impossible, since the normal is no longer a proper object of literary interest. Life under capitalism is, often rightly, presented as a distortion (a petrification or paralysis) of the human substance. But to present psycho-pathology as a way of escape from this distortion is itself a distortion. We are invited to measure one type of distortion against another and arrive, necessarily, at universal distortion. There is no principle to set against the general pattern, no standard by which the petty-bourgeois and the pathological can be seen in their social context. And these tendencies, far from being relativized with time, become ever more absolute. Distortion becomes the normal condition of human existence; the proper study, the formative principle, of art and literature.

I have demonstrated some of the literary implications of this ideology. Let us now pursue the argument further. It is clear, I think, that modernism must deprive literature of a sense of *perspective*. This would not be surprising; rigorous modernists such as Kafka, Benn and Musil have always indignantly refused to provide their readers with any such thing. I will return to the ideological implications of the idea of perspective later. Let me say here that, in any work of art, perspective is of overriding importance. It determines the course and content; it draws together the threads of the narration; it enables the artist to choose between the important and the superficial, the crucial and the episodic. The direction in which characters develop is determined by perspective, only those features being described which are material to their development. The more lucid the perspective – as in Molière or the Greeks – the more economical and striking the selection.

Modernism drops this selective principle. It asserts that it can dispense with it, or can replace it with its dogma of the *condition humaine*. A naturalistic style is bound to be the result. This state of affairs – which to my mind characterizes all modernist art of the past fifty years – is disguised by critics who systematically glorify the modernist movement. By concentrating on formal criteria, by isolating technique from content and exaggerating its importance, these critics refrain from judgement on the social or artistic significance of subject matter. They are unable, in consequence, to make the aesthetic distinction between *realism* and *naturalism*. This distinction depends on the presence or absence in a work of art of a 'hierarchy of significance' in the situations and characters presented. Compared with this, formal categories are of secondary importance. That is why it is possible to speak of the basically *naturalistic* character of modernist literature – and to see here the literary expression of an ideological continuity. This is not to deny that variations in style reflect changes in society. But the particular form this principle of naturalistic arbitrariness, this lack of hierarchic structure, may take is not decisive. We encounter it in the all-determining 'social conditions' of Naturalism, in Symbolism's impressionist methods and its cultivation of the exotic, in the fragmentation of objective reality in Futurism and Constructivism and the German *Neue Sachlichkeit*, or, again, in Surrealism's stream of consciousness.

These schools have in common a basically static approach to reality. This is closely related to their lack of perspective. Characteristically, Gottfried Benn actually incorporated this in his artistic programme. One of his volumes bears the title, *Static Poems*. The denial of history, of development, and thus of perspective, becomes the mark of true insight into the nature of reality.

> The wise man is ignorant
> of change and development
> his children and children's children
> are no part of his world.

The rejection of any concept of the future is for Benn the criterion of wisdom. But even those modernist writers who are less extreme in their rejection of history tend to present social and historical phenomena as static. It is, then, of small importance whether this condition is 'eternal', or only a transitional stage punctuated by sudden catastrophes (even in early Naturalism the static presentation was often broken up by these catastrophes, without altering its basic character). Musil, for instance, writes in his essay, *The Writer in our Age*: 'One knows just as little about the present. Partly, this is because we are, as always, too close to the present. But it is also because the present into which we were plunged some two decades ago is of a particularly all-embracing and inescapable character.' Whether or not Musil knew of Heidegger's philosophy, the idea of *Geworfenheit* is clearly at work here. And the following reveals plainly how, for Musil, this static state was upset by the catastrophe of 1914: 'All of a sudden, the world was full of violence. . . . In

European civilization, there was a sudden rift.' In short: thus static apprehension of reality in modernist literature is no passing fashion; it is rooted in the ideology of modernism.

To establish the basic distinction between modernism and that realism which, from Homer to Thomas Mann and Gorky, has assumed change and development to be the proper subject of literature, we must go deeper into the underlying ideological problem. In *The House of the Dead* Dostoevsky gave an interesting account of the convict's attitude to work. He described how the prisoners, in spite of brutal discipline, loafed about, working badly or merely going through the motions of work until a new overseer arrived and allotted them a new project, after which they were allowed to go home. 'The work was hard,' Dostoevsky continues, 'but, Christ, with what energy they threw themselves into it! Gone was all their former indolence and pretended incompetence.' Later in the book Dostoevsky sums up his experiences: 'If a man loses hope and has no aim in view, sheer boredom can turn him into a beast.' I have said that the problem of perspective in literature is directly related to the principle of selection. Let me go further: underlying the problem is a profound ethical complex, reflected in the composition of the work itself. Every human action is based on a presupposition of its inherent meaningfulness, at least to the subject. Absence of meaning makes a mockery of action and reduces art to naturalistic description.

Clearly, there can be no literature without at least the appearance of change or development. This conclusion should not be interpreted in a narrowly metaphysical sense. We have already diagnosed the obsession with psychopathology in modernist literature as a desire to escape from the reality of capitalism. But this implies the absolute primacy of the *terminus a quo*, the condition from which it is desired to escape. Any movement towards a *terminus ad quem* is condemned to impotence. As the ideology of most modernist writers asserts the unalterability of outward reality (even if this is reduced to a mere state of consciousness) human activity is, a priori, rendered impotent and robbed of meaning.

The apprehension of reality to which this leads is most consistently and convincingly realized in the work of Kafka. Kafka remarks of Josef K., as he is being led to execution: 'He thought of flies, their tiny limbs breaking as they struggle away from the fly-paper.' This mood of total impotence, of paralysis in the face of the unintelligible power of circumstances, informs all his work. Though the action of *The Castle* takes a different, even an opposite, direction to that of *The Trial*, this view of the world, from the perspective of a trapped and struggling fly, is all-pervasive. This experience, this vision of a world dominated by *angst* and of man at the mercy of incomprehensible terrors, makes Kafka's work the very type of modernist art. Techniques, elsewhere of merely formal significance, are used here to evoke a primitive awe in the presence of an utterly strange and hostile reality. Kafka's *angst* is the experience *par excellence* of modernism.

Two instances from musical criticism – which can afford to be both franker and more theoretical than literary criticism – show that it is indeed a universal experience with which we are dealing. The composer, Hanns Eisler, says of Schönberg: 'Long before the invention of the bomber, he expressed what people were to feel in the air raid shelters.' Even more characteristic – though seen from a modernist point of view – is Theodor W. Adorno's analysis (in *The Ageing of Modern Music*) of symptoms of decadence in modernist music: 'The sounds are still the same. But the experience of *angst*, which made their originals great, has vanished.' Modernist music, he continues, has lost touch with the truth that was its *raison d'être*. Composers are no longer equal to the emotional presuppositions of their modernism. And that is why modernist music has failed. The diminution of the original *angst*-obsessed vision of life (whether due, as Adorno thinks, to inability to respond to the magnitude of the horror or, as I believe, to the fact that this obsession with *angst* among bourgeois intellectuals has already begun to recede) has brought about a loss of substance in modern music, and destroyed its authenticity as a modernist art-form.

This is a shrewd analysis of the paradoxical situation of the modernist artist, particularly where he is trying to express deep and genuine experience. The deeper the experience, the greater the damage to the artistic whole. But this tendency towards disintegration, this loss of artistic unity, cannot be written off as a mere fashion, the product of experimental gimmicks. Modern philosophy, after all, encountered these problems long before modern literature, painting or music. A case in point is the problem of *time*. Subjective Idealism had already separated time, abstractly conceived, from historical change and particularity of place. As if this separation were insufficient for the new age of imperialism, Bergson widened it further. Experienced time, subjective time, now became identical with real time; the rift between this time and that of the objective world was complete. Bergson and other philosophers who took up and varied this theme claimed that their concept of time alone afforded insight into authentic, i.e. subjective, reality. The same tendency soon made its appearance in literature.

The German left-wing critic and essayist of the twenties, Walter Benjamin, has well described Proust's vision and the techniques he uses to present it in his great novel: 'We all know that Proust does not describe a man's life as it actually happens, but as it is remembered by a man who has lived through it. Yet this puts it far too crudely. For it is not actual experience that is important, but the texture of reminiscence, the Penelope's tapestry of a man's memory.' The connection with Bergson's theories of time is obvious. But whereas with Bergson, in the abstraction of philosophy, the unity of perception is preserved, Benjamin shows that with Proust, as a result of the radical disintegration of the time sequence, objectivity is eliminated: 'A lived event is finite, concluded at least on the level of experience. But a remembered event is infinite, a possible key to everything that preceded it and to everything that will follow it.'

It is the distinction between a philosophical and an artistic vision of the world. However hard philosophy, under the influence of Idealism, tries to liberate the concepts of space and time from temporal and spatial particularity, literature continues to assume their unity. The fact that, nevertheless, the concept of subjective time cropped up in literature only shows how deeply subjectivism is rooted in the experience of the modern bourgeois intellectual. The individual, retreating into himself in despair at the cruelty of the age, may experience an intoxicated fascination with his forlorn condition. But then a new horror breaks through. If reality cannot be understood (or no effort is made to understand it), then the individual's subjectivity – alone in the universe, reflecting only itself – takes on an equally incomprehensible and horrific character. Hugo von Hofmannsthal was to experience this condition very early in his poetic career:

> It is a thing that no man cares to think on,
> And far too terrible for mere complaint,
> That all things slip from us and pass away,
>
> And that my ego, bound by no outward force –
> Once a small child's before it became mine –
> Should now be strange to me, like a strange dog.

By separating time from the outer world of objective reality, the inner world of the subject is transformed into a sinister, inexplicable flux and acquires – paradoxically, as it may seem – a static character.

On literature this tendency towards disintegration, of course, will have an even greater impact than on philosophy. When time is isolated in this way, the artist's world disintegrates into a multiplicity of partial worlds. The static view of the world, now combined with diminished objectivity, here rules unchallenged. The world of man – the only subject-matter of literature – is shattered if a single component is removed. I have shown the consequences of isolating time and reducing it to a subjective category. But time is by no means the only component whose removal can lead to such disintegration. Here, again, Hofmannsthal anticipated later developments. His imaginary 'Lord Chandos' reflects: 'I have lost the ability to concentrate my thoughts or set them out coherently.' The result is a condition of apathy, punctuated by manic fits. The development towards a definitely pathological protest is here anticipated – admittedly in glamorous, romantic guise. But it is the same disintegration that is at work.

Previous realistic literature, however violent its criticism of reality, had always assumed the unity of the world it described and seen it as a living whole inseparable from man himself. But the major realists of our time deliberately introduce elements of disintegration into their work – for instance, the subjectivizing of time – and use them to portray the contemporary world more exactly. In this way, the once natural unity becomes a conscious, constructed unity (I have shown elsewhere that the device of the two temporal planes in Thomas Mann's *Doctor Faustus* serves to emphasize its historicity). But in modernist literature the disintegration of the world of man – and consequently the disintegration of personality – coincides with the ideological intention. Thus *angst*, this basic modern experience, this by-product of *Geworfenheit*, has its emotional origin in the experience of a disintegrating society. But it attains its effects by evoking the disintegration of the world of man.

To complete our examination of modernist literature, we must consider for a moment the question of allegory. Allegory is that aesthetic genre which lends itself *par excellence* to a description of man's alienation from objective reality. Allegory is a problematic genre because it rejects that assumption of an immanent meaning to human existence which – however unconscious, however combined with religious concepts of transcendence – is the basis of traditional art. Thus in medieval art we observe a new secularity (in spite of the continued use of religious subjects) triumphing more and more, from the time of Giotto, over the allegorizing of an earlier period.

Certain reservations should be made at this point. First, we must distinguish between literature and the visual arts. In the latter, the limitations of allegory can be the more easily overcome in that transcendental, allegorical subjects can be clothed in an aesthetic immanence (even if of a merely decorative kind) and the rift in reality in some sense be eliminated – we have only to think of Byzantine mosaic art. This decorative element has no real equivalent in literature; it exists only in a figurative sense, and then only as a secondary component. Allegorical art of the quality of Byzantine mosaic is only rarely possible in literature. Secondly, we must bear in mind in examining allegory – and this is of great importance for our argument – a historical distinction: does the concept of transcendence in question contain within itself tendencies towards immanence (as in Byzantine art or Giotto), or is it the product precisely of a rejection of these tendencies?

Allegory, in modernist literature, is clearly of the latter kind. Transcendence implies here, more or less consciously, the negation of any meaning immanent in the world or the life of man. We have already examined the underlying ideological basis of this view and its stylistic consequences. To conclude our analysis, and to establish the allegorical character of modernist literature, I must refer again to the work of one of the finest theoreticians of modernism – to Walter Benjamin. Benjamin's examination of allegory was a product of his researches into German Baroque drama. Benjamin made his analysis of these relatively minor plays the occasion for a general discussion of the aesthetics of allegory. He was asking, in effect, why it is that transcendence, which is the essence of allegory, cannot but destroy aesthetics itself.

Benjamin gives a very contemporary definition of allegory. He does not labour the analogies between modern art and the Baroque (such analogies are tenuous at best, and were much overdone by the fashionable criticism of the time). Rather, he uses the Baroque drama to criticize modernism, imputing the characteristics of the latter to the former. In so doing, Benjamin became the first critic to attempt a philosophical analysis of the aesthetic paradox underlying modernist art. He writes:

> In Allegory, the *facies hippocratica* of history looks to the observer like a petrified primeval landscape. History, all the suffering and failure it contains, finds expression in the human face – or, rather, in the human skull. No sense of freedom, no classical proportion, no human emotion lives in its features – not only human existence in general, but the fate of every individual human being is symbolized in this most palpable token of mortality. This is the core of the allegorical vision, of the Baroque idea of history as the passion of the world; History is significant only in the stations of its corruption. Significance is a function of mortality – because it is death that marks the passage from corruptibility to meaningfulness.

Benjamin returns again and again to this link between allegory and the annihilation of history:

> In the light of this vision history appears, not as the gradual realization of the eternal, but as a process of inevitable decay. Allegory thus goes beyond beauty. What ruins are in the physical world, allegories are in the world of the mind.

Benjamin points here to the aesthetic consequences of modernism – though projected into the Baroque drama – more shrewdly and consistently than any of his contemporaries. He sees that the notion of objective time is essential to any understanding of history, and that the notion of subjective time is a product of a period of decline. 'A thorough knowledge of the problematic nature of art' thus becomes for him – correctly, from his point of view – one of the hallmarks of allegory in Baroque drama. It is problematic, on the one hand, because it is an art intent on expressing absolute transcendence that fails to do so because of the means at its disposal. It is also problematic because it is an art reflecting the corruption of the world and bringing about its own dissolution in the process. Benjamin discovers 'an immense, anti-aesthetic subjectivity' in Baroque literature, associated with 'a theologically determined subjectivity'. (We shall presently show – a point I have discussed elsewhere in relation to Heidegger's philosophy – how in literature a 'religious atheism' of this kind can acquire a theological character.) Romantic – and, on a higher plane, Baroque – writers were well aware of this problem, and gave their understanding, not only theoretical, but artistic – that is to say allegorical – expression. 'The image,' Benjamin remarks, 'becomes a rune in the sphere of allegorical intuition. When touched by the light of theology, its symbolic beauty is gone. The false appearance of totality vanishes. The image dies; the parable no longer holds true; the world it once contained disappears.'

The consequences for art are far-reaching, and Benjamin does not hesitate to point them out: 'Every person, every object, every relationship can stand for something else. This transferability constitutes a devastating, though just, judgement on the profane world – which is thereby branded as a world where such things are of small importance.' Benjamin knows, of course, that although details are 'transferable', and thus insignificant, they are not banished from art altogether. On the contrary. Precisely in modern art, with which he is ultimately concerned, descriptive detail is often of an extraordinary sensuous, suggestive power – we think again of Kafka. But this, as we showed in the case of Musil (a writer who does not consciously aim at allegory) does not prevent the materiality of the world from undergoing permanent alteration, from becoming transferable and arbitrary. Just this, modernist writers maintain, is typical of their own apprehension of reality. Yet presented in this way, the world becomes, as Benjamin puts it, 'exalted and depreciated at the same time'. For the conviction that phenomena are *not* ultimately transferable is rooted in a belief in the world's rationality and in man's ability to penetrate its secrets. In realistic literature each descriptive detail is both *individual* and typical. Modern allegory, and modernist ideology, however, deny the *typical*. By destroying the coherence of the world, they reduce detail to the level of mere particularity (once again, the connection between modernism and naturalism is plain). Detail, in its allegorical transferability, though brought into a direct, if paradoxical connection with transcendence, becomes an abstract function of the transcendence to which it points. Modernist literature thus replaces concrete typicality with abstract particularity.

We are here applying Benjamin's paradox directly to aesthetics and criticism, and particularly to the aesthetics of modernism. And, though we have reversed his scale of values, we have not deviated from the course of his argument. Elsewhere, he speaks out even more plainly – as though the Baroque mask had fallen, revealing the modernist skull underneath:

> Allegory is left empty-handed. The forces of evil, lurking in its depths, owe their very existence to allegory. Evil is, precisely, the non-existence of that which allegory purports to represent.

The paradox Benjamin arrives at – his investigation of the aesthetics of Baroque tragedy has culminated in a negation of aesthetics – sheds a good deal of light on modernist literature, and particularly on Kafka. In interpreting his writings allegorically I am not, of course, following Max Brod, who finds a specifically religious allegory in Kafka's works. Kafka refuted any such interpretation in a remark he is said to have made to Brod himself: 'We are nihilistic figments, all of us; suicidal notions forming in God's mind.' Kafka rejected, too, the gnostic concept of God as an evil demiurge: 'The world is a cruel whim of God, an evil day's work.' When Brod attempted to give this an optimistic slant, Kafka shrugged off the attempt ironically: 'Oh, hope enough, hope without end – but not, alas, for us.' These remarks, quoted by Benjamin in his brilliant essay on Kafka, point to the general spiritual climate of his work: 'His profoundest experience is of the hopelessness, the utter meaninglessness of man's world, and particularly that of present-day bourgeois man.' Kafka, whether he says so openly or not, is an atheist. An atheist, though, of that modern species who regard God's removal from the scene not as a liberation – as did Epicurus and the Encyclopaedists – but as a token of the 'God-forsakenness' of the world, its utter desolation and futility. Jacobsen's *Niels Lyhne* was the first novel to describe this state of mind of the atheistic bourgeois intelligentsia. Modern religious atheism is characterized, on the one hand, by the fact that unbelief has lost its revolutionary *élan* – the empty heavens are the projection of a world beyond hope of redemption. On the other hand, religious atheism shows that the desire for salvation lives on with undiminished force in a world without God, worshipping the void created by God's absence.

The supreme judges in *The Trial*, the castle administration in *The Castle*, represent transcendence in Kafka's allegories: the transcendence of Nothingness. Everything points to them, and they could give meaning to everything. Everybody believes in their existence and omnipotence; but nobody knows them, nobody knows how they can be reached. If there is a God here, it can only be the God of religious atheism: *atheos absconditus*. We become acquainted with a repellent host of subordinate authorities; brutal, corrupt, pedantic – and, at the same time, unreliable and irresponsible. It is a portrait of the bourgeois society Kafka knew, with a dash of Prague local colouring. But it is also allegorical in that the doings of this bureaucracy and of those dependent on it, its impotent victims, are not concrete and realistic, but a reflection of that Nothingness which governs existence. The hidden, non-existent God of Kafka's world derives his spectral character from the fact that his own non-existence is the ground of all existence; and the portrayed reality, uncannily accurate as it is, is spectral in the shadow of that dependence. The only purpose of transcendence – the intangible *nichtendes Nichts* – is to reveal the *facies hippocratica* of the world.

That abstract particularity which we saw to be the aesthetic consequence of allegory reaches its high mark in Kafka. He is a marvellous observer; the spectral character of reality affects him so deeply that the simplest episodes have an oppressive, nightmarish immediacy. As an artist, he is not content to evoke the surface of life. He is aware that individual detail must point to general significance. But how does he go about the business of abstraction? He has emptied everyday life of meaning by using the allegorical method; he has allowed detail to be annihilated by his transcendental Nothingness. This allegorical transcendence bars Kafka's way to realism, prevents him from investing observed detail with typical significance. Kafka is not able, in spite of his extraordinary evocative power, in spite of his unique sensibility, to achieve that fusion of the particular and the general which is the essence of realistic art. His aim is to raise the individual detail in its immediate particularity (without generalizing its content) to the level of abstraction. Kafka's method is typical, here, of modernism's allegorical approach. Specific subject-matter and stylistic variation do not matter; what matters is the basic ideological determination of form and content. The particularity we find in Beckett and Joyce, in Musil and Benn, various as the treatment of it may be, is essentially of the same kind.

If we combine what we have up to now discussed separately we arrive at a consistent pattern. We see that modernism leads not only to the destruction of traditional literary forms; it leads to the destruction of literature as such. And this is true not only of Joyce, or of the literature of Expressionism and Surrealism. It was not André Gide's ambition, for instance, to bring about a revolution in literary style; it was his philosophy that compelled him to abandon conventional forms. He planned his *Faux-Monnayeurs* as a novel. But its structure suffered from a characteristically modernist schizophrenia: it was supposed to be written by the man who was also the hero of the novel. And, in practice, Gide was forced to admit that no novel, no work of literature could be constructed in that way. We have here a practical demonstration that – as Benjamin showed in another context – modernism means not the enrichment, but the negation of art.

12 Galvano Della Volpe
The Semantic Dialectic (1960)*

Galvano Della Volpe (1895–1968) joined the Italian Communist Party in 1944 and became its major Marxist philosopher. Within the distinct traditions of Italian Marxism, Della Volpe developed a materialist theory of scientific dialectic, notably in *Logic as a Positive Science* (1969; trans. 1980), which was anti-Hegelian in its emphasis on 'tauto-heterological identity'. His principal contribution to literary theory is his exposition of historical-materialist aesthetics in *Critique of Taste* (1960; trans. 1978). Taking issue with Plekhanov, Gramsci and Lukás, Della Volpe defended a socialist conception of realism. Arguing that materialist aesthetics had neglected the semantic or linguistic dimensions of poetry and art, he used Louis Hjelmslev's theory of glossematics to ground an aesthetic semiotics and an account of the realism of poetry. 'The Semantic Dialectic', from the section of *Critique of Taste* entitled 'Laocoon 1960', presents a summary of his argument. Describing the dialectic between the semantic values of univocal scientific language, polysemic poetry and ordinary language, he criticizes mystifications of the polysemic rationality of poetry. Accordingly, the maligned but material possibility of poetry in translation or paraphrase is especially revealing. Out of this analysis emerges an unusual critique of idealism and formalism in poetry criticism. His work has influenced critics such as Franco Moretti, notably in *Signs Taken For Wonders* (1983), to develop Marixst semiotics, but Della Volpe has not had much resonance outside Italian Marxism. Nevertheless, like Vološinov, he suggests a range of important but unsolved problems in materialist aesthetics of language. Della Volpe's other works include *Rousseau and Marx* (1964; trans. 1978). For discussion see D. Forgacs, 'The Aesthetics of Galvano Della Volpe', *New Left Review*, 117; and J. Fraser, *Introduction to the Thought of Galvano Della Volpe* (1977). Related translations of Italian Marxism include: S. Timpanaro, *On Materialism* (1975) and L. Colletti, *From Rousseau to Lenin* (1972) and *Marxism and Hegel* (1973).

We shall bring our discussion of poetry and literature to a close. Our analyses up to this point give us sufficient grounds for defining poetry as *polysemic characteristic typicality*. Science in general, or prose, can be defined as *univocal*

---

* From Galvano Della Volpe, *Critique of Taste*, trans. M. Caesar (London: NLB, 1978), 173–201.

characteristic typicality. Like that of poetry, we call the typicality of science *characteristic* because it too is unity-of-a-manifold or reason-and-sense. For, as we have seen above, and as the semantic need for a thing-sublanguage demonstrates, the very 'abstractness' of the physical sciences cannot be separated from a fundamental sense of the *qualities* of the world and from repeated contact with them.

We shall see in due course that this definition of poetry will *not* do as a blanket definition of all the other arts or art in general. But it does in the meantime provide us with an implicit definition of the poetic or literary symbol, whether it be literal or metaphorical in sense. The poetic symbol is a polysemic concrete concept, as opposed to the scientific symbol in general which is a univocal concrete concept. It is worth reiterating that it is an illusion, or to be more exact an epistemological error, to speak of 'universality' or 'truth' as belonging 'par excellence' to the scientific symbol. For our postulate of identity between thought and speech or signs in general means that the universality and omni-laterality – hence truth – proper to the scientific and philosophical symbol depends on, and is indissociable from, indeed we may say it is synonymous with, its omni-contextuality and univocality – in other words its ineliminable semantic aspect. Therefore, the poetic symbol cannot be considered any less uni-versal or omni-lateral, or any less true, simply because its semantic aspect is not omni-contextuality, but organic contextuality. We have seen in fact that the poetic symbol is no less unity-of-a-manifold, or thought, than is the scientific symbol. Thus universality or omni-laterality, and hence truth, are as much proper to the poetic symbol as they are to the scientific symbol.

Therewith we find further confirmation of the concept of literary or poetic *abstraction*, as synonymous with poetic symbol, along with that of scientific abstraction, as synonymous with scientific symbol. Both these abstractions are *determinate*, for both are characteristic typicality or, which comes to the same thing, concrete concept or discourse. We have seen that the discursive nature of the determinate abstraction, whether literary or scientific, is so real and concrete as to be actually dialectical. For it represents a semantic-formal transcendence of the literal-material in two directions: in that of the polysemic (literary abstraction or poetic symbol), and in that of the univocal (scientific symbolic abstraction).

On this point, it is perhaps worth underlining once again the semantic-dialectical *switch* that occurs between the equivocal, omni-textual thought of the literal-material and the polysemic or univocal. That switch represents the enunciation of values in the form of speech (signs), which are a very different matter from our traditional and simplistic, 'pure' values or thoughts or metaphysical 'forms', absolute and absolutist. Such forms are incapable of any 'transmutation' into each other: they remain locked into hermetic compartments of experience, as the 'spiritual forms' of fantasy or logic have shown us.

But speech-values – actual thoughts – circulate within each other naturally, because they have the same literal-material base. At the same time, however, their *specific differences* from one another are secured by virtue of their different semantic models: the polysemic and the univocal. These semantic models are indissociable from their corresponding values or thoughts exactly as means are from their ends, in the dialectic of ends and means which the identity between thought and speech or thought and sign has revealed itself as being.

It is not only in order to clarify the role of speech, or the sign in general, in both poetic (artistic) and scientific thought that we make this point. We are also interested, if we may put it this way, in a radical *emendatio* of idealist habits of mind. The idealists believe that they will be more firmly based in reality if they adhere to ends or values or forms that are 'pure' of all means or instrumentality or technique – in other words, if they adhere to hypostases, which are epistemologically without consistency and defective by definition. So we must try to accustom ourselves to the *epistemological import of the sign in general*. This is the only way we shall be able to explain rigorously, that is scientifically, the mobility and variety of reality-thought at the same time as its unity. Only thus can we distinguish a poetic metaphor from a historical fact or a physical or philosophical principle *without losing hold of what unites them*: reality-thought, the uni-versal.

For it is, as we know, undeniable that if metaphors as poetic genera or concepts are 'unreal', it is not in relation to reality or truth in general or *tout court*, but only in relation to scientific genera or concepts. Metaphors only become illegitimate if they are substituted for scientific concepts, with the result that two different orders of truth and reality are confused. The truth of the metaphor-concept 'adolescence the flower of our years' cannot take the place of the truth of a physiological or pedagogic concept of the age of maturation, and vice versa.

This being the case, it seems to us equally undeniable that the differential features of these two types of genera, the semantic organicity and necessity of the poetic genus, and the semantically disorganic scientific genus that is exempt from all semantic necessitation and fixity, enable us not to confuse the poetically credible with the historically or scientifically credible. While the former is defined and contained within the polysemic or 'stylistic' (not 'subjective'!) rigour which constitutes its semantic autonomy and its truth, the truth of the latter attains expression and definition only in the univocal rigour of its genera or concepts. What in fact constitutes the historically or scientifically credible is the semantic disorganicity and heteronomy of its concepts, those features which alone permit us a constant and repeated testing of them against the objectivity of the facts. But not only do they enable us to make this distinction. Since these differential features are not metaphysical, but semantic-epistemological, they also enable us to hold on to the *common nature* of the two kinds of genera or credibility: the fact that they are both reason or thought, that is, unity-of-a-manifold.

We have seen that semantic disorganicity and heteronomy, with its *open contexts*, is that kind of expressive articulation suited to the mind's vocation to experiment and documentation: those activities which characterize the appropriation of the reality and truth of things by science. The semantic-expressive component of thought which is suited to the appropriation of the reality and truth of things by poetry and art is the organic-contextual, with its autonomous or *closed* contexts. Now our analyses have already made plain that this semantic character must of itself expose the falsehood of the traditional, Aristotelian and idealist, preconception of the mere 'ideality' of poetic truth, as opposed to the 'factuality' of historical or scientific truth. For precisely the semantic dimension that is an indispensable component of poetic thought, lending it a real and scientifically verifiable character, renders poetic truth resistant to all metaphysical distinctions within thought itself – whether we call them hypostatic or abstract or absolutistic. Thought is always unity–multiplicity. At the same time the semantic character of poetic thought also effectively conceals it, directly or indirectly through its literal-material contents to what is called experience of the real or historicity in general. That connection of course is assured by a technique that differs from those of experiment and philosophical (-historical) argument – one that is semantically different as well. But our claim is borne out if we recollect that even the so-called 'free flights of fancy' of Pindar, Petrarch, Ariosto and Cervantes are artistic (have poetic value) in so far as they are credible because of the truth they express, and in so far as they are credible because they are *verifiable* by human experience, perhaps only indirectly or through contrast, but still verifiable. We must remember, in short, that the 'unreality' or 'ideality' of Pindar's hind (and Petrarch's) or Ariosto's hippogryph is not 'unreality' or 'ideality' in absolute terms. Each of these creatures has a well-defined and coherent sense, each of them is constituted by a rationale in the same way as any being in the real world. It is sufficient for this purpose that, however 'fantastic' they may be, they should not be Horace's human-head-on-a-horse's-neck. If they are 'unreal' or 'ideal', it is rather in the comparative sense in which metaphors and poetic symbols are 'unreal' general only in relation to scientific genera and *their* reality and truth, not in relation to reality and truth in general.

The whole import of the semantic-epistemological or scientific sense of the autonomy of poetry should by now have been clarified. This autonomy is to be understood as technical (semantic, precisely). It is not to be taken as a metaphysical autonomy, or as the autonomy of a hypostasis, the hypostasis of Art. There are two variants of the latter: the Aristotelian abstract rationalist hypostasis of the 'ideal' or the 'universal' (as opposed to a hypostasis of the 'factual' or the 'particular' that supposedly characterizes history); and the

Platonic, romantic and idealist hypostasis of the particular as 'enthusiasm' or 'raptus' or 'disinterested' feeling or 'intuition' or 'fantasy' (as opposed to a hypostasis of the universal or of 'logical form' that allegedly characterizes history and philosophy). Our exclusion applies to both.

Eduard Norden has rightly observed of Mommsen's *History of Rome* that, however great its intrinsic merits, as a work of science it 'passes over' (*vergehet*) into countless other histories: the truth of 'the knowledge that is gained therein', both in its 'development' and indeed in its very origins, does not come from the 'separate existence' or autonomy (*Sonder-existenz*) of the work. A poem, on the other hand, or a work of art, does not pass over into others in this sense; it 'lasts' on its own.[1] But Norden shares with romantic and idealist aesthetics the mistaken belief that the autonomy of poetry is the result of some mythicized 'individual *creative* force', some *subjective* or imaginative power. It is not. Rather its origin is the peculiar organic semantic structure of poetry, to which the aseity or semantic autonomy of the poem corresponds. The historical or scientific work, on the other hand, is semantically disorganic and hetero-nomous, and this both explains and confirms the need for it to pass over, forwards and backwards, into countless others. For it is in this way that its own scientific truth comes into being and takes shape. But Norden, not realizing this, is forced into self-contradiction, because at the same time as making his distinction he cannot help but acknowledge that there is a 'living creative force' with all its attributes (fantasy, etc.) not only in the poet, but also in the historian or scientist, in this case Mommsen. So that he nullifies the criterion of distinction between art and history which he had started by accepting.

Kant and the romantics made a fundamental error, which we are now in a position to see. We do not thereby mean to ignore their not inconsiderable merit in posing the problem of what was meant positively, anti-Platonically, by the autonomy of art. Nevertheless they committed the error, which has persisted in all their various successors and epigones down to the decadent aestheticists of our own day, of mistaking the *semantic immediacy* of poetic speech for a *synonymous immediacy of intuition* or *pure image*. That is, they took the immediacy which is to be attributed to the semantic un-relatedness and autonomy of poetic speech, in other words its *style qua* special technical epistemological condition of poetry and art in general, for an absolutized or abstract, generic aspect of poetry and art. This view rests on a hypostatic distinction between Art (as 'form', intuition, and so on) and non-Art. In short, they confused two things: on the one hand, a *specific* feature of art, which can be traced and identified critically and scientifically, namely the semantic organicity and autonomy of poetic and artistic thought or discourse; and on the other, a dogmatic, metaphysical notion of the abstract epistemological autonomy of a *generic* element (intuition or image) of that same poetic discourse or thought, which in fact *shares* with scientific discourse both intuition and concept.

The error of Kant, the romantics and the idealists arose then from the very proper modern need to give a positive explanation of the immediacy, or un-relatedness, of poetic or artistic values and hence their autonomy. But they could not meet the need to explain this immediacy, which is perceived ambiguously by ordinary aesthetic consciousness pre-eminently if not exclusively in emotional effects, except by drawing on the modern metaphysics of transcendental subjectivity (heir to neo-Platonic aesthetic motifs) and entrusting to the general epistemological category of feeling, that is immediacy or particularity, the task of finding a solution which it could not possibly provide. Since in fact what was being sought was the solution to the problem of *expressive* immediacy, the answer itself could only be found in a special, technical, epistemological examination of the semantic problematic of cognitive expression – in other words of actual concrete thought. A correct explanation of the epistemological phenomenon of expressive immediacy, as opposed to the myths of metaphysics, shows us that it is not at all the same thing as *cognitive immediacy*. The latter is a contradiction in terms, as Socrates and Plato, not to mention the Kant of the first *Critique*, have taught us.

Of course, there is a world of difference between demonstrating what we have just said and actually getting it into the vulgar aesthetic skull, still reverberating, more or less unconsciously, with the echoes of the romantic and mystical aspirations of modern metaphysical aesthetics. The facts that we owe the *truth* of certain unforgettable London fogs in Dickens (to take an example from narrative 'prose') solely to what Dickens *said*, that his statement is *sufficient to itself* (what statement uttered by a geographer or historian, a scientist in short, is sufficient to itself or true for itself?), that any critical account *explicates* Dickens' statement but does not *verify* it, because the statement contains its own verification in itself, since its verification comes from the *contextual dialectic* of a semantically *organic* discourse which brings the truth of that statement into being – these facts, and countless others of the same kind, are probably condemned to long obscurity yet at the hands of the myth-makers of the mysterious powers of 'pure intuition'.

We need to make two further points in order to clarify finally our concept of the poetic symbol. First, if metaphor (and its two extremes, hyperbole and simile), whether living or dead, is a cognitive value in general, whether poetic or ordinary, and if the sense of the poetic symbol or polysemic characteristic-typical concept can be either literal or metaphorical, it follows that the poetic symbol or concept is specified and delimited by its polysemic semantic aspect or character, and thus by its semantic autonomy. Secondly, therefore, poetic symbols in the fullest sense are those meanings, whether literal or metaphorical, whose semantic autonomy endows them with sufficient force – either directly or in combination with others – to develop and structure entire expressive worlds (literary works). The pattern of poetic symbols or semantically autonomous structural concepts in a text can be perceived at first glance, sometimes just from the title, as in those classic examples: *The Divine Comedy*, *The Waste Land*, *Les Parents Pauvres* (literal poetic symbol!), *Madame Bovary* (ditto), *Great Expectations* (ditto),[2] *War and Peace* (ditto), *Babbitt* (ditto), *Ghosts*, *Ulysses* (and it goes without saying that even a fragment of Sappho can be an expressive world, albeit in miniature).

But the notion of the literary or poetic work brings us back to another problem: that of its ascription to a superstructure and hence its relations to an infrastructure or socio-economic base. We have in fact been working towards a solution to this problem, perhaps unnoticed by the reader, in our conception of the dialectic of history and poetry as a semantic-formal dialectic and, connected to this, in the methodological theory of critical paraphrase. Both of these we have tried to substantiate in our analyses of literary works, while demonstrating, though not always explicitly, the inadequacy of the responses of present-day bourgeois taste, impressionistic and mysticizing, to the questions raised by them. Thus we have shown that the poetry, for example, of Sophocles' *Antigone* would be inconceivable and impossible without the language of the ethical and religious mythology of the caste-society of the poet's time and, implicitly, its associated primitive-economic organization; we have seen how unthinkable would be the poetry of the *Comedy* without the theological, tropological, language of Catholic culture in the Middle Ages and, by implication, an economic organization that was still partly feudal, partly communal; or that of *Faust* without the language of pantheism and idealism typical of bourgeois humanism in the age of Goethe, and the burgeoning free-enterprise economy associated with it; or that of *Lenin* without the language of the Marxist ideology of the October Revolution and the Soviet society, along with its socialist economy, to which the Revolution gave birth – and so on.

It is in fact becoming reasonably clear that a complex and materialist semantic dialectic, which supersedes the gratuitous metaphors of 'mirroring' and 'reflection', can provide us with an explanation or rational understanding of the way in which the substance of history passes over into poetry – how history actually conditions it in its specific nature as poetry. For that process occurs precisely through the medium of the literal-material and its associated omni-textuality, which is the infrastructural moment of the dialectic described above. By this I mean that it is through the medium of language-as-letter – a particular complex of instrumental forms and their respective thought-ends – that the whole ideological and cultural substance of a society comes to form the historical humus of the poetic work. The poem born from that humus will be inscribed in a superstructure and in the socio-economic infrastructure associated with it. Yet the poem comes into being by *developing* the thought-ends of the instrumental form (the 'form' of the letter) through which alone a historical humus is effective, and by *modifying* the instrument itself. Thus the literal-material is transcended, semantically-formally, into the polysemic or poetic value. *Mutatis mutandis*, the same dialectic – in the form of transcendence of the literal-material into the univocal – constitutes science, and inscribes it in a given superstructure.

All of this, incidentally, also confirms the fact that language – as a means which cannot by definition be dissociated from its thought-end – belongs in a general and a permanent way to the superstructure, rather than to any particular or privileged moment of the superstructure, Stalinist linguistics was in this respect at once right and wrong in its verdict on language.[3]

These questions were touched on at the beginning of our inquiry. When analysing *Antigone*, we sought to elucidate the poetic-structural complexes of the play and thereby to demonstrate why the literary character of Antigone and other similar characters could not have coexisted with Roberts and Co. The reasons for that fact are now clearer. Each of these poetic organisms refers back – in the name of its structural values or poetic meanings – to conditions which are not only historical, social, and by implication economic, but which are also *congruent* and *coherent* with the content-values of the work. In other words, they refer back to those particular circumstances, and not others; the conditions of ancient Greece, not those of the Middle Ages or our own times.

Marx wrote that Greek art presupposes 'not any mythology whatever, i.e. not an arbitrarily chosen unconsciously artistic reworking of nature, (here meaning everything objective, hence including society)', but Greek mythology – 'Egyptian mythology could never have been the foundation or the womb of Greek art', but 'in any case' there was needed '*a* mythology'. In the same way, Greek art pre-supposed a particular economy (primitive, pastoral, etc.) and not any other. Thus the undeveloped 'stage of society' [and economy] in which that art grew 'is not in contradiction' with the 'charm' which, as the art of a people from 'historic childhood', it holds over us. Rather, that charm 'is its *result* . . . and is inextricably bound up with the fact that the unripe social [and economic] conditions under which it arose, and could alone arise, can never return'.[4]

This is Marx's reply, by the way, to the commonly held, though abstract and superficial, view that 'in the case of the arts, it is well known that certain periods of their flowering are out of all proportion to the general development of society, hence also to the material foundation'. Careless bourgeois critics such as Wellek and Warren have attributed this view to Marx himself and assumed it to be significant in the sense that 'this passage appears to give up the Marxist position altogether'.[5] In fact, of course, Marx goes on immediately to say that 'the difficulty consists only in the general [i.e. historical-philosophical] formulation of these contradictions. As soon as they have been specified, they are already clarified' (*ibid.*).

Engels' position, already mentioned, is again relevant at this point. We refer to his perception that the 'median axis' of the cultural-historical curve of a given ideological or superstructural sphere (e.g. that of art) is all the more 'nearly parallel' to the axis of the historical curve of economic and material development 'the longer the [historical] period considered and the wider the [ideological] field dealt with'. He had already observed elsewhere that once discussion moves from the State and public and private law to ideological forms such as 'philosophy and religion' or art, the 'interconnection' [*Zusammenhang*] between ideas and their material conditions 'becomes more and more complicated, more and more obscured by intermediate links', but it nevertheless 'exists'.[6] It is in short characteristic of ideologies and cultures worthy of the name that their *universalism* should embrace *long periods*. During such periods, on the other hand, the corresponding kinds of economic forms can so to speak develop along their own lines, although in evident parallelism with the cultural or superstructural factors. (It is to suggest this parallelism and the problematic associated with it that we have used such expressions as 'implicit' or 'by implication' to characterize the nature of the relation between the ideology of poetic or literary ideas and the 'existent' economic conditions corresponding to them.)

In other words, only if we acknowledge the *intellectual* nature of poetry (concrete though it is), can we demonstrate its power to 'reflect' a society and hence its ideology. It is a flagrant contradiction to emphasize this power and still believe in art, as many self-styled Marxist philosophers persist in doing, as intuitive knowledge or knowledge 'through images', in abstract antithesis to science, understood as knowledge 'through concepts'.

The conception of poetry we have advanced in these pages leads to a way of appreciating the poem and understanding it historically whose philosophical and epistemological rationale has been shown in the critical paraphrase – as a true dialectical articulation of taste and decisive element in the practice of literary history. To clarify further this methodological criterion of the *dialectical paraphrase* of the poetic text, and to define more precisely the historical-materialist solution which we offer to the problem of literary criticism, we shall begin by comparing some of the traditional and more recent methods of literary history. Starting with positivism, we shall go on to examine idealism, present-day Marxism and neo-stylistics.

We shall take one example of the positivist method: Taine's comment on a famous line by Racine:

> Dans le fond des forêts votre image me suit
> (In the depth of the forests your image follows me),

of which he says: 'When Hippolyte speaks of the forests in which he lives, read the *grandes allées* of Versailles'.[7] Taine's overriding concern with the historical content of a poetic text is very obvious here, and on this occasion his interpretation is particularly external and gratuitous. Inevitably, his reading of the line misses the polysemic or poetic value of Racine's 'fond', which, as more attentive critics have noticed, expresses a two-fold depth, both physical and moral. The curious thing is, of course, that if one reads the *Phèdre* from within the text, that is, working through its organic-contextual or concrete stylistic values, its links with Racine's Christian-modern epoch are plentiful and obvious, as we have already had occasion to point out. (Our criticism is not intended to deny Taine's very considerable personal taste, which afforded him, in contradiction to his own method, some interesting insights on 'style' in his essay on *Stendhal*, and also on *Balzac*, riddled though these are with preconceptions of a moralistic and conventional character.)

We shall subdivide the idealist method into (a) the classical-idealist or Hegelian method, and (b) the romantic-idealist method. The limitations of the former lie in its interpretation of the poetic text in terms of its *philosophical content*, in homage to the principle of 'beautiful' form as the 'appearance' of the 'Idea'. The result is a concentration on eliciting the ethos of the text from its style that pays no attention to the style itself. In other words, the classical-idealist method is not concerned with the development of the form and content of the literal into the formality of the poetic or polysemic. An example is Hegel's philosophical reading of *Antigone*, cited above. The great merit of Hegel's approach, on the other hand, was that by distinguishing between classical and modern poetry it drew attention to the historical nature of poetry and art in general. For Croce, with his a-historical 'universality' of 'pure intuition', this was a defect.

The romantic-idealist method has been applied in various ways by Friedrich Schlegel, De Sanctis, Croce, and on to the epigones of post-romantic and decadent taste in general. Schlegel's method was to interpret a text philosophically, though with contradictory reliance on an idea of art as 'ironic fantasy', and hence 'beautiful *confusion*' – an *indistinct* unity of opposites. Thus he had a low estimation of French classical tragedy because 'it is empty formalism, without strength, charm or substance', as opposed to Shakespearean tragedy which is 'philosophical'.[8]

In De Sanctis, the method veers brilliantly between two opposite poles. On the one hand, he tended to devote particular attention to content, approaching it from an historicist and Hegelian point of view. This gives us such Desanctisian notions as the preconceived 'ideal', which is allegedly 'realized' by the work of art and yet always remains 'a beyond which is never attained'; and the idea of 'situation', which it has been noted is broader than the notion of 'figure-form', and aesthetically justifies abstract subject-matter by exalting 'stupendous situations'. On the other hand, De Sanctis tends towards a sensuous formalism, an idea of 'plasticity' based on the concept of art as 'fantasy' or 'vision' or 'figure'. Hence, for example, his pronouncement that the ethical 'concept' of Dante's *Inferno* was 'poetically superfluous, serving only to classify'. Further comment is unnecessary.[9]

In Croce's critical work, the method leads to a formalistic impressionism and aestheticism. The *Comedy* for example is reduced to a mosaic of 'lyrical' atoms. Every structural or conceptual element is regarded as 'extraneous' or extra-aesthetic. To judge poetry, furthermore, is simply 'to call attention to what is admirable at this or that point, admirable because it is admirable, not because it is clever syntax or a smart piece of style'.[10] Croce's 'monographic' approach to the history of art is a coherent methodological result of the criterion of form as 'pure cosmic *intuition*', which in turn is a distant echo of Kant's 'disinterested feeling', Schiller's idea of art as 'play', and Schlegel's notion of the 'freedom' (freedom from all 'interest') of creative 'ironic fantasy'.

Let us turn now to present-day Marxism, starting with the merits of its method. Firstly, it has replaced Hegel's philosophical interpretation of the work of art with a procedure that allows for more concrete interpretation. In the words of Plekhanov: 'As an adherent of the materialist conception of the world, I say that the first task of the critic is to translate the ideas of a work of art from the language of art into the language of sociology, to establish what might be called the sociological equivalent of a given literary phenomenon';[11] or in those of Lukács: artistic concentration 'is the maximum intensification in content of the *social* and human essence of a given situation'.[12] Secondly, it has brought about the modern rediscovery of the aesthetic problem of content and its importance in the internal economy of the work of art, as against the formalism of 'art for art's sake'. Plekhanov declared: 'the predominance of form over content produces works that are vacant and ugly; beauty lies in harmony of form and content'. Lukács writes: 'It is pointless to criticize a bad writer simply on the grounds of his formal defects. The contrast between an, empty and superficial representation and the actual reality of human and social life . . . will make it clear that formal defects are merely the consequence of a fundamental lack of content. The appeal to life is itself enough to expose the emptiness of insignificant artistic reproduction'. Thirdly, both Plekhanov and Lukács have from time to time applied these criteria successfully, when they have been deployed with circumspection. A case in point is Plekhanov's commentary on the novels of Balzac and their value for our knowledge of French society under the Restoration and Louis Philippe. Another example is Plekhanov on *Madame Bovary*. Lukács's essays on European and Russian realism, especially on Balzac, Stendhal, Zola and Tolstoy, should also be noted.[13]

But current Marxist method is also defective in certain respects. Its limitations are particularly obvious, firstly, where what Plekhanov calls the critic's 'second task', the 'necessary completion' of the first, is concerned: that is, 'the appreciation of the aesthetic values of the work under consideration'. The method runs into trouble here because the criterion of its appreciation or evaluation is whether the work of art contains, not so much an 'ideal content' or ideas in general, which would be acceptable ('art cannot live without ideas': Plekhanov), but, equally and even more importantly, an ideal content which is 'not false' – in other words, one which is progressive and not reactionary.

Plekhanov states: 'Not every idea can be expressed in a work of art' and 'false ideas harm a work of art', while for Lukács 'any false conception of the world "whatever" is unsuitable as the basis of realism.' Yet at the same time what do we find propping up this ponderous devotion to content but the old aesthetic epistemology of Kant and the romantics? Thus, according to Plekhanov, someone who proclaims ideas 'prefers to speak the *language of logic*', while the artist 'prefers to speak the *language of images*'. But to his credit Plekhanov then gets caught in a tangle of problems of some significance – a potentially productive one once freed of his premises. He remarks, *à propos* of Ibsen's 'sermons', that 'If an author thinks in images and figures, that is if he is an artist, the nebulousness of his preaching will inevitably render his artistic images indeterminate.' We might compare our own observations on the organic relation, assured by the dialectic of heterogeneities, between intellectual clarity or coherence of meaning and vividness of image. For Lukács, however, there is not the shadow of a doubt. 'Art makes us intuit sensibly' the 'dynamic unity' of the universal, particular and individual (the categories of Hegelian logic ever with us!), while science resolves this unity 'into its abstract elements and seeks to conceptualize the interaction of these elements'.

When these criteria are applied to actual literary history, and their inadequacies are not mitigated by the personal sensitivity of the critic (the usual rule, to which the previous cases are an exception), the limitations of the method become all the clearer. One example is Plekhanov's essentially mistaken interpretation of the poetry of Ibsen in *Ghosts*, *The Doll's House*, *The Pillars of the Community*, etc. Ibsen the artist is actually reproached for his (clear) bourgeois moral ideas – 'purity of will', ethical 'individualism' – and for his fundamental 'weakness' in not finding 'any way out of morals into politics' (meaning socially militant politics). *On this basis*, Plekhanov dismisses his dramatic moral speeches as incoherent and nebulous rhetoric and criticizes his poetic symbols for their 'abstractness', that is 'a witness to his poverty of *social* thought'. The only merit he can divine in Ibsen is as a satirist of the petty-bourgeoisie. Lukács is in this instance more felicitous, linking Ibsen to the 'preacher' Tolstoy, and remarking that 'Ibsen too . . . precisely through his didactic pathos excelled his contemporaries even from the purely artistic point of view'.[14]

On the other hand, we may note the failure of Lukács to understand *Madame Bovary*, a novel which he accuses of descriptivism for its own sake, in short, formalism. The faults of Lukács's fixation with content are exemplified when he complains that Flaubert tried to remedy the 'immobility', the 'empty and dispirited greyness' of his mediocre heroes 'by purely artistic and technical means' (*sic*). This attempt was 'bound to fail' because 'the mediocrity of the average man derives from the fact that the *social antinomies* which objectively determine his existence do not attain their highest degree of tension in him; on the contrary, they are obfuscated and attain a superficial equilibrium'. Flaubert is here condemned for giving artistic life to a social content which is not, for example, that of Zola and does not happen to square with the social ideas of his sociologist critic. But Lukács forgets how much he still owes Flaubert. What he owes him is all the poetic *truth* possessed by that 'mediocre pair', as Flaubert called them, in whom precisely everything, including first and foremost their consciousness of social antimonies, is shown to be *superficial*. Other misinterpretations by Lukács include his studies on Hölderlin, who is seen purely in his progressive or Enlightenment dimension to the exclusion, no less, of the romantic dimension into which it flowed and where it assumed its distinctive power and shape; or on Goethe, where much is lost of the figure of Mephistopheles, and too much is made of the 'small-holding' of Philemon and Baucis that is destined to be absorbed by Faust's large-scale industrial property; likewise his writings on Kleist.

The heroic Gramsci is one exception to this tradition of Marxist literary history. The critical jottings that he left and his notes on method are unfortunately brief, and he was never able to give them a firm foundation or work them systematically into an aesthetic epistemology. Even so, two themes come through strongly: the need to avoid stressing either content or form at the expense of the other, and the need to work towards a criticism that would be functional as well as materialist. It is enough to recall such observations on method as the following:

> Once the principle has been established that all we are looking for in the work of art is its artistic character, this in no way prevents us from inquiring into what mass of feelings, *what attitude towards life*, circulates within the work itself . . . What is not admissible is that a work should be beautiful because of its moral and political content to the exclusion of the form with which the abstract content has fused and become one.

> 'Content' and 'form' have an 'historical' as well as an 'aesthetic' meaning. 'Historical' form signifies a given *language*, as 'content' indicates a given *way of thinking* which is not only historical, but 'sober', expressive . . .

> Only by abstraction . . . can normative grammar be regarded as separate from living language.

(There is a residue of idealism in this too generous concession to Croce: 'The formal principle of the distinction of categories of the spirit and their unity of circulation does allow us, in spite of its abstractness, to grasp effectual reality.')

It is enough also to recall Gramsci's *structural* analysis of Dante's poetry in the Cavalcante episode (*Inferno* X, ll. 52–114). We quote his conclusions: 'The most important word in the line perhaps whom your Guido held in disdain (l. 63)

is not "whom" [Virgil] or "disdain" but simply the past definite "held" (*ebbe*)'. For 'the "aesthetic" and "dramatic" emphasis of the line falls on this word "held", which is the origin of the drama of Cavalcante, as interpreted in the "stage-directions" of Farinata: "catharsis" then follows' for 'the structural passage [the *concept* of the damned's foreseeing of the future and their ignorance of the present,] *is then not only structure, it is also poetry, a necessary element* in the *drama* which *has taken place*' (our emphases).

Let us finally turn to the neo-stylistic method. Its undoubted merits include the following. First, it is based on modern, scientific, Saussurean linguistics, rather than the linguistics of Humboldt and the romantics. In this it is different from and in opposition to the work of critics like Croce and Vossler. Spitzer is quite clear about the gulf between them when he observes that Vossler gives more consideration 'to "individual language" than "common language", *energeia* rather than *ergon*' in the belief that 'if he steeps himself in the soul of the great moulder of language, the poet, he will be in the presence of the creative act of language'. Secondly, it is well aware of the consequences of these linguistic premisses as they immediately affect aesthetic method and literary history. Thus, 'only after considerable refinement of the relevant disciplines' have we reached the point of 'regarding language as also *expression* and art as also *communication*' (Spitzer); and 'the greater the objective certainty at which a stylistic explanation may aim, the more we shall have overcome the *impressionism* which up to a short time ago seemed the only alternative to a positivistic study of literature' (Spitzer); and finally, 'even when we reach what in the abstract seems to be the same conclusion, it possesses a completely different degree of certainty if it has been arrived at on the basis of experimental stylistic evidence [i.e. "a non-formalist stylistic survey"] rather than by psychologistic procedures' (Contini). Thirdly, neo-stylistics has attempted, with Auerbach in particular, to point to the 'literary conquest of modern reality' in the texts themselves, preferably by analysing their semantic contents or meanings along with the relevant syntactic and stylistic modules. In this way, there has been a deepening of the stylistic approach, which has been brought closer and made more functional to the historical and social body and substance of the work of art.[15]

Against these merits of neo-stylistics are to be set its limitations, and these may be summed up in its unilateral tendency to force our perception of the literary fact into the Procrustean modules of linguistics and stylistics. In doing so, it affords us insights into poetic values which, unlike those of aestheticism and impressionism, are neither gratuitous nor unproductive. Even so, they remain at some distance from those values. They are not, in short, entirely in function of their respective texts. To give just a few examples: Spitzer's efforts to collate generic linguistic features and poetic 'spiritual' etymons (e.g. the verb 'voir' and Racinian tragedy, or 'complex disjunctions' and the reflective poetry of Proust); or some of Contini's writings on Dante, where the conclusions he reaches in the field of the history of Italian are more concerned with Dante's language than his poetry (e.g. his comments on the speech of Maestro Adamo). Contini tries to justify these conclusions with the 'cardinal theorem' that 'the [poetic] invention is not only functional, it is also possessed of an intense *linguistic* historicity'. Here one can clearly see a dangerous tendency to institute a distinction between form and content and to give abstract emphasis to the linguistic historicity of the poetic invention (or the historicity of its technical 'form') at the expense of the overall historicity of form and content together, from which, as we know, its poetic functionality is inseparable. The danger for both Spitzer and Contini is that of falling, even if in different ways, into historicist or philological formalism.

Auerbach, finally, oscillates between two poles. On the one hand, there is his tendency to misuse stylistic or rhetorical criteria, such as the mixture of high and low styles which he draws on to explain Christian and modern realism. Because these criteria have a fixed technical nature, they always risk being relatively external to *determinate* polysemic contents. On the other hand, he tends not to distinguish between poetic contents and historical or even purely diaristic contents in characterizing what he regards as a literary conquest of reality. So he falls out of the frying-pan of stylistic or rhetorical formalism into the fire of an historicist and moralistic criticism of content (the latter sanctioned by such transcendental and heterogeneous categories as 'existential realism' and the 'progress' of history).

Now, taking these observations as our starting point, we shall try to specify why it is that literary analysis based on the dialectical, and therefore critical, paraphrase of poetic texts is in a position to avoid both formalism and fixation on content. (We are still taking both these negative concepts in their traditional sense but see below.) To begin with the latter. We can see what 'content' criticism in general is, and thereby supersede it, if we bear the following points in mind. Firstly, once we can perceive the true nature of the so-called philosophical or sociological or historical equivalent of the poetic text, namely that it is a paraphrase (though an uncritical one) of the poetic thought or so-called 'content' in question, and thereby a reduction of it – a putting 'into simple language', one should say – to the thought or 'content' of the letter, or literal-material, or omni-textual (the common source of both science and poetry); then a comparison will necessarily be instituted between this paraphrase and the poetic thought or 'content' which it paraphrases. Why? Because a comparison of this sort is dictated, unavoidably, by a *quid* which separates, or at any rate distinguishes, the poetic thought from its paraphrase; the awareness of this distinguishing *quid* is precisely the beginning of taste, without it there is no literary criticism worthy of the name.

All the same – and this is the second point – the comparison thus instituted *is not immediate*. It is mediated, indeed is dialectical, in the precise sense that the distinguishing *quid* reveals itself to be a gap or switch – between poetic thought and paraphrase-equivalent – of a kind such that the poetic thought *both does not and yet does coincide* with itself in paraphrased form, or with itself, let us say, transferred *back* to the letter: in the same way as any thought which develops and potentiates another – as is the case here – does not and yet does coincide with the letter. The *way* in which a thought or 'content' develops lies, to be sure, in its 'form', but we should be more precise. For what in actual fact makes up 'form' is the same semantic, linguistic means as the means of thought (end) in general, whether the thought is in the act of developing another or is itself developable. Thus the 'form' of thought or 'content' in the act of developing another, in our case the 'form' of poetic thought, likewise *does not and yet does coincide* with the means or instrumental form of the 'content' to be developed, in other words with the form of the letter (language-as-letter or literal-material). It does not coincide in that, as the form of poetic thought, it is style-language – hence semantic organicity. It does coincide in that in the other form it exists in a paraphrase which presupposes the use of the same phonetic-grammatical constituents and exponents, and the same vocabulary, that is the *same* basic instrumental form or form of the letter. Thus the philosophical or sociological '*equivalent*' of the poetic thought is shown, in the light of this dialectic of language-means and thought-end which structures the relation of every form and every content, to be an *uncritical paraphrase*, in other words the *degradation* of a thought belonging to style-language to the omni-textual. Such an 'equivalent' is a *hybrid thought*, neither poetic nor scientific, neither polysemic nor univocal.

The cardinal epistemological theorem of the indissociability of means (language) and end (thought) is thereby decisively confirmed. The theorem, and the aesthetic corollary which follows from it, now read as follows:

(1) Since the semantic component of thought in general, in this instance the instrumental form of the letter, is an indissociable and therefore dialectical means of its end-thought, it is a component of the form, or aspiration to unity or value, which makes thought thought.

(2) It follows, for a semantic-epistemological or special reason as well as for a general one, that the aesthetic meaning traditionally given by Kantian romanticism and the idealists to the terms 'form' (i.e. disinterested feeling, pure image) and 'content' (i.e. ends, concepts) must be revised. For form is shown to be style-thought, while content is shown to be images, i.e. *matter*. Notice, however, that the literal-material coincides with matter only as regards the *imaginative, perceptual* aspects of its meanings, or virtual concrete concepts; while its phonetic-grammatical constituents and exponents, or instrumental form, come under the heading of the *form* or *unity* of its meanings.

It will not perhaps be superfluous to point out that we have so far been using the negative term 'content' provisionally, in the traditional sense of 'ideas': we shall therefore place it, like its opposite 'form', between inverted commas. Similarly, for the convenience of our analysis, we have spoken, again provisionally, of fixation on 'content' or 'ideas', in the post-romantic and idealist sense – meaning the abstract and mistaken attachment of 'ideas' or concepts to poetic 'form' without these 'contents' being properly 'immersed' in the form. This does not mean of course that we cannot go on using the notion of fixation on content as a negative term in criticism, but simply that its meaning will have to be revised in accordance with the revised sense of the related terms content and form. So it will now come to mean a *deficiency* of *ideas*, or *form*, in the work in question, an excessive amount, without measure or form, of fantasy-matter, and therefore a semantic tendency towards the equivocal and the banal. By the same token, *formalism* should be understood as meaning a *deficiency* of *fantasy*, or the prevalence of ideas or *conceptualism*, and therefore a semantic tendency towards the univocal.

It hardly needs adding at this stage that the critical method of dialectical paraphrase deals a decisive blow to formalism as well, whether taken in its traditional or its non-traditional sense. We shall touch briefly on the thoroughly traditional aesthetic-formalist method (which, being aestheticist, is fixated on 'content' in our sense) and then on the historicist-formalist method (which is formalist in our sense). Because of its inborn aesthetic mysticism and its indifference towards *la langue*, aesthetic formalism has never grasped the dialectical and therefore critical significance of paraphrase. On the contrary, it sees paraphrase merely as something pejorative, an abasement of the 'lyrical' or poetic to the level of prose, in one word a 'heresy'. So that while it sets out to exalt poetry, it actually lowers it to the level of the – gratuitous – play of fantasy or what-have-you. Croce's term is 'pure intuition', while Cleanth Brooks and other American New Critics talk about 'paradox' and 'irony', thereby meandering – for all their 'structural' analyses – in the now somewhat muddled tracks of Schlegel the theorizer of romantic 'ironic fantasy'.[16]

The historicist-formalist approach is taken by a considerable number of the neo-stylisticians. Although the starting-point of the method is modern, in that it acknowledges *la langue* as a positive aesthetic factor, it ultimately unbalances the relationship between language and poetry, by its abstract emphasis on the historicity of poetic language, its 'institutions' and sources, at the expense of the overall unitary historicity – and concreteness – of the *formed content* of poetry, of the polysemic.

On the other hand, there are two points certainly worth underlining in connection with the semantic dialectic which institutes literary criticism as paraphrase. In the first place, we should note the latitude of a paraphrase which has the literal-material or omni-textual as the base and reservoir of its dialectic – that is, the same technico-historical basis on which poetry or the polysemic is originally built. Secondly and most importantly, we should register the epistemological and real import not only of this basis, but also and more particularly of what critical paraphrase aims to elucidate, namely speech-as-style or the organic-contextual. For to that is entrusted, or better, in that consists, the *value* of the semantic switch – i.e. the development of thought from language-as-letter to language-as-style – in its dual differential relationship: what we might call the internal relation between poetic or polysemic thought and its rethinking in critical-paraphrastic terms; and the external relation between poetic thought and scientific, univocal thought.

Thus, for example, Pindar's styleme 'invidious misfortunes' is real, as an expressive fact, in two respects. Transcending its paraphrase 'hubris', etc., it is constituted as a peculiarly expressive polysemic meaning. But since its transcendence of the literal 'hubris' recalled by the paraphrase is dialectical, it remains – in and through its transcendence – within the uni-verse of communication (*langue*) which confers effective *validity* or universality on the peculiarly expressive meaning which it is. Finally it is related – through the *common* dialectical base of the literal 'hubris' – to all other possible peculiarly expressive meanings of the same letter, for instance, the scientific historical, or univocal, meaning of 'hubris', at the same time as it is differentiated from them. That is to say, one meaning delimits and is delimited by the other by virtue of the respective peculiarities of the ways in which the letter in question is dialectically transcended.

In other words, given the postulate of identity between thought and language (*sèma*) and our demonstration and specification of it in the sense of a dialectical identity of end and means, we are bound to acknowledge both the epistemological importance and the real significance of language-speech. The same acknowledgment cannot then be long delayed for those modes of the linguistic (semantic) dialectic which, as we believe we have shown in the case of the polysemic and the univocal, can be ascertained experimentally. Otherwise, the only alternative left – once we have excluded *a fortiori* any kind of positivism – seems to be that of metaphysics, with all the theoretical vitiation and methodological, practical impotence of its spiritual 'forms': 'artistic' form, 'logical' form, etc. Such is the meaning of the radical difference between a semantic dialectic – which, because it is semantic and has its basis in language-as-letter, is historical – and a dialectic of the Idea (specifically, a *beautiful*, sensuous, 'appearance' of the Idea) as in Hegel, or any other dialectic of Spirit or Being.

An obvious corollary of the historicity which is a feature of that dialectic, and of the associated rational character of the dialectically produced poetic symbol, is that poetic truth too is in its innermost being sociological truth. It is therefore always *realistic*. Or, which amounts to the same thing, it is always *verisimilitude*, whether direct or indirect, by analogy or through contrast. Verisimilitude is none other than the truth of ideas tested *by organic–semantic means* against the body of laws and probabilities – or *rationality* – which is the reality of experience and history. The criterion of verisimilitude has always been used, and always will be used, more or less consciously, by every literary critic. Thus, it is destined to survive the romantic revolution too. It is a criterion, whose inevitability is the simplest and surest proof of the rationality and historicity of poetry.

Two consequences follow from this: the feasibility of an aesthetic of literary realism, and hence – in virtue of the philosophical criterion – the validity of a poetic of socialist realism. For only when it has been demonstrated that there is *no* poetry *without ideas in general* will it be conceded that the dominant ideas of our time, those of socialism, also have the right to make poetry. It is a right for which we have the duty to struggle, and one way of doing so is by formulating a rigorous, normative concept of decadent poetry as distinct from contemporary democratic or revolutionary poetry. Our criterion, in other words, is one which enables us not to mistake the degree of artistic excellence in a poem of our times, in other words the semantic organicity of its ideas, while still identifying the degree of *contemporary historical import* or social reflection attained by it. Thus, as we have seen, Eliot's poetry tells us a good deal more, precisely as poetry, than does that of Valéry or Rilke. Which means, among other things, that we can no longer judge poetic value simply on the basis of one, abstract, aspect of form: the superficially semantic aspect of style, understood in a rhetorical sense. It must be judged on the basis of the validity of the *form*, as defined above, as it really functions in the poem: that is, according to the *complexity* or otherwise of the *ideas* which acquire *semantic organicity* and, by implication, the resultant *clarity* or otherwise of their imaginative *content*.

We would hope that it would thus be possible to do justice to all poetry, yet at the same time establish scales of values – though not, we hope, extrinsic ones. Let us take the example of the *decadent* poetry of T. S. Eliot. Eliot, though he is inspired by the Christian ideas of Dante, does not reproduce them, but rather rethinks them in a modern way, reflecting in their light the crisis of our times. (The mystical ideas of Rilke are a somewhat different case, for they are considerably less rich in historical resonance and therefore much less poetic; put another way, they give rise to a more schematic and therefore less complex and significant poetry.) Eliot *does not reproduce* traditional semantic modules either: and thus he achieves semantic organicity and originality in the expression of his ideas. Naturally, for a socialist in our times Eliot is not Mayakovsky. Yet the fact remains, if we may limit ourselves to this one point, that he helps us to understand the greatest communist poet through contrast with him (and is everything not contrast and dialectic in poetry too, if poetry is thought?), much better than do other poets who do not have the rich and profound coherence of that anguished reactionary. He makes us understand much better the *historical* necessity of the ideas which are the form of Mayakovsky's poetry: for example, the idea of socialist optimism – ideas which are forces in themselves, ideas-of-action, to a much greater extent than Eliot's own poetic ideas. For Eliot's ideas echo, even if they do not literally reproduce, other ideas whose historical springtide, so to speak, lies far back in time, and therefore, though they are poetic, they are also decadent.

All these are problems of a poetic of socialist realism based (the only way we can see that it could be based) on the philosophical foundation of an aesthetic of realism *tout court*.

It should now be clear, finally, that a semantic dialectic – inasmuch as it is a necessarily historical dialectic – cannot be the speculative dialectic of an idealistic a priori unity of opposites. Rather, it will be a real dialectic (=tauto-heterological identity), or dialectic of determinate abstractions, both polysemic and univocal: in short a systematic circle of heterogeneities, reason and matter. In this it follows the formula of a materialist, non-Kantian, critique of the a priori, which infers the positivity and indispensability of matter as co-element of thought for knowledge (and action) in general, not from an inexistent void but from the sterile and vicious plenitude of all a priori reasoning which does not take account of matter as extra-rational.

We can now, if we are not mistaken, proceed to a clarification of the *method* of our philosophical theory of literature, or the demonstrative analysis conducted up to this point. That method is one of epistemological *analysis* of the literary phenomenon in its specific components: characteristic typical abstraction, and then the semantically organic aspect of that abstraction, speech-as-style. At the same time, it is a method of *synthesis*, for it re-connects these elements in the category of *end-thought* and *means-sèma*, in other words in the concept of thought as unity of a manifold (or matter) and in this case language-speech as the indissociable, dialectical means of thought as end. But it should be noted that the method is also one of *experimental* analysis. Thus every theoretical or hypothetical statement concerning the specific elements of the literary phenomenon in general has been closely linked to a great variety of literary *exempla* or particular poetic instances, in which it has taken concrete form and by which it was verified. It is therefore also a method of *historical* synthesis.

The choice of such a method is dictated by the very nature of the theoretical theses or hypotheses which were our starting-point. For these acquire their sense first and foremost in and for the contemporary, post-romantic problematic of aesthetics in which the researcher is necessarily involved and committed. He is therefore bound to form a retrospective critical judgement – or more exactly, an historical-dialectical and therefore critical-synthetic judgement – of the philosophy and aesthetics that have preceded him. For he must test previous contributions by way of method to see how far they *are or are not at one* with the solutions advanced hypothetically to the questions that exercise contemporary aesthetics. The variety and complexity of the tools to be used in the demonstrative inquiry that will then ensue, ranging from those of epistemology and linguistics to those of literary exegesis or social history, further dictates the scientific-dialectical method of an historical-materialist theory of poetry and art in general.

Those who cannot stop fretting about a 'first and last principle' or absolute will obviously find no relief either in the experimental criterion of poetry as semantically organic concrete ideas or in the concept therein implied of a semantic dialectic. To start with the latter, it is quite natural that those who still accept the Hegelian concept of the dialectic of opposites – as a *circular* movement of negation and conservation of an original, meta-historical unity of opposites or Idea – will be unable to acquiesce in a dialectic of expressive facts (for example 'hubris' and 'invidious misfortunes') which is a real unity of the diverse because it is the unity of an actual manifold – the discrete. Thus to say that neither of the elements of the relation can be reduced absolutely to the other, and furthermore that neither absolutely excludes the other, is not the usual dialectician's game with words, for in effect they do circulate only *relatively* within each other, in the *diversified unity of an historical movement* – historical movement being the only non-mythical movement with which we are acquainted. That movement, it should be noted, is not circular, but rather one of both progression and regression from one element to the other. Therein lies the real, not invented, normative value of this historical-dialectical relation. To identify it we cannot use pure deduction nor an a priori or absolutizing synthetic procedure proper to metaphysics. We must instead use a scientific procedure, combining both analysis and synthesis – in other words, we must proceed by both *deduction and induction.*

Our imaginary metaphysician will also no doubt have got the impression that an experimental criterion of poetry gives him little more than the bare fact that the *Divine Comedy* and *Ulysses* exist, and he will probably charge us with constantly begging the question. No one who aspires to a purely deductive demonstration (deduction from an absolute 'universal' principle) will accept that a deductive-inductive circular procedure such as that we have tried to adopt here demonstrates anything. In particular, the metaphysician will demand a more 'profound', that is a more 'universal', aesthetic criterion. If it is not a Crocean eternal 'guise' or 'form' of the Spirit, it may well be along the lines of Hegel and Lukács, the 'sensible intuition' of the 'movement [of universal, particular and individual] in its living unity' and so forth.

But then we shall have to invite him once again to show what answers, if any, these 'universal' categories provide to the not inconsiderable number of real and particular problems that are raised again and again by works that are called poetic: poetic both for what they are in themselves and in relation to others that are called not poetic, and again in relation to others which are deemed equally artistic but not poetic. Since these categories explain everything in general and nothing in particular, he will have to think again, and consider with perhaps a little less impatience criteria such as those that we have here tried to put forward. For they are criteria of a scientific, general-historical or historical-dialectical, truth – a truth more sure, if less reassuring, than the metaphysical, eternal-dialectical truths of 'speculation', be it old or new.

NOTES

1 Eduard Norden, 'Geleitwort' to Theodor Mommsen, *Römische Geschichte* (Vienna-Leipzig, 1932), 13.
2 *Great Expectations* (1860–1) is a further example of literal poetic symbol (of Victorian bourgeois society). Harry Stone rightly comments: 'Pip's errors of vision, a result of his and society's upsidedown morality, are at the core of the fable'; *The Kenyon Review*, 24/4 (1962), 662–91.
3 Stalin, in his work on linguistics, was wrong to assert that 'language differs radically from the superstructure'. Not only was he wrong, but he contradicted himself, since he had already previously borrowed the principle from Marx that thought cannot exist in separation from language, to use it against Marx. This principle (discovered by Herder and Humboldt) implies that language too is to be located in the superstructure of a society at the same time as thought, given that the superstructure 'comprehends', as Stalin said, 'the political, juridical, religious, philosophical and artistic *ideas* of a society and their corresponding political, legal, etc. institutions'. Of course Stalin had no difficulty in showing against Marx that 'the Russian language has remained fundamentally the same as it was before the October Revolution', and in refuting the idea that it was ever the privileged product of 'a single class' of society, even a revolutionary class. See J. V. Stalin, *Marxism and Linguistics* (Moscow, 1951).
4 Marx, *Grundrisse* (Harmondsworth, 1973), 110–11
5 René Wellek and Austin Warren, *Theory of Literature* (London, 1963), 107 n.
6 Engels, 'Ludwig Feuerbach and the End of German Classical Philosophy', in *Marx–Engels Selected Works* (Moscow, 1968), 617.
7 Hippolyte Taine, *Nouveaux essais de critique et d'histoire* (Paris: Hachette, 1866), 227.
8 For his notion of poetry-as-irony (1797–8), see Friedrich Schlegel, *Kritische Schriften*, hrsgg. von Wolfdietrich Rasch (Munich, 1938), 10, 11, 60, 88, 93.
9 De Sanctis: as well as his *Storia della Letteratura Italiana* and *Saggi*, see for example the *Lezioni e Saggi su Dante* and *Scritti Critici*, a cura di Gianfranco Contini (Turin, 1949) (we have borne in mind Contini's introduction to this volume).
10 Croce, *La Critica e la Storia delle Arti Figurative* (Bari, 1946), 28.
11 See G. V. Plekhanov, *Kunst und Literatur* (Berlin, 1955).
12 Lukács, *Writer and Critic*, trans. A. Kahn (London, 1978).

13 Interest in Zola (as well as in Balzac and Stendhal as social novelists) has been reawakened by Erich Auerbach's magnificent book *Mimesis*. Auerbach has re-established the truth about Zola as a writer and as a stylist – and 'stylist' is the right word. That truth had been glimpsed by De Sanctis (see *Saggi Critici* (Bari, 1953) but then lost from sight by Croce in *Poesia e Non Poesia* (Bari, 1964) and even by Lukács (in his centenary essay in *Studies in European Realism*). Auerbach shows not only that Zola represents an enormous advance on the work of writers like the Goncourt brothers, but above all that Zola 'is one of the very few authors of the century who created their work out of the great problems of the age' (p. 512). In this respect, 'only Balzac can be compared with him', but 'Balzac wrote at a time when much of what Zola saw had not yet developed or was not yet discernible' (ibid.). That is to say, he does not simply give us a picture of social and political corruption under the Second Empire, as De Sanctis and Croce thought, neither is he simply 'the "historian of private life" under the Second Empire in France in the same way as Balzac was the historian of private life under the restoration and July monarchy' (Lukács). Zola's writing is always dry, fast, pitiless, material (sometimes, it is true, weighed down by emphasis, but not much more so than Balzac's): a modern poetic writing. It is the writing of one of the masters of Realism, in spite of the narrowness of his positivistic-scientist poetic, or, if you will, against his own theory. The fact is that in his artistic practice, his best works, while there are indeed *things* there is also *judgement*, and the two are inseparably fused in a critique at once of things and of society.

It is no good, finally, Lukács telling us that 'although his life-work is very extensive', Zola 'has never created a single character who grew to be a type, a by-word, almost a living being, such as for instance the Bovary couple . . . in Flaubert'. The criterion of artistic-proverbial universality, or the proverbially universal, is, to say the least, too trivial and empirical (in the bad sense). What are we to make, for example, of the 'unproverbiality' of Madame la présidente Tourvel, the character who is perhaps the most alive, and certainly the most moving and human, in Laclos's *Liaisons Dangereuses*, as against the Vicomte de Valmont who is certainly not artistically superior (in part because of the great precedent of Richardson's Lovelace) but is definitely proverbial? Anyway, isn't Tom Fool proverbial too?

14 Take, for example, the human and social richness of the discussion between consul Bernick and young Johan Tönnesen, just back from America, about Marta, the poor relation in the family in *The Pillars of the Community* (Act II). Is it a 'sermon', and a 'nebulous' one at that? Or is it not rather – beyond any doubt – one of the profoundest denunciations in poetic and dramatic form of bourgeois hypocrisy in family relations? The relation between poetry and moral and social reality, history, is immediate and organic in Ibsen, as can be seen in the subtle, and aesthetically functional, distinction-opposition between women's subjugation and humiliation in the family in liberal Europe and the freedom, even then, of their condition in democratic America – and the play was written in 1877!

15 See Leo Spitzer, *Critica Stilistica e Storia del Linguaggio* (Bari, 1954) and *Marcel Proust* (Turin, 1959); Contini, 'La stilistica di G. Devoto', *Lingua Nostra* 11 (1950); 'Introducione', De Sanctis, *Scritti Critici* (Turin, 1949).

16 Cleanth Brooks, 'The Language of Paradox', in *Critique and Essays in Criticism*, ed. R. Stallmann (New York: Ronald, 1949), 66 ff. 'The union which the creative imagination itself effects . . . is not logical' (p. 76); 'We must be prepared to accept the paradox of the imagination itself' (p. 78). Strangely enough, the example chosen as typical is Shakespeare's *The Phoenix and the Turtle*, a poem inspired by the neo-Platonic and mystical *concept* of love:

> Reason in it selfe confounded,
> Saw Division grow together,
> To themselves yet either neither,
> Simple were so well compounded.
>
> :
>
> Love hath Reason, Reason none,
> If what parts, can so remaine. . . .

Brooks in effect operates an aestheticist *hypostasis* of the characteristic paradox of metaphor or hyperbole (resemblance between things as 'far apart' as possible, in Aristotle's words, i.e. as dissimilar as possible). The result is an artificial and erroneous reduction of poetry to *metaphor* as romantically understood, that is to say as synonymous with every kind of 'fantastic' unity-of-opposites. The latter of course includes *Witz* or *Humor* or *Ironie* after the manner of Schlegel, as discussed above. Thus the noble metaphysical scheme of Friedrich Schlegel's aesthetic is annulled, or rendered merely latent, while its methodological criteria are still mobilized.

13 T. W. Adorno
Commitment (1962)*

A leading figure in what became known as the Frankfurt School, the work of T. W. Adorno (1903–69) embodies an attempt to think beyond conventional divisions of intellectual labour which finds its most symptomatic form in *Minima Moralia* (1951; trans. 1974). His principal philosophical works are: *Dialectic of Enlightenment*, written with Max Horkheimer (1944; trans. 1972); *Negative Dialectics* (1966; trans. 1973); and *Aesthetic Theory* (1970; trans. 1984). Better known for his writings on music, such as *Philosophy of Modern Music* (1948; trans. 1973), than as a literary critic, his work develops a conception of writing which is influenced by music, particularly Schonberg, Berg and Webern. This is reflected in the construction and titles of Adorno's writings, as in *Notes to Literature* (1974; trans. 1991–2), which collects most of his essays on literature. The opening essay of *Notes to Literature* argues for a conception of the essay evident in the argumentative form of 'Commitment' and influenced by the early Lukács and Walter Benjamin. Often caricatured as a defender of art against mass culture, Adorno's conception of the culture industry saw this split as an irreconcilable antagonism within the commodity fetishism of capitalism. Accordingly, he was critical of both avant-garde art and the products of the culture industry, while attempting to create a critical space for the social promise of cognitive and aesthetic negativity. 'Commitment' rethinks the tradition of committed literature through the work of Sartre and Brecht, to draw out the shape of contradictions in the politics of literature. On Adorno's work see G. Rose, *The Melancholy Science* (1978); F. Jameson, *Late Marxism* (1990); L. Zuidervaart, *Adorno's Aesthetic Theory* (1991); and S. Jarvis, *Adorno* (1995). For context see M. Jay, *The Dialectical Imagination* (1973) and R. Wiggershaus, *The Frankfurt School* (1994).

Since Sartre's essay *What is Literature?* there has been less theoretical debate about committed and autonomous literature. Nevertheless, the controversy over commitment remains urgent, so far as anything that merely concerns the life of the mind can be today, as opposed to sheer human survival. Sartre was

---

* 'Commitment', trans. Francis McDonagh, from Ernst Bloch and others, *Aesthetics and Politics* (London: NLB, 1977), 177–95.

moved to issue his manifesto because he saw – and he was certainly not the first to do so – works of art displayed side by side in a pantheon of optional edification, decaying into cultural commodities. In such coexistence, they desecrate each other. If a work, without its author necessarily intending it, aims at a supreme effect, it cannot really tolerate a neighbour beside it. This salutary intolerance holds not only for individual works, but also for aesthetic genres or attitudes such as those once symbolized in the now half-forgotten controversy over commitment.

There are two 'positions on objectivity' which are constantly at war with one another, even when intellectual life falsely presents them as at peace. A work of art that is committed strips the magic from a work of art that is content to be a fetish, an idle pastime for those who would like to sleep through the deluge that threatens them, in an apoliticism that is in fact deeply political. For the committed, such works are a distraction from the battle of real interests, in which no one is any longer exempt from the conflict between the two great blocs. The possibility of intellectual life itself depends on this conflict to such an extent that only blind illusion can insist on rights that may be shattered tomorrow. For autonomous works of art, however, such considerations, and the conception of art which underlies them, are themselves the spiritual catastrophe of which the committed keep warning. Once the life of the mind renounces the duty and liberty of its own pure objectification, it has abdicated. Thereafter, works of art merely assimilate themselves to the brute existence against which they protest, in forms so ephemeral (the very charge made against autonomous works by committed writers) that from their first day they belong to the seminars in which they inevitably end. The menacing thrust of the antithesis is a reminder of how precarious the position of art is today. Each of the two alternatives negates itself with the other. Committed art, necessarily detached as art from reality, cancels the distance between the two. 'Art for art's sake' denies by its absolute claims that ineradicable connection with reality which is the polemical a priori of the attempt to make art autonomous from the real. Between these two poles the tension in which art has lived in every age till now is dissolved.

Contemporary literature itself suggests doubts as to the omnipotence of these alternatives. For it is not yet so completely subjugated to the course of the world as to constitute rival fronts. The Sartrean goats and the Valéryan sheep will not be separated. Even if politically motivated, commitment in itself remains politically polyvalent so long as it is not reduced to propaganda, whose pliancy mocks any commitment by the subject. On the other hand, its opposite, known in Russian catechisms as formalism, is not decried only by Soviet officials or libertarian existentialists; even 'vanguard' critics themselves frequently accuse so-called abstract texts of a lack of provocation and social aggressivity. Conversely, Sartre cannot praise Picasso's *Guernica* too highly; yet he could hardly be convicted of formalist sympathies in music or painting.

He restricts his notion of commitment to literature because of its conceptual character: 'The writer deals with meanings.'[1] Of course, but not only with them. If no word which enters a literary work ever wholly frees itself from its meaning in ordinary speech, so no literary work, not even the traditional novel, leaves these meanings unaltered, as they were outside it. Even an ordinary 'was', in a report of something that was not, acquires a new formal quality from the fact that it was not so. The same process occurs in the higher levels of meaning of a work, all the way up to what once used to be called its 'Idea'. The special position that Sartre accords to literature must also be suspect to anyone who does not unconditionally subsume diverse aesthetic genres under a superior universal concept. The rudiments of external meanings are the irreducibly non-artistic elements in art. Its formal principle lies not in them, but in the dialectic of both moments – which accomplishes the transformation of meanings within it. The distinction between artist and *littérateur* is shallow: but it is true that the object of any aesthetic philosophy, even as understood by Sartre, is not the publicistic aspect of art. Still less is it the 'message' of a work. The latter oscillates unhappily between the subjective intentions of the artist and the demands of an objectively explicit metaphysical meaning. In our context, this meaning generally turns out to be an uncommonly practicable Being.

The social function of talk about commitment has meanwhile become somewhat confused. Cultural conservatives who demand that a work of art should say something, join forces with their political opponents against atelic, hermetic works of art. Eulogists of 'relevance' are more likely to find Sartre's *Huis Clos* profound, than to listen patiently to a text whose language challenges signification and by its very distance from meaning revolts in advance against positivist subordination of meaning. For the atheist Sartre, on the other hand, the conceptual import of art is the premiss of commitment. Yet works banned in the East are sometimes demagogically denounced by local guardians of the authentic message because they apparently say what they in fact do not say. The Nazis were already using the term 'cultural bolshevism' under the Weimar Republic, and hatred of what it refers to has survived the epoch of Hitler, when it was institutionalized. Today it has flared up again, just as it did forty years ago at works of the same kind, including some whose origins go a long way back and are unmistakably part of an established tradition.

Newspapers and magazines of the radical right constantly stir up indignation against what is unnatural, over-intellectual, morbid and decadent: they know their readers. The insights of social psychology into the authoritarian personality confirm them. The basic features of this type include conformism, respect for a petrified façade of opinion and society, and resistance to impulses that disturb its order or evoke inner elements of the unconscious that cannot be admitted. This hostility to anything alien or alienating can accommodate itself much more easily to literary realism of any provenance, even if it proclaims itself critical or socialist, than to works which swear allegiance to no political slogans, but whose mere guise is enough to disrupt the whole system of rigid coordinates that governs authoritarian personalities – to which the latter cling all the more fiercely, the less capable they are of spontaneous appreciation of anything not officially approved. Campaigns to prevent the staging of Brecht's plays in Western Germany belong to a relatively superficial layer of political consciousness. They were not even particularly vigorous, or they would have taken much crasser forms after 13 August.[2] By contrast, when the social contract with reality is abandoned, and literary works no longer speak as though they were reporting fact, hairs start to bristle. Not the least of the weaknesses of the debate on commitment is that it ignores the effect produced by works whose own formal laws pay no heed to coherent effects. So long as it fails to understand what the shock of the unintelligible can communicate, the whole dispute resembles shadow-boxing. Confusions in discussion of the problem do not indeed alter it, but they do make it necessary to rethink the alternative solutions proposed for it.

In aesthetic theory, 'commitment' should be distinguished from 'tendency'. Committed art in the proper sense is not intended to generate ameliorative measures, legislative acts or practical institutions – like earlier propagandist plays against syphilis, duels, abortion laws or borstals – but to work at the level of fundamental attitudes. For Sartre its task is to awaken the free choice of the agent which makes authentic existence possible at all, as opposed to the neutrality of the spectator. But what gives commitment its aesthetic advantage over tendentiousness also renders the content to which the artist commits himself inherently ambiguous. In Sartre the notion of choice – originally a Kierkegaardian category – is heir to the Christian doctrine 'He who is not with me is against me', but now voided of any concrete theological content. What remains is merely the abstract authority of a choice enjoined, with no regard for the fact that the very possibility of choosing depends on what can be chosen. The archetypal situation always cited by Sartre to demonstrate the irreducibility of freedom merely underlines this. Within a predetermined reality, freedom becomes an empty claim: Herbert Marcuse has exposed the absurdity of the philosophical theorem that it is always possible inwardly either to accept or to reject martyrdom.[3] Yet this is precisely what Sartre's dramatic situations are designed to demonstrate. But his plays are nevertheless bad models of his own existentialism, because they display in their respect for truth the whole administered universe which his philosophy ignores: the lesson we learn from them is one of unfreedom. Sartre's theatre of ideas sabotages the aims of his categories. This is not a specific shortcoming of his plays. It is not the office of art to spotlight alternatives, but to resist by its form alone the course of the world, which permanently puts a pistol to men's heads. In fact, as soon as committed works of art do instigate decisions at their own level, the decisions themselves become interchangeable. Because of this ambiguity, Sartre has with great candour confessed that he expects no real changes in the world from literature – a scepticism which reflects the historical mutations both of society and of the practical function of literature since the days of Voltaire. The principle of commitment thus slides towards the proclivities of the author, in keeping with the extreme subjectivism of Sartre's philosophy, which for all its materialist undertones, still echoes German speculative idealism. In his literary theory the work of art becomes an appeal to subjects, because it is itself nothing other than a declaration by a subject of his own choice or failure to choose.

Sartre will not allow that every work of art, at its very inception, confronts the writer, however free he may be, with objective demands of composition. His intention becomes simply one element among them. Sartre's question, 'Why write?', and his solution of it in a 'deeper choice', are invalid because the author's motivations are irrelevant to the finished work, the literary product. Sartre himself is not so far from this view when he notes that the stature of works increases, the less they remain attached to the empirical person who created them, as Hegel saw long ago. When he calls the literary work, in Durkheim's language, a social fact, he again involuntarily recalls its inherently collective objectivity, impenetrable to the mere subjective intentions of the author. Sartre therefore does not want to situate commitment at the level of the intention of the writer, but at that of his humanity itself.[4] This determination, however, is so generic that commitment ceases to be distinct from any other form of human action or attitude. The point, says Sartre, is that the writer commits himself in the present, 'dans le présent'; but since he in any case cannot escape it, his commitment to it cannot indicate a programme. The actual obligation a writer undertakes is much more precise: it is not one of choice, but of substance. Although Sartre talks of the dialectic, his subjectivism so little registers the particular other for which the subject must first divest itself to become a subject, that he suspects every literary objectification of petrifaction. However, since the pure immediacy and spontaneity which he hopes to save encounter no resistance in his work by which they could define themselves, they undergo a second reification. In order to develop his drama and novel beyond sheer declaration – whose recurrent model is the scream of the tortured – Sartre has to seek recourse in a flat objectivity, subtracted from any dialectic of form and expression, which is simply a communication of his own philosophy. The content of his art becomes philosophy, as with no other writer except Schiller.

But however sublime, thoughts can never be much more than one of the materials for art. Sartre's plays are vehicles for the author's ideas, which have been left behind in the race of aesthetic forms. They operate with traditional plots, exalted by an unshaken faith in meanings which can be transferred from art to reality. But the theses they illustrate, or where possible state, misuse the emotions which Sartre's own drama aims to express, by making them examples. They thereby disavow themselves. When one of his most famous plays ends with the dictum 'Hell is other people', it sounds like a quotation from *Being and Nothingness*, and it might just as well have been 'Hell is ourselves'. The combination of solid plot, and equally solid, extractable idea won Sartre great success and made him, without doubt against his honest will, acceptable to the culture industry. The high level of abstraction of such thesis-art led him into the mistake of letting some of his best works, the film *Les Feux sont Faits* or the play *Les Mains Sales*, be performed as political events, and not just to an audience of victims in the dark. In much the same way, a current ideology – which Sartre detests – confuses the actions and sufferings of paper leaders with the objective movement of history. Interwoven in the veil of personalization is the idea that human beings are in control and decide, not anonymous machinery, and that there is life on the commanding heights of society: Beckett's moribund grotesques suggest the truth about that. Sartre's vision prevents him from recognizing the hell he revolts against. Many of his phrases could be parroted by his mortal enemies. The idea that decision as such is what counts would even cover the Nazi slogan that 'only sacrifice makes us free'. In Fascist Italy, Gentile's absolute dynamism made similar pronouncements in philosophy. The flaw in Sartre's conception of commitment strikes at the very cause to which he commits himself.

Brecht, in some of his plays, such as the dramatization of Gorky's *The Mother* or *The Measures Taken*, bluntly glorifies the Party. But at times, at least according to his theoretical writings, he too wanted to educate spectators to a new attitude that would be distanced, thoughtful, experimental, the reverse of illusory empathy and identification. In tendency to abstraction, his plays after *Saint Joan* trump those of Sartre. The difference is that Brecht, more consistent than Sartre and a greater artist, made this abstraction into the formal principle of his art, as a didactic poetics that eliminates the traditional concept of dramatic character altogether. He realized that the surface of social life, the sphere of consumption, which includes the psychologically motivated actions of individuals, conceals the essence of society – which, as the law of exchange, is itself abstract. Brecht rejected aesthetic individuation as an ideology. He therefore sought to translate the true hideousness of society into theatrical appearance, by dragging it straight out of its camouflage. The people on his stage shrink before our eyes into the agents of social processes and functions, which indirectly and unknowingly they are in empirical reality. Brecht no longer postulates, like Sartre, an identity between living individuals and the essence of society, let alone any absolute sovereignty of the subject. Nevertheless, the process of aesthetic reduction that he pursues for the sake of political truth, in fact gets in its way. For this truth involves innumerable mediations, which Brecht disdains. What is artistically legitimate as alienating infantilism – Brecht's first plays came from the same milieu as Dada –

becomes merely infantile when it starts to claim theoretical or social validity. Brecht wanted to reveal in images the inner nature of capitalism. In this sense his aim was indeed what he disguised it as against Stalinist terror – realistic. He would have refused to deprive social essence of meaning by taking it as it appeared, imageless and blind, in a single crippled life. But this burdened him with the obligation of ensuring that what he intended to make unequivocally clear was theoretically correct. His art, however, refused to accept this *quid pro quo*: it both presents itself as didactic, and claims aesthetic dispensation from responsibility for the accuracy of what it teaches.

Criticism of Brecht cannot overlook the fact that he did not – for objective reasons beyond the power of his own creations – fulfil the norm he set himself as if it were a means to salvation. *Saint Joan* was the central work of his dialectical theatre. (*The Good Woman of Szechuan* is a variation of it in reverse: where Joan assists evil by the immediacy of her goodness, Shen Te, who wills the good, must become evil.) The play is set in a Chicago half-way between the Wild West fables of *Mahagonny* and economic facts. But the more preoccupied Brecht becomes with information, and the less he looks for images, the more he misses the essence of capitalism which the parable is supposed to present. Mere episodes in the sphere of circulation, in which competitors maul each other, are recounted instead of the appropriation of surplus-value in the sphere of production, compared with which the brawls of cattle dealers over their shares of the booty are epiphenomena incapable of provoking any great crisis. Moreover, the economic transactions presented as the machinations of rapacious traders are not merely puerile, which is how Brecht seems to have meant them; they are also unintelligible by the criteria of even the most primitive economic logic. The obverse of the latter is a political naïveté which could only make Brecht's opponents grin at the thought of such an ingenuous enemy. They could be as comfortable with Brecht as they are with the dying Joan in the impressive final scene of the play. Even with the broadest-minded allowance for poetic licence, the idea that a strike leadership backed by the Party could entrust a crucial task to a non-member is as inconceivable as the subsequent idea that the failure of that individual could ruin the whole strike.

Brecht's comedy of the resistible rise of the great dictator *Arturo Ui* exposes the subjective nullity and pretence of a fascist leader in a harsh and accurate light. However, the deconstruction of leaders, as with all individuals in Brecht, is extended into a reconstruction of the social and economic nexus in which the dictator acts. Instead of a conspiracy of the wealthy and powerful, we are given a trivial gangster organization, the cabbage trust. The true horror of fascism is conjured away; it is no longer a slow end-product of the concentration of social power, but mere hazard, like an accident or a crime. This conclusion is dictated by the exigencies of agitation: adversaries must be diminished. The consequence is bad politics, in literature as in practice before

1933. Against every dialectic, the ridicule to which Ui is consigned renders innocuous the fascism that was accurately predicted by Jack London decades before. The anti-ideological artist thus prepared the degradation of his own ideas into ideology. Tacit acceptance of the claim that one half of the world no longer contains antagonisms is supplemented by jests at everything that belies the official theodicy of the other half. It is not that respect for historical scale forbids laughter at house-painters, although the use of that term against Hitler was itself a painful exploitation of bourgeois class-consciousness. The group which engineered the seizure of power in Germany was also certainly a gang. But the problem is that such elective affinities are not extra-territorial: they are rooted within society itself. That is why the buffoonery of fascism, evoked by Chaplin as well, was at the same time also its ultimate horror. If this is suppressed, and a few sorry exploiters of greengrocers are mocked, where key positions of economic power are actually at issue, the attack misfires. *The Great Dictator* loses all satirical force and becomes obscene when a Jewish girl can hit a line of storm-troopers on the head with a pan without being torn to pieces. For the sake of political commitment, political reality is trivialized: which then reduces the political effect.

Sartre's frank doubt whether *Guernica* 'won a single supporter for the Spanish cause' certainly also applies to Brecht's didactic drama. Scarcely anyone needs to be taught the *fabula docet* to be extracted from it – that there is injustice in the world; while the moral itself shows few traces of the dialectical theory to which Brecht gave cursory allegiance. The trappings of epic drama recall the American phrase 'preaching to the converted'. The primacy of lesson over pure form, which Brecht intended to achieve, became a formal device itself. The suspension of form turns back against its own character as appearance. Its self-criticism in drama was related to the doctrine of objectivity [*Sachlichkeit*] in the applied visual arts. The correction of form by external conditions, with the elimination of ornament in the service of function, only increases its autonomy. The substance of Brecht's artistic work was the didactic play as an artistic principle. His method, to make immediately apparent events into phenomena alien to the spectator, was also a medium of formal construction rather than a contribution to practical efficacy. It is true that Brecht never spoke as sceptically as Sartre about the social effects of art. But, as an astute and experienced man of the world, he can scarcely have been wholly convinced of them. He once calmly wrote that, to be honest, the theatre was more important to him than any changes in the world it might promote. Yet the artistic principle of simplification not only purged politics of the illusory distinctions projected by subjective reflection into social objectivity, as Brecht intended, but it also falsified the very objectivity which didactic drama laboured to distil. If we take Brecht at his word and make politics the criterion by which to judge his committed theatre, then politics proves his theatre untrue. Hegel's *Logic* taught that essence must appear. If this is so, a representation of essence which ignores its relation to appearance must be as intrinsically false as the substitution of a lumpen-proletariat for the men behind fascism. The only ground on which Brecht's technique of reduction would be legitimate is that of 'art for art's sake', which his kind of commitment condemns as it does Lucullus.[5]

Contemporary literary Germany is anxious to distinguish Brecht the artist from Brecht the politician. The major writer must be saved for the West, if possible placed on a pedestal as an All-German poet, and so neutralized *au-dessus de la mêlée*. There is truth in this to the extent that both Brecht's artistic force, and his devious and uncontrollable intelligence, went well beyond the official credos and prescribed aesthetics of the People's Democracies. All the same, Brecht must be defended against this defence of him. His work, with its often patent weaknesses, would not have had such power, if it were not saturated with politics. Even its most questionable creations, such as *The Measures Taken*, generate an immediate awareness that issues of the utmost seriousness are at stake. To this extent Brecht's claim that he used his theatre to make men think was justified. It is futile to try to separate the beauties, real or imaginary, of his works from their political intentions. The task of immanent criticism, which alone is dialectical, is rather to synthesize assessment of the validity of his forms with that of his politics. Sartre's chapter 'Why write?' contains the undeniable statement that: 'Nobody can suppose for a moment that it is possible to write a good novel in praise of anti-Semitism.'[6] Nor could one be written in praise of the Moscow Trials, even if such praise were bestowed before Stalin actually had Zinoviev and Bukharin murdered.[7] The political falsehood stains the aesthetic form. Where Brecht distorts the real social problems discussed in his epic drama in order to prove a thesis, the whole structure and foundation of the play itself crumbles. *Mother Courage* is an illustrated primer intended to reduce to absurdity Montecuccoli's dictum that war feeds on war. The camp follower who uses the Thirty Years War to make a life for her children thereby becomes responsible for their ruin. But in the play this responsibility follows rigorously neither from the fact of the war itself nor from the individual behaviour of the petty profiteer; if Mother Courage had not been absent at the critical moment, the disaster would not have happened, and the fact that she has to be absent to earn some money, remains completely generic in relation to the action. The picture-book technique which Brecht needs to spell out his thesis prevents him from proving it. A socio-political analysis, of the sort Marx and Engels sketched in their criticism of Lassalle's play *Franz von Sickingen*, would show that Brecht's simplistic equation of the Thirty Years War with a modern war excludes precisely what is crucial for the behaviour and fate of Mother Courage in Grimmelshausen's novel. Because the society of the Thirty Years War was not the functional capitalist society of modern times, we cannot even poetically stipulate a closed functional system in which the lives and deaths of private individuals directly reveal economic laws. But Brecht needed the old lawless days as an image of his own, precisely because he saw clearly that the society of his own age could no longer be directly comprehended in terms of people and things. His attempt to reconstruct the reality of society thus led first to a false social model and then to dramatic implausibility. Bad politics becomes bad art, and vice versa. But the less works have to proclaim what they cannot completely believe themselves, the more telling they become in their own right; and the less they need a surplus of meaning beyond what they are. For the rest, the interested parties in every camp would probably be as successful in surviving wars today as they have always been.

Aporia of this sort multiply until they affect the Brechtian tone itself, the very fibre of his poetic art. Inimitable though its qualities may be – qualities which the mature Brecht may have thought unimportant – they were poisoned by the untruth of his politics. For what he justified was not simply, as he long sincerely believed, an incomplete socialism, but a coercive domination in which blindly irrational social forces returned to work once again. When Brecht became a panegyrist of its harmony, his lyric voice had to swallow chalk, and it started to grate. Already the exaggerated adolescent virility of the young Brecht betrayed the borrowed courage of the intellectual who, in despair at violence, suddenly adopts a violent practice which he has every reason to fear. The wild roar of *The Measures Taken* drowns out the noise of the disaster that has overtaken the cause, which Brecht convulsively tries to proclaim as salvation. Even Brecht's best work was infected by the deceptions of his commitment. Its language shows how far the underlying poetic subject and its message have moved apart. In an attempt to bridge the gap, Brecht affected the diction of the oppressed. But the doctrine he advocated needs the language of the intellectual. The homeliness and simplicity of his tone is thus a fiction. It betrays itself both by signs of exaggeration and by stylized regression to archaic or provincial forms of expression. It can often be importunate, and ears which have not let themselves be deprived of their native sensitivity cannot help hearing that they are being talked into something. It is a usurpation and almost a contempt for victims to speak like this, as if the author were one of them. All roles may be played, except that of the worker. The gravest charge against commitment is that even right intentions go wrong when they are noticed, and still more so, when they then try to conceal themselves. Something of this remains in Brecht's later plays in the linguistic *gestus* of wisdom, the fiction of the old peasant sated with epic experience as the poetic subject. No one in any country of the world is any longer capable of the earthy experience of South German muzhiks: the ponderous delivery has become a propaganda device to make us believe that the good life is where the Red Army is in control. Since there is nothing to give substance to this humanity as presented, which we have to take on trust,

Brecht's tone degenerates into an echo of archaic social relations, lost beyond recall.

The late Brecht was not so distant from official humanism. A journalistically minded Westerner could well praise *The Caucasian Chalk Circle* as a hymn to motherhood, and who is not touched when the splendid girl is finally held up as an example to the querulous lady beset with migraine? Baudelaire, who dedicated his work to the coiner of the motto *l'art pour l'art*, would have been less suited to such a catharsis. Even the grandeur and virtuosity of such poems as *The Legend of the Origin of the Book of Tao Te Ch'ing on Lao-Tzu's Journey into Exile* are marred by the theatricality of total plain-spokenness. What his classical predecessors once denounced as the idiocy of rural life, Brecht, like some existential ontologist, treats as ancient truth. His whole œuvre is a Sisyphean labour to reconcile his highly cultivated and subtle taste with the crudely heteronomous demands which he desperately imposed on himself.

I have no wish to soften the saying that to write lyric poetry after Auschwitz is barbaric; it expresses in negative form the impulse which inspires committed literature. The question asked by a character in Sartre's play *Morts sans sépulture*, 'Is there any meaning in life when men exist who beat people until the bones break in their bodies?', is also the question whether any art now has a right to exist; whether intellectual regression is not inherent in the concept of committed literature because of the regression of society. But Enzensberger's retort also remains true, that literature must resist this verdict, in other words, be such that its mere existence after Auschwitz is not a surrender to cynicism. Its own situation is one of paradox, not merely the problem of how to react to it. The abundance of real suffering tolerates no forgetting; Pascal's theological saying, *On ne doit plus dormir*, must be secularized. Yet this suffering, what Hegel called consciousness of adversity, also demands the continued existence of art while it prohibits it; it is now virtually in art alone that suffering can still find its own voice, consolation, without immediately being betrayed by it. The most important artists of the age have realized this. The uncompromising radicalism of their works, the very features defamed as formalism, give them a terrifying power, absent from helpless poems to the victims of our time. But even Schoenberg's *Survivor of Warsaw* remains trapped in the aporia to which, autonomous figuration of heteronomy raised to the intensity of hell, it totally surrenders. There is something embarrassing in Schoenberg's composition – not what arouses anger in Germany, the fact that it prevents people from repressing from memory what they at all costs want to repress – but the way in which, by turning suffering into images, harsh and uncompromising though they are, it wounds the shame we feel in the presence of the victims. For these victims are used to create something, works of art, that are thrown to the consumption of a world which destroyed them. The so-called artistic representation of the sheer physical pain of people beaten to the ground by rifle-butts contains, however remotely, the power to elicit enjoyment out of it. The moral of this art, not to forget for a single instant, slithers into the abyss of its opposite. The aesthetic principle of stylization, and even the solemn prayer of the chorus, make an unthinkable fate appear to have had some meaning; it is transfigured, something of its horror is removed. This alone does an injustice to the victims; yet no art which tried to evade them could confront the claims of justice. Even the sound of despair pays its tribute to a hideous affirmation. Works of less than the highest rank are also willingly absorbed as contributions to clearing up the past. When genocide becomes part of the cultural heritage in the themes of committed literature, it becomes easier to continue to play along with the culture which gave birth to murder.

There is one nearly invariable characteristic of such literature. It is that it implies, purposely or not, that even in so-called extreme situations, indeed in them most of all, humanity flourishes. Sometimes this develops into a dismal metaphysic which does its best to work up atrocities into 'limiting situations' which it then accepts to the extent that they reveal authenticity in men. In such a homely existential atmosphere the distinction between executioners and victims becomes blurred; both, after all, are equally suspended above the possibility of nothingness, which of course is generally not quite so uncomfortable for the executioners.

Today, the adherents of a philosophy which has since degenerated into a mere ideological sport, fulminate in pre-1933 fashion against artistic distortion, deformation and perversion of life, as though authors, by faithfully reflecting atrocities, were responsible for what they revolt against. The best example of this attitude, still prevalent among the silent majority in Germany, is the following story about Picasso. An officer of the Nazi occupation forces visited the painter in his studio and, pointing to *Guernica*, asked: 'Did you do that?' Picasso is said to have answered, 'No, you did.' Autonomous works of art too, like this painting, firmly negate empirical reality, destroy the destroyer, that which merely exists and, by merely existing, endlessly reiterates guilt. It is none other than Sartre who has seen the connection between the autonomy of a work and an intention which is not conferred upon it but is its own gesture towards reality. 'The work of art', he has written, '*does not have an end*; there we agree with Kant. But the reason is that it *is* an end. The Kantian formula does not account for the appeal which issues from every painting, every statue, every book.'[8] It only remains to add there is no straightforward relationship between this appeal and the thematic commitment of a work. The uncalculating autonomy of works which avoid popularization and adaptation to the market, involuntarily becomes an attack on them. The attack is not abstract, not a fixed attitude of all works of art to the world which will not forgive them for not bending totally to it. The distance these works maintain from empirical reality is in itself partly mediated by that reality. The imagination of the artist is not a creation *ex nihilo*; only dilettanti and aesthetes believe it to be so. Works of art that react against empirical reality obey the forces of that reality, which reject intellectual creations and throw them back on themselves. There is no material content, no formal category of artistic creation, however mysteriously transmitted and itself unaware of the process, which did not originate in the empirical reality from which it breaks free.

It is this which constitutes the true relation of art to reality, whose elements are regrouped by its formal laws. Even the avant-garde abstraction which provokes the indignation of philistines, and which has nothing in common with conceptual or logical abstraction, is a reflex response to the abstraction of the law which objectively dominates society. This could be shown in Beckett's works. These enjoy what is today the only form of respectable fame: everyone shudders at them, and yet no one can persuade himself that these eccentric plays and novels are not about what everyone knows but no one will admit. Philosophical apologists may laud his works as sketches from an anthropology. But they deal with a highly concrete historical reality: the abdication of the subject. Beckett's *Ecce Homo* is what human beings have become. As though with eyes drained of tears, they stare silently out of his sentences. The spell they cast, which also binds them, is lifted by being reflected in them. However, the minimal promise of happiness they contain, which refuses to be traded for comfort, cannot be had for a price less than total dislocation, to the point of worldlessness. Here every commitment to the world must be abandoned to satisfy the ideal of the committed work of art — that polemical alienation which Brecht as a theorist invented, and as an artist practised less and less as he committed himself more firmly to the role of a friend of mankind. This paradox, which might be charged with sophistry, can be supported without much philosophy by the simplest experience: Kafka's prose and Beckett's plays, or the truly monstrous novel *The Unnameable*, have an effect by comparison with which officially committed works look like pantomimes. Kafka and Beckett arouse the fear which existentialism merely talks about. By dismantling appearance, they explode from within the art which committed proclamation subjugates from without, and hence only in appearance. The inescapability of their work compels the change of attitude which committed works merely demand. He over whom Kafka's wheels have passed, has lost for ever both any peace with the world and any chance of consoling himself with the judgement that the way of the world is bad; the element of ratification which lurks in resigned admission of the dominance of evil is burnt away.

Yet the greater the aspiration, the greater is the possibility of foundering and failure. The loss of tension evident in works of painting and music which have moved away from objective representation and intelligible or coherent meaning, has in many ways spread to the literature known in a repellent jargon as 'texts'. Such works drift to the brink of indifference, degenerate insensibly into mere hobbies, into idle repetition of formulas now abandoned in other art-forms, into trivial patterns. It is this development which often gives substance to crude calls for commitment. Formal structures which challenge the lying positivism of meaning can easily slide into a different sort of vacuity, positivistic arrangements, empty juggling with elements. They fall within the very sphere from which they seek to escape. The extreme case is literature which undialectically confuses itself with science and vainly tries to fuse with cybernetics. Extremes meet: what cuts the last thread of communication becomes the prey of communication theory. No firm criterion can draw the line between a determinate negation of meaning and a bad positivism of meaninglessness, as an assiduous soldiering on just for the sake of it. Least of all can such a line be based on an appeal to human values, and a curse of mechanization. Works of art which by their existence take the side of the victims of a rationality that subjugates nature, are even in their protest constitutively implicated in the process of rationalization itself. Were they to try to disown it, they would become both aesthetically and socially powerless: mere clay. The organizing, unifying principle of each and every work of art is borrowed from that very rationality whose claim to totality it seeks to defy.

In the history of French and German consciousness, the problem of commitment has been posed in opposite ways. In France aesthetics have been dominated, openly or covertly, by the principle of *l'art pour l'art*, allied to academic and reactionary tendencies.[9] This explains the revolt against it. Even extreme avant-garde works have a touch of decorative allure in France. It is for this reason that the call to existence and commitment sounded revolutionary there. In Germany the situation is the other way round. The liberation of art from any external end, although it was a German who first raised it purely and incorruptibly into a criterion of taste, has always been suspect to a tradition which has deep roots in German idealism. The first famous document of this tradition is that senior masters' bible of intellectual history, Schiller's *Treatise on the Theatre as a Moral Institution*. Such suspicion is not so much due to the elevation of mind to an Absolute that is coupled with it – an attitude that swaggered its way to hubris in German philosophy. It is rather provoked by the aspect that any work of art free of an ulterior goal shows to society. For this art is a reminder of that sensuous pleasure of which even – indeed especially – the most extreme dissonance, by sublimation and negation, partakes. German speculative philosophy granted that a work of art contains within itself the sources of its transcendence, and that its inner meaning is always more than the work itself – but only therefore to demand a certificate of good behaviour from it. According to this latent tradition, a work of art should have no being for itself, since otherwise it would – as Plato's embryonic state socialism classically stigmatized it – be a source of effeminacy and an obstacle to action for its own sake, the German original sin. Killjoys, ascetics, moralists of the sort who are always invoking names like Luther and Bismarck, have no time for aesthetic autonomy; and there is also an undercurrent of servile heteronomy in the pathos of the categorical imperative, which is indeed on the one hand reason itself, but on the other an absolute datum to be blindly obeyed. Fifty years ago Stefan George and his school were still being attacked as Frenchifying aesthetes.

Today the curmudgeons whom no bombs could shake out of their complacency have allied themselves with the philistines who rage against the alleged incomprehensibility of the new art. The underlying impulse of these attacks is petty-bourgeois hatred of sex, the common ground of Western moralists and ideologists of Socialist Realism. No moral terror can prevent the side the work of art shows its beholder from giving him pleasure, even if only in the formal fact of temporary freedom from the compulsion of practical goals. Thomas Mann called this quality of art 'high spirits', a notion intolerable to people with morals. Brecht himself, who was not without ascetic traits – which reappear transmuted in the resistance of any great autonomous art to consumption – rightly ridiculed culinary art; but he was much too intelligent not to know that pleasure can never be completely ignored in the total aesthetic effect, no matter how relentless the work. The primacy of the aesthetic object as pure refiguration does not smuggle consumption, and thus false harmony, in again through the back door. Although the moment of pleasure, even when it is extirpated from the effect of a work, constantly returns to it, the principle that governs autonomous works of art is not the totality of their effects but their own inherent structure. They are knowledge as non-conceptual objects. This is the source of their nobility. It is not something of which they have to persuade men, because it has been given into their hands. This is why today autonomous rather than committed art should be encouraged in Germany. Committed works all too readily credit themselves with every noble value, and then manipulate them at their ease. Under fascism too, no atrocity was perpetrated without a moral veneer. Those who trumpet their ethics and humanity in Germany today are merely waiting for a chance to persecute those whom their rules condemn, and to exercise the same inhumanity in practice of which they accuse modern art in theory. In Germany, commitment often means bleating what everyone is already saying or at least secretly wants to hear. The notion of a 'message' in art, even when politically radical, already contains an accommodation to the world: the stance of the lecturer conceals a clandestine entente with the listeners, who could only be rescued from deception by refusing it.

The type of literature that, in accordance with the tenets of commitment but also with the demands of philistine moralism, exists for man, betrays him by traducing that which could help him, if only it did not strike a pose of helping him. But any literature which therefore concludes that it can be a law unto itself, and exist only for itself, degenerates into ideology no less. Art, which even in its opposition to society remains a part of it, must close its eyes and ears against it: it cannot escape the shadow of irrationality. But when it appeals to this unreason, making it a *raison d'être*, it converts its own malediction into a theodicy. Even in the most sublimated work of art there is a hidden 'it should be otherwise'. When a work is merely itself and no other thing, as in a pure pseudo-scientific construction, it becomes bad art – literally pre-artistic. The moment of true volition, however, is mediated through nothing other than the form of the work itself, whose crystallization becomes an analogy of that other condition which should be. As eminently constructed and produced objects, works of art, including literary ones, point to a practice from which they abstain: the creation of a just life. This mediation is not a compromise between commitment and autonomy, nor a sort of mixture of advanced formal elements with an intellectual content inspired by genuinely or supposedly progressive politics. The content of works of art is never the amount of intellect pumped into them: if anything, it is the opposite.

Nevertheless, an emphasis on autonomous works is itself socio-political in nature. The feigning of a true politics here and now, the freezing of historical relations which nowhere seem ready to melt, oblige the mind to go where it need not degrade itself. Today every phenomenon of culture, even if a model of integrity, is liable to be suffocated in the cultivation of kitsch. Yet paradoxically in the same epoch it is to works of art that has fallen the burden of wordlessly asserting what is barred to politics. Sartre himself has expressed this truth in a passage which does credit to his honesty.[10] This is not a time for political art, but politics has migrated into autonomous art, and nowhere more so than where it seems to be politically dead. An example is Kafka's allegory of toy guns, in which an idea of non-violence is fused with a dawning awareness of the approaching paralysis of politics. Paul Klee too has a place in any debate about committed and autonomous art; for his work, *écriture par excellence*, had its roots in literature and would not have been what it was without them – or if it had not consumed them. During the First World War or shortly after, Klee drew cartoons of Kaiser Wilhelm as an inhuman iron-eater. Later, in 1920, these became – the development can be shown quite clearly – the *Angelus Novus*, the angel of the machine, who, though he no longer bears any emblem of caricature or commitment, flies far beyond both. The machine angel's enigmatic eyes force the onlooker to try to decide whether he is announcing the culmination of disaster or salvation hidden within it. But, as Walter Benjamin, who owned the drawing, said, he is the angel who does not give, but takes.

NOTES

1 Jean-Paul Sartre, *What is Literature?* (London, 1967), 4.
2 Reference to the establishment of the Berlin Wall in 1961.
3 Reference to Marcuse's essay 'Sartre's Existentialism', included in *Studies in Critical Philosophy* (London, 1972), 157–90.
4 'Because he is a man'; *Situations* II (Paris, 1948), 51.
5 Reference to Brecht's last play on the Roman general Lucullus.
6 *What is Literature?*, 46
7 Reference to *The Measures Taken*, written in 1930, which contained an implicit justification in advance of the Moscow Trials. Zinoviev and Bukharin were condemned in 1938.
8 *What is Literature?*, 34.
9 'We know very well that pure art and empty art are the same thing and that aesthetic purism was a brilliant manœuvre of the bourgeois of the last century who preferred to see themselves denounced as philistines rather than as exploiters.' *What is Literature?*, 17.
10 See Jean-Paul Sartre, *L'Existentialisme est un humanisme* (Paris, 1946), 105.

14 Lucien Goldmann

Introduction to the Problems of a Sociology of the Novel (1963)*

Lucien Goldmann (1913–70) was born in Romania and studied in various parts of Europe before settling in Paris. He worked as assistant to Jean Piaget in Switzerland during the Nazi occupation of Paris. This influenced his theory of genetic structuralism and humanist science, though his primary influence was the early Lukács. Unlike Lukács, Goldmann was not politically active, and his Marxism is often attenuated to a politicized sociology of knowledge and cultural control. His major work, *The Hidden God* (1956; trans. 1964), is a study of Pascal and Racine. This study exemplifies his 'genetic' explanation of the fundamental relations of potential consciousness in historical structures of class consciousness. Rather than immanent cultural logics or individual psychology, the object of study for genetic structuralism is the world-view or pattern of feeling which unites a particular social group. This humanist and sociological approach to culture has similarities with Raymond Williams's work and his concept of structures of feeling. Goldmann also wrote sympathetically about contemporary writers such as Robbe-Grillet, Jean Genet and Nathalie Sarraute, using a similar methodology to that developed in *The Hidden God*. His work on the novel, collected in *Towards a Sociology of the Novel* (1964; trans. 1975), is generally considered less convincing, more like a vague sociology of literary expression than a Marxist account of literary production. Nevertheless, the opening chapter, 'Introduction to the Problems of a Sociology of the Novel', provides a succinct account of the qualities and problems of Goldmann's theoretical approach. Goldmann's other works include *The Human Sciences and Philosophy* (1969); *Racine* (1972); *Cultural Creation in Modern Society* (1976); and *Lukács and Heidegger* (1978). For discussion see Raymond Williams, 'Literature and Sociology', *Problems in Materialism and Culture* (1980); and Mary Evans, *Lucien Goldmann* (1981).

* From Lucien Goldmann, *Towards a Sociology of the Novel*, trans. A. Sheridan (London: Tavistock, 1975), 1–17.

Two years ago, in January 1961, the Institute of Sociology in the Free University of Brussels asked me to lead a research group into the sociology of literature, beginning with the novels of André Malraux. With a good deal of apprehension, I accepted. My work on seventeenth-century philosophy and tragedy in no way prejudiced me against the possibility of a similar study of the novel, even of a body of fiction so nearly contemporary as Malraux's. In fact, we spent the first year on a preliminary study of the problems of the novel as a literary form, taking as our starting-point Georg Lukács's already almost classic work – though still little known in France – *The Theory of the Novel*[1] and René Girard's recently published *Mensonge romantique et vérité romanesque*,[2] in which Girard – unknown to himself, as he later told me – discovered the Lukácsian analyses, while modifying them on several particular points.

Our study of *The Theory of the Novel* and Girard's book led me to formulate a number of sociological hypotheses that seem to me to be particularly interesting, and on the basis of which my later work on Malraux's novels was developed.

These hypotheses concern, on the one hand, the homology between the structure of the classical novel and the structure of exchange in the liberal economy and, on the other hand, certain parallels in their later evolutions.

Let us begin by tracing the outlines of the structure described by Lukács. This structure may not, as he believed, characterize the novel form in general, but it does characterize at least its most important aspects (and probably, from the genetic point of view, its primordial aspect). The novel form studied by Lukács is that characterized by a hero that he very felicitously calls the *problematic hero*.[3]

The novel is the story of a *degraded* (what Lukács calls 'demoniacal') search, a search for authentic values in a world itself degraded, but at an otherwise advanced level according to a different mode.

By authentic values, I mean, of course, not the values that the critic or the reader regards as authentic, but those which, without being manifestly present in the novel, organize in accordance with an *implicit* mode its world as a whole. It goes without saying that these values are specific to each novel and different from one novel to another.

Since the novel is an epic genre characterized, unlike the folk tale or the epic poem itself, by the insurmountable rupture between the hero and the world, there is in Lukács an analysis of the nature of two degradations (that of the hero and that of the world) that must engender both a *constitutive opposition*, the foundation of this insurmountable rupture, and an *adequate community* to make possible the existence of an epic form.

The radical rupture alone would, in effect, have led to tragedy or to lyric poetry; the absence of rupture or the existence of a merely accidental rupture would have led to the epic poem or the folk tale.

Situated between the two, the novel has a dialectical nature in so far as it derives specifically, on the one hand, from the fundamental community of the hero and of the world presupposed by all epic forms and, on the other hand, from their insurmountable rupture; the community of the hero and of the world resulting from the fact that they are both degraded in relation to authentic values, the opposition resulting from the difference of nature between each of these two degradations.

The *demoniacal* hero of the novel is a madman or a criminal, in any case, as I have said, a *problematic* character whose degraded, and therefore inauthentic, search for authentic values in a world of conformity and convention constitute the content of this new literary genre known as the 'novel' that writers created in an individualistic society.

On the basis of this analysis, Lukács develops a typology of the novel. Setting out from the relation between the hero and the world, he distinguishes three schematic types of the Western novel in the nineteenth century, to which is added a fourth that already constitutes a transformation from the novel form towards new modalities that would require a different type of analysis. In 1920, this fourth possibility seemed to him to be expressed pre-eminently in the novels of Tolstoy, which strive towards the epic. The three types of novel on which his analysis bears are as follows:

a) the novel of 'abstract idealism'; characterized by the activity of the hero and by his over-narrow consciousness in relation to the complexity of the world (*Don Quixote, Le Rouge et le noir*);

b) the psychological novel; concerned above all with the analysis of the inner life, and characterized by the passivity of the hero and a consciousness too broad to be satisfied by what the world of convention can offer him (*Oblomov* and *L'Éducation sentimentale*);

c) the *Bildungsroman*, which ends with a *self-imposed limitation*; although the hero gives up the problematic search, he does not accept the world of convention or abandon the implicit scale of values – a self-imposed limitation that must be characterized by the term 'virile maturity' (Goethe's *Wilhelm Meister* or Gottfried Keller's *Der grüne Heinrich*).

At a distance of forty years, René Girard's analyses are often very close to those of Lukács. For Girard, too, the novel is the story of a degraded search (which he calls 'idolatrous') for authentic values, by a problematic hero, in a degraded world. The terminology he uses is Heideggerian in origin, but he often gives it a content that is somewhat different from that of Heidegger himself. Without going into detail, we might say that Girard replaces Heidegger's duality of the ontological and the ontic by the obviously related duality of the ontological and the metaphysical, which correspond for him to the authentic and the inauthentic; but whereas, for Heidegger, any idea of progress and retreat is to be eliminated, Giarard confers on his terminology of the ontological and the metaphysical a content much closer to the positions of Lukács than to those of Heidegger, by introducing between the two terms a relation governed by the categories of progress and regression.[4]

Girard's typology of the novel is based on the idea that the degradation of the fictional world is the result of a more or less advanced ontological sickness (this 'more or less' is strictly contrary to Heidegger's thinking) to which corresponds, within the fictional world, an increase of metaphysical desire, that is to say, of degraded desire.

It is based therefore on the idea of degradation, and it is here that Girard introduces into the Lukácsian analysis a precision that seems to me particularly important. For him, indeed, the degradation of the fictional world, the progress of the ontological sickness, and the increase of metaphysical desire are expressed in a greater or lesser *mediatization* that progressively increases the distance between metaphysical desire and authentic search, the search for 'vertical transcendence'.

There are a great many examples of mediation in Girard's work, from the novels of chivalry that stand between *Don Quixote* and the search for chivalric values to the lover that stands between the husband and his desire for his wife, in Dostoevsky's *The Eternal Husband*. Incidentally, it does not seem to me that his examples are always as well chosen. Moreover, I am not at all sure that mediatization is as universal a category in the fictional world as Girard thinks. The term 'degradation' seems to me broader and more appropriate, on condition of course that the nature of this degradation is specified in each particular analysis.

Nevertheless, by introducing the category of mediation, and even by exaggerating its importance, Girard has elucidated the analysis of a structure that involved not only the most important form of degradation in the fictional world but also the form that is, from a genetic point of view, probably the first, that which gave birth to the literary genre of the novel, the novel itself having emerged as the result of other derived forms of degradation.

From this point on, Girard's typology is based first of all on the existence of two forms of mediation, external and internal, the first characterized by the fact that the mediating agent is external to the world in which the hero's search takes place (for example, the novels of chivalry in *Don Quixote*), the second by the fact that the mediating agent belongs to this world (the lover in *The Eternal Husband*).

Within these two qualitatively different groups, there is the idea of a progressive degradation that is expressed by the increasing proximity between the fictional character and the mediating agent, and the increasing distance between this character and *vertical transcendence*.

Let us now try to elucidate an essential point on which Lukács and Girard are in fundamental disagreement. As the story of a degraded search for authentic values in an inauthentic world, the novel is necessarily both a biography and a social chronicle. A particularly important fact is that the situation of the writer in relation to the world he has created is, in the novel, different from the situation in relation to the world of any other literary form. This particular situation, Girard calls *humour*; Lukács calls it *irony*. Both agree that the novelist must supersede the consciousness of his heroes and that this supersession (humour or irony) is aesthetically constitutive of fictional creation. But they diverge as to the nature of this supersession and, on this point, it is the position of Lukács that seems to me to be acceptable and not that of Girard.

For Girard, the novelist has left the world of degradation and rediscovered authenticity, vertical transcendence, at the moment he writes his work. This is why he thinks that most great novels end with a conversion of the hero to this vertical transcendence and that the abstract character of certain endings (*Don Quixote*, *Le Rouge et le noir*, one might also add *La Princesse de Clèves*) is either an illusion on the part of the reader, or the result of survivals from the past in the consciousness of the writer.

Such a notion is strictly contrary to Lukács's aesthetic, for which any *literary form* (and any great artistic form in general) is born out of the need to express an *essential* content. If the fictional degradation were really superseded by the writer, even through the ultimate conversion of a number of heroes, the story of this degradation would be no more than a mere incident and its expression would have at most the character of a more or less entertaining narrative.

And yet the writer's irony, his autonomy in relation to his characters, the ultimate conversion of the fictional heroes are undoubted realities.

However, Lukács thinks that precisely to the extent that the novel is the imaginary creation of a world governed by *universal* degradation, this supersession cannot itself be other than degraded, *abstract*, conceptual, and not experienced as a concrete reality.

According to Lukács the novelist's irony is directed not only on to the hero, whose demoniacal character he is well aware of, but also on the abstract, and therefore inadequate and degraded, character of his own consciousness. That is why the story of the degraded search, whether demoniacal or idolatrous, always remains the sole way of expressing essential realities.

The ultimate conversion of Don Quixote or Julien Sorel is not, as Girard believes, a discovery of authenticity, vertical transcendence, but simply an awareness of the vanity, the degraded character not only of the earlier search, but also of any hope, of any possible search.

That is why it is an end and not a beginning and it is the existence of this irony (which is always a self-irony, as well) that enables Lukács to make two related definitions that seem to me particularly appropriate to this form of the novel: '*the Way is begun, the journey is ended*', and '*the novel is the form of virile maturity'*, the second formula defining more specifically, as we have seen, the *Bildungsroman* of the *Wilhelm Meister* type, which ends with a self-imposed limitation (the hero gives up the problematic search, without accepting the world of convention or abandoning the explicit scale of values).

Thus the novel, in the sense given it by Lukács and Girard, appears as a literary genre in which authentic values, which are always involved, cannot be present in the work in the form of conscious characters or concrete realities. These values exist only in an abstract, conceptual form in the consciousness of the novelist in which they take on an *ethical* character. But abstract ideas have no place in a literary work, where they would form a heterogeneous element.

The problem of the novel, therefore, is to make what in the novelist's consciousness is *abstract* and *ethical* the essential element of a work in which reality can exist only in the mode of a non-thematized (Girard would say mediatized) absence or, which is equivalent, a degraded presence. As Lukács says, the novel is the only literary genre in which *the novelist's ethic becomes an aesthetic problem of the work*.

The problem of a sociology of the novel has always preoccupied sociologists of literature, though, as yet, no decisive step towards its elucidation has so far been attempted. Basically, the novel, for the first part of its history, was a biography and a social chronicle and so it has always been possible to show that the social chronicle reflected to a greater or lesser degree the society of the period – and one does not have to be a sociologist to see that.

On the other hand, a connection has also been made between the transformation of the novel since Kafka and the Marxist analyses of reification. Here, too, it has to be said that serious sociologists should have seen this as a problem rather than as an explanation. Although it is obvious that the absurd worlds of Kafka or Camus's *L'Étranger*, or Robbe-Grillet's world composed of relatively autonomous objects, correspond to the analysis of reification as developed by Marx and later Marxists, the problem arises as to why, when this analysis was elaborated in the second half of the nineteenth century and concerned a phenomenon that appeared in a still earlier period, this same phenomenon was expressed in the novel only at the end of World War I.

In short, all these analyses concern the relation between certain elements of the *content* of fictional literature and the existence of a social reality that they reflect almost without transposition or by means of a more or less transparent transposition.

But the first problem that a sociology of the novel should have confronted is that of the relation between the *novel form* itself and the *structure* of the social environment in which it developed, that is to say, between the novel as a literary genre and individualistic modern society.

It seems to me today that a combination of the analyses of Lukács and Girard, even though they were both developed without specifically sociological preoccupations, makes it possible, if not to elucidate this problem entirely, at least to make a decisive step towards its elucidation.

I have just said that the novel can be characterized as the story of a search for authentic values in a degraded mode, in a degraded society, and that this degradation, in so far as it concerns the hero, is expressed principally through the mediatization, the reduction of authentic values to the implicit level and their disappearance as manifest realities. This is obviously a particularly complex structure and it would be difficult to imagine that it could one day emerge simply from individual invention without any basis in the social life of the group.

What, however, would be quite inconceivable, is that a literary form of such dialectical complexity should be rediscovered, over a period of centuries, among the most different writers in the most varied countries, that it should have become the form *par excellence* in which was expressed, on the literary plane, the content of a whole period, without there being either a homology or a significant relation between this form and the most important aspects of social life.

This hypothesis seems to me particularly simple and above all productive and credible, though it has taken me years to find it.

The novel form seems to me, in effect, to be *the transposition on the literary plane of everyday life in the individualistic society created by market production.* There is a *rigorous homology* between the literary form of the novel, as I have defined it with the help of Lukács and Girard, and the everyday relation between man and commodities in general, and by extension between men and other men, in a market society.

The natural, healthy relation between men and commodities is that in which production is consciously governed by future consumption, by the concrete qualities of objects, by their *use-value.*

Now what characterizes market production is, on the contrary, the elimination of this relation with men's consciousness, its reduction to the implicit through the mediation of the new economic reality created by this form of production: *exchange-value.*

In other forms of society, when a man needed an article of clothing or a house, he had to produce them himself or obtain them from someone capable of producing them and who was under an obligation to provide him with them, either in accordance with certain traditional rules, or for reasons of authority, friendship, etc., or as part of some reciprocal arrangement.[5]

If one wishes to obtain an article of clothing or a house today, one has to find the money needed to buy them. The producer of clothes or houses is indifferent to the use-values of the objects he produces. For him, these objects are no more than a necessary evil to obtain what alone interests him, an exchange-value sufficient to ensure the viability of his enterprise. In the economic life, which constitutes the most important part of modern social life, every authentic relation with the qualitative aspect of objects and persons tends to disappear – interhuman relations as well as those between men and things – and be replaced by a mediatized and degraded relation: the relation with purely quantitative exchange-values.

Of course, use-values continue to exist and even to govern, in the last resort, the whole of the economic life; but their action assumes an *implicit character, exactly like that of authentic values in the fictional world.*

On the conscious, manifest plane, *the economic life* is composed of people orientated exclusively towards exchange-values, degraded values, to which are added in production a number of individuals – the creators in every sphere – who remain essentially orientated towards use-values and who by virtue of that fact are situated on the fringes of society and become *problematic individuals*; and, of course, even these individuals unless they accept the romantic illusion (Girard would say lie) of the *total* rupture between essence and appearance, between the inner life and the social life, cannot be deluded as to the degradations that their creative activity undergoes in a market society, when this activity is manifested externally, when it becomes a book, a painting, teaching, a musical composition, etc., enjoying a certain prestige, and having therefore a certain price. It should be added that as the ultimate consumer, opposed in the very act of exchange to the producers, any individual in a market society finds himself at certain moments of the day aiming at qualitative use-values that he can obtain only through the mediation of exchange-values.

In view of this, there is nothing surprising about the creation of the novel as a literary genre. Its apparently extremely complex form is the one in which men live every day, when they are obliged to seek all quality, all use-value in a mode degraded by the mediation of quantity, of exchange-value – and this in a society in which any effort to orientate oneself *directly* towards use-value can only produce individuals who are themselves degraded, but in a different mode, that of *the problematic individual.*

Thus the two structures, that of an important fictional genre and that of exchange, proved to be strictly homologous, to the point at which one might speak of one and the same structure manifesting itself on two different planes. Furthermore, as we shall see later, the *evolution* of the fictional form that corresponds to the world of reification can be understood only in so far as it is related to a *homologous history* of the structure of reification.

However, before making a few remarks about this homology between the two evolutions we must examine the problem, particularly important for the sociologist, of the process by which the literary form was able to emerge out of the economic reality, and of the modifications that the study of this process forces us to introduce into the traditional representation of the sociological conditioning of literary creation.

One fact is striking at the outset; the traditional scheme of literary sociology, whether Marxist or not, cannot be applied in the case of the structural homology just referred to. Most work in the sociology of literature established a relation between the most important literary works and the collective *consciousness* of the particular social group from which they emerged. On this point, the traditional Marxist position does not differ essentially from non-Marxist sociological work as a whole, in relation to which it introduces only four new ideas, namely:

a) The literary work is not the mere reflection of a real, given collective consciousness, but the culmination at a very advanced level of coherence of tendencies peculiar to the consciousness of a particular group, a consciousness that must be conceived as a dynamic reality, orientated towards a certain state of equilibrium. What really separates, in this as in all other spheres, Marxist sociology from positivistic, relativist or eclectic sociological tendencies is the fact that it sees the key concept not in the *real* collective consciousness, but in the constructed concept (*zugerechnet*) of *possible consciousness* which, alone, makes an understanding of the first possible.

b) The relation between collective ideology and great individual literary, philosophical, theological, etc. creations resides not in an identity of content, but in a more advanced coherence and in a homology of structures, which can be expressed in imaginary contents very different from the real content of the collective consciousness.

c) The work corresponding to the mental structure of the particular social group may be elaborated in certain exceptional cases by an individual with very few relations with this group. The *social* character of the work resides above all in the fact that an individual can never establish by himself a coherent mental structure corresponding to what is called a 'world view'. Such a structure can be elaborated only by a group, the individual being capable only of carrying it to a very high degree of coherence and transposing it on the level of imaginary creation, conceptual thought, etc.

d) The collective consciousness is neither a primary reality, nor an autonomous reality; it is elaborated implicitly in the overall behaviour of individuals participating in the economic, social, political life, etc.

These are evidently extremely important theses, sufficient to establish a very great different between Marxist thinking and other conceptions of the sociology of literature. Nevertheless, despite these differences, Marxist theoreticians, like positivistic or relativistic sociologists of literature, have always thought that the social life can be expressed on the literary, artistic or philosophical plane only through the intermediary link of the collective consciousness.

In the case we have just studied, however, what strikes one first is the fact that although we find a strict homology between the structures of economic life and a certain particularly important manifestation, one can detect no analogous structure at the level of the *collective consciousness* that seemed hitherto to be the indispensable intermediary link to realize either the homology or an intelligible, significant relation between the different aspects of social existence.

The novel analysed by Lukács and Girard no longer seems to be the imaginary transposition of the *conscious structures* of a particular group, but seems to express on the contrary (and this may be the case of a very large part of modern art in general) a search for values that no social group defends effectively and that the economic life tends to make implicit in all members of the society.

The old Marxist thesis whereby the proletariat was seen as the only social group capable of constituting the basis of a new culture, by virtue of the fact that it was not integrated into the reified society, set out from the traditional sociological representation that presupposed that all authentic, important cultural creation could emerge only from a fundamental harmony between the mental structure of the creator and that of a partial group of relative size, but universal ambition. In reality, for Western society at least, the Marxist analysis has proved inadequate; the Western proletariat, far from remaining alien to the reified society and opposing it as a revolutionary force, has on the contrary become integrated into it to a large degree, and its trade union and political action, far from overthrowing this society and replacing it by a socialist world, has enabled it to gain a relatively better place in it than Marx's analysis foresaw.

Furthermore, cultural creation, although increasingly threatened by the reified society, has continued to flourish. Fictional literature, as perhaps modern poetic creation and contemporary painting, are authentic forms of cultural creation even though they cannot be attached to the consciousness – even a potential one – of a particular social group.

Before embarking on a study of the processes that made possible and produced this *direct* transposition of the economic life into the literary life, we should perhaps remark that although such a process seems contrary to the whole tradition of Marxist studies of cultural creation, it confirms nevertheless, in a quite unexpected way, one of the most important Marxist analyses of bourgeois thought, namely the theory of the fetishization of merchandise and reification. This analysis, which Marx regarded as one of his most important discoveries, affirms in effect that in market societies (that is to say, in types of society in which economic activity predominates), the collective consciousness gradually loses all active reality and tends to become a mere reflection[6] of the economic life and, ultimately, to disappear.

There was obviously, therefore, between this particular analysis of Marx and the general theory of literary and philosophical creation of later Marxists, who presupposed an active role of the collective consciousness, not a contradiction but an incoherence. The latter theory never envisaged the consequences for the sociology of literature of Marx's belief that there survives in market societies a radical modification of the status of the individual and collective consciousness and, implicitly, relations between the infrastructure and the superstructure. The analysis of reification elaborated first by Marx on the level of everyday life, then developed by Lukács in the field of philosophical, scientific and political thought, finally taken up by a number of theoreticians in various specific domains, and about which I have myself published a study, would appear therefore, for the moment at least, to be confirmed by the facts in the sociological analysis of a certain fictional form.

Having said this, the question arises as to how the link between the economic structures and literary manifestations is made in a society in which this link occurs *outside the collective consciousness.*

With regard to this I have formulated the hypothesis of the convergent action of four different factors, namely:

a) The birth in the thinking of members of bourgeois society, on the basis of economic behaviour and the existence of exchange-value, of the *category of mediation* as a fundamental and increasingly developed form of thought, with an implicit tendency to replace this thought by a total false consciousness in which the mediating value becomes an absolute value and in which the mediated value disappears entirely or, to put it more clearly, with the tendency to conceive of the access to all values from the point of view of mediation, together with a propensity to make of money and social prestige absolute values and not merely mediations that provide access to other values of a qualitative character.

b) The survival in this society of a number of individuals who are essentially *problematic* in so far as their thinking and behaviour remain dominated by qualitative values, even though they are unable to extract themselves entirely from the existence of the degrading mediation whose action permeates the whole of the social structure.

These individuals include, above all, the creators, writers, artists, philosophers, theologians, men of action, etc., whose thought and behaviour are governed above all by the quality of their work even though they cannot escape entirely from the action of the market and from the welcome extended them by the reified society.

c) Since no important work can be the expression of a purely individual experience, it is likely that the novel genre could emerge and be developed only in so far as a *non-conceptualized*, affective discontent, an affective aspiration towards qualitative values, was developed either in society as a whole, or perhaps solely among the middle strata from which most novelists have come.[7]

d) Lastly, in the liberal market societies, there was a set of values, which, though not trans-individual, nevertheless, had a universal aim and, within these societies, a general validity. These were the values of liberal individualism that were bound up with the very existence of the competitive market (in France, liberty, equality and property, in Germany, *Bildungsideal*, with their derivatives, tolerance, the rights of man, development of the personality, etc.). On the basis of these values, there developed the category of *individual* biography that became the constitutive element of the novel. Here, however, it assumed the form of the *problematic* individual, on the basis of the following: (1) the personal experience of the problematic individuals mentioned above under (*b*); (2) the internal contradiction between individualism as a universal value produced by bourgeois society and the important and painful limitations that this society itself brought to the possibilities of the development of the individual.

This hypothetical schema seems to me to be confirmed among other things by the fact that, when one of these four elements, individualism, has gradually been eliminated by the transformation of the economic life and the replacement of the economy of free competition by an economy of cartels and monopolies (a transformation that began at the end of the nineteenth century, but whose qualitative turning-point most economists would place between 1900 and 1910), we witness a parallel transformation of the novel form that culminates in the gradual dissolution and disappearance of the individual character, of the hero; a transformation that seems to me to be characterized in an extremely schematic way by the existence of two periods:

a) The first, transitional period, during which the disappearance of the importance of the individual brings with it attempts to replace biography as the content of the work of fiction with values produced by different ideologies. For although, in Western societies, these values have proved to be too weak to produce their own literary forms, they might well give a new lease of life to an already existing form that was losing its former content. First and foremost, on this level, are the ideas of community and collective reality (institutions, family, social group, revolution, etc.) that had been introduced and developed in Western thinking by the socialist ideology.

b) The second period, which begins more or less with Kafka and continues to the contemporary *nouveau roman*, and which has not yet come to an end, is characterized by an abandonment of any attempt to replace the problematic hero and individual biography by another reality and by the effort to write the novel of the absence of the subject, of the non-existence of any ongoing search.[8]

It goes without saying that this attempt to safeguard the novel form by giving it a content, related no doubt to the content of the traditional novel (it had always been the literary form of the problematic search and the absence of positive values), but nevertheless essentially different (it now involves the elimination of two essential elements of the specific content of the novel: the psychology of the problematic hero and the story of his demoniacal search), was to produce at the same time parallel orientations towards different forms of expression. There may be here elements for a sociology of the theatre of absence (Beckett, Ionesco, Adamov during a certain period) and also of certain aspects of non-figurative painting.

Lastly, we should mention a problem that might and ought to be the subject of later research. The novel form that we have just studied is essentially critical and oppositional. It is a form of resistance to developing bourgeois society. An individual resistance that can fall back, within a group, only on *affective* and *non-conceptualized* psychical processes precisely because conscious resistances that might have elaborated literary forms implying the possibility of a positive hero (in the first place, a proletarian oppositional consciousness such as Marx had hoped for and predicted) had not become sufficiently developed in Western societies. The novel with a problematic hero thus proves, contrary to traditional opinion, to be a literary form bound up certainly with history and the development of the bourgeoisie, but not the expression of the real or possible consciousness of that class.

But the problem remains as to whether, parallel with this literary form, there did not develop other forms that might correspond to the conscious values and effective aspirations of the bourgeoisie; and, on this point, I should like to mention, merely as a general and hypothetical suggestion, the possibility that the work of Balzac – whose structure ought, indeed, to be analysed from this point of view – might constitute the only great literary expression of the world as structured by the conscious values of the bourgeoisie: individualism, the thirst for power, money and eroticism, which triumph over the ancient feudal values of altruism, charity and love.

Sociologically, this hypothesis, if it proves to be correct, might be related to the fact that the work of Balzac is situated precisely at a period in which individualism, ahistorical in itself, structured the consciousness of a bourgeoisie that was in the process of constructing a new society and found itself at the highest and most intense level of its real historical efficacity.

We should also ask ourselves why, with the exception of this single case, this form of fictional literature had only a secondary importance in the history of Western culture, why the real consciousness and aspirations of the bourgeoisie never succeeded again, in the course of the nineteenth and twentieth centuries, in creating a literary form of its own that might be situated on the same level as the other forms that constitute the Western literary tradition.

On this point, I would like to make a few general hypotheses. The analysis that I have just developed extends to one of the most important novel forms a statement that now seems to me to be valid for almost all forms of *authentic cultural creation*. In relation to this statement the only expression that I could see for the moment was constituted precisely by the work of Balzac,[9] who was able to create a great literary universe structured by purely individualistic values, at a historical moment when, concurrently, men animated by ahistorical values were accomplishing a considerable historical upheaval (an upheaval that was not really completed in France until the end of the bourgeois revolution in 1848). With this single exception (but perhaps one should add a few other possible exceptions that may have escaped my attention), it seems to me that there is valid literary and artistic creation only when there is an aspiration to transcendence on the part of the individual and a search for qualitative trans-individual values. 'Man passes beyond man', I have written, slightly altering Pascal. This means that man can be authentic only in so far as he conceives himself or feels himself as part of a developing whole and situates himself in a historical or transcendent trans-individual dimension. But bourgeois ideology, bound up like bourgeois society itself with the existence of economic activity, is precisely the first ideology in history that is both radically profane and ahistorical; the first ideology whose tendency is to deny anything sacred, whether the otherworldly sacredness of the transcendent religions or the immanent sacredness of the historical future. It is, it seems to me, the fundamental reason why bourgeois society created the first radically non-aesthetic form of consciousness. The essential character of bourgeois ideology, rationalism, ignores in its extreme expressions the very existence of art. There is no Cartesian or Spinozian aesthetics, or even an aesthetics for Baumgarten – art is merely an inferior form of knowledge.

It is no accident therefore if, with the exception of a few particular situations, we do not find any great literary manifestations of the bourgeois consciousness itself. In a society bound up with the market, the artist is, as I have already said, a problematic individual, and this means a critical individual, opposed to society.

Nevertheless reified bourgeois ideology had its thematic values, values that were sometimes authentic, such as those of individualism, sometimes purely conventional, which Lukács called false consciousness and, in their extreme forms, bad faith, and Heidegger's 'chatter'. These stereotypes, whether authentic or conventional, thematized in the collective consciousness, were later able to produce, side by side with the authentic novel form, a parallel literature that also recounted an individual history and, naturally enough, since conceptualized values were involved, could depict a positive hero.

It would be interesting to follow the meanderings of the secondary novel forms that might be based, quite naturally, on the collective consciousness. One would end up perhaps – I have not yet made such a study – with a very varied spectrum, from the lowest forms of the Delly type to the highest forms to be found perhaps in such writers as Alexandre Dumas or Eugène Sue. It is also perhaps on this plane that we should situate, parallel with the *nouveau roman*, certain best-sellers that are bound up with the new forms of collective consciousness.

However, the extremely schematic sketch that I have just traced seems to me to provide a framework for a sociological study of the novel form. Such a study would be all the more important in that, apart from its own object, it would constitute a not inconsiderable contribution to the study of the psychical structures of certain social groups, the middle strata in particular.

NOTES

1 Georg Lukács, *The Theory of the Novel*, trans. A. Bostock (London: Merlin, 1971).

2 René Girard, *Mensonge romantique et vérité romanesque* (Paris: Grasset, 1961).

3 I should say however that, in my opinion, the field of validity of this hypothesis must be contracted, for, although the hypothesis may be applied to such important works in the history of literature as Cervantes' *Don Quixote*, Stendhal's *Le Rouge et le noir*, and Flaubert's *Madame Bovary* and *L'Éducation sentimentale*, it can be applied only very partially to *La Chartreuse de Parme* and not at all to the works of Balzac, which occupy a considerable place in the history of the Western novel. As such, however, Lukács's analyses enable us, it seems to me, to undertake a serious sociological study of the novel form.

4 In Heidegger's thinking, as indeed in that of Lukács, there is a radical break between Being (for Lukács, Totality) and whatever may be spoken of in the indicative (a judgement of fact), or in the imperative (a judgement of value).

It is this difference that Heidegger designates as that of the ontological and the ontic. And, from this point of view, metaphysics, which is one of the highest and most general forms of thought in the indicative, remains in the final resort in the domain of the ontic.

While agreeing on the necessary distinction between the ontological and the ontic, totality and the theoretical, the moral and the metaphysical, the positions of Heidegger and Lukács are essentially different in the way these relations are conceived.

As a philosophy of history, Lukács's thought implies the idea of a coming-into-being (*devenir*) of knowledge, of a hope in progress, and a risk of regression. Now, for him, progress is the bringing together of positive thought and the category of totality; regression, the distancing of these two, ultimately inseparable, elements. The task of philosophy is precisely to introduce the category of totality as the basis of all partial research and of all reflection on positive data.

Heiddeger, on the other hand, establishes a radical separation (and, by the very fact, an abstract and conceptual one) between Being and the datum, between the ontological and the ontic, between philosophy and positive science, thus eliminating any idea of progress and regression. He, too, arrives in the end at a philosophy of history, but it is an abstract philosophy with two dimensions, the authentic and the inauthentic, openness to Being and oblivion of Being.

So, although Girard's terminology is Heideggerian in origin, the introduction of the catogories of progress and regression brings him closer to Lukács.

5 While ever exchange remains *sporadic* because it bears solely on surpluses or because it has the character of an exchange of use-values that individuals or groups cannot produce within an essentially natural economy, the mental structure of mediation does not appear or remains secondary. The fundamental transformation in the development of reification results from the advent of *market production.*

6 I speak of a 'consciousness-reflection' when the content of this consciousness and the set of relations between the different elements of the content (what I call its structure) undergo the action of certain other domains of the social life, without acting in turn on them. In practice, this situation has probably never been reached in capitalist society. This society creates, however, a tendency to the rapid and gradual diminution of the action of consciousness on the economic life and, conversely, to a continual increase of the action of the economic sector of the social life on the content and structure of consciousness.

7 There arises a problem here that is difficult to solve at the moment, but which might one day be solved by concrete sociological research. I mean the problem of the collective, affective, non-conceptualized 'sound-box' that made possible the development of the novel form.

Initially, I thought that reification, while tending to dissolve and to integrate in the overall society different partial groups, and, therefore, to deprive them to a certain extent of their specificity, had a character so contrary to both the biological and psychological reality of the individual human being that it could not fail to engender in *all* individual human beings, to a greater or lesser degree, reactions of opposition (or, if this reification becomes degraded in a qualitatively more advanced way, to reactions of evasion), thus creating a diffuse resistance to the reified world, a resistance that would constitute the background of fictional creation.

Later, however, it seemed to me that this hypothesis contained an unproved a priori supposition: that of the existence of a biological nature whose external manifestations could not be entirely denatured by social reality.

In fact, it is just as likely that resistances, even affective ones, to reification are circumscribed within certain particular social strata, which positive research ought to delimit.

8 Lukács characterized the time of the traditional novel by the proposition: 'We have started on our way, our journey is over.' One might characterize the new novel by the suppression of the first half of this statement. Its time might be characterized by the statement: 'The aspiration is there, but the journey is over' (Kafka, Nathalie Sarraute), or simply by the observation that 'the journey is already over, though we never started on our way' (Robbe-Grillet's first three novels).

9 A year ago, when dealing with the same problems and mentioning the existence of the novel with a problematic hero and of a fictional sub-literature with a positive hero, I wrote, 'Lastly, I shall conclude this article with a great question mark, that of the sociological study of the works of Balzac. These works, it seems to me,

constitute a novel form of their own, one that integrates important elements belonging to the two types of novels that I have mentioned and probably represents the most important form of fictional expression in history.'

The remarks formulated in these pages are an attempt to develop in greater detail the hypothesis hinted at in these lines.

15 Jean-Paul Sartre
The Objective Spirit (1972)*

Jean-Paul Sartre (1905–80) embodied a conception of the *philosophe* for which writing and literature are agents of liberation and enlightenment. Founding the socialist journal *Les Temps Modernes* after the war, his engaged approach to writing and human freedom was announced in *What is Literature?* (1948; trans. 1950). (See Adorno's critique in 'Commitment'.) The integrity and urgency of Sartre's engagement as a public intellectual, rejecting both bourgeois consensus and avant-garde isolation, necessitated his engagement with Marxism. He moved from an existentialist and socialist critique of the Stalinism of the French Communist Party to a mode of Marxism consolidated in his *Critique of Dialectical Reason* (1960; trans. 1976). Sartre wrote a number of influential essays, collected in *Situations*: such as 'Orphée Noir', his tribute to the poets of *négritude*, and his polemical introduction to Fanon's *The Wretched of the Earth*. The shift to Marxism can be traced in Sartre's three principal literary-critical studies: *Baudelaire* (1947); *Saint Genet* (1952; trans. 1963); and *The Family Idiot* (1971–2; trans. 1993). Of these, only *The Family Idiot*, a voluminous study of Gustave Flaubert, is recognizably Marxist, and it represents his most sustained contribution to Marxist literary theory. 'The Objective Spirit' – the pivotal chapter from this work – attempts to theorize the complex mediations between the lived experience of Flaubert as a writer, the objective malaise of literature and the material conditions of class consciousness and ideology. Helpful discussions of Sartre are provided by F. Jameson, *Marxism and Form* (1971); I. Mészáros, *The Work of Sartre* (1979); R. Aronson, *Jean-Paul Sartre* (1980); and H. E. Barnes, *Sartre and Flaubert* (1981).

Let us avoid any misunderstanding. At the beginning of the twentieth century, the long literary dream that began with Gustave at age 20 was completed with the last of the Symbolists. At that moment many young writers who wanted to preserve the heritage of the preceding generation and go beyond it toward a new classicism, influenced by the strange attitude of their fathers and older brothers, decided that neurosis was the necessary condition for genius, as Gide wrote of Dostoevsky. But this post–Symbolist generation was judging

* From Jean-Paul Sartre, *The Family Idiot: Gustave Flaubert, 1821–1857*, trans. Carol Cosman, 5 vols (Chicago and London: Chicago University Press, 1981–93), vol. 5 (1993), 33–56.

conditions necessary to the work of art according to those art demanded of their immediate predecessors. In this sense they were attesting to the fact that between 1850 and the end of the century you had to be mad to write. Quite true: their ideas only confirm my own. Only I cannot accept their *generalizing*, as if the meaning and function of literature – for the individual and society – were not constantly changing in the course of history; as if, depending on the period, art did not recruit its artists according to different criteria. It *is* true that from 1830 on, for reasons I shall enumerate, some of which are still valid today if less virulent, neurosis was the royal road to the masterpiece. But this doesn't seem to me to have been the case in the eighteenth century, and even less so in the seventeenth. In those times the author was chiefly required to be a 'respectable man', integrated into the society as long as he strictly observed certain rules. In this case, neurosis can exist – it does in Rousseau,[1] who may even have been psychotic, and probably in Pascal – but it is utilized *indirectly*, the writer writes *against his illness*, in spite of it, as Rousseau did, and not by virtue of it. In other authors it is certainly harmful: without it they would have done better or done more. In still other cases it takes its toll in different areas and so spares the literary realm. Every man, of course, is a totalization that is temporalized, and nothing can happen to him that does not affect him, one way or another, in all his parts. The point is that in integrated societies the psychoneurotic element, if it exists, is never regarded as the artist's aim, and even less as the reason for his art. I have said elsewhere that genius is a way out, the only one left when all is lost. I say so again, specifying that this way out is not neurotic and usually even allows one to spare oneself a neurosis. In a word, when literature does not appeal to psychopathology, neurotic accidents do not take place, or, if they are produced in an author, this fact – of prime importance for understanding the individual – is annulled in the Objective Spirit because it is a matter of chance, a non-meaning in relation to the meaning of that cultural moment. And although the substitution of one form for another is made *by men* and motivated by discomfort (there is a contradiction between the earlier form and content that asks to be treated in the present), there is no reason why this discomfort, which is of a specifically cultural order, should be experienced *neurotically, unless* the particular structures of the historical moment require it.

And this is precisely what happens around 1850, a moment in which the condition for creating art is to be neurotic.[2] Not in just any way but in a specific way, which we shall attempt to define; the objective movement that transforms culture on the basis of deeper transformations – but also as a function of traditions and laws proper to the cultural sector – produces such strict and contradictory norms that the contemporary moment of art cannot be realized as a determination of the Objective Spirit except in the form of *art-neurosis*. This does not mean that the works will be neurotic but that literary doctrines and the 'poetic arts' will be, and that artists will have to act, or actually be, neurotic. And because of the dual nature of the literary act, reading, while it is taking place, becomes the public's brief, induced neurosis.

This cannot be understood without several general clarifications regarding the Objective Spirit. We may well wonder if it isn't dangerous to preserve this suspect notion still bearing traces of its origins in Hegelian idealism. But there is some use in reviving it and indicating the instrumental function it can perform in the perspective of historical materialism. In fact, the Objective Spirit – in a defined society, in a given era – is nothing more than culture as practico-inert. Let us understand, first of all, that at the origin of culture is work, *lived, actual* work in so far as it surpasses and retains nature in itself by definition. Nature is the given environment during a specific period, and work reveals this environment as simultaneously that which presently exists *and* the field of possibles that can be made use of to give that environment a new being consonant with the goal fixed by the worker, in short, with a certain condition, called the environment, that does not yet exist. Thus work is by itself antiphysis; its definition is to be antinature nature, which is precisely the essence of every cultural phenomenon. It seeks knowledge in order to transform, which implies, elementary as the work might be, that for the worker it bears witness to a type of exploitation, to a regime and the class struggle, ultimately to an ideology. And for the worker himself immersed in this exploitation, work itself redounds upon him as an enemy force; being praxis, hence an illuminating surpassing of being toward an end (a surpassing of raw material toward the production of a change within the practical field), work is the internalization of the external and the re-externalization of the internal. As such, it is lived experience and consequently reveals both itself – as imposed, for example, and remaining external even while internalized – and, through it, the fundamental human relations proper to this mode of production (the kind of reciprocity established on the level of its concrete labour, the kind of non-reciprocity generated by the division of labour and possibly by the resulting exploitation). Moreover, this work is accomplished by means of an instrument – that would alone suffice to define society and man's relation to nature, at once antiphysis (which appears on the level of carved stone) and nature (appearing beyond antiphysis on the level of carved stone) and nature appearing beyond antiphysis and in it (even at the level of automation) as its internal and external limit, continually displaced. By the use he makes of it, the instrument therefore becomes the worker's *organ of perception*: it reveals the world and man in the world. Thus the most elementary praxis, in so far as it is actual and lived from the inside, already contains as an immediate condition of its later development and as a real moment of that development, *in the living state*, an intuitive, implicit and *non-verbal* knowledge, a certain direct and totalizing yet wordless understanding of contemporary man among men and in the world, hence an immediate grasp of the inhumanity of man and his subhumanity, the first seed of a *political* attitude of refusal. On this level all thought is given, but it is not posed for itself, and so in its extreme compression it escapes verbal elaboration. I have said enough about it, however, to make it clear that superstructures are not the site of this revealing but merely the upper levels of elaboration in which this practico-theoretical knowledge is isolated, posed for itself, and systematically made explicit, hence becoming theoretico-practical. Here we must take reflection as a starting-point, for reflection shapes lived experience according to its own ends, though that experience is originally unreflected and becomes reflected according to certain rules that themselves issue from certain reflexive needs. In other words, in the totality of praxis reflection isolates the moment of theory, which has never existed alone but only as a practical mediation determined by the end itself. Recourse to language thus becomes necessary. And language, on the one hand, isolates and transforms into a finished product the knowledge that existed implicitly in the worker's act. It provides names and hardens in the form of defined structures all the elements that have interpenetrated in the cultural revealing of work (mode of production, relations of production, institutional whole, mores, law, etc.). Named and thus perpetuated, these fragments of the real becoming fragments of knowledge are thereby falsified. Through this quality of false knowledge they come close to being a non-knowledge, which also exists on the elementary level of the living actualization of praxis – that set of opinions arising from pathos that are proffered, at this higher degree of elaboration, as learning from experience. In fact, these extrapolations are inseparable from lived experience, and they form, if you will, class subjectivity. After processing they will become the clearest of what we call ideologies. Thus, alongside false knowledge, whose origin is a practical and non-verbalized knowledge, ideologies that impose themselves on the worker – ideologies of his class, of the middle or ruling classes – are introduced or reintroduced into him in the form of recipes explicitly presented as a verbal exposé or a related set of determinations of discourse that would illuminate his condition and offer him the means to tolerate it. This involves chiefly, of course, a conception of the world and of men formed by the ruling class in taking possession of its environment through the systematic exercise of power, and inculcated – by familiar means – in the working classes as though it were a universal ideology, or a body of knowledge. In the worker, of course, these ideologies come into permanent conflict with *his own* ideology – which issues communally, like a myth, from his hopes, his despairs, the refusal to accept his condition as an inevitable destiny – and they have the upper hand as long as working-class ideology is not *verbalized*. Were it to be so, moreover, it might encourage a sudden awareness but might just as easily retard it: class consciousness appears only at the end of a theoretico-practical effort that aims at dissolving ideology into knowledge as much as possible. I will merely cite as an example the slow emancipation of the worker in the nineteenth century. Between 1830 and 1840, his ideas were so effectively confused that *L'Atelier*, the first proletarian newspaper, insisted on Catholicism, or at least Theism, in face of the Jacobin bourgeoisie who had deprived the worker of the consolation of God. He set his knowledge in the practical realm against alien ideologies – as did the Canuts in Lyon; when wages were lowered, he rebelled. But as soon as the revolt was either victorious or suppressed, he could think explicitly about this knowledge only through alien ideologies, words and phrases that did not apply to it – quite to the contrary – and that distorted it while claiming to articulate it.

Thus, elaborated ideologies are quite distinct from that intuitive and immediate constellation I have just described, which involves an implicit ideology spun around a kernel of knowledge, accompanied by myths and a system of values tacitly applied by agents who have never articulated its basis. Not only are these elaborated ideologies distinct from it but they are in conflict with it by providing immediate and non-verbalized thought with translations that conceal it from itself. Yet it will be observed that the force of these inadequate systems comes from their inertia. Primitive and immediate thought is none other than the practical behaviour of the worker in so far as it discloses in order to effect change and is necessarily accompanied by a non-positional consciousness of itself; this presupposes a constant 'syntony' of that tacit body and the real, whence its perpetual flexibility. It must exist as an act and as part of an act, or it does not exist at all. In other words, it issues from work and vanishes with it. On the other hand, *verbalized* value systems and ideologies remain in the mind, or at the very least in the memory, because language is matter and because their elaboration has given them material inertia. Written words are stones. Learning them, internalizing their combinations, we introduce into ourselves a mineralized thought that will subsist in us by virtue of its very minerality, until such time as some kind of material labour, acting on it from outside, might come to relieve us of it. I call these irreducible passivities *as a whole* the Objective Spirit. And this definition has no negative intent, no voluntary deprecation. In a society of exploitation, of course, these structured wholes are harmful to the exploited classes to the extent that they are introduced into everyone from the outside and recast in the memory as ramparts against any sudden awareness. But taken in themselves they simply manifest this necessity: matter is the mediating element between men to the same degree that through their praxis they become mediators between different states of matter. The Objective Spirit is culture itself but only in accordance with its becoming the practico-inert. That is valid for all its aspects, as much for the mode of production, defined by that particular wrought matter which is the instrument, as for relations between men as they are established as institutions and become lived institutionally. And the relational mode of wrought matter to the agent is, as I have proved elsewhere, imperative. Every object produced presents to me its directions for use as an order ('Shake contents before using', 'Slow, school zone', etc.). We understand that even if, as frequently happens, the sponsor of the object in question finds his interest in the imperative form – which guarantees the proper usage of the thing – he is not the source of that form. Strictly speaking, he can present his advice only in the form of a hypothetical imperative, such as: 'If you want to use this object, you must . . .', and so forth. For the real relation between men is actually reciprocity, which excludes orders. But whatever the object produced – even a machine – the utilization that Society or any such group recommends by way of it necessarily passes *through* and consequently undergoes the transformation imposed on it by the practico-inert. Its directions for use become an inert discourse participating in the inertia of matter. As such it imposes itself on the agent as *not to be* modified by any subjective intention – not because it represents the universal in the face of the particular, but because the practical seal imposed on the raw material participates in its materiality and is introduced into everyone as an inert thought that belongs to no one but must be preserved, whose practical consequences must be derived and applied on pain of seeing the practical thing burst out. In the internal structure of this thought, in any case, we encounter material inertia (for example, in a particular and mechanical relation between premises and consequences). In sum, it represents at once the beyond of matter here present and a kind of materialization of that beyond. And if there have always been men to give orders, they should rather be considered transmitters. Besides, the 'master' who commands, and usurps the inorganic minerality of the commandments given by the object, clearly plays an inorganic role in relation to the slave, and his orders obviously issue from a stone mouth, his own. Indeed, he commands as a function of his mineral being, of his interest, which is something imperative, and he augments its status as thing by depositing it into that other thing, discourse. In our view, the Objective Spirit represents culture as practico-inert, as the totality to this day (in any day) of the imperatives imposed on man by any given society.

But for our purpose, which is to study art-neurosis as an historically specific determination of the Objective Spirit, it is preferable to imagine only a sector of that spirit: the elaborated unity of ideologies, cosmogonies, ethico-aesthetic and confessional systems as they manifest themselves as the structuring of a discourse. We have no reason to consider them in themselves, as ideas that are institutionalized, but should consider them rather as they pose to language the question of their adequate expression, and thereby define literature in the abstract as a work of material production. We are at the top of a hierarchy, and thoughts seem almost dead. But they are merely exhausted along the way: they are neither reflections nor by-products of an infrastructural, unthinking reality but must simply be seen as the last avatars of total ideas, mute and practical, that are merely one at the outset with the act of work, of appropriation and exploitation, or a hundred other acts. This explosive combination of values, verities ideologies, myths and mystifications, contradicting each other in so far as they emanate from classes and – within classes – from different social strata, none the less poses itself as a multiple and contradictory comprehension of our species as the product of its history, of present circumstances, and of the future that it is preparing for itself 'on the basis of prior circumstances'. Enclosed in writing, it has become canned thought. But written language, by lending its material and institutional reality to those 'expressible' thoughts, has bent them to its laws. Intellection – and likewise comprehension – is surely a synthetic surpassing of signifying materiality toward signification. None the less, that surpassed matter is preserved in the act that transcends it, and it both limits and determines that act in spite of itself. Materialized in writing, culture – at this level – burdens thought with its own weight and does not derive its permanencies from a firm and sustained but still lively intention; quite to the contrary, they are the passive aspect of the idea. I am speaking, of course, of the written thing, and I am well aware that no judgement on it is ever definitive. Posterity will return to it and situate itself by situating it in new circumstances. Still, certain internal articulations, certain structures – manifest or implicit – are unvarying. Consequently, living thought as a surpassing is at once aroused, advanced and retarded by that opacity to be surpassed which is precisely the idea as written, 'thing-a-fied'. Indeed, this written idea has set its seal upon matter, but matter has in turn invaded the idea-seal, infected it with its heteronomy, better known as the principle of exteriority. It has broken the interiority of the original thought – a translucid presence of the all in the parts and the parts in the all – and substituted the *letter* in its place by penetrating even its minutest aspect with an external scattering. The idea becomes a thing: once imprinted, its tendency to persevere in its being is precisely that of the thing. When the library is deserted, thought dies; the thing alone remains, made of paper and ink.

Writing operates on a dual principle: one person writes, the other reads. Without the reader, nothing is left, not even signs – for their only function is to guide the project of transcendence. We might almost speak of an abstract virtuality, which does not come from the book itself but determines it from the outside in so far as it becomes the object of various intentions: of the librarian who arranges a catalogue, or of future readers who promise themselves that 'one day' they will read or reread the work. These considerations lead us to several conclusions.

1 *The Objective Spirit* while *never* on the side of pure lived experience and free thought, exists *as an act* only through the activity of men and, more precisely, through the activity of individuals. As far as we are concerned, it is clear that without readers it simply would not exist. On the other hand, in the intimacy of a room, in classrooms or libraries, millions of people read millions of books, each of which contains references to other works not consulted at

that moment. A detotalized totalization is thereby effected; each reader totalizes his reading in his own way, which is at once similar to and radically distinct from the totalization that another reader, in another town, another neighborhood, tries to realize with the same book. From this point of view, the multiplicity of individual totalizations (they are not all related to the same book but to different sectors of written knowledge, many implicitly referring to each other) seems irreducible. It would take too long to explain here how, despite the apparent atomization, this set of circumstances continually effects an exhaustive totalization without a totalizer. My point is, rather, that following generations will make today's lived present into a totality that is past, surpassed, still virulent in certain ways, and readers, individually or as a group, vaguely sense this. So they feel they must work their particular synthesis of one detail of a sector of knowledge in the stable and inherently dated milieu of accomplished totality. And this totality – as it appears to them, an invisible unity of the diverse, a transcendence that destroys their present immanence, a future that eradicates experience in men's hearts as it is being lived in the name of experience to be lived by future readers – represents for each of them the totalitarian objectivization of each one's particular efforts of acculturation. In this future objectivization, whose meaning is still unknown and which, as such, is aspired to only through empty intentions, they find their ineffable objective unity: it makes them, for themselves, representatives of the times. But as their praxis at this moment is reading – an effort, indeed, of acculturation – these living times that have already been fixed and described appear to them in their cultural aspect (the limits of knowledge, unresolved problems, areas of ignorance, established convictions to be revoked by the future). Seen from another angle, this is precisely the Objective Spirit of the age, an imperative constellation, unlimited but finite, whose thought cannot yet emerge.

2   However, although a gaze is needed to restore it by making it readable today, the Objective Spirit is characterized on this level by its position *outside*, not the present product of an effort of thought but first and foremost in books, in the writings of others. In this sense its materiality expresses at once its alterity (in relation to the reader) and its pastness (it bears a date, *it may already be dated*; recent works may be better informed, it may be challenged six months from now by works as yet unpublished). In any event, reading is an attempt to transform a thing into an idea. The eye must recover the ideative act of the other through its vestiges, gather up the scattering of signs, and discursively *recompose* according to learned codes what may formerly have been the object of flashes of intuition. Our concern, for the moment, is with the double character of the Objective Spirit, which can be a surpassing toward the idea *in us* only if it is *outside*, as worked matter. The guarantee of its permanence is its status as thing: it does not exist, it *is*, and the only dangers

threatening it come from outside, from great natural forces and social disorders. And when I transform the thing into an idea by reading, the metamorphosis is never complete; it is an idea-thing penetrating me because the reality of that hybrid being which I alone can revive is necessarily outside me as thought frozen in matter, and because that thought, even as I make it mine, remains definitively *other*, thought surpassed by another who orders me to revive it. Furthermore, the idea I appropriate is also, I know, appropriated by other readers at the same time; these are people I don't know, who are not like me, and who surpass the same material toward similar but perceptibly different significations. Thus every lexeme remains *within me* external to me to the extent that I perceive it as enriched by a thousand interpretations that escape me; the book, a finite mode of the Objective Spirit, appears both internal and external in relation to the reader. Reading is an internalization according to definite procedures, but the sentence is never entirely soluble. Its indestructible materiality derives at once from the frozen rigidity of the vestige and from its multiple relation – for every reader – to others. In other words, its *virtual* extension to a whole public and its current connections with series of readers or groups, or the two together. In this sense, writing gives us a glimpse of society as one of the elements of its essential duality. Or, if you will, the exteriority of writing makes it appear to every reader as a social object. This, indeed, is what it is. If apprehended in its relations to the seriality of readings, it seems to be a collective, a real index of social detotalization. Through it we measure the separation of individuals in an envisaged society; its mystery represents the false union of readers, each of whom is unaware of the other's thoughts. In our societies this may be the result of the creation of mass culture; in this case, as the words penetrate the person reading, that person internalizes his own solitude in the face of an impenetrable block of exigent sociality, without considering that this sociality is nothing but the detotalization of a collectivity as lived socially by each of its members. In short, the social opacity of the book and its institutional character refer quite simply to an indefinite number of other solitudes. In this way, the book as *collective* is, in a sense, a *sacred* object; its 'numinous' character is manifest most clearly when we imagine it in its occasional relations with uniformed people who read very little. When they approach a work – recommended by others whom they trust – they treat the text as if it were composed of *carmina sacra*, according it the same respect. In effect, they are dimly if inarticulately aware that by absorbing those little pointed black splinters we call words, they are about to swallow society whole. But they also know that it will remain *outside* as the collective character of the book, even as they are trying to install in themselves the content of the work as knowledge. Thus, through its exteriority the duality becomes a trinity: the relation reader–author refers to the usually serial relation among readers. The profundity of an *idea* I have *read*, as I have retained and understood it, *is others*: those significations that I have not grasped but that I know to have been awakened by the gaze of others as *underlying structures* of the legible object. Profundity is therefore an abstraction that haunts me, especially if I know and lament the gaps in my education, and it is an intention that misses its mark in so far as it escapes me in certain respects. It is a way of isolating myself with respect to society grasped through its culture, moreover, this abstract but present profundity defining the work in its objectivity comes to me as an imperative: I *must* understand what the author wanted to say as best I can, and in its totality, to the extent that others have exalted the meaning of the work and made those ideas-things incandescent. Obviously I will not complete this task – I know that well enough, and how far I get depends on my education, my greater or lesser degree of familiarity with abstractions, the time I have at my disposal, etc. But the imperative is to push as far as I can, to become integrated with new social strata; when I can go no further, the mysterious residue represents the unfathomable, indefinite social realm, or, more precisely, seriality.

If the work refers to a group – and it must be a sworn group – the imperatives are much more rigorous. For a young communist, the *Manifesto* of 1848 is at once the work of Marx, an objective description of reality, and the theory-practice that creates the unity of the Party to which he has just given his allegiance. The individual aspect of the work, its relation to the dead author, tends to be effaced (as does the relation of Carnot's principle, or some other discovery in the natural sciences, to the living man who invented it). On the other hand, the second characteristic is sustained and exalted by the third: the *processes* articulated by Marx and Engels, the events presented and illuminated by the class struggle, are not purely and simply facts for this neophyte. They are *also* facts and perhaps *primarily* facts, as we have just seen, in so far as knowledge absorbs such thinkers and eliminates them, but they are also what he *must* understand to realize a total integration with the group; and furthermore they are practical considerations which *must* illuminate his understanding of the current politics of his Party and his individual tasks. The book is structured as a collective to the extent that any group is necessarily penetrated by seriality (it may be that students or young workers meet regularly to read the book and discuss it. Only *this evening* the young man has gone to his room and reads without friends or witnesses). But while this ambiguous structure reminds the isolated reader *in this fashion* of his present solitude, it defines it not as a real and permanent state but as both a product of bourgeois society (therefore as a yoke to be thrown off) and a danger: all alone, I have no one to stop me from making a mistake. I must try to read as if I were *everyone together*. It is my vow – my commitment to the Party – that determines my reading; the book restores the group as the normative determination of my activities.

All these remarks, of course, derive from the fact that the work, something inert, continues to *be-there* passively, the way an object in motion continues to move indefinitely if nothing comes along to stop it. And the work presents itself to everyone in the name of that inertia as having existed before the current act of reading, existing elsewhere, in other libraries, and living on after the present reading. The book, whatever it is, and whether it conveys fact or fiction, virtually gives us the assertoric itself in the imperative form. Indeed, I distinguish two imperatives: the first – crude, obscure and solitary – is linked to seriality. We *must* read the Goncourts because everyone reads them and we should be able to discuss them; so we also *must* understand and judge them. The second imperative, which refers to the platoon and its unity, is the imperative of freedom – at least in principle. But in both we see that comprehension is not defined in each reader by the free play of his possibilities and the quiet recognition of their limits; rather it is required, and when at the end of his resources the reader halts midway, he feels guilty and regards his limits not as factual givens (linked to the empirical conditions of his intellectual development) but as a moral fault and a premeditated failure (in the past he *could* have learned more, even today he *should have been able* to concentrate more, to ask more of his intelligence – and of course none of this is true). In other words, when human intentions are addressed to us through worked matter, materiality renders them *other*; inert but indelible, they designate us as *other* than ourselves and our fellow citizens. Human reciprocity is broken by the mediation of the thing, and the frozen intention that summoned us *as others* can have only the structure of obligation. Thus the Objective Spirit – which is culture as practico-inert – can address itself to us, even in literature, only as an imperative. This is its very constitution, and it cannot be changed, even if we accomplish the task of intellection or comprehension prescribed to us, because of the indestructible residue of materiality that remains in us after reading, and which we apprehend as a failure or an unjustifiable halt in our mental operations. The Objective Spirit reveals our finitude and compels us to regard it as a fault.

These remarks, of course, are not meant to restore reading – or the transformation of the thing-idea into an idea-thing – into its plenitude. The syntheses of recomposition are in fact accomplished according to objective rules (the structures of language, the author's explicit and implicit intentions, the judgements on the author made by other authors we have already read, etc.) *and*, simultaneously, according to the idiosyncratic *habitus* of a singular internalization (oneirism, resonances, bad faith, ideological interests, etc.). As a result, the work, apprehended by a developed – at least partially closed – individuality, is never entirely taken for what it is; it is read in the light of the historical moment and of the cultural means at the reader's disposal (which indeed rank him in one social stratum or another); and at the same time the act of reading serves as a pretext for each reader to relive his own history and perhaps the primal scene. Be that as it may, under this subjective camouflage the skeleton of imperatives remains, directing the readerly thoughts as much as and more than they seem guided by the reader's oneiric (and purely factual) compliance.

3   This would be of little importance if, in the sector concerning us, the Objective Spirit as it is fundamentally materialized did not manifest itself to readers as the disparate contiguity of works belonging to all social categories and all periods. As soon as this atemporal juxtaposition is internalized and realized in me, it becomes explosive. I may have chosen *these* books and tried to digest them to satisfy my singular needs; as a systematic resurrection, reading constitutes me as the objective mediation between the cultural past and present, and between different conceptions to which contemporary works appeal. By awakening meanings through a totalizing movement whose source is my personal unity, I provoke collisions of ideas and feelings, and by lending them my time and my life I exalt and exacerbate innumerable contradictions. Now, given our earlier descriptions, we already know that these contradictions are written in stone: they are rooted in the inertia of thesis and antithesis. They coexist outside me in the pure, non-signifying being-there of the thing; internalized, they are revealed through my subjectivity, but still retain the rigidity that characterizes them on the outside. We are not, in effect, dealing with a flexible and fluctuating confrontation with an idea, which in a practical totalization would set the all against the part and the parts against each other. There is no whole; only disjunctures, contradictory theses, whose authors were often unaware they contradicted each other since they were unacquainted. Thus the oppositions are at once rigid and without real consistency, not having been generated by a rigorous totalization. The operation proposed to the reader here is the reverse: he must totalize and surpass toward a synthesis starting from those given contradictions revealed in contingency. I say he *must* totalize because, as we have seen, every idea of the Objective Spirit imposes itself as a demand as soon as it is invoked. Furthermore, when two ideas-demands are manifest at the same time in a reading, these contrary imperatives imply a third imperative: to reconcile or transcend toward a synthesis, to integrate these notions gleaned somewhat at random into the organic unity of a totalization that produces and surpasses them, and will itself be an imperative. Thus the Objective Spirit, an external-internal reality whose source – as far as we are now concerned – is the dual aspect of writing, is characterized both as a sum of inert demands and as a supreme, ubiquitous imperative that summons the reader to dissolve contradictions in the unity of an ongoing totalization. I say 'ongoing' because the Objective Spirit renews itself: every day it is enriched by new books, new demands. And these new writings can very well become integrated into one or another personal totalization effected by readers. But they can also set themselves against any such a totalization. In this case, everyone must get back to work again and break the determinations (the negations, the limits) of his totalization with respect to

the new work and its silent demand, so it can be included. And as the number of books published each day far surpasses the individual possibility of totalizing written culture, the perpetual addition of new material has the effect of preventing the totalization from closing in on itself and being transformed into a tranquil totality. This is what we will call the life of the Objective Spirit, a material detotalization internalized as a demand to be totalized which contradicts that dream of stone, totality in inertia, by the constant and nullifying appearance of new productions. The Objective Spirit of an age[3] is at once the sum of works published during a specific period and the multiplicity of totalizations effected by contemporary readers. As we know, thoughts are living things. They are born of original thought, which is merely practical behaviour as it reveals the environment from the totalizing perspective of its reorganization. When thoughts are in libraries, they are petrified by writing and therefore dead. The reader recomposes them, yet he does not reach the profound and naked life of the root-thought; the *lived* reality he confers by internalizing them cannot be a return to thought before writing: it assumes the written word and can merely animate the graphemes by binding them together in an interior synthesis. In this sense he is still distancing himself from primal spontaneity; his own personal, practical field is not defined by needs and physical dangers but is composed of books and words, and his work is the perpetual stirring up and reorganization of this field on command. Yet his practical thoughts are indeed spontaneous in that they represent his conscious behaviour (reflexive or unreflected) as a reader. Hence, whatever the content of the Objective Spirit as canned thoughts, we can say that every cultivated reader formally intuits it – totalizing it in the abstract in so far as that intuition simply illuminates the multiple aspects of reading.

Awakened significations do not demand only to be understood or even totalized: these engraved signs refer to the universe, to our being-in-the-world, and primarily to our conduct. We are led back to the real environment, full of surprising traps, that we left behind upon entering the library. Knowledge and ideas are – more or less directly – practical; so it is through our personal praxis that we must try to accomplish this veritable totalization demanded by books (through techniques, ethics, religions, etc.). Action, being the totalizing of doctrines, thus transforms us; we become representatives of a past or future group that we intuit behind the imposed practico-inert idea, or a group we will form by winning it over to our practical totalization. For the Objective Spirit tells us, contradictorily but imperatively, who we are: in other words, what we have to do.

We are chiefly concerned, however, with a category of specialized readers who read in order to write. In them, literature plays the role of recruiting officer. No doubt their choice to become writers represents a subjective way out of their difficulties and problems. We have seen this in Flaubert's case.

But just as you can become a shoemaker for accidental reasons and through particular events, and those reasons and events do not alter the objective need to know how to repair shoes according to current techniques and use an awl properly so every reader who reads in order to write will discover literature as it is in his time even before deciding to be an apprentice author. In short, none of them, in any age, invented or reinvented literature. We might say that it is reinvented in them as an obligation to write from the starting-point of literature already written. In every historical society in which an individual decides to be a writer – whatever the outcome – literature is given to him primarily as a totality he chooses to enter. This totality, of course, is not given to him in all its details, by which I mean in all works of literature; quite the contrary, the individual's approach to the All is variable. We have Flaubert's totality, Proust's – which might be called 'highly literate' – as well as that of the young shepherd whose writings were published by *Les Temps modernes*, who had read only almanacs, newspapers, and a few books by Victor Hugo. Yet none of them *invented* literature for his own ends. It existed, and each of those would-be writers, according to certain features of what I call literature-already-written, deemed it advisable to enter an apprenticeship and become a representative of literature-to-be-written. So literature seems to be a practical activity and manifests itself by the existing results of that activity, literary works, which the aspiring writer reads differently than a simple reader, in order to discover through inspection of the finished product the rules that aided its production and which he wants to know for his own use.

The difficulties he encounters are therefore of several kinds.

a) He reads each properly literary work as an All that defines literary activity. And as his major project is to write and the work read is a piece of writing, that writing becomes an obscure organization of imperatives he must assimilate that will provide him with rules. Early in his apprenticeship he does not envisage originality, or rather he conceives it as the production of a new work according to the old rules. For in some obscure way he feels new, of a new generation conditioned by the more or less profound changes of the society into which he was born. He imagines, therefore, that he will be original in any event through the new content he will give his books, for in them he will speak, according to tried and true methods, of new matters revealed to him by this set of circumstances. None of this is clear to him, but perhaps if he can treat a subject particular to *his time* by applying authorized rules, he will write a universal and singular book. Singular in its subject; universal in its formulas. In other words, conditioned by his prehistory and his protohistory he is in contradiction with the general rules of his profession (or the prevailing way of life), yet the imperatives engendered by the practico-inert are not diminished, and he fails to realize that his personality is no longer quite syntonic with past methods. The contradiction, moreover, varies according to periods and persons: in some it is veiled; in others it is visibly explosive. This problem, in short, recapitulates the generational struggle.

Thus, whatever the subjective motivations of the choice, *written* literature – that determination of the Objective Spirit – must be considered in every case the objective reason for the choice to write, for its continuation through other pens.

b) When reading is done *with* the intention of writing, it is prospective. Seeking and revealing in the narrative itself the norms that led the author to produce the work being read, it presents them to the future man of letters as aesthetic requirements and at the same time as formulas he will later apply. But more importantly, that conception of art read between the lines or sometimes clearly articulated by the author determines the adolescent in his future being, revealing to him and imposing on him a certain status. It defines the public to whom he must address himself, the kind of relationship he will have with it; and by so doing it classifies him, assigns him a rank in society, defines his powers. In this conception, literature defines its subject; not only does it sketch out themes he will have to develop, but by this very choice it orients his subjectivity, dictating feelings, emotions he will cultivate in particular, determining whether he must establish the predominance of reason over affect or, to the contrary, throw himself into passion, subject the reasons of reason to the reasons of the heart. A book read from the perspective of writing another book paints a portrait of the future artist which is none other than that of a dead author becoming the young reader's major imperative and his destiny. A few biographical details will do the rest; their very inertia will serve as a prophecy, surpassed, preserved, and surpassed again. Indeed, in this realm of the Objective Spirit the life of a writer is a book or a chapter, printed matter. It is set in words that perpetuate it, lending it with their material passivity a perennial quality that makes it both a particular affirmed essence – which its inert permanence tears away from that author's first affirmation and transports, moment by moment, as pure matter in itself – and an exemplary existence, a model to be imitated, through the reading of an adolescent who wants to write. It is not surprising that literature presents itself to the young reader who awakens it as form and content, a subject to be treated, a way and style of life, finally as the underlying determination of his idiosyncrasy – the all in the form of an imperative. It appears as a totality in any era we single out; economic, social and political conditions – historical circumstances – assign to the writer in one fell swoop his subject, his level of life, his place in society. These different features are together symbolic, and by *articulating each other* they reveal the place that a given community assigns to writing – its status and meaning, or, if you will, its public. It is, in fact, crucial whether the literary thing addresses itself to certain people or to everyone, to one class or another; this relation to the public is a fundamental given on the basis of which we can establish *what there is to say*, and *why*, and *by whom*. Thus through a literary work, whatever it is, the young reader grasps as his future a global and past reality he *must* restore. Naturally, this apprehension of the Other as a future self to be engendered often remains obscure – unless the author being read took care to articulate his poetic art; norms exist, they are guessed, but only through a vague intuition, opening the door to the apprentice-writer's phantasms and also his mistakes. Be that as it may, things will gradually become clear; it doesn't take long for an adolescent, especially if he continues his higher education, to grasp classical *order* as an irreducible whole (the social order, the order of life, the order of creation), and to detect in the 'century of Louis XV', beneath an apparent disorder, the writer's vigorous struggle against the powers that be – which implies a change of public and determines a new kind of life.

c) Everything would be fine if the function of literature were not in a constant state of flux, often from one generation to the next, as a function of the continual transformations of our historic societies. In the feudal centuries, despite extreme diversity in production, certain constants may be observed to which the reader could refer for his own peace of mind. For Ronsard and Racine, for example, the notion of glory is the same: the eternity of the work and the poet remain explicitly linked to the permanence of the monarchy. Only later does one write for the 'happy few' of the future, or hope to 'win on appeal'; the classical poets, like those of the Pleiad, mean to win glory in their lifetime, by the king's grace. The sovereigns succeeding him need merely take up his literary choices along with his sceptre and all his other attributes, for these are a dead man's final wishes and worthy of respect.

From the beginning of the eighteenth century, however, history accelerates; the public is continually transformed – generally growing but sometimes strangely retracting – and after the execution of Louis XVI, kings are an uncertain guarantee. In other words, the inert contiguity of books in libraries masks the upheaval that revolutions effected in all domains, and consequently in the written thing, which is merely the indirect projection of living culture in the practico-inert of writing. Doctrines succeed one another: they merely express the brutal transformations of the objective place and function which those societies in a permanent state of revolution assign to literary art. For the writer-apprentice who devours everything as it appears, these changes affect even the prose of his predecessors, those living authors who are still producing and who, addressing themselves to other readers, have other principles and other rules of life. If there were at least progress in the art of writing, historical duration would be restored, there would be no occasion to revive in the distant past the exemplary works and lives of the Greeks or Latins. Unfortunately, beauty does not make progress: we can conceive of it, indeed, only as a strict relation between form and the 'form of content'. Temporality, moreover, was long conceived as a process of degradation: the ancients were the best; after them, decadence began. An author could do no better than imitate them. This conception – familiar to the seventeenth century, abandoned by the bourgeois of the eighteenth century – was almost taken up again by the first generations of the nineteenth century, for quite different reasons. In sum, beauty seems non-temporal; and if there were temporalization, it would be a degeneration. These ideas – one, though illusory, seems to issue from authentic structures of the beautiful; the other is merely the projection in 1830 of political pessimism on the literary plane – exalt and actualize apparent contradictions that never really coexisted in time. For the young bookworm, Theocritus, Shakespeare and Hugo, as manifest through their works, are all equally present. Hence, the aesthetic conceptions made manifest in their works clash violently. And how is he to choose among them since they all participate equally in the beautiful? Even if one accepted the pessimism that makes temporality a form of degradation, these contradictions, no longer caught in the abstraction of a moment, would none the less remain insoluble. By granting the ancients – farthest removed from our concerns – an aesthetic perfection he denies to Hugo, who speaks directly to him of his daily life, his hopes, his enthusiasms and his sorrows, the adolescent might always condemn 'modernism', that is, any literature speaking to the contemporaries of today's world. Even as one would revive antiquity in the middle of the first industrial century, our lives would flow by in silence and the earth swallow them up, with no bard deigning to fix our passions in words – so different from the passions that moved Ulysses or a Sicilian shepherd – or to capture the flavour of our world. In fact, things did not go quite so far. A young reader of 1835, a future writer, becomes intoxicated with Hugo, Vigny, Musset; he finds in Goethe's *Faust* the mandate to totalize the universe; he may rank them inferior to Virgil, but despite this rigid, abstract judgement they speak to his deepest feelings.

Does he therefore take them as examples, making their essence, affirmed in their books, his imperative and his fate? That would seem the logical thing to do; although they are all still living, he comes immediately after them. But this is just why they contend with each other inside him when he internalizes them. These writers, sons of the Empire, were directly engaged with the seventeenth and eighteenth centuries, which they envisaged through the revolutionary outcome and from the viewpoint of the restored monarchy. For a young reader of 1835, their junior by ten or fifteen years, the situation is more complex. As he reads them, these writers reveal past centuries as they saw them, but he preserves – through that fissure characterizing the appearance of a new generation – a permanent possibility of becoming engaged directly with Voltaire, Corneille and Homer; he need merely read them. Hence the challenge is challenged. In his direct relations with past authors, the apprentice-writer discovers them to be different from the image given him by his older brothers, living literary figures. As if there were two Voltaires – the Voltaire of *Rolla* (and many other works) and the Voltaire who wrote *Candide*. Indeed, Musset, desolate at having nearly lost his faith, thought hideous the man who concluded his letters with the phrase 'Crush the Beast'. But as we have seen with Gustave, if the Postromantics regret the consolations of religion, they are none the less freer on this ground, and more bourgeois besides. When they read Voltaire directly, they find in him a relation to Christianity and a strain they can accept. So they are simultaneously for and against Voltaire. Thus the future writer is imperatively charged by every masterpiece he reads to reproduce in his century, through other masterpieces, the literature that produced those great books – as totality (art, social function, public, meaning and subject, life). But every imperative is contradicted by another established in him with equal rigour when he shifts from one author to another. He must call Boileau – as Hugo does – a 'has-been'! But if he reads *Art poétique*, he must bow before such taste and call him the 'legislator of Parnassus'. Boileau will be judged by Hugo and Hugo by Boileau, and the result will be a vacillating uncertainty that charges the future work with being romantic through a negation of the classics, and classical through the recovery and envelopment of Romanticism and its works in the name of rules and taste, in the name of a monarchical order definitively rejected by contemporary society. The trouble is that every literary form is internalized as a command-ment, the reader is penetrated with contradictory and frozen imperatives – that will be, for example, *Gargantua*, *Phèdre*, *Candide*, the *Confessions*, *Hermani*, each work becoming in the course of reading a singular imperative ('Create the society and consequently the public that will demand such a work from you and give you the kind of life that will allow you to produce it.') If you read for the sake of reading, eclecticism is possible, strictly speaking, but not comfortable. The reader will respond to these multiple contradictory demands simply with resignation; they will continue to clash in him and through him and while letting it happen he will not feel obliged to unify them – an obligation he does have, however, since the demands he has awakened are addressed in him only to himself. But things are quite different if he reads for the sake of writing. In every work, art as a whole affirms itself; none appears relative to a society, to a particular period, although it is entirely conditioned by it. Thus whatever he reads, the literary thing in him becomes a total demand: it induces him to write but demands that literary art as a whole should be manifest in each of his future writings – a totality present in each partial production – in such a way that this art requires him to be inside it. This is not a matter of either reconciling or explaining through historical relativism: the elements of these multiple contradictions being imperative, their surpassing in a unifying synthesis appears to be the absolute demand of literature in this future writer. Let us say that from this point of view, surpassing is writing. The demand to write, the distant and fixed summons art extends from the depths of the future, is merely the determination of a future enterprise by the recomposition of a past and reified activity. But this summons – expressed at the time by the words 'vocation' and 'genius' – is also past literature demanding to be reproduced whole in every future work. This means that every work read, by demanding to be reproduced as bearer of this totality, is challenged by others as much as it challenges them. Thus the literary imperative is double: the new work must restore the beautiful as the all of which it is a part through the ancient canon; it achieves the synthetic surpassing of contradictions, the artistic totality will be manifest in it only as a totalization (through concrete texture and not through doctrines) of all those dead totalities. In so far as the objective reason for this future activity is none other than the internalization of past literature, writing is not just writing anything. The meaning of the totalization to be attempted is objectively outlined as a solution to the revealed contradictions; the surpassing, of course, can only be invented, but in a way it will be from a perspective strictly defined by those contradictions themselves and so participating in their passive materiality. Thus in every age a sketchy outline is given of *what must be done*, given the imperative oppositions we internalize. Not just beginning with these, moreover, but also as a function of the place contemporary society reserves for the writer *compared* to the place literature already written claims for him through internalization. In other words, literature as a vocation induced by reading demands of the chosen writer that he affirm the literary thing through a new totalization – whether a drama, a novel without the slightest aesthetic commentary – which defines the society, the public and the place of the writer in the social fabric. But two principal factors can make this definition impossible: on the one hand, the contradictions can be such that no rational synthesis can surpass them; on the other hand, the situation created for living literature by the contemporary society can enter into conflict with the situation that is manifest to the apprentice writer as a synthetic demand of written works, so that the rational synthesis of these works, were it to be found, could not be lived as a real condition. But as I have just shown, the literary form and content of an era are inseparable from the real situation of the writer in society, and consequently from the function this society actually assigns to literature. From this perspective, the real task of the future writer, which imposes itself on him as a surpassing of contradictions read, may seem to him more or less incompatible with the conditions of life which contemporary society imposes on the artist and with the type of readers it offers him. This arises from the fact that every cultural sector is on its level the expression of the total society and at the same time develops according to its own rules, that is, from the practico-inert produced in it to this day. When these two oppositions are manifest *together*, when the objective imperative appears as a 'you must' which no 'you can' comes to sustain, this objective will lose none of its intransigence – indeed, its source lies in the materiality of the Objective Spirit. Yet those it solicits can satisfy it only in the dream, by a series of *unreal* behaviours with no correspondence to the objective structures of society and the possibilities they *actually* offer the writer. Hence the chosen writer's need to unrealize himself in order to write. At the same time, other determinations may compel the public, or one part of the public, to become unrealized in order to read (or to read to become unrealized); and this being the case, we could imagine that the Objective Spirit of the age, in contradiction to the general movement of the living society, would compel the future author to despair of his vocation and in the end renounce it; or force him to unrealize himself through the supposition that he has resolved the insoluble contradictions posed by written-literature, and by this resolution to play *as a role* for his own benefit the character demanded by the Objective Spirit and unwanted by the real society. He is, as we can see, doubly driven to neurosis. But that neurosis is itself objective, it is a way to write; a doubtful, suspect way, but unique. If the cultural practico-inert outlines a neurotic condition for the future artist as a sham, though a necessary subterfuge for producing *works in this time*, this necessary unrealization may be envisaged as an art-neurosis to the extent that art is not only the practico-inert set of works produced but the set of behaviours aimed at producing new ones. We need merely recapitulate briefly the givens that situate the future Postromantic writer in the culture between 1830 and 1850 to demonstrate that neurosis – we shall see more precisely what kind of neurosis – is an operational imperative for him. We will then be able to return to Flaubert – who lived those demands, as did all his contemporaries – and we shall try to establish the relationship that unites art-neurosis as a determination of objectivity to his subjective neurosis.

NOTES

1 Obviously, Rousseau's psychopathic state is a direct source of the *Confessions* (he had to defend himself against a conspiracy) and provides some of this autobiography's dominant themes. *Rousseau juge de Jean-Jacques*, on the other hand, can be described as a morbid work because it cannot be understood without reference to the author's illness. It should be observed, however, that that work, like the *Confessions*, is determined by the obsession with conspiracy. And conspiracy did exist. Not in the form of a rigorously organized cabal but rather as a tacit agreement between men who knew and understood each other well enough without direct contact or even correspondence, and certainly without a leader, to conduct

a well-organized campaign; when one of them came out into the open and struck, the others knew what they had to do. This is what gives the *Dialogues* their true dimensions; though the aggression is obviously exaggerated, its reality must never be forgotten. And I would contend that the three autobiographical works (in which I include *Les Rêveries*) are written *against* Rousseau's psychopathic state because they have a double aim: first, of course, to show his true self to readers, who might then judge fairly the calumnious accusations levelled against him; but also to know himself. Whence the profound states of heart and soul that were as yet unknown in Europe; whence the dialogue form, in *Rousseau juge de Jean-Jacques*, which has been foolishly cited as the onset of mental disintegration, when, quite to the contrary, this fiction was a guarantee for Rousseau of the distance necessary to all reflexive knowledge. As for the motive of this effort to know himself, it was doubtless from the outset a quest for serenity. He would find serenity in part in the 'Promenades', having accepted his fate. Thus, these three works together constitute at once a speech for the defence and the most sustained, the latest effort to grasp the meaning and value of a life in its fleeting, elusive flow that is often masked or deformed by the ravings of a suspicious soul. If the *Confessions* were merely an apology, we would long ago have ceased to read it. And in this sense we could speak of the work as neurotic: in it Rousseau would surrender to his phantasms. But this book is still alive after two centuries because it also contains the opposite tack: the author wants to use it to see clearly how to defend himself also against himself, and the apology finds its best arguments – even without using them explicitly – in that extraordinary, purifying investigation and in the decision to say *everything*. Thus – taking into account that other works offer rigorous *objective* contents – we can say that the admirable tension of style and ideas are generated in Rousseau not by his troubles but by his struggle against evil. He is a man of the eighteenth century, a citizen of Geneva, a doubly reasonable man attacked in his reason, who turns that reason on his adversary and, just as he appears to surrender to madness, devotes himself to the difficult enterprise of cleansing his understanding of the morbid infiltrations that might infect it. If literature was enriched by these invaluable works, which for the first time in centuries deliver up lived experience candidly, we owe this not only to the author's sensibility, but also and above all to the work of a reason that does not abdicate. Thus the illness is the source of the work only to the degree that Rousseau engages in single combat against it. And the normative principles that define the writing – and the whole book in its composition – are, in their rigorous rationality, the opposite of a neurotic art.

2 Edmond de Goncourt: 'Imagine, our work – and perhaps this is its originality – is dependent upon nervous illness.' Cited by Bourget, *Essais de psychologie contemporaine*, vol. 2, p. 162.

16 Raymond Williams

a) Tragedy and Revolution (1966)
b) Literature (1977)[*]

Briefly in the Communist Party as a student, Raymond Williams (1921–88) taught in the Workers' Educational Association and then at Cambridge University, where he became Professor of Drama. From a socialist humanist or Left-Leavisite approach, Williams's early critical distance from Marxism had, by the 1970s, developed into a more explicit *rapprochement* with Marxism. In *Culture and Society* (1958) and *The Long Revolution* (1961) he developed an approach, often called 'cultural materialism', which mediated between politics and aesthetics through a sociology of social forms. Williams's distinctive emphasis is on 'structures of feeling' as expressions of social relations between economic conditions and cultural life. Like Trotsky, he did not simply reject bourgeois culture, but argued for an expanded concept of culture, considering also the significance of new media such as film and television. Much of Williams's literary criticism addresses modern drama, notably in *Drama from Ibsen to Brecht* (1968) and *Modern Tragedy* (1966). 'Tragedy and Revolution', from *Modern Tragedy*, exemplifies his struggle to theorize the ideological and political significance of drama as a cultural form. His break with the privileging category of 'literature', exemplified by *The Country and the City* (1973), is theorized in 'Literature', from *Marxism and Literature* (1977). Williams has been criticized for the contrast between his insistence on material specificity and his often suggestive rather than historically detailed research. Doubts have also been expressed about the place of race and gender in his accounts of class and community. Williams's work and his responses to various criticisms are presented in a series of interviews collected in *Politics and Letters* (1979). Other works include *Keywords* (1976); *Problems in Materialism and Culture (1980); Towards 2000* (1983); and *Writing in Society* (1984). For discussion see A. O'Connor, *Raymond Williams* (1989); and *Raymond Williams*, ed. T. Eagleton (1989).

a) Tragedy and Revolution

The most complex effect of any really powerful ideology is that it directs us, even when we think we have rejected it, to the same kind of fact. Thus, when we try to identify the disorder which is at the root of our tragic experiences, we tend to find elements analogous to former tragic systems, as the ideology has interpreted them. We look, almost unconsciously, for a crisis of personal

[*] a) From Raymond Williams, *Modern Tragedy* (London: Chatto & Windus, 1966), 61–84; (b) from Raymond Williams, *Marxism and Literature* (Oxford: Oxford University Press, 1977), 45–54.

belief: matching a lost belief in immortality with a new conviction of mortality, or a lost belief in fate with a new conviction of indifference. We look for tragic experience in our attitudes to God or to death or to individual will, and of course we often find tragic experience cast in these familiar forms. Having separated earlier tragic systems from their actual societies, we can achieve a similar separation in our own time, and can take it for granted that modern tragedy can be discussed without reference to the deep social crisis, of war and revolution, through which we have all been living. That kind of interest is commonly relegated to politics, or, to use the cant word, sociology. Tragedy, we say, belongs to deeper and closer experience, to man not to society. Even the general disorders, which can hardly escape the most limited attention, and which equally can hardly be said to involve only societies and not men, can be reduced to symptoms of the only kind of disorder we are prepared to recognize: the fault in the soul. War, revolution, poverty, hunger; men reduced to objects and killed from lists; persecution and torture; the many kinds of contemporary martyrdom: however close and insistent the facts, we are not to be moved, in a context of tragedy. Tragedy, we know, is about something else.

Yet the break comes, in some minds. In experience, suddenly, the new connections are made, and the familiar world shifts, as the new relations are seen. We are not looking for a new universal meaning of tragedy. We are looking for the structure of tragedy in our own culture. Once we begin to doubt, in experience and then in analysis, the ordinary twentieth-century idea, other directions seem open.

Tragedy and Social Disorder

Since the time of the French Revolution, the idea of tragedy can be seen as in different ways a response to a culture in conscious change and movement. The action of tragedy and the action of history have been consciously connected, and in the connection have been seen in new ways. The reaction against this, from the mid-nineteenth century, has been equally evident: the movement of spirit has been separated from the movement of civilization. Yet even this negative reaction seems, in its context, a response to the same kind of crisis. The academic tradition, on the whole, has followed the negative reaction, but it is difficult to hear its ordinary propositions and feel that they are only about a set of academic facts. They sound, insistently, like propositions about contemporary life, even when they are most negative and most consciously asocial. The other nineteenth-century tradition, in which tragedy and history were consciously connected, seems then deeply relevant. In experience and in theory we have to look again at this relation.

We must ask whether tragedy, in our own time, is a response to social disorder. If it is so, we shall not expect the response to be always direct. The disorder will appear in very many forms, and to articulate these will be very complex and difficult. A more immediate difficulty is the ordinary separation of social thinking and tragic thinking. The most influential kinds of explicitly social thinking have often rejected tragedy as in itself defeatist. Against what they have known as the idea of tragedy, they have stressed man's powers to change his condition and to end a major part of the suffering which the tragic ideology seems to ratify. The idea of tragedy, that is to say, has been explicitly opposed by the idea of revolution: there has been as much confidence on the one side as on the other. And then to describe tragedy as a response to social disorder, and to value it as such, is to break, apparently, from both major traditions.

The immediate disturbance is radical, for the fault in the soul was a recognition of a kind; it was close to the experience, even when it added its ordinary formulas. From the other position, from the recognition of social disorder, there is a habit of easy abstraction which the scale of the disorder almost inevitably supports. As we recognize history, we are referred to history, and find it difficult to acknowledge men like ourselves. Before, we could not recognize tragedy as social crisis; now, commonly, we cannot recognize social crisis as tragedy. The facts of disorder are caught up in a new ideology, which cancels suffering as it finds the name of a period or a phase. From day to day we can make everything past, because we believe in the future. Our actual present, in which the disorder is radical, is as effectively hidden as when it was merely politics, for it is now only politics. It seems that we have jumped from one blindness to another, and with the same visionary confidence. The new connections harden, and no longer connect.

What seems to matter, against every difficulty, is that the received ideas no longer describe our experience. The most common idea of revolution excludes too much of our social experience. But it is more than this. The idea of tragedy, in its ordinary form, excludes especially that tragic experience which is social, and the idea of revolution, again in its ordinary form, excludes especially that social experience which is tragic. And if this is so, the contradiction is significant. It is not a merely formal opposition, of two ways of reading experience, between which we can choose. In our own time, especially, it is the connections between revolution and tragedy – connections lived and known but not acknowledged as ideas – which seem most clear and significant.

The most evident connection is in the actual events of history, as we all quite simply observe them. A time of revolution is so evidently a time of violence, dislocation and extended suffering that it is natural to feel it as tragedy, in the everyday sense. Yet, as the event becomes history, it is often quite differently regarded. Very many nations look back to the revolutions of their own history as to the era of creation of the life which is now most precious. The successful revolution, we might say, becomes not tragedy but epic: it is the origin of a people, and of its valued way of life. When the suffering is remembered, it is at once either honoured or justified. That particular revolution, we say, was a necessary condition of life.

Contemporary revolution is of course very different. Only a post-revolutionary generation is capable of that epic composition. In contemporary revolution, the detail of suffering is insistent, whether as violence or as the reshaping of lives by a new power in the state. But further, in a contemporary revolution, we inevitably take sides, though with different degrees of engagement. And a time of revolution is ordinarily a time of lies and of suppressions of truths. The suffering of the whole action, even when its full weight is acknowledged, is commonly projected as the responsibility of this party or that, until its very description becomes a revolutionary or counter-revolutionary act. There is a kind of indifference which comes early whenever the action is at a distance. But there is also an exposure to the scale of suffering, and to the lies and campaigns that are made from it, which in the end is also indifference. Revolution is a dimension of action from which, for initially honourable reasons, we feel we have to keep clear.

Thus the social fact becomes a structure of feeling. Revolution as such is in a common sense tragedy, a time of chaos and suffering. It is almost inevitable that we should try to go beyond it. I do not rely on what is almost certain to happen: that this tragedy, in its turn, will become epic. However true this may be, it cannot closely move us; only heirs can inherit. Allegiance to even a probable law of history, which has not, however, in the particular case, been lived through, becomes quite quickly an alienation. We are not truly responding to this action but, by projection, to its probable composition.

The living alternative is quite different in character. It is neither the rejection of revolution, by its simple characterization as chaos and suffering, nor yet the calculation of revolution, by laws and probabilities not yet experienced. It is, rather, a recognition; the recognition of revolution as a whole action of living men. Both the wholeness of the action, and in this sense its humanity, are then inescapable. It is this recognition against which we ordinarily struggle.

Revolution and Disorder

As we have reduced tragedy to the death of the hero, so we have reduced revolution to its crisis of violence and disorder. In simple observation, these are often the most evident effects, but in the whole action they are both preceded and succeeded, and much of their meaning depends on this fact of continuity. Thus it is strange that from our whole modern history revolution should be selected as the example of violence and disorder: revolution, that is, as the critical conflict and resolution of forces. To limit violence and disorder to the decisive conflict is to make nonsense of that conflict itself. The violence and disorder are in the whole action, of which what we commonly call revolution is the crisis.

The essential point is that violence and disorder are institutions as well as acts. When a revolutionary change has been lived through, we can usually see this quite clearly. The old institutions, now dead, take on their real quality as systematic violence and disorder; in that quality, the source of the revolutionary action is seen. But while such institutions are still effective, they can seem, to an extraordinary extent, both settled and innocent. Indeed they constitute, commonly, an order, against which the very protest, of the injured and oppressed, seems the source of disturbance and violence. Here, most urgently, in our own time, we need to return the idea of revolution, in its ordinary sense of the crisis of a society, to its necessary context as part of a whole action, within which alone it can be understood.

Order and disorder are relative terms, although each is experienced as an absolute. We are aware of this relativism, through history and comparative studies: intellectually aware, though that is often not much use to us, under the pressure of fear or interest or in the simple immediacy of our local and actual world. In the ideas of both tragedy and revolution, this dimension and yet also these difficulties are at once encountered. I have already argued that the relation between tragedy and order is dynamic. The tragic action is rooted in a disorder, which indeed, at a particular stage, can seem to have its own stability. But the whole body of real forces is engaged by the action, often in such a way that the underlying disorder becomes apparent and terrible in overtly tragic ways. From the whole experience of this disorder, and through its specific action, order is recreated. The process of this action is at times remarkably similar to the real action of revolution.

Yet revolution, at least in its feudal form as rebellion, is often, in many valued tragedies, the disorder itself. The restoration of 'lawful' authority is there literally the restoration of order. But the essential consideration lies deeper than this, below the false consciousness of feudal attitudes to rebellion. It is not difficult to see that the feudal definitions of lawful authority and rebellion are, at the political level, at worst timeserving, at best partisan. The majesty of kings is usually the political façade of successful usurpers and their descendants. What challenges it, as an action, is of the same human kind as what established it. Yet the investment of political power with religious or magical sanctions is also, in its most important examples, a vehicle for the expression of a fundamental conception of order, and indeed of the nature of life and of man. Characteristically, this is a conception of a static order, and of a permanent human condition and nature. Around such conceptions, real values are formed, and the threat to them overrides the temporary and arbitrary association of them with a particular figure or system. When connections of this kind are a living reality, the tragic action, whatever its local form, can have the widest human reference.

In its actual course, the tragic action often undercuts the ordinary association between fundamental human values and the acknowledged social system: the claims of actual love contradict the duties of family; the awakened individual consciousness contradicts the assigned social role. In the transition from a feudal to a liberal world, such contradictions are common and are lived out as tragedy. Yet the identification between a permanent order and a social system is still not really challenged. The contradictions and disorders are normally seen in terms of the identification, which has been blurred by human error but which the tragic action essentially restores. The figures of the true and false kings, of the lawful authority and his erring deputy, are dramatic modes of just this structure of feeling. There is a close relation between such dramatic modes and the type of argument common to political reformers and even political revolutionaries, in England in the seventeenth century, in which it was claimed that nothing new was being proposed or fought for, but only the restoration of the true and ancient constitution. This consciousness contained the most radical and even revolutionary actions. In tragedy, the stage was at last reached when there was scepticism about the possibility of any social order, and then resolution was seen as altogether outside the terms of civil society. A religious or quasi-religious withdrawal restored order by supernatural or magical intervention, and the tragic action came full circle.

Liberalism

Liberal tragedy inherited this separation between ultimate human values and the social system, but in a mode which it finally transformed. Slowly, in the development of liberal consciousness, the point of reference became not a general order but the individual, who as such embodied all ultimate values, including (in the ordinary emphasis of Protestantism) divine values. I shall trace the course of liberal tragedy to the point where new contradictions, in this absolute conception of the individual, led to deadlock and then to final breakdown (a breakdown of which I expect to see many further examples).

But the great current of liberalism had other effects, and is especially responsible for the sharp opposition between the idea of tragedy and the idea of revolution which we find so clearly in our own time. Liberalism steadily eroded the conceptions of a permanent human nature and of a static social order with connections to a divine order. From these erosions, and from the alternative conception of the possibility of human and social transformation, the early idea of revolution, in the modern sense, took its origins. Rebellion became revolution, and the most important human values became associated not with the received order but with development, progress and change. The contrast between the ordinary ideas of tragedy and of revolution seemed then quite stark. Revolution asserted the possibility of man altering his condition; tragedy showed its impossibility, and the consequent spiritual effects. On that opposition, we are still trying to rest.

Yet the essential history has already changed. The liberal idea of revolution and the feudal idea of tragedy are no longer the only alternatives, and to go on offering to choose between them is to be merely stranded in time. To understand this we must see what happened to the liberal idea of revolution.

It is at first sight surprising that so open and positive a movement as liberalism should ever have produced tragedy at all. Yet each of the literary movements which took their origins from liberalism came to a point where the most decisive choices were necessary, and where, while some chose, others merely divided. The nature of these choices is in the end essentially a matter of attitudes toward revolution. It is in this process that we are still engaged.

Naturalism

The literature of naturalism is the most obvious example. It seems now the true child of the liberal enlightenment, in which the traditional ideas of a fate, an absolute order, a design beyond human powers, were replaced by a confidence in reason and in the possibility of a continually expanding capacity for explanation and control. In politics this produced a new social consciousness of human destiny; in philosophy, analysis of the ideologies of religion and of social custom, together with new schemes of rational explanation; in literature, a new emphasis on the exact observation and description of the contemporary social world. But the literature of naturalism, finally, is a bastard of the enlightenment. Characteristically, it detached the techniques of observation and description from the purposes which these were intended to serve. What became naturalism, and what distinguished it from the more important movement of realism, was a mechanical description of men as the creatures of their environment, which literature recorded as if man and thing were of the same nature. The tragedy of naturalism is the tragedy of passive suffering, and the suffering is passive because man can only endure and can never really change his world. The endurance is given no moral or religious valuation; it is wholly mechanical, because both man and his world, in what is now understood as rational explanation, are the products of an impersonal and material process which though it changes through time has no ends. The impulse to describe and so change a human condition has narrowed to the simple impulse to describe a condition in which there can be no intervention by God or man, the human act of will being tiny and insignificant within the vast material process, universal or social, which at once determines and is indifferent to human destiny.

This naturalism, at once the most common theory and the most ordinary practice of our literature, began in liberalism but ends, ironically, as a grotesque version of the system originally challenged by liberalism, just as atheism ends as a grotesque version of faith. A living design became a mechanical fate, and the latter is even further from man than the former; more decisively alienated from any image of himself.

But then this development had real causes. It is, essentially, a deliberate arrest of the process of enlightenment, at the point of critical involvement. As such it corresponds to the deliberate arrest and subsequent decadence of liberalism, at the point where its universal principles required the transformation of its social programme, and where men could either go on or must go back. Everywhere in the nineteenth century we see men running for cover from the consequences of their own beliefs. In our own century, they do not even have to run; the temporary covers have become solid settlements. The universal principles of human liberation have become an embarrassment to men who, benefiting themselves from change of this kind, see before them an infinitely extending demand, of other classes and other peoples, which threatens to submerge and destroy their own newly won identity. A few men hold to their principles, and make their commitment, to a general social revolution. But the majority compromise, evade, or seek to delay, and the most destructive form of this breakdown – for simple reaction is easily recognized – is the characteristic substitution of evolution for revolution as a social model.[1]

The whole point of the new theories of social evolution, most evident in the theory of administered reform, was the separation of historical development from the actions of the majority of men, or even, in its extreme forms, from all men. Society, in this view, was an impersonal process, a machine with certain built-in properties. The machine might be described or regulated, but was not, ultimately, within human control. Social change, at its maximum, was the substitution of one group of fitters for another. Social description, at its best, was neutral and mechanical. The process, so to say, would build up, would evolve, and we must watch it, go with it, not get in its modernizing way. Any attempt to assert a general human priority, over the process as a whole, is then of course seen as childish: the mere fantasy of revolution.

The extent to which almost all our politics has been reshaped to this mechanical materialism hardly needs emphasis. But what has to be said is that this movement of mind, claiming its origins in reason, was theoretically and factually a mystification of real social activity, and as such discredited reason itself. It thus worked, finally, to the same effect as the other major movement which sought to express the values of liberalism but which seemed for so long to have so different a direction: the whole current of subjectivism and romanticism.

Romanticism

Utilitarianism, the most common English form of mechanical materialism, had sought liberal values in the reform of civil society. Romanticism, on the other hand, sought liberal values in the development of the individual. In its early stages, Romanticism was profoundly liberating, but, partly because of the inadequacy of any corresponding social theory, and partly because of the consequent decline from individualism to subjectivism, it ended by denying its own deepest impulses, and even reversing them. Almost all our revolutionary language in fact comes from the Romantics, and this has been a real hindrance as well as an incidental embarrassment. Romanticism is the most important expression in modern literature of the first impulse of revolution: a new and absolute image of man. Characteristically, it relates this transcendence to an ideal world and an ideal human society; it is in Romantic literature that man is first seen as making himself.

But of course when this is particularized, to social criticism and construction, it encounters fundamental obstacles. It is easier to visualize the ideal in an exotic or fabled community (or an historical community transformed by these elements). The existing social world is seen as so hostile to what is most deeply human that even what begins as social criticism tends to pass into nihilism. For more than a century, the fate of this Romantic tradition was uncertain. Some part of its force inspired the developing idea of total social revolution. A related part, while moving in this direction, got no further, finally, than the images of revolution: the flag, the barricade, the death of martyr or prisoner. But perhaps the major part went in a quite different direction, towards the final separation of revolution from society.

The decisive element, here, was the Romantic attitude to reason. In form, Romanticism can seem a negative reaction to the Enlightenment: its stress on the irrational and the strange seems an absolute contradiction of the stress on reason. But there is, here, a curious dialectic. Romanticism was not proposing what the Enlightenment had opposed; the one version of man was as new as the other. Yet, because this was not seen, the essential unity of these movements, as programmes for human liberation, was disastrously narrowed and confused. What the Romantics criticized as reason was not the reasoning activity, but the abstraction and final alienation of this activity, into what was called a rational but was in fact a mechanical system. Such criticism, and notably the English Romantic critique of utilitarianism, was not only humane; it was also on the side of man as a creative and active being. The eventual collapse to irrationalism can be understood only in terms of the earlier collapse to rationalism. The alienation of reason, from all the other activities of man, changed reason from an activity to a mechanism, and society from a human process to a machine. The protest against this was inevitable, but to stay with society as a human process involved commitments to social action which were indeed difficult to make. Under the pressure of difficulty and the disillusion of failure, the Romantic vision of man became in its turn alienated. The alienation of the rational, into a system of mechanical materialism, was matched by an alienation of the irrational, which has become complete only in our own century.

Thus, while one major part of the liberal idea of revolution had run into the mechanics of social evolution and administered reform, another major part had run into the parody of revolution, in nihilism and its many derivatives. To the former society was a machine, which would go its own predestined way in its own time. To the latter, society was the enemy of human liberation: man could free himself only by rejecting or escaping from society, and by seeing his own deepest activities, in love, in art, in nature, as essentially asocial and even anti-social. Ironically, just as mechanical materialism had produced a new kind of fate, the 'evolutionary' society from which man's activity and aspiration were shut out, so nihilism, also, produced a version of fate: the separation of humanity from society, but also the internalization of what had once been an external design. In its later variants, especially, nihilism emphasized and generalized the irrational as more powerful than social man. From its assumption of hostility between personal liberation and the social fact, it rationalized an irrationality, more dark and destructive than any known gods. In its last stages, the dream of human liberation was the nightmare of an ineradicable destructive instinct and the death-wish.

The End of Liberalism

The liberal idea of revolution was finally hemmed in on both sides: by its reduction to a mechanical and impersonal process, and by the channelling of personal revolt into an ideology which made social construction seem hopeless, because man as such was deeply irrational and destructive. In Western societies, the contrast of these positions is now normally offered as total, so that we see ourselves as having to choose between them. In politics we are offered not revolution, or even substantial change, but what is widely called modernization: that is, a separation of change from value. We are asked to go along with what is supposed to be an inevitable evolutionary process, or to bend, whatever its direction, to the 'wind of change' (which is an exact expression of just this alienation in that it blows from elsewhere and is rationalized as a natural force). Or, alternatively, we reject politics, and see the reality of human liberation as internal, private and apolitical, even under the shadow of politically willed war or politically willed poverty or politically willed ugliness and cruelty.

Yet in fact, since 1917, we have been living in a world of successful social revolutions. In this sense it is true to say that our attitude to the revolutionary societies of our own time is central and probably decisive in all our thinking. What our own ideology, in its many variants, has theoretically excluded, has happened or seems to have happened elsewhere. And then there are not really many choices left. We can actively oppose or seek to contain revolution elsewhere, as in national practice we have been continually doing. Militancy and indifference serve this tactic almost equally well. Or we can support revolution, elsewhere, in a familiar kind of romanticism, for which the images lie ready in the mind. Or, finally – I am stating my own position – we can work to understand and participate in revolution as a social reality: that is to say, not only as an action now in progress among real men, but also, and therefore, as an activity immediately involving ourselves.

It is here that the relation between revolution and tragedy is inescapable and urgent. It may still be possible, for some thinkers, to interpret actual revolution in the received ideology of rationalism. We can all see the constructive activity of the successful revolutionary societies, and we can take this as evidence of the simple act of human liberation by the energy of reason. I know nothing I welcome more than this actual construction, but I know also that the revolutionary societies have been tragic societies, at a depth and on a scale that go beyond any ordinary pity and fear. At the point of this recognition, however, where the received ideology of revolution, its simple quality as liberation, seems most to fail, there is waiting the received ideology of tragedy, in either of its common forms: the old tragic lesson, that man cannot change his condition, but can only drown his world in blood in the vain attempt; or the contemporary reflex, that the taking of rational control over our social destiny is defeated or at best deeply stained by our inevitable irrationality, and by the violence and cruelty that are so quickly released when habitual forms break down. I do not find, in the end, that either of these interpretations covers enough of the facts, but also I do not see how anyone can still hold to that idea of revolution which simply denied tragedy, as an experience and as an idea.

Socialism and Revolution

Socialism, I believe, is the true and active inheritor of the impulse to human liberation which has previously taken so many different forms. But in practice, I also believe, it is an idea still forming, and much that passes under its name is only a residue of old positions. I do not mean only such a movement as Fabianism, with its cast of utilitarianism and its mechanical conceptions of change. I mean also a main current in Marxism, which though Marx may at times have opposed it is also profoundly mechanical, in its determinism, in its social materialism, and in its characteristic abstraction of social classes from human beings. I can see that it is possible, with such habits of mind, to interpret revolution as only constructive and liberating. Real suffering is then at once non-human: is a class swept away by history, is an error in the working of the machine, or is the blood that is not and never can be rose water. The more general and abstract, the more truly mechanical, the process of human liberation is ordinarily conceived to be, the less any actual suffering really counts, until even death is a paper currency.

But then I do not believe, as so many disillusioned or broken by actual revolution have come to believe, that the suffering can be laid to the charge of the revolution alone, and that we must avoid revolution if we are to avoid suffering. On the contrary, I see revolution as the inevitable working through of a deep and tragic disorder, to which we can respond in varying ways but which will in any case, in one way or another, work its way through our world, as a consequence of any of our actions. I see revolution, that is to say, in a tragic perspective, and it is this I now seek to define.

Marx's early idea of revolution seems to me to be tragic in this sense:

> A class must be formed which has *radical chains*, a class in civil society which is not a class of civil society, a class which is the dissolution of all classes, a sphere of society which has a universal character because its sufferings are universal, and which does not claim a *particular redress* because the wrong which is done to it is not a *particular wrong* but *wrong in general*. There must be formed a sphere of society which claims no *traditional* status but only a *human* status . . . a sphere finally which cannot emancipate itself without emancipating itself from all the other spheres of society, without therefore emancipating all these other spheres; which is, in short, a *total loss* of humanity and which can only redeem itself by a *total redemption of humanity*.
>
> (*Zur Kritik der Hegelschen Rechts-Philosophie: Einleitung*)

So absolute a conception distinguishes revolution from rebellion, or, to put it another way, makes political revolution into a general human revolution:

> In all former revolutions the form of activity was always left unaltered, and it was only a question of redistributing this activity among different people, of introducing a new division of labour. The communist revolution, however, is directed against the former *mode* of activity, does away with *labour*, and abolishes all class rule along with the classes themselves . . .
>
> (*Die Deutsche Ideologie*)

The *social life* from which the worker is shut out . . . is *life* itself, physical and cultural life, human morality, human activity, human enjoyment, real human existence. . . . As the irremediable exclusion from this life is much more complete, more unbearable, dreadful, and contradictory, than the exclusion from political life, so is the ending of this exclusion, and even a limited reaction, a *revolt* against it, more fundamental, as *man* is more fundamental than the *citizen*, *human life* more than *political life*.

(Vorwärts, 1844)

This way of seeing revolution seems to me to stand. Whatever we have learned, since Marx wrote, about actual historical development, and thence about the agencies and tactics of revolution, does not affect the idea itself. We need not identify revolution with violence or with a sudden capture of power. Even where such events occur, the essential transformation is indeed a long revolution. But the absolute test, by which revolution can be distinguished, is the change in the *form* of activity of a society, in its deepest structure of relationships and feelings. The incorporation of new groups of men into the pre-existing form and structure is something quite different, even when it is accompanied by an evident improvement of material conditions and by the ordinary changes of period and local colour. In fact the test of a pre-revolutionary society, or of a society in which the revolution is still incomplete, is in just this matter of incorporation. A society in which revolution is necessary is a society in which the incorporation of all its people, *as whole human beings*, is in practice impossible without a change in its fundamental form of relationships. The many kinds of partial 'incorporation' – as voters, as employees, or as persons entitled to education, legal protection, social services and so on – are real human gains, but do not in themselves amount to that full membership of society which is the end of classes. The reality of full membership is the capacity to direct a particular society, by active mutual responsibility and co-operation, on a basis of full social equality. And while this is the purpose of revolution, it remains necessary in all societies in which there are, for example, subordinate racial groups, landless landworkers, hired hands, the unemployed, and suppressed or discriminate minorities of any kind. Revolution remains necessary, in these circumstances, not only because some men desire it, but because there can be no acceptable human order while the full humanity of any class of men is in practice denied.

The Tragedy of Revolution

This idea of 'the total redemption of humanity' has the ultimate cast of resolution and order, but in the real world its perspective is inescapably tragic. It is born in pity and terror: in the perception of a radical disorder in which the humanity of some men is denied and by that fact the idea of humanity itself is denied. It is born in the actual suffering of real men thus exposed, and in all the consequences of this suffering: degeneration, brutalization, fear, hatred, envy. It is born in an experience of evil made the more intolerable by the conviction that it is not inevitable, but is the result of particular actions and choices.

And if it is thus tragic in its origins – in the existence of a disorder that cannot but move and involve – it is equally tragic in its action, in that it is not against gods or inanimate things that its impulse struggles, nor against mere institutions and social forms, but against other men. This, throughout, has been the area of silence, in the development of the idea. What is properly called utopianism, or revolutionary romanticism, is the suppression or dilution of this quite inevitable fact.

There are many reasons why men will oppose such a revolution. There are the obvious reasons of interest or privilege, for which we have seen men willing to die. There is the deep fear that recognition of the humanity of others is a denial of our own humanity, as our whole lives have known it. There is the flight in the mind from disturbance of a familiar world, however inadequate. There is the terror, often justified, of what will happen when men who have been treated as less than men gain the power to act. For there will of course be revenge and senseless destruction, after the bitterness and deformity of oppression. And then, more subtly, there are all the learned positions, from an experience of disorder that is as old as human history and yet also is continually re-enacted: the conviction that any absolute purpose is delusion and folly, to be corrected by training, by some social ease where we are, or by an outright opposition to this madness which would destroy the world.

From all these positions, revolution is practically opposed, in every form from brutal suppression and massive indoctrination to genuine attempts to construct alternative futures. And all our experience tells us that this immensely complicated action between real men will continue as far ahead as we can foresee, and that the suffering in this continuing struggle will go on being terrible. It is very difficult for the mind to accept this, and we all erect our defences against so tragic a recognition. But I believe that it is inevitable, and that we must speak of it if it is not to overwhelm us.

In some Western societies we are engaged in the attempt to make this total revolution without violence, by a process of argument and consensus. It is impossible to say if we shall succeed. The arrest of humanity, in many groups and individuals, is still severe and seems often intractable. At the same time, while the process has any chance of success, nobody in his senses would wish to alter its nature. The real difficulty, however, is that we have become introverted on this process, in a familiar kind of North Atlantic thinking, and the illusions this breeds are already of a tragic kind.

Thus we seek to project the result of particular historical circumstances as universal, and to identify all other forms of revolution as hostile. The only consistent common position is that of the enemies of revolution everywhere, yet even they, at times, speak a liberal rhetoric. It is a very deep irony that, in ideology, the major conflict in the world is between different versions of the absolute rights of man. Again and again, men in Western societies act as counter-revolutionaries, but in the name of an absolute liberation. There are real complexities here, for revolutionary regimes have also acted, repeatedly and brutally, against every kind of human freedom and dignity. But there are also deep and habitual forms of false consciousness. Only a very few of us, in any Western society, have in fact renounced violence, in the way that our theory claims. If we believe that social change should be peaceful, it is difficult to know what we are doing in military alliances, with immense armament and weapons of indiscriminate destruction. The customary pretence that this organized violence is defensive, and that it is wholly dedicated to human freedom, is literally a tragic illusion. It is easy to move about in our own comparatively peaceful society, repeating such phrases as 'a revolution by due course of law', and simply failing to notice that in our name, and endorsed by repeated majorities, other peoples have been violently opposed in the very act of their own liberation. The bloody tale of the past is always conveniently discounted, but I am writing on a day when British military power is being used against 'dissident tribesmen' in South Arabia, and I know this pattern and its covering too well, from repeated examples through my lifetime, to be able to acquiesce in the ordinary illusion. Many of my countrymen have opposed these policies, and in many particular cases have ended them. But it is impossible to believe that as a society we have yet dedicated ourselves to human liberation, or even to that simple recognition of the absolute humanity of all other men which is the impulse of any genuine revolution. To say that in our own affairs we have made this recognition would also be too much, in a society powered by great economic inequality and by organized manipulation. But even if we had made this recognition, among ourselves, it would still be a travesty of any real revolutionary belief. It is only when the recognition is general that it can be authentic, for in practice every reservation, in a widely communicating world, tends to degenerate into actual opposition.

Our interpretation of revolution as a slow and peaceful growth of consensus is at best a local experience and hope, at worst a sustained false consciousness. In a world determined by the struggle against poverty and against the many forms of colonial and neo-colonial domination, revolution continually and inescapably enters our society, in the form of our own role in those critical areas. And here it is not only that we have made persistent errors, and that we comfort ourselves with the illusion of steady progress when the gap between wealth and poverty is actually increasing in the world, and when the consciousness of exploitation is rapidly rising. It is also that the revolutionary process has become, in our generation, the ordinary starting-point of war. It is very remarkable, in recent years, how the struggles for national liberation and for social change, in many different parts of the world, have involved the major powers in real and repeated dangers of general war. What are still, obtusely, called 'local upheavals', or even 'brushfires', put all our lives in question, again and again. Korea, Suez, the Congo, Cuba, Vietnam, are names of our own crisis. It is impossible to look at this real and still active history without a general sense of tragedy: not only because the disorder is so widespread and intolerable that in action and reaction it must work its way through our lives, wherever we may be; but also because, on any probable estimate, we understand the process so little that we continually contribute to the disorder. It is not simply that we become involved in this general crisis, but that we are already, by what we do and fail to do, participating in it.

There is, here, a strange contradiction. The two great wars we have known in Europe, and the widespread if still limited awareness of the nature of nuclear war, have induced a kind of inert pacifism which is too often self-regarding and dangerous. We say, understandably, that we must avoid war at all costs, but what we commonly mean is that we will avoid war at any cost but our own. Relatively appeased in our own situation, we interpret disturbance elsewhere as a threat to peace, and seek either to suppress it (the 'police action' to preserve what we call law and order; the fire brigade to put out the 'brushfire'), or to smother it with money or political manœuvres. So deep is this contradiction that we regard such activities, even actual suppression, as morally virtuous; we even call it peacemaking. But what we are asking is what, in a limited consciousness, we have ourselves succeeded in doing: to acquiesce in a disorder and call it order; to say peace where there is no peace. We expect men brutally exploited and intolerably poor to rest and be patient in their misery, because if they act to end their condition it will involve the rest of us, and threaten our convenience or our lives.

In these ways, we have identified war and revolution as the tragic dangers, when the real tragic danger, underlying war and revolution, is a disorder which we continually re-enact. So false a peacemaking, so false an appeal to order, is common in the action of tragedy, in which, nevertheless, all the real forces of the whole situation eventually work themselves out. Even if we were willing to change, in our attitudes to others and even more in our real social relations with them, we might still not, so late in the day, avoid actual tragedy. But the only relevant response, to the tragedy of this kind that we have already experienced, is that quite different peacemaking which is the attempt to resolve rather than to cover the determining tragic disorder. Any such resolution would mean changing ourselves, in fundamental ways, and our unwillingness to do this, the certainty of disturbance, the probability of secondary and unforeseen disorder, put the question, inevitably, into a tragic form.

The only consciousness that seems adequate in our world is then an exposure to the actual disorder. The only action that seems adequate is, really, a participation in the disorder, as a way of ending it. But at this point another tragic perspective opens. I find that I still agree with Carlyle, when he wrote in *Chartism*:

> Men who discern in the misery of the toiling complaining millions not misery, but only a raw material which can be wrought upon and traded in, for one's own poor hide-bound theories and egoisms; to whom millions of living fellow-creatures, with beating hearts in their bosoms, beating, suffering, hoping, are 'masses', mere 'explosive masses for blowing-down Bastilles with', for voting at hustings for *us*: such men are of the questionable species.

I have already argued the questionable nature of our many kinds of failure to commit ourselves to revolution. I would now repeat, with Carlyle, and with much real experience since he wrote, the questionable nature of a common kind of commitment. It is undoubtedly true that a commitment to revolution can produce a kind of hardening which even ends by negating the revolutionary purpose. Some people make the false commitment – the use of the misery of others – from the beginning. The most evident example is in Fascism, which is false revolution in just this sense. But, under real historical pressures, this hardening and negation occur again and again in authentic revolutionary activity, especially in isolation, under fire, and in scarcity so extreme as to threaten survival. The enemies of the revolutionary purpose then seize on the evidence of hardening and negation: either to oppose revolution as such, or to restore the convenient belief that man cannot change his condition, and that aspiration brings terror as a logical companion.

But this tragic aspect of revolution, which we are bound to acknowledge, cannot be understood in such ways. We have still to attend to the whole action, and to see actual liberation as part of the same process as the terror which appals us. I do not mean that the liberation cancels the terror; I mean only that they are connected, and that this connection is tragic. The final truth in this matter seems to be that revolution – the long revolution against human alienation – produces, in real historical circumstances, its own new kinds of alienation, which it must struggle to understand and which it must overcome, if it is to remain revolutionary.

I see this revolutionary alienation in several forms. There is the simple and yet bloody paradox that in the act of revolution its open enemies are easily seen as 'not men'. The tyrant, as he is killed, seems not a man but an object, and his brutality draws an answering brutality, which can become falsely associated with liberation itself. But it is not only a matter of the open enemies. Under severe pressure, the revolutionary purpose can become itself abstracted and can be set as an idea above real men. The decisive connection between present and future, which can only be a connection in experience and in continuing specific relations, is at once suppressed and replaced. There is then the conversion of actual misery and actual hope into a merely tactical 'revolutionary situation'. There is the related imposition of an idea of the revolution on the real men and women in whose name it is being made. The old unilinear model, by which revolution is abstractly known, is imposed on experience, including revolutionary experience. Often only this abstracted idea can sustain men, at the limits of their strength, but the need to impose it, in just such a crisis, converts friends into enemies, and actual life into the ruthlessly moulded material of an idea. The revolutionary purpose, born in what is most human and therefore most various, is negated by the single and often heroic image of revolutionary man, arrested at a stage in the very process of liberation and, persistent, becoming its most inward enemy.

In such ways, the most active agents of revolution can become its factual enemies, even while to others, and even to themselves, they seem its most perfect embodiment. But while we see this merely as accident, as the random appearance of particular evil men, we can understand nothing, for we are evading the nature of the whole action, and projecting its general meaning on to individuals whom we idealize or execrate. Elevating ourselves to spectators and judges, we suppress our own real role in any such action, or conclude, in a kind of indifference, that what has happened was inevitable and that there is even a law of inevitability. We see indeed a certain inevitability, of a tragic kind, as we see the struggle to end alienation producing its own new kinds of alienation. But, while we attend to the whole action, we see also, working through it, a new struggle against the new alienation: the comprehension of disorder producing a new image of order; the revolution against the fixed consciousness of revolution, and the authentic activity reborn and newly lived. What we then know is no simple action: the heroic liberation. But we know more also than simple reaction, for if we accept alienation, in ourselves or in others, as a permanent condition, we must know that other men, by the very act of living, will reject this, making us their involuntary enemies, and the radical disorder is then most bitterly confirmed.

The tragic action, in its deepest sense, is not the confirmation of disorder, but its experience, its comprehension and its resolution. In our own time, this action is general, and its common name is revolution. We have to see the evil and the suffering, in the factual disorder that makes revolution necessary, and in the disordered struggle against the disorder. We have to recognize this suffering in a close and immediate experience, and not cover it with names. But we follow the whole action: not only the evil, but the men who have fought against evil; not only the crisis, but the energy released by it, the spirit learned in it. We make the connections, because that is the action of tragedy, and what we learn in suffering is again revolution, because we acknowledge others as men and any such acknowledgement is the beginning of struggle, as the continuing reality of our lives. Then to see revolution in this tragic perspective is the only way to maintain it.

NOTE

1 Evolution in this Fabian sense is different again from both Darwinism and the competitive struggle for life. Yet it shares with the latter a metaphorical quality, still essentially unrelated to the scientific theory. For behind the idea of social evolution was an unconscious attachment to the development of a *single* form. Social development was unconsciously based on the experience of one type of Western society, and its imperialist contacts with more 'primitive' societies. The real social and cultural variation of human history was thus reduced to a single model: unilinear and predictable. Even Marxists took over this limited model, and its rigidity has been widely experienced in some twentieth-century communist practice. A more adequate understanding of both natural and cultural evolution would have made so mechanical and unilinear a model untenable, for it would have emphasized both variation and creativity and thus a more genuinely open and (in the full sense) revolutionary future.

b) Literature

It is relatively difficult to see 'literature' as a concept. In ordinary usage it appears to be no more than a specific description, and what is described is then, as a rule, so highly valued that there is a virtually immediate and unnoticed transfer of the specific values of particular works and kinds of work to what operates as a concept but is still firmly believed to be actual and practical. Indeed the special property of 'literature' as a concept is that it claims this kind of importance and priority, in the concrete achievements of many particular great works, as against the 'abstraction' and 'generality' of other concepts and of the kinds of practice which they, by contrast, define. Thus it is common to see 'literature' defined as 'full, central, immediate human experience', usually with an associated reference to 'minute particulars'. By contrast, 'society' is often seen as essentially general and abstract: the summaries and averages, rather than the direct substance, of human living. Other related concepts, such as 'politics', 'sociology' or 'ideology', are similarly placed and downgraded, as mere hardened outer shells compared with the living experience of literature.

The naïvety of the concept, in this familiar form, can be shown in two ways: theoretically and historically. It is true that one popular version of the concept has been developed in ways that appear to protect it, and in practice do often protect it, against any such arguments. An essential abstraction of the 'personal' and the 'immediate' is carried so far that, within this highly developed form of thought, the whole process of abstraction has been dissolved. None of its steps can be retraced, and the abstraction of the 'concrete' is a perfect and virtually unbreakable circle. Arguments from theory or from history are simply evidence of the incurable abstraction and generality of those who are putting them forward. They can then be contemptuously rejected, often without specific reply, which would be only to fall to their level.

This is a powerful and often forbidding system of abstraction, in which the concept of 'literature' becomes actively ideological. Theory can do something against it, in the necessary recognition (which ought hardly, to those who are really in contact with literature, to need any long preparation) that whatever else 'it' may be, literature is the process and the result of formal composition within the social and formal properties of a language. The effective suppression of this process and its circumstances, which is achieved by shifting the concept to an undifferentiated equivalence with 'immediate living experience' (indeed, in some cases, to more than this, so that the actual lived experiences of society and history are seen as less particular and immediate than those of literature) is an extraordinary ideological feat. The very process that is specific, that of actual composition, has effectively disappeared or has been displaced to an internal and self-proving procedure in which writing of this kind is genuinely believed to be (however many questions are then begged) 'immediate living experience' itself. Appeals to the history of literature, over its immense and extraordinarily various range, from the *Mabinogion* to *Middlemarch*, or from *Paradise Lost* to *The Prelude*, cause a momentary hesitation until various dependent categories of the concept are moved into place: 'myth', 'romance', 'fiction', 'realist fiction', 'epic', 'lyric', 'autobiography'. What from another point of view might reasonably be taken as initial definitions of the processes and circumstances of composition are converted, within the ideological concept, to 'forms' of what is still triumphantly defined as 'full, central, immediate human experience'. Indeed when any concept has so profound and complex an internal specializing development, it can hardly be examined or questioned at all from outside. If we are to understand its significance, and the complicated facts it partially reveals and partially obscures, we must turn to examining the development of the concept itself.

In its modern form the concept of 'literature' did not emerge earlier than the eighteenth century and was not fully developed until the nineteenth century. Yet the conditions for its emergence had been developing since the Renaissance. The word itself came into English use in the fourteenth century, following French and Latin precedents; its root was Latin *littera*, a letter of the alphabet. *Litterature*, in the common early spelling, was then in effect a condition of reading: of being able to read and of having read. It was often close to the sense of modern *literacy*, which was not in the language until the late nineteenth century, its introduction in part made necessary by the movement of *literature* to a different sense. The normal adjective associated with literature was *literate*. *Literary* appeared in the sense of reading ability and experience in the seventeenth century, and did not acquire its specialized modern meaning until the eighteenth century.

Literature as a new category was then a specialization of the area formerly categorized as *rhetoric* and *grammar*: a specialization to reading and, in the material context of the development of printing, to the printed word and especially the book. It was eventually to become a more general category than *poetry* or the earlier *poesy*, which had been general terms for imaginative composition, but which in relation to the development of *literature* became predominantly specialized, from the seventeenth century, to metrical composition and especially written and printed metrical composition. But *literature* was never primarily the active composition – the 'making' – which poetry had described. As reading rather than writing, it was a category of a different kind. The characteristic use can be seen in Bacon – 'learned in all literature and erudition, divine and humane' – and as late as Johnson – 'he had probably more than common literature, as his son addresses him in one of his most elaborate Latin poems'. *Literature*, that is to say, was a category of use and condition rather than of production. It was a particular specialization of what had hitherto been seen as an activity or practice, and a specialization, in the circumstances, which was inevitably made in terms of social class. In its first extended sense, beyond the bare sense of 'literacy', it was a definition of 'polite' or 'humane' learning, and thus specified a particular social distinction. New political concepts of the 'nation' and new valuations of the 'vernacular' interacted with a persistent emphasis on 'literature' as reading in the 'classical' languages. But still, in this first stage, into the eighteenth century, *literature* was primarily a generalized social concept, expressing a certain (minority) level of educational achievement. This carried with it a potential and eventually realized alternative definition of *literature* as 'printed books': the objects in and through which this achievement was demonstrated.

It is important that, within the terms of this development, literature normally included all printed books. There was not necessary specialization to 'imaginative' works. Literature was still primarily reading ability and reading experience, and this included philosophy, history and essays as well as poems. Were the new eighteenth-century novels 'literature'? That question was first approached, not by definition of their mode or content, but by reference to the standards of 'polite' or 'humane' learning. Was drama literature? This question was to exercise successive generations, not because of any substantial difficulty but because of the practical limits of the category. If literature was reading, could a mode written for spoken performance be said to be literature, and if not, where was Shakespeare? (But of course he could *now* be read; this was made possible, and 'literary', by *texts.*)

At one level the definition indicated by this development has persisted. Literature lost its earliest sense of reading ability and reading experience, and became an apparently objective category of printed works of a certain quality. The concerns of a 'literary editor' or a 'literary supplement' would still be defined in this way. But three complicating tendencies can then be distinguished: first, a shift from 'learning' to 'taste' or 'sensibility' as a criterion defining literary quality; second, an increasing specialization of literature to 'creative' or 'imaginative' works; third, a development of the concept of 'tradition' within national terms, resulting in the more effective definition of 'a national literature'. The sources of each of these tendencies can be discerned from the Renaissance, but it was in the eighteenth and nineteenth centuries that they came through most powerfully, until they became, in the twentieth century, in effect received assumptions. We can look more closely at each tendency.

The shift from 'learning' to 'taste' or 'sensibility' was in effect the final stage of a shift from a para-national scholarly profession, with its original social base in the church and then in the universities, and with the classical languages as its shared material, to a profession increasingly defined by its class position, from which essentially general criteria, applicable in fields other than literature, were derived. In England certain specific features of bourgeois development strengthened the shift; the 'cultivated amateur' was one of its elements, but 'taste' and 'sensibility' were essentially unifying concepts, in class terms, and could be applied over a very wide range from public and private behaviour to (as Wordsworth complained) either wine or poetry. As subjective definitions of apparently objective criteria (which acquire their apparent objectivity from an actively consensual class sense), and at the same time apparently objective definitions of subjective qualities, 'taste' and 'sensibility' are characteristically bourgeois categories.

'Criticism' is an essentially associated concept, in the same development. As a new term, from the seventeenth century, it developed (always in difficult relations with its general and persistent sense of fault-finding) from 'commentaries' on literature, within the 'learned' criterion, to the conscious exercise of 'taste', 'sensibility' and 'discrimination'. It became a significant special form of the general tendency in the concept of literature towards an emphasis on the use or (conspicuous) consumption of works, rather than on their production. While the habits of use or consumption were still the criteria of a relatively integrated class, they had their characteristic strengths as well as weaknesses. 'Taste' in literature might be confused with 'taste' in everything else, but, within class terms, responses to literature were notably integrated, and the relative integration of the 'reading public' (a characteristic term of the definition) was a sound base for important literary production. The reliance on 'sensibility', as a special form of an attempted emphasis on whole 'human' response, had its evident weaknesses in its tendency to separate 'feeling' from 'thought' (with an associated vocabulary of 'subjective' and 'objective', 'unconscious' and 'conscious', 'private' and 'public'). At the same time it served, at its best, to insist on 'immediate' and 'living' substance (in which its contrast with the 'learned' tradition was especially marked). It was really only as this class lost its relative cohesion and dominance that the weakness of the concepts *as concepts* became evident. And it is evidence of at least its residual hegemony that *criticism*, taken as a new conscious discipline into the universities, to be practised by what became a new para-national profession, retained these founding class concepts, alongside attempts to establish new abstractly objective criteria. More seriously, criticism was taken to be a natural definition of literary studies, themselves defined by the specializing category (printed works of a certain quality) of *literature*. Thus these forms of the concepts of *literature* and *criticism* are, in the perspective of historical social development, forms of a class specialization and control of a general social practice, and of a class limitation of the questions which it might raise.

The process of the specialization of 'literature' to 'creative' or 'imaginative' works is very much more complicated. It is in part a major affirmative response, in the name of an essentially general human 'creativity', to the socially repressive and intellectually mechanical forms of a new social order: that of capitalism and especially industrial capitalism. The practical specialization of work to the wage-labour production of commodities; of 'being' to 'work' in these terms; of language to the passing of 'rational' or 'informative' 'messages'; of social relations to functions within a systematic economic and political order: all these pressures and limits were challenged in the name of a full and liberating 'imagination' or 'creativity'. The central Romantic assertions, which depend on these concepts, have a significantly absolute range, from politics and nature to work and art. 'Literature' acquired, in this period, a quite new resonance, but it was not yet a specialized resonance. That came later as, against the full pressures of an industrial capitalist order, the assertion became defensive and reserving where it had once been positive and absolute. In 'art' and 'literature', the essential and saving *human* qualities must, in the early phase, be 'extended'; in the later phase, 'preserved'.

Several concepts developed together. 'Art' was shifted from its sense of a general human skill to a special province, defined by 'imagination' and 'sensibility'. 'Aesthetic', in the same period, shifted from its sense of general perception to a specialized category of the 'artistic' and the 'beautiful'. 'Fiction' and 'myth' (a new term from the early nineteenth century) might be seen from the dominant class position as 'fancies' or 'lies' but from this alternative position were honoured as the bearers of '*imaginative* truth'. 'Romance' and 'romantic' were given newly specialized positive emphases. 'Literature' moved with all these. The wide general meaning was still available, but a specialized meaning came steadily to predominate, around the distinguishing qualities of the 'imaginative' and the 'aesthetic'. 'Taste' and 'sensibility' had begun as categories of a social condition. In the new specialization, comparable but more elevated qualities were assigned to 'the works themselves', the 'aesthetic objects'.

But there was still one substantial uncertainty: whether the elevated qualities were to be assigned to the 'imaginative' dimension (access to a truth 'higher' or 'deeper' than 'scientific' or 'objective' or 'everyday' reality; a claim consciously substituting itself for the traditional claims of religion) or to the 'aesthetic' dimension ('beauties' of language or style). Within the specialization of literature, alternative schools made one or other of these emphases, but there were also repeated attempts to fuse them, making 'truth' and 'beauty', or 'truth' and 'vitality of language', identical. Under continuing pressure these arguments became not only positive assertions but increasingly negative and comparative, against all other modes: not only against 'science' and 'society' – the abstract and generalizing modes of other 'kinds' of experience – and not only against other kinds of writing – now in their turn specialized as 'discursive' or 'factual' – but, ironically, against much of 'literature' itself – 'bad' writing, 'popular' writing, 'mass culture'. Thus the category which had appeared objective as 'all printed books', and which had been given a social-class foundation as 'polite learning' and the domain of 'taste' and 'sensibility', now became a necessarily selective and self-defining area: not all 'fiction' was 'imaginative'; not all 'literature' was 'Literature'. 'Criticism' acquired a quite new and effectively primary importance, since it was now the only way of validating this specialized and selective category. It was at once a *discrimination* of the authentic 'great' or 'major' works, with a consequent grading of 'minor' works and an effective exclusion of 'bad' or 'negligible' works, and a practical realization and communication of the 'major' values. What had been claimed for 'art' and the 'creative imagination' in the central Romantic arguments was now claimed for 'criticism', as the central 'humane' activity and 'discipline'.

This development depended, in the first place, on an elaboration of the concept of 'tradition'. The idea of a 'national literature' had been growing strongly since the Renaissance. It drew on all the positive forces of cultural nationalism and its real achievements. It brought with it a sense of the 'greatness' or 'glory' of the native language, for which before the Renaissance there had been conventional apology by comparison with a 'classical' range. Each of these rich and strong achievements had been actual; the 'national literature' and the 'major language' were now indeed 'there'. But, within the specialization of 'literature', each was re-defined so that it could be brought to identity with the selective and self-defining 'literary values'. The 'national literature' soon ceased to be a history and became a tradition. It was not, even theoretically, all that had been written or all kinds of writing. It was a selection which culminated in, and in a circular way defined, the 'literary values' which 'criticism' was asserting. There were then always local disputes about who and what should be included, or as commonly excluded, in the definition of this 'tradition'. To have been an Englishman and to have written was by no means to belong to the 'English literary tradition', just as to be an Englishman and to speak was by no means to exemplify the 'greatness' of the language – indeed the practice of most English speakers was continually cited as 'ignorance' or 'betrayal' or 'debasement' of just this 'greatness'. Selectivity and self-defini-tion, which were the evident processes of 'criticism' of this kind, were, however, projected as 'literature' itself, as 'literary values' and even finally as 'essential Englishness': the absolute ratification of a limited and specializing consensual process. To oppose the terms of this ratification was to be 'against literature'.

It is one of the signs of the success of this categorization of literature that even Marxism has made so little headway against it. Marx himself, to be sure, hardly tried. His characteristically intelligent and informed incidental discus-sions of actual literature are now often cited, defensively, as evidence of the humane flexibility of Marxism, when they ought really to be cited with no particular devaluation) as evidence of how far he remained, in these matters, within the conventions and categories of his time. The radical challenge of the emphasis on 'practical consciousness' was thus never carried through to the categories of 'literature' and 'the aesthetic', and there was always hesitation about the practical application, in this area, of propositions which were held to be central and decisive almost everywhere else.

When such application was eventually made, in the later Marxist tradition, it was of three main kinds: an attempted assimilation of 'literature' to 'ideology', which was in practice little more than banging one inadequate category against another; an effective and important inclusion of 'popular literature' – the 'literature of the people' – as a necessary but neglected part of the 'literary tradition'; and a sustained but uneven attempt to relate 'literature' to the social and economic history within which 'it' had been produced. Each of these last two attempts has been significant. In the former a 'tradition' has been genuinely extended. In the latter there has been an effective reconstitution, over wide areas, of historical social practice, which makes the abstraction of 'literary values' much more problematical, and which, more positively, allows new kinds of reading and new kinds of questions about 'the works themselves'. This has been known, especially, as 'Marxist criticism' (a radical variant of the established bourgeois practice) though other work has been done on quite different bases, from a wider social history and from wider conceptions of 'the people', 'the language' and 'the nation'.

It is significant that 'Marxist criticism' and 'Marxist literary studies' have been most successful, in ordinary terms, when they have worked within the received category of 'literature', which they may have extended or even revalued, but never radically questioned or opposed. By contrast, what looked like fundamental theoretical revaluation, in the attempted assimilation to 'ideology', was a disastrous failure, and fundamentally compromised, in this whole area, the status of Marxism itself. Yet for half a century now there have been other and more significant tendencies. Lukács contributed a profound revaluation of 'the aesthetic'. The Frankfurt School, with its special emphasis on art, undertook a sustained re-examination of 'artistic production', centred on the concept of 'mediation'. Goldmann undertook a radical revaluation of the 'creative subject'. Marxist variants of formalism undertook radical re-definition of the processes of writing, with new uses of the concepts of 'signs' and 'texts', and with a significantly related refusal of 'literature' as a category. The methods and problems indicated by these tendencies will be examined in detail later in this book.

Yet the crucial theoretical break is the recognition of 'literature' as a specializing social and historical category. It should be clear that this does not diminish its importance. Just because it is historical, a key concept of a major phase of a culture, it is decisive evidence of a particular form of the social development of language. Within its terms, work of outstanding and perma-nent importance was done, in specific social and cultural relationships. But what has been happening, in our own century, is a profound transformation of these relationships, directly connected with changes in the basic means of production. These changes are most evident in the new technologies of language, which have moved practice beyond the relatively uniform and specializing technology of print. The principal changes are the electronic transmission and recording of speech and of writing for speech, and the chemical and electronic composition and transmission of images, in complex relations with speech and with writing for speech, and including images which can themselves be 'written'. None of these means cancels print, or even diminishes its specific importance, but they are not simple additions to it, or mere alternatives. In their complex connections and interrelations they com-pose a new substantial practice in social language itself, over a range from public address and manifest representation to 'inner speech' and verbal thought. For they are always more than new technologies, in the limited sense. They are *means of production*, developed in direct if complex relations with profoundly changing and extending social and cultural relationships: changes elsewhere recognizable as deep political and economic transformations. It is in no way surprising that the specialized concept of 'literature', developed in precise forms of correspondence with a particular social class, a particular organization of learning, and the appropriate particular technology of print, should now be so often invoked in retrospective, nostalgic or reactionary moods, as a form of opposition to what is correctly seen as a new phase of civilization. The situation is historically comparable to that invocation of the divine and the sacred, and of divine and sacred learning, against the new humanist concept of literature, in the difficult and contested transition from feudal to bourgeois society.

What can then be seen as happening, in each transition, is an historical development of social language itself: finding new means, new forms and then new definitions of a changing practical consciousness. Many of the active values of 'literature' have then to be seen, not as tied to the concept, which came to limit as well as to summarize them, but as elements of a continuing and changing practice which already substantially, and now at the level of theoretical redefinition, is moving beyond its old forms.

17 Louis Althusser

A Letter on Art in Reply to André Daspre (1966)[*]

Louis Althusser (1918–90) has been an important influence since *For Marx* (1965; trans. 1969) and *Reading 'Capital'* (1968; trans. 1970), though his work addresses Marx and philosophy rather than literature. Working with Etienne Balibar and Pierre Macherey, with whom he co-wrote *Reading 'Capital'*, Althusser suggested new 'symptomatic' ways of reading Marx. As his essay 'Freud and Lacan' (1969) implies, Althusser's return to Marx has affinities with Lacan's reworking of psychoanalysis through a return to Freud. Althusser rejected Hegelian, existentialist and humanist modes of Marxism, arguing that historical materialism provides a scientific theory of the overdetermined and decentred relations of reality. In his influential essay 'Ideology and State Apparatuses' – published in *Lenin and Philosophy and Other Essays* (1971) – he used Lacanian conceptions of the subject to describe how subjects are interpellated by social structures. According to Althusser human beings are not authors or subjects of social processes, but effects or symptoms of structural hierarchies. This seemed to offer a structuralist account of subjectivity which could be integrated with Marxism. But as the example of Slavoj Zizek indicates, such unstable compounds may metamorphose into Lacanian Hegelianism rather than anti-Hegelian Marxism. Althusser's work has been criticized for its inflated claims for theory, its lack of political specificity and its idealist relation to empiricism, notably in E. P. Thompson, *The Poverty of Theory* (1978). But Althusser's influence is still apparent in cultural studies, even if his Marxism is not. 'A Letter on Art' (1966) provides a brief discussion of how his theory of ideology might relate to literature. Later works include *Essays in Self-Criticism* (1976) and his memoir, *The Future Lasts a Long Time* (1993). Other attempts to combine Marxism, psychoanalysis and structuralism – such as the early work of Julia Kristeva, the Maoist phase of *Tel Quel*, or the work of Michel Pêcheux – present as many difficulties as solutions. For Althusserian literary criticism see Pierre Macherey, *A Theory of Literary Production* (1966; trans. 1978) and Terry Eagleton, *Criticism and Ideology* (1976). On Althusser

---

[*] From Louis Althusser, *Lenin and Philosophy and Other Essays*, trans. B. Brewster (London: NLB, 1971), 221–7.

in general, see A. Callinicos, *Althusser's Marxism* (1976); T. Benton, *The Rise and Fall of Structural Marxism* (1984); and *Althusser: A Critical Reader*, ed. G. Elliott (1994).

La Nouvelle Critique has sent me your letter.[1] I hope you will permit me, if not to reply to all the questions it poses, at least to add a few comments to yours in the line of your own reflections.

First of all, you should know that I am perfectly conscious of the *very schematic* character of my article on Humanism.[2] As you have noticed, it has the disadvantage that it gives a 'broad' idea of ideology without going into the analysis of details. As it does not mention art, I realize that it is possible to wonder whether art should or should not be ranked as such among ideologies, to be precise, whether art and ideology are one and the same thing. That, I feel, is how you have been tempted to *interpret* my silence.

The problem of the relations between art and ideology is a very complicated and difficult one. However, I can tell you in what directions our investigations tend. *I do not rank real art among the ideologies*, although art does have a quite particular and specific relationship with ideology. If you would like some idea of the initial elements of this thesis and the very complicated developments it promises, I advise you to read carefully the article Pierre Macherey has written on 'Lenin as a Critic of Tolstoy' in *La Pensée*, no. 121, 1965.[3] Of course, that article is only a beginning, but it does pose the problem of the relations between art and ideology and of the specificity of art. This is the direction in which we are working, and we hope to publish important studies on this subject in a few months time.

The article will also give you a first idea of the relationship between art and knowledge. Art (I mean authentic art, not works of an average or mediocre level) does not give us a *knowledge* in the *strict sense*, it therefore does not replace knowledge (in the modern sense: scentific knowledge), but what it gives us does nevertheless maintain a certain *specific relationship* with knowledge. This relationship is not one of identity but one of difference. Let me explain. I believe that the peculiarity of art is to 'make us see' (*nous donner à voir*), 'make us perceive', 'make us feel' something which *alludes* to reality. If we take the case of the novel, Balzac or Solzhenitsyn, as you refer to them, they make us *see*, *perceive* (but not *know*) something which *alludes* to reality.

It is essential to take the words which make up this first provisional definition literally if we are to avoid lapsing into an identification of what art gives us and what science gives us. What art makes us *see*, and therefore gives to us in the form of '*seeing*', '*perceiving*' and '*feeling*' (which is not the form of *knowing*), is the *ideology* from which it is born, in which it bathes, from which it detaches itself as art, and to which it *alludes*. Macherey has shown this very clearly in the case of Tolstoy, by extending Lenin's analyses. Balzac and Solzhenitsyn give us a 'view' of the ideology to which their work alludes and with which it is constantly fed, a view which presupposes a *retreat*, an *internal distantiation* from the very ideology from which their novels emerged. They make us 'perceive' (but not know) in some sense *from the inside*, by an *internal distance*, the very ideology in which they are held.

These distinctions, which are not just shades of meaning but specific differences, should *in principle* enable us to resolve a number of problems.

First the problem of the 'relations' between art and science. Neither Balzac nor Solzhenitsyn gives us any *knowledge* of the world they describe, they only make us 'see', 'perceive' or 'feel' the reality of the ideology of that world. When we speak of ideology we should know that ideology slides into all human activity, that it is identical with the 'lived' experience of human existence itself: that is why the form in which we are 'made to see' ideology in great novels has as its content the 'lived' experience of individuals. This 'lived' experience is not a *given*, given by a pure 'reality', but the spontaneous 'lived experience' of ideology in its peculiar relationship to the real. This is an important comment, for it enables us to understand that art does not deal with a reality *peculiar to itself*, with a *peculiar domain* of reality in which it has a monopoly (as you tend to imply when you write that 'with art, know-ledge becomes human', that the object of art is 'the individual'), whereas science deals with a *different domain* of reality (say, in opposition to 'lived experience' and the 'individual', the abstraction of structures). Ideology is also an object of science, the 'lived experience' is also an object of science, the 'individual' is also an object of science. The real difference between art and science lies in the *specific form* in which they give us the same object in quite different ways: art in the form of 'seeing' and 'perceiv-ing' or 'feeling', science in the form of *knowledge* (in the strict sense, by concepts).

The same thing can be said in other terms. If Solzhenitsyn does 'make us see' the 'lived experience' (in the sense defined earlier) of the 'cult of personality' and its effects, in no way does he give us a *knowledge* of them: this knowledge is the conceptual knowledge of the complex mechanisms which eventually produce the 'lived experience' that Solzhenitsyn's novel discusses. If I wanted to use Spinoza's language again here, I could say that art makes us 'see' 'conclusions without premises', whereas knowledge makes us pene-trate into the mechanism which produces the 'conclusions' out of the 'premises'. This is an important distinction, for it enables us to understand that a novel on the 'cult', however profound, may draw attention to its 'lived' effects, but *cannot give an understanding of it*; it may put the question of the 'cult' on the agenda, but it cannot *define the means* which will make it possible to remedy these effects.

In the same way, these few elementary principles perhaps enable us to point the direction from which we can hope for an answer to another question you pose: how is it that Balzac, despite his personal political options, 'makes us see' the 'lived experience' of capitalist society in a critical form? I do not believe one can say, as you do, that he '*was forced by the logic of his art to abandon certain of his political conceptions in his work as a novelist*'. On the contrary, we know that Balzac *never abandoned* his political positions. We know even more: his peculiar, reactionary political positions played a decisive part in the production of the content of his work. This is certainly a paradox, but it is the case, and history provides us with a number of examples to which Marx drew our attention (on Balzac, I refer you to the article by R. Fayolle in the special 1965 number of *Europe*). These are examples of a deformation of sense very commonly found in the dialectic of ideologies. See what Lenin says about Tolstoy (cf. Macherey's article): Tolstoy's personal ideological position is one component of the deep-lying causes of the *content* of his work. The fact that the content of the work of Balzac and Tolstoy is 'detached' from their political ideology and in some way makes us 'see' it from the *outside*, makes us 'perceive' it by a distantiation inside that ideology, *presupposes that ideology itself*. It is certainly possible to say that it is an 'effect' of *their art* as novelists that it produces this distance inside their ideology, which makes us 'perceive' it, but it is not possible to say, as you do, that art '*has its own logic*' which '*made Balzac abandon his political conceptions*'. On the contrary, *only because he retained them could he produce his work*, only because he stuck to his political ideology could he produce *in it* this internal 'distance' which gives us a critical 'view' of it.

As you see, in order to answer most of the questions posed for us by the existence and specific nature of art, we are forced to produce an adequate (scientific) *knowledge* of the processes which produce the 'aesthetic effect' of a work of art. In other words, in order to answer the question of the relationship between art and knowledge we must produce a *knowledge of art*.

You are conscious of this necessity. But you ought also to know that in this issue we still have a long way to go. The *recognition* (even the political recognition) of the existence and importance of art does not constitute *a knowledge of art*. I do not even think that it is possible to take as the beginnings of knowledge the texts you refer to,[4] or even Joliot-Curie, quoted by Marcenac.[5] To say a few words about the sentence attributed to Joliot-Curie, it contains a terminology – 'aesthetic *creation*, scientific *creation*' – a terminology which is certainly quite common, but one which in my opinion must be *abandoned* and replaced by another, in order to be able to pose the problem of the knowledge of art in the proper way. I know that the artist, and the art lover, *spontaneously* express themselves in terms of 'creation', etc. It is a 'spontaneous' language, but we know from Marx and Lenin that every 'spontaneous' language is an *ideological* language, the vehicle of an ideology, here the ideology of art and of the activity productive of aesthetic effects. Like all knowledge, the knowledge of art presupposes a preliminary *rupture* with the language of *ideological spontaneity* and the constitution of a body of scientific concepts to replace it. It is essential to be conscious of the necessity for this rupture with ideology to be able to undertake the constitution of the edifice of a knowledge of art.

Here perhaps, is where I must express a sharp reservation about what you say. I am not perhaps speaking about exactly what you *want* or *would like* to say, but about what you *actually* do say. When you counterpose '*rigorous reflection on the concepts of Marxism*' to '*something else*', in particular to what art gives us, I believe you are establishing a comparison which is either incomplete or illegitimate. Since art in fact provides us with *something else* other than science, there is not an opposition between them, but a difference. On the contrary, if it is a matter of *knowing* art, it is absolutely essential to begin with '*rigorous reflection on the basic concepts of Marxism*': there is no other way. And when I say, '*it is essential to begin . . .*', it is not enough to *say* it, it is essential to *do* it. If not, it is easy to extricate oneself with a passing acknowledgement, like '*Althusser proposes to return to a rigorous study of Marxist theory. I agree that this is indispensable. But I do not believe that it is enough.*' My response to this is the only real criticism: there is a way of declaring an exigency 'indispensable' which consists precisely of *dispensing with it*, dispensing with a careful consideration of all its implications and consequences – by the acknowledgement accorded it in order to move quickly on to 'something else'. Now I believe that the only way we can hope to reach a real knowledge of art, to go deeper into the specificity of the work of art, to know the mechanisms which produce the 'aesthetic effect', is precisely to spend a long time and pay the greatest attention to the '*basic principles of Marxism*' and not to be in a hurry to 'move on to something else', for if we move on too quickly to 'something else' we shall arrive not at a *knowledge* of art, but at an *ideology* of art: e.g., at the latent humanist ideology which may be induced by what you say about the relations between art and the 'human', and about artistic 'creation', etc.

If we must turn (and this demands slow and arduous work) to the 'basic principles of Marxism' in order to be able to pose correctly, in concepts which are not the *ideological* concepts of aesthetic spontaneity, but *scientific* concepts adequate to their object, and thus necessarily *new* concepts, it is not in order to pass art silently by or to sacrifice it to science: it is quite simply in order to *know* it, and to give it its due.

NOTES

1 See *La Nouvelle Critique*, 175 (April, 1966), 136–41.
2 *La Nouvelle Critique*, 164 (March, 1965); *For Marx* (London, 1969), 242–7.
3 Now in Pierre Macherey, *Pour une théorie de la production littéraire* (Paris, 1966), 125–57.
4 [Jean Marcenac, Elsa Triolet, Lukács, among others.]

5 [Jean Marcenac, *Les Lettres françaises*, 1966. 'I have always regretted the fact that F. Joliot-Curie never pursued the project he suggested to me at the time of Eluard's death, the project of a comparative study of poetic creation and scientific creation, which he thought might eventually prove an identity in their procedures.']

18 Etienne Balibar and Pierre Macherey

On Literature as an Ideological Form (1974)[*]

Etienne Balibar and Pierre Macherey teach philosophy at the University of Paris. Balibar and Macherey worked with Louis Althusser, and both contributed to *Lire le Capital* (1965), selections from which are translated as *Reading Capital* (1971). This work with Althusser was part of an attempt to redirect the Marxist ideology of the French Communist Party from within. Macherey also wrote *A Theory of Literary Production* (1966; trans. 1978): an early version of Althusserian literary criticism. *A Theory of Literary Production* applies Althusser's approach to 'symptomatic' reading to literary texts, seeking to articulate the way that the material conditions of a text's production are 'silently' inscribed within texts. Criticism attempts, accordingly, to unmask the hidden ideological contradictions held in resolution within the formal structures of a text. With the impact of events in May 1968 in Paris, and of Althusser's essay, 'On Ideology and Ideological State Apparatuses' (1969), Macherey's work shifted from this more formalist approach to an approach which stresses the place of literature within the material conditions of ideology and the state. This shifted attention from historical conditions of production to the conditions and ideological effects of a text's reproduction within society. Whereas Althusser had suggested that literature, while not scientific, had some autonomy from ideology, Balibar and Macherey reject the privileging of literature as a mode of discourse detached from its reproduction within a range of social practices. 'On Literature as an Ideological Form' prefaced Renée Balibar's *Les français fictifs* (1974), a study of the use of literature in the French education system. Macherey discusses his intellectual development in an interview published in *Red Letters*, 5 (1977). For critique see T. Eagleton, *Criticism and Ideology* (1976); and T. Eagleton, 'Macherey and Marxist Literary Theory' (1975) in *Against the Grain* (1986). Balibar's other works include: *On the Dictatorship of the Proletariat* (1977); *Race, Nation, Class*, with I. Wallerstein

[*] Trans. I. McLeod, J. Whitehead and A. Wordsworth, in *Untying the Text*, ed. R. Young (London: RKP, 1981), 79–99; first published in *Oxford Literary Review*, 3 (1978), 4–12.

(1991); and *Masses, Classes, Ideas* (1994). Macherey's most recent work is *The Object of Literature* (1995).

Is there a Marxist theory of literature? In what could it consist? This is a classic question, and often purely academic. We intend to reformulate it in two stages and suggest new propositions.

1 Marxist Theses on Literature and the Category of 'Reflection'

1.1 Can there be a 'Marxist aesthetic'?

It is not our intention to give an account of the attempts which have been made to substantiate this idea nor the controversies which have surrounded it. We will merely point out that to constitute an aesthetic (and particularly a literary aesthetic) has always presented Marxism with two kinds of problem, which can be combined or held separate: (*i*) How to explain the specific ideological mode for 'art' and the 'aesthetic' effect. (*ii*) How to analyse and explain the class position (or the class positions, which may be contradictory in themselves) of the author and more materially the 'literary text', within the ideological class struggle.

The first problem is obviously brought in, imposed on Marxism by the dominant ideology so as to force the Marxist critic to produce his own aesthetic and to 'settle accounts' with art, the work of art, the aesthetic effect, just like Lessing, or Hegel, or Taine, or Valéry, et al. Since the problem is imposed on Marxism from outside, it offers two alternatives: to reject the problem and so be 'proved' unable to explain, not so much a 'reality' as an absolute 'value' of our time, which is now supreme since it has replaced religious value; or to recognize the problem and therefore be forced to acknowledge aesthetic 'values', i.e., to submit to them. This is an even better result for the dominant ideology since it thereby makes Marxism concede to the 'values' of the dominant class within its own problematic – a result which has great political significance in a period when Marxism becomes the ideology of the working class.

The second problem meanwhile is induced from within the theory and practice of Marxism, on its own terrain, but in such a way that it can remain a formal and mechanical presentation. In this case the necessary criterion is that of practice. In the first place, of scientific practice: the question for Marxism should be, does the act of confronting literary texts with their class positions result in the opening of new fields of knowledge and in the first place simply in the siting of new problems? The proof of the right formulation would be whether it makes objectively clear within historical materialism itself whole sets of unsolved and sometimes as yet unrecognized problems.[1]

In the second place, of political practice itself, in so much as it is operative within literature. The least one should therefore ask a Marxist theory is that it should bring about real transformation, new practice, whether in the production of texts and 'works of art' or in their social 'consumption'. But is this a real transformation, even if at times it does have an immediate political effect – the simple fact of instilling the practitioners of art (writers and artists, but also teachers and students) with a Marxist ideology of the form and social function of art (even if this operation may sometimes have a certain immediate political interest)? Is it enough simply to give Marxism and its adherents their turn to taste and consume works of art in their own way? In effect experience proves that it is perfectly possible to substitute new 'Marxist' themes, i.e. formulated in the language of Marxism, for the ideological notions dominant in 'cultural life', notions that are bourgeois or petit-bourgeois in origin, and yet not alter at all the place of art and literature within social practice, nor therefore the practical relationship of individuals and classes to the works of art they produce and consume. The category of art in general dominates production and consumption, which are conceived and practised within this mode – whether 'committed', 'socialist', 'proletarian', or whatever.

Yet in the Marxist classics there were elements which can open a path [frayer la voie] – not an 'aesthetic', nor a 'theory of literature', any more than a 'theory of knowledge'. Yet through their mode of practising literature and the implications of a theoretical position based ultimately on revolutionary class practice, they pose certain theses about literary effects, which, worked within the problematic of historical materialism, make theses for a scientific and therefore historical analysis of literary effects.[2]

These very general premises are enough to show at once that the two types of problem between which Marxist attempts are divided, are really one and the same. To be able to analyse the nature and expression of class positions in literature and its output (the 'texts', 'works' perceived as literature) is simultaneously to be able to define and know the ideological mode of literature. But this means that the problem must be posed in terms of a theory of the history of literary effects, clearly showing the primary elements of their relation to their material base, their progressions (for they are not eternal) and their tendential transformations (for they are not immutable).

1.2 The materialist category of reflection

Let us be clear. The classic Marxist theses on literature and art set out from the essential philosophical category of the reflection. To understand this category fully is therefore the key to the Marxist conception of literature.

In the Marxist texts on this materialist concept, Marx and Engels on Balzac, Lenin on Tolstoy, it is *qua* material reflection, reflection of objective reality, that literature is conceived as an historic reality – in its very form, which scientific analysis seeks to grasp.

In the 'Talks at the Yenan Forum on Literature and Art', Mao Tse-tung writes, 'Works of literature and art, as ideological forms, are the product of the reflection in the human brain of the life of a given society.'[3] So the first implication of the category of reflection for Marxist theoreticians is to provide an index of reality of literature. It does not 'fall from the heavens', the product of a mysterious 'creation', but is the product of social practice (rather a particular social practice); neither is it an 'imaginary' activity, albeit it produces imaginary effects, but inescapably part of a material process, 'the product of the reflection . . . of the life of a given society'.

The Marxist conception thus inscribes literature in its place in the unevenly determined system of real social practices: one of several ideological forms within the ideological superstructures, corresponding to a base of social relations of production which are historically determined and transformed, and historically linked to other ideological forms. Be sure that in using the term ideological forms no reference to formalism is intended – the historical materialist concept does not refer to 'form' in opposition to 'content', but to the objective coherence of an ideological formation – we shall come back to this point. Let us note too that this first, very general but absolutely essential premiss, has no truck with queries about what ideological form is taken by literature within the ideological instance. There is no 'reduction' of literature to morality, religion, politics, etc.

The Marxist concept of reflection has suffered from so many misinterpretations and distortions that we must stop here for a moment. The conclusions reached by Dominique Lecourt through an attentive reading of Lenin's 'Materialism and Empiriocriticism' will be useful to us.[4]

Dominique Lecourt shows that the Marxist and Leninist category of reflection contains two propositions which are combined within a constitutive order – or better, two articulated successive problems. (Thus according to Lecourt there is not one simple thesis, but a double thesis of the reflection of things in thought.)

The first problem, which materialism always re-establishes in its priority, is the problem of the objectivity of the reflection. It poses the question: 'Is there an existent material reality reflected in the mind which determines thought?' And consequently it has the rider, 'Is thought itself a materially determined reality?' Dialectical materialism asserts the objectivity of the reflection and the objectivity of thought as reflection, i.e., the determinance of the material reality which precedes thought and is irreducible to it, and the material reality of thought itself.

The second problem, which can only be posed correctly on the basis of the first, concerns the scientific knowledge of the exactitude of the reflection. It poses the question, '*If* thought reflects an existent reality how accurate is its reflection?' or better, 'Under what conditions (i.e. historical conditions whereby the dialectic between 'absolute truth' and 'relative truth' intervenes) can it provide an accurate reflection?' The answer lies in the analysis of the relatively autonomous process of the history of science. In the context, it is clear that this second problem poses the question, 'What form does the reflection take?' But it only has a materialist implication once the first question has been posed and the objectivity of the reflection affirmed.

The result of this analysis, which we have only given in outline, is to show that the Marxist category of the 'reflection' is quite separate from the empiricist and sensualist concept of the image, reflection as 'mirroring'. The reflection, in dialectical materialism, is a 'reflection without a mirror'; in the history of philosophy this is the only effective destruction of the empiricist ideology which calls the relation of thought to the real a speculary (and therefore reversible) reflection. This is thanks to the complexity of the Marxist theory of 'reflection': it poses the separate nature of two propositions and their articulation in an irreversible order within which the materialist account is realized.

These observations are central to the problem of the 'theory of literature'. A rigorous use of this complex structure eliminates the seeming opposition of two contrary descriptions: that between formalism and the 'critical' or 'normative' use of the notion of 'realism'. That is, on one side an intention to study the reflection 'for itself', independent of its relationship to the material world; on the other, a confusion of both aspects and an assertion of the primacy of thought, a reversal of the materialist order.[5]

Hence the advantage of a rigorous definition like Lenin's, for it is then possible to articulate, in theory as in fact, two aspects which must be both kept separate and in a constitutive order: literature as an ideological form (amongst others), and the specific process of literary production.

1.3 Literature as an ideological form

It is important to 'locate' the production of literary effects historically as part of the ensemble of social practices. For this to be seen dialectically rather than mechanically, it is important to understand that the relationship of 'history' to 'literature' is not like the relationship or 'correspondence' of two 'branches', but concerns the developing forms of an internal contradiction. Literature and history are not each set up externally to each other (not even as the history *of* literature versus social and political history), but are in an intricate and connected relationship, the historical conditions of existence of anything like a literature. Very generally, this internal relationship is what constitutes the definition of literature as an ideological form.

But this definition is significant only in so far as its implications are then developed. Ideological forms, to be sure, are not straightforward systems of 'ideas' and 'discourses', but are manifested through the workings and history of determinate practices in determinate social relations, what Althusser calls the Ideological State Apparatuses (ISA). The objectivity of literary production therefore is inseparable from given social practices in a given ISA. More precisely, we shall see that it is inseparable from a given linguistic practice (there is a 'French' literature because there is a linguistic practice 'French', i.e. a contradictory ensemble making a national tongue), in itself inseparable from an academic or schooling practice which defines both the conditions for the consumption of literature and the very conditions of its production also. By connecting the objective existence of literature to this ensemble of practices, one can define the material anchoring points which make literature an historic and social reality.

First, then, literature is historically constituted in the bourgeois epoch as an ensemble of language – or rather of specific linguistic practices – inserted in a general schooling process so as to provide appropriate fictional effects, thereby reproducing bourgeois ideology as the dominant ideology. Literature submits to a threefold determination: 'linguistic', 'pedagogic', and 'fictive' [imaginaire] (we must return to this point, for it involves the question of a recourse to psychoanalysis for an explanation of literary effects). There is a linguistic determinance because the work of literary production depends on the existence of a common language codifying linguistic exchange, both for its material and for its aims – in so much as literature contributes directly to the maintenance of a 'common language'. That it has this starting-point is proved by the fact that divergences from the common language are not arbitrary but determined. In our introduction to the work of R. Balibar and D. Laporte, we sketched out an explanation of the historical process by which this 'common language' is set up.[6] Following their thought, we stressed that the common language, i.e. the national language, is bound to the political form of 'bourgeois democracy' and is the historical outcome of particular class struggles. Like bourgeois right, its parallel, the common national language is needed to unify a new class domination, thereby universalizing it and providing it with progressive forms throughout its epoch. It refers therefore to a social contradiction, perpetually reproduced via the process which surmounts it. What is the basis of this contradiction?

It is the effect of the historic conditions under which the bourgeois class established its political, economic and ideological dominance. To achieve hegemony, it had not only to transform the base, the relations of production, but also radically to transform the superstructure, the ideological formations. This transformation could be called the bourgeois 'cultural revolution' since it involves not only the formation of a new ideology, but its realization as the dominant ideology, through new ISA and the remoulding of the relationships between the different ISA. This revolutionary transformation, which took more than a century but which was preparing itself for far longer, is characterized by making the school apparatus the means of forcing submission to the dominant ideology – individual submission, but also, and more importantly, the submission of the very ideology of the dominated classes. Therefore in the last analysis, all the ideological contradictions rest on the contradictions of the school apparatus, and become contradictions subordinated to the form of schooling, within the form of schooling itself.

We are beginning to work out the form taken by social contradictions in the schooling apparatus. It can only establish itself through the formal unity of a unique and unifying educational system, the product of this same unity, which is itself formed from the coexistence of two systems or contradictory networks: those which, by following the institutional division of 'levels of teaching' which in France has long served to materialize this contradiction, we could call the apparatus of 'basic education' [primaire-professionnel] and that of 'advanced education' [secondaire-superieur].[7]

This division in schooling, which reproduces the social division of a society based on the sale and purchase of individual labour-power, while ensuring the dominance of bourgeois ideology through asserting a specifically national unity, is primarily and throughout based on a linguistic division. Let us be clear: there as well, the unifying form is the essential means of the division and of the contradiction. The linguistic division inherent in schooling is not like the division between different 'languages' observable in certain pre-capitalist social formations – those languages being a 'language of the common people' (dialect, patois or argot), and a 'language of the bourgeoisie' – on the contrary, the division presupposes a common language, and is the contradiction between different practices of the same language. Specifically, it is in and through the educational system that the contradiction is instituted – through the contradiction between the basic language [français élémentaire], as taught at primary school, and the literary language [français littéraire] reserved for the advanced level of teaching. This is the basis of the contradiction in schooling techniques, particularly between the basic exercise of 'rédaction – narration', a mere training in 'correct' usage and the reporting of 'reality', and the advanced exercise of comprehension, the 'dissertation – explication de textes', so-called 'creative' work which presupposes the incorporation and imitation of literary material. Hence the contradictions in schooling practice, and in ideological practice and in social practice. What thus appears as the basis of literary production is an unequal and contradictory relation to the same ideology, the dominant one. But this contradiction would not exist if the dominant ideology did not have to struggle all the time for its priority.

From this analysis, given in mere outline, there is an essential point to be grasped: the objectivity of literature, i.e. its relation to objective reality by which it is historically determined, is not a relation to an 'object' which it represents, is not representative. Nor is it purely and simply the instrument for using and transforming its immediate material, the linguistic practices determined within the practice of teaching. Precisely because of their contradictions, they cannot be used as a simple primary material: thus all use is an intervention, made from a standpoint, a declaration (in a general sense) from within the contradiction and hence a further development of it. So, the objectivity of literature is its necessary place within the determinate processes and reproduction of the contradictory linguistic practices of the common tongue, in which the effectivity of the ideology of bourgeois education is realized.

This siting of the problem abolishes the old idealist question, 'What is literature?', which is not a question about its objective determinance, but a question about its universal essence, human and artistic.[8] It abolishes it because it shows us directly the material function of literature, inserted within a process which literature cannot determine even though it is indispensable to it. If literary production has for its material and specific base the contradictions of linguistic practices in schooling taken up and internalized (through an indefinitely repeated labour of fiction), it is because literature itself is one of the terms of the contradiction whose other term is determinately bound to literature. Dialectically, literature is simultaneously product and material condition of the linguistic division in education, term and effect of its own contradictions. Not surprising therefore that the ideology of literature, itself a part of literature, should work ceaselessly to deny this objective base: to represent literature supremely as 'style', as individual genius, conscious or natural, as creativity, etc., as something outside (and above) the process of education, which is merely able to disseminate literature, and to comment on it exhaustively, though with no possibility of finally capturing it. The root of this constitutive repression is the objective status of literature as an historic ideological form, its relation to the class struggle. And the first and last commandment in its ideology is: 'Thou shalt describe all forms of class struggle, save that which determines thine own self.'

By the same token, the question of the relation of literature to the dominant ideology is posed afresh – escaping a confrontation of universal essences, in which many Marxist discussions have been trapped. To see literature as ideologically determined is not – cannot be – to 'reduce' it to moral ideologies or to political, religious, even aesthetic ideologies which are definable outside literature. Nor is it to make ideology the content to which literature brings form – even when there are themes and ideological statements which are more or less perfectly separable. Such a pairing is thoroughly mechanical, and, moreover, serves to corroborate the way in which the ideology of literature by displacement misconstrues its historic determinance. It merely prolongs the endless false dialectic of 'form' and 'content' whereby the artificially imposed terms alternate so that literature is sometimes perceived as content (ideology), sometimes as form ('real' literature). To define literature as a particular ideological form is to pose quite another problem: the specificity of ideological effects produced by literature and the means (techniques) of production. This returns us to the second question involved in the dialectical-materialist concept of reflection.

2 The Process of Production of Aesthetic Effects in Literature

By now, thanks to the proper use of the Marxist concept of reflection, we are able to avoid the false dilemma of the literary critic (should he analyse literature on its own ground — search out its essence, — or from an external standpoint — find out its function?). Once we know better than to reduce literature either to something other than itself or to itself, but instead analyse its ideological specificity,[9] helped by the conclusions of R. Balibar, we can attempt to trace the material concepts which appear in this analysis. Of course such a sketch has only a provisional value — but it helps us to see the consistency of the material concept of literature and its conceptual place within historical materialism.

As we see it, these concepts have three moments. They refer simultaneously to (i) the contradictions which ideological literary formations (texts) realize and develop; (ii) the mode of ideological identification produced by the action of fiction; and (iii) the place of literary aesthetic effects in the reproduction of the dominant ideology. Let us deal with each one schematically.

2.1 The specific complexity of literary formations — ideological contradictions and linguistic conflicts

The first principle of a materialist analysis would be: literary productions must not be studied from the standpoint of their unity which is illusory and false, but from their material disparity. One must not look for unifying effects but for signs of the contradictions (historically determined) which produced them and which appear as unevenly resolved conflicts in the text.

So, in searching out the determinant contradictions, the materialist analysis of literature rejects on principle the notion of 'the work' — i.e., the illusory presentation of the unity of a text, its totality, self-sufficiency and perfection (in both senses of the word: success and completion). More precisely, it recognizes the notion of 'the work' (and its correlative, 'the author') only in order to identify both as necessary illusions written into the ideology of literature, the accompaniment of all literary production. The text is produced under conditions which represent it as a finished work, providing a requisite order, expressing either a subjective theme or the spirit of the age, according to whether the reading is a naïve or a sophisticated one. Yet in itself the text is none of these things: on the contrary, it is materially incomplete, disparate and diffuse from being the outcome of the conflicting contradictory effect of superimposing real processes which cannot be abolished in it except in an imaginary way.[10]

To be more explicit: literature is produced finally through the effect of one or more ideological contradictions precisely because these contradictions cannot be solved within the ideology, i.e., in the last analysis through the effect of contradictory class positions within the ideology, as such irreconcilable. Obviously these contradictory ideological positions are not in themselves 'literary' – that would lead us back into the closed circle of 'literature'. They are ideological positions within theory and practice, covering the whole field of the ideological class struggle, i.e. religious, judicial and political, and they correspond to the conjunctures of the class struggle itself. But it would be pointless to look in the texts for the 'original' bare discourse of these ideological positions, as they were 'before' their 'literary' realizations, for these ideological positions can only be formed in the materiality of the literary text. That is, they can only appear in a form which provides their imaginary solution, or better still, which displaces them by substituting imaginary contradictions soluble within the ideological practice of religion, politics, morality, aesthetics and psychology.

Let us approach this phenomenon more closely. We shall say that literature 'begins' with the imaginary solution of implacable ideological contradictions, with the representation of that solution: not in the sense of representing, i.e. 'figuring' (by images, allegories, symbols or arguments), a solution which is really there (to repeat, literature is produced because such a solution is impossible) but in the sense of providing a 'mise en scène', a presentation as solution of the very terms of an insurmountable contradiction, by means of various displacements and substitutions. For there to be a literature, it must be the very terms of the contradiction (and hence of the contradictory ideological elements) that are enunciated in a special language, a language of 'compromise', realizing in advance the fiction of a forthcoming conciliation. Or better still it finds a language of 'compromise' which presents the conciliation as 'natural' and so both necessary and inevitable.

In *A Theory of Literary Production* with reference to Lenin's work on Tolstoy, and Verne and Balzac, the attempt was made to use materialist principles to show the complex contradictions which produce the literary text: in each case, specifically, what can be identified as the ideological project of the author, the expression of one determinate class position, is only one of the terms of the contradiction of whose oppositions the text makes an imaginary synthesis despite the real oppositions which it cannot abolish. Hence the idea that the literary text is not so much the expression of ideology (its 'putting into words' [sa mise en mots]) as its staging mise en scène, its display, an operation which has an inbuilt disadvantage since it cannot be done without showing its limits thereby revealing its inability to subsume a hostile ideology.

But what remained unclear in *A Theory* is the process of literary production, the textual devices which present the contradictions of an ideological discourse as the same as the fiction of its unity and its reconciliation, conditionally upon this same fiction. What still evades us, in other words, is the specific mechanism of the literary 'compromise', in so much as the materialist account is still too general. The work of R. Balibar makes it possible to surmount this difficulty and so not only complete the account but also to correct and transform it.

What does R. Balibar show us? That the discourse, literature's own special 'language', in which the contradictions are set out, is not outside ideological struggles as if veiling them in a neutral, neutralizing way. Its relation to these struggles is not secondary but constitutive; it is always already implicated in producing them. Literary language is itself formed by the effects of a class contradiction. This is fundamental, bringing us back to the material base of all literature. Literary language is produced in its specificity (and in all permitted individual variants) at the level of linguistic conflicts, historically determined, in the bourgeois epoch by the development of a 'common language' and of an educational system which imposes it on all, whether cultured or not.

This, schematically put, is the principle of the complex nature of literary formations, the production of which shares the material conditions necessary to the bourgeois social formation and transforms itself accordingly. It is the imaginary solution of ideological contradictions in so much as they are formulated in a special language which is both different from the common language and within it (the common language itself being the product of an internal conflict), and which realizes and masks in a series of compromises the conflict which constitutes it. It is this displacement of contradictions which R. Balibar calls 'literary style' and whose dialectic she has begun to analyse. It is remarkable dialectic, for it succeeds in producing the effect and the illusion of an imaginary reconciliation of irreconcilable terms by displacing the ensemble of ideological contradictions on to a single one, or a single aspect, the linguistic conflict itself. So the imaginary solution has no other 'secret' than the development, the redoubling of the contradiction: this is surely if one knows how to analyse it and work it out, the proof of its irreconcilable nature.

We are now ready to outline the principal aspects of the aesthetic effect of literature as an ideological device.

2.2 Fiction and realism: The mechanism of identification in literature

Here we must pause, even if over-schematically, to consider a characteristic literary effect which has already been briefly mentioned: the identification effect. Brecht was the first Marxist theoretician to focus on this by showing how the ideological effects of literature (and of the theatre, with the specific transformations that implies) materialize via an identification process between the reader or the audience and the hero or anti-hero, the simultaneous mutual constitution of the fictive 'consciousness' of the character with the ideological 'consciousness' of the reader.[11]

But it is obvious that any process of identification is dependent on the constitution and recognition of the individual as 'subject' – to use a very common ideological notion lifted by philosophy from the juridical and turning up under various forms in all other levels of bourgeois ideology. Now all ideology, as Althusser shows in his essay 'Ideology and Ideological State Apparatuses, must in a practical way 'hail or interpellate individuals as subjects': so that they perceive themselves as such, with rights and duties, the obligatory accompaniments. Each ideology has its specific mode: each gives to the 'subject' – and therefore to other real or imaginary subjects who confront the individual and present him with his ideological identification in a personal form – one or more appropriate names. In the ideology of literature, the nomenclature is: Authors (i.e. signatures), Works (i.e. titles), Readers and Characters (with their social background, real or imaginary). But in literature, the process of constituting subjects and setting up their relationships of mutual recognition necessarily takes a detour via the fictional world and its values, because that process (i.e. of constitution and setting-up) embraces within its circle the 'concrete' or 'abstract' 'persons' which the text stages. We now reach a classic general problem: what is specifically 'fictional' about literature? We shall preface our solution with a parenthesis.

Mostly when one speaks of fiction in literature it means the singling out of certain 'genres' privileged as fiction: the novel, tale, short story. More generally, it indicates something which, whatever its traditional genre, can be appealed to as novelistic, it 'tells a story', whether about the teller himself or about other characters, about an individual or an idea. In this sense, the idea of fiction becomes allegorically the definition of literature in general, since all literary texts involve a story or a plot, realistic or symbolic, and arrange in a 'time', actual or not, chronological or quasi-chronological, an unrolling of events which do or do not make sense (in formalist texts, order can be reduced to a verbal structure only). All description of literature in general, as of fiction, seems to involve a primary element: the dependence on a story which is analogous to 'life'.

But this characteristic involves another, more crucial still: the idea of confronting a model. All 'fiction', it seems, has a reference point, whether to 'reality' or to 'truth', and takes its meaning from that. To define literature as fiction means taking an old philosophical position, which since Plato has been linked with the establishing of a theory of knowledge, and confronting the fictional discourse with a reality, whether in nature or history, so that the text is a transposition, a reproduction, adequate or not, and valued accordingly and in relation to standards of verisimilitude and artistic licence.

No need to go further into details: it is enough to recognize the consistency which links the definition of literature as fiction with a particular appropriation of the category realism.

As everyone knows, realism is the key-word of a school: that in favour of a realist 'literature' in place of 'pure fiction', i.e. bad fiction. This too implies a definition of literature in general: all literature must be realist, in one way or another, a representation of reality, even and especially when it gives reality an image outside immediate perception and daily life and common experience. The 'shores' of reality can stretch to infinity.

And yet the idea of realism is not the opposite of fiction: it scarcely differs from it. It too has the idea of a model and of its reproduction, however complex that may be – a model outside the representation, at least for the fleeting instant of evaluation – and of a norm, even if it is nameless.

After this digression we can get back to the problem we had set ourselves. Marxist propositions, provisory and immature as they may be, are nevertheless bound to carry out a profound critical transformation of the classic idealist problematic. Let us have no doubt, for instance, that the classics of Marxism, no more than Brecht and Gramsci who can be our guides here, never dealt with literature in terms of 'realism'. The category of reflection, central to the Marxist problematic as we have shown, is not concerned with realism but with materialism, which is profoundly different. Marxism cannot define literature in general as fiction in the classic sense.

Literature is not fiction, a fictive image of the real, because it cannot define itself simply as a figuration, an appearance of reality. By a complex process, literature is the production of a certain reality, not indeed (one cannot over-emphasize this) an autonomous reality, but a material reality, and of a certain social effect (we shall conclude with this). Literature is not therefore fiction, but the production of fictions: or better still, the production of fiction-effects (and in the first place the provider of the material means for the production of fiction-effects).

Similarly, as the 'reflection of the life of a given society', historically given (Mao), literature is still not providing a 'realist' reproduction of it, even and least of all when it proclaims itself to be such, because even then it cannot be reduced to a straight mirroring. But it is true that the text does produce a reality-effect. More precisely it produces simultaneously a reality-effect and a fiction-effect, emphasizing first one and then the other, interpreting each by each in turn but always on the basis of their dualism.

So, it comes to this once more: fiction and realism are not the concepts for the production of literature but on the contrary the notions produced by literature. But this leads to remarkable consequences for it means that the model, the real referent 'outside' the discourse which both fiction and realism presuppose, has no function here as a non-literary non-discursive anchoring point predating the text. (We know by now that this anchorage, the primacy of the real, is different from and more complex than a 'representation'.) But it does function as an effect of the discourse. So, the literary discourse itself institutes and projects the presence of the 'real' in the manner of an hallucination.

How is this materially possible? How can the text so control what it says, what it describes, what it sets up (or 'those' it sets up) with its sign of hallucinatory reality, or contrastingly, its fictive sign, diverging, infinitesimally perhaps, from the 'real'? On this point too, in parts of their deep analysis, the works we have used supply the material for an answer. Once more they refer us to the effects and forms of the fundamental linguistic conflict.

In a study of 'modern' French literary texts, carefully dated in each case according to their place in the history of the common language and of the educational system, R. Balibar refers to the production of 'imaginary French' [français fictif]. What does this mean? Clearly not pseudo-French, elements of a pseudo-language, seeing that these literary instances do also appear in certain contexts chosen by particular individuals, e.g. by compilers of dictionaries who illustrate their rubrics only with literary quotations. Nor is it simply a case of the language being produced in fiction (with its own usages, syntax and vocabulary), i.e. that of characters in a narrative making an imaginary discourse in an imaginary language. Instead, it is a case of expressions which always diverge in one or more salient details from those used in practice outside the literary discourse, even when both are grammatically 'correct'. These are linguistic 'compromise formations', compromising between usages which are socially contradictory in practice and hence mutually exclude each other. In these compromise formations there is an essential place, more or less disguised but recognizable, for the reproduction of 'simple' language, 'ordinary' language, French 'just like that', i.e. the language which is taught in elementary school as the 'pure and simple' expression of 'reality'. In R. Balibar's book there are numerous examples which 'speak' to everyone, re-awakening or reviving memories which are usually repressed (it is their presence, their reproduction – the reason for a character or his words and for what the 'author' makes himself responsible for without naming himself – which produces the effect of 'naturalness' and 'reality', even if it is only by a single phrase uttered as if in passing). In comparison, all other expressions seem 'arguable', 'reflected' in a subjectivity. It is necessary that first of all there should be expressions which seem objective: these are the ones which in the text itself produce the imaginary referent of an elusive 'reality'.

Finally, to go back to our starting-point: the ideological effect of identification produced by literature or rather by literary texts, which Brecht, thanks to his position as a revolutionary and materialist dramatist, was the first to theorize. But there is only ever identification of one subject with another (potentially with 'oneself': 'Madame Bovary, c'est moi', familiar example, signed Gustave Flaubert). And there are only ever subjects through the interpellation of the individual into a subject by a Subject who names him, as Althusser shows: 'tu es Un tel, et c'est à toi que Je m'adresse'; 'Hypocrite lecteur, mon semblable, mon frère', another familiar example, signed Charles Baudelaire. Through the endless functioning of its texts, literature unceasingly 'produces' subjects, on display for everyone. So paradoxically using the same schema we can say: literature endlessly transforms (concrete) individuals into subjects and endows them with a quasi-real hallucinatory individuality. According to the fundamental mechanism of the whole of bourgeois ideology, to produce subjects ('persons' and 'characters') one must oppose them to objects, i.e. to things, by placing them in and against a world of 'real' things, outside it but always in relation to it. The realistic effect is the basis of this interpellation which makes characters or merely discourse 'live' and which makes readers take up an attitude towards imaginary struggles as they would towards real ones, though undangerously. They flourish here, the subjects we have already named: the Author and his Readers, but also the Author and his Characters, and the Reader and his Characters via the mediator, the Author – the Author identified with his Characters, or 'on the contrary' with one of their Judges, and likewise for the Reader. And from there, the Author, the Reader, the Characters opposite their universal abstract subjects: God, History, the People, Art. The list is neither final nor finishable: the work of literature is by definition to prolong and expand it indefinitely.

2.3 The aesthetic effect of literature as ideological domination-effect

The analysis of literature (its theory, criticism, science, etc.) has always had as its given object either – from a spiritualist perspective – the essence of Works and Authors, or better of the Work (of Art) and of Writing, above history, even and especially when seeming its privileged expression; or – from an empiricist (but still idealist) perspective – the ensemble of literary 'facts', the supposedly objective and documentary givens which lend biographical and stylistic support to 'general facts', the 'laws' of genres, styles and periods. From a materialist point of view, one would analyse literary effects (more precisely, aesthetic literary effects) as effects which cannot be reduced to ideology 'in general' because they are particular ideological effects, in the midst of others (religious, juridical, political) to which they are linked but from which they are separate.

This effect must finally be described at a threefold level, relating to the three aspects of one social process and its successive historical forms: (1) its production under determinate social conditions; (2) its moment in the reproduction of the dominant ideology; (3) and consequently as in itself an ideological domination-effect. To demonstrate this: the literary effect is socially produced in a determined material process. This is the process of constitution, i.e. the making and composing of texts, the 'work' of literature. Now, the writer is neither supreme creator, founder of the very conditions to which he submits (in particular, as we have seen, certain objective contradictions within ideology), nor its opposite – expendable medium, through whom is revealed the nameless power of inspiration, or history, or period, or even class (which comes to the same thing). But he is a material agent, an intermediary inserted in a particular place, under conditions he has not created, in submission to contradictions which by definition he cannot control, through a particular social division of labour, characteristic of the ideological superstructure of bourgeois society, which individuates him.[12]

The literary effect is produced as a complex effect, not only, as shown, because its determinant is the imaginary resolution of one contradiction within another, but because the effect produced is simultaneously and inseparably the materiality of the text (the arrangement of sentences), and its status as a 'literary' text, its 'aesthetic' status. That is, it is both a material outcome and a particular ideological effect, or rather the production of a material outcome stamped with a particular ideological effect which marks it ineradicably. It is the status of the text in its characteristics – no matter what the terms, which are only variants: its 'charm', 'beauty', 'truth', 'significance', 'worth', 'profundity', 'style', 'writing', 'art', etc. Finally, it is the status of the text *per se*, quite simply, for in our society only the text is valid in itself, revealer of its true form; equally, all texts once 'written' are valid as 'literary'. This status extends as well to all the historic dissimilar modes of reading texts: the 'free' reading, reading for the pure 'pleasure' of letters, the critical reading giving a more or less theorized, more or less 'scientific' commentary on form and content, meaning, 'style', 'textuality' (revealing neologism!) – and behind all readings, the explication of texts by academics which conditions all the rest.

Therefore, the literary effect is not just produced by a determinate process, but actively inserts itself within the reproduction of other ideological effects: it is not only itself the effect of material causes, but is also an effect on socially determined individuals, constraining them materially to treat literary texts in a certain way. So, ideologically, the literary effect is not just in the domain of 'feeling', 'taste', 'judgement', and hence of aesthetic and literary ideas; it sets up a process itself: the rituals of literary consumption and 'cultural' practice.

That is why it is possible (and necessary) when analysing the literary effect as produced *qua* text and by means of the text, to treat as equivalents the 'reader' and the 'author'. Equivalent too are the 'intentions' of the author – what he expresses whether in the text itself (integrated within the 'surface' narrative) or alongside the text (in his declarations or even in his 'unconscious' motives as sought out by literary psychoanalysis) – and the interpretations, criticism and commentaries evoked from readers, whether sophisticated or not.

It is not important to know whether the interpretation 'really' identifies the author's intention (since the latter is not the cause of literary effects but is one of the effects). Interpretations and commentaries reveal the (literary) aesthetic effect, precisely, in full view. Literariness is what is recognized as such, and it is recognized as such precisely in the time and to the extent that it activates the interpretations, the criticisms and the 'readings'. This way a text can very easily stop being literary or become so under new conditions.

Freud was the first to follow this procedure in his account of the dream-work and more generally in his method of analysing the compromise formations of the unconscious; he defined what must be understood by the 'text' of the dream. He gave no importance to restoring the manifest content of the dream – to a careful isolated reconstruction of the 'real' dream. Or at least he accedes to it only through the intermediary of the 'dream narrative', which is already a transposition through which via condensation, displacement and dream symbolism, repressed material makes its play. And he posited that the text of the dream was both the object of analysis and explanation simultaneously, through its own contradictions, the means of its own explanation: it is not just the manifest text, the narrative of the dream, but also all the 'free' associations (i.e., as one well knows, the forced associations, imposed by the psychic conflicts of the unconscious), the 'latent thoughts' for which the dream (or symptom) can serve as a pretext and which it arouses.

In the same way, criticism, the discourse of literary ideology, an endless commentary on the 'beauty' and 'truth' of literary texts, is a train of 'free' associations (in actuality forced and predetermined) which developed and realizes the ideological effects of a literary text. In a materialist account of the text one must take them not as located above the text, as the beginnings of its explication, but as belonging to the same level as the text, or more precisely to the same level as the 'surface' narrative whether that is figurative, allegorically treating with certain general ideas (as in the novel or autobiography) or straightforwardly 'abstract', non-figurative (as in the moral or political essay). They are the tendential prolongation of this façade. Free from all question of the individuality of the 'writer', the 'reader' or the 'critic', these are the same ideological conflicts, resulting in the last instance from the same historic contradictions, or from their transformations, that produce the form of the text and of its commentaries.

Here is the index of the structure of the process of reproduction in which the literary effect is inserted. What is in fact 'the primary material' of the literary text? (But a raw material which always seems to have been already transformed by it.) It is the ideological contradictions which are not specifically literary but political, religious, etc.; in the last analysis, contradictory ideological realizations of determinate class positions in the class struggle. And what is the 'effect' of the literary text? (at least on those readers who recognize it as such, those of the dominant cultured class). Its effect is to provoke other ideological discourses which can sometimes be recognized as literary ones but which are usually merely aesthetic, moral, political, religious discourses in which the dominant ideology is realized.

We can now say that the literary text is the agent for the reproduction of ideology in its ensemble. In other words, it induces by the literary effect the production of 'new' discourses which always reproduce (under constantly varied forms) the same ideology (with its contradictions). It enables individuals to appropriate ideology and make themselves its 'free' bearers and even its 'free' creators. The literary text is a privileged operator in the concrete relations between the individual and ideology in bourgeois society and ensures its reproduction. To the extent that it induces the ideological discourse to leave its subject-matter which has always already been invested as the aesthetic effect, in the form of the work of art, it does not seem a mechanical imposition, forced, revealed like a religious dogma, on individuals who must repeat it faithfully. Instead it appears as if offered for interpretations, a free choice, for the subjective private use of individuals. It is the privileged agent of ideological subjection, in the democratic and 'critical' form of 'freedom of thought'.[13]

Under these conditions, the aesthetic effect is also inevitably an effect of domination: the subjection of individuals to the dominant ideology, the dominance of the ideology of the ruling class.

It is inevitably therefore an uneven effect which does not operate uniformly on individuals and particularly does not operate in the same way on different and antagonistic social classes. 'Subjection' must be felt by the dominant class as by the dominated but in two different ways. Formally, literature as an ideological formation realized in the common language, is provided and destined for all and makes no distinctions between readers but for their own differing tastes and sensibilities, natural or acquired. But concretely, subjection means one thing for the members of the educated dominant class: 'freedom' to think within ideology, a submission which is experienced and practised as if it were a mastery, another for those who belong to the exploited classes: manual workers or even skilled workers, employees, those who according to official statistics never 'read' or rarely. These find in reading nothing but the confirmation of their inferiority: subjection means domination and repression by the literary discourse of a discourse deemed 'inarticulate' and 'faulty' and inadequate for the expression of complex ideas and feelings.

This point is vital to an analysis. It shows that the difference is not set up after the event as a straightforward inequality of reading power and assimilation, conditioned by other social inequalities. It is implicit in the very production of the literary effect and materially inscribed in the constitution of the text.

But one might say, how is it clear that what is implicit in the structure of the text is not just the discourse of those who practise literature but also, most significantly, the discourse of those who do not know the text and whom it does not know; i.e. the discourse of those who 'write' (books) and 'read' them, and the discourse of those who do not know how to do it although quite simply they 'know how to read and write' – a play of words and a profoundly revealing double usage. One can understand this only by reconstituting and analysing the linguistic conflict in its determinant place as that which produces the literary text and which opposes two antagonistic usages, equal but inseparable, of the common language: on one side, 'literary' French which is studied in higher education [l'enseignment secondaire et supérieur] and on the other 'basic', 'ordinary' French which far from being natural, is also taught at the other level [à l'école primaire]. It is 'basic' only by reason of its unequal relation to the other, which is 'literary' by the same reason. This is proved by a comparative and historical analysis of their lexical and syntactical forms – which R. Balibar is one of the first to undertake systematically.

So, if in the way things are, literature can and must be used in secondary education both to fabricate and simultaneously dominate, isolate and re-press the 'basic' language of the dominated classes, it is only on condition that that same basic language should be present in literature, as one of the terms of its constitutive contradiction – disguised and masked, but also necessarily given away and exhibited in the fictive reconstructions. And ultimately this is because literary French embodied in literary texts is both tendentially distinguished from (and opposed to) the common language and placed within its constitution and historic development, so long as this process characterizes general education because of its material importance to the development of bourgeois society. That is why it is possible to assert that the use of literature in schools and its place in education is only the converse of the place of education in literature, and that therefore the basis of the production of literary effects is the very structure and historical role of the currently dominant ideological state apparatus. And that too is why it is possible to denounce as a denial of their own real practice the claims of the writer and his cultured readers to rise above simple classroom exercises, and evade them.

The effect of domination realized by literary production presupposes the presence of the dominated ideology within the dominant ideology itself. It implies the constant 'activation' of the contradiction and its attendent ideological risk – it thrives on this very risk which is the source of its power. That is why, dialectically, in bourgeois democratic society, the agent of the reproduction of ideology moves tendentially via the effects of literary 'style' and linguistic forms of compromise. Class struggle is not abolished in the literary text and the literary effects which it produces. They bring about the reproduction, as dominant, of the ideology of the dominant class.

NOTES

1 [In the Althusserian formulation, 'science' is distinguished from 'ideology' not so much by what it 'knows' as by the fact that it produces new 'problematics', new objects of possible knowledge and new problems about them. The effect of ideology, according to Althusser, is the reverse of this; it contains any problems or contradictions by masking them with fictional or imaginary resolutions.]

2 Lenin shows this clearly in his articles on Tolstoy. [Lenin's articles on Tolstoy, written 1908–11, are reprinted as an appendix to Macherey's *A Theory of Literary Production*. (London: RKP, 1978).]

3 *Selected Readings from the Works of Mao Tse-Tung (A)* (Peking: Foreign Language Press, 1971), 250.

4 Dominique Lecourt, 'Une crise et son enjeu (Essai sur la position de Lénine en philosophie)', collection Théorie (Paris: Maspero, 1973).

5 [Macherey and Balibar here refer to structuralism (and also, by implication, to the journal *Tel Quel*), and to the concept of realism, as espoused by Lukács.]

6 R. Balibar and D. Laporte, *Le français national (constitution de la langue nationale commune à l'époque de la révolution démocratique bourgeoise)* (Paris: Hachette, 1974). [Introduced by E. Balibar and P. Macherey.]

7 Readers are referred to the first two chapters of J. Baudelot and R. Establet, *L'Ecole capitaliste en France* (Paris: Maspero, 1972).

8 [Macherey and Balibar are referring here to Sartre's *What is Literature?* (1948). In the *Red Letters* interview, Macherey adds

He was looking for a definition, a theory of what literature *is*, and in my view, this sort of enterprise is really very traditional and not very revolutionary. The question 'what is literature?' is as old as the hills; it revives . . . an idealist and conservative aesthetic. If I had a single clear idea when I began my work, it was that we must abandon this kind of question because 'what is literature?' is a false problem. Why? Because it is a question which already contains an answer. It implies that literature is *something*, that literature exists as a *thing*, as an eternal and unchangeable thing with an essence.]

9 See Macherey, *A Theory of Literary Production*.

10 Rejecting the mythical unity and completeness of a work of art does not mean adopting a reverse position – that of seeing the work of art as anti-nature, a violation of order (as in *Tel Quel*). Such reversals are characteristic of conservative ideology: 'For oft a fine disorder stems from art' (Boileau)!

11 [See *Brecht on Theatre*, trans. John Willett (London: Methuen, 1964).]

12 [On the category of the author, see also Michel Foucault, 'What Is an Author?', in *Language, Counter-Memory, Practice*, ed. and trans. Donald F. Bouchard (Ithaca: Cornell, 1977), 113–38; and Roland Barthes, 'The Death of the Author', in *Image-Music-Text*, essays selected and translated by Stephen Heath (London: Fontana, 1977), 142–8.]

13 One could say that there is no proper religious literature; at least there was not before the bourgeois epoch, by which time religion had been instituted as a form (subordinant and contradictory) of the bourgeois ideology itself. Rather, literature

itself and the aesthetic ideology played a decisive part in the struggle against religion, the ideology of the dominant feudal class.

19 Terry Eagleton

Towards a Science of the Text (1976)[*]

Terry Eagleton (1943–) is a Professor of English Literature at the University of Oxford and one of the leading figures in English Marxist literary criticism. His work emerged as part of the broader range of engagement with European Marxism associated with *New Left Review* which saw the translation of numerous Marxist writings previously unavailable in English. This theoretical diversification distinguishes Eagleton from the more specifically 'English' literary and historical studies associated with Raymond Williams and E. P. Thompson. Eagleton developed his approach through polemical engagements with these English traditions, notably against Raymond Williams, and through critiques of the more Hegelian Marxism associated with Lukács and Jameson. His work achieved prominence as an Althusserian approach to literature with *Criticism and Ideology* (1976). 'Towards a Science of the Text', from *Criticism and Ideology* exemplifies this Althusserian phase, but needs to be read through the complicated historical overlap with Macherey's subsequently revised theoretical approach in 'On Literature as an Ideological Form' (ch. 18 above). Eagleton himself has since extended his theoretical coordinates, engaging with poststructuralism to develop a materialist mode of criticism open to diverse intellectual currents, an approach exemplified by *The Ideology of the Aesthetic* (1990). Eagleton has argued that polemic and satire are essential modes for politically revolutionary writing. His critical style reflects this in an essayistic approach which combines the critical spirit of Brecht and Benjamin, notably in *Walter Benjamin* (1981) and *Against the Grain* (1986). Eagleton has also engaged with a broader readership through influential introductory texts such as *Marxism and Literary Criticism* (1976); *Literary Theory* (1983); and *The Function of Criticism* (1984). Other works include *Shakespeare and Society* (1967); *Exiles and Emigrés* (1970); *Myths of Power* (1976); *The Rape of Clarissa* (1982); and *Ideology* (1991). *The Significance of Theory* (1990) contains a helpful bibliography.

[*] From Terry Eagleton, *Criticism and Ideology* (London: NLB, 1976), 64–101.

Adam Smith's contradictions are of significance because they contain problems which it is true he does not resolve, but which he reveals by contradicting himself.

(Karl Marx, *Theories of Surplus Value*)

I have examined the process whereby the literary text is produced by an interaction of structures. It is now necessary to work in reverse, to take our standpoint within the text itself, and to analyse its relations to ideology and to history.

The literary text is not the 'expression' of ideology, nor is ideology the 'expression' of social class. The text, rather, is a certain *production* of ideology, for which the analogy of a dramatic production is in some ways appropriate. A dramatic production does not 'express', 'reflect' or 'reproduce' the dramatic text on which it is based; it 'produces' the text, transforming it into a unique and irreducible entity. A dramatic production is not to be judged by its fidelity to the text in the sense that a mirror-image can be judged faithfully to reflect its object; text and production are not commensurable formations to be laid out alongside one another, their distance or relation measured as one measures the distance between two physical objects. Text and production are incommensurate because they inhabit distinct real and theoretical spaces. Nor is the dramatic production to be conceived of as an 'interpenetration' of these two spaces, textual and theatrical, or as a 'realization' or 'concretization' of the text. The relation between text and production is not imaginable as that of an essence to an existence, soul to body: it is not simply a question of the production 'bringing the text alive', revitalizing and de-reifying it, releasing it from its suspended animation so that the imprisoned life it contains becomes fluid and mobile. The production is not in this sense the soul of the text's corpse; nor is the converse relation true, that the text is the informing essence of the production. The text does not contain, *in potentia*, dramatic 'life': the life of the text is one of literary significations, not a typographical 'ghosting' of the flesh of production. The text is not the production 'in rest', nor is the production the text 'in action'; the relation between them cannot be grasped as a simple binary opposition (rest/motion, soul/body, essence/existence), as though both phenomena were moments of a single reality, distinct articulations of a concealed unity. The notion of binary opposition here is, indeed, a curious one, since it includes the possibility of a passage, a transition, from one phenomenon to another, while at the same time in Cartesian fashion rendering that passage mysteriously inexplicable – the miracle of resurrection, reanimation or realization, of the word becoming flesh. It is only by the materialist concept of productive labour, as the definitive relation between text and production, that such a notion can be demystified, and the myth of a 'passage' eradicated. For the idea of a passage between text and production implies that they are congruent realities, adjacently situated on a single terrain;

and it is no escape from this to claim, more suavely, that the passage between them is complex and difficult – that the relation is 'deflected' or 'refracted' rather than direct. One does not escape from reflectionist models by imagining a somewhat more complicated mirror. Nor is it a question of the dramatic production 'enacting' the text; the metaphor of enactment is itself a misleading one, suggesting as it does a simple miming of the pre-existent. An actor in the theatre does not 'enact'; rather, he *acts* – functions, performs, behaves. He 'produces' his role, not as a conjurer produces a playing card, but as a carpenter produces a chair. The relation between text and production is a relation of *labour*: the theatrical instruments (staging, acting skills and so on) transform the 'raw materials' of the text into a specific product, which cannot be mechanically extrapolated from an inspection of the text itself. The question of two different productions of the same dramatic text is relevant here; for two such productions can vary to the point where the question of in what precise sense we are dealing with the 'same' text becomes pertinent. Of course in a literal sense the text is in both cases identical; but the productions to which it gives rise may diverge to the point where we can speak, figuratively, of the production of a 'different' text in each case – where the *Othello* of one director is not the *Othello* of another. The character of the text will determine the nature of the production, but conversely, the production will determine the character of the text – will, by a process of selection, organization and exclusion, define 'which' text is actually being put to work. The theatrical mode of production in no sense merely 'mediates' the text; on the contrary, its practices and conventions 'operate' the textual materials according to an internal logic of their own.

This relative autonomy of the theatrical mode of production is, in fact, historically variable. Certain theatrical modes will display in their very structure an ideology of the 'faithful representation' of the text; others will view the text as rewritable raw material, dethroning it from its privileged status as absolute arbitrator. No single, unalterable relation is in question here: certain texts will confer greater or lesser degrees of relative autonomy on theatrical practice, while certain theatrical practices will unilaterally constitute the text as licensing such autonomy. Yet what is not variable is the fact that text and production are distinct formations – different material modes of production, between which no homologous or 'reproductive' relationship can hold. They are not two aspects of the same discourse – the text, as it were, thought or silent speech and the production thought-in-action, articulate language; they constitute distinct kinds of discourse, between which no simple 'translation' is possible. For translation can occur only between two categorially comparable systems, and this is not the case here. There can be no more question of 'translating' text into production than there can be of 'translating' stone into a sculpture, or cotton into a shirt. The text–production relationship is not to be theorized as one between thought and word; it is more analogous to the relation between grammar and speech. Speech is a product, not a reproduction, of grammar; grammar is the determining structure of discourse, but the character of discourse cannot be mechanically derived from it. The analogy is obviously imperfect, since grammar is a formal, abstract corpus of rules whereas speech is 'concrete'; and the text–production relationship cannot be considered in terms of an abstract concrete opposition, which could only be Platonic or empiricist. Indeed the whole problem arises because the text is as 'concrete' as the production itself, but in its own distinct mode. The text is not a mere set of abstract notations, a skeletal framework which 'inspires', 'cues' or 'intimates' the production, a threadbare score on which the production improvises. If this were so then the relations between text and production would be obvious – the former as the map of the real terrain of the latter, the text as the mere enabling conditions of the production, or as the 'deep structure' of its contingent speech. Such a conception abolishes the problem by effectively abolishing the materiality of the text, dwindling it to a ghostly presence, and so reverting to the essence/existence duality which belongs also to the opposing error of fetishizing the text. The text's determination of the dramatic performance is considerably more rigorous than such metaphors would suggest: in the conventional way, every line, every gesture, every item of the text must be produced on stage. Directorial 'freedom', once the production is in hand, is the freedom of *producing* this text, not of producing *this* text; for once the initial decision for the text is taken, the text is ineluctable. In studying the relations between text and performance, then, we are studying a mode of determination which is precise and rigorous, yet which cannot be accounted for in terms of a 'reflection' or 'reproduction'. We are examining, in short, the conditions of a *production*.

Before we proceed to apply this analogy to the relations between literary text and ideology, it is worth pursuing briefly another potentially suggestive aspect of it. The dramatic performance is a production of the dramatic text; but the text itself is not a terminus. It exists in some complex relation to history which has yet to be determined – but in any case, if our analogy of dramatic production–literary text is correct, we may say that the dramatic text is itself a production. What is at issue here, then, is the *production of a production*. The dramatic text is the determinate product of a particular history; and in considering its relations to the dramatic performance, we are thus dealing with two complexly articulated sets of determinants. The dramatic production, as I have argued, is an operation, a *mise-en-scène*, of the text; but in so producing it, it simultaneously produces the text's internal relations to its object. The dramatic production, in other words, can never simply be the production of the text as autotelic artefact, as an exhibition of jewellery might display a necklace; it is, inevitably, a production of the text as *product* – of the text in its relations to what it speaks of. It does not simply 'give' us those relations, in the manner in which the text itself conceives them; the production does not merely 'double' the text's self-understanding but constructs an interpretation of that self-understanding, an ideology of that ideology. In doing so, it can alert us to the text's ignorance and miscomprehension, to modes of sense intimated but suppressed by the text itself. A dramatic production may, indeed, take this as its conscious end – Brecht's *Coriolanus*, for example – or, as more generally with 'epic theatre', seek those modes of theatrical production which display the product precisely as product. But it is not such conscious demystification which is in the first place at issue here. For every dramatic production fashions a relationship between itself and the text by fashioning a relationship between the text and what it speaks of. The determining basis of that relationship is, naturally, the text's own self-comprehension; for if that were thrown completely aside, discarded and abolished, there would be no play to produce. But if the production cannot absolutely transcend its text, it can at least round on it, torture and interrogate it with a critical rigour which, since it exists only in the *relation* of production to text, can be shown but not stated. The production moves now with, now athwart the ideology of its text, in a double movement constituted at once by the aesthetic logic of its ideologically determinate productive techniques and the ideological demands which determine those aesthetic devices. Some productions move almost wholly 'with' their texts, as with the naturalist performance of naturalist drama; but the apparent homology of text and performance here is merely the illusory concealment of a labour. One might imagine at the other extreme a naturalist text produced by 'epic' or expressionist techniques, and so radically 'defamiliarized' to yield up conflicts and absences unknown to itself. And one can imagine, too, a whole hierarchy of possible productions intermediate between these poles, in which the relations between mode of production, 'ideology of production' and 'ideology of text' are precisely determinable.

The parallel I am pursuing, then, may be schematised as follows:

history/ideology ⟶ dramatic text ⟶ dramatic production
history ⟶ ideology ⟶ literary text

The literary text, that is to say, produces ideology (itself a production) in a way analogous to the operations of dramatic production on dramatic text. And just as the dramatic production's relation to its text reveals the text's internal relations to its 'world' under the form of its own *constitution* of them, so the literary text's relation to ideology so constitutes that ideology as to reveal something of its relations to history.

Such a formulation instantly raises several questions, the first of which concerns the relation of the text to 'real' history. In what sense is it correct to maintain that *ideology*, rather than *history*, is the object of the text? Or, to pose the question slightly differently: In what sense, if any, do elements of the historically 'real' enter the text? Georg Lukács, in his *Studies in European Realism*, argues that Balzac's greatness lies in the fact that the 'inexorable veracity' of his art drives him to transcend his reactionary ideology and perceive the real historical issues at stake. Ideology, here, clearly signifies a 'false consciousness' which blocks true historical perception, a screen interposed between men and their history. As such, it is a simplistic notion: it fails to grasp ideology as an inherently complex formation which, by inserting individuals into history in a variety of ways, allows of multiple kinds and degrees of access to that history. It fails, in fact, to grasp the truth that some ideologies, and levels of ideology, are more false than others. Ideology is not just the bad dream of the infrastructure: in *deformatively* 'producing' the real, it nevertheless carries elements of reality within itself. But it is not enough, therefore, to modify the image of 'screen' to that of 'filter', as though ideology were a mesh through which elements of the real could slip. Any such 'interventionist' model of ideology holds out the possibility of looking behind the obstruction to observe reality; but in the capitalist mode of production, what is there to be observed is certainly not the real. The real is by necessity empirically imperceptible, concealing itself in the phenomenal categories (commodity, wage-relation, exchange-value and so on) it offers spontaneously for inspection. Ideology, rather, so produces and constructs the real as to cast the shadow of its absence over the perception of its presence. It is not merely that certain aspects of the real are illuminated and others obscured; it is rather that the presence of the real is a presence constituted by its absences, and vice versa. Balzac was indeed able to achieve partial insight into the movement of real history, but it is mistaken to image such insight as a transcendence of ideology into history. No such displacement of realms occurs: it is rather that Balzac's insights are the effect of a specific conjuncture of his mode of authorial insertion into ideology, the relations of the ideological region he inhabited to real history, the character of that stage of capitalist development, and the 'truth-effect' of the particular aesthetic form (realism) he worked. It is by force of this conjuncture that he was able to be at once exceedingly deluded and extraordinarily percipient. There is no more question of Balzac's texts having 'by-passed' the ideological and established a direct relation to history than there is of Shakespeare's drama having launched its critique of bourgeois individualism from outside a highly particular ideological standpoint.

The notion of a direct, spontaneous relation between text and history, then, belongs to a naïve empiricism which is to be discarded. For what would it mean to claim that a text was *directly* related to its history? The text can no more be conceived as directly denoting a real history than the meaning of a word can be imagined as an object correlated with it. Language, among other things, certainly denotes objects; but it does not do so in some simple relationship, as though word and object stood adjacent, as two poles awaiting the electric current of interconnection. A text, naturally, may speak of real history, of Napoleon or Chartism, but even if it maintains empirical historical accuracy this is always a *fictive* treatment – an operation of historical data according to the laws of textual production. Unless real history can be read as fiction in such a case, we are dealing not with literary but with historiographical discourse. To say that the 'historical' literary work must operate as fiction is not, of course, to suppress the relevance of the particular history with which it deals, as though this might be *any* history. It is to claim that *this* particular history is being fictionalized – construed in terms of an ideological production of its agents' modes of ideological insertion into it, and so rendered as *ideology to the second power*.

It is not that the text, in allowing us access to ideology, swathes us in simple illusion. Commodities, money, wage-relations are certainly 'phenomenal forms' of capitalist production, but they are nothing if not 'real' for all that. It is not that Jane Austen's fiction presents us merely with ideological delusion; on the contrary, it also offers us a version of contemporary history which is considerably more revealing than much historiography. And this is not just the effect of Austen's aesthetic forms, which so 'distantiate' ideology as to light up the shady frontiers where it abuts, by negation, onto real history. If ideology is indeed mere illusion, then it would certainly demand some such formal, unilateral operation to embarrass it into a betrayal of truth. But if Austen's forms do this, it is because they themselves are the product of certain ideological codes which, in permitting us access to certain values, forces and relations, yield us a sort of historical knowledge. It is not, to be sure, knowledge in the strict scientific sense; but epistemology does not divide neatly down the middle between strict science and sheer illusion. If Austen's texts can be spoken of as partly veridical, it is because the capacity of their aesthetic devices to yield complex, historically significant perceptions is determined by their productive relation to an ideological conjuncture which itself 'feels' more of the historical real than, say, *Gryll Grange*. It is not, however, a question of 'degrees of knowledge', in the sense that the more 'knowledgeable' text (let us say, *Caleb Williams*) necessarily achieves the more valuable perceptions. On the contrary, the value of Austen's fiction thrives quite as much on its ignorance as on its insight: it is because there is so much the novels cannot possibly know that they know what they do, and in the *form* they do. It is true that Austen, because she does not *know*, only 'knows'; but what she 'knows' is not thereby nothing at all, cancelled to a cypher by the exclusion of the real. For without the exclusion of the real as it is known to historical materialism, there could be for Austen nothing of the ethical discourse, rhetoric of character, ritual of relationship or ceremony of convention which she presents – nothing, in short, of those elements for which we find her fiction 'valuable'. These rituals and discourses are not just the vacant spaces left by the withdrawal of the real; there is nothing 'unreal' about the fierce ideological combats they encode. It is because the ideological is 'real' (if not in the strongest sense) that it is not always essential for it to submit to a formal, quasi-scientific self-distantiation for it to hint at history. It is true that this is what happens when ideology enters fiction; but it is not always merely by virtue of this 'fiction-effect' that the ideological may be waylaid into delivering up its historical truth. For it depends on the ideological conjuncture in question, and on the character of the forms which go to work upon it. The mode of a text's insertion into an ideological sub-ensemble, the mode of that sub-ensemble's insertion into the dominated ensemble of ideologies, the ideological character of its formal devices: these articulations, determined in the last instance by the historical real, are simultaneously what determine the nature, degree and quality of textual access to itself which that historical real permits.

History, then, certainly 'enters' the text, not least the 'historical' text; but it enters it precisely *as ideology*, as a presence determined and distorted by its measurable absences. This is not to say that real history is present in the text but in disguised form, so that the task of the critic is then to wrench the mask from its face. It is rather that history is 'present' in the text in the form of a *double-absence*. The text takes as its object, not the real, but certain significations by which the real lives itself – significations which are themselves the product of its partial abolition. Within the text itself, then, ideology becomes a dominant structure, determining the character and disposition of certain 'pseudo-real' constituents. This inversion, as it were, of the real historical process, whereby in the text itself ideology seems to determine the historically real rather than vice versa, is itself naturally determined in the last instance by history itself. History, one might say, is the *ultimate* signifier of literature, as it is the ultimate signified. For what else in the end could be the source and object of any signifying practice but the real social formation which provides its material matrix? The problem is not that such a claim is false, but that it leaves everything exactly as it was. For the text presents itself to us less as historical than as a sportive flight from history, a reversal and resistance of history, a momentarily liberated zone in which the exigencies of the real seem to evaporate, an enclave of freedom enclosed within the realm of necessity. We know that such freedom is largely illusory – that the text is *governed*; but it is not illusory merely in the sense of being a false perception of our own. The text's illusion of freedom is part of its very nature – an effect of its peculiarly *overdetermined* relation to historical reality.

One might express this sense of freedom by saying that the literary text, in contrast with, say, historiography, appears to have no determinate object. Historiography, whatever its ideological mode, has such an object: history itself. But what is the precise object of the literary text? What does the text 'denote'? For even those empathetic, hermeneutical forms of historiography which seek to reconstruct real history out of the categories of the 'lived' –

which, in short, take as their object history-as-ideology – none the less thereby take as their indirect object history itself. But the literary text seems rather to produce its own object, which is inseparable from its modes of fashioning it – which is an *effect* of those modes rather than a distinct entity. In so far as it presents itself as its own product, the text appears to be *self-producing*. It is possible, certainly, to draw a theoretical distinction between the text's means of production and what is produced: the former would include those aesthetic categories relatively independent of specific contents (*genres*, forms, conventions and so on), while the latter might encompass particular themes, plots, characters, 'situations'. But this distinction is clearly not of the same kind as the material and temporal distinction between a power-loom and its products. A power-loom, for one thing, is not altered by its products (I leave aside the question of the value it transfers to them) in the way that a literary convention is transformed by what it textually works. The text appears to produce itself in the sense that, within its space, producer, mode of production and product seem coterminous and indissociable. In textual analysis, propositions about the authorial producer are properly reducible to descriptions of textual operations, which are in turn merely an alternative metaphor for what is being textually operated. 'Product' and 'producer' appear thus merely figurative abstractions for that self-generative process of the production of meanings which *is* the text.

That the text is *in a certain sense* self-producing is, as I shall argue later, a valid claim. Yet the notion that the text is simply a ceaselessly self-signifying practice, without source or object, stands four square with the bourgeois mythology of individual freedom. Such freedom is not mythological because it does not, after a fashion, exist, but because it exists as the precise effect of certain determinants which enforce their own self-concealment. The text's 'freedom', similarly, is the precise effect of its ineluctable relation to history, the phenomenal form of its real necessity. A comparison with the historiographical work may clarify the point. Historiography conventionally organizes its significations so as to yield an 'objective' account of the real; that it does not typically do so is because of an ideological construction of that real which is *contingent* to its character as a discourse. It is, however, intrinsic to the character of literary discourse that it does not take history as its immediate object, but works instead upon ideological forms and materials of which history is, as it were, the concealed underside. Literary and historiographical texts are thus 'ideological' in quite distinct senses. The literary text does not *take* history as its object, even when (as with 'historical' fiction) it believes itself to do so; but it does, nevertheless, *have* history as its object in the last instance, in ways apparent not to the text itself but to criticism. It is this *distantiation* of history, this absence of any particular historical 'real', which confers on literature its air of freedom; unlike the historiographical work, it seems to be liberated from the need to conform its meanings to the exigencies of the actual. But this liberation is merely the other face of an internal necessity. The text, we may say, gives us certain socially determined representations of the real cut loose from any particular real conditions to which those representations refer. It is in this sense that we are tempted to feel that it is self-referential, or conversely (the twin idealist error) refers to 'life' or the 'human condition', since if it denotes no concrete state of affairs it must denote either itself, or states of affairs in general. But it is precisely in this absence of the particular real that the text most significantly refers – refers, not to concrete situations, but to an ideological formation (and hence, obliquely, to history) which 'concrete situations' have actually produced. The text gives us such ideology without its real history alongside it, as though it were autonomous – gives us states of affairs which are imaginary, pseudo-events, since their meaning lies not in their material reality but in how they contribute to fashioning and perpetuating a particular process of signification. In this sense, as history is distantiated, becoming, so to speak, more 'abstract', the signifying process assumes greater dominance, becoming more 'concrete'. The literary work appears free – self-producing and self-determining – because it is unconstrained by the necessity to reproduce any particular 'real'; but this freedom simply conceals its more fundamental determination by the constituents of its ideological matrix. If it seems true that at the level of the text's 'pseudo-real' – its imaginary figures and events – 'anything can happen', this is by no means true of its ideological organization; and it is precisely because *that* is not true that the free-wheeling contingency of its pseudo-real is equally illusory. The pseudo-real of the literary text is the product of the ideologically saturated demands of its modes of representation.

History, then, operates upon the text by an ideological determination which within the text itself privileges ideology as a dominant structure determining its own imaginary or 'pseudo' history. This 'pseudo' or 'textual' real is not related to the historical real as an imaginary 'transposition' of it. Rather than 'imaginatively transposing' the real, the literary work is the production of certain produced representations of the real into an imaginary object. If it distantiates history, it is not because it transmutes it to fantasy, shifting from one ontological gear to another, but because the significations it works into fiction are already representations of reality rather than reality itself. The text is a tissue of meanings, perceptions and responses which inhere in the first place in that imaginary production of the real which is ideology. The 'textual real' is related to the historical real, not as an imaginary transposition of it, but as the product of certain signifying practices whose source and referent is, in the last instance, history itself.

The literary text, accordingly, is characterized by a peculiar conjuncture of 'concrete' and 'abstract'. It resembles historiography in its density of texture, yet is analogous to philosophical discourse in the 'generality' of its object.[1] It differs from both in taking this 'abstract' object as concrete. The text strikes us with the arresting immediacy of a physical gesture which turns out to have no precise object – as though we were observing the behaviour of a man urgently gesticulating, and so *intimating* an actual state of affairs, only to realize that his gestures were in some sense mere ritual and rehearsal – learnt, studied actions which indicated nothing immediate in his environment, but revealed, rather, the *nature* of an environment which could motivate such behaviour. Our mistake was to search his environment for an object to correlate with his gesture, rather than to grasp his gesturing as a relationship to the environment itself. (As though we thought he was pointing, when in fact he was dancing.) What may seem gratuitous in such a man's behaviour, removed as it is from any 'concrete' motivation, then appears, on the contrary, as the rehearsed and calculated behaviour of an actor; it seems gratuitous, not because it is spontaneous, but precisely because it is not. The ambivalent status of the text, located, so to speak, between phenomenological historiography and philosophy, arises from its specific relation to ideology. As a production of the 'lived' it approximates to the former; as a production of the 'lived' shorn of particular real conditions, it resembles the latter. Philosophy, of course, deals with the lived not as 'spontaneous' response and perception but in terms of the general categories underlying it – categories which may or may not be ideological, or more or less entwined with ideology. In this sense it differs from literature, whose aim is to give us the lived as it were spontaneously; but literature none the less resembles it in so far as this 'spontaneity' is in fact phenomenal. Literature, too, as I shall argue, reveals more or less indirectly the categories of the lived; it is merely that it typically produces those categories so as to conceal them, dissolving them in the 'concrete'. (Pope's *Essay on Man* presents certain categorial propositions, but in so far as the rhetorical strategy of its form is to induce an *experience* of them, it is a literary rather than philosophical text.)

To say that the text 'concretizes the abstract', however, would be an inadequate formulation. It would be more accurate to say that what I have provisionally termed the 'abstraction' of the 'textual real', its lack of identity (or purely fortuitous identity) with any particular historical real, produces, and is the product of a peculiar overdetermination of the text's significatory devices. It is in that overdetermination – in the complex concentration of its many determinants – that the text's 'concretion' inheres. (When Marx speaks in the *Grundrisse* of '*rising*' from the abstract to the concrete he abolishes a whole tradition of philosophy in a single verb.) For the literary text behaves as though it fashions its 'real' in order the more concretely (in Marx's sense) to fashion its representational modes; or, to put it conversely, as though the very rigorousness of its ideological determinations necessitated, paradoxically, a certain flexibility and provisionality of its 'textual real'. This is not, after all, to suggest that in the text anything can happen; it is rather to indicate that 'textual reals' are dissolved, displaced, condensed and conflated by the predominant demands of textual ideology, and that this provisionality is then typically *naturalized*. Such a claim should not be mistaken for the Formalist doctrine that the text selects only such 'contents' as will reinforce its form; for as I shall argue later, the forms which 'select' such content are themselves selected from that always preformed content which is ideology. An example of the dominance within the text of 'ideology' over the 'pseudo-real', of the relation of *production* between them, can be found in the so-called 'typicality' of the figures and events in the lineage of realist fiction. What is meant by the Hegelian proposition that such characters and situations appear at once as irreducibly individual and historically representative is that they are overdetermined products – that by a certain displacement and conflation of multiple 'pseudo-real' components they assume, reciprocally, an unusually intense degree of concretion, concentrating those diverse determinants within themselves.

It is true that some texts seem to approach the real more closely than others. The level of the 'textual real' in *Bleak House* is considerably more predominant than it is in, say, Burns's lyric, *My love is like a red, red rose*. The former seeks to illuminate, among other things, a highly localized history; the latter has an extremely abstract referent. Yet whereas it is obvious that Burns's poem refers us to certain modes of ideological signification rather than to a 'real' object, so that whether he had a lover at all is, of course, entirely irrelevant (and is *intimated* to be so by the poem's very form), the same is true, if not so obviously, of Dickens's novel. It is simply that Dickens deploys particular modes of signification (realism) which entail a greater foregrounding of the 'pseudo-real'; but we should not be led by this to make direct comparisons between the imaginary London of his novel and the real London. The imaginary London of *Bleak House* exists as the product of a representational process which signifies, not 'Victorian England' as such, but certain of Victorian England's ways of signifying itself. Fiction does not trade in imaginary history as a way of presenting real history; its 'history' is imaginary because it negotiates a particular ideological *experience* of real history. It is useful in this respect to think of the text not merely as the *product* of ideology, but as a *necessity* of ideology – not in an empirical sense, since ideologies without literature have certainly existed, but theoretically, in that fiction is the term we would give to the fullest self-rendering of ideology, the only logical form that such a complete rendering could assume. And this is not, of course, because fiction is 'untrue', and so a fit vehicle for 'false consciousness', but rather that in order to reconstruct a society's self-representations we would finally encounter the need to cut them loose from particular 'reals' and mobilize them in the form of situations which, because imaginary, would allow for the range, permutation, economy and flexibility denied to a mere reproduction of the routinely lived.

The literary text's lack of a real direct referent constitutes the most salient fact about it: its fictiveness. There are familiar problems here, over predominantly fictive texts with much 'factual' material, or preponderantly 'factual' texts with significant fictive elements. But it is enough for the present to say that fictiveness is the most general constituent of the literary text, and that this refers not at all to the *literal* fictiveness of the text's events and responses (for they may happen to be historically true), but to certain modes of producing such materials. A poet's biographical experience becomes 'fictive' when produced in poetic form – when a specific mode of production gives rise to a different *object*, enforces our attention not to the biographical accuracy or significance of the experience but to its function as part of a structure of representations of a more general history. (It is from this fact, among others, that the conventional notion of the 'universality' of major art doubtless arises.) The primary constituent of this aesthetic mode of production is, as I have suggested, a certain dominance (or 'excess') of the signifying practice over the signified – so that as the signified becomes more 'abstract', putative or virtual, the signifying process is correspondingly thrown into a certain relief. What might be conventionally called 'typical' literary discourse – at least what is commonly thought of as such discourse: the 'poetic' – is characterized by such a 'disturbance' of the normative relations between signifier and signified. The effect of this disturbance is so to highlight and intensify the signifying practice itself as to produce, in Formalist parlance, a 'defamiliarization' of experience. This is not the case with every kind of literary discourse: it is not true, for example, of much realist or any naturalistic language. But 'poetic' language none the less reveals a relation between signifier and signified shared also, if less obviously, by the realist or naturalist text. I mean simply that a statement such as 'Thou still unravished bride of quietness' *self-evidently* belongs to literary discourse, whereas a statement such as 'After a while I went out and left the hospital and walked back to the hotel in the rain' may or may not do so, depending on its context. Both statements in fact belong to literary discourses which lack a real particular referent; it is simply that in the first case this absence inscribes itself in the very letter of the text, which proclaims its lack of a real object in its very internal disproportionment of elements, flaunts its relative autonomy of the real in the formal structures of its proposition. It is the very eloquence of the 'poetic' which alludes to a kind of silence. Realist prose, on the other hand, 'pretends' to a real particular referent in its every phrase, only to unmask that pretence in its status as a complete discourse ('novel'). The 'poetic' is in this sense its concealed truth, parading in its very microstructures the macrostructural character of the realist work.

The literary relations between signifier and signified are not, of course, given once and for all as an invariable absolute. On the contrary, they shift and mutate in response to the determinations of aesthetic ideology, as Roland

Barthes demonstrates for a particular span of French literary history in *Le Degré zéro de l'écriture*. A text may so 'foreground' its signifiers as to radically deform, distantiate and defamiliarize its signified; or it may strictly curb such excess, in apparent humble conformity to the logic of its 'content'. This aesthetic contrast should not be misread as a political one, as though the former text were necessarily 'progressive' and the latter inevitably 'reactionary'. Defamiliarization may revitalize an ideology for reactionary ends, and the conformist, 'transparent' text is in part to be judged in the light of that to which it 'conforms'. But the contrast is in any case misleading if it suggests that some texts *really* distantiate their object while others really conform to it. Both statements are metaphorical descriptions of alternative aesthetic effects: they do not articulate a changed general relation between text, ideology and history. No text literally 'conforms itself to its content', adequates its signifiers to some signified distinct from them; what is in question is not the relation between the text and some separable signified, but the relation between textual signification (which is both 'form' and 'content') and those more pervasive significations we name ideology. This is not a relation which can be gauged simply by the degree to which the text *overtly* foregrounds its significations, even though such a practice in particular texts may well produce, and be produced by, a peculiar relation to ideology. For, to repeat, even the 'prosaic' text reproduces – although not in its every phrase – that dominance of signifier over signified paraded by the poem. It reproduces it in its entire structure – in that internal distribution of its elements, characterized by a high degree of relative autonomy, which is possible only because it has no real particular referent.

It remains to resolve a possible ambiguity as to what precisely constitutes the literary work's 'signified'. The signified *within the text* is what I have termed its 'pseudo-real' – the imaginary situations which the text is 'about'. But this pseudo-real is not to be directly correlated with the historically real; it is, rather, an effect or aspect of the text's whole process of signification. What that whole process signifies is ideology, which is itself a signification of history. The relations in question here can be clarified by a simple diagram:

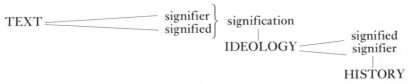

The 'disturbance' of relation between signifier and signified in 'prototypical' literary discourse is an effect of the relation between that discourse as a whole and ideology. It is because the text's materials are ideological rather than historical – because, as it were, the text exists in the 'hollow' it has scooped out between itself and history – that it lacks a real particular referent, and displays that lack in the relative autonomy of its structuration. The 'poetic' text displays it also in its disproportioning of signifier and signified, whereby the absence of a concrete historical object is proclaimed, made manifest, in the very predominance of the signifying process over the 'pseudo-real'.

We need, however, to be more precise both about the ideology which the text works, and the process of that working. To formulate the issue in this way is already to risk falsification, for the text, as I shall argue later, does not simply 'take' ideological materials which are extrinsic to it. Ideology pre-exists the text; but the *ideology of the text* defines, operates and constitutes that ideology in ways unpremeditated, so to speak, by ideology itself. The particular production of ideology which we may term the 'ideology of the text' has no pre-existence: it is identical with the text itself. What is in question here, indeed, is a double relation – not only the objectively determinable relation between text and ideology, but also (and simultaneously) that relation as 'subjectively' flaunted, concealed, intimated or mystified by the text itself. Every text implicitly manifests a relation to its pre-existent materials, suggesting (contrast Trollope and Mallarmé) how far they pre-exist it. Nor is this relation necessarily a single one: for a work may acknowledge its dependence on the pre-existent in some of its elements only to assert a pure autonomy in others.

'Pre-textual' ideology presents itself to the work in diverse forms: in 'ordinary language', accredited symbol and convention, codes of perceptual habit, other artefacts. It offers itself also in more formalized ways: in those particular aesthetic, political, ethical and other formulae which may at once permeate 'ordinary language' yet emerge from it as distinct crystallizations of meaning. That the work may establish a relatively direct relation to such formulae is not to be overlooked. It is true that ideology most typically presents itself to the text as 'life' rather than category, as the immediate stuff of experience rather than as system of concepts. But much of the literature of Christendom, neo-classicism, Stalinism allows ideology to enter the text in relatively 'pure' form, rehearsing its categories in ways which to some degree disengage them from the contingencies of the 'lived'. In such cases we can observe unusually direct relations between:

1   'General' ideological categories
2   'General' ideological discourses
3   Aesthetic ideological categories
4   Aesthetic ideological discourses
5   Text

In the case of Stalinism, for example, aesthetic categories ('socialist realism') bear a peculiarly direct relation to 'general ideology', producing modes of aesthetic discourse which seem merely to mime 'general' ideological modes. Even with such a work, however, there can be no question of *reducing* textual to ideological discourse. The categories of an ideology produce a series of ideological significations which form the immediate materials of the text; and those significations can be seen as a concrete 'production' of the ideological categories. The study of the text is a study of the production of such produced categories – an analysis of ideological production to the second power. In the relatively 'pure' ideological work, ideological discourses are so produced as to appear 'inverted back' into the categories which give rise to them. This is not to be understood in Hegelian fashion as the text 'universalizing' its materials, discovering the general within the particular. It is not in 'raising' the particular to the general that such a work reveals its ideology, but in the very particularity of its operations upon it – in a precise set of mutations and displacements which produces the effect of a simple 'miming'.

There are other texts, however, where the materials appropriated for production are more obviously those of ideology 'at work' – as spontaneously secreted in immediate experience, and so as 'unconscious' of its categorical structure. Ideology here comes to the text intensively *worked*, ready-made for the text's transformative operations. The relation of the literary work to 'ordinary language' is relevant here, for it is in 'ordinary language' that ideology is produced, carried and naturalized, and the text's relation to it is a crucial index of its ideological character. Apart from the case of works whose 'relation' to ordinary language is one of direct negation – those, for example, written in the alien language of an imperial ruling class – every text bears some relation to the common discourse of its society. But there is a clear difference between the text which seems to reproduce it ('seems', since this too is a convention – we have to *learn* how to read such a text) and the work whose devices radically transmute such speech. Nor is it only a question of language in the strict sense: for to say that everything that happens in the text happens in terms of language is equivalent to saying that everything happens in the world because of God. Such a statement is so pervasively applicable as to cancel itself out and leave everything exactly as it was. The linguistic devices of *The Faerie Queene* or *Finnegans Wake* signal a set of mutations of ideological 'discourses' in a wider sense – perceptions, assumptions, symbolizations. Here, by the working of aesthetic ideology, a production of already-produced categories is achieved; and it can be claimed that it is in this production to the second power that the true relation of the text to ideology inheres. The text, through its formal devices, establishes a transformative relation between itself and ideology which allows us to perceive the usually concealed contours of the ideology from which it emerges.

It is this position which Louis Althusser argues, in a well-known passage in *Lenin and Philosophy*:

> *I do not rank real art among the ideologies*, although art does have a quite particular and specific relationship with ideology. . . . Art (I mean authentic art, not works of an average or mediocre level) does not quite give us a *knowledge* in

the *strict sense*, it therefore does not replace knowledge (in the modern sense: scientific knowledge), but what it gives us does nevertheless maintain a certain specific *relationship* with knowledge. This relationship is not one of identity but one of difference. Let me explain. I believe that the peculiarity of art is to 'make us see', 'make us perceive', 'make us feel' something which *alludes* to reality. . . . What art makes us *see* . . . is the ideology from which it is born, in which it bathes, from which it detaches itself as art, and to which it *alludes*. . . . Balzac and Solzhenitsyn give us a 'view' of the ideology to which their work alludes and with which it is constantly fed, a view which presupposes a *retreat*, an *internal distantiation* from the very ideology from which their novels emerge. They make us 'perceive' (but not know) in some sense *from the inside*, the very ideology in which they are held. . . .[2]

This is a suggestive, radically unsatisfactory statement. To begin with, there is the notable evasion of 'real' and 'authentic' art, as ambiguous in its own way as Lucien Goldmann's concept of the 'valid' text. In both cases, an evaluative judgement is illegitimately inserted into (or snatched out of) what purports to be a scientific account of the structures of art as such. Is it *constitutive* of aesthetic 'authenticity' that the process described here occurs, or does it merely follow from works whose 'authenticity' is to be assessed by other, unexamined criteria? Is the work 'real' because it permits us to perceive the ideology in which it bathes, in which case how, precisely, is this an *aesthetic* judgement? Or is that distantiation one effect of a value which has other determinants? And how, exactly, is this distantiation achieved? Pierre Macherey elaborates the argument by suggesting that it is the effect of the form which the text bestows on ideology;[3] but to leave the matter there is merely to stand convicted of formalism. For if it is true that the text's relation to ideology is crucially effected by its forms, it is not the whole truth. Althusser and Macherey appear to want to *rescue* and *redeem* the text from the shame of the sheerly ideological; yet in these passages they can do so only by resorting to a nebulously figurative language ('allude', 'see', 'retreat') which lends a merely rhetorical quality to the distinction between 'internal distantiation' and received notions of art's 'transcendence' of ideology. It is as though the aesthetic must still be granted mysteriously privileged status, but now in embarrassedly oblique style. If 'real' art is not to be ranked among the ideologies, does it then form a distinct region within the social formation, additional to the Althusserian categories of the economic, political, ideological and scientific? That indeed would seem a considerable – one might think, excessive – privilege to confer on it. The fact is that Macherey in particular is forced into his quasi-formalist position by the logic of his view of ideology itself. For if ideology is spoken of as 'illusion' (Macherey's term), then it would indeed only be by virtue of some formal *mise-en-scène* that it could approximate to the status of a knowledge. But if ideology is not knowledge, it is not pure fantasy either. The text establishes a relationship with ideology by means of its forms, but does so on the basis of the *character* of the ideology it works. It is the character of that ideology, *in conjunction with* the transmutative operations of the literary forms it produces or enables, which determines the degree to which the text achieves significant or nugatory perceptions. Engels does not attribute Balzac's valid perceptions, nor Lenin Tolstoy's, nor Trotsky Mayakovsky's, merely to the inherently realizing, revelatory function of form. The process of the text is the process whereby ideology produces the forms which produce it, thus determining in general both the instruments and devices which work it, and the nature of the work-process itself. It is true that in producing ideology the text grants it a form, but that form is not merely arbitrary, as Macherey's discussion of the text 'giving ideology a form' might suggest. For the form which is given is determined in the last instance by the 'form' of the problematic which the text operates. This is not, to be sure, a *rigorous* determination, for the same ideology may be produced by a variety of literary forms; but it will, none the less, enable a series of possible forms and disable others. The 'materials' worked by the text already offer themselves to it in a certain 'form', as more or less coherently ranked and organized significations which partly constitute what Fredric Jameson has called the 'logic' of the text's content.[4] It is not, naturally, as though form vanquished the inchoateness of ideology – a proposition parallel to the bourgeois critical assumption that art orders the 'chaos' of experience. Ideology is a relatively coherent formation, which thus broadly determines those structural definitions and distributions of meaning we term literary form; but the forms of the text are not, on the other hand, mere epiphenomena of an ideological 'content'. The form of the ideological content – the categorial structure of the ideological problematic – has a *generally* determining effect of the form of the text, not least in the determination of *genre*. But the form of the text itself is not, of course, identical with its *genre*: it is, rather, a unique production of it.

If the literary work can be seen as an ideological production to the second power, it is possible to see how that double-production may, as it were, partly cancel itself out, invert itself back into an analogue of knowledge. For in producing ideological representations, the text reveals in peculiarly intense, compacted and coherent form the categories from which those representations are produced. 'Reveals' is perhaps a misleading term here, for not every text displays its ideological categories on its surface: the visibility of those categories depends on the text's precise modes of working them, as well as on the nature of the categories themselves. Indeed in most literary works it is an effect of the productive modes to conceal and 'naturalize' ideological categories, dissolving them into the spontaneity of the 'lived'. In this sense, what ideology does to history the literary work raises to the second power, producing as 'natural' the significations by which history naturalizes itself; but the work simultaneously reveals (to criticism, if not to the casually inspecting glance) how that naturalness is the effect of a particular production. If the text displays itself as 'natural', it manifests itself equally as constructed artifice; and it is in this duality that its relation to ideology can be discerned.

It is essential, then, to examine in conjuncture two mutually constitutive formations: the nature of the ideology worked by the text and the aesthetic modes of that working. For a text may operate an ideology which contains elements of the real and simultaneously 'dissolve' those elements, in whole or part, by the manner of its working. Conversely, a notably 'impoverished' ideology may be transmuted by aesthetic forms into something approximating to knowledge. More complex situations are also possible. One might say, for example, that a poem like *The Waste Land* emerges from a potentially more 'productive' problematic, in terms of the range and complexity of the questions it is able to pose, than, say, Georgian poetry, but that this potential is 'blocked' or repressed by the peculiar effect of its mythological forms. But it could also be claimed that those forms inhere in the problematic itself, and that it is the poem's dislocatory, experimental devices which transmute that problematic into perceptions normally beyond its scope. Ideology and mode of aesthetic production are both typically complex formations, between whose elements multiple particular relations of homology and contradiction are possible.

A further weakness of Althusser's formulation is what might be called its consumer-centredness. It is as if the *reader* were the final guarantor of the validity of the text – as if it were 'our' (whose?) 'seeing' and 'feeling' the ideology in which the work 'bathes' (ominously gestural terms) which ensures its 'authenticity'. True, it is the work itself which produces such an effect; but because the mechanisms of this process are left unexamined, the focus shifts to the 'reader's response'. The liberal humanist problematic is preserved in different form: it is just that it is now ideology, rather than reality, which is revealed to us in a privileged moment of insight. It is surely necessary here to return to the productive process of the text itself. I have suggested that the relatively 'pure' ideological text so produces ideological discourses as to 'invert them back' into the categories which give rise to them. But other relations between text and ideology are clearly possible: there is no question of a fixed, historically immutable relationship here. Other texts so produce ideological discourses as to display variable degrees of internal conflict and disorder – a disorder produced by those displacements and mutations of ideology enforced upon the text by the necessity to arrive, in accordance with the laws of its aesthetic production, at a 'solution' to its problems. In such a text, the relative coherence of ideological categories is revealed under the form of a concealment – revealed by the very *incoherence* of the text, by the significant disarray into which it is thrown in its efforts to operate its materials in the interests of a 'solution'.

It is important not to take the term 'solution' too literally here. I do not mean by 'solution' simply the determinate answer to an articulate question, which is palpably not the case with much modernist and postmodernist literature. In a less literal sense of the terms, every text can be seen as a 'problem' to which a 'solution' is to be found; and the process of the text is the process of problem-solving. Every text, that is to say, proposes an initial situation which then undergoes some mutation; in every text, something *happens*. This is most obvious in narrative, the simplest structure of which is $a–b–c$, where b intervenes to mutate a into c; but it is true also of non-narrative works, true even of the tersest Imagist poem. By 'problem', I mean the initial given elements of the text, of which something is to be *made*; and it is only in certain texts (narrative in particular) that this making is formally figured as diachronic. The initial given elements of the text need not be *temporally* initial; and even if they are, this is merely the formal or generic index of a problem-solving which is essentially 'synchronic'. The narrative structure of *Tom Jones* mutates Tom's initial situation at Paradise Hall into a series of episodes which are then 'resolved' by the novel's final settlement. But this diachronic axis is no more than the index of a 'synchronic' resolution of certain persistent ideological conflicts (liberty/authority, fraternity/hierarchy, charity/prudence and so on) which in adjacent texts of the time – Pope's *Moral Essays*, for example – assume such directly 'synchronic' form. This is not to argue that the diachronic axis is merely contingent, a purely phenomenal level of the text; on the contrary, it is ideologically significant that at a certain conjuncture the 'problem' must be 'chronologized', put in train. But 'problem' and 'solution' are always given together, as alternative descriptions of the work's modes of operation on its ideology. It is not, to repeat, that the text necessarily provides a definite answer to a specific question; but the nature of a 'non-solution' is as significant as the nature of a 'solution'. No text lacks a resolution in the sense of merely stopping: if it is to be a 'finished' text – and strictly speaking there are no others, for that the text is complete as we have it is part of its definition – its 'non-solution' must signify. It is still *this* 'non-solution' rather than that which is at issue – a 'non-solution' determined by the way in which the 'problem' has been posed. In this sense, every text is the answer to its own question, proposing to itself only such problems as it can resolve, or leave unresolved without radically interrogating the terms of its problematic. Problem and solution are synchronic in the sense that the text so works upon its materials as to cast them from the outset into 'resolvable' (or *acceptably* unresolvable) form in the very act of trying to resolve them. It is therefore important to read the text, as it were, backwards – to examine the nature of its 'problems' in the light of its 'solutions'. Given the initial elements of the work, we can already construct from them a typology of ideologically permissible 'solutions'; and this is one of the senses in which it can be said that the work 'determines itself'. Within a certain conjuncture of 'general' and 'aesthetic' ideology, only certain permutations of textual elements will be possible: having posited a, the text may then posit either b or c but not x. It is, indeed, in the dual character of the text which results from this – in its combination of suspense and internal logic, openness and closure, free-play and fixity, the provisional and the determinate, that the characteristic experience of *reading* lies.

It is important to grasp here the closeness of relation between the 'ideological' and the 'aesthetic'. The text does not merely 'take' ideological conflicts in order to 'resolve' them aesthetically, for the character of those conflicts is itself overdetermined by the textual modes in which they are produced. The text's mode of resolving a particular ideological conflict may then produce textual conflicts elsewhere – at other levels of the text, for example – which need in turn to be 'processed'. But here the work is 'processing' ideological conflict under the form of resolving specifically *aesthetic* problems, so that the problem-solving process of the text is never merely a matter of its reference outwards to certain pre-existent ideological cruxes. It is, rather, a matter of the 'ideological' presenting itself in the form of the 'aesthetic' and vice versa – of an 'aesthetic' solution to ideological conflict producing in its turn an aesthetic problem which demands ideological resolution, and so on. It is not simply that ideology furnishes the 'materials' for the text's formal aesthetic operations; the textual process is, rather, a complex mutual articulation of the two, whereby aesthetic modes so define and determine ideological problems as to be able to continue to reproduce themselves, but only within the limits and subject to the problems which their own overdetermination of the ideological sets. This is one sense in which the processes of conflict and resolution are synchronic rather than diachronic. Every phrase, every image of the text, in so far as it is both in general determined by and exerts a determination on the whole, in so far as it is always both product and producer, destination and departure, is at once an 'answer' and a 'question', mobilizing new possibilities of conflict in the very moment of taking the weight of a provisional 'solution'. We may say, then, that the text in this sense 'produces itself' – but produces itself in constant relation to the ideology which permits it such relative autonomy, so that this ceaseless elaboration and recovery of its own lines of meaning is simultaneously the production of a determining ideology. One might say, too, that the text's *relation to itself* is problematical because it is simultaneously a relation to certain ideological problems. The text is thus never at one with itself, for if it were it would have absolutely nothing to say. It is, rather, a process of *becoming* at one with itself – an attempt to overcome the problem of itself, a problem produced by the fact that the text itself is the production, rather than reflection, of an ideological 'solution'.

It may be useful to refer once more at this point to the work of Pierre Macherey. Macherey claims that literary works are internally dissonant, and that this dissonance arises from their peculiar relation to ideology. The distance which separates the work from ideology embodies itself in the internal distance which, so to speak, separates the work from itself, forces it into a ceaseless difference and division of meanings. In putting ideology to work, the text necessarily illuminates the absences, and begins to 'make speak' the silences, of that ideology. The literary text, far from constituting some unified plenitude of meaning, bears inscribed within it the marks of certain determinate absences which twist its various significations into conflict and contradiction. These absences – the *'not-said'* of the work – are precisely what bind it to its ideological problematic: ideology is present in the text in the form of its eloquent silences. The task of criticism, then, is not to situate itself within the same space as the text, allowing it to speak or completing what it necessarily leaves unsaid. On the contrary, its function is to install itself in the very incompleteness of the work in order to *theorize* it – to explain the ideological necessity of those *'not-saids'* which constitute the very principle of its identity. Its object is the *unconsciousness* of the work – that of which it is not, and cannot be, aware. What the text 'says' is not just this or that meaning, but precisely their difference and separation: it articulates the space which both divides and binds together the text's multiple senses. It is criticism's task to demonstrate how the text is thus 'hollowed' by its relation to ideology – how, in putting that ideology to work, it is driven up against those gaps and limits which are the product of ideology's relation to history. An ideology exists because there are certain things which must not be spoken of. In so putting ideology to work, the text begins to illuminate the absences which are the foundation of its articulate discourse. And in doing this, it helps to 'liberate' us from the ideology of which that discourse is the product.

It is worth noting here that these formulations of Macherey suggest the possibility of an encounter between Marxist criticism and the great scientist who has so often figured within such criticism merely as an eloquent silence: Freud. In his *The Interpretation of Dreams* and elsewhere, Freud argues that the analyst of dreams must penetrate the manifest content of the dream to uncover its latent content. But this is not a simple hermeneutical exercise, since the analyst's task is not only to lay bare the meaning of a distorted text, but to expose *the meaning of the text-distortion itself.* Psychoanalysis, that is to say, must reconstruct what Freud calls the *'dream-work'* – the actual process of production of the dream. The 'truth' of the dream lies precisely in its distortion. The analyst must indeed strip off what Freud terms the 'uppermost dream layer', which is the result of a secondary elaboration of the dream by consciousness after the dreamer awakes; but this is simply preparatory to tackling the 'depth' layer of the dream, the symbols which express a latent content in disguised form.

Freud's 'uppermost dream layer' exists to systematize the dream, fill in its gaps and smooth over its contradictions, produce from it a relatively coherent text. But beneath this lies the real, incomplete, self-divided, mutilated text of the dream itself, which resists interpretation – a resistance manifest in the patient's hesitating and circuitous associating, his forgetting of portions of his text. This pressure of resistance, Freud believes, is at the very root of the genesis of the dream, responsible for the 'gaps, obscurities and confusions which may interrupt the continuity of even the finest of dreams'. The dream, as distorted and mutilated text, is a conflict and compromise between unconscious material seeking expression, and the intervention of an ideological censor. The typical consequence of this is that the unconscious is able to say what it wanted, but not in the way it wanted to say it – only in softened, distorted, perhaps unrecognizable form. This dissonance is especially apparent in the dream's gaps: 'the breaks in the text', Freud remarks, 'are places where an interpretation has prevailed which is ego-alien even though a product of the ego.'

Freud's 'uppermost dream layer' corresponds, perhaps, to what Macherey terms 'normative' criticism: that criticism which *refuses* the text as it is, 'corrects' it against a rounded, ideal construction of what it 'might' be, rejects the determinate nature of its partial, conflictual presence. Grasping the text as a mere fictive rehearsal of an ideal object which 'precedes' it, an ideal present within the text as an abiding truth or essence from which it deviates, the typical gesture of 'normative' criticism is to inscribe a 'Could do better' in the work's margin. The 'normative' critical illusion, as such, is merely a displacement of the empiricist fallacy which simply 'receives' the work as a spontaneous given: it is just that 'normative' criticism intervenes to treat and modify the text so that it can be better consumed. The uppermost dream layer, then, is analogous to the literary text as defined by 'normative' criticism, and as defined, as it were, by itself – the text as it would 'want' to appear, as spontaneous, complete and so as ideological. The 'real' dream-text, by contrast, corresponds to the literary text as defined by scientific criticism, and so as 'unconscious' of itself, constituted by that *relation* to ideology which it cannot speak of directly but can only manifest in its mutilations. Both Freud and Macherey explain the text's lacunae and hiatuses by referring the discourse in question to the conditions of its production: indeed Macherey himself draws this parallel, when he comments that Freud situates the meaning of the dream *elsewhere*, outside of itself, in the structure of which it is the product. In the case of both dream and literary text, that structure is not 'microcosmically' present within the discourse, but is precisely what ruptures that discourse into asymmetry; ideology appears 'in' the text as a mode of disorder. The task of both criticism and dream analysis, then, is to articulate that of which the discourse speaks-without-saying-it – or, more precisely, to examine the distortion mechanisms which produce that ruptured discourse, to reconstruct the work-process whereby the text suffers an internal displacement by virtue of its relations to its conditions of possibility.

Freud's 'uppermost dream layer' may be taken, perhaps, to correspond to what could be termed the 'phenomenal' text – that self-coherent plenitude of sense which 'spontaneously' offers itself to the inspecting glance as continuously 'readable' discourse. It is this phenomenal presence of the text which, within bourgeois ideology, plays its part in constituting the reader as equivalently self-coherent 'subject', centred in the privileged space of an entirely appropriable meaning. But 'athwart' that phenomenal presence may be constructed the 'real' text, the discourse which the 'phenomenal' text exists to conceal by its constant suturing. The critic is not, of course, a *therapist* of the text: his task is not to cure or complete it, but to explain why it is as it is. Nevertheless, the analogy between criticism and the analysis of dreams is a suggestive one, not least because of the resemblances between text and dream as modes of discourse. The problematical relation between them and their conditions of production results in both cases in an inherently *ambiguous* discourse, such that the terms in which Freud characterizes the devices of dream suggest 'literariness' – dream as a degrammaticized language with shifting semantic emphases, operating through 'loosely related compressions', blendings and condensations of its materials which may entail the suspension of elementary logical rules. It is an ambiguity appropriate to the displacement and elision of meaning, and it is therefore an equally appropriate mode for the literary text. I have argued already that the text's high degree of relative autonomy of the real produces its typical *concretion*, its peculiarly overdetermined concentration of meanings; but this concentration also gives rise to the prototypically ambiguous, polysemic nature of literary language. Because literary discourse has no real particular referent, its significations remain multiple and partly 'open' in a way which enables those displacements and elisions of meaning occasioned by its relation to ideology.

Macherey's conception of the text–ideology relation is a fertile, suggestive one; but it is also, it must be said, partial. The central concept of *absence* behaves in his work as a theoretical nexus between Marxist and structuralist elements of thought: it allows him, in short, to preserve a high degree of autonomy of the artefact while simultaneously relating it to history. It is, in other words, an absolutely necessary concept if an essentially formalist theory of literary language is to cohabit with historical materialism – if the Russian literary debates of the 1920s are to be transcended at a stroke. But there is not only something curiously Hegelian about conceiving of the work's identity as wholly constituted by what it is not; it is also that an essentially *negative* conception of the text's relation to history, while doubtless posing a salutary countercheck to those heavily 'positive' models employed by some neo-Hegelian and 'vulgar' Marxist theory, runs the danger of its own kind of dogmatism. For it is not invariably true that a text is thrown into grievous internal disarray by its relation to ideology, or that such a relation consists simply in the text's forcing ideology up against the history it denies. We have seen already that there are texts which establish a less 'fraught' relation to ideology, without thereby merely 'reproducing' it. Pope's *Essay on Man* is a highly 'produced' version of an ideology which is not thereby thrown into conflict with itself – where the *acceptable* contradictions ('paradoxes') inherent in the ideology can be negotiated without notable self-mutilation. There are other texts which in working, displacing and transmuting ideological components in the name of a 'solution' display a set of dissonances which do not, however, twist them into severe self-contradiction. In such texts, the ideological discourses selected are often more 'innocent' of direct ideological determination, more impure and ambiguous from this viewpoint, and so, in needing to be produced more rigorously, betray in this act a certain index of recalcitrance to the mode of production. It is as if the ideological categories at issue here do not 'spontaneously' determine their appropriate discourses, but rather 'present' to the aesthetic operation a number of alternatives and indeterminacies – indeterminacies of which they must be 'shorn', but which to a greater or lesser degree may remain clustered around them in the final product. Some of Pope's poetry is again exemplary here: for part of the particular 'aesthetic effect' of that work is the constant dramatic visibility of the mechanisms of aesthetic transmutation, a visibility which is in the same act concealed and 'naturalized'. The text, that is to say, parades an illusion of limited 'freedom' in its materials, as though their specific weight and allusiveness might allow them to escape from submission to aesthetic processing, only to demonstrate that such submission is after all inexorable. Words and phrases gesture to their places in 'pre-textual' discourses only to yield up the inevitability of their textual locus, and so of their place in its specific ideological formation. Or, once again, there are texts where, as Macherey argues, the *mis-en-scène* of ideology produces severe self-divisions of meaning – a work like *The Prelude*, for example, in which an organicist evolutionary ideology is ruptured by starkly epiphanic 'spots of time', recalcitrant material which refuses to be absorbed. Here the 'official' ideology of the text is in contradiction with its modes of producing it, what is said at odds with what is shown. In so far as *The Prelude* draws back from the tragic brink to which its isolated epiphanies allude, its 'official' ideology might be said to triumph; but the reverse might be said of one or two of the 'Lucy' poems, where certain obscure pressures of feeling force their way through to throw the 'official' ideology into radical question. There are, in other words, conflicting ways in which ideology presses the text into disorder; and even here we must discriminate between disorder of *meaning* (or levels of meaning) and disorder of *form*. *The Prelude* is *formally* fissured by its ideological contradictions, unable to rise to the seamless impersonal epic it would wish itself to be: its generic uncertainty, unevenness of texture, haltings and recoveries of narrative and shifts of standpoint are at odds with the consoling evolutionism of its outlook, indices of its lack of unity with itself. But the ideological conflicts of some of the 'Lucy' poems, by contrast, are illuminated precisely by the unruffled intactness of their form.

To argue for differential relations between text and ideology is not to argue for eclecticism. It is to claim that those relations are historically mutable – as mutable as 'general' and 'aesthetic' ideologies themselves – and therefore demand specific historical definition. Indeed such variability can be traced in the career of a single author: I have in mind Thomas Hardy. *Under The Greenwood Tree* produces a 'pastoral' ideology and in doing so displays its limits, dramatizing forms of social mobility, disruption and dissolution which such an ideology cannot encompass. But these elements are not permitted radically to subvert the pastoral form, which, as the novel's partly self-ironic subtitle suggests ('A Rural Painting of the Dutch School'), preserves itself by a certain distantiation of what it is unable to absorb. *Far from the Madding Crowd* is a more overtly ironic title, appropriate for a novel which brings more intensively realist techniques to bear on 'pastoral' ideology, throws it into radical self-question yet uncertainly endorses it in its final refusal of tragedy. The formal dissonances of *The Return of the Native* and *The Mayor of Casterbridge*, typically 'impure' Hardyesque compounds of pastoral, mythology, 'classical' tragedy and fictional realism, are the product of a definitive ideological transcendence of pastoral which is still to find its complete formal consummation – as in *The Woodlanders* and *Tess of the D'Urbervilles* – in a fully elaborated realism. No sooner does Hardy consummate such a relation, however, than he begins in *Jude the Obscure* to force it into self-contradiction by pressing beyond it into fictional modes which highlight the limits of realism itself. The dramatic internal dislocations and contradictions of *Jude the Obscure* are indeed the effect of its forcing the ideology it operates to an extreme limit; but before Hardy reaches this point, his fiction demonstrates a series of alternative relations between text and ideology.

Macherey insists that the contradictions of the text are not to be grasped as the reflection of real historical contradictions. On the contrary: textual contradictions result precisely from the *absence* of such a reflection – from the contortive effect on the work of the ideology which interposes itself between the work and history. But if the text's internal conflicts are not the reflection of historical contradictions, neither are they the reflection of ideological ones. For strictly speaking there can be no contradiction *within* ideology, since its function is precisely to eradicate it. There can be contradiction only between ideology and what it occludes – history itself. Textual dissonances, then, are the effect of the work's *production* of ideology. The text *puts* the ideology into contradiction, discloses the limits and absences which mark its relation to history, and in doing so puts itself into question, producing a lack and disorder within itself. But there is a danger here of lapsing into too expansionist and 'totalitarian' a conception of ideology. For it is not as though ideology is always and everywhere a seamless imaginary whole – always and everywhere 'at its best'. Ideology, seen from within, has no outside; in this sense one does not transgress its outer limits as one crosses a geographical boundary. The threshold of ideology is also an internal limit: ideological space is curved like space itself, and history lies beyond it as only God could lie beyond the universe. It is not possible to effect a 'passage' from the heart of ideology beyond its boundaries, for from that vantage-point there are no boundaries to be transgressed; ideology curves back upon itself, creating outside of itself a void which cannot be explored because it is, precisely, nothing. If it is impossible to cross its frontiers from within, it is because those frontiers – since nothing lies beyond them – have no existence. To travel indefinitely along any one track of ideological meaning is not to encounter an ultimate threshold of articulation but to describe an arc which returns one inexorably to one's starting-point. In discovering its demarcations, ideology discovers its self-dissolution; it cannot survive the 'culture shock' consequent on its stumbling into alien territory adjacent to itself. In discovering such territory, ideology finds its *homeland*, and can return to it only to die. It cannot survive the traumatic recognition of its own repressed parentage – the truth that it is not after all self-reproductive but was historically brought to birth, the scandal that, before it ever was, history existed. Such a recognition may be forced upon ideology by the unwelcome discovery of a rival sibling – an antagonistic ideology which reveals to it the secret of its own birth. That secret may be spoken directly; but it may also be that ideology, in discerning the moment when its rival emerged from the womb of history, is thereby constrained to acknowledge itself as an offspring of the same parent. It is not, in other words, simply by virtue of ideology being forced up against the wall of history by the literary text that it is terrorized into handing over its secrets. Its contradictions may be forced from it by its historically determined encounter with another ideology, or ideological sub-ensemble; indeed it is possible to claim that it is in such historical conjunctures that the moment of genesis of much major literature is to be found. It is true that Shakespearean drama does not merely 'reproduce' a conflict of historical ideologies; but neither does it merely press a particular ideology to the point where it betrays its significant silences. Rather, it produces, from a specific standpoint within it, the severe contradictions of an ideological formation characterized by a peculiarly high degree of 'dissolution' – dissolution produced by a conflict of antagonistic ideologies appropriate to a particular stage of class struggle.

The guarantor of a scientific criticism is the science of ideological formations. It is only on the basis of such a science that such a criticism could possibly be established – only by the assurance of a knowledge of ideology that we can claim a knowledge of literary texts. This is not to say that scientific criticism is merely an 'application' of historical materialism to literature. Criticism is a specific element of the theory of superstructures, which studies the particular laws of its proper object; its task is not to study the laws of ideological formations, but the laws of the production of ideological discourses as literature.

If literary texts were reducible to their ideological formations, then criticism would indeed be no more than a specific application of the science of those formations. The more notorious forms of such reductionism have largely disappeared from Marxist criticism; but there have arisen more sophisticated, and so more tempting versions of the method to take their place. To conceive of the literary work as an enigmatic 'message' whose 'code' is to be deciphered is one such contemporary version, resting, as Pierre Macherey has argued, on an essentially Platonic notion of the artefact. If the text is an encoded message then it operates merely as an intermediary, as the simulacrum of a concealed structure; and certain kinds of structuralist analysis, in elaborating a 'copy' of that structure, hence become the simulacrum of a simulacrum. The writer's production is merely the *appearance* of a production, since its true object lies behind or within it; to criticize, therefore, is to reduce the 'externality' of the text to the structure secreted in its 'interior'.

But the text is not the phenomenon of an ideological essence, the microstructure of a macrostructure; the ideology to which the text belongs does not figure within it as its 'deep structure'. The problematic of Lucien Goldmann's 'genetic structuralism' presses such an error to an exemplary extreme: for here the most 'valid' work is that which most 'purely' transposes to the plane of 'imaginary creation' the structure of the 'world view' of a social group or class. The text, in Goldmann's hands, is rudely robbed of its materiality, reduced to no more than the microcosm of a mental structure. Not only is it untrue, *pace* Goldmann, that historically disparate works may 'express' the same 'world view'; it is not necessarily true by any means that the works of the same author will belong to the same ideology. And even texts which do belong to the same ideology will not 'give' it in the same way – indeed may give it in such divergent ways that we can properly speak of the 'ideology of the text', as a uniquely constituted world of representations. Such a world, far from reflecting ideology in miniature, actively extends and elaborates it, becoming a constitutive element of its self-reproduction. In this sense, to speak of the 'relation' between text and ideology is itself to risk posing the issue too extrinsically. For it is less a question of two externally related phenomena than of a 'relationship of difference' established by the text *within* ideology – a relationship which, *precisely because* it produces in the text a high degree of relative autonomy, enables it to become an inherent constituent of ideological reproduction. One might even risk saying that the text is the process whereby ideology enters into a mode of relation with itself peculiarly enabling of its self-reproduction. Such a formulation can easily be misunderstood in Hegelian terms – the text as a point where the spirit of ideology enters upon material incarnation only to reappropriate itself, literature as a mere passage or transaction within ideology itself. It is to avoid such a misconception that we need to speak of a relation of production between text and ideology; but it is equally important not to grasp that relation as merely external. An analogy may perhaps be found in the relation of ideology itself to the capitalist mode of production. Ideology is not merely a 'set of representations' externally related to that mode of production: on the contrary, it has its base in those very economic forms which cannot but conceal the truth of capitalist production in their phenomenal presence. The relation between ideology and mode of production, then, is an *internal* one; but at the same time ideology, by virtue of an 'internal distantiation', constitutes itself as a relatively autonomous formation. In a parallel way, the literary text is constituted as a relatively autonomous formation on the basis of the internal bonds which leash it to ideology.

This complex relation of text to ideology, whereby the text is neither an epiphenomenon of ideology nor a wholly autonomous element, is relevant to the question of the text's 'structure'. The text can be spoken of as having a structure, even if it is a structure constituted not by symmetry but by rupture and decentrement. For this itself, in so far as the distances and conflicts between its diverse elements are determinate rather than opaque, constitutes a structure of a specific kind. Yet this structure is not to be seen as a microcosm or cryptogram of ideology; ideology is not the 'truth' of the text, any more than the dramatic text is the 'truth' of the dramatic performance. The 'truth' of the text is not an essence but a practice – the practice of its relation to ideology, and in terms of that to history. On the basis of this practice, the text constitutes itself as a structure: it destructures ideology in order to reconstitute it on its own relatively autonomous terms, in order to process and recast it in aesthetic production, at the same time as it is itself destructured to variable degrees by the effect of ideology upon it. In this destructuring practice, the text encounters ideology as a relatively structured formation which presses upon its own particular valencies and relations, confronts it with a 'concrete logic' which forms the outer perimeter of the text's own self-production. The text works, now with, now against the variable pressure of these valencies, finding itself able to admit one ideological element in relatively unprocessed form but finding therefore the need to displace or recast another, struggling against its recalcitrance and producing, in that struggle, new problems for itself. In this way the text disorders ideology to produce an internal order which may then occasion fresh disorder both in itself and in the ideology. This complex movement cannot be imaged as the 'structure of the text' transposing or reproducing the 'structure of the ideology': it can only be grasped as a ceaseless reciprocal *operation* of text on ideology and ideology on text, a mutual structuring and destructuring in which the text constantly overdetermines its own determinations. The structure of the text is then the *product* of this process, not the reflection of its ideological environs. The 'logic of the text' is not a discourse which doubles the 'logic of ideology'; it is, rather, a logic constructed '*athwart*' that more encompassing logic.

Yet if textual structure does not reproduce ideological structure, it is important on the other hand to avoid falling into a fresh empiricism of the literary object. There is, as I have argued, a particular 'ideology of the text', reducible to neither 'general' nor 'authorial' ideologies, which in any two texts would be the same only if those texts were verbally identical. In this sense it is appropriate to speak of every author, and each text of every author, as yielding a 'different' ideology. The ideology of Wycherley is not that of Etheredge, nor is the ideology of *The Country Wife* that of *The Plain Dealer*. Yet there is nothing to be gained in the end by arguing that there are as many ideologies as there are texts – a claim as vacuous as the proposition that there are as many ideologies as there are individual subjects in class-society. We may recircle at this point to the analogy of text and dramatic performance with which we began. It is true, figuratively speaking, that two different productions of *Othello* yield different texts; but the critical analysis of those productions is possible only if they are placed in relation to the one determinate Shakespearean text. Similarly, it is not a *reduction* of the works of Wycherley and Etheredge to situate them on the same ideological terrain: it is only by doing so that their differences, and so their unique identities, can be established. An empiricism of the literary text entails, inevitably, a nominalism of ideology.

The relation between text and ideology, then, can be generally summarized as follows. Ideology presents itself to the text as a set of significations which are already articulated in a certain *form* or series of forms, displaying certain general structural relations. Ideology also presents to the text a determinate series of specific modes and mechanisms of aesthetic production – an ideologically determined set of possible modes of aesthetically producing ideological significations. These specific modes are themselves generally determined by the structural forms 'naturally' assumed by ideology: they stand in determinate relations of degrees of conflict or homology with the general forms of perception and representation inherent in the structure of the ideological significations themselves. They may be historically and ideologically 'given together' with those general forms, as a particular mode of narrative is given together with a general ideological form of representing 'individual progress', or they may be historically and ideologically non-synchronous with such general representational forms. Since the text is generally a complex unity of such modes of aesthetic production, it may therefore incorporate a set of differential, mutually conflictual relations to the general forms given to it by the structure of its significations. It may not, in this sense, be historically identical with itself. These aesthetic modes of production, on the basis of the determination of the general representational forms of the ideology, then 'produce' a set of ideological significations which are themselves the product of certain general ideological categories – categories which articulate such significations in a certain form. In producing such significations, the productive forms at once 'pre-constitute' them – that is to say, partly determine *which* significations are to be produced – and so operate on those selected as to displace, recast and mutate them according to the relatively autonomous laws of its own aesthetic modes, on the basis of those modes' ideological determination and of the specific form and character of the ideological significations put to work. This process of displacement and mutation, whereby the 'aesthetic' produces the 'ideological' on the basis of an ideological determination overdetermined by the aesthetic itself, reveals itself to criticism as a complex series of transactions between text and ideology – transactions which figure in the text as a process of more or less visible conflicts produced, resolved and thereby reproduced. It is in this process that something of the general structure of that process of the production of social significations which is ideology is laid bare. In yielding up to criticism the ideologically determined conventionality of its modes of constructing sense, the text at the same time obliquely illuminates the relation of that ideology to real history.

Literature, one might argue, is the most revealing mode of experiential access to ideology that we possess. It is in literature, above all, that we observe in a peculiarly complex, coherent, intensive and immediate fashion the workings of ideology in the textures of lived experience of class-societies. It is a mode of access more immediate than that of science, and more coherent than that normally available in daily living itself. Literature presents itself in this sense as 'midway' between the distancing rigour of scientific knowledge and the vivid but loose contingencies of the 'lived' itself. Unlike science, literature appropriates the real as it is given in ideological forms, but does so in a way which produces an illusion of the spontaneously, unmediatedly real. It is thus more removed from the real than science, yet appears closer to it. Like science, literature appropriates its object by the deployment of certain categories and protocols – in its case, *genre*, symbol, convention and so on. As with science, these categories are themselves the elaborated product of perception and representation; but in the case of literature that elaboration is not carried to the point of producing *concepts* – rather to the point of certain forms which, while performing an *analogous* function to that of conceptual categories in science, tend simultaneously to conceal and naturalize them-selves, standing in apparently intimate, spontaneous relation to the 'materials' they produce. That relation is itself ideologically variable; but it is a prototypical effect of literature to partly 'dissolve' its modes of production into the 'concrete life' which is their product. Like private property, the literary text thus appears as a 'natural' object, typically denying the determinants of its productive process. The function of criticism is to refuse the spontaneous presence of the work – to deny that 'naturalness' in order to make its real determinants appear.

NOTES

1 One is happy to observe here a remarkable consonance of viewpoints between materialist criticism and Sir Philip Sidney's *Apology for Poetry*.
2 *Lenin and Philosphy* (London, 1971), 203–4.
3 *Pour une Théorie de la production littéraire* (Paris, 1974), 77–83.
4 See his *Marxism and Form* (Princeton, 1971), 327–40.

20 The Marxist-Feminist Literature Collective

Women's Writing: *Jane Eyre, Shirley, Villette, Aurora Leigh* (1978)*

The 'unhappy marriage' of Marxism and feminism has mostly consisted of divorce proceedings, despite the deep, if contradictory, historical affinities evident from F. Engels, *The Origin of the Family, Private Property and the State* (1884; trans. 1942) and Alexandra Kollontai, to Kate Millett, *Sexual Politics* (1970) and Juliet Mitchell, *Women: The Longest Revolution* (1984). Although working with shared critiques of the family and the dependence of marriage and patriarchy on property relations, one half of the Marxist- feminist compound is usually prioritized. Specific struggles often subsume gender within class alliances, or subsume class alliances within struggles to forge gendered political identities. Despite a long tradition of socialist-feminism – see Barbara Taylor, *Eve and the New Jerusalem: Socialism and Feminism in the Nineteenth Century* (1983) – there is little specifically Marxist-feminist literary theory. The major exception is the period of the 1970s and 1980s. The 'triple alliance' of Althusserian Marxism, structuralism and psychoanalysis produced a range of theoretical innovations focused on discourse, film and the ideological interpellation of subjects within capitalist patriarchy. This can be traced in the early work of Julia Kristeva; in the work of film theorists such as Laura Mulvey and Stephen Heath; and in journals such as *Screen, m/f, Feminist Review* and *New Formations*. Perhaps the most productive theoretical developments concerned commodity fetishism, the social organization of desire, and the hegemony of discourses of power and knowledge. Amid the increasing fragmentation of antagonistic identity politics, however, the struggles of new social movements in such theoretical compounds threaten to devolve into hierarchies of oppression and formalist rhetoric. The Marxist-Feminist Literature Collective's essay introduces the aims and identity of the Collective. Taking issue with the way Marxists such as Terry Eagleton prioritize class struggle over

* From *Ideology & Consciousness*, 3 (spring, 1978), 27–48.

feminist themes, the essay attempts to develop a revised Marxist-feminist methodo-logy. Many of those in the Collective have since produced notable work as individuals, but often the engagement with Marxism has diminished in favour of psychoanalysis or the work of Michel Foucault. See for example Michèle Barrett's retrospective preface to the revised *Women's Oppression Today: The Marxist/Feminist Encounter* (1988); and Cora Kaplan, *Sea Changes* (1986).

Who Are We?

This paper arises from the work of a group which has been meeting in London for one and a half years (though some of its members joined more recently). It was presented at the Essex Literature Conference in July 1977, by the whole Collective, whose members at the time were Cheris Kramer, Cora Kaplan, Helen Taylor, Jean Radford, Jennifer Joseph, Margaret Williamson, Maud Ellmann, Mary Jacobus, Michèle Barrett and Rebecca O'Rourke.

The cumbersome title – Marxist-Feminist Literature Collective – covers (or perhaps conceals), on one side of the hyphen – in the adjective 'Marxist' – a diversity of positions in relation to Marxism. On the other side of the hyphen, the adjective 'feminist' points, among other things, to an important aspect of our practice. A major contribution of the women's movement has been the organizational principle of collective work; for all of us, the method of work within the group has been a departure from and a challenge to the isolated, individualistic ways in which we operate in academic spheres. Our paper, in its polylogic structure and presentation, draws on the continuing play of ideas and debate from within which we speak, and challenges the monologic discourse of patriarchal literary criticism.

Theoretical Introduction

A Marxist-feminist critical practice proposes to account for the inadequacies of a standard Marxist approach to literature and ultimately to transform this approach. In this paper we discuss the articulation of class and gender in terms both of the historical conjuncture of 1848 and of the problems of a Marxist-feminist method in theorizing literature. Literary texts are assumed to be ideological in the sense that they cannot give us a knowledge of the social formation; but they do give us something of equal importance in analysing culture, an imaginary representation of real relations.

A Marxist-feminist approach, by focusing on gender as a crucial determin-ant of literary production, can provide a better understanding of literature as a gender-differentiated signifying practice. This is not to privilege gender over class, but to challenge the tradition in which women's writing has often been hived off from the mainstream of male writing and criticism.

Both Marxism and feminism have rightly taken considerable interest recently in the possibility of an integration between Marxist and psychoanalytic thought. Both Marxism and psychoanalysis propose their methods as exhaustive; but we argue that it is only through a synthesis of these two, problematic though that is, that we can unfold the crucial interdependence between class structure and patriarchy.

Lukács argued that coherent literary works could only be produced by a unified, ascending social class, and in this context he stressed 1848 as the date at which the bourgeoisie as a class and realism as a literary form began to decline. The limitations of this approach are notorious, and too numerous to list here. What we shall do is not only, using the ideas of Jacques Lacan, Pierre Macherey and others,[1] analyse the incoherences and contradictions in the texts we discuss, but also relate these precisely to the marginal position of female literary practice in this period.

Central to our analysis of these texts is a recognition of the marginality of their authors to the public discourse of mid-nineteenth-century society. The partial exclusion of women from the public literary world is one aspect of the general marginality of women in this period, as instanced by their exclusion from the exercise of political power and their separation from production. This congruence between the marginality of women writers and the general position of women in society is represented in the situation of many female characters in the texts.

The period of protest which culminated in the political events of the 1840s marked the transition from a manufacturing economy to the industrial capitalist mode of production – developments which had serious consequences for women and the family. Working–class women were drafted into production as a source of cheap labour; bourgeois women remained in the home and were separated from production. In both cases women were excluded from ownership of the means of production, distribution and exchange.

However, the inadequacy of a solely economic mode of analysis is shown by Engels' optimistic claim in 1884 that, because of working-class women's entry into the industrial labour process, 'the last remnants of male domination in the proletarian home have lost all foundation'.[2] It is clearly necessary also to analyse the contemporary ideological formation in terms of the hegemony of patriarchal attitudes. Such attitudes are represented for example in the double standard of sexual morality, whereby women were either madonnas or whores, and middle-class women in particular were subject to the constraints of the ideology of domesticity and the angel in the house. The ideology of romantic love, while masking the economic basis of bourgeois marriage in this period as the exchange of women, shows by its persistence that it exists autonomously, independent of its specific economic functions in a given historical conjuncture.

The four texts under consideration foreground these questions. *Jane Eyre* (1847), *Shirley* (1849), *Villette* (1853) and *Aurora Leigh* (1857) can be read as a discussion of gender definition, kinship structures, and to some extent the relation between these and social class. The texts of Charlotte Bronte and Elizabeth Barrett Browning refuse to reproduce contemporary economic and ideological determinations; instead they represent a systematic evasion or interrogation of the Law of these determinations. Althusser has stressed its inescapability: 'The Law cannot be "ignored" by anyone, least of all by those ignorant of it, but may be evaded or violated by everyone.'[3]

We argue that this 'evasion' of the law occurs in the texts in the interrelated areas of social class, kinship and Oedipal socialization. The necessary connections between these three areas are represented in the texts' presentation of two key points of articulation – the institution of marriage and the role of the *pater familias*.

All the major female characters of the texts have an extremely marginal and unstable class position, and all display an obvious discrepancy between their class position and their alleged rightful status; their status is bourgeois, but they are all orphans and most of them are without financial independence. Comparing these texts with those of Jane Austen, the lack of determinancy of class background is striking.

The bourgeois kinship structure of the period, predicated on the exchange of women, is similarly evaded. None of the heroines have fathers present to give them away in marriage. More importantly, we can analyse marriage itself as the crucial point of articulation between class and kinship structures. This can be seen in two ways: on one hand, the only women in the texts who are free to exercise choice in marrying – Jane Eyre, Aurora Leigh, Shirley and Polly de Bassompierre – have, or miraculously acquire, some degree of financial independence.

On the other hand, the example of Caroline Helstone demonstrates with great force the law which Charlotte Brontë otherwise evades, in that her marriage to Robert Moore can only take place when the repeal of the Orders in Council has enabled him to be a successful capitalist. Without this repeal, he would have emigrated to Canada and she would have been an Old Maid!

The evasion of Oedipal determination, so crucial to gender definition in this period, will be discussed in more detail in its most striking manifestation, in *Aurora Leigh*. But in all these texts the devised absence of the father represents a triple evasion of all the areas we have so far mentioned – class structure, kinship structure and Oedipal socialization. Its consequences are that there is no father from whom the bourgeois woman can inherit property, no father to exchange her in marriage, and no father to create the conditions for typical Oedipal socialization.

The subversiveness of this evasion was recognized by contemporary reviewers, for in 1848 Lady Eastlake wrote in the *Quarterly Review*:

> We do not hesitate to say that the tone of mind and thought which has overthrown authority and violated every code human and divine abroad, and fostered chartism and rebellion at home, is the same which has also written *Jane Eyre*.[4]

In discussing literary texts, it is important to look at the way women's access to language is ideologically determined. One of the effects of the lack of access to education of which women writers complain is to exclude them from the discourses of institutions such as universities, law, politics and finance which structure their oppression. Women, who are speaking subjects but partially excluded from culture, find modes of expression which the hegemonic discourse cannot integrate. Whereas the eruptive word cannot make the culturally inaccessible accessible, it can surely speak its absence. Kristeva has classified these modes of expression as 'semiotic' as opposed to 'symbolic'.

Inevitably, the work of Kristeva has been considered for its obvious bearing on our analysis. Her notion of the semiotic comprised the repressed, pre-linguistic elements which are located in the tonal, rhythmic, expressive and gestural qualities of poetic discourse. In our view, her association of these qualities with the feminine is fallacious; she has used a cultural ascription of feminity to describe pre-linguistic elements which are in fact universal, and she thus risks privileging and feminizing the irrational. But as we all know, intuition is still the short-change given women by the patriarchy. Not only are there limitations from a feminist perspective, but by calling the feminine, or the semiotic, subversive, she formulates an anarchic revolutionary poetics which is politically unsatisfactory. Her argument, seductive as it is, idealizes and romanticizes the discursive ruptures of the avant-garde. Her failure to locate these notions historically also tends to eternalize the social exaggeration of biological difference. Nevertheless, her suggestive writings have polyphonic resonances in our work, which alludes to, sometimes even dwells on, the explosive and temporarily liberating dissonance within the texts.

Introduction to the Texts: Gender and Genre

In 1859, Charlotte Brontë made a final, impatient plea to Lewes:

> I wish you did not think me a woman. I wish all reviewers believed 'Currer Bell' to be a man; they would be more just to him. . . . I cannot, when I write, think always of myself and what you consider elegant and charming in femininity.[5]

Criticism of women writers is in general divided between the extremes of gender-disavowal and gender-obsession. The second tendency, which Brontë struggles against in Lewes, patronizes women writers as outsiders to literary history, without justifying this apartheid. The Brontës are considered important 'women novelists', not simply novelists. This kind of 'gender criticism' subsumes the text into the sexually defined personality of its author, and thereby obliterates its literarity. To pass over the ideology of gender, on the other hand, ignores the fact that the conditions of literary production and consumption are articulated, in the Victorian period, in crucially different ways for women and men. Any rigorous Machereyan analysis must account for the ideology of gender as it is written into or out of texts by either sex. Women writers, moreover, in response to their cultural exclusion, have developed a relatively autonomous, clandestine tradition of their own.

Gender and genre come from the same root, and their connection in literary history is almost as intimate as their etymology. The tradition into which the women novelist entered in the mid-nineteenth century could be polarized as at once that of Mary Wollstonecraft and of Jane Austen, with the attendant polarization of politics – between revolutionary feminism and conservatism – and of genre – between romanticism and social realism. Wollstonecraft and Austen between them pose the central question of access to male education and discourse on the one hand, on the other the annexing of women's writing to a special sphere, domestic and emotional.

Austen's refusal to write about anything she didn't know is as undermining to the patriarchal hegemony as Wollstonecraft's demand for a widening of women's choices: the very 'narrowness' of her novels gave them a subversive dimension of which she herself was unaware, and which has been registered in critics' bewilderment at what status to accord them.

Bourgeois criticism should be read symptomatically: most of its so-called 'evaluation' is a reinforcement of ideological barriers. Wollstonecraft's, and later Brontë's, ambivalent relation to Romanticism, usually described as clumsy Gothicism, is bound up with their feminism. Romanticism becomes a problem for women writers because of its assumptions about the 'nature of femininity'. The tidal rhythms of menstruation, the outrageous visibility of pregnancy, lead, by a *non sequitur* common to all sexual analogy, to the notion that women exist in a state of unreflective bios, the victims of instincts, intuitions and the mysterious pulsations of the natural world. Intuition is held to be a prelapsarian form of knowledge, associated especially with angels, children, idiots, 'rustics' and women. These excluded, or fabulous, groups act for the patriarchy as a mirror onto which it nostalgically projects the exclusions of its discourse. As a glorified, but pre-linguistic communion with nature, intuition lowers women's status while appearing to raise it.

While Wollstonecraft and Brontë are attracted to Romanticism because reluctant to sacrifice, as women writers, their privileged access to feeling, both are aware that full participation in society requires suppression of this attraction. The drive to female emancipation, while fuelled by the revolutionary energy at the origins of Romanticism, has an ultimately conservative aim – successful integration into existing social structures. Romanticism, after the disappointments of the French Revolution, was gradually depoliticized, and it is only in the mid-nineteenth century, in a period of renewed revolutionary conflict, that it once again becomes a nexus of ideological tension where gender, genre, politics and feminism converge.

Jane Eyre: Her Hand in Marriage

Charlotte Brontë's second preface to *Jane Eyre* states her authorial project as to 'scrutinise and expose' what she calls 'narrow human doctrines' of religion and morality.[6] Our reading of *Jane Eyre* identifies Charlotte Brontë's interrogation of the dominant ideology of love and marriage; but also suggests the Machereyan 'not-said' of the novel – what it is not possible for her to 'scrutinise and expose', woman as a desiring subject, a sexual subject seeking personal fulfilment within the existing structures of class and kinship, i.e. in a patriarchal capitalist society. *Jane Eyre* is *about* kinship, *about* the fact that the social position of a woman, whether rich or poor, pretty or plain, is mediated through the family – to which she may or may not belong. _ *but she ra family*

The text of *Jane Eyre* speaks that desire in the interstices of the debate on woman's social role, between the romance/realism divide, the conflict between Reason and Imagination in her heroine's consciousness. It speaks of women's sexuality in Victorian England, opening the locked room of a tabooed subject – just as that part of the text which concerns Bertha Mason/Rochester disrupts the realistic narrative of Jane's search for an adequate kinship system, i.e. an opening into the family structure from which she is excluded. Charlotte Brontë's general fictional strategy is to place her heroines in varying degrees of marginality to the normative kinship patterns. Frances Henri, Crimsworth (a female surrogate), Jane, Shirley, Caroline Helstone and Lucy Snowe, all have a deviant socialization, all confront the problem of a marriage not negotiated by a *pater familias*.

Why? By excluding them from a conventional family situation in which their socialization and their exchange in marriage cannot follow the practice of Victorian middle-class women, Charlotte Brontë's fiction explores the constraints of the dominant ideology as they bear on female sexual and social identity.

'At the centre of Charlotte Brontë's novels is a figure who either lacks or deliberately cuts the bonds of kinship' (Eagleton, *Myths of Power*). But Eagleton, although stressing this structural characteristic, discusses it primarily in terms of class mobility. This treatment of Jane Eyre herself as an asexual representative of the upwardly mobile bourgeoisie leads to a reductionist reading of the text. It neglects gender as a determinant, by subsuming gender under class. The meritocratic vision of 'individual self-reliance', as Eagleton puts its, *cannot* be enacted by a woman character in the same way as it can be by a male. For a woman to become a member of the 'master–class' depends on her taking a sexual master whereby her submission brings her access to the dominant culture.

The social and judicial legitimacy of this relationship – its encoding within the law – is of primary importance; hence Jane's rejection of the role of Rochester's mistress. She would not merely *not* acquire access – she would forfeit the possibility of ever doing so. The structure of the novel, Jane's development through childhood and adolescence into womanhood, does not simply represent an economic and social progression from penniless orphan to member of the landed gentry class; it represents a woman's struggle for access to her own sexual and reproductive potential – in other words, her attempts to install herself as a full subject within a male-dominated culture.

For example, the structure of the five locales of the novel is customarily seen as the articulation of the heroine's progress – a progress described in liberal criticism as the moral growth of the individual, in vulgar sociological terms as 'upward social mobility'. To foreground kinship provides a radically different reading.

Jane's progress is from a dependent orphan to the acquisition of the family necessary for her full integration into mid-nineteenth-century culture as a woman. Her cousins, the Rivers, and the Madeira uncle who intervenes twice – once via his agent, Bertha's brother, to save her from becoming a 'fallen woman' as Rochester's bigamous wife, and again at the end of the novel with a legacy which is in effect a dowry – provide Jane with the necessary basis for her exchange into marriage.

Each of the five houses through which the heroine passes traces the variety and instability of a kinship structure at a transitional historical period, and the ideological space this offers to women.

At Gateshead, as the excluded intruder into the Reed family and at Thornfield as the sexually tabooed and socially ambiguous governess, Jane's lack of familial status renders her particularly vulnerable to oppression and exploitation. At Lowood, she acquires a surrogate sister and mother in Helen Burns and Miss Temple – only to lose them through death and marriage. The instability of kinship relations is imaged in the patterns of gain and loss, acceptance and denial, enacted at each 'home' – most dramatically in the loss of a lawful wedded husband, spiritually and sexually akin but socially tabooed. The subsequent flight from Thornfield reduces her to a homeless vagrant lacking both past and identity. Throughout the text, the symmetrical arrangement of Reed and Rivers cousins, the Reed and Eyre uncles, the patterns of metaphors about kinship, affinity and identification articulate the proposition that a woman's social identity is constituted within familial relationships. Without the kinship reading, the Rivers' transformation into long-lost, bonafide blood relations at Moor End appears a gross and unmotivated coincidence. This apparently absurd plot manipulation is in fact dictated by the logic of the not-said.

Like such violations of probability, the Gothic elements in the novel are neither clumsy interventions to resolve the narrative problems nor simply the residues of the author's earlier modes of discourse, the childhood fantasies of Angria. Their main function is to evade the censorship of female sexuality within the signifying practice of mid-Victorian realism. For the rights and wrongs of women in social and political terms, there existed a rationalist language, a political rhetoric, inherited from Mary Wollstonecraft. But for the 'unspeakable' sexual desires of women, Charlotte Brontë returned on the one hand to Gothic and Romantic modes, on the other to a metonymic discourse of the human body – hands and eyes for penises, 'vitals' or 'vital organs' for women's genitalia – often to comic effect:

> I am substantial enough – touch me.' . . .
> He held out his hand, laughing. 'Is that a dream?' said he, placing it close to my eyes. He had a rounded, muscular, and vigorous hand, as well as a long, strong arm.[7]

The tale told of women's sexual possibilities is a halting, fragmented and ambivalent one. The libidinal fire of Jane Eyre's 'vital organs' is not denied, not totally repressed, as the refusal of St John Rivers suggests:

> At his side, always and always restrained, always checked – forced to keep the fire of my nature continually low, to compel it to burn inwardly, and never utter a cry, though the imprisoned flame consume vital after vital.[8]

The marriage proposed here, significantly, is an inter-familial one which denies the heroine's sexuality. If women's sexuality is to be integrated, reconciled with male patriarchal Law, a compromise must be achieved with the individual Law-bearer, in this case through a return to Edward Rochester.

The alternative to either repression or integration is examined through that part of text concerned with Bertha Mason/Rochester. Her initial intervention, the uncanny laughter after Jane surveys from the battlements of Thornfield the wider world denied her as a woman, signifies the return of the repressed, the anarchic and unacted desires of women. Bertha's appearances constitute a punctuating device or notation of the not-said – the Pandora's box of unleashed female libido. Bertha's tearing of the veil on the eve of Jane's wedding, for example, is a triumphant trope for the projected loss of Jane's virginity unsanctioned by legitimate marriage. Thus while other spectres were haunting Europe, the spectre haunting Jane Eyre, if not Victorian England, was the insurgence of women's sexuality into the signifying practice of literature.

The myth of unbridled male sexuality is treated through Rochester, whose name evokes that of the predatory Restoration rake, here modified by Byronic sensibility. In the vocabulary of Lacanian psychoanalysis, his maiming by the author is not so much a punitive castration, but represents his successful passage through the castration complex. Like all human subjects he must enter the symbolic order through a necessary acceptance of the loss of an early incestuous love object, a process he initially tries to circumvent through bigamy. His decision to make Jane his bigamous wife attempts to implicate the arch-patriarch, God himself ('I know my maker sanctions what I do'). The supernatural lightning which this presumption provokes is less a re-establishing of bourgeois morality than an expression of disapproval by the transcendental phallic signifier of Rochester's Oedipal rivalry. It is God at the end of the novel who refuses to sanction Jane's marriage to St John Rivers when invoked in its support, and who sends Rochester's supernatural cry to call Jane to him; and it is God's judgement which Rochester, in his maimed condition, finally accepts with filial meekness.

By accepting the Law, he accepts his place in the signifying chain and enters the Symbolic order, as bearer rather than maker of the Law. Sexuality in a reduced and regulated form is integrated – legitimized – within the dominant kinship structure of patriarchy and within the marriage which he (by Bertha's death-by-fire), and Jane (by her acquisition of a family) is now in a position to contract. *Jane Eyre* does not attempt to rupture the dominant kinship structures. The ending of the novel ('Reader, I married him') affirms those very structures. The feminism of the text resides in its 'not-said', its attempt to inscribe women as sexual subjects within this system.

Shirley: Piercing cries . . .

Shirley, Charlotte Brontë's only social-realist novel, is regarded as a failure of structure, theme and characterization by liberal and Marxist critics alike – though for different reasons. Liberal critics favour Winifred Gerin's explanation of the dislocated plot and inferior 'artistic independence and wholeness';[9] that Charlotte Brontë varied her style and tone at different stages of the novel in accordance with her personal circumstances (volume 1, confident, after the success of *Jane Eyre*, volume 2 grave and reflective, because Emily was dying, etc. etc.). Eagleton's Marxist study of the Brontë novels[10] is refreshingly free of such schmaltz. He explains the failure of the novel primarily in terms of Brontë's central concern with the contradictions within the ruling class, which resulted in grotesque caricatures of the working class. He sees the novel's 'central dramatic incident', the mill attack, as 'curiously empty' because 'at the point of its most significant presence in the novel, the working class is wholly invisible'.

Eagleton argues a strong case for the novel's 'unspoken subject' – Chartism. Yet he focuses on the class-struggle elements of the book almost to the exclusion of the equally prominent feminist theme – and seems not to notice that Shirley is a woman (he even calls her a 'paternalist'). Neither he nor anyone else has explained the dislocations and structural awkwardness of the novel in terms of the originality of a conception which attempts to foreground class and gender as problems of equal weight and complexity.

Because it is attempting a critique of the male hegemony in relation to both the working class and women, the novel abounds with dislocations and contradictions. Yet its two central subjects, class and gender, are remarkable for the invisibility of their representatives. If the proletariat is 'invisible' at the moment of its most significant presence, it's worth remembering that the two women, through whose eyes the mill attack is observed, are also invisible – not only to the male ruling class but also, ironically, to the working-class men whose impotence and vulnerability mirror their own.

This is Brontë's only novel to focus on an exclusively male world, that of work and political struggle. But whereas Mrs Gaskell – who attempted a similar task in *Mary Barton* – often retreats into timid authorial apology ('I am not sure if I can express myself in the technical terms of either masters or workmen')[11] Brontë uses an original narrative technique: examination of male proletarian struggle from the perspective of, and by analogy with, oppressed bourgeois women. The analogies are potentially so revolutionary that they cannot be spoken, but must lurk disguised within a text which is then read as structurally deficient.

Shirley is a novel which conceals its feminist argument within an historical framework – the Napoleonic Wars and Luddism – with the result that Brontë's contemporaries and modern critics alike have failed to acknowledge the thematic complexity which Brontë ambitiously attempted in this work.

After the success of *Jane Eyre* in 1847 Brontë wrote often in her letters about the 'condition of women' question, especially about the plight of single women without work. Many critics point to the half-hearted liberalism of her feminist statements in the letters as an indication of her reactionary beliefs – which they find substantiated in the conventionally happy endings of three of her four novels. Yet in Brontë's fiction the contradictions of her politics, especially her feminism, are writ large – as contemporary criticism testified. For example, while the feminist radical Mary Taylor wrote to Charlotte Brontë of *Jane Eyre*, 'Has the world gone so well with you that you have no protest to make against its absurdities?', Mrs Oliphant saw it as a 'wild declaration of the "Rights of Woman"'.[12]

Shirley, unlike *Jane Eyre* and *Villette*, has two heroines, used by the author to reflect different crises for women in a male world itself in crisis.

Just as Charlotte Brontë jealously guarded her masculine *nom de plume* long after her true identity was common knowledge, so Shirely cherishes for much of the novel the bisexual possibilities inherent in her position. She enjoys her title, Captain Keeldar; whistles and moves like a man; discusses politics with her tenant Moore. Nevertheless, like the androgyny of Charlotte Brontë/Currer Bell, it is a fantasy and – when bourgeois and proletarian men meet in bloody confrontation – Shirley, for all her position as landowner, banker and gun-toter, must be firmly relegated to the silent invisible world of women who are expected to live through the mill attack 'asleep in [their] beds – unconscious'. Shirley embodies the contradictions of a woman endowed with male privilege and economic independence, yet still defined as a 'lady' within patriarchal culture. She expresses resentment at the constrictions her femininity imposes upon her, yet fully accedes to the marginality of women in social and political life, and at no point identifies politically with other women. While flaunting her independence of men and fantasizing about an allegorical female omnipotence, ultimately she wants to be mastered, and gets it from a man who chides her with being 'womanish' and 'childish' and with whom the final declaration of love is spoken as 'My pupil' 'My master'. Her androgyny is a game, an impossibility. Imprisoned within her time, Brontë couldn't imagine what else a woman landowner could do with wealth and independence but give them to the man she chose to love.

That is, except become a writer. Like Emily Brontë, Shirley has the imaginative power to 'make earth an Eden, life a poem'. But Brontë waxes censorious over Shirley's incapacity to 'possess' what she can create, through 'indolence, recklessness and ignorance'. For Brontë, writing was a way of acquiring property, thus status where most women had none. The knowledge of her worth as an artist was the means she used to place herself in a world which, since she rejected the idea of teaching, offered her no other role. It's therefore not surprising that the first time Shirley has a fantasy of female omnipotence – the woman-Titan/Eve vision – Bronte reduces it sharply to size by reminders of patriarchal supremacy: the sight of six soldiers riding by, followed by conversations with two working men about 'starving folk' in which they scorn Shirley's attempt to talk politics.

Eagleton finds Shirley's visionary outburst 'embarrassing', yet Brontë did too – for different reasons. She undermines its power by reminding us both of Shirley's privilege in class terms (Farren and Scott have no time in their lives for poetry) but also of her irrelevance, in gender terms, to patriarchy. Joe Scott quotes St Paul, reminding her 'Adam was first formed, then Eve'. A vision of Eve's omnipotence is valid among poetic women, but in real terms Adam rules OK.

Yet although Shirley is progressively diminished by her author until she joins the silent ranks of propertyless, Sunday-school-teaching wives, it is not she who carries the full burden of the gender question. It is Caroline who stands for Womankind. Caroline appears to be the classic Victorian young lady: Brontë's only unemployed heroine of no independent means, she spends her time sewing for the Jew basket and learning appropriate female skills; she lives – and almost dies – for love. Everyone around her confirms the appropriateness of a life which she finds intolerable. Authorial comment on her life – and on Victorian woman's life in general – comes from the caricature of Hortense, with her endless drawer-tidying; from Rose Yorke, who sees Caroline's life as a 'long, slow death'; and from the spectres of three old maids with their lives of 'terrible hollowness, mockery, want, craving'. Caroline Helstone speaks the oppression of women within patriarchal society by the very silence to which she is constantly reduced.

Brontë's critique of the hegemony of patriarchy and capitalism is couched in the 'piercing cries for relief' to Heaven which, in her letters,[13] she defends as the right of women and 'operatives' when their lot becomes intolerable. The cry of the operatives is heard in the threats they pose throughout the novel to the safety of property and lives; their destruction of machinery; the attack on the mill, and the wounding of Robert Moore. The cry of the women is carried within the novel in Brontë's portrayal of Caroline's passive endurance in the face of ill treatment by parents, uncle and lover; her illness and near-death; and her complete dependence on Moore to pop the question to save her from a fate worse than death – becoming an old maid.

But the cry to Heaven is also voiced as a recurrent argument throughout, with Brontë speaking in her own thinly disguised voice, often through Caroline. Brontë's tirades against the injustices done to women rupture women's silence by speech about the unspeakable. But within the text they cannot provoke a transformation of women's conditions; outside monologue and her expressed desire to become a governess, Caroline is denied access to culture, given few possibilities of full speech.

Analogies between the two oppressed groups can be spoken only sentiment-ally and metaphorically. Caroline feels warmly towards children and workers at the mill, defending their rights against Moore's dismissive 'mob' label, drawing admonitory parallels with *Coriolanus*. Moore calls her a 'little demo-crat', yet hers is the democracy of the weak, intuitive and powerless who ally themselves with others similarly handicapped, but who, in the last analysis, fear for nothing more than their own skins and the maintenance of the *status quo*. Caroline and William forge their closest alliance only in a metaphoric Eden – the garden round which the ex-millworker, now gardener, wheels the convalescent woman, while they discuss 'minute observations on points of natural history'.

Incompletely articulated, falteringly narrated, this is Brontë's reactionary view of class struggle, seen primarily in Christian, sentimental terms. But the fully spoken political subject of the novel is the urgent plight of dependent women. At least Luddism and Chartism provided organized, powerful modes of speech for working men; all Brontë can offer on the gender question are 'piercing cries for relief' to Heaven, and a double wedding, at least ensuring for her heroines some right of access to speech through formal alliances with their oppressors.

Villette: The Phantom of Feminism

> Is this enough? Is it to live? . . . Does virtue lie in abnegation of self? I do not believe it. . . . Each human being has his share of rights.

Caroline Helstone's assertion of the inalienable rights of self, in *Shirley*, provides the germ of *Villette* – a novel in which repression returns vengefully on the self-estranged heroine in the form of a ghostly nun. But *Villette* is not simply about the perils of repression: it is a text fissured and distorted by its own repressions, concealing a buried letter. Lucy Snowe writes two letters to Graham Bretton, one dictated by 'Reason' the other by 'Feeling'. In the same way the narrative and representational conventions of Victorian realism are threatened and disrupted by an incompletely repressed Romanticism. Satanic revolt and supernatural haunting, delusion and dream, function discursively in a text which can give no formal recognition to Romantic and Gothic modes, and which is haunted by the unacknowledged phantom – the Machereyan 'not-said' of feminism itself.

Lucy Snowe's haunted self-estrangement encodes the novel's alienation from the literary and ideological forces which constitute its ghostly subtext. Arnold saw in *Villette* nothing but Charlotte Brontë's own 'hunger, rebellion and rage'.[14] It is easy enough to dismiss the unmediated relationship proposed here between author and work. But the assumption that autobiographical release fuels the novel is natural enough. Belonging as it does to the Rousseauist tradition of the *roman personnel* (the lived fiction), *Villette* invites its readers to make just such an identification between Charlotte Brontë and her creation – and then frustrates it. This is its real oddity. The novel perversely withholds its true subject by an act of repression which mimics Lucy's own. Lucy lies to us. Her deliberate ruses, omissions and falsifications break the unwritten contract of first-person narrative, unsettling our faith in the reliability of the text. 'I, Lucy Snowe, plead guiltless of that curse, an overheated and discursive imagination' she tells us; but the same sentence goes on to speak of the infant Paulina's grief 'haunting' the room as Lucy herself will later be haunted by the imagination she denies.

We learn about Lucy only at one remove, through the displacement which is a central feature of Charlotte Brontë's narrative technique – Paulina's abandonment as a child and her premature love for Graham Bretton, Miss Marchmont's confinement and erotic arrest, the cretin who becomes her 'strange, deformed companion' during her long vacation ordeal-by-solitude. It hardly needs emphasizing that the heart-sick Miss Marchmont and the mind-sick cretin are symptoms of Lucy's repression (as Paulina is a symptom of her loss). Lucy's regression from child to invalid to cretin parodies the *bildungsroman* or Romantic quest for self which is the hidden 'plot' (the conspiracy of silence) of *Villette*, 'Who *are* you, Miss Snowe?'

Lucy's invisibility is an aspect of her oppression: Vashti's spectacular performance is an aspect of her revolt. Earlier, Lucy has crossed the divide between onlooker and actress, at the same time breaching the sexual divide; impersonating a man while clad as a woman from the waist down, she discovers in herself 'a keen relish for dramatic expression' – liberated in an unorthodox inter-sexual drama. Vashti too is an iconoclast and breacher of sexual convention, an importantly female version of the central Romantic protagonist, the satanic rebel and fallen angel whose exclusion and damnation is a function of divine tyranny:

> Pain, for her, has no result in good; tears water no harvest of wisdom: on sickness, on death itself, she looks with the eye of a rebel. Wicked, perhaps, she is, but also she is strong. . . . Her hair, flying loose in revel or war, is still an angel's hair, and glorious under a halo. Fallen, insurgent, banished, she remembers the heaven where she rebelled. Heaven's light, following her exile, pierces its confines, and discloses their forlorn remoteness.[15]

Villette can only be silent about the true nature and origin of Lucy's oppression – that is, the enshrining of marriage and the home in Victorian ideology and its consequences for women. But the ideological not-said is eloquently inscribed in the margin of the text – in the 'discursive' activity of Lucy's (over-) heated imagination. Here we witness also, in contrast to Lucy's fascination, Graham Bretton's sexual judgement on 'a woman, not an artist: it was a branding judgement'. 'Branded' as a fallen woman, a rebel against conventional morality, Vashti is at once excluded from the home and thereby permitted to retain her potency – a daemonic symbol of sexual energy and revolt, created by a woman (actress/author) in contrast to the static, male-fabricated icons of women exhibited in an earlier chapter: Cleopatra or the Jeune Fille/Mariéee/Jeune Mère/Veuve (woman as sexual object or bearer of ideology).

> Where was the artist of the Cleopatra? Let *him* come and sit down and study this different vision. (our italics)

The role of Gothicism is crucial in *Villette*, deconstructing, in a Derridean sense, the hierarchy of true/false, real/fictive, challenging the monopolistic claims of realism on truth, and rendering its representationalism no less fictive and arbitrary than the Gothic and Romantic modes commonly viewed as parasitic. A realist reading of *Villette* must relegate the nun to the level of inept machinery. But she is indispensable to its symbolic level. The legend of the nun, buried alive for 'some sin against her vow' lies dormant until passion threatens to reassert itself in the living. The first apparition, summoned up by Lucy's love for Graham Bretton, occurs when she plunges into the vault-like attic to read his letter, daring us to label her mad:

> Say what you will, reader – tell me I was nervous, or mad . . . this I vow – I saw there – in that room – on that night – an image like – a NUN.[16]

The second apparition marks the burial of Graham's letters, and Lucy's love for him, on the very spot where the nun is rumoured to have been entombed. The third apparition is provoked by M. Paul's declaration of his and Lucy's affinity; the birth of love and the turbulent reactivation of repression occur simultaneously. 'Who are you? and why do you come to me?' asks Lucy. Too easily identified as the spectre of repression or as the double of her repressed self, the nun remains recalcitrantly other – the Lacanian Other which no image can mirror, only the structure of language itself, by its ceaseless play of difference hollowing being into desire. In banishing the seductive mirroring conventions of representational realism, with its illusory coalescence of signifier and signified, the nun thus banishes the Lacanian 'Imaginary' and reinstates the 'Symbolic' realm. Like the purloined letter in Lacan's reading of the Poe story,[17] she is the joker in the pack, the free-floating signifier which derives its significance from its place in the signifying chain (meaning one thing to Lucy, another to M. Paul, and another again to the clandestine lovers, Ginevra and de Hamal). Her 'uncanniness' lies in validating Romantic and Gothic modes, not as 'discursive' or parasitic, but – because shifting, arbitrary and dominated by desire – as the system of signification which can properly articulate the subject.

This is not to say that the meaning of *Villette* lies in its ghostly sub-text; rather, the relationship between the two levels points to the real conditions of its literary possibility. Charlotte Brontë's imagination was nurtured on a Romanticism to be repressed in the interests of Victorian realism:

> When I first began to write . . . I restrained imagination, eschewed romance, repressed excitement.[18]

The resulting distortions and mutilations are part of the novel's meaning, like those of a dream-text. Its triumphant evasion of a 'normalized' reading, designed to correct it into false coherence, is especially evident in the closing movement – in the coda-like sequence of Lucy's drugged expedition to the park, for instance, and in the double ending. In the park, Lucy is returned to her old role of excluded and invisible onlooker, while the characters of the novel parade before her in their family parties. But this time she is 'metteur en scène' in a drama of her own making. The self-imposed fiction of M. Paul's improbable engagement to his young ward at once denies reality and expresses an essential 'truth', Lucy's imaginative apprehension of her inevitable single-ness. Designed to underline this inevitability, the double ending further exposes the uneasy relationship between the Romantic imagination and the Victorian novel – here, the 'romance' that is the complement of its realism. Fittingly, the deconstruction is effected by metaphors drawn from the Romantic paradox of creation-in-destruction – the Shelleyan storms which throughout the novel punctuate significant phases in Lucy's quest for self. There is thus a profound ambiguity in the Romantic cataclysm which shipwrecks Lucy's educational idyll with M. Paul and undermines the transparent compromise with the novel-reader:

> Trouble no quiet, kind heart . . .

By admitting to the incompatibility of Romanticism and Victorian 'ro-mance', creative potency and marriage as defined by Victorian ideology, Lucy at last becomes a truly reliable narrator – single and double at the same time.

Lucy's two letters express a duality articulated elsewhere in the novel, in the visionary passage in which Reason plays the part of wicked and 'envenomed' step-mother, while Imagination is celebrated as the succouring, nourishing, consoling 'daughter of heaven'. It is within this primal relationship that the novelist herself is constituted as woman and writer – nurtured on Romanti-cism, fostered by an uncongenial Reason. The split re-enacts that felt by a woman writer of an earlier revolutionary period. Mary Wollstonecraft's attack on Rousseau's infantilizing ideal of feminine 'sensibility' and her demand for access to Enlightenment Reason ('sense') coexist with highly autobiographical novels which – even as they anatomize the constitution of feminity within the confines of 'sensibility' – cannot escape its informing influence. The legacy of Romanticism is similarly divisive for Charlotte Brontë, at once fuelling unstated feminist demands and risking confining her to irrationality. A feminist critique of her writing, by illuminating the margins of her text, not only relocates it in the mainstream of Victorian literary production and its hidden problematic (the presence of an incompletely repressed Romanticism), but, at the same time, insists on its otherness – on the centrality of gender as a distinguishing, not merely overdetermining, aspect of Charlotte Brontë's achievement as a woman writer: the phantom which haunts her fiction and its criticism.

Aurora Leigh: Curse and Write

Villette was published in the year Elizabeth Barrett Browning began work on her 'intensely modern . . . poetic art-novel', *Aurora Leigh*. Most of Barrett Browning's mature work has overt, traditional political content, and expresses a fiery Romantic individualism mixed with passionate concern for the oppressed poor, suppressed nationality (Italy), the slave and women. Romantic individualism is not suppressed or mediated by the author's gender or by gender concerns in Barrett Browning's poetry. Speaking directly from the female position, she proposes political syntheses which include demands for the reconstruction of social and political relations in forms other than those offered by reformist or conservative patriarchal ideologies. Unlike most other women writers in England, Barrett Browning expressed her consciousness of 1848 as a revolutionary moment which was an appropriate subject for art. Her disillusionment with the political resolutions of 1848 is articulated in *Aurora Leigh* (1857) through a mode of discourse which is only intermittently homologous with the political feminism of the day, but consistently hostile to existing patriarchal discourses and institutions.

The most significant way in which *Aurora Leigh* takes up the issue of gender difference in bourgeois culture is through its focus on the woman as poet. Barrett Browning argued that Victorian feminists privileged the ideological over the practical: 'By speaking we prove only that we can speak.' She attempts to resolve the contradiction implicit in her own speech by seeing poetry as action: 'The artist's part is both to be and do . . . turning outward, with a sudden wrench . . . the thing [s/he] feels inmost.' On this Moebius strip we too as Marxist-feminist critics and writers inscribe ourselves.

The unrepressed Romanticism of Barrett Browning's politics and aesthetic theory throws into relief the question of women's access to full subjectivity in culture in *Aurora Leigh*. Marriage as a way of finding a vocation through a man's work, as an attempt to annul class difference, as a means of class mobility, as a way for women to gain protection, as a repair for male violence, as *anything* but the union of two desiring subjects, is attacked in the poem. The conflicts about kinship and marriage, and the oppressive rules of femininity, which dominate Austen's and Brontë's work are produced with a difference in *Aurora Leigh*. Romney and Aurora are second cousins, and their union is a partial defiance both of Victorian prescriptions about sex roles and of the rules of exogamy. By making marriage the resolution of problems about neither women's place in culture nor their place in class, *Aurora Leigh* projects those problems back on to the independent activity of women themselves. The first and most central activity is that of writing itself.

Thus the question posed in *Aurora Leigh*, openly, discursively, rather than invisibly stitched into the design of the poem, is this: can woman be at once the speaker/writer of her own discourse and a desiring, choosing subject in her own right? In any text written by a woman the author has tacitly assumed the role of speaker. Female literary production breaks the cultural taboo against women as public speakers, a taboo felt by almost all women who defined themselves as writers in the nineteenth century. Instead of weeping Barrett Browning urged women: 'Curse and write.' Yet the social and public silence of women after puberty was central to the construction of femininity, a term Elizabeth Barrett Browning hated. The central contradiction for female authors as producers of their own speech is suppressed or displaced in the work of Austen and Brontë. By making her heroine a poet Barrett Browning breaks what is virtually a gentlemen's agreement between women writers and the arbiters of high culture in Victorian England that stated that women could write if they would only shut up about it.

In *Aurora Leigh* the contradiction of women speaking and women silent is partially dissolved in the first lines of the poem:

> Of writing many books there is no end;
> And I who have written much in prose and verse
> For others' uses, will write now for mine.

Writing as a creative expression of the self for a public audience is here asserted as the 'given' of the protagonist's history. In *Villette* the writing even of letters is a problem, in *Shirley* writing is an unfulfilled talent. Speaker and woman are conventionally joined at the beginning of the poem. At the end this unity is queried; and the dissonance and lack hinted at throughout is exposed as the suppression of Aurora's love for Romney and the error of her youthful passion 'to exalt/The artist's instinct in me at the cost/of putting down the woman's'. Both lives have been distorted through denial of love, but Aurora does not now reject her art; on the contrary, love completes her original presentation of self. The condition for Aurora's marriage which Barrett Browning sets in the narrative is that she retain her position as speaking subject. A woman poet is the speaker throughout the poem even when it is the authorial voice and not Aurora who seems to be speaking. This doubled female voice is strengthened too by the choice of genre. The lyricization of blank verse in Romanticism demands a first-person singular speaker.

The verse form, its constantly reflexive quality and the irresistible congruence between the female poet/producer and female poet/speaker make the Romantic mode dominant, bringing with it feminized organic metaphors of nourishing and succouring:

> I drew the elemental nutriment and heat
> From nature as earth feels the sun at nights
> Or as a babe sucks surely in the dark.

There is a new force here in the equation between creativity and the mother–child relationship.

Crucial to Aurora's installation in the poem as a poet is the way in which Barrett Browning revises the experience of orphaning. Aurora loses her mother at the Oedipal moment – age four – and her father as she attains the menarch. ('I was just thirteen,/ . . . and suddenly awoke/to full life and life's needs and agonies . . . beside/A stone-dead father.') Aurora thus avoids the usual social experience of Oedipalization – she does not have to realize her mother as a rival or come to terms with her own lack of masculine power; instead she projects on to her mother's portrait a composite and shifting image of women as they are glassed in Western culture. Meanwhile her father has taught her that male discourse is to be challenged ('He taught me all the ignorance of men . . .'). Conveniently he dies before the intense father–daughter relationship becomes sexually dangerous. Aurora's socialization is presented as an alternative to, or circumvention of, Victorian childhood. Aurora remains female but not feminine. Her early education equips her to enter and criticize patriarchal discourse: orphaned, she is uniquely placed to rebel, and as an adult she takes over and professionalizes her mother's function of 'kissing full speech into empty words'.

Barrett Browning thought *Villette* a strong book, better than *Shirley*, possibly better than *Jane Eyre*. In correspondence with a friend about the parallels between Rochester and Romney's blinding she comments: 'The hero was monstrously disfigured and blinded in a fire the particulars of which escape me.' Romney is merely 'mulcted in his natural sight'. The semi-suppressed source and the significance of the revision are both obvious. The mulcting of Romney's sight leads to a clear-sighted abandonment of his misguided social projects – 'mapping out of masses to be saved' – and leaves room for Love and Art, Aurora's project. In a democratic marriage work and love become shared activities involving no sexual division of labour, 'Art', the poem itself in its real and fictional existence, making the syn-thesis possible. The blinding of Romney removes him as an independent actor, weakens his alignment with the dominant male culture, increases his dependence on Aurora and makes it impossible for him to see her as a sexual object.

The conclusion of the poem produces all the contradictions endemic to feminist reformism within an essentially bourgeois and 'romantic' problematic. Barrett Browning has instituted companionate marriage in place of the traditional Victorian family. However she goes further than this, suggesting that Marian and Aurora could support each other without men if necessary, and making Marian refuse Romney at the end of the poem not because she thinks herself defiled by rape but because she no longer loves him, and because she prefers to claim her child for the mother–child dyad rather than accept a surrogate paternity. Paradoxically, male violence in its most brutal form – the unknown rapist – has made her independent. Thus the poem's conclusion asserts a new definition of reform: the restructuring of male–female relations as an alternative to male political discourse and theory: 'Fourier's void,/And Comte absurd – and Cabet puerile.' (Shades of the Webbs, and the utopian sexual politics of 1968.) We may call this resolution ideological and/or utopian but there is no doubt that it constitutes a significant revision of social and gender relations. Throughout Brontë's work the basic need of women is to make a love-match. By excluding the importance of the self-expression of which her novels are themselves the practice, Brontë also excludes her own solution, that of being a professional woman writer. Only Barrett Browning is able to inscribe this radical alternative within the text itself, and to centre it in the structure of her narrative.

Writing for women represents a kind of repair. For Elizabeth Barrett Browning it was an act of imagination which expanded the stunted and fragmented image of self demanded by conventional sexual and social rela-tions; she speaks of her poetry as the 'Escape from pangs of heart and bodily weakness – when you throw off *yourself* – what you feel to be *yourself* – into another atmosphere and into other relations where your life may spread its wings out new'. The androgynous Romantic bird image effects the transfor-mation of woman into poet. *Aurora Leigh* itself is one of the first great works by a woman to insist on a reading that privileges gender and asserts women's right to the pen. The silk handkerchief of gender cannot be pulled out of the text by the critic as the kicking phallic rabbit of class.

The Open End

Our aim here has not been to rescue these works, nor to celebrate them. It has been to take issue with a selective literary tradition in which certain works have been installed in the canon and others excluded. A tradition out of which some works have been misread and some not read at all. This is a matter not solely of critical, but also of material reproduction. *Aurora Leigh*, for instance, has been virtually unavailable since 1897. Only recently has a feminist press decided to reprint it.

In dealing with the texts we had necessary recourse to the wider theoretical debate in Marxism, feminism and psychoanalysis. Our reading of the texts was predicated upon our insistence that class, kinship, gender and socialization are related in both material and ideological terms, and that these relations must be theorized and historicized.

We do not wish to see the inscription of psychoanalysis within historical materialism without the transformation of both by feminist theory. Historical materialism has obscured the specific social relations of reproduction and kinship in its analysis of the general mode of production, whereas the problem with Lacanian psychoanalysis is that the concept of the symbolic order consolidates as it theorizes patriarchal structures. Thus Althusser, in the 'ISA's' essay and in 'Freud and Lacan', develops the category of an ungendered human subject. We would argue that Marxist critics must confront the proposition that all subjects are gendered and that all literary discourse is gender specific. In this paper we have signalled the silence of women within public discourse. What has enabled us to break that silence is the political practice of the Women's Movement.

NOTES

1 Relevant works by Lacan, Macherey and others are as follows: L. Althusser, 'Ideology and Ideological State Apparatuses', in *Lenin and Philosophy and Other Essays* (London: NLB, 1971); T. Eagleton, *Myths of Power: A Marxist Study of the Brontës* (London: Macmillan, 1975); J. Kristeva, *La Révolution du langage poétique*, collections Tel Quel (Paris: Seuil, 1976), and 'Signifying Practice and Mode of Production', trans. and intro. G. Nowell-Smith, *Edinburgh Film Festival Magazine*, 1 (1976); J. Lacan, *Ecrits*, trans. A. Sheridan (London: Tavistock, 1977); P. Macherey, *Pour une Théorie de la production littéraire* (Paris: Maspero, 1970), and an interview trans. and intro. J. Radford and C. Mercer, *Red Letters*, 5 (1977).

2 F. Engels, *The Origins of Family, Private Property and the State* (New York: Pathfinder, 1972), 80.

3 Althusser, 'Freud and Lacan', in *Lenin and Philosophy*, 195.

4 Lady Eastlake, review of *Jane Eyre*, *Quarterly Review*, 84 (Dec. 1848), 174. (Quoted in J. Stern, 'Women and the Novel', *Women's Liberation Review*, 1 (Oct. 1972).)

5 T. J. Wise and J. A. Symington (eds), *The Brontës: Their Lives, Friendships and Correspondence*, 4 vols (London: Shakespeare Head, 1932), vol. 3, 31.

6 Currer Bell, Preface to the 2nd edn of *Jane Eyre* (London: Smith, Elder & Co., 1847).

7 *Jane Eyre* (Harmondsworth: Penguin, 1966), 306–7.

8 Ibid., 433.

9 W. Gérin, *Charlotte Brontë: The Evolution of Genius* (Oxford: Oxford University Press, 1967), 390.

10 Eagleton, *Myths of Power*, 45–60.

11 Mrs Gaskell, *Mary Barton* (Dutton: Everyman's Library, 1911), 160.

12 Mary Taylor to Charlotte Brontë in Wise and Symington, *The Brontës*, vol. 2, 235; Margaret Oliphant, *Blackwoods Magazine*, 77 (1855), 557–9.

13 Charlotte Brontë to W. S. Williams in Wise and Symington, *The Brontës*, vol. 2, 202.

14 See M. Allott, *The Brontës: The Critical Heritage* (London, 1974), 201.

15 *Villette* (London: Dent, 1977), 235.
16 Ibid., 222.
17 'Seminar on "The Purloined Letter" ', trans. J. Mehlman, *Yale French Studies*, 48 (1972), 38–72.
18 Wise and Symington, *The Brontës*, vol. 2, 152.

21 Fredric Jameson
On Interpretation (1981)*

Since the early 1970s Fredric Jameson (1934–) has been considered the leading American Marxist literary critic. This reputation was consolidated by *Marxism and Form* (1971) and *The Prison-House of Language: A Critical Account of Structuralism and Russian Formalism* (1972). Jameson's most original contributions to Marxist literary theory were first developed in *The Political Unconscious: Narrative as a Socially Symbolic Act* (1981). In this work Jameson synthesizes the approaches of Lukács, particularly *History and Class Consciousness* (1923; trans. 1971) and Althusser, with a range of insights and approaches to interpretation drawn from semiotics, psychoanalysis and poststructuralism. 'On Interpretation' is the final section of the opening theoretical introduction to Jameson's exposition of his theory of narrative. The rest of the book develops this through close readings of Balzac, Gissing and Conrad. For Jameson, history is the necessary horizon of interpretation. Interpretation grasps literary works as symbolic practices which provide imaginary and ideological solutions to otherwise unresolved socio-political contradictions. Criticism, accordingly, seeks to reveal these historical and ideological subtexts as the political unconscious of literary forms. Jameson's subsequent work includes an influential essay on postmodernism. This is part of ongoing studies on the cultural logic of contemporary capitalism which has involved Jameson in analyses of film and so-called 'third world' culture. Jameson has been criticized as a depoliticized Hegelian Marxist whose theoretical eclecticism tends towards totalizing gestures and master-codes. This tendency is evident in Jameson's awkward construction of collective political subjects, such as feminism and 'third world' social movements, and the generality of his use of categories such as 'postmodernism'. Aspects of such criticisms are developed in the sections in this anthology by Aijaz Ahmad and Alex Callinicos, and in Terry Eagleton, *Against the Grain* (1986). Jameson's other works include *Sartre* (1961); *Fables of Aggression* (1979); *The Ideologies of Theory*, 2 vols (1988); *Late Marxism* (1990); *Signatures of the Visible* (1990); *Postmodernism* (1991); *The Geopolitical Aesthetic* (1992); and *The Seeds of Time* (1994).

* From Fredric Jameson, *The Political Unconscious* (London: Methuen, 1981), 74–102.

At this point it might seem appropriate to juxtapose a Marxist method of literary and cultural interpretation with those just outlined, and to document its claim to greater adequacy and validity. For better or for worse, however, as I warned in the preface, this obvious next step is not the strategy projected by the present book, which rather seeks to argue the perspectives of Marxism as necessary preconditions for adequate literary comprehension. Marxist critical insights will therefore here be defended as something like an ultimate *semantic* precondition for the intelligibility of literary and cultural texts. Even this argument, however, needs a certain specification: in particular we will suggest that such semantic enrichment and enlargement of the inert givens and materials of a particular text must take place within three concentric frameworks, which mark a widening out of the sense of the social ground of a text through the notions, first, of political history, in the narrow sense of punctual event and a chroniclelike sequence of happenings in time; then of society, in the now already less diachronic and time-bound sense of a constitutive tension and struggle between social classes; and, ultimately, of history now conceived in its vastest sense of the sequence of modes of production and the succession and destiny of the various human social formations, from prehistoric life to whatever far future history has in store for us.[1]

These distinct semantic horizons are, to be sure, also distinct moments of the process of interpretation, and may in that sense be understood as dialectical equivalents of what Frye has called the successive 'phases' in our reinterpretation – our rereading and rewriting – of the literary text. What we must also note, however, is that each phase or horizon governs a distinct reconstruction of its object, and construes the very structure of what can now only in a general sense be called 'the text' in a different way.

Thus, within the narrower limits of our first, narrowly political or historical, horizon, the 'text', the object of study, is still more or less construed as coinciding with the individual literary work or utterance. The difference between the perspective enforced and enabled by this horizon, however, and that of ordinary *explication de texte*, or individual exegesis, is that here the individual work is grasped essentially as a *symbolic act*.

When we pass into the second phase, and find that the semantic horizon within which we grasp a cultural object has widened to include the social order, we will find that the very object of our analysis has itself been thereby dialectically transformed, and that it is no longer construed as an individual 'text' or work in the narrow sense, but has been reconstituted in the form of the great collective and class discourses of which a text is little more than an individual *parole* or utterance. Within this new horizon, then, our object of study will prove to be the *ideologeme*, that is, the smallest intelligible unit of the essentially antagonistic collective discourses of social classes.

When finally, even the passions and values of a particular social formation find themselves placed in a new and seemingly relativized perspective by the ultimate horizon of human history as a whole, and by their respective positions in the whole complex sequence of the modes of production, both the individual text and its ideologemes know a final transformation, and must be read in terms of what I will call the *ideology of form*, that is, the symbolic messages transmitted to us by the coexistence of various sign systems which are themselves traces or anticipations of modes of production.

The general movement through these three progressively wider horizons will largely coincide with the shifts in focus of the final chapters in this book, and will be felt, although not narrowly and programmatically underscored, in the methodological transformations determined by the historical transformations of their textual objects, from Balzac to Gissing to Conrad.

We must now briefly characterize each of these semantic or interpretive horizons. We have suggested that it is only in the first narrowly political horizon – in which history is reduced to a series of punctual events and crises in time, to the diachronic agitation of the year-to-year, the chroniclelike annals of the rise and fall of political regimes and social fashions, and the passionate immediacy of struggles between historical individuals – that the 'text' or object of study will tend to coincide with the individual literary work or cultural artefact. Yet to specify this individual text as a symbolic act is already fundamentally to transform the categories with which traditional *explication de texte* (whether narrative or poetic) operated and largely still operates.

The model for such an interpretive operation remains the readings of myth and aesthetic structure of Claude Lévi-Strauss as they are codified in his fundamental essay 'The Structural Study of Myth'.[2] These suggestive, often sheerly occasional, readings and speculative glosses immediately impose a basic analytical or interpretive principle: the individual narrative, or the individual formal structure, is to be grasped as the imaginary resolution of a real contradiction. Thus, to take only the most dramatic of Lévi-Strauss's analyses – the 'interpretation' of the unique facial decorations of the Caduveo Indians – the starting-point will be an immanent description of the formal and structural peculiarities of this body art; yet it must be a description already pre-prepared and oriented toward transcending the purely formalistic, a movement which is achieved not by abandoning the formal level for something extrinsic to it – such as some inertly social 'content' – but rather immanently, by construing purely formal patterns as a symbolic enactment of the social within the formal and the aesthetic. Such symbolic functions are, however, rarely found by an aimless enumeration of random formal and stylistic features; our discovery of a text's symbolic efficacity must be oriented by a formal description which seeks to grasp it as a determinate structure of still properly formal *contradictions*. Thus, Lévi-Strauss orients his still purely visual analysis of Caduveo facial decorations toward this climactic account of their contradictory dynamic: 'the use of a design which is symmetrical but yet lies across an oblique axis . . . a complicated situation based upon two contradictory forms of duality, and resulting in a compromise brought about by a secondary opposition between the ideal axis of the object itself [the human face] and the ideal axis of the figure which it represents'.[3] Already on the purely formal level, then, this visual text has been grasped as a contradiction by way of the curiously provisional and asymmetrical resolution it proposes for that contradiction.

Lévi-Strauss's 'interpretation' of this formal phenomenon may now, perhaps overhastily, be specified. Caduveo are a hierarchical society, organized in three endogamous groups or castes. In their social development, as in that of their neighbours, this nascent hierarchy is already the place of the emergence, if not of political power in the strict sense, then at least of relations of domination: the inferior status of women, the subordination of youth to elders, and the development of a hereditary aristocracy. Yet whereas this latent power structure is, among the neighbouring Guana and Bororo, masked by a division into moieties which cuts across the three castes, and whose exogamous exchange appears to function in a non-hierarchical, essentially egalitarian way, it is openly present in Caduveo life, as surface inequality and conflict. The social institutions of the Guana and Bororo, on the other hand, provide a realm of appearance, in which real hierarchy and inequality are dissimulated by the reciprocity of the moieties, and in which, therefore, 'asymmetry of class is balanced . . . by symmetry of "moieties"'.

As for the Caduveo,

> they were never lucky enough to resolve their contradictions, or to disguise them with the help of institutions artfully devised for that purpose. On the social level, the remedy was lacking . . . but it was never completely out of their grasp. It was within them, never objectively formulated, but present as a source of confusion and disquiet. Yet since they were unable to conceptualize or to live this solution directly, they began to dream it, to project it into the imaginary . . . We must therefore interpret the graphic art of Caduveo women, and explain its mysterious charm as well as its apparently gratuitous complication, as the fantasy production of a society seeking passionately to give symbolic expression to the institutions it might have had in reality, had not interest and superstition stood in the way.[4]

In this fashion, then, the visual text of Caduveo facial art constitutes a symbolic act, whereby real social contradictions, insurmountable in their own terms, find a purely formal resolution in the aesthetic realm.

This interpretive model thus allows us a first specification of the relationship between ideology and cultural texts or artefacts: a specification still conditioned by the limits of the first, narrowly historical or political horizon in which it is made. We may suggest that from this perspective, ideology is not something which informs or invests symbolic production; rather the aesthetic act is itself ideological, and the production of aesthetic or narrative form is to be seen as an ideological act in its own right, with the function of inventing imaginary or formal 'solutions' to unresolvable social contradictions.

Lévi-Strauss's work also suggests a more general defence of the proposition of a political unconscious than we have hitherto been able to present, in so far as it offers the spectacle of so-called primitive peoples perplexed enough by the dynamics and contradictions of their still relatively simple forms of tribal organization to project decorative or mythic resolutions of issues that they are unable to articulate conceptually. But if this is the case for pre-capitalist and even pre-political societies, then how much more must it be true for the citizen of the modern *Gesellschaft*, faced with the great constitutional options of the revolutionary period, and with the corrosive and tradition-annihilating effects of the spread of a money and market economy, with the changing cast of collective characters which oppose the bourgeoisie, now to an embattled aristocracy, now to an urban proletariat, with the great fantasms of the various nationalisms, now themselves virtual 'subjects of history' of a rather different kind, with the social homogenization and psychic constriction of the rise of the industrial city and its 'masses', the sudden appearance of the great transnational forces of communism and fascism, followed by the advent of the superstates and the onset of that great ideological rivalry between capitalism and communism, which, no less passionate and obsessive than that which, at the dawn of modern times, seethed through the wars of religion, marks the final tension of our now global village? It does not, indeed, seem particularly far-fetched to suggest that these texts of history, with their fantasmatic collective 'actants', their narrative organization, and their immense charge of anxiety and libidinal investment, are lived by the contemporary subject as a genuine politico-historical *pensée sauvage* which necessarily informs all of our cultural artefacts, from the literary institutions of high modernism all the way to the products of mass culture. Under these circumstances, Lévi-Strauss's work suggests that the proposition whereby all cultural artefacts are to be read as symbolic resolutions of real political and social contradictions deserves serious exploration and systematic experimental verification. It will become clear in later chapters of this book that the most readily accessible formal articulation of the operations of a political *pensée sauvage* of this kind will be found in what we will call the structure of a properly political *allegory*, as it develops from networks of topical allusion in Spenser or Milton or Swift to the symbolic narratives of class representatives or 'types' in novels like those of Balzac. With political allegory, then, a sometimes repressed ur-narrative or master fantasy about the interaction of collective subjects, we have moved to the very borders of our second horizon, in which what we formerly regarded as individual texts are grasped as 'utterances' in an essentially collective or class discourse.

We cannot cross those borders, however, without some final account of the critical operations involved in our first interpretive phase. We have implied that in order to be consequent, the will to read literary or cultural texts as symbolic acts must necessarily grasp them as resolutions of determinate contradictions; and it is clear that the notion of contradiction is central to any Marxist cultural analysis, just as it will remain central in our two subsequent horizons, although it will there take rather different forms. The methodological requirement to articulate a text's fundamental contradiction may then be seen as a test of the completeness of the analysis: this is why, for example, the conventional sociology of literature or culture, which modestly limits itself to the identification of class motifs or values in a given text, and feels that its work is done when it shows how a given artefact 'reflects' its social background, is utterly unacceptable. Meanwhile, Kenneth Burke's play of emphases, in which a symbolic act is on the one hand affirmed as a genuine *act*, albeit on the symbolic level, while on the other it is registered as an act which is 'merely' symbolic, its resolutions imaginary ones that leave the real untouched, suitably dramatizes the ambiguous status of art and culture.

Still, we need to say a little more about the status of this external reality, of which it will otherwise be thought that it is little more than the traditional notion of 'context' familiar in older social or historical criticism. The type of interpretation here proposed is more satisfactorily grasped as the rewriting of the literary text in such a way that the latter may itself be seen as the rewriting or restructuration of a prior historical or ideological *subtext*, it being always understood that that 'subtext' is not immediately present as such, not some common-sense external reality, nor even the conventional narratives of history manuals, but rather must itself always be (re)constructed after the fact. The literary or aesthetic act therefore always entertains some active relationship with the Real; yet in order to do so, it cannot simply allow 'reality' to persevere inertly in its own being, outside the text and at distance. It must rather draw the Real into its own texture, and the ultimate paradoxes and false problems of linguistics, and most notably of semantics, are to be traced back to this process, whereby language manages to carry the Real within itself as its own intrinsic or immanent subtext. In so far, in other words, as symbolic action – what Burke will map as 'dream', 'prayer' or 'chart'[5] – is a way of doing something to the world, to that degree what we are calling 'world' must inhere within it, as the content it has to take up into itself in order to submit it to the transformations of form. The symbolic act therefore begins by generating and producing its own context in the same moment of emergence in which it steps back from it, taking its measure with a view toward its own projects of transformation. The whole paradox of what we have here called the subtext may be summed up in this, that the literary work or cultural object, as though for the first time, brings into being that very situation to which it is also, at one and the same time, a reaction. It articulates its own situation and textualizes it, thereby encouraging and perpetuating the illusion that the situation itself did not exist before it, that there is nothing but a text, that there never was any extra- or con-textual reality before the text itself generated it in the form of a mirage. One does not have to argue the reality of history: necessity, like Dr Johnson's stone, does that for us. That history – Althusser's 'absent cause', Lacan's 'Real' – is *not* a text, for it is fundamentally non-narrative and non-representational; what can be added, however, is the proviso that history is inaccessible to us except in textual form, or in other words, that it can be approached only by way of prior (re)textualization. Thus, to insist on either of the two inseparable yet incommensurable dimensions of the symbolic act without the other: to over-emphasize the active way in which the text reorganizes its subtext (in order, presumably, to reach the triumphant conclusion that the 'referent' does not exist); or on the other hand to stress the imaginary status of the symbolic act so completely as to reify its social ground, now no longer understood as a subtext but merely as some inert given that the text passively or fantasmatically 'reflects' – to overstress either of these functions of the symbolic act at the expense of the other is surely to produce sheer ideology, whether it be, as in the first alternative, the ideology of structuralism, or, in the second, that of vulgar materialism.

Still, this view of the place of the 'referent' will be neither complete nor methodologically usable unless we specify a supplementary distinction between several types of subtext to be (re)constructed. We have implied, indeed, that the social contradiction addressed and 'resolved' by the formal prestidigitation of narrative must, however reconstructed, remain an absent cause, which cannot be directly or immediately conceptualized by the text. It seems useful, therefore, to distinguish, from this ultimate subtext which is the place of social *contradiction*, a secondary one, which is more properly the place of ideology, and which takes the form of the *aporia* or the *antinomy*: what can in the former be resolved only through the intervention of praxis here comes before the purely contemplative mind as logical scandal or double bind, the unthinkable and the conceptually paradoxical, that which cannot be unknotted by the operation of pure thought, and which must therefore generate a whole more properly narrative apparatus – the text itself – to square its circles and to dispel, through narrative movement, its intolerable closure. Such a distinction, positing a system of antinomies as the symptomatic expression and conceptual reflex of something quite different, namely a social contradiction, will now allow us to reformulate that co-ordination between a semiotic and a dialectical method, which was evoked in the preceding section. The operational validity of semiotic analysis, and in particular of the Greimassian semiotic rectangle, derives, as was suggested there, not from its adequacy to nature or being, nor even from its capacity to map all forms of thinking or language, but rather from its vocation specifically to model ideological closure and to articulate the workings of binary oppositions, here the privileged form of what we have called the antinomy. A dialectical re-evaluation of the findings of semiotics intervenes, however, at the moment in which this entire system of ideological closure is taken as the symptomatic projection of something quite different, namely of social contradiction.

We may now leave this first textual or interpretive model behind, and pass over into the second horizon, that of the social. The latter becomes visible, and individual phenomena are revealed as social facts and institutions, only at the moment in which the organizing categories of analysis become those of social class. I have in another place described the dynamics of ideology in its constituted form as a function of social class:[6] suffice it only to recall here that for Marxism classes must always be apprehended relationally, and that the ultimate (or ideal) form of class relationship and class struggle is always dichotomous. The constitutive form of class relationships is always that between a dominant and a labouring class: and it is only in terms of this axis that class fractions (for example, the petty bourgeoisie) or ec-centric or dependent classes (such as the peasantry) are positioned. To define class in this way is sharply to differentiate the Marxian model of classes from the conventional sociological analysis of society into strata, subgroups, professional elites and the like, each of which can presumably be studied in isolation from one another in such a way that the analysis of their 'values' or their 'cultural space' folds back into separate and independent *Welt-anschauungen*, each of which inertly reflects its particular 'stratum'. For Marxism, however, the very content of a class ideology is relational, in the sense that its 'values' are always actively in situation with respect to the opposing class, and defined against the latter: normally, a ruling class ideology will explore various strategies of the *legitimation* of its own power position, while an oppositional culture or ideology will, often in covert and disguised strategies, seek to contest and to undermine the dominant 'value system'.

This is the sense in which we will say, following Mikhail Bakhtin, that within this horizon class discourse – the categories in terms of which individual texts and cultural phenomena are now rewritten – is essentially *dialogical* in its structure.[7] As Bakhtin's (and Vološinov's) own work in this field is relatively specialized, focusing primarily on the heterogeneous and explosive pluralism of moments of carnival or festival (moments, for example, such as the immense resurfacing of the whole spectrum of the religious or political sects in the English 1640s or the Soviet 1920s) it will be necessary to add the qualification that the normal form of the dialogical is essentially an *antagonistic* one, and that the dialogue of class struggle is one in which two opposing discourses fight it out within the general unity of a shared code. Thus, for instance, the shared master code of religion becomes in the 1640s in England the place in which the dominant formulations of a hegemonic theology are reappropriated and polemically modified.[8]

Within this new horizon, then, the basic formal requirement of dialectical analysis is maintained, and its elements are still restructured in terms of *contradiction* (this is essentially, as we have said, what distinguishes the relationality of a Marxist class analysis from static analysis of the sociological type). Where the contradiction of the earlier horizon was univocal, however, and limited to the situation of the individual text, to the place of a purely individual symbolic resolution, contradiction here appears in the form of the dialogical as the irreconcilable demands and positions of antagonistic classes. Here again, then, the requirement to prolong interpretation to the point at which this ultimate contradiction begins to appear offers a criterion for the completeness or insufficiency of the analysis.

Yet to rewrite the individual text, the individual cultural artefact, in terms of the antagonistic dialogue of class voices is to perform a rather different operation from the one we have ascribed to our first horizon. Now the individual text will be refocused as a *parole*, or individual utterance, of that vaster system, or *langue*, of class discourse. The individual text retains its formal structure as a symbolic act: yet the value and character of such symbolic action are now significantly modified and enlarged. On this rewriting, the individual utterance or text is grasped as a symbolic move in an essentially polemic and strategic ideological confrontation between the classes, and to describe it in these terms (or to reveal it in this form) demands a whole set of different instruments.

For one thing, the illusion or appearance of isolation or autonomy which a printed text projects must now be systematically undermined. Indeed, since by definition the cultural monuments and masterworks that have survived tend necessarily to perpetuate only a single voice in this class dialogue, the voice of a hegemonic class, they cannot be properly assigned their relational place in a dialogical system without the restoration or artificial reconstruction of the voice to which they were initially opposed, a voice for the most part stifled and reduced to silence, marginalized, its own utterances scattered to the winds, or reappropriated in their turn by the hegemonic culture.

This is the framework in which the reconstruction of so-called popular cultures must properly take place – most notably, from the fragments of essentially peasant cultures: folk songs, fairy tales, popular festivals, occult or oppositional systems of belief such as magic and witchcraft. Such reconstruction is of a piece with the reaffirmation of the existence of marginalized or oppositional cultures in our own time, and the reaudition of the oppositional voices of black or ethnic cultures, women's and gay literature, 'naïve' or marginalized folk art, and the like. But once again, the affirmation of such non-hegemonic cultural voices remains ineffective if it is limited to the merely 'sociological' perspective of the pluralistic rediscovery of other isolated social groups: only an ultimate rewriting of these utterances in terms of their essentially polemic and subversive strategies restores them to their proper place in the dialogical system of the social classes. Thus, for instance, Bloch's reading of the fairy tale, with its magical wish-fulfilments and its Utopian fantasies of plenty and the *pays de Cocagne*,[9] restores the dialogical and antagonistic content of this 'form' by exhibiting it as a systematic deconstruction and undermining of the hegemonic aristocratic form of the epic, with its sombre ideology of heroism and baleful destiny; thus also the work of Eugene Genovese on black religion restores the vitality of these utterances by reading them, not as the replication of imposed beliefs, but rather as a process whereby the hegemonic Christianity of the slave-owners is appropriated, secretly emptied of its content and subverted to the transmission of quite different oppositional and coded messages.[10]

Moreover, the stress on the dialogical then allows us to reread or rewrite the hegemonic forms themselves; they also can be grasped as a process of the reappropriation and neutralization, the co-optation and class transformation, the cultural universalization, of forms which originally expressed the situation of 'popular', subordinate or dominated groups. So the slave religion of Christianity is transformed into the hegemonic ideological apparatus of the medieval system; while folk music and peasant dance find themselves transmuted into the forms of aristocratic or court festivity and into the cultural visions of the pastoral; and popular narrative from time immemorial – romance, adventure story, melodrama and the like – is ceaselessly drawn on to restore vitality to an enfeebled and asphyxiating 'high culture'. Just so, in our own time, the vernacular and its still vital sources of production (as in black language) are reappropriated by the exhausted and media-standardized speech of a hegemonic middle class. In the aesthetic realm, indeed, the process of cultural 'universalization' (which implies the repression of the oppositional voice, and the illusion that there is only one genuine 'culture') is the specific form taken by what can be called the process of legitimation in the realm of ideology and conceptual systems.

Still, this operation of rewriting and of the restoration of an essentially dialogical or class horizon will not be complete until we specify the 'units' of this larger system. The linguistic metaphor (rewriting texts in terms of the opposition of a *parole* to a *langue*) cannot, in other words, be particularly fruitful until we are able to convey something of the dynamics proper to a class *langue* itself, which is evidently, in Saussure's sense, something like an ideal construct that is never wholly visible and never fully present in any one of its individual utterances. This larger class discourse can be said to be organized around minimal 'units' which we will call *ideologemes*. The advantage of this formulation lies in its capacity to mediate between conceptions of ideology as abstract opinion, class value and the like, and the narrative materials with which we will be working here. The ideologeme is an amphibious formation, whose essential structural characteristic may be described as its possibility to manifest itself either as a pseudo-idea – a conceptual or belief system, an abstract value, an opinion or prejudice – or as a protonarrative, a kind of ultimate class fantasy about the 'collective characters' which are the classes in opposition. This duality means that the basic requirement for the full description of the ideologeme is already given in advance: as a construct it must be susceptible to both a conceptual description and a narrative manifestation all at once. The ideologeme can of course be elaborated in either of these directions, taking on the finished appearance of a philosophical system on the one hand, or that of a cultural text on the other; but the ideological analysis of these finished cultural products requires us to demonstrate each one as a complex work of transformation on that ultimate raw material which is the ideologeme in question. The analyst's work is thus first that of the identification of the ideologeme, and, in many cases, of its initial naming in instances where for whatever reason it had not yet been registered as such. The immense preparatory task of identifying and inventorying such ideologemes has scarcely even begun, and to it the present book will make but the most modest contribution: most notably in its isolation of that fundamental nineteenth-century ideologeme which is the 'theory' of *ressentiment*, and in its 'unmasking' of ethics and the ethical binary opposition of good and evil as one of the fundamental forms of ideological thought in Western culture. However, our stress here and throughout on the fundamentally narrative character of such ideologemes (even where they seem to be articulated only as abstract conceptual beliefs or values) will offer the advantage of restoring the complexity of the transactions between opinion and protonarrative or libidinal fantasy. Thus we will observe, in the case of Balzac, the generation of an overt and constituted ideological and political 'value system' out of the operation of an essentially narrative and fantasy dynamic; the chapter on Gissing, on the other hand, will show how an already constituted 'narrative paradigm' emits an ideological message in its own right without the mediation of authorial intervention.

This focus or horizon, that of class struggle and its antagonistic discourses, is, as we have already suggested, not the ultimate form a Marxist analysis of culture can take. The example just alluded to – that of the seventeenth-century English revolution, in which the various classes and class fractions found themselves obliged to articulate their ideological struggles through the shared medium of a religious master-code – can serve to dramatize the shift whereby these objects of study are reconstituted into a structurally distinct 'text' specific to this final enlargement of the analytical frame. For the possibility of a displacement in emphasis is already given in this example: we have suggested that within the apparent unity of the theological code, the fundamental difference of antagonistic class positions can be made to emerge. In that case, the inverse move is also possible, and such concrete semantic differences can on the contrary be focused in such a way that what emerges is rather the all-embracing unity of a single code which they must share and which thus characterizes the larger unity of the social system. This new object – code, sign system or system of the production of signs and codes – thus becomes an index of an entity of study which greatly transcends those earlier ones of the narrowly political (the symbolic act), and the social (class discourse and the ideologeme), and which we have proposed to term the historical in the larger sense of this word. Here the organizing unity will be what the Marxian tradition designates as a *mode of production*.

I have already observed that the 'problematic' of modes of production is the most vital new area of Marxist theory in all the disciplines today; not paradoxically, it is also one of the most traditional, and we must therefore, in a brief preliminary way, sketch in the 'sequence' of modes of production as classical Marxism, from Marx and Engels to Stalin, tended to enumerate them.[11] These modes, or 'stages' of human society, have traditionally included the following: primitive communism or tribal society (the horde), the *gens* or hierarchical kinship societies (neolithic society), the Asiatic mode of production (so-called Oriental despotism), the *polis* or an oligarchical slave holding society (the ancient mode of production), feudalism, capitalism and communism (with a good deal of debate as to whether the 'transitional' stage between these last – sometimes called 'socialism' – is a genuine mode of production in its own right or not). What is more significant in the present context is that even this schematic or mechanical conception of historical 'stages' (what the Althusserians have systematically criticized under the term 'historicism') includes the notion of a cultural dominant or form of ideological coding specific to each mode of production. Following the same order these have generally been conceived as magic and mythic narrative, kinship, religion or the sacred, 'politics' according to the narrower category of citizenship in the ancient city-state, relations of personal domination, commodity reification, and (presumably) original and as yet nowhere fully developed forms of collective or communal association.

Before we can determine the cultural 'text' or object of study specific to the horizon of modes of production, however, we must make two preliminary remarks about the methodological problems it raises. The first will bear on whether the concept of 'mode of production' is a synchronic one, while the second will address the temptation to use the various modes of production for a classifying or typologizing operation, in which cultural texts are simply dropped into so many separate compartments.

Indeed, a number of theorists have been disturbed by the apparent convergence between the properly Marxian notion of an all-embracing and all-structuring mode of production (which assigns everything within itself – culture, ideological production, class articulation, technology – a specific and unique place), and non-Marxist visions of a 'total system' in which the various elements or levels of social life are programmed in some increasingly constricting way. Weber's dramatic notion of the 'iron cage' of an increasingly bureaucratic society,[12] Foucault's image of the gridwork of an ever more pervasive 'political technology of the body',[13] but also more traditional 'synchronic' accounts of the cultural programming of a given historical 'moment', such as those that have variously been proposed from Vico and Hegel to Spengler and Deleuze – all such monolithic models of the cultural unity of a given historical period have tended to confirm the suspicions of a dialectical tradition about the dangers of an emergent 'synchronic' thought, in which change and development are relegated to the marginalized category of the merely 'diachronic', the contingent or the rigorously non-meaningful (and this, even where, as with Althusser, such models of cultural unity are attacked as forms of a more properly Hegelian and idealistic 'expressive causality'). This theoretical foreboding about the limits of synchronic thought can perhaps be most immediately grasped in the political area, where the model of the 'total system' would seem slowly and inexorably to eliminate any possibility of the *negative* as such, and to reintegrate the place of an oppositional or even merely 'critical' practice and resistance back into the system as the latter's mere inversion. In particular, everything about class struggle that was anticipatory in the older dialectical framework, and seen as an emergent space for radically new social relations, would seem, in the synchronic model, to reduce itself to practices that in fact tend to reinforce the very system that foresaw and dictated their specific limits. This is the sense in which Jean Baudrillard has suggested that the 'total-system' view of contemporary society reduces the options of resistance to anarchist gestures, to the sole remaining ultimate protests of the wildcat strike, terrorism and death. Meanwhile, in the framework of the analysis of culture also, the latter's integration into a synchronic model would seem to empty cultural production of all its antisystemic capacities, and to 'unmask' even the works of an overtly oppositional or political stance as instruments ultimately programmed by the system itself.

It is, however, precisely the notion of a series of enlarging theoretical horizons proposed here that can assign these disturbing synchronic frameworks their appropriate analytical places and dictate their proper use. This notion projects a long view of history which is inconsistent with concrete political action and class struggle only if the specificity of the horizons is not respected; thus, even if the concept of a mode of production is to be considered a synchronic one (and we will see in a moment that things are somewhat more complicated than this), at the level of historical abstraction at which such a concept is properly to be used, the lesson of the 'vision' of a total system is for the short run one of the structural limits imposed on praxis rather than the latter's impossibility.

The theoretical problem with the synchronic systems enumerated above lies elsewhere, and less in their analytical framework than in what in a Marxist perspective might be called their infrastructural regrounding. Historically, such systems have tended to fall into two general groups, which one might term respectively the hard and soft visions of the total system. The first group projects a fantasy future of a 'totalitarian' type in which the mechanisms of domination – whether these are understood as part of the more general process of bureaucratization, or on the other hand derive more immediately from the deployment of physical and ideological force – are grasped as irrevocable and increasingly pervasive tendencies whose mission is to colonize the last remnants and survivals of human freedom – to occupy and organize, in other words, what still persists of Nature objectively and subjectively (very schematically, the Third World and the Unconscious).

This group of theories can perhaps hastily be associated with the central names of Weber and Foucault; the second group may then be associated with names such as those of Jean Baudrillard and the American theorists of a 'post-industrial society'.[14] For this second group, the characteristics of the total system of contemporary world society are less those of political domination than those of cultural programming and penetration: not the iron cage, but rather the *société de consommation* with its consumption of images and simulacra, its free-floating signifiers and its effacement of the older structures of social class and traditional ideological hegemony. For both groups, world capitalism is in evolution toward a system which is not socialist in any classical sense, on the one hand the nightmare of total control and on the other the polymorphous or schizophrenic intensities of some ultimate counter-culture (which may be no less disturbing for some than the overtly threatening characteristics of the first vision). What one must add is that neither kind of analysis respects the Marxian injunction of the 'ultimately determining instance' of economic organization and tendencies: for both, indeed, economics (or political economy) of that type is in the new total system of the contemporary world at an end, and the economic finds itself in both reassigned to a secondary and non-determinant position beneath the new dominant of political power or of cultural production respectively.

There exist, however, within Marxism itself precise equivalents to these two non-Marxian visions of the contemporary total system: rewritings, if one likes, of both in specifically Marxian and 'economic' terms. These are the analyses of late capitalism in terms of *capitalogic*[15] and of *disaccumulation*,[16] respectively; and while this book is clearly not the place to discuss such theories at any length, it must be observed here that both, seeing the originality of the contemporary situation in terms of systemic tendencies *within* capitalism, reassert the theoretical priority of the organizing concept of the mode of production which we have been concerned to argue.

We must therefore now turn to the second related problem about this third and ultimate horizon, and deal briefly with the objection that cultural analysis pursued within it will tend toward a purely typological or classificatory operation, in which we are called upon to 'decide' such issues as whether

Milton is to be read within a 'pre-capitalist' or a nascent capitalist context, and so forth. I have insisted elsewhere on the sterility of such classificatory procedures, which may always, it seems to me, be taken as symptoms and indices of the repression of a more genuinely dialectical or historical practice of cultural analysis. This diagnosis may now be expanded to cover all three horizons at issue here, where the practice of homology, that of a merely 'sociological' search for some social or class equivalent, and that, finally, of the use of some typology of social and cultural systems, respectively, may stand as examples of the misuse of these three frameworks. Furthermore, just as in our discussion of the first two we have stressed the centrality of the category of contradiction for any Marxist analysis (seen, within the first horizon, as that which the cultural and ideological artefact tries to 'resolve', and in the second as the nature of the social and class conflict within which a given work is one act or gesture), so too here we can effectively validate the horizon of the mode of production by showing the form contradiction takes on this level, and the relationship of the cultural object to it.

Before we do so, we must take note of more recent objections to the very concept of the mode of production. The traditional schema of the various modes of production as so many historical 'stages' has generally been felt to be unsatisfactory, not least because it encourages the kind of typologizing criticized above, in political quite as much as in cultural analysis. (The form taken in political analysis is evidently the procedure which consists in 'deciding' whether a given conjuncture is to be assigned to a moment within feudalism – the result being a demand for bourgeois and parliamentary rights – or within capitalism – with the accompanying 'reformist' strategy – or, on the contrary, a genuine 'revolutionary' moment – in which case the appropriate revolutionary strategy is then deduced.)

On the other hand, it has become increasingly clear to a number of contemporary theorists that such classification of 'empirical' materials within this or that abstract category is impermissible in large part because of the level of abstraction of the concept of a mode of production: no historical society has ever 'embodied' a mode of production in any pure state (nor is *Capital* the description of a historical society, but rather the construction of the abstract concept of capitalism). This has led certain contemporary theorists, most notably Nicos Poulantzas,[17] to insist on the distinction between a 'mode of production' as a purely theoretical construction and a 'social formation' that would involve the description of some historical society at a certain moment of its development. This distinction seems inadequate and even misleading, to the degree that it encourages the very empirical thinking which it was concerned to denounce, in other words, subsuming a particular or an empirical 'fact' under this or that corresponding 'abstraction'. Yet one feature of Poulantzas' discussion of the 'social formation' may be retained: his suggestion that every social formation or historically existing society has in fact consisted in the overlay and structural coexistence of *several* modes of production all at once, including vestiges and survivals of older modes of production, now relegated to structurally dependent positions within the new, as well as anticipatory tendencies which are potentially inconsistent with the existing system but have not yet generated an autonomous space of their own.

But if this suggestion is valid, then the problems of the 'synchronic' system and of the typological temptation are both solved at one stroke. What is synchronic is the 'concept' of the mode of production; the moment of the historical coexistence of several modes of production is not synchronic in this sense, but open to history in a dialectical way. The temptation to classify texts according to the appropriate mode of production is thereby removed, since the texts emerge in a space in which we may expect them to be criss-crossed and intersected by a variety of impulses from contradictory modes of cultural production all at once.

Yet we have still not characterized the specific object of study which is constructed by this new and final horizon. It cannot, as we have shown, consist in the concept of an individual mode of production (any more than, in our second horizon, the specific object of study could consist in a particular social class in isolation from the others). We will therefore suggest that this new and ultimate object may be designated, drawing on recent historical experience, as *cultural revolution*, that moment in which the coexistence of various modes of production becomes visibly antagonistic, their contradictions moving to the very centre of political, social and historical life. The incomplete Chinese experiment with a 'proletarian' cultural revolution may be invoked in support of the proposition that previous history has known a whole range of equivalents for similar processes to which the term may legitimately be extended. So the Western Enlightenment may be grasped as part of a properly bourgeois cultural revolution, in which the values and the discourses, the habits and the daily space, of the *ancien régime* were systematically dismantled so that in their place could be set the new conceptualities, habits and life forms, and value systems of a capitalist market society. This process clearly involved a vaster historical rhythm than such punctual historical events as the French Revolution or the Industrial Revolution, and includes in its *longue durée* such phenomena as those described by Weber in *The Protestant Ethic and the Spirit of Capitalism* – a work that can now in its turn be read as a contribution to the study of the bourgeois cultural revolution, just as the corpus of work on romanticism is now re-positioned as the study of a significant and ambiguous moment in the resistance to this particular 'great transformation', alongside the more specifically 'popular' (pre-capitalist as well as working-class) forms of cultural resistance.

But if this is the case, then we must go further and suggest that all previous modes of production have been accompanied by cultural revolutions specific to them of which the neolithic 'cultural revolution', say, the triumph of patriarchy over the older matriarchal or tribal forms, or the victory of Hellenic 'justice' and the new legality of the *polis* over the vendetta system are only the most dramatic manifestations. The concept of cultural revolution, then – or more precisely, the reconstruction of the materials of cultural and literary history in the form of this new 'text' or object of study which is cultural revolution – may be expected to project a whole new framework for the humanities, in which the study of culture in the widest sense could be placed on a materialist basis.

This description is, however, misleading to the degree to which it suggests that 'cultural revolution' is a phenomenon limited to so-called 'transitional' periods, during which social formations dominated by one mode of production undergo a radical restructuration in the course of which a different 'dominant' emerges. The problem of such 'transitions' is a traditional crux of the Marxian problematic of modes of production, nor can it be said that any of the solutions proposed, from Marx's own fragmentary discussions to the recent model of Etienne Balibar, are altogether satisfactory, since in all of them the inconsistency between a 'synchronic' description of a given system and a 'diachronic' account of the passage from one system to another seems to return with undiminished intensity. But our own discussion began with the idea that a given social formation consisted in the coexistence of various synchronic systems or modes of production, each with its own dynamic or time scheme – a kind of meta-synchronicity, if one likes – while we have now shifted to a description of cultural revolution which has been couched in the more diachronic language of systemic transformation. I will therefore suggest that these two apparently inconsistent accounts are simply the twin perspectives which our thinking (and our presentation or *Darstellung* of that thinking) can take on this same vast historical object. Just as overt revolution is no punctual event either, but brings to the surface the innumerable daily struggles and forms of class polarization which are at work in the whole course of social life that precedes it, and which are therefore latent and implicit in 'pre-revolutionary' social experience, made visible as the latter's deep structure only in such 'moments of truth' – so also the overtly 'transitional' moments of cultural revolution are themselves but the passage to the surface of a permanent process in human societies, of a permanent struggle between the various coexisting modes of production. The triumphant moment in which a new systemic dominant gains ascendancy is therefore only the diachronic manifestation of a constant struggle for the perpetuation and reproduction of its dominance, a struggle which must continue throughout its life course, accompanied at all moments by the systemic or structural antagonism of those older and newer modes of production that resist assimilation or seek deliverance from it. The task of cultural and social analysis thus construed within this final horizon will then clearly be the rewriting of its materials in such a way that this perpetual cultural revolution can be apprehended and read as the deeper and more permanent constitutive structure in which the empirical textual objects know intelligibility.

Cultural revolution thus conceived may be said to be beyond the opposition between synchrony and diachrony, and to correspond roughly to what Ernst Bloch has called the *Ungleichzeitigkeit* (or 'non-synchronous development') of cultural and social life.[18] Such a view imposes a new use of concepts of periodization, and in particular of that older schema of the 'linear' stages which is here preserved and cancelled all at once. We will deal more fully with the specific problems of periodization in the next chapter: suffice it to say at this point that such categories are produced within an initial diachronic or narrative framework, but become usable only when that initial framework has been annulled, allowing us now to co-ordinate or articulate categories of diachronic origin (the various distinct modes of production) in what is now a synchronic or meta-synchronic way.

We have, however, not yet specified the nature of the textual object which is constructed by this third horizon of cultural revolution, and which would be the equivalent within this dialectically new framework of the objects of our first two horizons – the symbolic act, and the ideologeme or dialogical organization of class discourse. I will suggest that within this final horizon the individual text or cultural artefact (with its appearance of autonomy which was dissolved in specific and original ways within the first two horizons as well) is here restructured as a field of force in which the dynamics of sign systems of several distinct modes of production can be registered and apprehended. These dynamics – the newly constituted 'text' of our third horizon – make up what can be termed *the ideology of form*, that is, the determinate contradiction of the specific messages emitted by the varied sign systems which coexist in a given artistic process as well as in its general social formation.

What must now be stressed is that at this level 'form' is apprehended as content. The study of the ideology of form is no doubt grounded on a technical and formalistic analysis in the narrower sense, even though, unlike much traditional formal analysis, it seeks to reveal the active presence within the text of a number of discontinuous and heterogeneous formal processes. But at the level of analysis in question here, a dialectical reversal has taken place in which it has become possible to grasp such formal processes as sedimented content in their own right, as carrying ideological messages of their own, distinct from the ostensible or manifest content of the works; it has become possible, in other words, to display such formal operations from the standpoint of what Louis Hjelmslev will call the 'content of form' rather than the latter's 'expression', which is generally the object of the various more narrowly formalizing approaches. The simplest and most accessible demonstration of this reversal may be found in the area of literary genre. Our next chapter, indeed, will model the process whereby generic specification and description can, in a given historical text, be transformed into the detection of a host of distinct generic messages – some of them objectified survivals from older modes of cultural production, some anticipatory, but all together projecting a formal conjuncture through which the 'conjuncture' of coexisting modes of production at a given historical moment can be detected and allegorically articulated.

Meanwhile, that what we have called the ideology of form is something other than a retreat from social and historical questions into the more narrowly formal may be suggested by the relevance of this final perspective to more overtly political and theoretical concerns; we may take the much-debated relation of Marxism to feminism as a particularly revealing illustration. The notion of overlapping modes of production outlined above has indeed the advantage of allowing us to short-circuit the false problem of the priority of the economic over the sexual, or of sexual oppression over that of social class. In our present perspective, it becomes clear that sexism and the patriarchal are to be grasped as the sedimentation and the virulent survival of forms of alienation specific to the oldest mode of production of human history, with its division of labour between men and women, and its division of power between youth and elder. The analysis of the ideology of form, properly completed, should reveal the formal persistence of such archaic structures of alienation – and the sign systems specific to them – beneath the overlay of all the more recent and historically original types of alienation – such as political domination and commodity reification – which have become the dominants of that most complex of all cultural revolutions, late capitalism, in which all the earlier modes of production in one way or another structurally coexist. The affirmation of radical feminism, therefore, that to annul the patriarchal is the most *radical* political act – in so far as it includes and subsumes more partial demands, such as the liberation from the commodity form – is thus perfectly consistent with an expanded Marxian framework, for which the transformation of our own dominant mode of production must be accompanied and completed by an equally radical restructuration of all the more archaic modes of production with which it structurally coexists.

With this final horizon, then, we emerge into a space in which History itself becomes the ultimate ground as well as the untranscendable limit of our understanding in general and our textual interpretations in particular. This is, of course, also the moment in which the whole problem of interpretive priorities returns with a vengeance, and in which the practitioners of alternate or rival interpretive codes – far from having been persuaded that History is an interpretive code that includes and transcends all the others – will again assert 'History' as simply one more code among others, with no particularly privileged status. This is most succinctly achieved when the critics of Marxist interpretation, borrowing its own traditional terminology, suggest that the Marxian interpretive operation involves a thematization and a reification of

'History' which is not markedly different from the process whereby the other interpretive codes produce their own forms of thematic closure and offer themselves as absolute methods.

It should by now be clear that nothing is to be gained by opposing one reified theme – History – by another – Language – in a polemic debate as to ultimate priority of one over the other. The influential forms this debate has taken in recent years – as in Jürgen Habermas' attempt to subsume the 'Marxist' model of productions beneath a more all-embracing model of 'communication' or intersubjectivity,[19] or in Umberto Eco's assertion of the priority of the Symbolic in general over the technological and productive systems which it must organize as *signs* before they can be used as *tools*[20] – are based on the misconception that the Marxian category of a 'mode of production' is a form of technological or 'productionist' determinism.

It would seem therefore more useful to ask ourselves, in conclusion, how History as a ground and as an absent cause can be conceived in such a way as to resist such thematization or reification, such transformation back into one optional code among others. We may suggest such a possibility obliquely by attention to what the Aristotelians would call the generic satisfaction specific to the form of the great monuments of historiography, or what the semioticians might call the 'history-effect' of such narrative texts. Whatever the raw material on which historiographic form works (and we will here only touch on that most widespread type of material which is the sheer chronology of fact as it is produced by the rote-drill of the history manual), the 'emotion' of great historiographic form can then always be seen as the radical restructuration of that inert material, in this instance the powerful reorganization of otherwise inert chronological and 'linear' data in the form of Necessity: why what happened (at first received as 'empirical' fact) had to happen the way it did. From this perspective, then, causality is only one of the possible tropes by which this formal restructuration can be achieved, although it has obviously been a privileged and historically significant one. Meanwhile, should it be objected that Marxism is rather a 'comic' or 'romance' paradigm, one which sees history in the salvational perspective of some ultimate liberation, we must observe that the most powerful realizations of a Marxist historiography – from Marx's own narratives of the 1848 revolution through the rich and varied canonical studies of the dynamics of the Revolution of 1789 all the way to Charles Bettelheim's study of the Soviet revolutionary experience – remain visions of historical Necessity in the sense evoked above. But Necessity is here represented in the form of the inexorable logic involved in the determinate failure of all the revolutions that have taken place in human history: the ultimate Marxian presupposition – that socialist revolution can only be a total and world-wide process (and that this in turn presupposes the completion of the capitalist 'revolution' and of the process of commodification on a global scale) – is the perspective in which the failure or the blockage, the contradictory reversal or functional inversion, of this or that local revolutionary process is grasped as 'inevitable', and as the operation of objective limits.

History is therefore the experience of Necessity, and it is this alone which can forestall its thematization or reification as a mere object of representation or as one master-code among many others. Necessity is not in that sense a type of content, but rather the inexorable *form* of events; it is therefore a narrative category in the enlarged sense of some properly narrative political unconscious which has been argued here, a retextualization of History which does not propose the latter as some new representation or 'vision', some new content, but as the formal effects of what Althusser, following Spinoza, calls an 'absent cause'. Conceived in this sense, History is what hurts, it is what refuses desire and sets inexorable limits to individual as well as collective praxis, which its 'ruses' turn into grisly and ironic reversals of their overt intention. But this History can be apprehended only through its effects, and never directly as some reified force. This is indeed the ultimate sense in which History as ground and untranscendable horizon needs no particular theoretical justification: we may be sure that its alienating necessities will not forget us, however much we might prefer to ignore them.

NOTES

1 A useful discussion of the phenomenological concept of 'horizon' may be found in Hans-Georg Gadamer, *Truth and Method*, trans. G. Barden and J. Cumming (New York: Seabury, 1975), 216–20, 267–74. It will become clear in the course of my subsequent discussion that a Marxian conception of our relationship to the past requires a sense of our radical difference from earlier cultures which is not adequately allowed for in Gadamer's influential notion of *Horizontverschmelzung* (fusion of horizons). This is perhaps also the moment to add that from the perspective of Marxism as an 'absolute historicism', the stark antithesis proposed by E. D. Hirsch, Jr., between Gadamer's historicist 'relativism' and Hirsch's own conception of a more absolute interpretive validity, will no longer seem particularly irreconcilable. Hirsch's distinction between *Sinn* and *Bedeutung*, between the scientific analysis of a text's intrinsic 'meaning' and what he is pleased to call our 'ethical' evaluation of its 'significance' for us (see, for example, *The Aims of Interpretation*, Chicago: University of Chicago Press, 1976), corresponds to the traditional Marxist distinction between science and ideology, particularly as it has been retheorized by the Althusserians. It is surely a useful working distinction, although in the light of current revisions of the idea of science one should probably make no larger theoretical claims for it than this operative one.

2 Claude Lévi-Strauss, *Structural Anthropology*, trans. C. Jacobson and B. G. Schoepf (New York: Basic, 1963), 206–31. The later four-volume *Mythologiques* reverse the perspective of this analysis: where the earlier essay focused on the individual mythic *parole* or utterance, the later series models the entire system or

langue in terms of which the various individual myths are related to each other. *Mythologiques* should therefore rather be used as suggestive material on the historical difference between the narrative mode of production of primitive societies and that of our own: in this sense, the later work would find its place in the third and final horizon of interpretation.

3 Claude Lévi-Strauss, *Tristes tropiques*, trans. John Russell (New York: Atheneum, 1971), 176.

4 Ibid., 179–80.

5 Kenneth Burke, *The Philosophy of Literary Form* (Berkeley: University of California Press, 1973), 5–6; and see also my 'Symbolic Inference; or, Kenneth Burke and Ideological Analysis', *Critical Inquiry*, 4 (spring, 1978), 507–23.

6 *Marxism and Form* (Princeton: Princeton University Press, 1974), 376–82. The most authoritative contemporary Marxist statement of this view of social class is to be found in E. P. Thompson, *The Making of the English Working Classes* (New York: Vintage, 1966), 9–11; in *The Poverty of Theory*, Thompson has argued that his view of classes is incompatible with 'structural' Marxism, for which classes are not 'subjects' but rather 'positions' within the social totality (see, for the Althusserian position, Nicos Poulantzas, *Political Power and Social Classes*, trans. T. O'Hagan (London: New Left Books, 1973)).

7 Mikhail Bakhtin, *Problems of Dostoyevsky's Poetics*, trans. R. W. Rotsel (Ann Arbor: Ardis, 1973), 153–69. See also Bakhtin's important book on linguistics, written under the name of V. N. Vološinov, *Marxism and the Philosophy of Language*, trans. L. Matejka and I. R. Titunik (New York: Seminar Press, 1973), 83–98; and Bakhtin's posthumous collection, *Esthétique et théorie du roman*, trans. Daria Olivier (Paris: Gallimard, 1978), esp. 152–82.

8 See Christopher Hill, *The World Turned Upside Down* (London: Temple Smith, 1972).

9 Ernst Bloch, 'Zerstörung, Rettung des Mythos durch Licht', in *Verfremdungen* I (Frankfurt: Suhrkamp, 1963), 152–62.

10 Eugene Genovese, *Roll Jordan Roll* (New York: Vintage, 1976), 161–284.

11 The 'classical' texts on modes of production, besides Lewis Henry Morgan's *Ancient Society* (1877), are Karl Marx, *Pre-Capitalist Economic Formations*, a section of the *Grundrisse* (1857–8) published separately by Eric Hobsbawm (New York: International, 1965), and Friedrich Engels, *The Family, Private Property, and the State* (1884). Important recent contributions to the mode of production 'debate' include Etienne Balibar's contribution to Althusser's collective volume, *Reading Capital*, trans. B. Brewster (London: New Left Books, 1970); Emmanuel Terray, *Marxism and 'Primitive' Societies*, trans. M. Klopper (New York: Monthly Review, 1972); Maurice Godelier, *Horizon: trajets marxistes en anthropologie* (Paris: Maspéro, 1973); J. Chesneaux (ed.), *Sur le mode de production asiatique* (Paris: Editions Sociales, 1969); and Barry Hindess and Paul Hirst, *Pre-Capitalist Modes of Production* (London: Routledge & Kegan Paul, 1975).

12 'The Puritan wanted to work in a calling; we are forced to do so. For when asceticism was carried out of monastic cells into everyday life, and began to dominate worldly morality, it did its part in building the tremendous cosmos of the modern economic order. This order is now bound to the technical and

economic conditions of machine production which today determine the lives of all the individuals who are born into this mechanism, not only those directly concerned with economic acquisition, with irresistible force. Perhaps it will so determine them until the last ton of fossilized coal is burnt. In Baxter's view the care for external goods should only lie on the shoulders of the saint "like a light cloak, which can be thrown aside at any moment". But fate decreed that the cloak should become an iron cage.' *The Protestant Ethic and the Spirit of Capitalism*, trans. T. Parsons (New York: Scribners, 1958), 181.

13 Michel Foucault, *Surveiller et punir* (Paris: Gallimard, 1975), 27–8 and *passim*.

14 Jean Baudrillard, *Le Système des objets* (Paris: Gallimard, 1968); *La Société de consommation* (Paris: Denöel, 1970); *Pour une économie politique du signe* (Paris: Gallimard, 1972). The most influential statement of the American version of this 'end of ideology'/consumer society position is, of course, that of Daniel Bell: see his *Coming of Post-Industrial Society* (New York: Basic, 1973) and *The Cultural Contradictions of Capitalism* (New York: Basic, 1976).

15 See, for a review and critique of the basic literature, Stanley Aronowitz, 'Marx, Braverman, and the Logic of Capital', *Insurgent Sociologist*, 8, no. 2/3 (fall, 1978), 126–46; and see also Hans-Georg Backhaus, 'Zur Dialektik der Wertform', in A. Schmidt (ed.), *Beiträge zur marxistischen Erkenntnistheorie* (Frankfurt: Suhrkamp, 1969), 128–52; and Helmut Reichelt, *Zur logischen Struktur des Kapitalbegriffs bei Karl Marx* (Frankfurt: Europäische Verlagsanstalt, 1970). For the Capitalogicians, the 'materialist kernel' of Hegel is revealed by grasping the concrete or objective reality of Absolute Spirit (the Notion in-and-for-itself) as none other than capital (Reichelt, 77–8). This tends, however, to force them into the post-Marxist position for which the dialectic is seen as the thought-mode proper only to capitalism (Backhaus, 140–1): in that case, of course, the dialectic would become unnecessary and anachronistic in a society that had abolished the commodity form.

16 The basic texts on 'disaccumulation theory' are Martin J. Sklar, 'On the Proletarian Revolution and the End of Political-Economic Society', *Radical America*, 3, no. 3 (May–June, 1969), 1–41; Jim O'Connor, 'Productive and Unproductive Labor', *Politics and Society*, 5 (1975), 297–336; Fred Block and Larry Hirschhorn, 'New Productive Forces and the Contradictions of Contemporary Capitalism', *Theory and Society*, 7 (1979), 363–95; and Stanley Aronowitz, 'The End of Political Economy', *Social Text*, 2 (1980), 3–52.

17 Poulantzas, *Political Power and Social Classes*, 13–16.

18 Ernst Bloch, 'Nonsynchronism and Dialectics', *New German Critique*, 11 (spring, 1977), 22–38; or *Erbschaft dieser Zeit* (Frankfurt: Suhrkamp, 1973). The 'non-synchronous' use of the concept of mode of production outlined above is in my opinion the only way to fulfil Marx's well-known programme for dialectical knowledge 'of rising from the abstract to the concrete' (1857 Introduction, *Grundrisse*, 101). Marx there distinguished three stages of knowledge: (1) the notation of the particular (this would correspond to something like empirical history, the collection of data and descriptive materials on the variety of human societies); (2) the conquest of abstraction, the coming into being of a properly 'bourgeois' science or of what Hegel called the categories of the Understanding (this moment, that of the construction of a static and purely classificatory concept

of 'modes of production', is what Hindess and Hirst quite properly criticize in
Pre-capitalist Modes of Production); (3) the transcendence of abstraction by the
dialectic, the 'rise to the concrete', the setting in motion of hitherto static and
typologizing categories by their reinsertion in a concrete historical situation (in the
present context, this is achieved by moving from a classificatory use of the
categories of modes of production to a perception of their dynamic and contradictory coexistence in a given cultural moment). Althusser's own epistemology,
incidentally – Generalities I, II and III (*Pour Marx* (Paris: Maspéro, 1965), 187–90)
– is a gloss on this same fundamental passage of the 1857 Introduction, but one
which succeeds only too well in eliminating its dialectical spirit.

19 See Jürgen Habermas, *Knowledge and Human Interests*, trans. J. Shapiro (Boston:
Beacon, 1971), esp. Part I.

20 Umberto Eco, *A Theory of Semiotics* (Bloomington: Indiana University Press,
1976), 21–6.

22 Aijaz Ahmad

Jameson's Rhetoric of Otherness and the 'National Allegory' (1987)*

Aijaz Ahmad is Professorial Fellow at the Centre of Contemporary Studies, Nehru Memorial Museum and Library, New Delhi. Ahmad's work emerges as a resistance to the way intellectuals have migrated from the so-called 'Third World' and developed theories of 'colonial' and 'post-colonial' discourse. A range of essays collected in *In Theory: Classes, Nations, Literatures* (1992) develops a theoretical approach to the intellectual trajectories of writers such as Edward Said and Salman Rushdie. Ahmad traces the way the academic industry of the metropolitan 'West' has configured writers around questions of empire, colony, migrancy and postcolonial identity politics. Against this, Ahmad restates a Marxist account of relations between imperialism, decolonization and the struggle for socialism. 'Jameson's Rhetoric of Otherness and the "National Allegory" ', first published in *Social Text*, 17 (1987), takes issue with Jameson's conception of 'national allegory' as the determinate form of cultural production in the 'Third World'. Ahmad takes Jameson's work as a representative and theoretically sophisticated statement of literary radicalism which nevertheless needs to be criticized, not for its lack of postcolonial authenticity, but for its lack of Marxist rigour. Ahmad stresses the way that postcolonial history developed through the dominance of distinct national bourgeois formations in specific nation-states, a history itself overdetermined by the international division of labour organized by imperialism. His critical Indian Marxist perspective on cultural nationalism, postcolonial theory and the category of 'Third World' literature is part of ongoing Marxist debates about internationalism and the global struggle for socialism. Accordingly, Ahmad's work needs to be distinguished from the work of African Marxists such as Chidi Amuta; from the tradition of 'Black' American Marxism – see Cedric J. Robinson, *Black Marxism* (1983); the work of 'migrant' Asian intellectuals such as Gayatri Spivak; and in relation to traditions of Marxism in Europe and North and South America.

* From Aijaz Ahmad, *In Theory: Classes, Nations, Literatures* (London: Verso, 1992), 95–122.

In assembling the following notes on Fredric Jameson's 'Third World Literature in the Era of Multinational Capital'[1] I find myself in an awkward, position. If I were to name the *one* literary critic/theorist writing in the USA today whose work I generally hold in the highest regard, it would surely be Jameson. The plea that generates most of the passion in his text – that the teaching of literature in the US academy be informed by a sense not only of 'Western' literature but of 'world literature'; that the so-called literary canon be based not upon the exclusionary pleasures of dominant taste but upon an inclusive and opulent sense of heterogeneity – is, of course, entirely salutary. And I wholly admire both the knowledge and the range of sympathies he brings to the reading of texts produced in distant lands.

But this plea for syllabus reform – even his marvellously erudite reading of Lu Xun and Ousmane – is conflated with – indeed, superseded by – a much more ambitious undertaking which pervades the entire text but is explicitly announced only in the last sentence of the last footnote: the construction of 'a theory of the cognitive aesthetics of third-world literature'. This 'cognitive aesthetics' rests, in turn, upon a suppression of the multiplicity of significant difference among and within both the advanced capitalist countries on the one hand and the imperialized formations on the other. We have, instead, a binary opposition of what Jameson calls the 'First' and the 'Third' worlds. It is in this passage from a plea for syllabus reform to the enunciation of a 'cognitive aesthetics' that most of the text's troubles lie. These troubles are, I might add, quite numerous.

There is doubtless a personal, somewhat existential side to my encounter with this text, which is best clarified at the outset. I have been reading Jameson's work now for roughly fifteen years, and at least some of what I know about the literatures and cultures of Western Europe and the USA comes from him; and because I am a Marxist, I had always thought of us, Jameson and myself, as birds of the same feather, even though we never quite flocked together. But then, when I was on the fifth page of this text (specifically, on the sentence starting with 'All third-world texts are necessarily . . .' etc.), I realized that what was being theorized was, among many other things, myself. Now, I was born in India and I write poetry in Urdu, a language not commonly understood among US intellectuals. So I said to myself: '*All? . . . necessarily?*' It felt odd. Matters became much more curious, however. For the further I read, the more I realized, with no little chagrin, that the man whom I had for so long, so affectionately, albeit from a physical distance, taken as a comrade was, in his own opinion, my civilizational Other. It was not a good feeling.

I

I too think that there *are* plenty of very good books written by African, Asian and Latin American writers which are available in English and which must be taught as an antidote to the general ethnocentricity and cultural myopia of the Humanities as they are presently constituted in these United States. If some label is needed for this activity, one may call it 'Third World Literature'. Conversely, however, I also hold that this term, 'the Third World', is, even in its most telling deployments, a polemical one, with no theoretical status whatsoever. Polemic surely has a prominent place in all human discourses, especially in the discourse of politics, so the use of this term in loose, polemical contexts is altogether valid. But to lift it from the register of polemics and claim it as a basis for producing theoretical knowledge, which presumes a certain rigour in constructing the objects of one's knowledge, is to misconstrue not only the term itself but even the world to which it refers. I shall argue in context, then, that there is no such thing as a 'Third World Literature' which can be constructed as an internally coherent object of theoretical knowledge. There are fundamental issues – of periodization, social and linguistic formations, political and ideological struggles within the field of literary production, and so on – which simply cannot be resolved at this level of generality without an altogether positivist reductionism.

The mere fact, for example, that languages of the metropolitan countries have not been adopted by the vast majority of the producers of literature in Asia and Africa means that the vast majority of literary texts from those continents are unavailable in the metropolises, so that a literary theorist who sets out to formulate 'a theory of the cognitive aesthetics of third-world literature' will be constructing ideal-types, in the Weberian manner, duplicating all the basic procedures which Orientalist scholars have historically deployed in presenting their own readings of a certain tradition of 'high' textuality as *the* knowledge of a supposedly unitary object which they call 'the Islamic civilization'. I might add that literary relations between the metropolitan countries and the imperialized formations are constructed very differently from such relations among the metropolitan countries themselves. Rare would be a literary theorist in Europe or the USA who does not command a couple of European languages besides his or her own; and the frequency of translation, back and forth, among European languages creates very fulsome channels for the circulation of texts, so that even a US scholar who does not command much beyond English can be quite well grounded in the various metropolitan traditions. Linguistic and literary relations between the metropolitan countries and the countries of Asia and Africa, on the other hand, offer three sharp contrasts to this system of textual exchanges among the metropolitan countries. Rare would be a modern intellectual in Asia or Africa who does not know at least one European language; equally rare would be, on the other side, a major literary theorist in Europe or the United States who has ever bothered with an Asian or African language; and the enormous industry of translation which circulates texts among the advanced capitalist countries grinds erratically and slowly when it comes to translation from Asian or African languages. The upshot is that major literary traditions – such as those of Bengali, Hindi, Tamil, Telegu and half a dozen others from India alone – remain, beyond a few texts here and there, virtually unknown to the American literary theorist.

One consequence, then, is that the few writers who happen to write in English are valorized beyond measure. Witness, for example, the characterization of Salman Rushdie's *Midnight's Children* in the *New York Times* as 'a Continent finding its voice' – as if one has no voice if one does not speak in English. Or Richard Poirier's praise for Edward Said in *Raritan* which now adorns the back cover of a recent book of Said's: 'It is Said's great accomplishment that thanks to his book, Palestinians will never be lost to history.'[2] This is the upside-down world of the *camera obscura*: not that Said's vision is itself framed by the Palestinian experience, but that Palestine would have no place in history without Said's book! The retribution visited upon the head of an Asian, an African, an Arab intellectual who is of any consequence and writes in English is that he or she is immediately elevated to the lonely splendour of a representative – of a race, a continent, a civilization, even the 'Third World'. It is in this general context that a 'cognitive theory of third-world literature' based upon what is currently available in languages of the metropolitan countries becomes, to my mind, an alarming undertaking.

I shall return to some of these points presently, especially to the point about the epistemological impossibility of a 'third-world literature'. Since, however, Jameson's own text is so centrally grounded in a binary opposition between a First and a Third World, it is impossible to proceed with an examination of his particular propositions regarding the respective literary traditions without first asking whether or not this characterization of the world is itself theoretically tenable, and whether, therefore, an accurate conception of *literature* can be mapped out on the basis of this binary opposition. I shall argue later that since Jameson defines the so-called Third World in terms of its 'experience of colonialism and imperialism', the political category that necessarily follows from this exclusive emphasis is that of 'the nation', with nationalism as the peculiarly valorized ideology; and, because of this privileging of the nationalist ideology, it is then theoretically posited that 'all third-world texts are necessarily . . . to be read as . . . national allegories'. The theory of the 'national allegory' as the metatext is thus inseparable from the larger Three Worlds Theory which permeates the whole of Jameson's own text. We too have to begin, then, with some comments on 'the Third World' as a theoretical category and on 'nationalism' as the necessary, exclusively desirable ideology.

II

Jameson seems to be aware of the difficulties in conceptualizing the global dispersion of powers and populations in terms of his particular variant of the

Three Worlds Theory ('I take the point of criticism', he says). And after reiterating the basic premiss of that theory ('the capitalist first world'; 'the socialist bloc of the second world'; and 'countries that have suffered colonialism and imperialism'), he does clarify that he does not uphold the specifically Maoist theory of 'convergence' between the United States and the Soviet Union. The rest of the difficulty in holding this view of the world is elided, however, with three assertions: that he cannot find a 'comparable expression'; that he is deploying these terms in 'an essentially descriptive way'; and that the criticisms are at any rate not 'relevant'. The problem of 'comparable expression' is a minor matter, which we shall ignore; 'relevance', on the other hand, is the central issue, and I shall return to it presently. First, however, I want to comment briefly on the matter of 'description'.

More than most critics writing in the USA today, Jameson should know that when it comes to a knowledge of the world, there is no such thing as a category of the 'essentially descriptive'; that 'description' is never ideologically or cognitively neutral; that to 'describe' is to specify a locus of meaning, to construct an object of knowledge, and to produce a knowledge that will be bound by that act of descriptive construction. 'Description' has been central, for example, in the colonizing discourses. It was by assembling a monstrous machinery of descriptions – of our bodies, our speech acts, our habitats, our conflicts and desires, our politics, our socialities and sexualities, in fields as various as ethnology, fiction, photography, linguistics, political science – that those discourses were able to classify and ideologically master colonial subjects, enabling the transformation of descriptively verifiable multiplicity and difference into the ideologically felt hierarchy of value. To say, in short, that what one is presenting is 'essentially descriptive' is to assert a level of facticity which conceals its own ideology, and to prepare a ground from which judgements of classification, generalization and value can be made.

As we come to the substance of what Jameson 'describes', I find it significant that First and Second Worlds are defined in terms of their production systems (capitalism and socialism, respectively), whereas the third category – the Third World – is defined purely in terms of an 'experience' of externally inserted phenomena. That which is constitutive of human history itself is present in the first two cases, absent in the third case. Ideologically, this classification divides the world between those who make history and those who are mere objects of it; elsewhere in the text, Jameson would significantly reinvoke Hegel's famous description of the master–slave relation to encapsulate the First–Third World opposition. But analytically, this classification leaves the so-called Third World in limbo; if only the First World is capitalist and the Second World socialist, how does one understand the Third World? Is it pre-capitalist? Transitional? Transitional between what and what? But then there is also the issue of the location of particular countries within the various 'worlds'.

Take, for example, India. Its colonial past is nostalgically rehashed on US television screens in copious series every few months, but the India of today has all the characteristics of a capitalist country: generalized commodity production, vigorous and escalating exchanges not only between agriculture and industry but also between Departments I and II of industry itself, and technical personnel more numerous than those of France and Germany combined. It is a very miserable kind of capitalism, and the conditions of life for over half the Indian population – roughly four hundred million people – are considerably worse than what Engels described in *The Condition of the Working Class in England*. But India's steel industry did celebrate its hundredth anniversary a few years ago, and the top eight of her multinational corporations are among the fastest-growing in the world, active as they are in numerous countries, from Vietnam to Nigeria. This economic base is combined, then, with unbroken parliamentary rule of the bourgeoisie since Independence in 1947, a record quite comparable to the length of Italy's modern record of unbroken bourgeois-democratic governance, and superior to the fate of bourgeois democracy in Spain and Portugal, two of the oldest colonizing countries. This parliamentary republic of the bourgeoisie in India has not been without its own lawlessnesses and violences, of a kind and degree now not normal in Japan or Western Europe, but a bourgeois political subjectivity *has* been created for the populace at large. The corollary on the Left is that the two communist parties (CPI and CPI–M) have longer and more extensive experience of regional government, within the republic of the bourgeoisie, than all the Eurocommunist parties combined, and the electorate that votes ritually for these two parties is probably larger than the communist electorates in all the rest of the capitalist world.

So – does India belong in the First World or the Third? Brazil, Argentina, Mexico, South Africa? And . . .? But we *know* that countries of the Pacific rim, from South Korea to Singapore, constitute the fastest-growing region within global capitalism. The list could be much longer, but the point is that the binary opposition which Jameson constructs between a capitalist First World and a presumably pre- or non-capitalist Third World is empirically ungrounded in any facts.

III

I have said already that if one believes in the Three Worlds Theory – hence in a 'Third World' defined exclusively in terms of 'the experience of colonialism and imperialism' – then the primary ideological formation available to a left-wing intellectual will be that of nationalism; it will then be possible to assert – surely with very considerable exaggeration, but possible to assert none the less – that 'all third-world texts are necessarily ... *national allegories*' (original emphasis). This exclusive emphasis on the nationalist ideology is there even in the opening paragraph of Jameson's text, where the only choice for the 'Third World' is said to be between its 'nationalisms' and a 'global American postmodernist culture'. Is there no other choice? Could not one join the 'Second World', for example? There used to be, in Marxist discourse, a thing called 'socialist and/or communist culture' which was neither nationalist nor postmodernist. Has that vanished from our discourse altogether, even as the name of a desire?

Jameson's haste in totalizing historical phenomena in terms of binary oppositions (nationalism/postmodernism, in this case) leaves little room for the fact, for instance, that the only nationalisms in the so-called Third World which have been able to resist US cultural pressure and have actually produced any alternatives are those which are already articulated to and assimilated within the much larger field of socialist political practice. Virtually all the others have had no difficulty in reconciling themselves with what Jameson calls 'global American postmodernist culture'; in the singular and sizeable case of Iran (which Jameson forbids us to mention on the grounds that it is 'predictable' that we shall do so), the anti-communism of the Islamic nationalists has produced not social regeneration but clerical fascism. Nor does the absolutism of that opposition (postmodernism/nationalism) permit any space for the simple idea that nationalism itself is not some unitary thing with some predetermined essence and value. There are hundreds of nationalisms in Asia and Africa today; some are progressive, others are not. Whether or not a nationalism will produce a progressive cultural practice depends, to put it in Gramscian terms, upon the political character of the power bloc which takes hold of it and utilizes it, as a material force, in the process of constituting its own hegemony. There is neither theoretical ground nor empirical evidence to support the notion that bourgeois nationalisms of the so-called Third World will have any difficulty with postmodernism; they *want* it.

Yet there *is* a very tight fit between the Three Worlds Theory, the overvalorization of the nationalist ideology, and the assertion that 'national allegory' is the primary, even exclusive, form of narrativity in the so-called Third World. If this 'Third World' is *constituted* by the singular 'experience of colonialism and imperialism', and if the only possible response is a nationalist one, then what else is there that is more urgent to narrate than this 'experience'? In fact, there is *nothing else* to narrate. For if societies here are defined not by relations of production but by relations of intra-national domination; if they are forever suspended outside the sphere of conflict between capitalism (First World) and socialism (Second World); if the motivating force for history here is neither class formation and class struggle nor the multiplicities of intersecting conflicts based upon class, gender, nation, race, region, and so on, but the unitary 'experience' of national oppression (if one is merely the *object* of history, the Hegelian slave), then what else *can* one narrate but that national oppression? Politically, we are Calibans all. Formally, we are fated to be in the poststructuralist world of Repetition with Difference; the same allegory, the nationalist one, rewritten, over and over again, until the end of time: 'all third-world texts are necessarily. . . .'

IV

But one could start with a radically different premiss: namely, the proposition that we live not in three worlds but in one; that this world includes the experience of colonialism and imperialism on both sides of Jameson's global divide (the 'experience' of imperialism is a central fact of all aspects of life inside the USA, from ideological formation to the utilization of the social surplus in military-industrial complexes); that societies in formations of backward capitalism are as much constituted by the division of classes as are societies in the advanced capitalist countries; that socialism is not restricted to something called 'the Second World' but is simply the name of a resistance that saturates the globe today, as capitalism itself does; that the different parts of the capitalist system are to be known not in terms of a binary opposition but as a contradictory unity – with differences, yes, but also with profound overlaps. One immediate consequence for literary theory would be that the unitary search for 'a theory of cognitive aesthetics for third-world literature' would be rendered impossible, and one would have to forgo the idea of a metanarrative that encompasses all the fecundity of real narratives in the so-called Third World. Conversely, many of the questions that one would ask about, let us say, Urdu or Bengali traditions of literature may turn out to be rather similar to the questions one has asked previously about English/American literatures. By the same token, a *real* knowledge of those other traditions may force the US literary theorists to ask questions about their own tradition which they have not asked heretofore.

Jameson claims that one cannot proceed from the premiss of a real unity of the world 'without falling back into some general liberal and humanistic universalism'. That is a curious idea, coming from a Marxist. One would have thought that the world was united not by liberalist ideology – that the world was not at all constituted in the realm of an Idea, be it Hegelian or humanist – but by the global operation of a single mode of production, namely the capitalist one, and the global resistance to this mode, a resistance which is itself unevenly developed in different parts of the globe. Socialism, one would have thought, was not by any means limited to the so-called Second World (the socialist countries) but is a global phenomenon, reaching into the farthest rural communities in Asia, Africa and Latin America, not to speak of individuals and groups within the United States. What gives the world its unity, then, is not a humanist ideology but the ferocious struggle between capital and labour which is now strictly and fundamentally global in character. The prospect of a socialist revolution has receded so much from the practical horizon for so much of the metropolitan Left that the temptation for the US Left intelligentsia is to forget the ferocity of that basic struggle which in our time transcends all others. The advantage of coming from Pakistan, in my own case, is that the country is saturated with capitalist commodities, bristles with US weaponry, borders on China, the Soviet Union and Afghanistan, suffers from a proliferation of competing nationalisms, and is currently witnessing the first stage in the consolidation of the communist movement. It is difficult, coming from there, to forget that primary motion of history which gives our globe its contradictory unity. None of this has anything to do with liberal humanism.

As for the specificity of cultural difference, Jameson's theoretical conception tends, I believe, in the opposite direction – namely, that of homogenization. Difference between the First World and the Third is absolutized as an Otherness, but the enormous cultural heterogeneity of social formations within the so-called Third World is submerged within a singular identity of 'experience'. Now, countries of Western Europe and North America have been deeply tied together over roughly the last two hundred years; capitalism itself is so much older in these countries; the cultural logic of late capitalism is so strongly operative in these metropolitan formations; the circulation of cultural products among them is so immediate, so extensive, so brisk, that one could sensibly speak of a certain cultural homogeneity among them. But Asia, Africa and Latin America? Historically, these countries were never so closely tied together; Peru and India simply do not have a common history of the sort that Germany and France, or Britain and the United States, have; not even the singular 'experience of colonialism and imperialism' has been in specific ways the same or similar in, say, India and Namibia. These various countries, from the three continents, have been assimilated into the global structure of capitalism not as a single cultural ensemble but highly differentially, each establishing its own circuits of (unequal) exchange with the metropolis, each acquiring its own very distinct class formations. Circuits of exchange among them are rudimentary at best; an average Nigerian who is literate about his own country would know infinitely more about England and the United States than about any country of Asia or Latin America or, indeed, about most countries of Africa. The kind of circuits that bind the cultural complexes of the advanced capitalist countries simply do not exist among countries of backward capitalism, and capitalism itself, which is dominant but not altogether universalized, does not yet have the same power of homogenization in its cultural logic in most of these countries, except among the urban bourgeoisie.

Of course, great cultural similarities also exist among countries that occupy analogous positions in the global capitalist system, and there are similarities in many cases that have been bequeathed by the similarities of socio-economic structures in the pre-capitalist past. The point is not to construct a typology that is simply the obverse of Jameson's, but rather to define the material basis for a fair degree of cultural homogenization among the advanced capitalist countries and the lack of that kind of homogenization in the rest of the capitalist world. In context, therefore, one is doubly surprised at Jameson's absolute insistence upon Difference and the relation of Otherness between the First World and the Third, and his equally insistent idea that the 'experience' of the 'Third World' could be contained and communicated within a single narrative form. By locating capitalism in the First World and socialism in the Second, Jameson's theory freezes and dehistoricizes the global space within which struggles between these great motivating forces actually take place. And by assimilating the enormous heterogeneities and productivities of our life into a single Hegelian metaphor of the master–slave relation, this theory reduces us to an ideal-type and demands from us that we narrate ourselves through a form commensurate with that ideal-type. To say that all Third World texts are necessarily this or that is to say, in effect, that any text originating within that social space which is *not* this or that is not a 'true' narrative. It is in this sense above all that the category of 'Third World Literature' which is the site of this operation, with the 'national allegory' as its metatext as well as the mark of its constitution and difference, is, to my mind, epistemologically an impossible category.

V

Part of the difficulty in engaging with Jameson's text is that there is a constant slippage, a recurrent inflation, in the way he handles his analytic categories. The specificity of the First World, for example, seems at times to be predicated upon the postmodernist moment, which is doubtless of recent origin; but at other times it appears to be a matter of the capitalist mode of production, which is a much larger, much older thing; and, in yet another range of formulations, this First World is said to be coterminous with 'Western civilization' itself, obviously a rather primordial way of being, dating back to Antiquity ('Graeco-Judaic', in Jameson's phrase) and anterior to any structuration of productions and classes as we know them today. *When* did this First World become First: in the pre-Christian centuries, or after World War II?

And at what point in history does a text produced in countries with 'experience of colonialism and imperialism' become a *Third World text*? In one kind of reading, only texts produced *after* the advent of colonialism could be so designated, since it is colonialism/imperialism which constitutes the Third World as such. But in speaking constantly of 'the West's Other'; in referring to the tribal/tributary and Asiatic modes as the theoretical basis for his selection of Lu Xun (Asian) and Sembene (African) respectively; in characterizing Freud's theory as a 'Western or First World reading' as contrasted with ten centuries of specifically Chinese distributions of the libidinal energy which are said to frame Lu Xun's texts – in deploying these broad epochal and civilizational categories, Jameson also suggests that the difference between the First World and the Third is itself primordial, rooted in things far older than capitalism as such. So, if the First World is the same as 'the West' and the 'Graeco-Judaic', one has, on the other hand, an alarming feeling that the *Bhagavad-Gita*, the edicts of Manu, and the Qur'an itself are perhaps Third World texts (though the Judaic elements of the Qur'an are quite beyond doubt, and much of the ancient art in what is today Pakistan is itself Graeco-Indic).

But there is also the question of *space*. Do all texts produced in countries with 'experience of colonialism and imperialism' become, by virtue of geographical origin, 'third-world texts'? Jameson speaks so often of '*all* third-world texts', insists so much on a singular form of narrativity for Third World Literature, that not to take him literally is to violate the very terms of his discourse. Yet one knows of so many texts from one's own part of the world which do not fit the description of 'national allegory' that one wonders why Jameson insists so much on the category, '*all*'. Without this category, of course, he cannot produce *a* theory of Third World Literature. But is it also the case that he means the opposite of what he actually says: not that '*all* third-world texts are to be read . . . as national allegories' but that *only* those texts which give us national allegories can be admitted as authentic texts of Third World Literature, while the rest are by definition excluded? So one is not quite sure whether one is dealing with a fallacy ('all third-world texts are' this or that) or with the Law of the Father (you must write *this* if you are to be admitted into my theory).

These shifts and hesitations in defining the objects of one's knowledge are based, I believe, on several confusions, one of which I shall specify here. For if one argues that the Third World is constituted by the 'experience of colonialism and imperialism', one must also recognize the two-pronged action of the colonial/imperialist dynamic: the forced transfers of value *from* the colonialized/imperialized formations, and the intensification of capitalist relations *within* those formations. And if capitalism is not merely an externality but also a shaping force within those formations, then one must conclude also that the separation between the public and the private, so characteristic of capitalism, has occurred there as well, at least in some degree and especially among the urban intelligentsia which produces most of the written texts and is itself caught in the world of capitalist commodities. With this bifurcation must have come, at least for some producers of texts, the individuation and personalization of libidinal energies, the loss of access to 'concrete' experience, and the consequent experience of the self as an isolated, alienated entity incapable of real, organic connection with any collectivity. There must be texts, perhaps numerous texts, that are grounded in this desolation, bereft of any capacity for the kind of allegorization and organicity that Jameson demands of them. The logic of Jameson's own argument – that the Third World is constituted by the 'experience of colonialism and imperialism' – leads necessarily to the conclusion that at least some of the writers of the Third World itself must be producing texts characteristic not of the so-called tribal and Asiatic modes but of the capitalist era as such, much in the manner of the so-called First World. But Jameson does not draw that conclusion.

And he does not draw that conclusion at least partially because this so-called Third World is to him suspended outside the modern systems of production (capitalism and socialism). He does not quite say that the Third World is pre- or non-capitalist, but that is clearly the implication of the contrast he establishes – as, for example, in the following formulation:

> one of the determinants of capitalist culture, that is, the culture of the western realist and modernist novel, is a radical split between the private and the public, between the poetic and the political, between what we have come to think of as the domain of sexuality and the unconscious and that of the public world of classes, of the economic, and of secular political power: in other words, Freud versus Marx . . .

> I will argue that, although we may retain for convenience and for analysis such categories as the subjective and the public or political, the relations between them are wholly different in third-world culture. (p. 69)

It is noteworthy that 'the radical split between the private and the public' is distinctly located in the capitalist mode here, but the *absence* of this split in so-called Third World culture is not located in any mode of production – in keeping with Jameson's very definition of the Three Worlds. But Jameson knows what he is talking about, and his statements have been less ambiguous in the past. Thus we find the following in his relatively early essay on Lukács in *Marxism and Form*:

> In the art works of a preindustrialized, agricultural or tribal society, the artist's raw material is on a human scale, it has an immediate meaning. . . . The story needs no background in time because the culture knows no history; each generation repeats the same experiences, reinvents the same basic human situations as though for the first time . . . The works of art characteristic of such societies may be called concrete in that their elements are all meaningful from the outset . . . in the language of Hegel, this raw material needs no *mediation*.

> When we turn from such a work to the literature of the industrial era, everything changes . . . a kind of dissolution of the human sets in. . . . For the unquestioned ritualistic time of village life no longer exists; there is henceforth a separation between public and private. (pp. 165–7)

Clearly, then, what was once theorized as a difference between the pre-industrial and the industrialized societies (the unity of the public and the private in one, the separation of the two in the other) is now transposed as a difference between the First and Third Worlds. The idea of the 'concrete' is now rendered in only slightly different vocabulary: 'third-world culture . . . must be situational and materialist despite itself.' And it is perhaps that other idea – namely that 'preindustrialized . . . culture knows no history; each generation repeats the same experience' – which is at the root of now suspending the so-called Third World outside the modern modes of production (capitalism and socialism), encapsulating the experience of this Third World in the Hegelian metaphor of the master–slave relation, and postulating a unitary form of narrativity (the national allegory) in which the 'experience' of this Third World is to be told. In both texts, the theoretical authority that is invoked is, predictably, that of Hegel.

Likewise, Jameson insists over and over again that the *national* experience is central to the cognitive formation of the Third World intellectual, and that the narrativity of that experience takes the form exclusively of a 'national allegory'. But this emphatic insistence on the category 'nation' itself keeps slipping into a much wider, far less demarcated vocabulary of 'culture', 'society', 'collectivity', and so on. Are 'nation' and 'collectivity' the same thing? Take, for example, the two statements which seem to enclose the elaboration of the theory itself. In the beginning, on page 69, we are told:

> All third-world texts are necessarily, I want to argue, allegorical, and in a very specific way: they are to be read as what I will call *national allegories*, even when, or perhaps I should say, particularly when their forms develop out of predominantly western machineries of representation, such as the novel.

But at the end, on pages 85–6, we find the following: '. . . the telling of the individual story and the individual experience cannot but ultimately involve the whole laborious telling of the experience of the collectivity itself.'

Are these two statements saying the same thing? The difficulty of this shift in vocabulary is that one may indeed connect one's personal experience to a 'collectivity' – in terms of class, gender, caste, religious community, trade union, political party, village, prison – combining the private and the public, and in some sense 'allegorizing' the individual experience, without involving the category of 'the nation' or necessarily referring back to the 'experience of colonialism and imperialism'. The latter statement would then seem to apply to a much larger body of texts, with far greater accuracy. By the same token, however, this wider application of 'collectivity' establishes much less radical difference between the so-called First and Third Worlds, since the whole history of realism in the European novel, in its many variants, has been associated with ideas of 'typicality' and 'the social', while the majority of the written narratives produced in the First World even today locate the individual story in a fundamental relation to some larger experience.

If we replace the idea of the 'nation' with that larger, less restrictive idea of 'collectivity', and if we start thinking of the process of allegorization not in nationalistic terms but simply as a relation between private and public, personal and communal, then it also becomes possible to see that allegorization is by no means specific to the so-called Third World. While Jameson overstates the presence of 'us', the 'national allegory', in the narratives of the Third World, he also, in the same sweep, understates the presence of analogous impulses in the US cultural ensembles. For what else are, let us say, Pynchon's *Gravity's Rainbow* or Ellison's *The Invisible Man* but allegorizations of individual – and not so individual – experience? What else could Richard Wright and Adrienne Rich and Richard Howard mean when they give their books titles like *Native Son* or *Your Native Land, Your Life* or *Alone With America*? It is not only the Asian or the African but also the American writer whose private imaginations must *necessarily* connect with experiences of the collectivity. One has only to look at Black and feminist writing to find countless allegories even within these postmodernist United States.

VI

I also have some difficulty with Jameson's description of 'third-world literature' as 'non-canonical', for I am not quite sure what that *means*. Since the vast majority of literary texts produced in Asia, Africa and Latin America are simply not available in English, their exclusion from the US/British 'canon' is self-evident. If, however, one considers the kind of texts Jameson seems to have in mind, one begins to wonder just what mechanisms of canonization there *are* from which this body of work is so entirely excluded.

Neruda, Vallejo, Octavio Paz, Borges, Fuentes, García Márquez et al – that is to say, quite a few writers of Latin American origin – *are* considered by the American academy to be major figures in modern literature. They, and even their translators, have received the most prestigious awards (the Nobel for García Márquez, for instance, or the National Book Award for Eshleman's translation of Vallejo) and they are *taught* quite as routinely in Literature courses as their German or Italian contemporaries might be – perhaps more regularly, in fact. Soyinka was recently canonized through the Nobel Prize, and Achebe's novels are consistently more easily available in the US book market than are, for example, Richard Wright's. Edward Said, a man of Palestinian origin, has received virtually every honour the US academy has to offer, with distinct constituencies of his own; *Orientalism*, at least, is taught very widely, across several disciplines – more widely, it seems, than any other left-wing literary/cultural work in this country. V. S. Naipaul is now fully established as a major English novelist, and he does come from the Caribbean; he *is*, like Borges, a 'third-world writer'. Salman Rushdie's *Midnight's Children* was awarded the most prestigious literary award in England, and *Shame* was immediately reviewed as a major novel, almost always favourably, in virtually all the major newspapers and literary journals in Britain and the USA. Rushdie is a major presence on the British cultural scene and a prized visitor to conferences and graduate departments on both sides of the Atlantic. The blurbs on the Vintage paperback edition of *Shame*, based partly on a quotation from the *New York Times*, compare him with Swift, Voltaire, Sterne, Kafka, Grass, Kundera and Márquez. I am told that a doctoral dissertation has already been written about him at Columbia.[3] What else *is* canonization, when it comes to modern, contemporary, and in some cases (Rushdie, for example) relatively young writers?

My argument is not that these reputations are not well deserved (Naipaul, of course, is a different matter), nor that there should not be *more* such canonizations. But the representation of this body of work in Jameson's discourse as simply 'non-canonical' – that is, as something that has been altogether excluded from the contemporary practices of high textuality in the US academy – does appear to overstate the case considerably.

Jameson speaks of 'non-canonical forms of literature such as that of the third world', compares this singularized *form* to 'another non-canonical form' in which Dashiell Hammett is placed, and goes on to say:

> Nothing is to be gained by passing over in silence the radical difference of non-canonical texts. The third-world novel will not offer the satisfactions of Proust or Joyce; what is more damaging than that, perhaps, is its tendency to remind us of outmoded stages of our own first-world cultural development and to cause us to conclude that 'they are still writing novels like Dreiser and Sherwood Anderson'.

Now, I am not sure that realism, which appears to be at the heart of Jameson's characterization of 'Third World Literature' in this passage, is quite as universal in *that* literature or quite as definitively superseded in what Jameson calls 'first-world cultural development'. Some of the most highly regarded US fictionists of the present cultural moment, from Bellow and Malamud to Grace Paley and Robert Stone, seem to write not quite 'like Dreiser and Sherwood

Anderson' but surely within the realist mode. On the other hand, Césaire became so popular among the French Surrealists because the terms of his discourse were contemporaneous with their own, and Neruda has been translated by some of the leading US poets because he is even formally not 'outmoded'. Novelists like García Márquez or Rushdie have been so well received in US/British literary circles precisely because they do not write like Dreiser or Sherwood Anderson; the satisfactions of their outrageous texts are not those of Proust or Joyce but are surely of an analogous kind, delightful to readers brought up on modernism and postmodernism. Césaire's *Return to the Native Land* is what it is because it combines what Jameson calls a 'national allegory' with the formal methods of the Parisian avant-garde of his student days. Borges, of course, is no longer seen in the USA in terms of his Latin American origin; he now belongs to the august company of the significant moderns, much like Kafka.

To say that the canon simply does not admit any Third World writers is to misrepresent the way bourgeois culture works – through selective admission and selective canonization. Just as modernism has now been fully canonized in the museum and the university, and as certain kinds of Marxism have been incorporated and given respectability within the academy, certain writers from the 'Third World' are also now part and parcel of literary discourse in the USA. Instead of claiming straightforward exclusion, it is perhaps more useful to inquire how the principle of selective incorporation works in relation to texts produced outside the metropolitan countries.

VII

I want to offer some comments on the history of Urdu literature – not in the form of a cogent narrative, less still to formulate a short course in that history, but simply to illustrate the kind of impoverishment that is involved in the a priori declaration that 'All third-world texts are necessarily . . . to be read as national allegories'.

It is, for example, a matter of some considerable curiosity to me that the Urdu language, although one of the youngest linguistic formations in India, had nevertheless produced its first great poet, Khusrow (1253–1325), in the thirteenth century, so that a great tradition of poetry got going; but then it waited for roughly six centuries before beginning to assemble the first sizeable body of prose narratives. Not that prose itself had not been there; the earliest prose texts in Urdu date back to the fifteenth century, but those were written for religious purposes and were often mere translations from Arabic or Farsi. Non-seminarian and non-theological narratives – those that had to do with the pleasures of reading and the etiquettes of civility – began appearing much, much later, in the last decade of the eighteenth century. Then, over two dozen

were published during the next ten years. What inhibited that development
for so long, and why did it happen precisely at that time? Much of that has
to do with complex social developments that had gradually led to the
displacement of Farsi by Urdu, as the language of educated, urban speech
and of prose writing in certain regions and groupings of Northern India.

That history we shall ignore, but a certain material condition of that
production can be specified: many – though by no means all – of those prose
narratives of the opening decades of the nineteenth century were written and
published for the simple reason that a certain Scotsman, John Gilchrist, had
argued within his own circles that employees of the East India Company could
not hope to administer their Indian possessions on the basis of Farsi alone,
and certainly not English, so that Fort William College was established in 1800
for the education of the British in Indian languages. For some time Farsi
remained the most popular of all the languages taught at the College, but
Gilchrist fancied himself as a scholar and exponent of the indigenous
vernaculars, Urdu among them. He hired some of the most erudite men of his
time and got them to write whatever they wanted, so long as they wrote in
accessible prose. It was a stroke of luck even more than genius, for what came
out of that enterprise was the mobilization of the whole range of speech
patterns and oral vocabularies existing at that time (the *range* of vocabularies
was in keeping with the pedagogical purpose) and the construction of
narratives which either transcribed the great classics of oral literature or
condensed the fictions that already existed in Arabic or Farsi and were
therefore part of the cultural life of the North Indian upper classes. Thus the
most famous of these narratives, Meer Amman's *Bagh-o-Bahaar*, was a
condensation, in superbly colloquial Urdu, of the monumental *Qissa-e-
Chabaar-Dervish*, which Faizi, the great scholar, had composed some centuries
earlier in Farsi for the amusement of Akbar, the Mughal king who was almost
an exact contemporary of the British Queen Elizabeth I.

But that was not the only impulse, and the publishing house of the Fort
William College was in any case closed soon thereafter. A similar development
was occurring in Lucknow, outside the British domains, at exactly the same
time; some of the Fort William writers had themselves come from Lucknow,
looking for alternative employment. Rajab Ali Beg Saroor's *Fasaana-e-Aja'ib*
is the great classic of this other tradition of Urdu narrativity (these were
actually not two different traditions but parts of the same, some of which were
formed in the British domains, some not). In 1848, eight years before it fell
to British guns, the city of Lucknow had twelve printing presses, and the
consolidation of the narrative tradition in Urdu is inseparable from the history
of those presses. The remarkable thing about all the major Urdu prose
narratives which were written during the half-century in which the British
completed their conquest of India is that there is nothing in their contents, in
their way of seeing the world, which can reasonably be connected with the

colonial onslaught or with any sense of resistance to it; by contrast, there is a large body of *letters* as well as poetry which documents that colossal carnage. It is as if the establishment of printing presses and the growth of a reading public for prose narratives gave rise to a kind of writing whose only task was to preserve in books at least some of that Persianized culture and those traditions of orality which were fast disappearing. It is only in this negative sense that one could, by stretching the terms a great deal, declare this to be a literature of the 'national allegory'.

The man who gave the language its first great publishing house, Munshi Naval Kishore, came somewhat later, however. His grandfather had been employed, like many upper-caste Hindus of the time, in the Mughal Ministry of Finance; his own father was a businessman, genteel and affluent but not rich. Naval Kishore himself had a passion for the written word; but like his father and grandfather, he also understood money. He started his career as a journalist, then went on to purchasing old handwritten manuscripts and publishing them for wider circulation. Over time he expanded into all sorts of fields, all connected with publishing, and gave Urdu its first great modern archive of published books. Urdu, in turn, showered him with money; at the time of his death in 1895, his fortune was estimated at one crore rupees (roughly half a million British pounds). He *had* to publish, I might add, more than national allegories, more than what came out of the experience of colonialism and imperialism, to make that kind of money.

But let me return to the issue of narration. For it is also a matter of some interest to me that the emergence of what one could plausibly call a novel came more than half a century *after* the appearance of those early registrations of the classics of the oral tradition and the rewriting of Arabic and Farsi stories. Sarshar's *Fasaana-e-Azaad*, the most opulent of those early novels, was serialized during the 1870s in something else that had begun in the 1830s: regular Urdu newspapers for the emergent middle classes. Between the traditional tale and the modern novel, then, there were other things, such as newspapers and sizeable reading publics, much in the same way as one encounters them in a whole range of books on English literary history, from Ian Watt's *The Rise of the Novel* to Lennard J. Davis's more recent *Factual Fictions*. And I have often wondered, as others have sometimes wondered about Dickens, if the structure of Sarshar's novel might not have been very different had it been written not for serialization but for direct publication as a book.

Those other books, independent of newspapers, came too. One very prolific writer, whose name as it appears on the covers of his books is itself a curiosity, was Shams-ul-Ulema Deputy Nazir Ahmed (1831–1912). The name was actually Nazir Ahmed. 'Shams-ul-Ulema' literally means 'a Sun among the scholars of Islam', and indicates his distinguished scholarship in that area; 'Deputy' simply refers to the fact that he had no independent income and had joined the colonial Revenue Service. His training in Arabic was rigorous and immaculate; his knowledge of English was patchy, since he had had no formal training in it. He was a prolific translator of everything: the Indian Penal Code, the Indian Law of Evidence, the Qur'an, books of astronomy. He is known above all as a novelist, however, and he had one overwhelming anxiety: that girls should get a modern education (in this he represented the emergent urban bourgeoisie) but that they should nevertheless remain good, traditional housewives (a sentiment that was quite widespread, across all social boundaries). It was this anxiety that governed most of his fiction.

It is possible to argue, I think, that the formative phase of the Urdu novel and the narrativities that arose alongside that novel, in the latter part of the nineteenth century and the first decades of the twentieth, had to do much less with the experience of colonialism and imperialism as such and much more with two other kinds of pressures and themes: the emergence of a new kind of petty bourgeois who was violating all established social norms for his own pecuniary ends (Nazir Ahmed's own *Ibn-ul-Vaqt* – 'Time-Server', in rough English approximation – is a classic of that genre); and the status of women. Nazir Ahmed, of course, took conservative positions on both these themes, and was prolific on the latter, but there were others as well. Rashid-ul- Khairi, for example, established a very successful publishing house, the Asmat Book Depot, which published hundreds of books for women and children, as well as four of the five journals that came into my family over two generations: *Asmat, Khatoon-e-Mashriq, Jauhar-e-Nisvan, Banaat* and *Nau-Nehaal*. English approximations for the last four titles are easy to provide: 'Woman of the East', 'Essence of Womanhood', 'Girls' (or 'Daughters') and 'Children'. But the first title, *Asmat*, is harder to render in English, for the Urdu usage of this word has many connotations, from 'Virginity' to 'Honour', to 'Propriety', in a verbal condensation which expresses interrelated preoccupations. That these journals came regularly into my family for roughly forty years is itself significant, for mine was not, in metropolitan terms, an educated family; we lived in a small village, far from the big urban centres, and I was the first member of this family to finish high school or drive a car. The fact that two generations of women and children in such a family would be part of the regular readership of such journals shows the social reach of this kind of publishing. Much literature, in short, revolved around the issues of femininity and propriety, in a very conservative sort of way.

But then there were other writers, such as Meer Hadi Hassan Rusva, who challenged the dominant discourse and wrote his famous *Umrao Jan Ada* about those women for whom Urdu has many words, the most colourful of which can be rendered as 'women of the upper chamber': women to whom men of property in certain social milieux used to go for instruction in erotic play, genteel manners, literary taste and knowledge of music. The scandal of

Rusva's early-twentieth-century text is its proposition that since such a woman depends upon no one man, and because many men depend on her, she is the only relatively free woman in our society. He obviously did not like Nazir Ahmed's work, but I must also emphasize that the ironic and incipient 'feminism' of this text is not a reflection of any Westernization. Rusva was a very traditional man, and he was simply tired of certain kinds of moral posturing. Meanwhile, the idea that familial repressions in our traditional society were so great that the only women who had any sort of freedom to make fundamental choices for themselves were those who had no 'proper' place in that society – this subversive idea was to reappear in all kinds of ways when the next major break came in the forms of Urdu narrativity, in the 1930s, under the banner not of nationalism but of the Progressive Writers' Association, which was a cultural front for the Communist Party of India and had come into being directly as a result of the United Front Policy of the Comintern after 1935.

Critical Realism became the fundamental form of narrativity thereafter, for roughly two decades. 'Nation' was certainly a category used in this narrative, especially in non-fiction, and there was an explicit sense of sociality and collectivity, but the categories one deployed for that sense of collectivity were complex and several, for what Critical Realism demanded was that a critique of others (anti-colonialism) be conducted in the perspective of an even more comprehensive, multifaceted critique of ourselves: our class structures, our familial ideologies, our management of bodies and sexualities, our idealisms, our silences. I cannot think of a single novel in Urdu between 1935 and 1947, the crucial year leading up to decolonization, which is in any direct or exclusive way about 'the experience of colonialism and imperialism'. All the novels I know from that period are predominantly about other things: the barbarity of feudal landowners, the rapes and murders in the houses of religious 'mystics', the stranglehold of moneylenders upon the lives of peasants and the lower petty bourgeoisie, the social and sexual frustrations of schoolgirls, and so on. The theme of anti-colonialism is woven into many of those novels, but never in an exclusive or even a dominant emphasis. In fact, I do not know of *any* fictional narrative in Urdu, in roughly the last two hundred years, which is of any significance and any length (I am making an exception for a few short stories here) in which the issue of colonialism or the difficulty of a civilizational encounter between the English and the Indian has the same primacy as, for example, in Forster's *A Passage to India* or Paul Scott's *The Raj Quartet*. The typical Urdu writer has had a peculiar vision, in which he or she has never been able to construct fixed boundaries between the criminalities of the colonialist and the brutalities of all those indigenous people who have had power in our own society. We have had our own hysterias here and there – far too many, in fact – but there has never been a sustained, powerful myth of a primal innocence, when it comes to the colonial encounter.

The 'nation' indeed became the primary ideological problematic in Urdu literature only at the moment of Independence, for our Independence too was peculiar: it came together with the Partition of our country, the biggest and possibly the most miserable migration in human history, the worst bloodbath in the memory of the subcontinent: the gigantic fratricide conducted by Hindu, Muslim and Sikh communalists. Our 'nationalism' at this juncture was a nationalism of mourning, a form of valediction, for what we witnessed was not just the British policy of divide and rule, which surely was there, but our own willingness to break up our civilizational unity, to kill our neighbours, to forgo that civic ethos, that moral bond with each other, without which human community is impossible. A critique of others (anti-colonial nationalism) receded even further into the background, entirely overtaken now by an even harsher critique of ourselves. The major fictions of the 1950s and 1960s – the shorter fictions of Manto, Bedi, Intezar Hussein; the novels of Qurrat ul Ain, Khadija Mastoor, Abdullah Hussein – came out of that refusal to forgive what we ourselves had done and were still doing, in one way or another, to our own polity. No quarter was given to the colonialist; but there was none for ourselves either. One *could* speak, in a general sort of way, of 'the nation' in this context, but not of 'nationalism'. In Pakistan, of course, there was another, overriding doubt: were we a nation at all? Most of the left wing, I am sure, said 'No'.

VIII

Finally, I also have some difficulty with the way Jameson seems to understand the epistemological status of the Dialectic. For what seems to lie at the heart of all the analytic procedures in his text is a search for – the notion that there *is* – a unitary determination which can be identified, in its splendid isolation, as the source of all narrativity: the proposition that the 'Third World' is a *singular* formation, possessing its own unique, unitary force of determination in the sphere of ideology (nationalism) and cultural production (the national allegory).

Within a postmodernist intellectual milieu where texts are to be read as the utterly free, altogether hedonistic plays of the Signifier, I can well empathize with a theoretical operation that seeks to locate the production of texts within a determinate, knowable field of power and signification, but the idea of a *unitary* determination is in its *origins* a pre-Marxist idea. I hasten to add that this idea is surely present in a number of Marx's own formulations as well as in a number of very honourable, highly productive theoretical formations that have followed, in one way or another, in Marx's footsteps. It is to be seen in action, for example, even in so recent a debate as the one that followed the famous Dobb–Sweezy exchange and came to be focused on the search for a 'prime mover' (the issue of a unitary determination in the rise of the capitalist mode of production in Western Europe). So when Jameson implicitly invokes this particular understanding of the Dialectic, he is in distinguished company indeed.

But there is, I believe, a considerable space where one could take one's stand between (a) the postmodernist cult of utter non-determinacy and (b) the idea of a unitary determination which has lasted from Hegel up to some of the most modern of the Marxist debates. For the main thrust of the Marxist Dialectic, as I understand it, comprises a *tension*, a mutually transformative relation, between the problematic of a final determination (of the ideational content by the life-process of material labour, for example) and the utter historicity of multiple, interpenetrating determinations, so that – in Engels's words – the 'outcome' of any particular history hardly ever corresponds to the 'will' of *any* of those historical agents who struggle over that outcome. Thus, for example, I have said that what constitutes the unity of the world is the global operation of the capitalist mode of production and the resistance to that mode which is ultimately socialist in character. But this constitutive fact does not operate in the same way in all the countries of Asia and Africa. In Namibia, the imposition of the capitalist mode takes a directly colonial form, whereas the central fact in India is the existence of stable and widespread classes of capitalist society within a postcolonial bourgeois polity; in Vietnam, which has already entered a post-capitalist phase – albeit in a context of extreme devastation of the productive forces – the character of this constitutive dialectic is again entirely different. So while the problematic of a 'final determination' is surely active in each case, it is constituted differently in different cases, and in each case literary production will, in principle, be differently constituted.

What further complicates this dialectic of the social and the literary is that most literary productions, whether of the 'First World' or the 'Third', are not always available for that kind of direct and unitary determination by any one factor, no matter how central that factor is in constituting the social formation as a whole. Literary texts are produced in highly differentiated, usually overdetermined contexts of competing ideological and cultural clusters, so that any particular text of any complexity will always have to be placed within the cluster that gives it its energy and form, before it is totalized into a universal category. This fact of overdetermination does not mean that individual texts merely float in the air, or that 'Totality' as such is an impossible cognitive category. But in any comprehension of Totality, one would always have to specify and historicize the determinations which constitute any given field; with sufficient knowledge of the field, it *is* normally possible to specify the principal ideological formations and narrative forms. What is not possible is to operate with the few texts that become available in the metropolitan languages and then to posit a complete singularization and transparency in the process of determinacy, so that all ideological complexity is reduced to a single ideological formation and all narrativities are read as local expressions of a metatext. If one does that, one produces not the knowledge of a Totality, which I too take to be a fundamental cognitive category, but an idealization, either of the Hegelian or the positivist kind.

What I mean by multiple determinations at work in any text of considerable complexity can be specified, I believe, by looking briefly at the problem of the cultural location of Jameson's own text. This is, ostensibly, a First World text; Jameson is a US intellectual and identifies himself as such. But he is a US intellectual of a certain kind: not everyone is able to juxtapose Ousmane and Deleuze so comfortably, so well; and he debunks the 'global American culture of postmodernism' which, he says, is *the* culture of his country. His theoretical framework, moreover, is Marxist, his political identification is socialist – which would seem to place this text in the Second World. But the particular energy of his text – its thematics, its relation with those other texts which give it its meaning, the very narrative upon which his 'theory of cognitive aesthetics' rests – takes him deep into the Third World, valorizing it, asserting it, filiating himself with it, as against the politically dominant and determinant of his own country. Where (in what *world?*) should *I*, who do not believe in the Three Worlds Theory, place his text: in the First World of his origin, the Second World of his ideology and politics, or the Third World of his filiation and sympathy? And, if 'all third-world texts are necessarily' this or that, how is it that his own text escapes an exclusive location in the First World? I – being who I am – shall place it *primarily* in the global culture of socialism – Jameson's Second World, my name for a global resistance – and I shall do so not by suppressing the rest (his US origins, his Third World sympathies) but by identifying that which has been central to all his theoretical undertakings for many years.

These are obviously not the only determinations at work in Jameson's text. I shall mention only two others, both of which are indicated by his silences. His is, among other things, a *gendered* text. It is inconceivable to me that *this* text could have been written by a US *woman* without some considerable statement, probably a full-length discussion, of the fact that the bifurcation of the public and the private, and the necessity to reconstitute that relation where it has been broken – which is so central to Jameson's discussion of the opposition between First World and Third World cultural practices – is indeed a major preoccupation of First World women writers today, on both sides of the Atlantic. And Jameson's text is also determined by a certain *racial* milieu. For it is equally inconceivable to me that *this* text could have been written by a *Black* writer in the USA who would not also insist that Black Literature of this country possesses the unique Third World characteristic that it is replete with national allegories (more replete, I personally believe, than is Urdu literature).

I point out these obvious determinations of Jameson's text for three reasons. One is to strengthen my proposition that the ideological conditions of a text's production are never singular but always several. Second, even if I were to accept Jameson's division of the globe into three worlds, I would still have to insist, as my references not only to feminism and Black Literature but to Jameson's own location would indicate, that there is right here, within the belly of the First World's global postmodernism, a veritable Third World, perhaps two or three of them. Third, I want to insist that within the unity that has been bestowed upon our globe by the irreconcilable struggle between capital and labour, there are more and more texts which cannot easily be placed within this or that world. Jameson's is not a First World text; mine is not a Third World text. We are not each other's civilizational Others.

NOTES

1 *Social Text* (fall, 1986), 65–88.
2 Edward W. Said, *After the Last Sky: Palestinian Lives* (New York: Pantheon, 1986).
3 Timothy Brennan's *Salman Rushdie and the Third World: Myths of the Nation* (New York: St Martin's Press, 1989), based upon that dissertation, appeared after the publication of this chapter in *Social Text*.

23 Chidi Amuta

The Materialism of Cultural Nationalism: Achebe's *Things Fall Apart* and *Arrow of God* (1989)[*]

In *The Theory of African Literature* (1989), Chidi Amuta confronts the hegemony of Western interpretations of African culture and the necessary failure of attempts to resuscitate pre-colonial African cultures as alternatives, focusing instead on the role of literature in national liberation and anti-imperialist struggles. Amuta's work emerges from debates among the Ife-Ibadan School of Marxist critics in Nigeria. Amuta argues against Chinweizu and others, *Towards the Decolonization of African Literature* (1980); against the obfuscatory mythology of writers such as Wole Soyinka; and against Western discourses of postcolonial theory. Amuta insists on the defining role of the socio-economic, political and ideological contradictions of African experience, in a Marxist theory of African literature whose 'conceptual inspiration' is, as Amuta puts it, 'derived from Marx, Engels, Plekhanov, Mao, Trotsky, Eagleton, Fanon, Onoge, Ngugi, Cabral and kindred spirits'. Amuta is critical of Western neo-imperialist appropriations of African literature, in the guises of cultural anthropology and comparative criticism, and of attempts to annex African writing as 'new' literatures of England in diaspora. Critical also of orthodox Marxist interpretations of African culture, Amuta uses Frantz Fanon, *The Wretched of the Earth* (trans. 1967); Amilcar Cabral, *Unity and Struggle* (1980); and Ngugi Wa Thiong'o, *Decolonising the Mind* (1986) as 'springboards' for a theory of the literary text as a 'prismatic dialectical image' of Africa. In this extract, Amuta's analysis of Achebe seeks to show how theoretical reorientation has implications for practical criticism. Amuta has also published *Towards a Sociology of African Literature* (1986); and essays in *Ufahamu, Critical Arts* and *The Journal of African Marxists*.

The impulse for a materialist reconsideration of Achebe's novels set in pre-colonial Igbo society is an act of rebellion against their systematic

[*] From Chidi Amuta, *The Theory of African Literature: Implications for Practical Criticism* (London: Zed, 1989), 130–6.

appropriation into the metaphysical aesthetics of traditionalist scholarship.[1] *Things Fall Apart* and *Arrow of God* have since become axiomatic reference points for diverse interests and opinions intent on rediscovering and commenting on 'traditional African society' and 'the culture conflict' inaugurated by the advent of colonialism, stock concepts which have since been adumbrated into a mini-catechism. Gradually also, these works have become part of the cultural raw material for the definition of an immutable African world. Little or no effort, however, has so far been made to situate analyses of the novels in the context of the specific socio-economic formation that characterized pre-colonial Igbo (African) societies and to understand the series of conflicts explored in the novels in terms of the collusion between that socio-economic formation and another one ushered in by the colonial encounter.

The contention being entered here is that both works constitute realistic depictions of social experience in the context of a pre-literate communal socio-economic formation at its point of impact with a nascent Western imperialist capitalist formation. It is precisely this unequal collision that provides the basis for conflict in the novels and also furnishes the ground rules for the resolution of the experiential conflicts through form.

In this respect, *Things Fall Apart* serves to furnish, albeit fictionally, the essential aspects of pre-literate communalism. Its fictional world is one in which the basic unit of social organization is the village which also serves as the locus for communal life and values. The village economy is essentially agrarian, depending for its subsistence on land as the principal means of production. Manual labour applied through basic iron tools – such as hoes or machetes – defines the dominant mode of production while production relations are essentially communalistic, characterized by co-operation and mutual assistance. Accordingly, because of the low level of mastery of nature and its laws, man is very much subject to the whims and caprices of elemental forces. If the rains do not come early or come in torrents, man's very survival is threatened as the possibility of a rich harvest is inextricably tied to the continued existence of the community.

It is this general background that animates and informs the realism in *Things Fall Apart*. Consequently, the Umuofia society is one in which a very high premium is placed on work – manual work. A man's social estimation is very much determined by the strength of his arm as manifested in his ability to cultivate the land and defeat his opponents in fights and wrestling matches. This accounts for society's adverse estimation of Unoka, Okonkwo's father. In a society where there is no conscious separation between artistic and manual labour, the individual who insists on being identified purely as an artist is doomed to public scorn, open condemnation and alienation. This, precisely, is the tragedy of Unoka's plight, for in the context of twentieth-century Western society, Unoka would be a superstar! In Umuofia society, however, the indicators of social success are a full barn and a brimming household and the ability to prove one's mettle through physical prowess. These are qualities which Unoka lacks and which consign his efforts to the domain of 'unproductive' labour.

On the contrary, Okonkwo's meteoric rise to fame and prosperity is almost exclusively predicated on his strength and will. And society measures his reputation in purely material productive terms: 'He was a wealthy farmer and had two barns full of yams.' Because there is as yet no conscious division of labour, Okonkwo is simultaneously a farmer, wrestler, warrior and leading political figure.

> Okonkwo was clearly cut out for great things. He was still young but he had won fame as the greatest wrestler in the nine villages . . . To crown it all he had taken two titles and had shown incredible prowess in two inter-tribal wars.[2]

Achebe's depiction of pre-colonial Igbo society as an essentially patriarchal one is largely realistic to the extent that it is based on a recognition of physical strength as a decisive factor in social life. Men and women are engaged in productive labour but the more exerting functions are reserved for the menfolk. Achebe is nevertheless critical of the excesses of this male-dominated society.

From this economic base arise certain beliefs, customs and practices which accord legitimacy and coherence to social experience. The *ozo* title, for instance, into which men of oustanding achievement are admitted, becomes a political–cum–juridical instrument not only for rewarding achievement but also for preserving social morality among its most privileged members. In addition, the religious beliefs and practices of the people arise from a purely instrumental conception of deity rather than from a blind self-surrender to the whims of immutable and inscrutable supernatural agencies. In the world of Umuofia, belief in the supernatural is a product of man's incomplete control over nature and his limited understanding of its mechanisms. This terrain is the breeding ground of fear and superstition and therefore of animistic worship.

> Darkness held a vague terror for these people, even the bravest among them. Children were warned not to whistle at night for fear of evil spirits. Dangerous animals became even more sinister and uncanny in the dark. A snake was never called by its name at night, because it would hear. It was called string.[3]

Nevertheless, man's conception of deity is essentially humanistic. Gods have a human face and their actions are predicated on human needs and necessities. For instance, when Okonkwo's lazy father, Unoka, resorts to augury to find an explanation for his poor harvests, the retort of the oracle is a direct reflection of society's work ethic with its premium on hard work: 'when a man is at peace with his gods and his ancestors, his harvest will be good or bad according to the strength of his arm. Go home and work like a man.' In this instrumental and symbiotic relationship between man and the gods, the gods that are accorded primacy are those that have a direct relevance to the land which is the principal means of production, hence the importance of the earth goddess:

> Ani played a greater part in the life of the people than any other deity. She was the ultimate judge of morality and conduct . . . The feast of the New Yam was held every year before the harvest began, to honour the earth goddess and the ancestral spirits of the clan.

It is perhaps in *Arrow of God* that Achebe gives the greatest stridency to the cultural dimension of pre-literate communal Igbo (African) society. This is not, however, to undermine Achebe's intense gaze on the material basis of cultural and spiritual life in his referent society. On the contrary, the various ideological and institutional mechanisms of that society are placed in sharp focus in order to place the colonial haemorrhage in bolder relief. Thus, the humanistic bias of this society is the first condition for its proper under-standing. While in the Judaeo-Christian world-view, deity precedes human existence: in the world of Umuaro, man creates god to serve his social and economic needs. Here, it needs to be pointed out that the supreme deity, Ulu, is a 'synthetic' deity, fashioned by the peoples of the six villages that make up Umuaro to meet their need for collective security against the ravages of slave raiders.

> In the very distant past, . . . the hired soldiers of Abam used to strike in the dead of night, set fire to the houses and carry men, women and children into slavery. Things were so bad for the six villages that their leaders came together to save themselves. They hired a strong team of medicine-men to install a common deity for them. This deity which the fathers of the six villages made was called Ulu . . . from that day they were never again beaten by an enemy.[4]

In effect, the gods did not *exist* as objective entities but were essentially mental projections of human possibilities. In the world of these novels also, the physical approximations and mental pictures of the various gods are humanistic. For instance, when Ezeulu's son, Obika, returns home late at night to report that he had seen an apparition, Ezeulu quickly interprets the apparition as the god of wealth. It is instructive that the mental picture of Eru, the god of wealth, held by the community is an approximation of the physical attributes and material paraphernalia of wealth in the society. The god is said to be 'dressed like a wealthy man', with 'an eagle's feather in his red cap' and 'carried a big [elephant] tusk across his shoulder'. The point remains that Obika had merely been frightened by a flash of lightning in the dark at a particular place which the collective unconscious has grown to associate with the presence of Eru. It is the consciousness of Ezeulu as an older member of the society and, therefore, a custodian of the mythic and spiritual heritage of the society that fleshes out the young man's fear of darkness into a mental picture. The important point here, however, is that this mental picture of the god of wealth is rendered in human terms. In this socio-economic setting therefore, man creates god in his own image ('one day the men of Okperi made a powerful deity and placed their market in its care', p. 19).

Accordingly, the communal mode of production necessitates a broad republican political arrangement. In both Umuofia and Umuaro, political authority is vested in the council of elders and indeed the collectivity of the community. This point is much more pungently registered in the social setting of *Things Fall Apart* in which political and judicial decisions ranging from the declaration of war to inter-family adjudication are taken collectively. In *Arrow of God*, on the other hand, the historical necessity created by the slave raids necessitates a certain separation of secular authority from the purely religious functions. Ezeulu's significance is intricately tied to the psycho-social necessity that created his patron deity, Ulu. When he tries to mistake his otherwise purely religious functions for political ones, he runs into trouble with his community which quickly reasserts the supremacy of its communal will over Ezeulu's nascent individualism.

If, therefore, cultural nationalism defines the sensibility within which these novels are created, the culture which is being reaffirmed must be seen as the totality of the foregoing economic base and its legitimizing beliefs, practices and structures. Against this background, the historic clashes between both Umuofia and Umuaro on one hand and the forces of colonialism on the other must be seen as confrontations between two antithetical production formations. The Europeans were forcing capitalist structures down the throats of members of a pre-literate communal society. Both the production relations and the superstructural set-up necessitated by the two formations are grossly antithetical.

Consequently, a primary source of conflict between the respective indigenous societies and their British invaders is the question of land. This comes out in the land dispute between Okperi and Umuaro. When the white man intervenes on the side of Okperi against Umuaro, the latter society witnesses a major crisis, for land as the only means of production is organically entwined with the very life of the people. Similarly, when the Christian missionaries approach the elders of Umuofia for land to erect their church on, they are offered the evil forest which is not normally cultivated by the community. To meddle with the land and its people is to assault their very social and cultural institutions. It is in these terms that the colonialists' introduction of Christianity, courts, etc. can be understood.

Against this background, it is an underestimation to insist that Achebe is mainly concerned with culture clash in these novels. He is in fact very keenly aware of and consistently exposes the economic exploitation which the colonialist assault entailed. In *Things Fall Apart*, the narrative voice insists:

> The white man had indeed brought a lunatic religion, but he had also built a trading store and for the first time palm-oil and kernel became things of great price, and much money flowed into Umuofia.[5]

The point, however, is that Achebe's depiction of the economic aspect of the colonial experience is embedded in critical suggestions while the experiences of his characters constantly reaffirm the centrality of economic factors in the life of his referent society.

To grasp the essence of the internal materialism of these works is to evoke questions about the literary/artistic strategies by means of which they are realized.

In this respect, the centralization of Aristotelian-type monumentalized heroes in these novels is an attempt to employ the strategy of typification to concretize the historical issues at stake. At first sight, both Okonkwo and Ezeulu would appear decontextualized as individuals in a society where the community wields the decisive will. On the contrary, if we view them as instances of typification as an artistic strategy, they are essentially specific characters through whose experiences the crucial issues of the epoch are fictionally distilled and examined. The theoretical anchor for this contention is brilliantly articulated by the Soviet aesthetic theoretician, A. Bazhenova in the following terms:

> The typical character is a concentration of the unique thoughts, feelings and actions of an individual who becomes, due to the artist's creative power and his penetration of that character, one of the equivalents of a society, an age, a people, a nation, a class, a profession.[6]

Okonkwo, therefore, must be understood as an embodiment of the spirit of his age and the dramatization of the response of that *spirit* to forces hostile to the stability of his society and its culture. His decisive and heroic response to the colonialists must also be seen as a revolutionary anti-colonialist stance. When he stands up in open arrogant defiance of the colonialists, he is not defending culture as a superstructural proposition but the totality of the socio-economic formation and therefore cultural identity of his people. In this respect, his revolutionary stature must be seen in terms of Cabral's contention that in the colonial situation, the cultural values that would energize the national liberation struggle are lodged in the countryside and among the peasantry.[7] Okonkwo embodies the *spirit* of those values. Jean-Paul Sartre, in his preface to Fanon's *The Wretched of the Earth*, captures the legitimacy of the Okonkwo reflex when he writes:

> When the peasant takes a gun in his hands, the old myths grow dim and the prohibitions are one by one forgotten. The rebel's weapon is the proof of his humanity. For in the first days of the revolt you must kill: to shoot down a European is to kill two birds with one stone, to destroy an oppressor and the man he oppresses at the same time: there remain a dead man, and a free man.[8]

Ezeulu presents a somewhat more complex subtilization of the tragic implications of the colonialist assault. To the extent that his social significance (as a priest) is rooted in the superstructural realm of the social totality, he is more of an embodiment of the cultural values of his society than Okonkwo. As the personification of the spiritual values of Umuaro, Ezeulu is eminently placed to reflect the crisis of consciousness inaugurated in the society by the colonial intervention. Consequently, his psyche becomes the battleground for the reconciliation of the two conflicting value systems and their supporting institutions. He saves himself Okonkwo's kind of terminal tragedy by adopting a somewhat more 'liberal' and dynamic attitude to the prevailing historical exigency without, however, severing his links with his patron deity and its sustaining society. Although he sends his son, Oduche, to the white man's school, he will not accept to be the white man's warrant chief. Even in adopting what could be regarded as a moderate position, Ezeulu prepares himself for a tragic role. Thus, while his society sees him as an ambitious, even treacherous man, the white man, Winterbottom, sees him as a stubborn tribal chieftain. It is the indignation attendant on being caught in between these antithetical expectations that defines the tragic essence of *Arrow of God* in general.

A proper appreciation of the tragic affiliations of this novel (and even *Things Fall Apart*) must be predicated on a clear epistemological distinction. Unlike the traditional Aristotelian concept, tragedy in *Arrow of God* is a function of human action (or inaction) at the material level which is complicated or made problematic by a given historical situation. In effect, Achebe's sense of the tragic in these novels compels a materialist epistemology which underlines the very instrumentality of the relationship between man and his gods in pre-colonial Africa.

In a society where the decisive political will is communal, it can be argued that Ezeulu's principal flaw consists in a certain egocentricity which places individual self-assertion above the will of the collectivity and even the imperatives of public office. But in the context of the historical conjunctures of the moment, what constitutes his undoing is that he responds to the pressures of colonialism (which are collective in nature) in a rather individual-istic manner. His tragedy, then, is essentially one of a basic dislocation between individual action and the demands of a historical imperative requiring collective assertion.

At the level of structure, Achebe's mastery of novelistic art finds expression in a certain sense of balance which presents the experiences in their dialectical essence. Just as the structure and institutional practices of pre-colonial society are presented in their contradictory essence so also are the motivations and values of colonialism exposed. This feature is perhaps more pronounced in *Arrow of God*, a novel in which the colonial presence has become entrenched. Captain Winterbottom furnishes a typification of the stock prejudices at the core of colonialist ideology. His personal responses to his African (Nigerian) environment are permeated by prejudices which are reminiscent of Joseph Conrad's *Heart of Darkness*. He is perennially haunted by his obsession with the primitivity of the native and his customs: 'He would wonder what unspeakable rites went on in the forest at night, or was it the heart-beat of the African darkness?' (p. 29). In his racist psyche, the Nigerian land is one vast expanse of unrelieved primitivity perennially haunted by uncanny and male-volent presences: 'This dear old land of waking nightmares!' Accordingly, he frowns at European officials interacting with 'natives' and sees his African workers and subjects as lower animals. Of his servant, Boniface, he says: 'He's a fine specimen, isn't he? He's been with me four years. He was a little boy of about thirteen – by my own calculation, they've no idea of years – when I took him on. He was absolutely raw' (p. 35).

Without, however, diminishing the place of racial bigotry in colonialist ideology, Achebe relieves Winterbottom's excesses through another white character, Tony Clark, who adopts a more liberal attitude to the natives. Mr Clark interacts freely with Africans and accords some measure of respect to their institutions. But his individual 'progressive' stance does not diminish the assumptions and prejudices that underlie the British policy of Indirect Rule.

One aspect of these novels that has attracted excited comments is the use of language. Achebe's creative use of the grammatical features and rhythm of Igbo speech and elements of Igbo oral lore has been variously interpreted and richly described. What remains unfinished, however, is to proffer a sociological explanation of the place of language in Achebe's referent society. Like in all pre-literate communal societies, language in the societies of *Things Fall Apart* and *Arrow of God* is not just a means of communication. It is, on the contrary, the expression of what Lukács calls the immanence of meaning in being. These are societies in which language serves as a veritable accompaniment to the process of production of material life. Art (poetry, folk-tales, etc.), philosophy, science and politics are all embedded in the matrix of social language because there is as yet no overt fragmentation of experience into different specializations each requiring its own mode of discourse. This, according to Lukacs, 'is a homogeneous world, and even the separation between man and world, between "I" and "you", cannot disturb its homogeneity'.[9]

Language in this social totality becomes a purveyor of the 'metaphysical' nature of experience. Thus between the world of the folk-tale and that of real life, there is a certain contiguity. Thus when in *Things Fall Apart*, Achebe weaves folk-tales into the plot structure, he is merely reiterating this basic contiguity.

From the foregoing then, the importance of Achebe's portrayal of pre-colonial society in these novels lies in his ability to deploy the realistic essence of novelistic fiction to recover and expose the dynamism of preliterate African communalism at an important historical moment.

NOTES

1 For typical positions in this critical fashion, see Bernth Lindfors (ed.), *Critical Perspectives on Chinua Achebe* (London: Heinemann, 1979).

2 Chinua Achebe, *Things Fall Apart* (London: Heinemann, 1985), 13.

3 Ibid., 31.

4 Achebe, *Arrow of God* (London: Heinemann, 1974), 14–15. All further page references are to this edition.

5 Achebe, *Things Fall Apart*, 126.

6 A. Bazhenova, 'The Creative Process and Typification', in *Marxist-Leninist Aesthetics and the Arts* (Moscow: Progress, 1980), 243.

7 See Amilcar Cabral, *Return to the Source* (New York: Monthly Review Press, 1973), 39–56; 57–74.

8 Jean-Paul Sartre, Introduction to Frantz Fanon, *The Wretched of the Earth* (Harmondsworth: Penguin, 1967), 19.

9 Georg Lukács, *The Theory of the Novel* (Cambridge, Mass: MIT Press, 1978), 32.

24   Alex Callinicos
The Jargon of Postmodernity (1989)[*]

Alex Callinicos is a Reader in Politics at the University of York, a leading figure in the Socialist Workers Party, and a member of the editorial board of *International Socialism*. His books include *Althusser's Marxism* (1976); *Is There a Future for Marxism?* (1982); *Marxism and Philosophy* (1983); *The Revolutionary Ideas of Karl Marx* (1983); *Making History* (1987); *Against Postmodernism* (1989); *The Revenge of History* (1991); and *Theories and Narratives* (1995). Literary theory is not an important component in his work, though there are discussions of ideology and poststructuralist theories of language in *Is There a Future for Marxism?* and *Marxism and Philosophy*. 'The Jargon of Postmodernity', the first chapter from *Against Postmodernism*, offers an example of literary theory within a classical Marxist perspective tackling the ideology of a contemporary social formation. The chapter's title echoes Adorno's attack on the ideology of phenomenology in *The Jargon of Authenticity* (1964). While essays by Marxists such as Jameson's 'Postmodernism, or the Cultural Logic of Late Capitalism' (1984) have been instrumental in putting postmodernism at the centre of critical debates, Callinicos suggests that postmodernism should be understood as a symptom. Elsewhere in *Against Postmodernism* he argues that postmodernism is rooted in the combination of Western disillusionments after the events of 1968, and the life-style opportunities contemporary capitalism offers upper white-collar strata, such as intellectuals. Context and comparisons with Callinicos are provided by Jürgen Habermas's *The Philosophical Discourse of Modernity* (1985); and J.-F. Lyotard, *The Postmodern Condition* (1979; trans. 1984).

> We live, I regret to say, in an age of surfaces.
>
> *Oscar Wilde*

[*] From Alex Callinicos, *Against Postmodernism: A Marxist Critique* (Cambridge: Polity, 1989), 9–28.

1.1 The Enlightenment and All That

'Postmodernity' and revolution: the subject of this book may be summed up by these two words apparently with little in common. In fact, they share at least one feature: both lack a referent in the social world. But the two words fail to refer in quite different ways. Socialist revolution is the outcome of historical processes at work throughout the present century which have produced a series of major social and political convulsions, and on one occasion – Russia in October 1917 – the actual emergence, albeit short lived, of a workers' state. The absence of successful socialist revolution is a contingent historical fact. Postmodernity by contrast is merely a theoretical construct, of interest primarily as a symptom of the current mood of the Western intelligentsia (hence the quotation marks around 'postmodernity' above, which should be treated as invisibly surrounding every other occurrence of the word in this book). Postmodernity and revolution are, however, connected. Not only does belief in a postmodern epoch generally go along with rejection of socialist revolution as either feasible or desirable, but it is the perceived failure of revolution which has helped to gain widespread acceptance of this belief.

Lyotard treats the rejection of revolution as an instance of a more general phenomenon constitutive of the postmodern, namely the collapse of the 'grand narratives'. These he associates especially with the Enlightenment, that is, with those primarily French and Scottish thinkers of the eighteenth century who sought to extend the methods of theoretical inquiry they believed to be characteristic of the seventeenth-century scientific revolution from the explanation of the physical to that of the social world as part of a broader attempt by human beings to gain rational control of their environment. The philosophy of history which tended to issue from this approach is well expressed by the title of Condorcet's famous essay, *Sketch of the Progress of the Human Mind*: in the evolution of society can be traced the progressive improvement of the human condition. Lyotard plainly regards Hegel and Marx as, in this respect at least, the successors of the *philosophes*.

But now, he claims, the entire Enlightenment project has foundered:

> This idea of progress as possible, probable or necessary was rooted in the certainty that the development of the arts, technology, knowledge and liberty would be profitable to mankind as a whole.
>
> After two centuries, we are more sensitive to signs that signify the contrary. Neither economic nor political liberalism, nor the various Marxisms, emerge from the sanguinary last two centuries free from the suspicion of crimes against mankind ... What kind of thought is able to sublate (*Aufheben*) Auschwitz in a general (either empirical or speculative) process towards a universal emancipation?[1]

Lyotard calls this thought 'trivial'; a better word would be 'old'. What Georg Lukács called 'Romantic anti-capitalism' had already emerged by the end of the eighteenth century to challenge the Enlightenment and the bourgeois social order which it appeared to sanction in the name of an idealized pre-capitalist past.[2] Hegel and Marx can be seen as responding to the Romantic critique of the Enlightenment, seeking to integrate it into a more complex understanding of historical development than that offered by Condorcet and the other *philosophes*. Rejection of the Enlightenment, frequently claiming inspiration from Nietzsche, was notoriously a staple of *fin-de-siècle* European thought. Perhaps the most celebrated (and complex) recent example of this tradition is Max Horkheimer's and Theodor Adorno's *Dialectic of Enlightenment* (1944), where the urge to dominate nature, sanctioned by the *philosophes*, culminates in the 'totally administered world' of late capitalism, in which the repressed returns in the barbarous and irrational form of fascism.

'Incredulity towards metanarratives' seems therefore to be at least as old as the Enlightenment which was so productive of grand narratives in the first place. The *fin-de-siècle* recognition of what Sorel called the illusions of progress seems especially embarrassing for those who want to associate distinctively Postmodern art with this incredulity. For the leading figures of the heroic era of Modernism at the beginning of the century generally rejected the notion of historical progress. Thus T. S. Eliot in his famous 1923 review of *Ulysses* describes Joyce's use of myth as 'simply a way of controlling, of ordering, of giving a shape and a significance to the immense panorama of futility and anarchy that is contemporary history'.[3] Frank Kermode argues that what he calls 'the sense of an ending', the feeling of being at the end of an epoch, 'the mood of end-dominated crisis' is 'endemic to what we call modernism'.[4]

Nevertheless an apocalyptic conception of postmodernity as the site of the final catastrophe of Western civilization is fairly commonplace. Thus Arthur Kroker and David Cooke write: 'Ours is a *fin-de-millennium* consciousness, which, existing at the end of history in the twilight time of ultramodernism (of technology) and hyperprimitivism (of public moods), uncovers a great arc of disintegration and decay against the background radiation of parody, kitsch, and burnout.'[5] But postmodernists tend not simply to claim this apocalyptic consciousness (quite a common feature of Western thought, according to Kermode, since the Middle Ages) for their own,[6] but to counterpose it to Modernism, which tends to be conceived as itself an example of the Enlightenment. Thus Linda Hutcheon ascribes to Modernism '[f]aith in the rational, scientific mastery of reality' – precisely what was distinctive to the Enlightenment project.[7]

Russell Berman points out that both postmodernists and defenders of the Enlightenment project such as Habermas assert that the concepts of modernity and modernism which are at stake correspond to the cultural formations of humanism that have prevailed in the West since the Renaissance or at least the ninteenth century. Hence the apparent similarity of contemporary polemics to the confrontation between the Enlightenment and its Romantic opposition, so often repeated during the past two centuries. The consequence of this epochal definition of modernity is the relative denigration of the aesthetic revolution at the end of the nineteenth century and the beginning of the twentieth century and the emergence of what is commonly known as 'modern art' or 'modernist literature' in contrast to the traditional and conventional forms of the preceding decades.[8]

We shall return to this lack of historical specificity in section 1.4 below, but let us first consider the other side of this assimilation of Modernist *art* to the Enlightenment, namely the appropriation of features of Modernism in order to give Postmodern art its distinctive identity.

1.2 The Evisceration of Modernism

Compare these two passages:

> In the multidimensional and slippery space of Postmodernism anything goes with anything, like a game without rules. Floating images such as those we see in the painting of David Salle maintain no relationship with anything at all, and meaning becomes detachable like the keys on a key ring. Dissociated and decontextualized, they slide past one another failing to link up into a coherent sequence. Their fluctuating but not reciprocal interactions are unable to fix meaning.[9]

> [T]he nature of our epoch is multiplicity and indeterminacy. It can only rest on *das Gleitende* [the moving, the slipping, the sliding], and is aware that what other generations believed to be firm is in fact *das Gleitende*.[10]

The first passage comes from a talk given by the art critic Suzy Gablik in Los Angeles in 1987, the second was written by the poet Hugo von Hofmannsthal in 1905. Both depict the world as plural and polysemic, but for Gablik such a view is distinctive to Postmodern art. A conception of reality of ultimately Nietzschean provenance which was fairly widespread among the intelligentsia of *Mitteleuropa* at the end of the last century and which is often present in the work of major Modernist figures such as Hofmannsthal is presented as peculiarly *Post*modernist.

But this kind of appropriation of Modernist motifs is absolutely typical of accounts of Postmodernist art. The force of this point can only be established by considering first the nature of Modernism itself. Eugene Lunn offers an excellent definition:

'1   *Aesthetic Self-Consciousness or Self-Reflexiveness.*' The process of producing the work of art becomes the focus of the work itself: Proust, of course, provided the definitive example in *A la recherche du temps perdu*.

'2   *Simultaneity, Juxtaposition, or "Montage".*' The work loses its organic form and becomes an assemblage of fragments, often drawn from different discourses or cultural media. Cubist and Surrealist collages come to mind, along with the practice of cinematic montage developed by Eisenstein, Vertov and other revolutionary Russian film-makers.

'3   *Paradox, Ambiguity, and Uncertainty.*' The world itself ceases to have a coherent, rationally ascertainable structure, and becomes, as Hofmannsthal says, multiple and indeterminate. Klimt's great paintings 'Philosophy', 'Medicine' and 'Jurisprudence', commissioned for the University of Vienna but rejected because of the scandal their dark and ambiguous images represented to Enlightenment thought, exemplify this vision.

'4   *"Dehumanization" and the Demise of the Integrated Individual Subject or Personality.* 'Rimbaud's famous declaration *'JE est un autre'* ('I am another') finds its echoes in the literary explorations of the unconscious inaugurated by Joyce and pursued by the Surrealists.[11]

Oddly enough, the authors of two of the most interesting recent discussions of Modernism, Perry Anderson and Franco Moretti, both deny that there is any relatively unified set of artistic practices which can be captured by a definition such as Lunn's. Anderson writes: 'Modern*ism* as a notion is the emptiest of cultural categories. Unlike Gothic, Renaissance, Baroque, Mannerist, Romantic, or Neoclassical, it designates no describable object in its own right at all; it is completely lacking in positive content.'[12] Anderson perhaps places excessive faith in the traditional categories of art history, terms whose origins are often arbitrary and use uncertain and shifting.[13] Moretti is rather more concrete in the way he expresses his scepticism about the label 'Modernism':

> 'Modernism' is a portmanteau word that perhaps should not be used too often. But I don't think I would classify Brecht as a modernist . . . I just cannot think of a meaningful category that could include, say, surrealism, *Ulysses*, and something by Brecht. I can't think what the common attributes of such a concept could be. The objects are too dissimilar.[14]

But in fact Brecht's plays can be seen quite plausibly to fall under the 'common attributes' of Lunn's definition: the alienation (*Verfremdung*) effect is intended precisely to make the audience realize that they are in a theatre and not eavesdropping on real life; Brecht explicitly gives montage as a defining feature of his epic theatre; the plays are constructed in part to deny the spectator the satisfaction of an unequivocal meaning; and the narratives they unfold no longer treat the individual subject as the sovereign and coherent author of events. This is not to deny the considerable variations within Modernism: one of the merits of Lunn's account is the contrast it draws between the confident rationalism of Cubism in France before 1914, and, on the one hand, the 'langorous aestheticism' of Vienna, and, on the other, the 'nervous, agitated and suffering' art produced by German Expressionism.[15] Nor is it to ignore the very important differences within Modernism concerning the status of art itself. 'Nevertheless, Lunn's definition does, in my view, capture the distinctive features of the art which emerged across Europe at the end of the nineteenth century.

The advantages of having some such conception of Modernism becomes plain when one considers the definitions offered of Postmodernism, for example by Charles Jencks: 'To this day I would define Postmodernism as . . . *double-coding: the combination of Modern techniques with something else (usually traditional building) in order for architecture to communicate with the public and a concerned minority, usually other architects.*'[16] This definition gets its purchase from the attempts by architects over the last couple of decades to get away from the elongated slabs characteristic of the International Style, with which architectural Modernism is identified. But if (as it is intended to be) it is taken as a *general* characterization of Postmodern art,[17] then it is hopelessly inadequate. 'Double-coding' – what Lunn calls 'Simultaneity, Juxtaposition, or "Montage" ' – is a defining feature of Modernism. Thus Peter Ackroyd writes of *The Waste Land*:

> Eliot found his own voice by first reproducing that of others – as if it was only through his reading of, and response to, literature that he could find anything to hold onto, anything 'real'. That is why *Ulysses* struck him so forcibly, in a way no other novel ever did. Joyce had created a world which exists only in, and through, the multiple uses of language – through voices, through parodies of style . . . Joyce had a historical consciousness of language and thus of the relativity of any one 'style'. The whole course of Eliot's development would lead him to share such a consciousness . . . In the closing sequence of *The Waste Land* itself he creates a montage of lines from Dante, Kyd, Gérard de Nerval, the *Pervigilium Veneris* and Sanskrit . . . There is no 'truth' to be found, only a number of styles and interpretations – one laid upon another in an endless and apparently meaningless process.[18]

Eliot is a particularly relevant example to take in the light of Jencks' claim that Postmodernism represents a 'return to the larger Western tradition' after Modernism's 'fetish of discontinuity'.[19] For one of Eliot's main preoccupations – expressed, for example, in 'Tradition and the Individual Talent' – was the relationship of both continuity and discontinuity between his own work and the broader European tradition:

> the historical sense compels a man to write not merely with his own generation in his bones, but with a feeling that the whole literature of Europe from Homer

and within it the whole literature of his own country has a simultaneous existence and composes a simultaneous order. This historical sense, which is a sense of the timeless as well as of the temporal and of the timeless and the temporal together, is what makes a writer traditional. And it is at the same time what makes a writer most acutely conscious of his place in time, of his own contemporaneity.[20]

Eliot is in no sense exceptional among the major Modernists in this concern for placing himself with respect to 'the larger Western tradition', as any acquaintance with the work, say, of Joyce or Schoenberg or Picasso will confirm. It is, therefore, difficult to be persuaded by Linda Hutcheon's claim that 'postmodernism goes beyond self-reflexivity to situate discourse in a broader context'.[21] She uses what she calls 'historiographic metafiction', a number of contemporary novels, in order to illustrate this thesis, but the examples she gives – Salman Rushdie's *Midnight's Children*, John Fowles' *The French Lieutenant's Woman*, Julian Barnes' *Flaubert's Parrot* and E. L. Doctorow's *Ragtime* among others – seem fairly heterogeneous, and united chiefly by their use, for various ends and in different modes, of the Modernist fictional devices pioneered by Conrad, Proust, Joyce, Woolf and others at the beginning of the century.

Hutcheon's argument is one among a number of manœuvres used to deal with the embarrassing fact that both the definitions given and the examples cited of Postmodern art place it most plausible as a continuation of and not a break from the *fin-de-siècle* Modernist revolution. Another popular move is to treat Modernism as essentially elitist. Thus Hutcheon talks of '[t]he obscurity and hermeticism of modernism',[22] while even Andreas Huyssen (who is usually above such things) tells us that 'the most significant trends within postmodernism have challenged modernism's relentless hostility to mass culture'.[23] Taken as claims about the internal construction of Modernist art these are far too strong. Even the forbiddingly mandarin Eliot loved the London music hall and sought to integrate its rhythms into some of his poetry, especially *Sweeney Agonistes*.[24] Stravinsky wrote not only *Le Sacre du printemps* but also *L'Histoire du soldat*, which draws heavily on ragtime. If directed at the great Modernists' Aestheticism, their tendency to view art as refuge from 'the immense panorama of futility and anarchy that is contemporary history', the accusation of elitism does strike home, but even here those committed to the idea of a radically novel Postmodern art must confront the development of avant-garde movements such as Dadaism, Constructivism and Surrealism which deployed Modernist techniques to overcome the separation between art and life as part of a broader struggle to revolutionize society itself. This is a question which I consider in the next chapter: however, the arguments presented so far seem to me sufficient to cast doubt on the claims made for the novelty of Postmodern art.

1.3 The Search for Precursors

There are nevertheless considerably more subtle attempts to establish the existence of a distinctively Postmodern art than any considered so far. These conceive Postmodernism as a tendency within Modernism itself. Such an approach clearly involves a retreat from, or the rejection of the idea that Modernism and Postmodernism can be correlated in any very strong sense with distinctive stages of social development – say, respectively, industrial and post-industrial society.

Confusingly enough Lyotard, who helped to get the hare of a new, postmodern epoch running in the first place, also argues that treating the '"post-" in the term "postmodernist"' . . . in the sense of a simple succession, of a diachrony of periods, each of them clearly identifiable' is 'totally modern . . . Since we are beginning something completely new, we have to re-set the hands of the clock at zero.' But the idea of a total break with tradition 'is, rather, a manner of forgetting or repressing the past. That's to say of repeating it. Not overcoming it.'[25]

If Postmodernism isn't a movement beyond Modernism, what is it? 'It is undoubtedly a part of the modern', Lyotard replies.[26] To develop his point he draws here on Kant's conception, elaborated in the *Critique of Judgement* as part of his aesthetics, of the sublime, which 'is to be found in an object even devoid of form, so far as it immediately involves, or its presence provokes, a representation of *limitlessness*, yet a superadded thought of its totality'. The particular philosophical significance of the sublime is that it offers us an experience of nature 'in its chaos, or in its wildest and most irregular disorder and desolation', which, 'provided it gives signs of magnitude and power', leads us to formulate ideas of pure reason, in particular that of the physical world as a unified and purposive order, which, according to Kant, cannot be found in sense experience. The feeling, therefore, of the sublime is a form of aesthetic experience which breaks the boundaries of the sensuous. And, 'though the imagination, no doubt, finds nothing beyond the sensible world to which it can lay hold, still this thrusting aside of the sensible barriers gives it a feeling of being unbounded and this removal is thus a presentation of the infinite'. Kant suggests that there may be 'no more sublime passage' than the Mosaic ban on graven images.[27]

The essential for Lyotard is less the religio-metaphysical connotations of the sublime for Kant but rather 'the incommensurability of reality to concept which is implied in the Kantian philosophy of the sublime'. He emphasizes, not the 'superadded thought of . . . totality' which Kant says is inherent in the feeling of the sublime, but rather our inability to experience this totality. Lyotard distinguishes between two different attitudes towards 'the sublime relation between the presentable and the conceivable', the Modern and the Postmodern:

> modern aesthetics is an aesthetic of the sublime, though a nostalgic one. It allows the unpresentable to be put forward only as the missing contents; but the form, because of its recognizable consistency, continues to offer to the reader or viewer matter for solace or pleasure ... The postmodern would be that which, in the modern, puts forward the unpresentable in presentation itself; that which denies itself the solace of good forms, the consensus of a good taste which would make it possible to share collectively the nostalgia for the unattainable; that which searches for new presentations, not in order to enjoy them but in order to impart a stronger sense of the unpresentable.[28]

Postmodern art therefore differs from Modernism in the attitude it takes up towards our inability to experience the world as a coherent and harmonious whole. Modernism reacts to 'the immense panorama of futility and anarchy that is contemporary history' by looking back nostalgically to a time before our sense of totality was lost, as Eliot does when he claims that in the Metaphysical poets of the seventeenth century there was 'a direct sensuous apprehension of thought, or a recreation of thought into feeling', which disappeared after the 'dissociation of sensibility' already evident in Milton and Dryden.[29] Postmodernism, by contrast, ceases to look back. It focuses instead 'on the power of the faculty to conceive, on its "inhumanity" so to speak (it was the quality Apollinaire demanded of modern artists)' and 'on the increase of being and jubilation which result from the invention of new rules of the game, be it pictorial, artistic, or any other'.[30]

This conception of Postmodernism effectively abandons the attempt to ascribe to it structural characteristics such as 'double-coding' in order to differentiate it from Modernism. Indeed, as Fredric Jameson observes, Lyotard's argument has 'something of the celebration of modernism as its first ideologues projected it – a constant and ever more dynamic revolution in the languages, forms and tastes of art'.[31] Similarly Jencks complains that 'Lyotard continues in his writings to confuse Post-Modernism with the latest avant-gardism, that is Late Modernism.'[32] Jencks has in mind in particular some of the Minimalist art of the 1960s and 1970s, and indeed it does seem that Lyotard is inclined to favour such work, as is suggested by the exhibition, *Les Immatériaux*, which he organized at the Pompidou Centre. The main thrust of Lyotard's argument, however, involves the claim that Postmodernism is a tendency within Modernism characterized by its refusal to mourn, and indeed its willingness to celebrate our inability to experience reality as an ordered and integrated totality. Minimalist art may fall under this definition, but a perhaps more interesting question concerns the exemplars of Postmodernism during the heroic era of Modernism at the beginning of the century.

Lyotard offers one rather unconvincing example. He argues that Proust's work is plainly Modernist, since although 'the hero is no longer a character but the inner consciousness of time, . . . the unity of the book, the odyssey of that consciousness, even if it is deferred from chapter to chapter, is not seriously challenged'. By contrast 'Joyce allows the unpresentable to become perceptible in his writing itself, in the signifier. The whole range of available narrative and even stylistic operators is put into play without concern for the unity of the whole, and new operators are tried.'[33] But surely, despite the variety of styles and voices present in *Ulysses*, an implicit coherence is achieved through Joyce's use of myth? And is not this order even more evidently at work in *Finnegans Wake* in the cyclical pattern traced by both the book and history?[34]

Joyce is placed firmly in the Modernist camp by Jameson in his brilliant study of Wyndham Lewis, the most sustained attempt to show Postmodernist impulses at work within Modernism. Lewis's significance for Jameson lies in his rejection of the 'impressionistic aesthetic' characteristic of 'Anglo-American modernism'. Pound, Eliot, Joyce, Lawrence and Yeats all pursued 'strategies of inwardness, which set out to reappropriate an alienated universe by transforming it into personal styles and private languages'. Nothing could be more different than 'the prodigious force with which Wyndham Lewis propagates his bristling mechanical sentences and hammers the world into a forbidding cubist surface', the relentless externality of his style, in which the human, the physical and the mechanical are shattered and assimilated to each other. In a daring and imaginative move for a Marxist to take, Jameson argues that the writing of Lewis − fascist, sexist, racist, elitist − must be seen, precisely because of its distinctive formal 'expressionism', as a particularly powerful 'protest against the reified experience of an alienated social life, in which, against its own will, it remains formally and ideologically locked'.[35]

The difficulty lies not so much with Jameson's reading of Lewis, which is essentially a particularly bold example of what Frank Kermode calls the 'discrepancy theory', in accord with which Marxist criticism seeks to uncover in texts an unconscious meaning often at odds with their author's intentions,[36] but with the picture of main-stream Modernism which he contrasts with Lewis's writing. Modernism on this account is especially concerned with the time of private, subjective experience, what Bergson called *durée*, time as the individual person lives it, at once fragmented and operating at quite different rhythms from the homogeneous and linear 'objective' time of modern society.[37] Perhaps this will do when applied to Proust, but it fits Lewis's great English-speaking contemporaries rather badly. To take (yet again) the case of Eliot, we saw above that he conceived the entire European tradition as composing 'a simultaneous order' with his own writing. Indeed, it has been argued more generally that literary Modernism is characterized precisely by the *spatialization* of writing, the juxtaposition of fragmentary images torn out of any temporal sequence.[38] In 'Tradition and the Individual Talent' Eliot also makes the celebrated claim that '[p]oetry is not a turning loose of emotion, but an escape from emotion; it is not the expression of personality, but an escape from personality.'[39] Such statements seem to fit poems like *The Waste Land* better than the claim that they represent a 'strategy of inwardness', a retreat into the 'inner consciousness of time'. Eliot approvingly described *Ulysses* as a return to Classicism that uses the materials provided by modern life rather than rely on a sterile academicism; interestingly Lewis claimed that the 'Men of 1914', by which he meant Eliot, Pound, Joyce and himself, represented 'an attempt to get away from romantic into classical art' comparable to Picasso's revolution in painting.[40]

Jameson, the author after all of a book called *The Political Unconscious*, might argue that such professions by Eliot and others of a commitment to an impersonal, spatialized art very different from the 'impressionist aesthetic' which he ascribes to them are less important than what is revealed by the formal construction of their work. But without entering into such a formal analysis, it is worth observing how much less plausible Jameson's interpretation becomes when applied to the broader currents of Modernism beyond the English-speaking world. Where, for example, does Expressionism fit in – a highly subjective kind of art which nevertheless *externalized* inner anguish, projecting it on to and thereby distorting the objective environment of the personality? Or Cubism, which systematically dismantled the objects of common-sense experience, spreading out before the viewer their internal structure and external relationships?[41] Or the *Neue Sachlichkeit* of Weimar Germany, which reacted against the extravagances of Expressionism in favour of cool, matter-of-fact (*sachlich*), sometimes avowedly Neo-Classical art, but combined this with a critical, if not revolutionary attitude towards existing society – an art whose greatest achievement was perhaps Brecht's 'theatre for a scientific age'?[42]

More generally, Jameson's attempt to counterpose Lewis's 'expressionism' with the 'impressionistic aesthetic' supposedly typical of Modernism occludes what is best understood as a dialectical relationship between interiority and exteriority. The exploration of the peculiar rhythms of subjective experience is undoubtedly one of the major themes of Modernist writing: think of Proust, Woolf, Joyce. The paradox is that the deeper one probes beyond even fragmentary inner consciousness into the unconscious, the more one threatens to crack the subject open, and to confront the external forces which traverse and constitute the ego.

This is the trajectory taken by Freud: the unravelling of unconscious desires led him face to face with history – not simply the history of the individual subject, but the historical processes which produced the social institutions, above all the family, subtending the odyssey of the self. Deleuze and Guattari argue that Freud's fault was that he did not take the process far enough, relying instead on the mythologized history which rendered the bourgeois family eternal.[43] However that may be, the point stands that the logic of depth psychology, the exploration of inner consciousness, is to disintegrate the subject, and display its fragments as directly related to the social and natural environment supposedly external to the self. One can see this logic at work, for example, in two of the great figures of Viennese Modernism, Klimt and Kokoschka. Klimt's paintings are suffused with an inner unease and pervasive eroticism which are still held in control in a harmonious, indeed stylized relationship of the parts of the whole; in Kokoschka the tensions which Klimt was still able more or less to manage have exploded, distorting and disorganizing the subjects of his paintings, which are traversed by an anarchic psychic energy.[44]

One might argue that Postmodernism is nothing but the outcome of this dialectic of interiority and exteriority, an art of the surface, the depthless, even the immediate. Thus Scott Lash proposes that we see Postmodernism as 'a figural, as distinct from discursive, regime of signification. To signify via figures rather than words is to signify iconically. Images or other figures which signify iconically do so through their resemblance to the referent.' Consequently Postmodern art involves 'de-differentiation', so that, on the one hand, the signified (meaning) tends 'to wither away and the signifier to function as a referent', and, on the other hand, 'the referent functions as a signifier'. Contemporary film (*Blue Velvet*) and criticism (Susan Sontag's attack on interpretation) provide Lash with examples of this essentially Imagist art, but, like Lyotard, he sees Postmodernism as immanent within Modernism, particularly in the shape of Surrealism, which 'understood reality to be composed of signifying elements. Thus Naville enthused that we should get pleasure from the streets of the city in which kiosks, autos and lights were in a sense already representations, and Breton spoke of the world itself as "automatic writing".'[45]

One obvious difficulty with this analysis is that it offers no account of how Postmodernism thus understood differs from those arts – for example, painting and cinema – which are necessarily iconic. John Berger has claimed recently that painting is distinguished by the way it 'offers palpable, instantaneous, unswerving, continuous, physical presence. It is the most immediately sensuous of the arts.'[46] It is at least arguable that one of the main thrusts of Modernist painting is to release this immediate sensuous charge inherent in painting from both aesthetic ideologies of form and representation and broader social ideologies subordinating art to organized religion and the state. One can see the resulting sense of liberation at work, for example, in Matisse's paintings. The attempt to achieve something like the same effect in poetry was a crucial impulse in the Modernist literary revolution: Pound called Imagism the 'sort of poetry where painting or sculpture seems as if it were "just coming over into speech" '.[47] If the figural is the defining characteristic of Postmodernism, then the latter is a far more pervasive feature of Modernism than Lash appears to believe.

Matters are not much improved if we focus on Surrealism, as Lash does. It is quite true that the Surrealists had a magical conception of reality according to which chance events in the daily life of the city offered occasions of what Walter Benjamin called 'profane illumination'. In this sense reality did indeed function for them as a signifier. But by the mid-1920s what had originally been a primarily Aestheticist project intended to realize Rimbaud's injunction that '[t]he poet makes himself a *seer* by a long, prodigious and rational *disordering of all the senses*' had developed into a broader political commitment to social revolution which led most leading Surrealists to join the Communist Party (in most cases rather briefly) and Breton to a life-long involvement in the anti-Stalinist left. ' "Transform the world", Marx said; "change life", Rimbaud said – these two watch-words are for us one and the same', Breton told the Congress of, Writers for the Defence of Culture in 1935.[48]

This conjoining of political and aesthetic revolution makes it difficult to see the Surrealists as precursors of Postmodernism. For most accounts of Postmodern art tend to emphasize its rejection of revolutionary political change. Lyotard associates 'the nostalgia of the whole and one, . . . the reconciliation of the concept and the sensible, of the transparent and the communicable experience' with 'terror, . . . the fantasy to seize reality'.[49] The thought is presumably the traditional liberal one that any attempt at total social change will lead straight to the Gulag. One consideration behind the frequent claims made for Postmodern 'wit' and 'irony' seems to be that the collapse of belief in the possibility or desirability of global political transformation leaves us with nothing better to do than playfully to parody what we can no longer take seriously. Parody is, however, so pervasively present in the great Modernists – Eliot and Joyce, for example – that any attempt to claim it exclusively for Postmodernism just seems implausible; indeed, Franco Moretti's claims that irony is a constitutive feature of Modernism. Jameson suggests that matters have gone a stage further – that while Modernist parody retains some conception of a norm from which one is deviating, Postmodernism is distinguished by pastiche, the 'neutral practice of mimicry, without any of parody's ulterior motives, amputated of the satiric impulse, devoid of laughter and of any conviction that alongside the abnormal tongue you have momentarily borrowed, some healthy linguistic normality still exists.'[50]

How can Surrealism, which united Rimbaudian artistic experimentation with Marxist revolutionary socialism, be plausibly regarded as a precursor of Postmodernism, which sees revolution as, at best a joke, at worst a disaster? Lash doesn't help matters by drawing on Benjamin's discussion of post-auratic art. Benjamin used the term 'aura' in order to capture the properties of uniqueness and unapproachability which he argues are characteristic of the traditional work of art. '[T]he unique value of the "authentic" work of art has its basis in ritual', he claims, 'the location of its original use value.' The aura preserves this 'ritual function' even after the decline of organized religion in the shape of the 'secular cult of beauty, developed during the Renaissance' and the 'negative theology' of art involved in nineteenth-century Aestheticism (*l'art pour l'art*). The contemporary development of the mass reproduction of art by mechanical means reaching its climax in cinema, however, causes the aura to decay, both by destroying the uniqueness of images and by altering their mode of consumption – the reception of the work of art is no longer a matter of individual absorption in the image, but – above all in the film theatre – is 'consummated by a collectivity in a state of distraction'.[51]

Now Lash claims that Modernism is typically auratic, Postmodernism post-auratic, the latter shattering the organic unity of the work of art 'through pastiche, collage, allegory and so on'.[52] Lash doesn't explain how Postmodernism's use of collage and the like distinguishes it from a paradigmatically Modernist movement like Cubism. More to the point, his argument involves a serious misunderstanding of Benjamin's account of post-auratic art. Benjamin argued that decay of the aura achieved by mass media such as cinema was the explicit objective of avant-garde movements such as Dada. 'What they intended and achieved was a relentless destruction of the aura of their creations . . . Dadaistic activities actually assured a rather vehement distraction by making works of art the centre of scandal.' But the kinds of shock effects sought by the Dadaists with their meaningless poems and assaults on their audiences are achieved on a much larger scale by film, whose rapid succession of shots interrupts the spectator's consciousness, preventing her from sinking into a state of absorbed contemplation.[53]

The significance of the resulting changes in the mode of reception was for Benjamin political. The decline of the aura means that art is no longer 'based on ritual' but 'begins to be based on another practice – politics'. 'Reception in a state of distraction' allows the audience to adopt a more detached and critical attitude: 'The public is an examiner, but an absent- minded one.'[54] This new mode of reception, Benjamin believed, would lead the mass consumers of mechanically reproduced art to adopt a critical stance not merely towards what they saw but towards the capitalist society that produced it. Adorno argued that this belief involved a naïve technological determinism, detaching the new physical means of mass reproduction from the bourgeois social relations of their use.[55] Whatever one thinks of this, Benjamin was certainly right to detect a political dynamic at work within avant-garde movements' attempts to alter the mode of reception of art. This is true even of the Dadaists, who were not the apolitical jokers depicted by postmodernists eager to appropriate them. The Berlin group in particular emerged in a context defined by the First

World War, the Russian Revolution of October 1917 and the German Revolution of November 1918. Its leading figures – Richard Huelsenbeck, Wieland Herzefelde, John Heartfield, George Grosz – saw themselves, like the Surrealists a few years later, as political as well as aesthetic revolutionaries, and were sympathizers or members of the German Communist Party. 'Dada is German Bolshevism', Huelsenbeck said.[56] Grosz – whose savage assaults on the German bourgeoisie in works like *The Face of the Ruling Class* have permanently fixed our image of the Weimar republic – later wrote: 'I came to believe, however fleetingly, that art divorced from political struggle was pointless. My own art would be my rifle, my sword; all brushes and pens not dedicated to the great fight for freedom were no more use than empty straws.'[57]

The relationship between the Modernist avant-garde and revolutionary politics is in fact complex and problematic, as we shall see in chapter 2. Nevertheless, Benjamin's chief example of artistic practice consciously directed at achieving the same effects as are produced in cinema – Brecht's epic theatre – represents perhaps the most sustained attempt to unite aesthetic Modernism and revolutionary Marxism. Thus Benjamin argues that the 'forms of epic theatre correspond to the new technical forms – cinema and radio'. Brecht's aim, he says, is to create an audience that is relaxed rather than absorbed, so that 'instead of identifying itself with the hero' it will 'learn to be astonished at the circumstances within which he has his being'. Brechtian alienation, the 'making strange' of social conditions we normally take for granted, produces a detached audience involved in a process of active discovery rather than fixed in a passive condition of identification with actors whose participation in a piece of fiction the conventions of theatrical Naturalism seek to conceal.[58] Benjamin's adoption of epic theatre as a prime example of post-auratic art, however, does not sit well with Lash's argument, since Lash cites Sontag's rejection of Brecht's 'theatre of dialogue' for Artaud's 'theatre of the senses' as a key instance of the shift towards Postmodernism. There have, in fact, been some attempts to claim Brecht for Postmodernism,[59] but these are highly implausible. Brecht's emphasis on epic theatre as 'theatre for instruction', directed towards 'an audience of the scientific age', concerned to encourage its consumers to reflect on, and develop a rational, critical understanding of the world, is so plainly intended to achieve a theatre of *enlightenment* that it is hard to imagine his plays fitting easily into a Postmodernist canon.[60] Lash's attempt to use Benjamin's aesthetics to characterize Postmodern art does therefore seem rather to confirm Andreas Huyssen's sardonic comment: 'Given the ravenous eclecticism of postmodernism, it has recently become fashionable to include Adorno and Benjamin in the canon of postmodernism *avant la lettre* – truly a case of the critical text writing itself without the interference of any historical consciousness whatsoever.'[61]

1.4 The Abolition of Difference

The abiding impression left by the various claims made for Postmodern art surveyed in the preceding pages is their contradictory character. Postmodernism corresponds to a new historical stage of social development (Lyotard) or it doesn't (Lyotard again). Postmodern art is a continuation of (Lyotard), or a break from (Jencks) Modernism. Joyce is a Modernist (Jameson) or a Postmodernist (Lyotard). Postmodernism turns its back on social revolution, but then practitioners and advocates of a revolutionary art like Breton and Benjamin are claimed as precursors. No wonder that Kermode calls Postmodernism 'another of those period descriptions that help you to take a view of the past suitable to whatever it is you want to do'.[62]

What runs through all the various – mutually and often internally inconsistent – accounts of Postmodernism is the idea that recent aesthetic changes (however characterized) are symptomatic of a broader, radical novelty, a sea-change in Western civilization. A little before the postmodern boom got into full swing Daniel Bell noted the widespread 'sense of an ending' among the Western intelligentsia 'symbolized . . . in the widespread use of the word *post* . . . to define, as a combined form, the age into which we are moving'. Bell illustrated this proliferation of 'posts-' by listing the following examples: post-capitalist, post-bourgeois, post-modern, post-civilized, post-collectivist, post-Puritan, post-Protestant, post-Christian, post-literature, post-traditional, post-historical, post-market society, post-organization society, post-economic, post-scarcity, post-welfare, post-liberal, post-industrial . . .[63]

For postmodernists the decisive break is usually with the Enlightenment, with which, as we saw in section 1.1 above, Modernism tends to be identified. Sometimes this involves the most astonishing claims, such as the following: 'Modernism in philosophy goes back a long way: Bacon, Galileo, Descartes – pillars of the modernist conception of the fashionable, the new and the innovative'[64] – a statement so ignorant as almost to invite one's admiration. How can thinkers committed to a representational epistemology most fully articulated by Locke, in which the sensory qualities of objects are signs of their rationally ascertainable inner structure, be assimilated to an artistic movement whose products affronted common-sense expectations often in the belief that the scientific knowledge of reality was neither possible or even desirable? The point of such assertions seems to be less their factual content, which is slight, than the attempt to establish the novelty of Postmodernism, usually characterized in terms borrowed from Modernism, by treating the latter as merely the latest exemplar of Western rationalism.

This operation tends to involve conceiving Postmodernism's break with the Enlightenment in apocalyptic terms, so that it becomes the revelation of the fundamental flaw inherent in European civilization for centuries if not millenia. Perhaps the silliest example of this mode of thinking is provided by Kroker and Cook, who claim that 'since Augustine nothing has changed in the deep, structural code of Western experience', so that *De Trinitate* offers 'special insight into the modern project, at the very moment of its inception and from inside out'. Indeed, not simply the 'modern project' but the 'postmodern scene . . . begins in the fourth century . . . everything since the Augustinian refusal has been nothing but a fantastic and grisly implosion of experience as Western culture itself runs under the signs of passive and suicidal nihilism'. The apocalyptic 'sense of an ending' which postmodernism supposedly articulates loses any historical specificity, becoming instead the chronic condition of Western civilization since the fall of Rome. Here indeed is the night Hegel spoke of when criticizing Schelling, in which all cows are black, in which Augustine, Kant, Marx, Nietzsche, Parsons, Foucault, Barthes and Baudrillard have all been analysing the same 'postmodern scene'.[65]

Kroker's and Cook's vacuous parlour nihilism is in fact the *reductio ad absurdum* of a style of thinking with rather more distinguished antecedents. Both Nietzsche and Heidegger see Western metaphysics as founded upon a constitutive fault traversing its entire history – respectively Plato's reduction of the plurality of reality to phenomenal manifestations of the essential realm of the Forms, and the oblivion at the time of the Presocratics of the originary ontological difference between Being and beings. The subsequent history of European thought consists of variations on and elaborations of this founding error, which reaches its climax in the philosophy of self-constituting subjectivity founded by Descartes and thereby serves to legitimize the rationalized domination of both nature and humanity characteristic of modernity. Habermas highlights the contradiction which Nietzsche and Heidegger, as well as their successors – notably Foucault and Derrida – face in using the tools of rationality – philosophical argument and historical analysis – in order to carry out the critique of reason as such.[66] More relevant for present purposes is the way in which so sweeping a dismissal of Western civilization as founded since antiquity upon error encourages precisely the kind of dissolution of historical differences into repetitions of this original sin which we saw above to be typical of postmodernism.

As it happens, this tendency of the Nietzscheo-Heideggerian tradition, so embarrassing for self-proclaimed philosophers of difference, has been subjected to the most probing of critiques by Hans Blumenberg. Blumenberg's particular concern is with the 'secularization thesis', the treatment of modern beliefs, institutions and practices as secularized versions of Christian motifs, and specifically with the theory, elaborated by Karl Löwith, that the Enlightenment conception of historical progress was merely the translation into pseudo-scientific vocabulary of the Christian notion of divine providence. As Blumenberg observes, the 'secularization of Christianity that produces modernity becomes for Löwith a comparatively unimportant differentiation' compared to the earlier 'turning away from the pagan cosmos of antiquity' with its cyclical conception of time which Judaism and Christianity perform by conceiving human history as the unfolding of God's plan of salvation. It is impossible here to do justice to the wealth of historical knowledge which Blumenberg displays in order to demonstrate the distinctive character of modern thought and the qualitative break which it represents with respect to Christian theology. He traces the origins of this break to the nominalist critique of Aristotelian metaphysics in the later Middle Ages, which in particular disenchanted the physical world, expelling from it any hint of divine purpose and reducing it to the purely contingent result of God's exercise of his will. The nominalist denial of any worldly intimation of divine order, intended to highlight the absolute perfection and power of the 'hidden God' (*deus absconditus*), had the paradoxical effect of creating a space within which took shape what for Blumenberg is the distinctively modern attitude of 'self-assertion': 'The more indifferent and ruthless nature seemed to be with respect to man, the less it could be a matter of indifference to him, and the more ruthlessly he had to materialize, for his mastering grasp, even that was pregiven to him as nature.' Nature could no longer be contemplated as a hierarchy of purposes by the 'blissful onlooker' inherited by medieval scholasticism from Plato and Aristotle. The nominalist 'postulate that man had to behave as though God were dead . . . induces a restless taking stock of the world which can be designated as the motive power of the age of science'. Curiosity ceases to be the vice it was for Christian theology and becomes systematized in the methodical interference in nature characteristic of Galilean science. The scholastic conception of the world as a finite and definitively knowable order is supplanted by 'the reality–concept of the open context, which anticipates reality as the always incomplete result of a realization, as dependability constituting itself successively, as never definitive and absolutely granted consistency'. This conception of reality as open and incomplete in turn underlies the Enlightenment conception of progress which, unlike Christian eschatology, does not focus on 'an event breaking into history . . . that transcends as is heterogeneous to it', but 'extrapolates from a structure present in every moment to a future that is immanent in history'. Thus 'the idea of progress is . . . the continuous self-justification of the present by means of the future that it gives itself, before the past, with which it compares itself.'[67]

Blumenberg provides a rich and powerful critique of the style of thinking inaugurated by Nietzsche and continued by Heidegger, one in which, according to Löwith's secularization thesis, 'things must remain the same as they were made' by 'Christianity's intervention in European history (and through European history in world history)', 'so that even a post-Christian atheism is actually an intra-Christian mode of expression of negative theology, and a materialism is the continuation of the Incarnation by other means'.[68] But

Blumenberg's preoccupation with the distinctive character of modernity also highlights the question implicit in this whole chapter. Postmodernism in its various manifestations defines itself by contrast with Modernist art and more generally with the 'modern age' which we have supposedly now left behind us. The main thrust of this chapter has been negative – to demonstrate both the weight attached by postmodernists to Postmodern art and their inability to come up with a plausible and coherent account of its distinguishing characteristics. The reader might, however, quite reasonably demand a positive account of the nature of modernity and of the Modernist art which is presumably its critical reflex. I attempt to meet this demand in chapter 2 [of *Against Postmodernism*], and to do so in a way that, unlike the postmodernist theories critically surveyed in this chapter, gives its proper due to the historical specificity of the phenomena under examination.

NOTES

1 J.-F. Lyotard, 'Defining the Postmodern', *ICA Documents* 4 (1985), 6.
2 See R. Sayre and M. Löwy, 'Figures of Romantic Anti-capitalism', *New German Critique* 32 (1984).
3 T. S. Eliot, *Selected Prose*, ed. F. Kermode (London, 1975), 177.
4 F. Kermode, *The Sense of an Ending* (Oxford, 1968), 98.
5 A. Kroker and D. Cooke, *The Postmodern Scene*, 2nd edn (Houndmills, 1988), 8.
6 See Kermode, *Sense*, esp. ch. 1.
7 L. Hutcheon, *A Poetics of Postmodernism* (London, 1988), 28.
8 R. A. Berman, 'Modern Art and Desublimation', *Telos* 62 (1984–5), 33–4.
9 S. Gablik, 'The Aesthetics of Duplicity', *Art & Design* 3, 7/8 (1987), 36.
10 Quoted in C. Schorske, *Fin-de-Siècle Vienna* (New York, 1981), 19.
11 See E. Lunn, *Marxism and Modernism* (London, 1985), 34–7.
12 P. Anderson, 'Modernity and Revolution', in C. Nelson and L. Grossberg (eds), *Marxism and the Interpretation of Culture* (Houndmill, 1988), 332.
13 Compare F. Kermode, *History and Value* (Oxford, 1988), ch. 6.
14 F. Moretti, 'The Spell of Indecision' (discussion), in Nelson and Grossberg, *Marxism*, p. 346.
15 Lunn, *Marxism*, 58; see generally 33–71.
16 C. Jencks, *What is Postmodernism?* (London, 1986), 14.
17 See, for example, ibid., 3–7.
18 P. Ackroyd, *T. S. Eliot* (London, 1985), 118–19.
19 Jencks, *Postmodernism?*, 43.
20 Eliot, *Selected Prose*, 38.
21 Hutcheon, *Poetics*, 41.
22 Ibid., 32.
23 A. Huyssen, 'Mapping the Postmodern', *New German Critique* 33 (1984), 16.
24 Ackroyd, *Eliot*, 105, 145–8.
25 Lyotard, 'Defining', 6.

26 J.-F. Lyotard, *The Postmodern Condition* (Manchester, 1984), 79.

27 I. Kant, *Critique of Judgement* (Oxford, 1973), I, 90, 92, 127.

28 Lyotard, *The Postmodern Condition*, 79, 81. As Huyssen observes, Lyotard's 'turn to Kant's sublime forgets that the 18th-century fascination with the sublime of the universe, the cosmos, expresses precisely the very desire of totality and representation which Lyotard so abhors and persistently criticizes in Habermas's own work'; 'Mapping', p. 46. See also my discussion of the sublime in 'Reactionary Postmodernism?', in R. Boyne and A. Rattansi (eds), *Postmodernism and Social Theory* (Houndmills, forthcoming).

29 Eliot, *Selected Prose*, 63–4. Jencks apparently believes that Eliot 'located [the dissociation of sensibility] in the nineteenth century' (!), *Postmodernism?*, 33.

30 Lyotard, *The Postmodern Condition*, 79–80.

31 F. Jameson, Foreword to ibid., p. xvi.

32 Jencks, *Postmodernism?*, 42.

33 Lyotard, *The Postmodern Condition*, 80.

34 G. Deleuze and F. Guattari, *Mille plateaux* (Paris, 1980), 12.

35 F. Jameson, *Fables of Aggression* (Berkeley and Los Angeles, 1979), 2, 81, 2, 14.

36 Kermode, *History*, 98 ff. Perhaps the most elaborated account of the 'discrepancy theory' is P. Macherey, *A Theory of Literary Production* (London, 1978), esp. part I.

37 Jameson, *Fables*, ch. 7.

38 J. Frank, 'Spatial Form in Modern Literature', in *The Widening Gyre* (New Brunswick, 1963).

39 Eliot, *Selected Prose*, 43.

40 Ibid., 176–7; W. Lewis, *Blasting & Bombardiering* (London, 1967), 250.

41 See J. Berger, *The Success and Failure of Picasso* (Harmondsworth, 1965), 47 ff.

42 See J. Willett, *The New Sobriety 1917–1933* (London, 1978).

43 G. Deleuze and F. Guattari, *L'Anti-Oedipe* (Paris, 1973), ch. 2.

44 See Schorske, *Fin-de-Siècle Vienna*, chs 5 and 8.

45 S. Lash, 'Discourse or Figure?', *Theory, Culture & Society* 5, 2/3, 320, 331–2.

46 J. Berger, 'Defending Picasso's Late Work', *International Socialism* 2, 40 (1988), 113.

47 Quoted in N. Zach, 'Imagism and Vorticism', in M. Bradbury and J. McFarlane (eds), *Modernism 1890–1930* (Harmondsworth, 1976), 234.

48 M. Nadeau, *A History of Surrealism* (Harmondsworth, 1973), 212 n. 5. See also W. Benjamin, 'Surrealism', in *One-Way Street and Other Writings* (London, 1979). Rimbaud defined the task of the poet in his letter to Paul Demeny of 15 May 1871, translated by Oliver Bernard in *Collected Poems* (Harmondsworth, 1969), 10.

49 Lyotard, *The Postmodern Condition*, 82.

50 F. Jameson, 'Postmodernism, or the Cultural Logic of Late Capitalism', *New Left Review* 146 (1984), p. 45.

51 W. Benjamin, *Illuminations* (London, 1970), 226, 241.

52 S. Lash and J. Urry, *The End of Organized Capitalism* (Cambridge, 1987), 286–7.

53 Benjamin, *Illuminations*, 239–40.

54 Ibid., 226, 242–3.

55 E. Bloch et al., *Aesthetics and Politics* (London, 1977), 100–41, with a Presentation by Perry Anderson.

56 Quoted in C. Russell, *Poets, Prophets and Revolutionaries* (New York, 1985), 117. See more generally ibid., 114–18; and H. Richter, *Dada* (London, 1965), ch. 3.

57 G. Grosz, *A Small Yes and a Big No* (London, 1982), 91–2. See also Count Harry Kessler's report of his meeting with Grosz on 5 Feb. 1919: 'Grosz argued that art as such is unnatural, a disease, and the artist a man possessed . . . He [Grosz] is really a Bolshevist in the guise of a painter', *The Diaries of a Cosmopolitan 1918–1937* (London, 1971), 64.

58 W. Benjamin, *Understanding Brecht* (London, 1977), 6, 18.

59 See, for example, Hutcheon, *Poetics*, 35.

60 See J. Willett (ed.), *Brecht on Theatre* (London, 1964): the emphasis laid by Brecht in later writings – for example, in 'A Short Organum for the Theatre' – on the role of pleasure as well as instruction in epic theatre involves a modification rather than the abandonment of his earlier views.

61 Huyssen, 'Mapping', 42.

62 Kermode, *History*, 132.

63 D. Bell, *The Coming of Post-Industrial Society* (London, 1974), 51–4.

64 J. Silverman and D. Welton, editors' introduction to *Postmodernism and Continental Philosophy* (Albany, 1988), 2.

65 Kroker and Cooke, *Postmodern Scene*, 8, 76, 127, 129, 169.

66 J. Habermas, *The Philosophical Discourse of Modernity* (Cambridge, 1987), esp. Lecture IV.

67 H. Blumenberg, *The Legitimacy of the Modern Age* (Cambridge, Mass., 1983), 28, 30, 32, 182, 346, 423. Compare K. Löwith, *Meaning in History* (Chicago, 1949).

68 Blumenberg, *Legitimacy*, 115. Jean Baudrillard provides a good example of this style of thinking: he tells us that political economy, within whose categories Marxism is trapped, is 'only a kind of actualization' of 'the great Judaeo–Christian dissociation of the soul and Nature', *The Mirror of Production* (St Louis, 1975), 63, 65.

Index

Figures in **bold** denote authorship